Massacre Along the Medicine Road

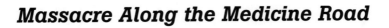

Massacre Along the Medicine Road

A Social History of the Indian War of 1864 in Nebraska Territory

Ronald Becher

CAXTON PRESS
Caldwell, Idaho
1999

Library of Congress Cataloging-in-Publication Data

Becher, Ronald, 1943 –
Massacre along the Medicine Road : a social history of the Indian War of 1864 in Nebraska Territory / Ronald Becher.
p. cm.
Includes bibliographical references and index.
ISBN 0-87004-389-7. – ISBN 0-87004-387-0 (pbk.)
1. Cheyenne Indians--Wars, 1864. 2. Cheyenne Indians--Wars--Nebraska. 3. Frontier and pioneer life--Nebraska--History--19th century. I. Title.
E99.C53B43 1999
973.7'37 – dc21 98-48924
CIP

Lithographed and bound in the United States of America by
CAXTON PRESS
Caldwell, Idaho
164332

DEDICATION

In memory of my parents,

June and Hugo,

with love and gratitude.

CONTENTS

Illustrations x
List of Maps xi
Preface xiii
Acknowledgments xix

PART ONE

Chapter 1 – A Day in August 2
Chapter 2 – "They had no hope to keep any land" 5
Chapter 3 – "Bad management or some untoward misfortune" . . 14
Chapter 4 – "They have been deceived so often by the whites" . . . 30
Chapter 5 – "A smothered passion for revenge" 37
Chapter 6 – "God bless our home" 46
Chapter 7 – "The settlers in our county viewed the future with anxiety" 60
Chapter 8 – "The shortest road to the people's hearts" 78
Chapter 9 – "An expensive Indian war is about to take place" . . 100
Chapter 10 – "All quiet on the Platte" 114
Chapter 11 – "Ash Hollow will be nowhere" 122
Chapter 12 – August 6, 1864 128

PART TWO

Chapter 1 – The Little Blue River Valley. 132
Chapter 2 – The Raid on the Little Blue 148
Sunday, August 7, 1864 148
Monday, August 8 164
Tuesday, August 9 171
Wednesday, August 10 182
Thursday, August 11 187

Friday, August 12 .190
Saturday, August 13 .194
Sunday, August 14 .197
Monday, August 15 .201
Tuesday, August 16 .203
Wednesday, August 17 .206
Thursday, August 18 .208
Friday, August 19 .210
Chapter 3 – The raid on the Martin family .223
Chapter 4– The Great Platte River Road and its people .242
Chapter 5 – The war along the Platte .251

PART THREE

Chapter 1 – The defense of Grand Island .274
Chapter 2 – The fortification of Columbus .279
Chapter 3 – Panic in Omaha .284
Chapter 4 – The Denver Road .290
Chapter 5 – The press covers the war .293
Chapter 6 – General Curtis' second Indian campaign .302
Chapter 7 – The odyssey of the captives .312
Chapter 8 – The trail laid waste — by the White Man .334
Chapter 9 – The stages roll again .338
Chapter 10 – The close of 1864 .342
Chapter 11 – The ordeal of Nancy Morton .355
Chapter 12 – The ordeal of Lucinda Eubank .369

PART FOUR

Chapter 1 – "Reflect on times that are past" .380
Chapter 2 – "Well, what more could we do?" .394
Chapter 3 – "Her mind is somewhat impared" .410
Chapter 4 – "We felt very sad when we went through our old roaming place" .435
Chapter 5 – "This has been a glorious day for me" .444

Epilogue 449
Appendix A 451
Appendix B 454
List of Abbreviations 458
Bibliography 458
Index 468
The author 475

ILLUSTRATIONS

PART I

Bull train in Nebraska City 111
General Samuel Ryan Curtis 112
Colonel John Milton Chivington 112
General Robert B. Mitchell 112
Henson Wiseman 113

PART II

Indian Hollow 219
Drawing of the Roper cabin 220
Joseph B. Roper 220
Erastus Comstock in 1858 220
The ascent to Nine Mile Ridge 221
Oregon-California Trail seen from the Eubank homesite 222
Martin Ranch in 1866 240
George Martin 240
Ann Martin 240
Robert and Nathaniel Martin 241
Nathaniel Martin and the arrows which wounded him 241
Nancy Fletcher Morton at age 15 271
Thomas Frank Morton 271
Colonel Samuel Summers 271
Plum Creek massacre site 272

PART III

The cannon left by General Curtis at Fort Independence 330
Luther North 330

Colonel Robert Livingston 331

Frank North 331

Colonel Thomas Moonlight 331

Laura Roper and the children in Denver 332

Lucinda Eubank 332

Major Wynkoop and chiefs at the Camp Weld council 333

PART IV

Laura Roper Vance returns to The Narrows, January 13, 1929 447

The site of Laura Roper's capture at the Narrows, 1998 447

William Eubank 448

Portrait of Laura Roper Vance, 1929 448

Dedication of the monument at Oak Grove, 1918 448

LIST OF MAPS

Hostilities in Eastern Nebraska Territory prior to August 7, 1864 95

The Little Blue Valley . . . . .Foldout

Vicinity of The Narrows 154

Bob Emery's stagecoach chase, August 9, 1864 174

Major trails in eastern Nebraska Territory 225

The odyssey of the Martin Family 235

Platte Valley ranches, stations, and military posts 246

Vicinity of the Plum Creek Massacre 257

PREFACE

What author George Hyde called "the worst Indian raid in Nebraska history" occurred during three desperate days, August 7-9, 1864. Those who survived the attacks always counted those days as the most momentous of their entire lives. Yet, in terms of human destruction, these raids did not begin to approach the scale of the massacres that took place in colonial times at Jamestown or during King Philip's War, or on the Pennsylvania frontier following the defeat of Braddock. Moreover, the number killed in the Nebraska raids amounted to about seven percent of the total deaths suffered in the Minnesota Uprising just two years earlier. The attacks had no apparent effect upon Nebraska statehood or the construction of the transcontinental railroad, or even upon the Civil War, which provided the dark background against which they occurred. Why, then, should we blow the dust of 130 years from events which seemed to have so little import for our national life?

Actually, they were not unimportant to the nation at the time. The startling events in Nebraska and Colorado territories were news from coast-to-coast. The Indian War of 1864 began at the very zenith of the Oregon-California Trail, the white man's Medicine Road. It disrupted transcontinental communication through the valley of the Platte River, and spawned economic adversity, with ripple effects that were felt even in the large metropolitan areas of the East. It proved to be the opening scene of the final act of an American tragedy that wasted millions of dollars and scores of human lives—a tragedy which ended only with the complete subjugation of the Indian peoples of the plains.

The incidents of these raids also make wonderfully exciting stories. There are some touches moviemakers would love: a thrilling stagecoach chase, a howling war party attacking an unprepared wagon train, bodies bristling with arrows, and lots of blood. Over the years, these incidents became famous in their localities, unfortunately accumulating a barnacle-like crust of half truths and legends. It is time to revisit these events, strip away the accretions of time, and set them down as truthfully as possible.

It is the reason *why* these raids took place that most often escapes the story tellers. The Indian people did not go to war simply because they had nothing better to do with their time. Rather, the attacks were the result of a bewildering complexity of factors that had been a long time building. Incredibly, they had been specifically predicted over a number of years by the most knowledgeable individuals on the frontier. It has been my aim to summarize these factors, relating causes, reactions, and consequences in a holistic fashion.

The history of any conflict should be much more than a sterile recitation of facts, dates, regimental tactics, and body counts. In the words of Ora Clement (Secretary, Native Sons and Daughters of Nebraska), "History, if it is to have any meaning for us, must have its skeleton of facts clothed in a living tissue of human experience." And Eugene Ware defended his account of life along the great trails by saying, "Well, it is history, and future times will want to know what manner of men wrought out the surprising details of that age."

For me personally, the story of the Indian War of 1864 is a study of the human beings who wrought out the surprising details of the developing frontier of Nineteenth Century America—how they lived, the values they held most dear, and how they behaved under circumstances which we today can hardly imagine. I have tried to get as close to them as possible over the gulf of more than a century, and I had a great desire to solve some of the mysteries surrounding their fates. In all this I fear I have been only partly successful.

In assembling the story of these raids, I determined to work from original sources as far as possible—a noble objective, but also a frustrating one. Very few of those who were in the midst of the action ever committed their experiences to paper, and then not until many years afterward. Some of their accounts are so distorted and impossible of harmonization as to make them virtually worthless. Others, thankfully, proved quite reliable. Even so, many details of those frantic August days were never recorded and are now lost for all time.

Why did this occur?

There are several likely reasons. Most, but not all, the people in our story were quite literate. But the days following the attacks were a time of paralyzing confusion as the frontier people floated numbly eastward with the wreckage of what had been an industrious and secure society. The months and years to follow were times of backbreaking toil as they struggled to keep their families fed, sheltered, and together. They were literally starting from scratch, and they had neither the time nor energy to write a record of their experiences.

They talked about the disaster, of course. Ed Lemmon recalled that Indian raid stories were popular fare around his family hearth and table for many years to come. The survivors were happy to be interviewed and they answered questions to the best of their recollection. But, by the time their lives and fortunes had returned to a reasonable state of tranquillity, the task of writing down a detailed history of their experiences was simply too daunting. Consequently, we read in their letters phrases such as, "I can't put it all on paper," or "I could tell you if I could see you," or "I could show you if I was there."

Other factors have also contributed to a sparseness of primary source material. Strong personal feelings were considered too private to be shared in print. The pioneer people did not bother to record details of everyday life which they felt were mundane or common knowledge. Even private land transactions were not always entered into the county record books. Surveyors and census workers sometimes botched their assignments through drunkenness, negligence, or incompetence. Land records became lost through fire and transfer, and the land itself has in some places been changed by leveling and cultivation.

Incredibly, I discovered several living links with those people of 1864. In a comfortable home overlooking the California coast lives Mrs. Virginia Leasure, a granddaughter of Laura Roper who was captured by the Cheyennes. Virginia knew her famous grandmother quite well (she was fourteen years old when Laura died) and has a remarkable memory of all she saw and heard, both from Laura, and from her own mother, Nellie Vance Peak. Laura Roper may well be the most enigmatic personality in this narrative, and Virginia has formed a very realistic appraisal of her grandmother's life and character. She was also kind enough to share with me her memories and materials from her family album.

Dewey Ellis lives with his wife, Sonja, in Loveland, Colorado. It was Dewey's grandfather, William Eubank, who was carried into captivity by the Cheyennes when only six months old. The Ellises have devoted much time and patience to the study of the Eubank family, which was nearly decimated along the Little Blue River, and they granted me a very cordial interview as they were passing through Omaha on vacation.

On the original family farm in southern Hall County, Nebraska, I found Howard and Twyla Weavers. Howard's grandfather was a half brother to the Martin boys who suffered so terribly from the arrows of the Sioux. Howard has vivid memories of "Uncle Nat" showing his scars and telling his story to children in a nearby elementary school. And, even though I was a perfect stranger who showed up at their door unannounced, they bade me come in and patiently answered my questions about the old Martin place for several hours.

South of Lexington, Nebraska, I found Clyde Wallace. Clyde isn't exactly a living link with the past, but he comes mighty close. For most of his ninety-plus years, he has walked every foot of the Platte

Valley in the vicinity of the Plum Creek Massacre, and talked with the old pioneers who came to the area shortly after the raids of 1864. It was a hot, sticky day when the two of us rode around the scene of the action with Clyde drawing on his voluminous knowledge of the Oregon-California Trail to furnish a nonstop narration. At last he urged me to drive up into the bluffs south of his farm where we parked overlooking the valley which shimmered in a pastel haze below. "Isn't that just beautiful?" he remarked several times. "The most beautiful place in the world." And so it was, at least to the two of us who had been born and raised in the valley.

How often must a band of Sioux or Cheyenne or Pawnee braves sat their ponies on this same spot, looking out over the valley with its tortuously braided river, feeling the same mixture of peace and admiration that we felt? For the Indian people, too, this valley was their birthplace. From it they took their food and shelter. In it they found solace and rest, at least between raids on each other's villages. By 1864, this good life had become, for the Indians, mostly a memory. There would be a few days of rage, a short season of fear; then the Indian would be gone.

On a more technical note: In assembling this story, I found that many necessary facts and details were simply not available in any source. Many of these I have derived by charting the movements and times of individuals and wagon trains, extrapolating schedules for the Atchison-Denver stagecoaches, charting phases of the moon, adapting sunrise and sunset tables, and examining the topography of the land itself. On occasions when I was forced to speculate, I have tried to make clear in the text that I did so. What little dialogue is included was not invented, but copied verbatim from primary sources.

In times of stress, human beings tend to be emotional rather than rational creatures. With the exception of Nancy Morton, the people in our story gave only the barest indications of their personal feelings. For the sake of clothing my skeleton of facts "in a living tissue of human experience," I have attempted in a limited way to get inside their heads and hearts. This is a risky business for which I have relied upon my background in human development and special education psychology to use what information is available to make my inferences—and I have tried to be careful not to exceed my own level of expertise.

I have also attempted to describe certain events and locales so as to create for the reader a vivid mental image. However, no word painting, no photographs can create the same feelings and understandings that can be obtained by simply visiting the scenes where the events took place, whether it be the back roads of western Missouri, the ascent up onto Nine Mile Ridge, or the bluffs south of old Julesburg. In the same way, one can only comprehend the terror generated by the guerilla bushwhackers in the Kansas-Missouri border region by reading the St. Joseph newspapers from 1864 and the dispatches in *Official Records*. For those who really want to relive this story, such activities are well worth the trouble.

The problem of time was an ever present bugaboo. The system of standard time as we know it came into use in 1883, adopted by the nation's railroads out of necessity. It was not legalized until 1918 when Congress directed the Interstate Commerce Commission to establish standard time zones. Prior to 1883, each community kept its own time which was determined by the passage of the sun across the local meridian. Since there is a longitudinal difference of ten degrees between Atchison and Denver, this amounted to a differential of about forty minutes. Also, when we realize that most of the people did not carry watches in their workaday lives; that coaches and trains made the trip from Denver to Atchison faster than vice versa; that mule trains were faster than bull trains; and that speeds were generally faster in summer than in winter, it can be seen that determining times of events was a perfect joy. Happily, the sun has remained constant, for all practical purposes, in its times of rising and setting over the centuries, helping to stabilize the fluidity of frontier time.

In noting and crediting sources, I have used a dual system which will surely bring down the wrath of professional historians everywhere. For direct quotations, ideas, or material borrowed from the work of others, I have given credit in conventional endnotes. But the narratives in Parts 2 and 3 are built up from such a multitude of sources that nearly every other sentence would require multiple credits; and to spell out the logical proofs and sources for derived details would make the notes more voluminous than the text, and the reader's task prohibitively tedious. Therefore, in addition to the endnotes, I have simply listed my sources of information at the end of each subsection in Parts 2, 3, and 4.

A few terms deserve explanation. By *High Plains* I refer to that area of Oklahoma, Kansas, Colorado, Nebraska, and the Dakotas lying between the Rocky Mountains and the 100th meridian, which is a line drawn roughly between Pierre, South Dakota and Dodge City, Kansas. *Great Plains* refers to the central United States west of the Mississippi River. In referring to the Indian people, I have used the terms *aboriginal* and *indigenous* according to their dictionary sense, which means simply the people who were there (on the plains) first.

The term *wild tribes* applies to the Cheyennes, Sioux, Comanches, Arapahoes, and other warlike nomadic tribes of the High Plains, as opposed to the more sedentary tribes such as the Pawnees and Omahas. It is a term used by George Bent, himself a half-breed Cheyenne, when he writes, "The Indians were wild people in those days" (Hyde, *Life of George Bent,* 139).

A few terms are archaic, such as *horse equipments*. I have kept them because they occur in the primary sources and are not difficult to understand. For those who are curious, I ought also to say that *mountain howitzers* were light brass cannons, having short barrels that weighed about 220 pounds. Normally mounted on a carriage with small wheels, they could be easily disassembled for transport on the backs of pack animals. Little used by the Civil War armies in the east, they were of great utility on the plains because of their mobility.

ACKNOWLEDGEMENTS

It was inevitable that, during the seven years I spent working on this project, I would lose some of my helpers. Thus it was a sad day for western historians and friends of the old trail when Clyde Wallace passed away in November 1996. Also, I had planned, just for sentimental reasons, to make my final photo tour of the Little Blue Valley on August 7, 1996—the 132nd anniversary of the great Sunday raid. Instead, I spent the forepart of the day at the bedside of my mother, who was coming to the end of a long period of suffering from Alzheimer's Disease. She left me shortly before noon—another reason why August 7 will always be a special day for me.

All my research began with the foundation prepared by others who have gone before, particularly George Bird Grinnell, George Hyde, John Ellenbecker, and Addison Sheldon, the former director of the Nebraska State Historical Society. In addition to the "living links" aforementioned, many other people and institutions have willingly cooperated in locating materials for this study. They deserve to be recognized, for without them, this book would be no more than a pamphlet. My sincere thanks to the cordial and competent personnel of the following:

Adair County Courthouse; Kirksville, Missouri
Gage County Courthouse; Beatrice, Nebraska
Hall County Courthouse; Grand Island, Nebraska
Henry County Courthouse; Cambridge, Illinois
McHenry County Courthouse; Woodstock, Illinois
Moniteau County Courthouse and Office of the City Clerk; California, Missouri
Nemaha County Courthouse; Seneca, Kansas
Otoe County Courthouse; Nebraska City, Nebraska
Platte County Courthouse; Columbus, Nebraska
Pottawattamie County Courthouse; Council Bluffs, Iowa

I owe a further debt of gratitude to the following institutions and individuals:

Bob Wallace, former director, Dawson County, Nebraska, Historical Society

Carol Green, Director, Genoa, Nebraska Historical Society
Catherine Renschler, Director, Adams County, Nebraska Historical Society
Colorado Historical Society, Stephen H. Hart Library
Gage County, Nebraska Historical Society
Illinois Historical Museum
Iowa State Historical Society
Kansas State Historical Society
Marshall County, Kansas Historical Society
Missouri State Archives
Montana Historical Society
National Archives; Washington, D. C. and Kansas City, Missouri
Nebraska State Historical Society
United Methodist Research Center; Lincoln, Nebraska
Wyoming Historical Society
Bennett Martin Public Library; Lincoln, Nebraska
Council Bluffs , Iowa Public Library
Crown Point, Indiana Community Library
Denver Public Library, Western History Department
The Depot Museum; Julesburg, Colorado
Hastings, Nebraska Museum
Marysville, Kansas Public Library
Midcontinent Public Library; Independence, Missouri
Missouri Valley Room, Kansas City, Missouri Public Library
Morton-James Public Library; Nebraska City, Nebraska
Ottumwa, Iowa Public Library
Quincy, Illinois Public Library
St. Bonaventure Catholic Parish; Columbus, Nebraska
Seneca, Kansas Public Library
Stuhr Museum of the Prairie Pioneer; Grand Island, Nebraska, and Russ Czaplewski
W. Dale Clark Library; Omaha, Nebraska

I also received assistance from a number of people possessing specific areas of knowledge. Dr. Gene Brott of Concordia College in Seward, Nebraska, worked out a computer program which gave me the lunar tables for the year 1864. Mr. Gene Hughes of the Stuhr Museum accompanied me to the banks of the Wood River on a pleasant March afternoon. There, still togged out in his Civil War uniform following a re-enactment for some youngsters, Gene paced back and forth with his witching rods until he had "confirmed" the location of the grave which holds the remains of the Smith and Anderson victims of 1862. If, in fact, we really did find a grave, it wasn't that of the

Smith and Anderson people. Local citizens pinpointed the supposed site nearly a half mile away. Rob Bozell, archaeologist with the Nebraska Museum of History, was kind enough to attempt a confirmation of the site, with the permission of Mr. Gene Monson, who farms the property. On a cold, rainy afternoon, we all gathered on the banks of the Wood River to find the Smiths and Andersons, but our probing was inconclusive. Probably in the end, it really doesn't matter where their bones are resting. What's done is done. But I would still like to know who or what, if anything, is buried beneath the first site.

Russ Genung is a native of Oak, Nebraska, and president of the Nebraska chapter of the Oregon-California Trails Association. His guided tours of the area around The Narrows helped me to pinpoint significant locations and landmarks from which I developed my maps.

It was also my good fortune to find temporary employment with two people who literally grew up on top of the Oregon-California Trail near the site of Little Blue Station. Glenn Cederberg and Joyce Vannier, both employees of the Lincoln Public Schools, contributed a great deal of time in reading portions of the manuscript and in helping me to understand the topography of the area.

In order to see that topography from a different perspective, I enlisted the aid of one of my former teachers, Mr. Charles Krutz, now retired from the faculty of Concordia Teachers College. A gifted musician, creative teacher, golfer, tennis player, and modern day Renaissance man, Krutz is also a skilled pilot. Armed with a pile of county grid maps, and with son Jim Krutz along as navigator, the three of us flew over the Little Blue Valley to take aerial photos of some of the historic sites along the old trail. Other than encountering a few white-knuckle thermals, it was an enjoyable experience too soon ended.

Some of my most pleasant hours of research were spent at the Historical Research Center of the Stuhr Museum in Grand Island, Nebraska. It seems like every time I stopped there, the weather was brutally cold. Inside, though, I knew Tom Anderson would be ready and willing to lead the way to the coffeepot. Tom is a journalist turned local historian who was then working as curator of photographs at the museum. He provided most of my information, both print and oral tradition, about the events which occurred along the Grande Ile of the Platte; and it was Tom who cheerfully assured me that no one had ever yet written a perfect book, and I was not about to be the first to do so.

I also found, in the early stages of my research, that wherever I went, it seemed like Lyn Ryder had been there before me, asking many of the same questions. After seeing her *Tragedy on the Little*

Blue, I decided she could be very helpful, so I gave her a call. That was the beginning of a very fruitful collaboration. For several years we have exchanged bits and pieces of information, Lyn working in Denver and I in Nebraska. Much of what I know about the Eubank and Uhlig families is a direct result of her work; for Lyn believes, as do I, that those people really *are* the story and deserve to be remembered.

At last I was ready to write my rough draft, which was typed on a 1940 Underwood. Several drafts and countless revisions later, I definitely needed some wizardry to help me put the manuscript into an electronic format. To the rescue came the Reverend Jeffrey McPike—one of my former fifth grade students who, in his present life, is a computer whiz, friend, and associate pastor of a large Lutheran church. Now Jeff became the teacher and I the novice, a reversal of roles which I enjoyed thoroughly.

It is my fervent wish that all of us working together have been able to produce a document which does some justice to the human beings who are its subjects—people whose existence we seek to understand more fully, and whose actions we seek to view more compassionately. We can but hope that the historians of 2150 A.D. will write our stories with the same grace.

Part I

But why should I mourn at the untimely fate of my people?
Tribe follows tribe, and nation follows nation, like the waves of the sea.
It is the order of nature, and regret is useless.

Seattle, Chief of the Dwamish, 1854

Part I
Chapter One

A day in August

On a promontory of the low bluffs, the watchers stood motionless, silent, and very uncomfortable in the August heat. Below them spread the panorama of the Little Blue Valley, its cottonwoods, wild plums, and elderberries wearing a thousand values of forest green and spotted here and there by splashes of red sumac. The far side of the valley shimmered in a velvety blue haze while among the trees, the grey-brown waters of the Little Blue River tumbled between low banks. Under a brassy sun, trees and river floated serenely on a light green ocean of native bluestem and buffalo grass. The sweltering day was relieved only by occasional puffs of breeze that wandered fitfully among the eroded bluffs.

The watchers fixed their attention on a pastoral scene taking place in the valley below. There, rather inconspicuous in the world of grass and riverbank brush, a small group of travelers ambled along the old Oregon Trail. The two women wore long sleeved dresses and bonnets, while the man following closely behind wore the loose, dull garb of a pioneer farmer. One of the women carried an infant, while a small girl toddled alongside, slowing the progress of the group to a crawl. But then, they seemed to be in no hurry as they laughed and talked among themselves, obviously enjoying the walk and each other's company.

The first warnings came as the travelers drew even with the bluff—savage, guttural yells and piercing screams from back down river, cutting through the buoyant air. The travelers turned and stood still for a second or two, wrestling with their indecision. Then, women and children scurried toward the river to take shelter in the thick brush, while the man sprinted back the way they had come. He had run no more than a few yards when several dusky, half-naked horsemen appeared from around a bend in the trail. At their first war cries, the man turned to run desperately toward the river, only to be struck down violently on the grassy bank.

As the terrible riders continued upriver, the little girl gave a high, childish scream from the hiding place. In an instant, the horsemen flushed the women and children from cover. The chase was pitifully short. From atop the bluffs, the women's bodies appeared doll-like alongside the powerful animals. Roughly, the survivors were thrust up onto the horses, and the group turned back downriver. The distant screaming ceased, and as horses and riders were swallowed up among the oaks and cottonwoods at the bend of the trail, peace returned to the valley. Where seconds before there had been a carefree group of friends walking idly along, there was now only an empty silence and the tortured body of the man, lying like a pile of old rags on the riverbank.

The watchers on the bluff had not moved. The drama had taken place so quickly they had scarcely time to draw more than a dozen breaths. Now, slowly, they began to turn away from the quiet valley, walking mostly in silence, absorbed in the meaning of what they had just witnessed, disturbed by the "death" of the pioneer farmer who even now was coming back to life on the riverbank, and would soon join the watchers and the "Indians" at a barbecue.

What had taken place in the valley of the Little Blue that day was a re-enactment of the 1864 massacre of settlers by Cheyenne, Sioux, and Arapaho Indians. The drama is staged periodically by residents in the area of Oak, Nebraska, some of whom are descendants of those first settlers in the valley.

It was a small action, as such things are measured—a brief, opening act in the drama of the Indian War of 1864—a conflagration which eventually extended from the Rocky Mountains to the Missouri River, and from the Niobrara to the Arkansas and beyond. As with every war, there is really no way to accurately measure its cost in lives and property destroyed. Many of its victims remain nameless. Yet, the killing of the farmer on the riverbank and the capture of his wife and children has been remembered because we know their names and something of their personal sagas. In their experiences are distilled all the agonies of all the human victims of every war ever fought.

The people who died that day, and those who survived, were rather ordinary folk: a self-righteous preacher; a bluff, hard-working rancher who was just a little fond of strong drink; a redheaded teamster; a Mormon couple traveling through; pregnant women, infants, children, teenagers, hired hands. They were Irish, English, and German—people with names such as Uhlig, Kelley, Hunt, Comstock, and Gilbert. They were in the valley that day because opportunity had led them there—opportunity and their dreams of having a place of their own on which to find happiness and security in the labors of their hands. They were a tough, remarkable people.

The re-enactment at Oak is held in commemoration of their lives, particularly those lives that ended that August 7, 1864. For most of them, there are no graves to be decorated on Memorial Day, no tombstones by which to lay a small bouquet. But who, for that matter, knows the place where lie the bones of Lean Bear and Star and Little Heart? Who can recite the names of the Cheyenne innocent done to death at Cedar Canyon or along Sand Creek? Their only floral tributes are the meadow rose and smartweed of the prairies; their last resting place is known only to God.

Part of the tragedy of those remembered dead, and of those who loved them, is that, in their lifetimes, they never fully understood why they became victims, or why there had to be a war at all. It is left to us, the watchers on the bluff, to puzzle out the answer, in the faith that every individual who understands *why* contributes a small measure to the endless struggle toward human nobility.

Perhaps there would have been no violence along the Little Blue River that hot August day, nothing to watch from the bluffs so many years later, if it had not been for the forces that caused those people to leave their former homes: economic hardship, social turmoil, and civil war. Drawn westward by ambition, enterprise, free land, and a mystical national sentiment known as Manifest Destiny, they came to the prairie on a road driven through the homelands of an indigenous people who, at the end, were left no real choice between physical and cultural extinction.

More than a decade earlier, the Indian people had watched the awesome procession of wagons crawling along that road, the Oregon-California Trail; and, sensing the irresistible power of the westward migration, they had christened it the White Man's Medicine Road. So, in our quest to understand *why*, we must begin by revisiting the forces which brought the Medicine Road into being.

Part I
Chapter Two
"They had no hope left to keep any land"

It really wasn't much of a trail in the early years—hardly more than a few buffalo paths and matted tracks in the tall bluestem grass and some scratches on rocky ridges. From its origin at Independence, Missouri, the Oregon Trail found its way across the northeast corner of present Kansas to the south bank of the Platte River in central Nebraska. Following the Platte and North Platte across Nebraska and Wyoming, it jumped to the Snake River in southern Idaho and thence across the Blue Mountains to the Columbia, arriving in Oregon's Willamette Valley after an odyssey of 2,020 miles, give or take a few.

First traveled from west to east in 1812-1813 by Robert Stuart, an employee of John Jacob Astor's fur company, the route remained little used until the early 1840s. By that time, changes in the national life were causing Americans to turn their eyes toward the West in search of a new life untrammeled by rampant urbanization and industrialization. A financial panic in 1837 deepened into a national depression By 1842, crop prices in Missouri and neighboring states had sunk so low that farmers were burning their corn and bacon for fuel.

Early adventurers sent back glowing reports from the far Oregon Country, singing the praises of its rich soil, temperate climate, and bountiful resources, all there just for the taking. Financially strapped farmers and others who just plain resented being hemmed in looked to the West and thought to themselves, "Why not Oregon? If so-and-so made it, so can I."

There was also a nationalistic motive driving the mass removal to Oregon. Following the Revolutionary War, negotiations between the infant United States and Great Britain never quite settled the question of Canadian boundaries. In the far West, the United States insisted on a boundary at fifty-four degrees forty minutes north latitude while Britain held out for the forty-ninth parallel. In the absence of more creative statesmanship, the two nations, in 1818, signed an agreement to occupy the Northwest Country jointly, thus forestalling the day of reckoning. No one argued that Great Britain had the right of ownership by virtue of first possession. But that nation appeared less interested in settlement than in the fur trade. It was apparent that the question of national ownership would eventually be decided simply by whichever country had the most citizens living in the disputed territory. Thus by his removal to Oregon Country, a man might not only improve living conditions for himself and his family, but he could also do his part in gaining this fertile, timbered land for his nation so recently forged in the fires of revolution.

So the westward migration began. Following in the footsteps of missionaries and fur traders, the first organized party of sixty-nine settlers left the rendezvous on the Missouri border in 1841, guided by mountain man Tom Fitzpatrick. Though about half their number left the trail in southern Idaho for California, the remainder continued on to Oregon. From that time, the yearly migrations increased in size, and the letters that the new settlers sent back to friends and family in "the states" continued to fuel the engine of emigration. Folks whose grandparents left New England for Pennsylvania; whose parents moved on to Tennessee or Kentucky or Missouri, piled their earthly possessions into farm wagons and steeled themselves for the six-month journey across plains and mountains to a new home in a rich, if disputed, land.[1]

The land which lay between Missouri and Oregon was not uninhabited. Aboriginal peoples had dwelt in the plains and mountains for many hundreds of years. As the first wagon trains struggled through their country, these native people were friendly, even admirous of the early wayfarers, quite oblivious to the impact which this society of robust, white-skinned adventurers would have upon their own.

The first hundred miles of the Oregon Trail wound through the lands of the Shawnees, Delawares, and Wyandottes, people whose history bore eloquent testimony to that impact. It was not a history whose lessons were well understood as yet by the Indian people of the far West.

The Europeans who founded Jamestown in the tidewater region of Virginia encountered a native population confederated under Chief Powhatan, and quickly proved themselves as inept in their dealings with the Indians as they were in their own domestic affairs. Relations between the English and Indians sputtered along uncertainly with interludes of revolting brutality until 1614, when Powhatan's daughter, Pocahontas, took up the Christian faith and married colonist John Rolfe. A period of tranquility followed until the death of Powhatan in 1618. Under his successor, Opechancanough, the peace deteriorated sharply.

On March 22, 1622 (ironically, Good Friday), Opechancanough's warriors spread out among the James River plantations, supposedly on trading expeditions. In a sudden, barbarous uprising, they massacred 347 white colonists (black slaves were unharmed)—nearly one of every four settlers in the tidewater region. A war of revenge quite naturally followed, and the Indian tribes were greatly weakened. Again in 1644, an aged Opechancanough orchestrated the massacre of 500 more colonists. This time the reprisals wrought the end of the Powhatan confederation and its chief. An outraged militiaman shot the captive Opechancanough in the back.

Affairs between Indians and colonists began more peacefully in New England, due chiefly to the fact that the Puritans and Separatists were a more disciplined people on what they viewed as a more noble mission. From the very first, the Pilgrims of Plymouth Plantation formed a sort of mutual aid society with the neighboring Wampanoags and their sachem, Massasoit. By combining deft negotiations with an often illusory show of armed might, the Pilgrims maintained a peace with the Wampanoags which endured for forty years. Sadly, such forthright and positive diplomacy proved the exception rather than the rule in New England.

On May 25, 1637, a force of Puritans and friendly Narragansett allies, acting on ill-founded suspicions, attacked a Pequot Indian fortress on the Mystic River. At slight loss to themselves, the Puritans managed to kill between 500 and 700 Pequots. Many of the Indians were burned to death inside their flaming fortress, and the affair was so ghastly that the Narragansetts begged the whites to stop the killing.

In time, even the amicable relations between Plymouth and the Wampanoags began to fray at the edges. As a second generation of leaders assumed control of both societies, the Pilgrims came to view their Indian neighbors with increasing suspicion. Massasoit died about 1660 and was succeeded first by his eldest son, Wamsutta, and then by his younger son, Metacomet, whom the English had named King Philip. The racial and political atmosphere continued to thicken with suspicions, charges, and provocations, and in 1675, the Indians laid their grievances before a delegation of mediators from Rhode Island colony:

> *They said they had been the first in doing good to the English, and the English in doing wrong . . . if twenty of their honest Indians testified that an Englishman had done them wrong, it was as nothing, and if but one of their worst Indians testified against any Indian or their king (sachem), when it pleased the English that was sufficient . . . They did not want any of their Indians to be called or forced to be Christian Indians . . . when their kings sold land, the English would later say it was more than they agreed to . . . some being given to drunkenness were made drunk by the English and then cheated in the bargaining . . . now they had no hopes left to keep any land.*[2]

It was an eloquent plaint but all for naught. From 1675 to 1678, King Philip's War raged across New England, leaving more than 6,000 Indians and 3,000 white colonists dead. In terms of percentage of population killed, this was the most severe conflict ever to be fought on the North American continent.[3] When it ended, only fifty-eight years after Plymouth Colony had been planted among the Wampanoags, the power and society of the New England Indians was shattered. But, as author Russell Bourne pointed out, even though the conflict was largely between red people and white, "it is difficult to find in New England of the seventeenth century a pattern of built-in racial murderousness, on either side. There was simply not the confidence and wisdom and political skill to make one culture of two that were not that different."[4] Be that as it may, the pattern had been cut for the conquest of all the aboriginal peoples of the United States.

Following the catastrophe which befell the Indians of New England, the tide of colonization swept westward to engulf the tribes of the old Northwest—the Delawares, Shawnees, Eries, Ottawas, Hurons, Chippewas, and Pottawattamies. From 1689 to 1763, these people found themselves embroiled, along with their eastern cousins, in the four Colonial Wars (French and Indian Wars), confusing affairs in which at times everyone seemed to be fighting everyone else. When the major North American action ended in 1760, the Indians of the Ohio Valley and Great Lakes region found themselves hemmed in by a network of British forts, and infiltrated by the inevitable migration of white settlers over the Appalachian Mountains. Disgusted with the broken promises of the English, their arrogance and seizure of Indian lands, an Ottawa chief named Pontiac incited the trans-Allegheny tribes to a bloody rebellion in 1763. In a grim reprise of King Philip's War, the insurgents captured every British post in the Ohio Valley except Pittsburgh and Detroit. The wilderness regions of Virginia, Maryland, and Pennsylvania were ravaged, and the line of white settlement rolled back beyond the Appalachians. But aid from the recently-vanquished French proved to be only Pontiac's hopeful illusion, and following Colonel Henry Bouquet's victory at the Battle of Bushy Run, the rebellion fell to pieces.

When, little more than a decade later, the colonists' quarrel with the mother country turned to revolution, the native peoples decided to sit this one out. "This is a Quarrell between Father and Children," proclaimed the powerful Iroquois nation. "We shall not meddle with it."[5] But the hostility of the frontiersmen and the pressure of their settlements upon Indian territory eventually forced the Delawares, Shawnees, Cherokees, Chippewas, Mohawks, and Senecas into the war on the side of Great Britain. As before, the Indian people came out the poorer for their allegiance. As the conflict ground to a halt, the majority of the survivors of the once-proud Six Nations of the Iroquois fled to British protection in Canada.

With the adoption of a constitution and the election of a government, the new United States of America began putting its house in order. During these formative years, there arose among the Shawnees a mighty prophet whose ambitious dream was the confederation of all the aboriginal peoples from the Great Lakes to Florida to halt further cession of Indian lands to the white people. Tecumseh's message found willing ears among the tribes, but his dream began to go sour in 1811 when General William Henry Harrison claimed a triumph over the Shawnees at the Battle of Tippecanoe. The dream faded completely when Harrison's soldiers killed Tecumseh in Ontario during the War of 1812.

Throughout this period, the uncontrolled and unofficial policy of westward migration had the practical effect of forcing the Indian people westward as well. It required but little effort to turn this movement into official government policy. During his presidency, Thomas Jefferson proposed the removal of all eastern Indians to regions west of the Mississippi River where white settlement was considered impractical. As Secretary of War in the Monroe administration, John C. Calhoun suggested that the Indians be given vocational training so that, once relocated on the Central Plains, they might subsist themselves as did the white man. Finally, in 1825, President James Monroe presented Congress with a plan calling for the removal of all eastern Indians to the plains west of the Mississippi.

When Andrew Jackson acceded to the presidency, he brought with him a frontiersman's hostility to the Indians, and a determination to rid the eastern United States of their presence. In 1830, the Indian Removal Act passed Congress, and negotiators went out among the tribes to obtain their legal consent. Between 1829 and 1837, the United States concluded no less than ninety-four treaties with the affected tribes.[6]

Some resisted. Sauk Chief Black Hawk fought a desperate war against the settlers of Illinois country until he had only a handful of people left. In the south, the Five Civilized Tribes, which had actually come quite far on the road to assimilation into white society, were forced to move anyway. Throughout the latter 1830s, the Choctaws, Creeks, Chickasaws, and Cherokees were pushed westward along the "Trail of Tears" into Indian Territory in present day Oklahoma. The Seminoles would have none of it, however. Under Chief Osceola, they conducted a protracted and costly war until 1842, when they, too, were overcome and sent west. With the relocation of the broken tribes of the old Northwest—the Shawnees, Delawares, Ottawas, Pottawattamies, and their cousins—to the Missouri River Valley, the Indian problems of the developing nation had been neatly settled, or so it seemed at the time.

In the 1830s, no one was thinking in terms of a continental United States. Previous explorations had pronounced the High Plains uninhabitable for white people, and beyond the plains lay the forbidding ranges of the Rocky Mountain system. It only made sense to push the Indians into this wasteland where they might remain untroubled by white invaders, and incidentally form a barrier against surprise incursions from Mexico.

Of course the Mississippi River proved to be no barrier to the westward migration, nor did the Missouri. Thus it was that the first miles of the Oregon Trail wound through the country of a people who had been thoroughly trampled by the westward sweep of the young nation. After reaching the Platte River, the trail continued its climb toward the Rockies, passing now through the lands of aboriginal people for whom the old process of conquest and removal had barely begun.

Throughout the 1840s, the reaction of the Indians to the Oregon migration remained benign, even friendly. But, unlike the intermingled and co-dependent societies of settler and Indian in Seventeenth Century New England, the cultural and racial differences between emigrants and Indians on the High Plains were formidable. With the increasing numbers and size of the wagon trains came increasing friction between the races. Small incidents became insults, misunderstandings over trifles became major irritants, and letters soon began flowing to congressional delegations demanding a military presence along the trail to cow the obstreperous Indians into proper submission.

In 1829, the government began sending infantry escorts with the freight caravans traversing the Santa Fe Trail.[7] Captain Henry Wharton's company of sixty dragoons, which escorted the 1834 train to Santa Fe, was the first U.S. cavalry unit to serve on the western plains.[8] As attention began to focus on the route to Oregon, the army was directed to send Lieutenant John C. Fremont to find the best possible routes for the annual migration. Fremont's report of 1842 concluded that a military show of force was indeed necessary to maintain a respectful attitude among the plains tribes, and that the area near the fur trading post of Fort Laramie would be an ideal location for an army post as well.

When James K. Polk became president in 1845, he immediately dispatched an expedition under Colonel Stephen Watts Kearny along the Oregon Trail to intimidate the wild tribes by a show of might that included mountain howitzers and military rockets.[9] Kearny's mission seems to have accomplished its purpose, and it was his opinion that such an expedition along the trail every two or three years would be sufficient to keep the Indians properly submissive. President Polk disagreed, and recommended to Congress that stockades and blockhouses be erected along the trail from the Missouri River all the way to the Rockies.[10] Thomas Hart Benton pushed through the enabling legislation in 1846, and work began on Fort Kearny on the Missouri (at present day Nebraska City). The choice of a site was not well thought out, and from the first it was clear that a fort along the middle Missouri was too far east to protect anybody from anything. In 1848, the post was moved nearer the junction of the Oregon Trail with the Platte River at the head of the Grande Ile. The following year, the government purchased Fort Laramie from the American Fur Company for $4,000; the Mounted Riflemen established Cantonment Loring near the fur trading post of Fort Hall; and the U. S. Army had established its presence along the Oregon Trail.

The army found itself very busy indeed, for the years 1849 and 1850 witnessed emigrations of 30,000 and 50,000 wayfarers along the trail, most of whom left it at Soda Springs to angle southwestward to the gold fields of California.[11] So great was the impact of the gold rush that the name "Oregon Trail" gave way to "California Road," although the army maintained the term "Oregon Route" until 1854.[12]

The effect of the emigrations of these years upon the plains Indians was nothing less than shock and dismay. Under the ceaseless milling of ironshod hooves and wheels, the Oregon-California Trail became an ugly, bare scar across the face of the earth. For a mile or more on either side, the white men's cattle nibbled the prairie grass down to the ground. Where the Indians made their campfires with windfalls and driftwood from the rivers, the emigrants chopped down the scarce timber wherever they found it. The trail corridor itself became a vast trash dump as travelers discarded heavy plows, stoves, tools, and furniture that overburdened their wagons and wore out their draft animals. Most alarming of all, the whites wantonly slaughtered the buffalo they found near the trail, using little for food and leaving the rest to rot. By 1850, the buffalo had begun to move farther back from the trail, slowly parting to form great northern and southern herds. Since the plains Indians' very existence depended upon these animals, the Oregon-California Trail made it increasingly difficult for them to procure the necessary food and shelter.

Awestruck and mystified by the force of the emigration, the Indians coined their own term for the trail: the White Man's Medicine Road. And they wondered: Were there still any white people left in the East? And why had those blue coated soldiers come to build their camps along the Medicine Road?[13] True, there had been some thievery and intimidation of the emigrants, mostly the work of a few hotheaded young warriors; but, other than this, the Sioux and Cheyenne people allowed the white-topped caravans to pass through their country unmolested. Evidently, the soldiers had come to police the emigrants, and were doing a rather poor job of it. Therefore, the Indians would take their concerns to the agent which the white man's government had appointed to manage its contacts with the wild tribes. Perhaps the agent could make the whites understand how these thousands of travelers with their wagons and cattle were causing great hardships and ill will among the Indian people.

In truth, that agent had for several years been exerting himself in behalf of his Indian charges. He had traveled ceaselessly across the plains, waging a one-man public relations campaign to placate the aroused tribes, and he championed their cause in official Washington. He realized that the situation could not long continue as it was. The nation needed to make some effort to compensate the Indians for the loss of their livelihood and address their grievances. On their part, the tribes needed to adapt themselves to the changes being wrought around them. From his farsighted concern came one of the most remarkable events ever to occur on the High Plains.

Chapter Two notes

[1] Excellent general sources on the Oregon Trail are Irene Paden's *The Wake of the Prairie Schooner* and Jay Monaghan's *The Oregon Trail.* Franzwa's *The Oregon Trail Revisited* is sprightly and readable, and Lavender's *Westward Vision* concentrates on the period from the discovery of the New World until 1846.

[2] Easton, John. "A Relacion of the Indyan Warre." In Charles Lincoln, ed., *Narratives of the Indian Wars, 1675 - 1699.* n.p., New York, 1913. A more lengthy quotation appears in Horowitz, *The First Frontier*, Page 63.

[3] Bourne, *The Red King's Rebellion*, jacket, 242.

[4] Ibid., 246.

[5] Horowitz, *The First Frontier*, 225.

[6] Lavender, *Bent's Fort*, 165.

[7] Ibid., 92.

[8] Ibid., 164.

[9] Grinnell, *The Fighting Cheyennes*, 99.

[10] Nadeau, *Fort Laramie*, 61.

[11] Mattes, *The Great Platte River Road*, 23.

[12] Post returns from Fort Kearny, Nebraska Territory.

[13] McFarling, *Exploring the Northern Plains*, 217.

Part I
Chapter Three

"Bad management or some untoward misfortune"

There never had been a gathering quite like it. For nearly four weeks in September 1851 some 10,000 Indians, many of them traditional enemies, camped, feasted, and counciled together on the plains below Fort Laramie. In and amongst the tribes were some three hundred white soldiers, frontiersmen, and government officials, men who would bring the words of the Great Father to his red children.

The "Big Talk" was the brainchild of Tom Fitzpatrick, who had charge of the Upper Platte and Arkansas Agency created by the government in 1846. Fitzpatrick's qualifications were excellent. Born in Ireland in 1799, he ascended the Missouri River in 1822 with Ashley's Hundred. He went on to become a major partner in the Rocky Mountain Fur Company, guided the westward migrations of '41 and '42 and served as chief guide with Kearny's 1845 expedition. From his agency at Bent's Fort on the Arkansas, Fitzpatrick had the awesome task of administering the affairs of the Cheyennes, Arapahoes, Commanches, Kiowas, and a portion of the Sioux nation. His unofficial partnership with the trader, William Bent, brought to the agency a wealth of knowledge and experience unsurpassed by any other two white men on the frontier. Both knew that the old ways of tribal life had begun to pass away with the advent of the first white traders, and could never be restored.

In 1848, Fitzpatrick conceived the notion of holding a massive peace conference with the wild tribes of the plains. The meeting would be an attempt to bring a halt to the intertribal wars by reserving specific areas for hunting and roaming for each tribe. It would attempt to end friction between emigrants and Indians by restricting white emigration to certain corridors which guaranteed safe passage through Indian hunting grounds, and would also offer compensation in goods to offset the losses and damage already suffered by the tribes. The goals of the Big Talk were certainly idealistic, but it was an idealism born of desperation. The tide of white emigration had become irresistible and the Indian was left no choice but to adapt or disappear.

Even though Fitzpatrick won the earnest support of David Mitchell, Superintendent of Indian Affairs, Congress did not approve funds for the conference until the spring of 1851. The council itself was scheduled to begin at Fort Laramie on September 1 of that year.[1]

The Commanches, Kiowas, and Apaches refused to come so far north to camp among so many enemies. Even so, the vast throng that assembled included Brule and Ogalala Sioux, Arapahoes, Cheyennes, Assiniboins, Gros Ventres, Mandans, Shoshones, Crows, interpreters, mountain men, three troops of cavalry, a company of infantry, and agents, including Mitchell and Fitzpatrick. Even Jim Bridger and the ubiquitous Father Pierre De Smet were on hand.

The hunting had not gone well that summer. The Indians attending the council were poor and hungry, and plainly realized their dependence on the white man. Eventually, the participants reached an accord that allotted to each tribe a certain domain between the Platte and Arkansas Rivers. Because the buffalo were being forced away from their traditional grazing areas, all the tribes would be allowed to hunt anywhere in the region. For its part, the government agreed to protect the Indians from the depredations of ruthless white men and to pay annuities valued at $50,000 per year for the next fifty years. To facilitate communication and responsibility, Mitchell insisted that each tribe choose one chief who could speak in behalf of his people. The tribes complied except for the Sioux, who found the request so alien to their culture that they were unable to agree on a candidate. At last Mitchell proposed a Brule chief known as Conquering Bear, or Scattering Bear, and the Sioux rubber-stamped his decision.

There seems to have been a curious psychology at work among the Indians at the council. As the days passed, a mood of peace and brotherhood took root among the people. Even when Mitchell moved the council site downriver to Horse Creek, there was little grumbling or dissension. Such traditional enemies as Sioux and Shoshones treated each other with a kindly solicitude and spoke of the old wars as times to be buried and forgotten. As the council broke up and the Indians went their various ways, there was in the air a heady conviction that an unprecedented era of peace was dawning on the High Plains.

Father De Smet, all aglow over his spectacular achievement of baptizing 1,194 Indian and half breed children, confidently predicted that the treaty signed at Horse Creek would "be the commencement of a new era for the Indians—an era of peace. In future, peaceable citizens may cross the desert unmolested, and the Indian will have little to dread from the bad white man, for justice will be rendered to him."[2]

The Indians may not have seen things quite that way. Their chiefs allowed themselves to be lectured, and frankly confessed their poverty and dependence. In the end, they agreed to the treaty because they had no better choice. The agreement had been imperfectly conceived and was probably unworkable even before it was consummated, but Mitchell and Fitzpatrick had no better choice, either. In a desperate attempt to prevent the inevitable plains war, they were grasping at straws and probably got the best that could be had, thanks in part to the forbearance of the Indians. In his report to the commissioner in Washington, Mitchell stressed that the Indians had demonstrated their good faith in signing the treaty, and warned: "Nothing but bad management or some untoward misfortune can ever break it."[3]

In less than thirteen years, the treaty would be a dead letter. The plains would be aflame, and the Oregon-California Trail would be smeared with blood and smudged with the smoking ruins of wagons and road ranches.

How did things go so very wrong?

Perhaps the course of history could not have been denied; however, the dreary saga of the unraveling of the peace obtained at Horse Creek is a complex mechanism of factors, all of which can be classed as either "bad management" or "untoward misfortune." To properly understand the roots of the Indian War of 1864, it is instructive to examine the circumstances, incidents, and personalities in this saga, to witness from the distance of a century and a third how they all conspired together to wreck the new era of peace and brotherhood which flamed so briefly in the camps along Horse Creek. At the heart of the disintegration of this new era was the incompatibility which existed in every phase of the red and white cultures—their mores and manners, modes of subsistence, social organization, and concepts of property rights and land ownership. This cultural mismatch would prove so profound that the two peoples simply could not, or would not accommodate each other.

When the first Europeans landed on the east coast, they were armed with patents issued by their governments. In their eyes, legal title to lands in the New World had already been established by virtue of the discovery of these lands by a Christian monarch. Therefore, they had a perfect right to settle wherever they pleased within the bounds of their patents.

In addition to the "right of discovery," there existed in their culture a right of possession over lands not already settled or cultivated. Wrote Governor John Winthrop of Massachusetts Bay Colony, "As for the Natives of New England, they enclose noe land, neither have any setled habytation, nor any tame Cattle to improve the land by . . . Soe as if we leave them sufficient for their use, we may lawfully take the rest."[4]

There existed a third method by which land might be acquired, namely the right of purchase. In this way, lands already settled or cultivated by the Indians could be had in exchange for material goods which they desired.

Closely related to the rights of land ownership was the concept of property rights. The colonists arrived in the New World with well-defined ideas regarding the sanctity of private property, ideas which had evolved over centuries and which still form the basis of our system of laws. They recognized that, while a property owner may have had a moral obligation to share his worldly goods with those in need (especially if he was a Christian), he had no legal obligation to do so. The right of the owner was preeminent over the needs of society in all but the most serious of occasions. Also, the taking of property without the consent of the owner was an offense, not against the owner, but against the society or the state.

These foregoing conventions meant nothing to the Indians. In their culture, no one could ever really own the land, its wildlife, or its waters. The Great Spirit had made these things for all his people, though it was possible to reserve (by force, if necessary) a portion of the creation for the exclusive use of an individual tribe or band. Purchase of the creation was a concept alien to their belief system; but, since it seemed to please the whites and save a lot of fuss and bother, the Indians found it expedient to "touch the pen" to proffered treaties. In this way, many tracts of woods, fields, and valleys were exchanged for trinkets, knives, or tobacco. But, while the Indians never took such treaties seriously, to the whites, the agreements were inviolable.

Although the individual had certain property rights within the Indian culture, the needs of the community took precedence over the rights of the individual. Sharing with others was not an option, but a duty. Food was always the common property of all, no matter in whose pot it might be cooking, and the taking of food by one in need of sustenance was never considered theft. While the taking of goods belonging to someone outside the community (white emigrants, for example) was not considered theft, the taking of goods from within the community was an offense, not against the society, but against the individual owner. Oddly enough, such thievery could be punished by social ridicule or even ostracism.[5]

If the Indians were bewildered by the whites' concepts of property rights, they found the sheer numbers of white people incomprehensible. Often they described the emigrants as being like a plague of locusts, numerous as the blades of grass or the needles of the pines–the only analogies the Indian could think of to express the inexpressible. Even those tribal leaders who had seen something of the eastern cities were hesitant to relate their revelations to their people for fear of being ridiculed. In a vain attempt to explain away the crush of traffic on the Oregon-California Trail, even the astute Spotted Tail, of the Brule Sioux, convinced himself that the white people were driving their wagons around in a great circle–up the Platte and back down the Smoky Hill—to trick the Indians into believing the whites were more numerous than they really were.[6]

As the wagons continued to roll up the Platte (but not back down the Smoky Hill), the more thoughtful whites increasingly realized that their overwhelming numbers spelled doom for the prairie Indians' way of life. Humanitarians, particularly in the eastern states, recognized that the Indians' only hope of avoiding extinction was in adaptation. This meant adopting to a large degree the white culture: working for a living (farming or herding), giving up fighting and horse stealing, and becoming more "socially acceptable."

Advocates of agriculture could see no reason why the Indians would not cheerfully turn to tilling the soil, giving up the old hand-to-mouth lifestyle for a sedentary, agrarian existence. They could point with pride to the Five Civilized Tribes that had adapted themselves so well to the white man's culture. Of course, they lost their eastern homelands anyway, but the theory was still valid. It was also true that some of the plains Indians had already become settled and agricultural people. But these were mainly the tribes of the Missouri Valley–the Mandans, Poncas, Omahas, and Otoes—and even these people continued to hunt for a portion of their subsistence. Few of these well-meaning whites took into account the fact that the growing of crops on the High Plains was, even for white farmers, a whole lot more difficult than it was in the Shenandoah Valley, or even the Missouri Valley, for that matter. Mostly the idea never got beyond the talking stage, for a number of good reasons.

The tribal lore of the Cheyennes recalled days in the previous century when that tribe had extensively raised crops. So, when in 1846, William Bent discussed with their headmen the necessity of once again becoming an agricultural society, the Cheyennes seized upon the idea with some excitement. Chief Yellow Wolf spent the entire winter selling his band on the rewards of farming. But there were great obstacles to be overcome.

First and foremost, the younger men who would carry the burden of the fieldwork refused to give up hunting and horse stealing. If they refused to work, the fields would have to be tilled by those who were the most defenseless: the women, the very old, and the very young. To protect the farms and workers from such ancient enemies as the Utes and Pawnees, it would be necessary to build fortified strongholds, an idea which made the soldiers of the Great Father very unhappy. And though the government gave lip service to the agricultural domestication of the Cheyennes, it never provided the necessary supplies of seed and implements. By the spring of 1847, the Cheyennes' excitement over corn and pumpkins had evaporated.[7]

The growing of corn and vegetables on the High Plains would have required a prodigious effort, anyhow. In later years, the Cheyennes' agent admitted that, although the land on their reservation was fertile, crops could not be grown there without irrigation, and no one in those years seemed to have had much experience with that.[8] Far to the northwest, the Mormons were beginning to construct their extensive water distribution system, but their society was highly structured and authority was centralized. Without massive government funding and expertise, such a project would have been impossible for the Indians of the High Plains. Even had they been living in a second Eden, the whole notion of farming was, for the wild tribes, completely unacceptable because it was hard work with no glory in it. There was, however, a great deal of glory in fighting.

In 1818, a number of fur trading interests in the Pacific Northwest met the local Indian tribes in council. The purpose of the talks was to smooth the local business climate by promoting peace among tribes which were perpetually at war with one another. As this became clear, an Owyhee chief named Tum-A-Tap-Um, brandishing a collection of scalps, stood and addressed the assembly: "If we make peace, how shall I employ my young men? They delight in nothing but war, and besides, our enemies, the Snakes, never observe a peace. Look! Am I to throw all these trophies away? Shall Tum-A-Tap-Um forget the glories of his forefathers and become a woman?"[9]

Years later, Colorado Territorial Governor John Evans heard the same objections from the High Plains Cheyennes and Arapahoes, testifying:

> *I thought it would be a very humane and good idea to get those Indians to quit fighting one another, and I gave them a great many lectures on the improprieties of these war parties but I found, after I had done it, that it gave a great deal of offense to them. One of them said he had been brought up to war, and to quit fighting was a thing he could not think of, and he thought it an unworthy interference on my part.*[10]

Not farming, but hunting and fighting—those were the only proper vocations of the young warriors who fought, not only to protect their homes and people, but to exhibit their courage; for bravery was the most important attribute in their society. Beyond this, there was simply the joy of battle and the spice of personal danger. Of course, it was inevitable that in battle some would be killed, but that was not a consequence the Indian feared. Rather, the warrior who died in battle was considered fortunate because he "went out while he was on top," so to speak. A glorious death in battle (and entrance into the spirit world) while at the peak of physical prowess was much preferred to growing old and infirm, no longer able to enjoy the hunt and the warpath, and no longer of much use to anyone.

Understandably, such a philosophy produced a splendid and formidable warrior who held the fighting qualities of white men in derision. While the Indian was swift, stealthy, and magnificently mounted, the white soldiers walked or rode large, heavy animals that required great quantities of grain. The soldiers were clumsy and noisy, and they raised great clouds of dust which advertised their every movement. The Sioux and Cheyennes could only smile slyly at the ineptitude of the whites, for they themselves "were always proud of their prowess as warriors and it was never their opinion that the white soldiers were their equals as fighters . . . To them, no man who required another man to tell him to pick up his gun, to stand, run, halt, salute, and march into the foe could possibly be a good warrior."[11] If becoming civilized meant giving up the thrill of the hunt and the glory of fighting, the young warriors wanted no part of it.

Adapting to the ways of the white man, however, would require much more of the Indian than merely giving up the warpath for the plow. He must become socially acceptable in manners and customs as well. The great majority of emigrants and homesteaders on the frontier had little or no experience with the Indians' capacity for violence, at least until the 1860s. But they were all too often witnesses to behaviors which they found downright repulsive. In modern terms, we might say they suffered culture shock. They were annoyed at having Indians underfoot in camp; by their habit of grabbing at bright, shiny objects which excited their wonder; and by their constant begging and petty thievery. Of the Santees who frequently barged into her home, Abigail Gardner Sharp wrote:

> *It is impossible to express my abhorrence for those repulsive and ferocious looking beings, as they entered our house and began at once to ask for something to eat; nor did they ask for victuals alone, but whatever they thought serviceable, or what pleased their fancy, they persistently demanded, all the while jabbering their Indian jargon. To get rid of them as soon as possible they were fed bountifully, and what they asked for was given them, if it could be spared.*[12]

Lieutenant Eugene Ware was highly irritated that the Pawnees had no better manners than to stare at him through the windows of the council chamber,[13] and at least one pioneer housewife drove some uninvited Indians from her sod home by threatening to drench them with the hot grease in which she was frying doughnuts.[14] Pioneer stomachs were revolted when Indians displayed scalps or appendages cut from the bodies of vanquished foes or ate the offal of butchered animals. The Pawnees were notorious for their lack of personal hygiene, and emigrant women were embarrassed by prepubescent Sioux children of both sexes running around nude.[15]

Government officials were bothered, not so much by the Indians' uncouth manners, as by their inability to organize politically; for, to the bureaucratic mind, elected leadership and a hierarchy of responsibility were as natural as breathing. An Indian chief, they felt, ought to have total control over his band or tribe. His word should be binding on all.

Among the plains tribes there was no such concept. The Indian of the plains acted as an individual responsible only to himself. He was willing to follow those whom he perceived to have special leadership and personal qualities, and his actions could be tempered by social pressure, but his decisions were strictly his own. Violations of tribal codes were punished more by public disapproval than by the chief, and the decisions of councils were often enforced by soldier societies. The office of chief was a position of great honor, often conferred for acts of heroism or other outstanding personal attributes, but it held no real power of command. The chief ruled mostly by force of personality, and when he put his signature to a treaty, it bound no one but himself, for he had no power of decision over any other individual.

Thus, while the impulse to ensure the survival of the wild tribes by making them economically viable and socially acceptable in the white man's world was noble and humanitarian, nobody quite knew how to go about doing it. The civilizing process required the unwilling Indians to make all the concessions. Worse, it overlooked some uncomfortable truths about the white man's culture, and the fact that the intermingling of societies could be potentially deadly for the red people of the plains.

Debauchment of the aboriginal peoples had made a small beginning already in 1628 when Thomas Morton defied the pious Pilgrims by serving up strong drink to the local Indians at "Merie Mount." During the Colonial Wars, liquor was used freely by both English and French to purchase the allegiance of the indigenous tribes. So severe were the ravages of alcohol among the Indian people that Pontiac, in his surrender message to General Amherst, stated that, if the English wished to punish the insurrectionists further, "it may easily be done without any expense to the Crown, by permitting a free sale of rum, which will destroy them more effectually than fire and sword."[16]

In the early 1800s, the fur traders introduced alcohol to the tribes of the mountains and High Plains with the same catastrophic results. Some of the traders were absolutely shameless in their use of liquor to lubricate their dealings (and enhance their profits), knowing that the Indians, being ignorant of its dangers, would sell anything and everything for a drink of the magical beverage.

The business usually began when the trader entered a village and opened a keg. A good buffalo robe bought nine gills of raw alcohol, diluted with water and often sugared to enhance the taste.[17] As a brave became more and more drunk, his drinks became more and more diluted. This continued until the Indian became so insensate that he was slyly being served nothing more than plain water hopped up with a little red pepper and tobacco.

Wiser heads among the tribes realized that the liquor trade would only hasten the decay of their way of life. When Joseph La Flesche became chief of the Omahas, he ordered the public flogging of any member of the tribe who used alcohol. His action was controversial, but the effects were salutary: during his years as chief, La Flesche nearly eradicated drunkenness within the tribe.[18]

Similar measures could have benefitted the tribes of the High Plains. In 1835, Colonel Henry Dodge observed the effects of Mexican liquor on a village of Cheyennes camped south of the Arkansas River. The alcohol flowed freely, wrote Dodge, until men, women, and even children were staggering about, frothing and naked.[19] In such debauches, whites and Indians alike were sometimes killed, and on at least one occasion, a liquor-peddling trader was roasted alive over a campfire by his overly enthused patrons.

The more responsible traders such as Bent, St. Vrain and Company realized that an uncontrolled flow of liquor would soon lead to the total debauchment of the tribe and a corresponding curtailment of the buffalo robe trade. To remain competitive, William Bent sometimes used alcohol sparingly, but at the same time he wrote numerous letters to government officials, protesting their failure to enforce restrictions on the alcohol suppliers. Finally, in 1844, Bent, accompanied by a Cheyenne named Slim Fox, made a trip to St. Louis in a personal attempt to impress upon the Indian Superintendent the dangers posed by the liquor being smuggled to the tribes. Bent's long journey yielded no results.[20]

Although alcohol was a serious threat to the health and moral fiber of the unsophisticated Indian people, it was at least tangible and could be potentially countered. The white man's diseases, however, were invisible—stealthy, malevolent visitors, completely undeterred by bravery or medicine ceremonies. Even before the arrival of the Pilgrims in 1620, whole tribes along the eastern seacoast had been wiped out by deadly, European diseases contracted from fishing and exploring parties. At the very time when the Massachusetts Indians were beginning to resist the pressure of the Bay Colony, a fearsome illness wiped out thousands of the New England natives. The Puritans, quite naturally, saw the divine hand in the catastrophe, noting that "God ended the controversy by sending the Small-pox amongst the Indians." Governor Winthrop drew the logical Calvinistic conclusion: "If God were not pleased with our inheriting these parts, why did he drive out the natives before us and why doth he still make roome for us, by diminishinge them as we increase?"[21] Throughout the mid Nineteenth Century, great numbers of white people were carried off the earth by the ravages of measles, smallpox, and cholera, both in the eastern cities and along the western trails. But, once given a foothold among the Indians, who had not acquired the slightest immunity, the scourge ran with the ferocity of a range fire.

As the Indian people became more hungry, dependent, and demoralized, the "social diseases" contributed to the accelerating pattern of decay. Prostitution had been unknown among the plains tribes prior to the surge of westward expansion, but the practice grew along with the white population, particularly in the vicinity of military posts. Young soldiers, faced with the monotony of their masculine society and long, lonely nights in a buffalo robe bed, were able to set aside cultural and racial differences long enough to satisfy their urges. The result was a spread of gonorrhea within the ranks and throughout the native population. Strike-The-Ree complained:

> *Before the soldiers came along we had good health; but once the soldiers came along they go to my squaws and want to sleep with them, and the squaws being hungry will sleep with them in order to get something to eat, and will get a bad disease, and then the squaws turn to their husbands and give them the bad disease.*[22]

The officers were aware of the dangers which such liaisons presented to the morale of the troops and Indians alike. During his tenure as commander of the District of Nebraska, General Robert B. Mitchell summarily dismissed several officers who frequented the squaw camps around Fort Laramie, and enjoined the rest to set good examples for their men.[23] But, though the general took pains to halt such improper relations, his efforts could hardly put a stop to practices which have followed conquering armies since the beginning of time.

It was the function of the Indian Bureau to address these problems and to administer the blessings of white civilization among the native tribes. The field representative of the bureau was the agent, who served as the communication pipeline between the tribes and the Great Father's chiefs. The agent in charge of a group of tribes (agency) was to concern himself with the well-being of the Indian people, their adherence to the treaties they had signed, and the equitable distribution of annuity goods delivered to them under the terms of those treaties. In theory, the concept was workable. In reality, the agency system was a swamp of greed and mismanagement. Official oversight of agents in the field was throttled by distance, difficulties of communication, and the power of political patronage, especially in the context of the exigencies of the Civil War.

The abuse of their positions for personal gain followed a theme upon which the individual agents improvised endless variations. Distilled to its essence, the most common scheme involved the annuity goods which were supposed to be distributed among the Indian people, but were often sold by the agent who pocketed the cash. Sometimes the Indians were forced to "buy" their own annuities by offering robes and furs in exchange for what was rightfully theirs. Since the agent also licensed the traders who worked among the Indians, it became common practice to appoint loyal henchmen, thereby eliminating competition and driving down the prices paid the Indians for furs, and increasing the spoils of thievery.

A typical example of this thievery was John Loree, appointed as Agent for the Upper Platte in April, 1862. As a farmer living outside St. Joseph, Missouri, Loree had been instrumental in maintaining

Union loyalty in a crucial region of the border state. By disenfranchising established traders, and by unabashed cheating and thieving, Loree managed to antagonize everyone at the agency, red and white alike. The clever opposition of Colonel William O. Collins and the rising indignation of the Sioux finally drove him from his post in 1864.[24]

The Upper Platte Agency had been riddled with graft even before Loree's arrival. Since much of the agent's "gratuities" depended upon the supply of annuity goods, it was vital to keep those goods flowing into the warehouses. When the Sioux mounted a war against the Crows in violation of the Treaty of 1851, Loree's predecessor continued to report that all was peaceful, so the goods supposedly destined for the Sioux continued to arrive.[25]

The damage done by Loree in his two years on the plains might have been contained if his case had been exceptional. But similar fraud had been going on for years on the agencies for the Minnesota Sioux and lower plains tribes. When Samuel Colley took over the Agency of the Upper Arkansas, he licensed his son, Dexter, to trade with the Indians there. William Bent later described how Dexter, who arrived at the agency with a net personal worth of only $1,500, bragged that he had cleared between $25,000 and $30,000 in the three years he had been doing business. For his part, Samuel Colley simply culled out the most desirable items from each year's annuity shipments, piled the rest on the ground for distribution, and induced several compliant chiefs to sign vouchers for the complete lot. He then sold the items withheld and pocketed the receipts.[26]

Viewed from a time of enhanced social consciousness, it seems incredible that the odoriferous workings of the Indian Bureau could have been tolerated for so long with so little public outcry. But by 1860, the country had already entered upon what has been called the "Age of Exploitation." The land was vast, its resources seemingly unbounded, and the economic muscle generated by the Industrial Revolution had created a sense of complacency regarding the methods by which wealth was accumulated. Still ahead lay the era of Credit Mobilier and the railroad robber barons; of trusts and holding company pyramids and interlocking directorships; of child labor and the shameless human exploitation practiced by the mining and meat packing industries. In the moral climate of the times, the corrupt agents were viewed as merely seizing the advantages of their positions, using sharp business heads to increase their wealth. Besides, if the deflection of annuity goods for the agents' personal gain was a bit tawdry, what right had the Indians to complain? They stole horses, didn't they?

President Lincoln was well aware of the corruption of the agency system, but he and his government were stretched paper thin by the war effort. The Indian problems inherited by his administration had been a long time building. Matters were coming to a head in 1860 because the Indians had been pushed westward as far as they could go–to the Great American Desert—and now the white people wanted that as well. The problems which had been so conveniently shunted aside for three decades could be ignored no longer. Even the Congress was coming to recognize this reality; but it would not be until 1867, with the Civil War ended and the transcontinental railroad rushing toward completion, that this reality was articulated by Congressman Lot Morrill:

> *As population has approached the Indian we have removed him beyond population. But population now encounters him on both sides of the continent, and there is no place on the continent to which he can be removed beyond the progress of population.*[27]

At the time of passage of the Indian Removal Act, no one seemed to worry much about the exact relation of the aboriginal peoples to the national government. By 1860, however, the increasing militancy of the red people (and just possibly, a national conscience troubled over the status of black people) was forcing the question: Were the Indian tribes sovereign powers, possessing all the rights usually accorded to foreign countries? Were the Indians citizens by virtue of being born into a territory which the federal government claimed as its own? Or were they conquered peoples, to be disarmed, policed, and administered by an occupying army?

While eastern humanitarians, Indian agents, government officials, and emigrants debated the Indians' status, the fact remained that their potential for causing trouble was of growing concern on the frontier. Therefore, since taking up station along the Oregon Trail in 1848, the United States Army found itself playing an increasingly important role in maintaining the peace presumed to have been assured by the Treaty of 1851.

Now, by its very nature, an army is a force of fighting men. Such were the regulars sent west to guard the overland trails. Their officers, fresh from the military academy, carried visions of martial glory in their heads—dreams of grenadiers in great, hollow square formations; of glittering cavalry squadrons wheeling, charging to glory, shaking the earth with the mighty thunder of their swift steeds. They had been wholly infused with the tactics of Frederick the Great,

Napoleon, Marshal Ney, and Wellington. But on the bleak plains around Laramie, surrounded by the dusky and generally pacific people of a stone age culture, beset by thousands of noisy and troublesome emigrants, the soldiers' visions of glory shriveled like the prairie shortgrass in a rainless summer. True, Napoleon had endured the trackless wastes of Russia—but at least he had been fighting. The officers and men of Sixth Infantry had been hung out to dry in godforsaken Nebraska Territory—fighting men sent to keep the peace at Fort Boredom. It is understandable that they were moved to stir up a little action now and then at the expense of the Indians.

This was even more true of the volunteer forces which manned the posts after the regulars had been called east in 1861. In general, the regular soldiers had behaved as professionals doing the business of their government. The volunteers, having been recruited from the frontier population at large, were different. They often harbored bitter memories of past Indian outrages and were inclined to view the Indians as less than human. As a result, they fought with a special viciousness. Of these volunteers, Grinnell writes,

> *It was undoubtedly the coming of these troops that brought on the war with the plains tribes in 1864. Red Cloud always used to say 'The white soldiers always want to make a war,' and there was a good deal of truth in that statement.*[28]

Illustrative of the mindset of the typical volunteer fighting man was Hervey Johnson, of the Eleventh Ohio Cavalry. From his post at Deer Creek Station, he penned wordy letters of observation and complaint back to his family. He did not spare them his feelings about Indians:

> *I do believe that of all the specimens of humanity I ever saw, the Indian(s) around here are the most low-lived, dirty, sneaking, and impudent . . . I believe I hate them worse every day. I could shoot an Indian with as much coolness as I would a dog, and I will do it (if) I can(.) Nothing but a war of extermination will ever rid the country of their depredations, they pay no regard to treaties, and as their disease is severe, the remedy should be in proportion.*[29]

Lieutenant Ware records that the favorite slang term for an Indian was "abbrigoin," (a corruption of "aborigine") and adds,

> *The Indians were a wild, bloodthirsty set of barbarians, and one half, at least, of them deserved killing as much as the wolves which barked around their tepees.*[30]

Many volunteer officers held racial opinions as corrosive as those of the enlisted men. Major Scott Anthony, of the First Colorado Cavalry, wrote:

> *The Indians are all very destitute this season, and the government will be compelled to subsist them to a great extent, or allow them to starve to death, which would probably be much the easier way of disposing of them.*[31]

Anthony's fellow major, Jacob Downing, proclaimed,

> *I think and earnestly believe the Indians to be an obstacle to civilization, and should be exterminated.*[32]

Not all officers held views as extreme as those of the First Colorado men, of course, and many of them, by virtue of being better educated than the private soldiers, struggled with their own personal "world views" of the red race, and with their own roles on the frontier. Their feelings were often confused and contradictory, influenced by the popular eastern conception of the "noble savage;" by conditions on the frontier; by personal experience and conscience; and by the supposed superiority of white society whose "vices influenced Indians more profoundly than did its virtues."[33]

This, then, is a summary of the factors which contributed to the extinguishing of that light of promise which had flared so hopefully in the camps along Horse Creek. Cultural divergence, racial intolerance, and the vices of white society would prove in short order to be more formidable than the treaty signed in 1851. The breakup began just two years later with the Sioux.

Chapter three notes

[1] Lavender, *Bent's Fort*, 342.

[2] Chittenden and Talbot, *Life of Father De Smet*, 684.

[3] This analysis of the council at Horse Creek and Mitchell's quote are taken from Nadeau, *Fort Laramie*, 82.

[4] Horowitz, *The First Frontier*, 38.

[5] For this sketch of concepts regarding property rights, I have relied on Skogen, *Indian Depredation Claims*, 4-6.

[6] Ware, *The Indian War of 1864*, 116.

[7] Lavender, *Bent's Fort*, 288.

[8] U. S. Congress, "Massacre of Cheyenne Indians," 34.

[9] Ross, *Fur Hunters of the Far West*, 171.

[10] U. S. Congress, "Massacre of Cheyenne Indians," 44.

[11] Standing Bear, *Land of the Spotted Eagle*, 173.

[12] Sharp, *History of the Spirit Lake Massacre*, 25.

[13] Ware, *The Indian War of 1864*, 20.

[14] According to family oral tradition, the brave lady was the author's great-great grand-mother, but I have read variations of this tale in other sources.

[15] Reading, "The Journal of Pierson Barton Reading," 154; also Ellen Tootle, "Diary," in Holmes, Ed., *Covered Wagon Women*, Vol. 8.

[16] Horowitz, *The First Frontier*, 188.

[17] Lavender, *Bent's Fort*, 159-160.

[18] Fletcher and La Flesche, *The Omaha Tribe*, 618-619.

[19] Lavender, *Bent's Fort*, 173.

[20] Ibid., 247.

[21] Horowitz, *The First Frontier*, 37-38.

[22] Nadeau, *Fort Laramie*, 161.

[23] Ware, *The Indian War of 1864*, 214.

[24] Nadeau, *Fort Laramie*, 161-167.

[25] Grinnell, *The Fighting Cheyennes*, 85.

[26] U. S. Congress, "Massacre of Cheyenne Indians," 93.

[27] Utley, *Frontier Regulars*, 4.

[28] Grinnell, *The Fighting Cheyennes*, 6.

[29] Unrau, Ed., *Tending the Talking Wire*, 61, 150, 210.

[30] Ware, *The Indian War of 1864*, 147.

[31] O.R. Vol. 22, Part 2, 571.

[32] U.S. Congress, "Massacre of Cheyenne Indians," 70.

[33] Smith, *The View From Officers' Row*, 27.

Part I
Chapter Four

"They have been deceived so often by the whites"

The Sioux Nation, at the middle of the Nineteenth Century, ranged over an extensive domain from central Minnesota westward through Wyoming and Montana and southward into western Nebraska. The Indian people who occupied this vast territory were loosely organized in three major divisions.[1] Easternmost were the Santee Sioux, or Dakotas, as they called themselves, consisting of four subtribes: Sisseton, Wahpeton, Mdewkanton, and Wahpekute. Basically a woodland people who lived in permanent villages and engaged in limited agriculture, the Dakotas were forced from their original homeland in northern Minnesota by the Chippewas. In 1857, they ceded all their lands east of the Mississippi River to the government and were assigned a reservation along the Minnesota River in the southwestern part of the state.

Ranging along the Missouri River in present North and South Dakota were the Nakota people, consisting of the subtribes known as Yanktons and Yanktonnaise. The Yanktons also ceded their lands to the United States in 1857, yet remained generally docile and friendly toward the whites. The same could not be said of the Yanktonnaise, who responded to white pressure and maltreatment by becoming exceedingly dangerous.

The westernmost division of the Sioux nation was the Teton, or Lakota Sioux, of which there were seven subtribes: Brule, Ogalala, Hunkpapa, Minneconjou, Sans Arc, Two Kettle, and Blackfoot. All remained generally friendly to the whites through the 1840s and

1850s; yet it was upon these people, especially upon the Ogalalas and Brules, that the flood of emigration along the Oregon-California Trail placed a severe physical and cultural strain. This tension was exacerbated by the establishment of a military post at Fort Laramie and its subsequent mismanagement. Having made a commitment to post military garrisons along the trail, a parsimonious government belatedly discovered that the cost of an armed presence on the High Plains was enormous. Several not-too-creative cost cutting measures were soon adopted.

Cavalry horses eat grain—lots of it. Through the decades of the forties and fifties, that grain had to be hauled out to the Oregon Trail posts from Fort Leavenworth, Kansas. The haul to Fort Kearny was expensive enough, but on the trek to Laramie, the draft animals ate more grain than they delivered. In 1850, the War Department calculated that it cost $34.24 per month to feed a single cavalry mount at Fort Laramie.[2] Economics thus dictated that Laramie be garrisoned entirely by infantry with perhaps only a small detachment of cavalry for courier duty. Mounted troops were also kept to a minimum at Fort Kearny.[3]

Unfortunately, even infantrymen have to eat, and the necessary coffee, flour, sugar, and vegetables, like the grain, had to be freighted out from Leavenworth. This problem was addressed by cutting the garrisons to the bare minimum necessary to maintain the posts. Since fewer soldiers required fewer officers, Fort Laramie continued to be downgraded in importance until at last the post commander was only a second lieutenant in rank.

If the Sioux had been awed by Colonel Kearny's military show in 1845, they were contemptuous of the feeble garrisons in the forts. Far from being the protectors of the Overland Road, the forts existed at the benign sufferance of the Indians, and everyone knew it. With no palisades and maintained by a handful of soldiers, Fort Laramie (and Fort Kearny as well) could have been wiped off the map by the Sioux at their leisure. They did not do so because they continued to hope that the bluecoats would help to control the depredations of the emigrants.

Agent Tom Fitzpatrick saw trouble ahead and continually protested the policy of maintaining tiny garrisons at Laramie and along the Arkansas River. He ridiculed the notion that foot soldiers were of any use against the splendid horsemanship of the plains warriors, and suggested that mounted forces of at least 300 troopers be maintained both on the upper Platte and along the Arkansas—forces free to travel at will, showing their muscle to the tribes. As his solution was expensive, his protests went unheeded.[4]

It is hardly surprising, therefore, that the Treaty of 1851 did not bring an era of peace to the plains. Instead of the fifty-year term to which all parties had agreed, Congress approved a period of only fifteen years and gave the president authority to reduce that to ten. As a sop to the Indians, the annuity payments were increased, and the amended document was returned to Fitzpatrick, who was expected to present it to the Indians a second time for their approval. Despite the fact that the emigration of 1852 was one of the largest in trail history, and that the Indians near the trail continued to suffer from the shortage of buffalo, events around Laramie remained deceptively peaceful.

In the spring of 1853, a band of Minneconjou Sioux rode down from their haunts north of the Black Hills to join their Ogalala and Brule brothers around Laramie. The Minneconjou were strangers in the territory and had established no friendly ties with the local traders. They were also a very belligerent lot, badgering the passing emigrant trains, extorting presents and "tribute" from the greenhorns in the caravans. They also bullied the soldiers at the fort, and in a dispute over the use of a ferryboat, they fired several shots at a sergeant. In the army's attempt to identify and arrest the culprit, a brief firefight broke out with the Minneconjou, and two of the band were killed. Though the Brules and Ogalalas had nothing to do with the matter, all the Sioux were much agitated by the affair.[5]

The year 1854 brought tragedy. The cavalry which had been temporarily assigned to Fort Laramie was withdrawn. First Lieutenant Richard Garnett was also transferred, leaving the fort under the command of Second Lieutenant Hugh Fleming, who had been involved in the skirmish with the Minneconjou the year before. Eighteen fifty-four was also the year that Tom Fitzpatrick died. His experience and judgment would be sorely missed in the perilous times ahead; for the Minneconjou were once again making their presence known, and friendly Sioux warned that their hearts were bad toward the whites.

Finally, 1854 was the year of the stray Mormon cow and the infamous Grattan Affair. Briefly recounted, the Sioux and Cheyennes were camped near Fort Laramie that August, waiting to receive their annuity goods. A Danish Mormon emigrant lost or abandoned a footsore cow near the camps, and a visiting Minneconjou named High Forehead butchered the animal to make a feast for his hosts.[6] The Mormon continued on to the fort where he demanded restitution for his lost cow. The Indians offered several times to compensate the emigrant, but he felt their offers were too little. Under the Treaty of 1851, satisfaction for a proven offense could be obtained by withholding some of the annuity goods. Disregarding this provision, a troublesome second lieutenant named Grattan led a detachment into the Sioux camp to demand the surrender of High Forehead. Chief Conquering Bear was perplexed and indecisive, Grattan was overly excited, the interpreter was drunk, and High Forehead understandably refused to surrender. As the troops opened fire, Conquering Bear went down mortally wounded, and the enraged Brules charged, killing or mortally wounding every man of the detachment. The angry warriors then turned to attack Fort Laramie, which was held just then by only ten soldiers, but trader James Bordeaux and tribal leaders were able to abort their designs. Realizing that all their annuity goods would probably be withheld now, the Brules broke into the government warehouses and took what they wanted, before moving their camps northward. The Cheyennes remained and were given the goods due them, but they burned with indignation, feeling that their Lakota cousins had been grievously wronged.[7]

The following November, five warriors from Conquering Bear's band, including Spotted Tail, Red Leaf, and Long Chin, attacked a mail wagon west of Horse Creek, killing two drivers and a passenger. A second party attacked a trading post west of Laramie. Over the winter, the tribes laid plans to return to the Oregon-California Trail in the spring and, barring any response from the puny garrison at the fort, continue their raiding all summer.[8]

A few days after Lieutenant Grattan's defeat, Agent John Whitfield arrived at Fort Laramie and began taking statements from witnesses. He reported to his superiors that the little band of infantry at the fort was perfectly useless—large enough to stir up trouble, but too feeble to give any aid to emigrants who were being forced to pay tribute to the Sioux for the privilege of passing along the road unmolested, as guaranteed in the Treaty of 1851.[9]

Major Hoffman of the Sixth Infantry also wrote to his headquarters protesting the placement of a handful of soldiers under inexperienced officers deep in Indian country.[10] His accusations of wrongdoing on the part of Lieutenant Grattan were supported by Representative Thomas Hart Benton and by David Mitchell, who had negotiated the treaty at Horse Creek three years earlier. The resulting firestorm of charges and countercharges threatened to tear apart the army, which always maintained that the Sioux were the aggressors. The only thing upon which everyone could agree was that peace between the white man and the Sioux had come to a violent end.

In the winter camps, the war talk of the Brules won over to their cause some bands of Yanktons, Hunkpapas, Sans Arcs, and Blackfoot Sioux. But the long-planned summer raids amounted to little more than horse stealing, for the Sioux were very much divided. The

Ogalalas and many of the Brules wanted nothing to do with the raids, and their conduct remained exemplary.

The army's response to the Grattan Affair came in September 1855 when General William Harney and a force of more than 700 infantry, cavalry, and light artillery forced a fight on the reluctant Chief Little Thunder on Bluewater Creek.[11] The Indians suffered about one hundred killed, including the inevitable toll of women and children. After learning the particulars of the Grattan Affair from the people at Fort Laramie, Harney labored to show the Sioux some justice and to reestablish the harmony which had existed at the time of the Big Talk. His report to Secretary of War Jefferson Davis showed evidence of his newfound respect for the Sioux, and a fervent hope that a true era of peace between white men and Indians would now follow.[12] Harney's report concluded:

> *They (the Indians) have been deceived so often by the whites that they would never again give them their confidence . . . It is not yet too late for us to requite, to some degree, this unfortunate race for their many sufferings . . . With proper management a new era will dawn upon such of the Indians as yet remain.*[13]

But the pressure of the westward movement refused to abate. The passage of the Kansas-Nebraska Act in 1854 had thrown open to settlement a vast territory and forced the Yanktons, Poncas, Omahas, and Pawnees to cede their homelands to the government. On the western plains, the news of the cessions threw the Lakotas into a panic. During the summer of 1857, they came together at Bear Butte, on the northern edge of the Black Hills, to hold a Big Talk of their own. There they pledged to resist any further white explorations through their sacred lands; to deny the white people permission to build any more roads; to refuse all future annuity payments; and to refuse asylum to homeless Yanktons who had been foolish enough to cede their land to the government.

After the conference broke up, a party of Minneconjous, Hunkpapas, and Blackfoot Sioux rode west on the hunt to lay in a winter supply of meat and robes. They were stalking a large buffalo herd when they stumbled across a survey party out of Fort Laramie, led by Lieutenant Gouvernor Kemble Warren, an army topographical engineer who had been with Harney at Bluewater. The Indians firmly told Warren that his presence there was a violation of the treaty they had made with General Harney and, if his expedition continued, it would scare the nearby buffalo herd far away to the west, making their winter preparations much more difficult. Besides, they knew Warren was only looking for places to build more roads through their sacred Black Hills, and these they refused to give up. Warren admitted the truth in all they had said. With a mixture of sympathy for the Sioux and uncertainty of his party's ability to withstand an attack, he wisely turned back and skirted the southern edge of the black Hills.[14]

In 1859 the government tried again, sending a topographical party under Captain William Raynalds up the Missouri to the Yellowstone country and back down river to Omaha. The Raynalds expedition survived early spring snows and floods, threats by the Sioux and attacks by the Crows, and it succeeded in thoroughly irritating the plains tribes. Agent Thomas Twiss warned the government that widespread hostilities were a very real possibility.

In an attempt to prevent such hostilities, Twiss held a treaty council at his Deer Creek Agency in September, 1859. The Sioux, Northern Cheyenne, and Arapaho people wearily agreed to settle on reserves north of the North Platte River and make an attempt to live and farm like the white people. Their sincerity may have been disingenuous, but it was the only way they could see to avoid eventual extinction.[15] Despite their unprecedented concessions, the Deer Creek Treaty was rejected in the Senate. Thus it appeared that, in the future, military force would be the only option left in dealing with the wild tribes.

Actually, except for Harney's attack on Little Thunder, the Sioux had managed fairly well to avoid disaster at the hands of the whites. The events which would eventually draw them into full scale war were occurring in the meantime, not on the northern plains, but among their cousins and allies farther south, the Cheyenne and Arapaho people.

Chapter Four notes

1 As with many other areas pertaining to the plains tribes, it is difficult for white people to arrive at an exact understanding of their social organization, i.e. tribe, subtribe, band, or society. This organization of the Sioux nation is probably the most prevalent. Others, including Lieutenant G. K. Warren in his 1857 report, have grouped them differently.

2 Hyde, *A Life of George Bent*, 95.

3 Hyde, *Red Cloud's Folk.*

4 Ibid., 69.

5 Ibid., 70-71; Grinnell, *The Fighting Cheyennes*, 105.

6 Hyde (*Spotted Tail's Folk*) reminds us that High Forehead may not have been so innocent in the matter. It must be recalled that the Minneconjou had a bad attitude toward the whites, and probably needed no excuse to stir up a little trouble.

7 McCann, "The Grattan Massacre," 6.

8 Hyde, *Red Cloud's Folk*, 77.

9 Ibid., 76.

10 Grinnell, *The Fighting Cheyennes*, 105.

1 Ibid., 108-110.

12 Hyde, *Red Cloud's Folk*, 80.

13 Nadeau, *Fort Laramie*, 130.

14 McFarling, *Exploring the Northern Plains*, 280-283.

15 Nadeau, *Fort Laramie*, 144-145.

Part I
Chapter Five
"A smothered passion for revenge"

The Cheyennes were an Algonquian speaking people who, prior to the 1800s, had inhabited the area between the upper Mississippi Valley and the shores of Lake Superior.[1] In those days they were a docile, agricultural folk who, finding themselves pressured by the more aggressive Chippewa, Sioux, Cree, and Assiniboin peoples, migrated westward and south, eventually establishing themselves on the High Plains.

The acquisition of horses somewhere along the way allowed the tribe to transform itself from a sedentary to a nomadic society whose subsistence was based on hunting, primarily buffalo. Tribal lore recounts how the Cheyennes wearied of the attacks of their neighbors and became more aggressive, eventually becoming a High Plains people renowned for their fighting capabilities. At some point in their wanderings they became associated with the Arapahoes, and it was these latter people who were consistently in the van of the march.

Cheyenne society was regulated by organizations formed within the tribe and generally known as soldier societies. Nearly every able-bodied male belonged to one of these groups: Kit Foxes, Elkhorn Scrapers, Red Shields, or Dog Soldiers. The Dog Soldiers were practically a nation and a law unto themselves. They kept their own camps and acted as rear guard when the tribes were on the march. Many of the highly militant Dog Soldiers were half Sioux; in fact, a pure-blood Cheyenne was almost unknown due to the tribe's practice of intermarriage with other peoples and the adoption of children captured in war. Frontiersmen came to know the Cheyennes as a tall, noble, well-favored people whose women were extremely neat housekeepers.

The Cheyenne and Arapaho removal to the High Plains was completed sometime during the late 18th century. Berthrong noted that, already in 1805, they were reported living in the area of Scotts Bluff (Nebraska) and had forsaken their traditional pottery for utensils of hide and iron goods purchased from traders. The establishment of the Oregon Trail through their territory tended to divide the Cheyenne and Arapaho peoples into a northern group (generally ranging north of the Platte River) and a southern group (between the North Platte and the Arkansas).

There was constant friction between the Southern Cheyennes and the Commanches, but the Cheyennes learned to give as good as they got and generally held their own. It was in 1829 that two Cheyenne braves, hotly pursued by a Comanche war party, stumbled upon the camp of a white trading and trapping expedition. At considerable personal risk, the young trader in charge hid the two among the camp equipment and sent the pursuers away empty-handed. By this courageous act, William Bent earned the undying gratitude of the tribe, and was on his way to becoming the one white man on the plains whom the Cheyennes trusted completely. Bent, in turn, became their most empathic advocate. Throughout these early decades the Cheyenne remained on friendly terms with the few white people they encountered on the High Plains.

This peaceful coexistence was severely strained by the hordes of Forty-niners who pushed up the Platte and Arkansas Rivers on their way to the gold fields of California. Caught between two streams of migration, the Cheyennes and Arapahoes were dismayed to find their traditional campsites fouled and stripped of grass. The grass would grow back, of course, but the scarce groves of trees being wantonly chopped up for campfires were irreplaceable on the arid plains.

With the throngs of gold seekers came disease. In particular, the Forty-niners brought cholera, which the Cheyennes called "cramps." Both the Sioux and Cheyennes were the hardest hit of all the plains tribes because they were the closest to the great trails and had the most contact with the white emigrants. In 1854 the Cheyennes also contracted smallpox, possibly from the Kiowas. William Bent spent much time doctoring the sick, and only one Cheyenne is known to have died from the disease.[2]

The tribe also struggled with alcoholism, said to have begun when the trader, John Gantt, began using alcohol as a trade tool sometime around 1830. Like the Sioux to the north, so also the Cheyennes and Arapahoes came to realize that the white people and their culture posed a substantial threat to their health, tribal organization, and way of life. Soon the young braves began to commit minor depredations. To guarantee the safety of the trade caravans, a line of military posts sprang up through the heart of Cheyenne country, increasing the likelihood for more serious clashes between white and Indian cultures.

In 1853, Lean Bear was visiting the whites at Fort Atkinson (near present Dodge City, Kansas). Entranced by the sparkling ring which he saw on the finger of an officer's wife, he impulsively grabbed her hand, the better to admire such a thing of beauty. The lady was quite naturally frightened, and her husband came rushing to her defense, striking Lean Bear with a whip. With his honor badly bruised, Lean Bear returned to camp, painted for war, and attempted to get up a war party. The chiefs talked him out of the idea and the crisis passed.[3]

A more serious incident involving the Northern Cheyennes occurred in the spring of 1856. At that time, the people were still indignant over the treatment of their Sioux allies in retaliation for the Grattan Affair nearly two years before. That April, a party of Cheyennes found some stray horses on the prairie near Platte Bridge Crossing (near present Casper, Wyoming). The military commander at Platte Bridge Station ordered the Indians to return the horses, as they belonged to some white men in the vicinity. The Cheyennes were willing to do this, with the exception of one brave, who steadfastly maintained that the horse in question had belonged to him for quite some time. The commander refused to give in, and ordered his men to take four Cheyenne captives to force the return of the horse.

The Cheyennes did not understand the concept of "prisoner" or "hostage." When adult males fell into their hands in the course of a fight, the Cheyennes always made a quick end to the affair by killing them. Taking a Cheyenne warrior prisoner was the same, to their way of thinking, as announcing his imminent execution. Therefore, the Platte Bridge hostages, having nothing to lose, quite naturally attempted to escape. The guards opened fire, killing one of the four, and Wolf Fire was overpowered and recaptured. (Even though Wolf Fire had taken no part in the affair of the stray horses, he was kept in the guardhouse for several years until he died there.) His clan fled toward the Black Hills, killing an old trapper named Ganier in retaliation. When soldiers destroyed their village, many of the northern Cheyennes moved south with their brethren between the Platte and the Arkansas, carefully avoiding whites and refraining from further raiding.[4]

In August 1856, a war party of Cheyennes headed north to take renewed vengeance on the Pawnees who had caused them so much grief in the past. They had no quarrel with the white soldiers, and even stopped by Fort Kearny to visit for a time. Continuing down the

Platte, they made evening camp a few miles below the post. Finding themselves out of tobacco, two young men, one of them a half-breed, attempted to flag down a passing mail coach to beg for some chew. The driver of the coach panicked, and fired several pistol shots at the two, who responded by loosing several arrows after the fleeing coach, slightly wounding the driver. Feeling disappointed but justified, they stalked back to camp, making no effort to move on.

The following day, Captain George Stewart and troopers of the First Cavalry made a surprise charge on the camp, killing ten of the Cheyennes. The surviving warriors crossed to the north side of the Platte and vented their outrage on a Utah-bound Mormon train of four wagons encamped near the mouth of the Wood River. During the attack, the Cheyennes killed two men and a child and abducted a woman whom they later killed when her strength gave out. Five days later, on August 30, a small war party killed an emigrant woman near Cottonwood Springs and drove off livestock from another small train. About September 5, Cheyennes killed Utah Congressional Delegate Almon Babbitt and two other men in their camp along the Council Bluffs Road 120 miles west of Fort Kearny. On September 6, another war party attacked a group of Mormons killing two men, a woman, and a child. Yet another attack was made on a party of emigrants along the Little Blue River. By this time, not only the sparse frontier population, but newspapers in the river cities were demanding that the government "exterminate" the warlike Cheyennes to guarantee the safety of the trails.[5]

Not long after these incidents had occurred, a party of Cheyennes stopped briefly at Fort Kearny. Among the members of the group was a Sioux brave, who was asked to identify several arrows brought in from the scene of the attack along the Little Blue. He told the officers that the arrows were indeed Sioux, and was promptly placed under arrest. His Cheyenne companions escaped amid a hail of bullets and raided the horse herds, recovering a number of Cheyenne ponies which had been captured by Captain Stewart's troopers.

In response to the accelerating pattern of depredations by the young Cheyennes, the government determined to send a punitive expedition to the western plains. But, thanks to a penny-pinching Congress, there were no troops available for such a campaign just then. The only units capable of a lengthy expedition were the companies of Colonel Edwin Vose Sumner's First Cavalry, most of which were stationed at Fort Leavenworth. But the colonel and his men were already on active duty in the Kansas-Missouri border region, trying to enforce a peace in the "Wakarusa War" then being fought out between

Jayhawkers and bushwhackers. The Cheyennes would have to wait their turn to be punished.

Over the winter of 1856-1857, nearly all the Cheyennes gathered in encampments on the Solomon River in western Kansas. There, around the lodge fires, the old stories of the white soldiers' treachery and injustice were endlessly recounted, and the young men of the tribe dedicated themselves to widening the action during the coming summer. They reckoned that the time was propitious, since the whites were fighting among themselves in eastern Kansas and many of the soldiers were occupied there.

From a pair of medicine men named White Bull (Ice) and Dark came wonderful news: The two had succeeded in making a medicine of great power by which the warriors could be made immune to the bullets which came from the white men's guns. By using the prescribed rituals and incantations, the bullets could be made to fall directly from the muzzles to the ground. With opportunity, motivation, and a secret weapon on their side, the young Cheyennes were spoiling for a fight.

The federal government was eager to accommodate them. Having effected a cease fire in the border troubles, Colonel Sumner organized a punitive expedition at Fort Leavenworth. Hoping to catch the Cheyennes in a vise, he ordered Major John Sedgwick up the Arkansas with half the force, while the colonel himself took the remaining troops up the Platte. From Bent's Fort, Sedgwick turned north to meet Sumner, who was coming down from Fort Laramie. Failing to find any war parties, Sedgwick and Sumner met on the South Platte, where they combined their forces and marched eastward down the Solomon.

The Southern Cheyennes had taken little part in the troubles of the previous year, and were not at all convinced that war with the white soldiers was a good idea. While some of them had gone south to consult with William Bent, the rest were camped with their northern brothers along the Solomon. On July 29, Sumner's force of six troops of cavalry, trailed by three companies of infantry, ran into the warriors from the combined camps, strung out in a long battle line, eager to meet the bluecoats. They had among them a few old guns, but their medicine was strong and their quivers filled with arrows. Today the guns of the white soldiers would be useless.

Sumner wheeled his troopers into a battle line facing the Cheyennes, gave the order to draw sabers, and charged. It was a command decision which he never really explained. Possibly he had heard of the gallant charge of the Light Brigade in the Crimea the year before, or maybe the old dragoon simply could not resist the chance to perform a classic cavalry maneuver. It was a decision for which he was later criticized in military circles; but it was a decision which caused the complete disintegration of the Cheyenne warfront. The Indians stood their ground for a few moments, loosing a few ineffectual arrows. And then they remembered: Their medicine was only for use against the white men's guns. It was worthless against all those flashing "long knives." Like a flock of starlings, the Cheyenne braves broke formation and ran, desperately urging their ponies to gain distance on Sumner's heavy cavalry mounts. Each side suffered several casualties, but the fighting was all but over for the summer.[6]

Tactically, the battle had decided very little. But Sumner's destruction of the Cheyenne camp left the tribe poorly prepared for the winter. The colonel had planned to follow up his victory, but once again his plans were derailed by civil unrest. President Buchanan's troubles with the Mormons had reached an impasse, and the War Department ordered Sumner to break up his Cheyenne expedition and send most of his cavalry off to Utah Territory. Further punishment of the Cheyennes would have to wait. Even though they had escaped disaster, the tribesmen found their thirst for battle cooling. With the departure of Sumner's forces, a measure of peace returned to the High Plains.

As matters turned out, Sumner's cavalry did not go to Utah, but were ordered back to eastern Kansas to guard against riots in the upcoming election. Sumner and some of his troopers reached Fort Leavenworth on September 16, while the remainder returned in October. Though no one was aware of it at the time, the expedition had brought with it a tiny seed whose germination would bring unforseen changes to the High Plains and hasten the dissolution of the Cheyenne and Arapaho nations. That seed was a small bag of gold dust.

Fall Leaf, one of Sumner's Delaware Indian guides, had obtained the gold from a party of white men who had gathered it near the confluence of Cherry Creek and the South Platte River. Whether or not he understood the import of his actions, Fall Leaf exhibited the gold dust around Leavenworth and told his incredulous listeners where he had gotten it. In the spring of 1858, the first would-be miners were scrambling across the plains to Cherry Creek to seek the fortune in gold which they were certain could be had for a few days work.

The Treaty of 1851 had guaranteed the Indians that no whites would be allowed to settle on the buffalo range between the North Platte and the Arkansas Rivers, and for several years the white people had kept their part of the agreement. The arid, desolate land had no readily apparent value except as a hunting ground for the Indians. Now the rush for Colorado gold would prove stronger than any treaty.

In the spring of 1859, an estimated 125,000 to 150,000 gold seekers came stampeding up the Platte.[7] Others trailed along the Smoky Hill or up the Arkansas. Most of these men were not experienced plainsmen, and a number of them lost their way. The Cheyennes found them wandering dazed and aimless, took them to their villages, cared for them, and sent them on their way to Cherry Creek.[8] Many other whites turned back before reaching the gold fields, and of course, many died en route. It is probably safe to say that more than 80,000 eventually made it to the diggings. When they discovered that the tales of easy riches had been much exaggerated, some 40,000 angry and disappointed men went trooping back through the heart of Indian country, raising as much hell as they felt like, and greatly exciting the tribes.[9]

Some gold was found, of course, and some men did become rich—enough so that Kansas Governor Denver organized Arapaho County, which reached all the way to the mountains. The search for gold continued to filter westward into the Front Range, but the miners kept on coming. Throughout 1860-1863, an estimated 90,000 people would journey westward up the Platte, about half of them going on to the confluence of Cherry Creek and the South Platte where Denver City was growing rapidly.

The Indians never ceased to be astonished by the gold rush. They knew about the yellow metal, of course, but placed no value on it. A thousand Arapahoes were camped right in the heart of Denver City, and Chief Left Hand maintained his good humor amid all the commotion. But he also did his best to remind the white people that the territory really belonged to the Indians and he hoped they would leave as soon as they had found all the gold they wanted.

Most of the Indians were greatly agitated by the antics of the whites. In November 1858 a delegation of Cheyennes and Arapahoes visited William Bent and asked him to beg the Great Father to do something to stop these insane people from cutting down all the trees and ruining the hunting and camping grounds. Bent passed their concerns along to A. M. Robinson, Superintendent of Indian Affairs, whose reaction was unanticipated: He appointed William Bent as agent for the tribes.[10]

Bent was not pleased with his new responsibility and did not formally accept the position until May 1859. He had already resigned himself to the accelerating decay of the Cheyenne and Arapaho people, and determined once again to induce those who were amenable to become farmers. Many of the Indians agreed that farming might well be their only course of action to avoid eventual starvation, and a few were even enthusiastic about the idea. Alas, Bent was unable to procure the necessary funds for implements and seed.

Although on the surface, Indians and whites appeared to be living amicably amongst each other on Cherry Creek, Denver City was now a going concern, and there was a nagging propriety about the Indians' title to the land under the Treaty of 1851. As the Cheyennes and Arapahoes endeavored mightily to keep the peace with their raucous white neighbors, sharp minds began searching for ways to extinguish the Indians' entitlement. William Bent probably understood the tribes better than any other white man living, and he shrewdly perceived the undercurrent of tension which they were trying so hard to keep under control. In October 1859, he wrote:

> *A smothered passion for revenge agitates these Indians, perpetually fomented by the failure of food, the encircling encroachment of the white population, and the exasperating sense of decay and impending extinction with which they are surrounded . . . A desperate war of starvation and extinction is imminent and inevitable, unless prompt measures shall prevent it.*[11]

Those "prompt measures" included another treaty, much like the one Twiss had negotiated at Deer Creek, withdrawing the tribes from the Cherry Creek area in favor of a new reserve along the Arkansas where they could be transformed into an "agricultural and pastoral people."

Feeling completely impotent to effect needed change, Bent wanted out of his position badly. However, he remained until the government sent Commissioner A. B. Greenwood to negotiate a treaty which would, in effect, make the land grab of Denver City legal. Most of the Cheyennes were off hunting, but a few minor chiefs arrived on September 18 and tentatively agreed to the new compact. Bent resigned his office the very next day, and turned over the task of obtaining the additional necessary signatures to the new agent, his old Westport friend, Albert Gallatin Boone.

Boone did his best, but his dealings with the reserve Indians of eastern Kansas had not prepared him to deal with the wild tribes of the High Plains, and his inexperience led him to commit a number of gaffes which totally forfeited their confidence. Nevertheless, on February 18, 1861, the Treaty of Fort Wise completed the legal surround which the Cheyennes and Arapahoes had dreaded for so long. Many of the tribesmen, including the militant Dog Soldiers, would have nothing to do with the matter, preferring death to being cooped up on a reservation.

Thus it was that Fall Leaf and his little bag of gold unwittingly did more toward the subjection of the Cheyenne and Arapaho people than had been accomplished by the rest of the Sumner expedition. Moreover, the effects of the Colorado gold rush were not confined merely to the South Platte-Cherry Creek area. The thousands of people living on the Colorado frontier had to be provisioned entirely from the Missouri River ports, giving rise to the burgeoning business of wagon freighting. The Oregon-California Trail, originally a pathway for emigrants to the west coast, now branched off onto the Denver Road along the South Platte, and entered its last decade as a great, dirt superhighway—a bidirectional artery of commerce as well as emigration. Triggered by the rush for gold in Colorado and later in Idaho, by anticipation of a national homestead act, by the Civil War, and by plain old American capitalistic enterprise, an avalanche of humanity rolled over the trails, spawning a line of roadside supply stations. In the final analysis, these so-called "road ranches" and their accompanying influx of homesteaders would have a more profound effect on the aboriginal peoples than would all the skirmishes fought by the United States Army.

Chapter Five notes

1 This capsule background of the Cheyenne people is distilled from these sources:
Berthrong, *The Southern Cheyennes.*
Grinnell, *The Fighting Cheyennes.*
Lavender, *Bent's Fort.*
Moore, *The Cheyenne Nation.*

2 Lavender, *Bent's Fort*, 353.

3 Hyde, *The Life of George Bent*, 98.

4 Ibid., 100.

5 Grinnell, *The Fighting Cheyennes*, 113; Chalfant's *Cheyennes and Horse Soldiers* also has an excellent account of this episode.

6 Lavender, *Bent's Fort*, 355; also Chalfant, op. cit.

7 Mattes, "The South Platte Trail," 8-9.

8 Grinnell, *The Fighting Cheyennes*, 125. In a note, Grinnell attributes this information to George Bent.

9 Ibid., 124-125.

10 Lavender, *Bent's Fort*, 364-365.

11 Ibid., 367-368.

Part I
Chapter Six

"God bless our home"

Fall Leaf had told the truth, as far as he knew it. There was indeed gold to be found along Cherry Creek. The first significant color was panned there by the vanguard of the miners in 1858. The big rush itself took place during the 1859 trail season, and by the end of the year, a new city had materialized. Of course, everything from flour and sugar to window glass and pianos for the saloons had to be transported from the Missouri River ports over 650 miles distant. This quite naturally drove prices through the roof.

But it is an ill wind that blows no one any good, and it did not take long for folks with a flair for enterprise to figure out that the real money was to be made, not in mining gold, but in supplying the miners. In places like Omaha and Nebraska City, it seemed as if every man who could scrape together the cash to purchase a wagon and several yoke of oxen was in competition with large freighting firms such as Byram and Howe, or Russell, Majors and Waddell for a share of the Denver City trade. The symbiotic relationship between the wagon freighters and the Colorado frontier enabled Denver City to grow spectacularly, and the federal treasury to remain solvent; for gold mining and ore processing operations require great quantities of water which could be had only during the summer months. Without the freighters, the miners would have found it necessary to trek back to the Missouri ports during the warm months to obtain their supplies. The loss of working time would have curtailed the production of gold during the Civil War—a time when the economy of the Union states required vast, new resources of gold. "Had it not been for the high plains wagon freighter, the development of Colorado and Denver would have been delayed for at least a decade, if not much longer."[1]

Others who witnessed the variety and volume of travel along the Oregon-California-Denver Road foresaw a potential bonanza to be made in supplying the suppliers. From the first days of the gold rush, a series of private supply houses sprouted up all along the road from the Kansas-Nebraska border to Denver City—the "convenience stores" of the trail. Charles Dawson writes:

> *Men with foresight grasped the situation, and began to establish stations along the trail in what is now Nebraska where the overland people might camp and secure feed for their beasts of burden and other supplies. These ranchers cut hay, planted corn and gardens, and bought their supplies at the river towns, thus becoming the first agriculturists and storekeepers.*[2]

These supply stations, no matter how humble or grand, became known as road ranches; and because of their uniqueness and importance to the white man's conquest of the High Plains, they need to be described through the eyes of those who saw them.

Maurice Morris, an Englishman who traveled west in 1864, scoffed at the term "ranch," saying,

> *It must not be supposed that these ranches imply farming on any scale whatever; they are simply business stations to meet the wants of the emigrants and travelers westward, and therefore each mainly consists of one room, which serves for store, grog shop, and bedroom by night. In the smaller ones, and they are far the most numerous, the stock in hand may be set down as consisting of much pork and ham, a few pounds of coffee, salt, pepper, vinegar, pearl-ash, soda, flour, butter, eggs, dried apples, peaches in tins, and oysters also, with a Falstaffian proportion of a vile compound of whiskey and I know not what, which is palpably known as "bust head," or "forty rod," because the unfortunate imbiber is seriously affected in either brain or legs, or even in both, before he has gone that distance.*
>
> *Winter is the harvest time for these ranches, for then they have to feed the passing stock on corn and hay, which they retail at enormous prices . . . But one of their great sources of wealth lay in "trading" oxen. For this purpose they begin with a few of their own, and when a man passes with a foot-sore*

ox which can go no further, they sell the traveler a fresh one at their own rate . . . Under these circumstances it will not be surprising that these "rancheros" make their pile pretty quickly.[3]

Contrary to Morris' cynical assertions, some of the ranchers did in fact raise their own crops, especially along the Little Blue River, where land and climate were favorable. A Little Blue rancher named James Bainter, who had ten acres planted in corn, wrote:

The profits of the ranch business were wonderfully good; everything sold by the pound; potatoes sold for five cents per pound, the same for hay and other things in proportion.[4]

The family on nearby Buffalo Ranch also planted corn and kept a garden, mainly for their own use. Their chief business staple, hence the name of the ranch, was buffalo meat. Several hunters were hired to harvest the buffalo which still roamed the vicinity. Forequarters were sold for three cents a pound and hindquarters for five cents. Meat, tallow, and hides were taken to Brownville on the Missouri River to be exchanged for food staples and clothing.

Along the Platte, Moses Sydenham and Washington Hinman, as well as the German settlers of Grand Island City, raised experimental gardens from which they sold produce at outrageous prices to travelers starved for fresh vegetables and melons.

But as the ranches became located farther from the Missouri, the gardens became fewer and poorer, and prices climbed accordingly. Louisa Cook noted in 1862 that potatoes sold for $1.50 a bushel, corn about the same, while sugar was twenty-five cents per pound and flour six cents. She wrote with some amusement that "all the houses, whether fenced in or not, are called ranches," and observed that none of the ranches west of Fort Kearny had gardens.[5]

Frank Root was constantly up and down the trail throughout 1863, and he also wrote:

I don't think there was as much as a respectable-sized garden spot under cultivation at any of the various ranches along the Platte between Fort Kearny and a few miles east of the mountains.[6]

The ranchmen were hardly to blame. After journeying up the Platte Valley in 1820, Major Stephen Long had confirmed Zebulon

Pike's 1806 report that the region was a wasteland fit only for the nomadic savages who inhabited it. Wrote Long:

> *It is a region destined, by the barrenness of its soil, the inhospitable character of its climate, and by other physical disadvantages, to be the abode of perpetual desolation."*

In spite of this dreary evaluation, a few halting attempts at agriculture were made. Lieutenant Colonel Ludwell Powell, the first commander of Fort Kearny, planted trees and gardens in order to make the post a more pleasant place for his soldiers. Most of his trees died, and the gardens never produced enough to feed more than a fraction of the men on duty.[8] In 1851 Captain Henry Wharton tried again, reporting that, with a good growing season and the labor of an entire company of infantry, "I should feel confident of raising here corn(,) oats and all kinds of vegetables . . ." [9] But good growing seasons were rare, and by 1854 the garden initiative had been abandoned at Fort Kearny. When Lieutenant Ware first saw the fort in 1863, another attempt at gardening had begun. A small irrigation well had been dug and the plot fertilized with manure hauled from the stables, but "the result was very feeble, and outside of that nothing was raised."[10] It is a simple fact of geography that, under the dominance of the Rocky Mountain rainshadow, farming on the High Plains is a difficult business, especially without adequate irrigation, and those early road ranchers hadn't quite gotten the knack of it.

Though they may have been lacking in fresh produce, most of the ranches nevertheless carried a considerable variety of goods. In addition to those items listed by Morris, Margaret Carrington mentioned stocks of nutmeg and peppermint, ready-made clothing, pipes, whips, camp kettles, and frying pans.[11] According to Ware, the ranches west of Kearny stocked supplies of goggles, something like large spectacles, for protecting the eyes from blowing dust and alkali.[12]

The road ranches were also protective havens for man and beast when the unpredictable plains weather turned ugly. Mrs. Carrington left a vivid description of her stay at a sheltering ranch amid the snow and biting cold of a November storm: Stage passengers stood warming themselves by the stove, gobbled huge platters of bacon and cabbage, breakfasted on pork and eggs, and washed everything down with mugs of hot coffee. At night, she noted, everyone lay down to sleep on the floor like a row of ten pins. In spite of the discomforts, it was Mrs. Carrington's opinion that the ranchmen were "some of the best and bravest hearted men of any race or people."[13]

Well, perhaps not all of them. John Collins found that, along the Omaha-Fort Kearny Military Road, a freighter seeking shelter and feed for his mules was forced to pay as much as a dollar per span for a single night.

> *If you did not patronize these ranches, the alternative was to camp where you could and wake up in the morning to find one or two head of stock gone . . . The stray stock was sometimes found in the corral of the ranchman with a charge of $5.00 to $10.00 for recovering it.*[14]

Jack Morrow's Junction Ranch, at the forks of the Platte River, was the acme of variety, size, and sheer skullduggery. The unscrupulous Morrow constructed his two and one-half story ranch house and a row of nearby pilgrim huts from cedar logs, and populated his place with a weird collection of loafers, hunters, traders, and drifters. In a nearby squaw camp were several hundred "bad Indians" and a number of white squawmen whose work it was to stampede the emigrants' stock and hide the animals in the rugged canyons south of the ranch. To make sure that travelers were unable to bypass his place, Morrow had his employees dig what might be called an antiwagon ditch and dike which ran all the way from the ranch to the southern bluffs. The flamboyant badman carried an impressive stock of goods for sale to the unwary. In later years he expanded his activities to include supplying railroad ties, a freighting operation between Fort Laramie and Salt Lake City, and even a soft coal mine in Wyoming. Mrs. Carrington was completely taken in by Morrow, calling him "the prince of ranchmen, and a king of good fellows." Had her husband not been a colonel of cavalry, her opinion might have been far different, for Morrow was always careful to remain on good terms with the army.[15]

Other road ranches were not nearly as pretentious as Junction Ranch, and their buildings followed certain patterns according to locality. Along the Little Blue River, where there were groves of oaks and cottonwoods, the ranch-store was usually built of logs, mortised at the corners, chinked with clay, and enclosing a board floor. Buffalo Ranch was quite small, requiring only three wagon loads of logs. Its roof was made of small logs laid closely together and covered with thick slough grass, which was then topped by two, thick courses of sod. The owners reported the little house to be warm in winter, cool in summer, and entirely leakproof.[16]

But along the Platte, the only timber to be had were the scrawny trees which dotted the islands in the river. In the absence of logs for building, the ranchmen turned to the tough prairie sod for their houses and corrals, the only wooden components being roof supports and window and door casings. In all cases, these sod huts were gloomy and cramped, but warm in winter and, as events were to prove, highly resistant to fire and arrows.

As the line of road ranches became firmly established along the trail, their supplies of hay and feed grain enabled the wagon freighters to extend the trail season to virtually twelve months, though the cost was high. Once assured of adequate supplies of shelled corn, many freighters switched from oxen to mule power, increasing the number of freighting runs which could be made during the year. All this had the effect of leveling prices in Denver City, particularly on foodstuffs, although the cost of hay and corn to the freighter maintained those prices at inflated levels. Only the coming of the railroad in 1870 decreased and steadied prices for good, ending a fabulous decade for the High Plains wagon freighter.

The road ranches also proved a boon to the Pony Express in 1860, and to the organization of Ben Holladay's stagecoach empire in 1862. The best and most strategically located ranches were expanded to serve as home or swing stations. The owners and their families went on Holladay's payroll as cooks, agents, and stock tenders for the line. Mail dropped at designated stations was collected by the coaches which maintained daily schedules between Atchison, Kansas and Salt Lake City. Along with business and personal mail, the coaches carried the latest newspapers from Atchison, Nebraska City, Omaha, and Denver. Unlike the people of the first migration in 1841, the travelers of the 1860s were never far from communication with "the states." Once they reached the Platte River, their communication was instantaneous, for after 1862, the transcontinental telegraph line followed the trail from Fort Kearny westward.

Thus the road ranches made possible the growth of Denver City and also spearheaded a wave of settlement along the route of the trail corridor. The settler who operated a trailside store was virtually guaranteed a profit as he and his family struggled to build their new home in Nebraska Territory. The road ranch became a mechanism of survival for whole families desiring an escape from poverty, overcrowded conditions, unyielding cropland, and civil unrest. Moreover, in moving to secure a better life for his loved ones, which has been the heart's desire of mankind from antiquity, the road rancher-homesteader was also responding to a great national impulse known as Manifest Destiny.

In the great burst of nationalism which followed the Revolution, the young nation began to push settlements far over the Appalachian Mountains and onto the central plains. Gradually, it began to dawn upon Americans that the entire width of the continent was to be theirs to explore, to tame, and to exploit. And what a continent it was! The reports of Lewis and Clark were convincing evidence that North America was much larger than anyone had dared to imagine. There was seemingly endless land and resources beyond belief—a fantastically beautiful country to be forged into a showcase of democracy, to become a haven for the oppressed peoples of Europe. Every new step westward reinforced the confidence of Americans in themselves as the new chosen people of God, whose duty it was to subdue and populate this wondrous land. This growing conviction was given a name by the journalist John L. O'Sullivan, who wrote in 1845 that nothing must be allowed to interfere with "the fulfillment of our manifest destiny to overspread the continent allotted by Providence for the free development of yearly multiplying millions."[17]

It was a doctrine which struck a sympathetic chord in the national psyche. And when the German painter, Emanuel Leutze, was commissioned by Congress to execute one of his heroic, overblown canvasses commemorating the hardy pioneer spirit, he borrowed a line from the British philosopher, George Berkely, for his title: *Westward the Course of Empire Takes its Way*. The painting, which owed more to Moses and the Israelites looking over into the promised land than to any actual event of the trail, placed the imprimatur of Divine Providence upon the course of empire by mystically depicting a large cross hovering over a dying emigrant.

There was, to be sure, a slight problem over the ownership of this vast territory. The indigenous people who claimed it were loosely organized into hundreds of tribal units, many of them fiercely antagonistic to one another. None of them had surveyed or marked or recorded just exactly which part of the continent they claimed as their own. In the words of Governor Winthrop, they had enclosed "noe land, neither have any setled habytation." Moreover, many of those tribal units claimed land which they themselves had wrested by force or intimidation from other tribes. The Sioux and Cheyennes had taken over a territory which had "belonged" at various times to the Crows, Pawnees, Assiniboins, Comanches, and others—and who had claimed the land even before those people? Leutze's painting reminded Americans that God's chosen people had ample precedent for the outright seizure of territory from heathen tribes (and, to the pioneers, the Indians were assuredly heathen). The Israelites of Old Testament times had conquered their promised land from the likes of the Amelikites and the Hittites, Jebusites and Canaanites. It required but a simple step in logic to see that a Christian people had the right, even the duty to take control of this rich land in the continent's interior.

Americans had the will, the technology, and the divine mandate to cause this wonderful land to flower and produce, to yield up its vast cornucopia of riches. The aboriginal people would benefit greatly if they became Christianized and gave up their old lifestyle to join in this subduing of the land. But, if they objected, the thing would be done anyway and they would be simply pushed aside.

Even with the promise of free land, rich harvests, and the profits of commerce as their cause; with Manifest Destiny and the rights of free Americans as their armament, the homesteaders found that subduing the land could be a fearfully hard and downright dangerous enterprise. Their greatest challenge was the land itself.

For want of water and communication, the early settlers who came into the prairie country clustered along its streams and trails. They wrote glowing letters to friends and kin back east about the kaleidoscope of wildflowers which perfumed the limitless sea of grass; about the rich, stone-free soil and the variety and abundance of wild game. To new arrivals, the plains seemed at first to be a garden of earthly delights.

It did not take long for the less delightful features of the broad, new country to make themselves known. There was the blasting heat of summer, that shriveled the pitiful crops and browned the prairie grasses, which made men sick and drove animals mad. Winter brought brittle cold that froze exposed skin within minutes, and slashing blizzards in which a man no more than a few yards from his home might lose his way only to freeze to death in a swirling, stinging world of icy whiteness.

In dry years, there came clouds of grasshoppers that darkened the sky and devoured everything green. The hoppers formed clusters as large as a man's hat atop fenceposts and their chewing could be plainly heard on a still evening. Wet years brought clouds of gnats and swarms of mosquitoes that ate at the eyes and nostrils of the draft animals and swarmed through screenless windows and doors, biting and stinging until the inhabitants, with swollen and painful faces, sought shelter under their mosquito netting.

There were the unpredictable prairie rattlesnakes, capable of striking thrice in a second, whose venom could kill a man and sicken an ox. There were the violent storms of summer, blowing up in less than twenty minutes, lancing the earth with fire from the heavens, battering and killing with tornadic winds and huge hailstones. There were prairie fires that could outrun a man as they raced through the winter killed grasses, incinerating rabbits and prairie hens and snakes, leaving hard-earned haystacks in cinders.

And always there was the unceasing wind, generating a low, moaning, rushing sound as it swept over the billows of grass that stretched from horizon to horizon. Many Easterners, accustomed to great tracts of forests and gentle mountains, discovered that the open, treeless plains caused psychological torments in the form of uneasiness and apprehension.

Many homesteaders hung on grimly in the face of these curses. Others were broken, physically and mentally, by the rigors of the harsh land. As they retreated eastward, exhausted and heartsick, they left behind them the grubby ruins of what were to have been their dream homes. One abandoned claim on the south edge of the Platte Valley was reportedly marked by a sign which proclaimed,

> *This claim for sale. Four miles to the nearest neighbor. Seven miles to the nearest schoolhouse. Fourteen miles to the nearest town. Two hundred feet to the nearest water. God bless our home! For further information address Thomas Ward, Oskaloosa, Iowa.*[18]

Those who persevered eventually found ways of living in harmony with the land. They came, in time, to love its rich smells and the feel of its loamy earth. They swelled with pride over their first harvests and their expanding houses. And all too often they laid their young children to rest beneath its protecting sod. It became a part of them, and they would fight for it against the savages which roamed over the country, whose behaviors were unpredictable and uncouth. And, in those uncertain years before 1861, the land became their security in the midst of frightening social and economic currents which threatened to make a mockery of the noble premises of Manifest Destiny, which left the very future of the American nation in gathering gloom.

If the signers of the Declaration of Independence had really believed that "all men are created equal," they would have dropped their quills and rushed home to free their slaves. This they did not do, of course, and the incongruity of slavery in a free society prevailed through years of ineffectual compromise to be settled by civil war. The people who came in the latter 1850s and early 1860s to homestead along the route of the overland trails were much affected by the growing national unrest. Many came to the Indian frontier to escape what they saw as an impending storm in which they could discern no ray of hope. In understanding their world and their reactions to it, it is helpful to pay brief attention to the events which generated this climate of national disaffection.[19]

The passage of the Kansas-Nebraska Act in 1854 threw open these two future states to settlement. The act also repealed the Missouri Compromise, leaving the status of slavery in Kansas and Nebraska to be determined by popular vote. Immediately, men on both sides of the issue began flooding into eastern Kansas, establishing "freesoil towns" or "slave towns" which were little more than armed camps. In May 1855, a proslavery posse of Missourians attacked the freesoil town of Lawrence, and the "Wakarusa War" (so named because most of the fighting occurred along the Wakarusa River) became a shooting war. Every possible stratagem, legal or illegal, was used by both sides to influence the farcical election, and matters were only stabilized by the arrival of Colonel Edwin Vose Sumner and several companies of his First U. S. Cavalry Regiment.

In May 1856, the violence spread into the halls of the United States Senate with the vicious beating of abolitionist Senator Charles Sumner by an offended Congressman from South Carolina. Thereafter, members of the Congress began to attend sessions with weapons at their sides.

Two days after the beating of Senator Sumner, a radical abolitionist named John Brown led a few mangy followers on a night raid along Pottawattamie Creek in eastern Kansas, during which they murdered five proslavery settlers.

In March 1857, James Buchanan became President of the United States. Buchanan desired nothing more for his administration than tranquility at home and abroad. He would have none. Several days after his inauguration, the Supreme Court handed down its decision in the Dred Scott case, affirming that slaves were indeed the property of their owners. The year 1857 drew to a close with financial panic deepening into depression.

Eighteen fifty-seven was also the year Buchanan sent a military force to Utah Territory to show the Mormons who was boss. After some frantic negotiating and compromise on both sides, the "Mormon War" ended in 1858 without a shot being fired. Militarily it had been a fiasco, proving only that the U.S. Army was ill-equipped for a campaign even within its own country.

In October of 1859, the "Kansas Tornado," John Brown, attempted to incite a slave rebellion by capturing the federal arsenal at Harpers Ferry, (West) Virginia. He was captured and hanged for his trouble, becoming an example to some, a martyr to others. His trial served only to focus the glare of national attention on the slavery question which had now gone beyond useful debate anyhow.

Completely eclipsed by these ponderous events of national importance were several small, local disturbances having nothing to do with slavery, which occurred on the plains and proved to be portents of larger eruptions to come. Near Clear Lake, Iowa, in 1855, a party of Santee Sioux in search of a few Winnebagoes to kill, became sidetracked by the chase of a lordly rooster in the farmyard of a Mr. Dickerson. During their comic pursuit, the Indians knocked over the man's grindstone. Failing to see the humor of the situation, Mr. Dickerson grabbed a piece of the broken stone and brained one of the warriors with it. The rest of the band then turned on him and robbed him of some household possessions. A posse of armed settlers tracked down the band a short time later, and the chief sent out a flag of truce for a parley. Restitution was made, and the "Grindstone War" ended peaceably, although tensions were high enough that many settlers in Cerro Gordo County left their homes for a time.[20]

The excitement had barely abated when, in the fall of 1856, an outlaw Wahpekute chief named Inkpaduta led a few followers in perpetrating the Spirit Lake Massacre. Trouble began when several of the Indians stole some corn and killed a farmer's dog and were caught and whipped for their misdeeds. Throughout the winter and into the spring of 1857, Inkpaduta's band took revenge on the white settlers around Lake Okoboji in northern Iowa (only one man was actually killed west of Spirit Lake) and several women were kidnapped. Five companies of the Tenth Infantry were sent in pursuit of the renegades, and Chief Little Crow and his Mdewkanton tribesmen were coerced to join the chase by a threat to withhold their annuity payments.

No sooner did the military forces begin to move, when orders came for the infantry to cease pursuit of the Indians and join Colonel Albert Sidney Johnston's command headed for Utah to prosecute the Mormon War. After the departure of the regulars, citizen volunteers from northern Iowa and southern Minnesota joined with Little Crow's Santees to track down the fugitives on Yellow Medicine River. Inkpaduta's son was killed in the fight, but the old, smallpox-scarred chief escaped. The volunteers returned home feeling cheated of justice, and the entire episode accomplished little more than to increase the ill will between settlers and Santees.[21]

In Nebraska Territory also, there was trouble with a tribe which, like the Santees, had been on generally friendly terms with the white people. The Pawnees were Caddoan-speaking Indians who migrated northward from near Mexico sometime in the early 1600s. Eventually imposing themselves between the Sioux to the west and the sedentary Missouri River tribes to the east, the Pawnees exercised hegemony over a large region between the Niobrara and the Smoky Hill Rivers, and from the forks of the Platte to the Missouri. Their northward migration had taken them away from the contesting Spanish and

French, but had placed them directly astride the central Platte Valley route, hence directly in the path of the "course of empire." Increasing contact with the white man weakened the once numerous Pawnees until, by the late 1850s, there were only about 3,000 left.[22]

From their permanent villages along the Platte and Loup Rivers, the Pawnees maintained peaceable relations with the Omahas, Otoes, and Poncas, as well as with the white men who were coming into their country in increasing numbers. With their Sioux and Cheyenne neighbors, however, the Pawnees were continually at war by reason of their unprovoked attack upon a village of Republican River Sioux during the northward migration.

In 1857, the Pawnees ceded their lands to the government by the Treaty of Table Creek. Under its terms, the tribe agreed to move to a new reservation encompassing land on both sides of the Loup River west of Looking Glass Creek, where stood the Mormon way settlement of Genoa. Not only would this remove the Pawnees from the Platte Valley corridor, but it would also remind the recalcitrant Brigham Young in Salt Lake City that the government could apply pressure to conform in all sorts of creative ways.

For its part, the United States promised to build an agency for the Pawnees, complete with storehouses, a gristmill, sawmill, and school. It also promised to protect them from their ancient enemies as they worked their fields and tended their stock.

Those ancient enemies, the Sioux and Cheyennes, must have been delighted with the Pawnees' new reservation. Not only had their hated foes been moved some four days travel closer, but the valley of the Loup and its tributaries provided convenient and secluded invasion routes leading from the desolate Nebraska sandhills directly to the Pawnee Agency. The move was certain to simplify the business of intertribal warfare.

The Pawnees were apprehensive about their new reserve, located as it was on the site of an aboriginal village which had been attacked and burned nearly two centuries before. Their mood soured even more when a party of whites ransacked and burned their village of Pahuk (directly south of present Fremont, Nebraska) shortly after they left on their spring hunt. Continuing northwestward up the valley of the Elkhorn River, some of the young Pawnees committed a string of depredations upon the property of white settlers, attacked and robbed a man near Fontanelle, and reportedly wounded a homesteader near West Point. After a brief gunbattle between a party of citizens and some of the Pawnee braves, the settlers of the Elkhorn Valley became alarmed over possible reprisals and petitioned Territorial Governor Samuel Black to call out the militia to chasten the tribe.

Governor Black was at his home in Nebraska City, accessible from Omaha only by sending a mounted messenger down the Iowa side of the Missouri River. In his absence, Secretary of State J. Sterling Morton assumed the reins of government and, on July 4, 1859, issued orders for militia units to respond to the emergency. He also called upon the commander at Fort Kearny to send federal troops, and Lieutenant Beverly Robertson was sent north with a company of Second Dragoons to join militia units from Omaha and Columbus under the command of General John Thayer.[23] On the second day of the march, Thayer's men were joined by an aging politician, Samuel Ryan Curtis—a graduate of West Point and current congressman from Iowa's First District. Not long after, Governor Black also caught up to the militia companies and, as commander in chief, assumed command of the expedition. It was soon discovered that the governor was far too intoxicated to command anything. After ordering Lieutenant Robertson (over whom he had no authority) to return to Columbus for twenty barrels of whiskey and four sacks of flour, he was placed under "tent arrest" by General Thayer, and the march continued.

The Pawnees, meanwhile, had been joined by some Omahas, and the troops located their joint camp on a small tributary of the Elkhorn some ten miles west of the present town of Norfolk. Thayer formed his men into line of battle, trained the dragoons' fieldpiece on the Indian camp, and gave the order to charge.

The Pawnee War ended with all the anticlimax of the Grindstone War. The Indians came running toward the advancing troops, waving flags, and shouting "Good Indian!" Thayer withheld the order to fire, the charge was halted, and a peace agreement was reached. There was only one casualty—not a rooster this time, but a horse belonging to one of the Omahas, accidentally shot by a careless militiaman. Restitution was made, and the affair came to an end. The damages done to the settlers of the Elkhorn Valley remained to be addressed, however, and their claims would bedevil the agent for the Pawnees for the next several years.[24]

Like the first mutterings of some long-quiescent volcano, these small disturbances should have been significant of the current of resentment which was building, even within tribes that had long been reconciled to the advance of white civilization. Perhaps in a time of national tranquillity, they would have been taken more seriously. But to a nation tearing at its own vitals, beset with growing pains both economic and moral, they went virtually unnoticed, except in their immediate localities. The residue of these small "wars" would survive as a toxin in the minds of white homesteaders in southern Minnesota and along the trails through Nebraska, breeding resentment and mistrust which would greatly color their reactions when the aboriginal people of the frontier finally reached the breaking point.

Chapter Six notes

1 Already in 1860 the volume of freight which left the Missouri River ports is reckoned at 15,900,000 pounds. Walker, *The Wagonmasters*, 194, 199.

2 Dawson, *Pioneer Tales*, 28.

3 Morris, *Rambles in the Rocky Mountains*, 47-48.

4 *Biographical and Historical Memoirs*, 345.

5 Holmes, Ed., *Covered Wagon Women*, Vol. 8, 37.

6 Root and Connelley, *Overland Stage*, 246.

7 Major Long's report quoted in *Nebraska–A Guide to the Cornhusker State* (WPA), 50.

8 Wilson, *Fort Kearny*, 29.

9 Captain Henry Wharton to the Adjutant General, July 6, 1851, in *Fort Kearny Letterbook*.

10 Ware, *The Indian War of 1864*, 34.

11 Carrington, *Absaraka*, 60.

12 Ware, *The Indian War of 1864*, 131.

13 Carrington, *Absaraka*, 60.

14 Collins, *Across the Plains in '64*, 10.

15 Carrington, *Absaraka*, 58; also Miller, *Shutters West*, 107.

16 Ellenbecker, *The Indian Raids on the Upper Little Blue*, 9.

17 Garraty, *The American Nation*, 312-313.

18 WPA, *Nebraska–A Guide*, 290.

19 An excellent general source on this period of American history is Catton, *This Hallowed Ground.*

20 Sharp, *History of the Spirit Lake Massacre*, 25.

21 Ibid.

22 Grinnell, *Two Great Scouts*, 51; also Papers of Frank North.

23 Ironically, the Civil War resulted in General Thayer and Lieutenant Robertson serving on opposite sides–Thayer as a division commander with Grant in the southwest, Robertson as a general of cavalry with Lee in Virginia.

24 Grinnell, *Two Great Scouts*, 8-9; Thayer, "The Pawnee War of 1859;" NSHS, *Transactions* Vol. 2 (1887), 181-185; Wilson, *Fort Kearny*, 153.

Part I
Chapter Seven

"The settlers in our country viewed the future with anxiety"

Throughout the 1840s and 1850s, the regular army saw hard use. It fought the Seminoles in Florida, the Mexicans, the Sioux, and the Cheyennes. It was called upon to explore regions in the Black Hills and Rocky Mountains. It guarded seacoasts and the Mexican border, the Santa Fe and Oregon-California Trails. It enforced peace in eastern Kansas and rattled the saber in far Utah Territory. Yet, at the time of the attack on Fort Sumter in April, 1861, the army was woefully under strength, numbering barely 16,000 officers and men. Of its 198 companies, 183 of them were on duty in the West—approximately one soldier for every 120 square miles.[1]

In the days following the surrender of Fort Sumter, the great majority of these troops were called east for duty in the national crisis. Within months, nearly a third of the officer corps had resigned to serve the Confederacy, though virtually all the enlisted men remained loyal to the government. For all practical purposes, the army had ceased to protect the frontier.[2]

Along the trails and over the settlements swept the fear that the plains Indians would take advantage of the army's departure by ravaging the frontier and rolling back the line of settlement all the way to the Missouri–yet nothing happened. Rather, the beginning of the Civil War found the wild tribes occupied with hunting and trading, carrying on their normal activities.[3] Hard things had passed between Indian and white people since the Big Talk in 1851, but the tribes simply had no intention of attacking the settlers. At the same time, their "normal activities" included a great many attacks on their old enemies, the Pawnees, whom the white man had conveniently softened up for them.

The year before Fort Sumter found the Pawnees settling in on their new reservation, and the Sioux and Cheyennes preparing a warm welcome for them.[4] On June 22, 1860, an estimated force of 300 hostile warriors attacked the Pawnees, killing two squaws outside the village. Agent Gilles, at great personal risk, mounted and rode out among the attackers for a talk. Both Sioux and Cheyennes were much opposed to harming white people at this time if they could possibly avoid doing so, and after a brief exchange of arguments and threats, the attackers withdrew. It proved to be only a temporary respite, for a few days later, the reservation was attacked a second time with a loss of twelve more people. The Pawnees and their agent were incensed. Where, they wanted to know, was the protection promised them in the Treaty of Table Creek?

That protection was at Fort Kearny, nearly 100 miles away, in the person of a mixed bag of Second Dragoons and Second Infantry. Unless the lives of whites were endangered, no one seemed to think it necessary to send a military force to protect the reservation.

Agent Gilles strenuously protested this breach of the treaty to Major Charles May and Captain Alfred Sully at Fort Kearny, to no avail. On July 5, with most of the Pawnee warriors gone hunting to the south, the Sioux and Cheyennes returned for a third attack. Mostly the aged and infirm Pawnees had been left behind, and these were hidden by Agent Gilles in two large root cellars near his residence. The attackers burned twenty lodges, destroyed crops, and managed to scalp one squaw. Again on July 11, they attacked the agency, killing oxen and stealing the millwright's tools.

Finally, on the last day of August, a force of twenty dragoons and thirty infantrymen arrived on the reservation, just in the nick of time, as things turned out. On the very next day, the Cheyennes raided the horse herds and the cavalry turned out in pursuit. Moreover, the Pawnees were not hunting this time, and their enraged warriors joined the chase during which the Cheyenne camp was captured and two of the attackers killed. Although Captain Sully received orders to withdraw the troops at the end of August, the raids came to an end for the year.

The continuing hostilities between the Pawnees and the Sioux and Cheyennes were potentially dangerous to the whites, yet the wild tribes had, to this time, scrupulously avoided harming the frontier people. Though the settlers remained wary of their warring red neighbors, they were not overly alarmed by their presence. In the summer of 1860, the tribes fought a noisy battle on the Grande Ile of the Platte. Nearby, a group of homesteaders from the German Settlements continued to haul in their cut hay, though they were within sight and sound of the fight.[5] The Germans, like most of the homesteaders along the trails, had developed a "live-and-let-live" policy toward all the tribes. For the time being, it seemed to be working well enough that the handful of regular cavalry left at Fort Kearny were deemed adequate for the task at hand. Indeed, most of the army's troubles in 1860-1862 seem to have been caused by the white people along the trail.

When Captain John Thompson and his men of the Fourth Cavalry came to Fort Kearny in late 1861, the officer found that he had not nearly enough manpower to guard government property at the post from "lawless, lecherous, thievish, unscrupulous villains—old discharged soldiers, citizens of Kearny City, who seek and take every opportunity to pilfer, not only from the post, but from emigrants on the road . . ."[6]

Given the skeleton military presence along the trails, the mounting pressure from emigrants and homesteaders, and the inattention of a government preoccupied by civil war, the continuing absence of hostilities on the part of the plains tribes seemed too good to be true. It was. The turning point came early in 1862.

Joseph P. Smith and his brother-in-law, James Anderson, were in their early fifties when they brought their families from Crown Point, Indiana, to homestead in Nebraska Territory. A native of New York, one-time captain of private militia companies, and wealthy farmer, Smith anticipated that the Homestead Act, when signed into law, would qualify his family for a bonanza in free government land. As he and Anderson were well aware, many of their neighbors had already joined others from Illinois, Indiana, Wisconsin, and Ohio in emigrating to the valleys of the Big and Little Blue, Platte, and Loup Rivers, so the combined families decided to make their move. Though Smith and Anderson were of an advanced age to withstand the rigors of pioneering, they were nevertheless healthy and accustomed to hard work.

In the summer of 1861, James Anderson took his Scotch-born wife and two sons through Omaha and westward along the Military Road to a point about twelve miles west of the German Settlements along the Grand Island of the Platte. There, on the banks of the lazy Wood River and several hundred yards north of the trail, the Andersons put up a log cabin which served as both home and road ranch.

The area was not exactly unsettled. Some of their neighbors living along the Wood River were Mormons recently displaced from their community of Genoa when the Pawnee Reservation was relocated there. Even as the Andersons arrived, many of these people were preparing to move westward to their new Zion on the Great Salt Lake. There would be an abundance of land to be claimed under preemption rights when the Homestead Act was finally signed into law.

In the fall of the year, the Smith family also left Crown Point. By the last week in October, they reached Omaha, where they outfitted themselves for the frontier. After sending back word to friends that everything was alright thus far, Joseph Smith took his family west along the Military Road, out onto the prairie, destined for one last, great pioneering adventure.

The little cabin begun by the Andersons must have been cramped for so many people that first winter, and the families used every available opportunity to build additional space. On February 5, 1862, Smith and Anderson left their home for the north channel of the Platte, about two and one-half miles south, to cut cottonwood logs. The day was seasonably cold and the ground was covered with snow, so the men took two wagon sleds on which to haul the timber. Joseph Smith took along his two sons—ten-year-old Willie and eight-year-old Charles—while James Anderson was accompanied by his oldest son, Alexander, who was thirteen. The five of them cut and loaded logs until around ten o'clock in the morning, when Anderson drove the first sled home to unload. It was nearly noon when he returned to the Platte with his empty sled.

All was quiet. The second sled stood alone with a half load of timber. The team was gone and there was no sign of Smith or the boys. Scattered around the sled lay the harness, which had been cut to pieces. Cautiously, Anderson began walking toward the river channel.

Not far away, three men were making their way along the Military Road, driving several wagons loaded with shelled corn for Fort Kearny. The oxen were finding it a tough pull as they crunched through the snow, and Charles Boehl and Henry and John Thomsson were driving slowly. They were within a quarter mile of the Smith and Anderson homestead when they heard James Anderson yelling wildly. Off to the southwest, they saw the empty sled careening over the snow, Anderson whipping his team and shouting like a man gone berserk. The women had emerged from the cabin before he reached the dooryard, and the men on the loaded wagons could see him waving his arms wildly. By the time Boehl and the Thomssons reached the cabin, all the women were crying hysterically. From Anderson, the men learned that Smith and the children were dead, and they immediately started for the Platte to see for themselves.

On the ice of the narrow channel, just below the low riverbank, they found the body of the former militia captain. In one side, just below the armpit, an arrow was buried up to its feathers. A short distance away they found Smith's two sons. Little Charles was lying face down in the snow. His arms and skull had been crushed by a heavy club and the work had been finished off with an ax. Willie had an arrow through his wrist, and his skull had been cleft with the ax. His lower jaw had been cut away from the corner of his mouth to one ear. All around the small bodies, the snow was crimsoned and trampled, and the boys' heads and clothing were soaked with their blood.

Word of the atrocity spread quickly among the Wood River settlers, and neighbors began arriving on the scene to search the riverbank for the missing Alexander. His body was soon found among the trees a short distance from the others. Alexander had also been hacked to death and his skull crushed.

The murders infuriated the Wood River people, and a party of eighteen men, including Boehl and the Thomsson brothers, followed a set of snowy tracks westward along the Wood River. Jesse Eldridge, who lived two and one-half miles east of the Smith-Anderson place, led a second party of men westward along the north channel.

The winter night came early. The temperature dropped and snow began to fall. Soon all the tracks were covered over. Ill prepared for the pursuit, the Wood River party turned back.

The Eldridge group had better luck. About eighteen miles east of Fort Kearny, they discovered some twenty Sioux warriors, sheltering themselves from the bitter weather in a rude tent they had constructed from poles and blankets. The Sioux were armed with bows and arrows, but they surrendered these to the angry posse. Then the settlers marched the warriors through the storm to the fort. On the way, some of the Sioux were badly frostbitten, and all suffered greatly from the cold. Upon their arrival at the fort, the men turned their captives over to Captain John Thompson, who began an immediate investigation. Some evidence which remains unrecorded proved the Sioux to be innocent. Whatever it was, it was so convincing that even the settlers could find no fault with it, and the warriors were allowed to leave the fort.

Then Captain Thompson's frustration with his job got the best of his public relations skills. He reportedly warned the settlers to leave well enough alone, adding that he would rather see twenty farmers killed than one Indian, if that would prevent a general Indian war. There was nothing left for Jesse Eldridge and his men to do but swallow their resentment and turn for home. They might have recalled that, when the Civil War broke out only ten months earlier, the officers at Fort Kearny had warned them to leave the country, as the Sioux would probably begin attacking white settlers along the trails.

In all likelihood, the murders on the north channel of the Platte were done by several malcontents, a random, senseless act committed upon people who had no thought for danger and were vulnerable targets of opportunity. Nevertheless, the "live-and-let-live" policy had suffered serious damage, and it was inevitable that the white settlers would begin to view their wandering red neighbors with fear and mistrust. After February 5, 1862, as one of the German homesteaders wrote, "the settlers in our county viewed the future with anxiety."[7]

The Wood River people buried Joseph Smith and the three boys under the naked boughs of a large, spreading elm tree on the banks of the Wood River. Before the month was out, the sad news had reached friends and acquaintances in Crown Point. James Anderson took the wives and daughters and his nine-year-old son, William, who was the only remaining male child of the two families, away from the homesteading frontier and back to Indiana. Behind them they left their hopes and dreams buried with the bodies of their loved ones on the abandoned homestead, with only the great elm to mark the place where their journeys had come to an end.[8]

In the months following the killing of the Smith and Anderson people, a pattern of expanding violence began to spread all across the plains. Even though the Deer Creek Treaty engineered by Agent Thomas Twiss was rejected by the Senate, the Sioux and Cheyennes generally remained on their good behavior throughout 1861, prompting the government to reduce the garrison at Fort Laramie to little more than a hundred men. At the same time, the depletion of the buffalo herds was making ammunition for hunting more and more essential; yet, when the annuities were delivered to the wild tribes, they included no powder or lead. No doubt this omission was caused by the necessity of arming the volunteer armies massing in the east, but to the Indians it was an unforgivable breach of the Treaty of 1851. With opportunity and necessity both present, young Sioux braves began turning their energies to war.[9]

In April 1862, they began attacks on stations and coaches along the Oregon-California trail west of Fort Laramie. Within a short time they had effectively closed the road. Mail and passenger coaches were withdrawn, and telegraphic communication with California was severed. To shore up the military presence along the route, California volunteers began patrolling the western sections, and Ohio volunteers were diverted from the war in Missouri to guard the road between Laramie and South Pass.

In June, Captain Thompson was replaced at Fort Kearny by Colonel Edmund Alexander of the Tenth Infantry. The army's weakness along the Platte was, of course, well known to the Sioux and Cheyennes ranging through Nebraska. It was reasonable to assume that, if the commanders at Fort Kearny were having trouble maintaining their own post, they would certainly have little interest in protecting the Pawnee Reservation. Secure in this awareness, the hostile warriors twice attacked the Pawnees during the summer. In their raid of June 29, they killed nine women whom they caught working in the fields and chased young Luther North, an employee at the agency, to shelter in the home of a nearby Mormon settler. North lost his hat during his wild ride to safety. The hat turned up several weeks later at Fort Kearny—on the head of one of Spotted Tail's Brule Sioux warriors.[10] But the really shocking story of that summer took place, not at Genoa or along the western trails, but along the Minnesota River. There, not quite five years after Inkpaduta's depredations, the rumblings of discontent exploded into full scale warfare.

At the beginning of the Civil War, relations between the Minnesota settlers and the Santees were still roiled as a result of the Spirit Lake Massacre. As large numbers of able-bodied men left the Minnesota settlements to join the volunteer army, Copperheads and disloyal traders began spreading news of Union military reverses, often adding a few embellishments of their own. Among the Santees there grew apprehensions that the southern soldiers might battle their way into Minnesota to enslave the red people as they had the blacks. There were also rumors that the war was costing the Great Father so much money that soon he would have none left for the Indians' annuities. When the 1862 annuity goods failed to arrive on schedule, those rumors appeared to be well-founded. Some of the Santees proposed that they sell their land in the Minnesota River Valley and seek aid from the British, but nothing came of those farfetched ideas.

The cultural tensions, hunger, rumors, and late annuities made the situation in southern Minnesota terribly volatile. The spark which ignited the explosion occurred on Sunday, August 17, 1862. Several young braves, acting on a dare, killed white settlers near Acton, Minnesota. The Santees, feeling that their relations with the whites were now lost beyond recall, erupted in a furious uprising. As was the case with the western Sioux, the Santees were much divided, and even those who went to war refused to follow the strategies proposed by Chief Little Crow. Many of the Santees remained peaceable, and a number of whites who had befriended the Indians were spared or warned away from the disaster. The uprising eventually claimed the lives of as many as 757 soldiers and settlers.[11]

The revolt failed, as Little Crow feared it would. The federal government responded to Minnesotans' pleas for help by placing General John Pope in charge of the Department of the Northwest, which included Minnesota, Iowa, Wisconsin, and Dakota Territory. Governor Ramsey placed Henry Hastings Sibley, an experienced fur trader, in command of the state militia. Sibley assembled a force of more than 1,400 men, including elements of the Third, Sixth, and Seventh Regiments, and slowly advanced up the Minnesota River, driving the Sioux before him, pushing them over into Dakota.

The Dakota settlers were greatly alarmed, to say the least. Within a week after the uprising began, a party of Indians killed several settlers on the outskirts of Sioux Falls. That town was abandoned, and by mid September, most of the settlers in eastern Dakota had concentrated at Fort Randall or at the agency of the friendly Yanktons. Many also fled to Sioux City, where residents frantically erected a stockade complete with blockhouses.[12]

News of the Minnesota revolt spread quickly across Nebraska Territory, increasing the anxiety among the settlements and road ranches along the Platte route. Minnesota Sioux were supposedly seen lurking everywhere, and in October the Second Nebraska Volunteer Cavalry was mustered to help guard the homefront. Captain Henry Edwards and Company D were dispatched to guard the beleaguered Pawnee Agency, and four other companies were strung out along the Oregon-California Trail. The remainder of the regiment was sent north to bolster the campaign which General Alfred Sully, the former captain at Fort Kearny, was preparing against the Yanktonnaise and Santees.

At last the tumultuous year 1862 drew to a close, heavy with foreboding. General McClellan's magnificent Army of the Potomac had been forced to withdraw from the very gates of the rebel capital at Richmond, and, before his reassignment to the Department of the Northwest, General Pope had been stymied at Cedar Mountain and shamefully beaten in a second battle at Bull Run. There had been some federal successes along the Mississippi River, but General Grant's victory at Shiloh and McClellan's at Antietam had been so narrowly won and at such appalling cost that they seemed utterly cheerless.

The situation on the plains was cheerless, too. The Santees had shocked the Department of the Northwest with their unexpected revolt; Sioux had killed settlers, including children, on the Wood

River; Brules and Ogalalas had continued their attacks on the Pawnee Reservation, while Minneconjous and Brules had closed the Oregon-California Trail west of Fort Laramie. Even the Cheyennes, who had been quiet ever since Sumner's 1857 expedition, were reported to be stealing stock and looting ranches along the Arkansas River. And for protection from the danger which seemed to be everywhere, the people of Nebraska Territory had only the five companies of the Second Nebraska, and they were due to be mustered out the following September. Clearly the territory needed much greater protection if the homesteads and commerce of the trails were to be kept secure.

The winds and snows of winter put an effective end to the Indian unrest for the balance of 1862, while the frontier people holed up in their cabins and soddies and stoked their iron stoves. In their enforced idleness, they found occasion to discuss with travelers and friends their suspicions that the Indian outrages of the past season had been incited by the Confederate government. This supposed rebel involvement in the troubles with the plains tribes became a popular source of indignation among the settlers, in part because human nature always demands a bogeyman, and also because it made such perfect sense.

Aside from comparatively trifling incidents such as the Grindstone War and the Spirit Lake Massacre, there had never been any trouble with the Santee people. The western Sioux and the Cheyennes had been peaceful since 1855 and 1857 respectively. All had remained quiet when the regulars were called away from the West in the spring of 1861. But the South had indeed put together a government and a military establishment, and without warning, the Santees had soaked the Minnesota Valley in blood and the High Plains tribes had begun to commit depredations from Laramie to South Pass and along the Arkansas. The coincidence was too great to be ignored: There was quite evidently a baleful influence at work among the Indians. It could only be the government of the Confederate States of America.

The usefulness of the Indian tribes to the southern war effort had not been hidden from officials of the rebel government. Barely a month after the surrender of Fort Sumter, Francis Marshall, a pioneer businessman and founder of Marysville, Kansas, wrote to the newly-elected president of the Confederacy, Jefferson Davis, of his plan to use the tribes of Indian Territory to capture Forts Laramie and Wise. The plan was designed to bring Colorado, Kansas, and Missouri into the Confederacy, to cut communications between California and the eastern states, and possibly to wangle an appointment for Mr. Marshall in the southern army.[13]

The Davis government was way ahead of Francis Marshall. It had already dispatched General Albert Pike to Indian Territory to recruit regiments among the Five Civilized Tribes. Many of the Indians there were slaveholders themselves, and presumably harbored some sore feelings toward the federal government which had forced them over their "Trail of Tears" nearly thirty years before. It was a fact that, ever since the election of Abraham Lincoln to the presidency, the Five Civilized Tribes had been in a practical and philosophical stew over their possible involvement in the white man's war.

In February, 1861, the Choctaws decided to cast their lot with the southern states and the Chickasaws soon followed suit. The Cherokees, Creeks, and Seminoles contained strong Unionist factions and were badly divided. For a time, the Cherokees attempted to remain neutral, but the Union defeat at Wilson's Creek placed the secessionist faction in the ascendancy. Finding themselves in the minority, and faced with threats from the Davis government, the loyal groups of Cherokees, Creeks, and Seminoles banded together under the leadership of Hopoeithleyohola, a Creek chieftain. Beginning in December, 1861, the loyalists were repeatedly attacked by their secessionist kinsmen and white Confederate forces, and were finally driven from Indian Territory into the state of Kansas. The weather turned bitterly cold during their exodus and snow accumulated on the ground. Some of the loyal Indians froze to death on the march. The people of Kansas were much affected by their suffering and mounted an energetic relief effort to supply them with food and clothing until such time as Union forces were strong enough to reconquer their homeland. The internal dissension and suffering caused by Confederate activity among the tribes of Indian Territory remain a little known horror of the Civil War.[14]

General Albert Pike proved to be an effective organizer of Indian troops for the southern cause. As a well-educated and restless youth from Massachusetts, Pike had come to the southwest along the Santa Fe Trail with Charles Bent's experimental ox train in the boom year of 1831. By the time of the Civil War, he had become an old hand along the trail, well acquainted with the peoples of Indian Territory. Some 3,500 Indians of Pike's regiments, organized along tribal lines, fought for the Confederacy at the battle of Pea Ridge. They also accounted for some ugly charges of scalping. Pike promptly issued stern orders against the scalping of enemy dead, reasoning that it would only bring Yankee reprisals. He even sent a copy of his order to the federal commander, General Samuel Ryan Curtis, who was unimpressed by Pike's sincerity.[15]

In all, an estimated 10,000 Indians fought during the Civil War, serving Union and Confederate causes west of the Mississippi.[16] The Battle of Pea Ridge, fought in March, 1862, remains the most widely known example of the participation of Indian regiments during the conflict.

General Pike also attempted to expand his recruitment beyond Indian Territory to the reserve tribes of eastern Kansas and to the wild tribes of the southern plains, sending emissaries among the Comanches, Kiowas, Cheyennes, and Arapahoes. The Comanches and Kiowas had long harbored a hatred of "Texans," as all southern whites were known, and refused to listen. The Cheyennes and Arapahoes, greatly angered by the invasion of the Colorado gold seekers, gave the Confederate proposals their attention, but were unable to reach a consensus. In their indecision, they sought the advice of the "Little Whiteman," William Bent, whom they trusted implicitly. Bent advised them that, for their own peace and safety, they should remain out of the white man's quarrel. With his quiet wisdom, Pike's chances of forging a coalition of Indians of the southern plains went up in smoke.[17]

Little of this was known among the people along the Oregon-California-Denver Trails that winter of 1862-1863. Neither could they know that the new year would find the Union noose tightening around the neck of the rebellion, moving the Confederacy to renew its solicitation of the plains tribes. This time even the Cheyennes and Arapahoes would refuse to listen, so southern recruitment efforts would be diverted northward to the reserve Indians—the Osages, Caddoes, Delawares, Wichitas, Kichais, Wacoes, Shawnees, and Kickapoos. These Indians would prove their loyalty by slaughtering to a man a group of Confederate officers riding northward on a recruiting mission.[18] And when Quantrill and his guerilla army withdrew from their orgy of destruction in Lawrence, Kansas, they would be pursued by a band of reserve Indians led by Shawnee Chief Charles Blue Jacket and Delaware Chief White Turkey.[19]

Nevertheless, the specter of a Confederate-forged alliance of plains tribes continued to haunt the frontier until 1865 when there was no more Confederacy. It was always an empty fear. Grinnell writes, "There was thus some ground for the well-nigh universal alarm concerning a Confederate plot to bring about a rising among the plains Indians . . . Those better acquainted with these primitive people would have understood that there was so little cohesion among Indians and so little idea of united action that there never was any danger of general uprising."[20]

The return of warm weather to the Oregon-California Trail brought the greening of the prairie grass and the homing of songbirds and butterflies and Sioux on the prowl. Two of them chased a lone Pawnee into Hackney's Station on the Little Blue. There, in full view of the proprietor and a visiting neighbor, they shot him dead.[21] Later a Sioux war party stopped the westbound coach near Oak Grove Ranch on the Little Blue and demanded information on a group of Pawnees which had stolen some of their horses.[22]

It should be remembered that so far the Sioux, as a matter of "official" policy, had avoided harming any white people. But they definitely meant business. On June 23, they opened the new raiding season with a major attack on the Pawnee Reservation. Agent Benjamin Lushbaugh and Captain Edwards gave chase. Lushbaugh suddenly found himself surrounded by several warriors who warned him to go back. The agent turned his horse around just in time to see an arrow glance off Captain Edwards' forehead, laying open the flesh above the officer's right eye down to the skull.[23] With blood streaming into his eyes, the captain turned back to the agency for medical assistance while Lieutenant Henry Gray continued the pursuit of the Sioux with a portion of the company. After a chase of nearly fifteen miles, the Sioux stopped running and confronted Gray with a battle line which he estimated at 400 warriors. The Sioux opened fire and the few Pawnees which had accompanied the troops fled for home. Lieutenant Gray and his thirty-five men stood their ground for a time, but even when reinforced by their wounded captain and twenty more troopers, they were at a decided disadvantage. With the approach of dusk, Captain Edwards, having already lost two men, called it quits and fell back to the agency. It was clear that the Sioux, if pressed, would attack white soldiers as readily as they would Pawnees. And, if their number was anything close to that stated by Captain Edwards in his report, Company D was fortunate to regain its camp that evening. The Sioux retired to their camp, too, but nobody considered the raids ended.

On July 17, Lieutenant Colonel Sapp, of the Second Nebraska, arrived in Omaha from an inspection tour of the Pawnee Reservation. There were reports, the officer told the press, that the Sioux were massing 5,000 warriors along the Republican River, and the Pawnees and some of the Omahas were putting together a war party to go down and fight them there.[24] Apparently, the great expedition never got off the ground, and it was less than a week later that the nerves of the frontier people were jarred by another barbarous incident reminiscent of the Smith-Anderson murders nearly eighteen months before.

Henson Wiseman was forty years old when he brought his wife and six children to St. James, Cedar County, Nebraska Territory. After their marriage in Parkersburg, (West) Virginia, the Wisemans moved west to Burlington, Iowa. But, like so many other Americans of the time, they were drawn ever westward toward the frontier, going next to Des Moines, on to Sioux City, and finally to a homestead in Cedar County. And, like so many other Americans, the Wisemans' personal version of Manifest Destiny was accompanied by tragedy: Of the eight children born to the couple in Iowa, two died. Within the year following their arrival in Cedar County, death also claimed their eighteen-year-old son, Benjamin. When the next eldest son, John, answered President Lincoln's call for volunteers by enlisting in the Union Army, there were five children left in the Wiseman home.

As a result of the Minnesota uprising, the Second Nebraska Volunteer Cavalry was recruited to help guard the line up the Platte and Missouri Rivers. Henson Wiseman and fifty of his neighbors (which was about all of them that were fit) enlisted with the understanding that their company would be utilized as a home guard. But no sooner had the men been mustered in as Company I, when they were ordered north into Dakota to join General Sully's expedition. The Cedar County men protested vehemently that their removal would leave their families defenseless against potential attacks by small bands of aroused Santees or Yanktonnaise. They were given some vague promises that their homes would be guarded by other forces soon to be sent northward.

While her husband was gone with his regiment, Phoebe Wiseman found it necessary to journey to Yankton to purchase some supplies. She set off on July 21, leaving her five children alone on the homestead. Returning late on the rainy afternoon of July 23, she was startled to see the front door of the cabin ajar and smeared with blood. All was silent as she crept forward to peer inside. On the floor lay the body of an Indian warrior. Panicked, she ran around to the back of the cabin to find eight-year-old William dead in the grass, shot through with buckshot and ball. The gruesome discovery so terrified Phoebe Wiseman that she ran the three miles to St. James through thickets of dripping weeds and brush, fearing that Indians might be lying in wait along the road. The few men who were left in the settlement listened to her anguished story, but it was quite dark by then, and nobody was willing to return with her to the scene until daylight.

In the early morning, an armed party made its way cautiously to the Wiseman cabin. Inside, they found four-year-old Loren still alive, though he had been stabbed savagely in the side. He could only say, "The Indians scared me," which he repeated over and over again.

Fourteen-year-old Hannar, the only daughter, was also still alive and, though conscious, was unable to speak a word. It appeared to the rescuers that her mouth had been torn apart by having a rifle shell exploded inside it, and arrows had been shot into her pubic region from below, the points protruding from above her hips on each side. Ten-year-old Andrew was also dead, having been stabbed repeatedly. Fifteen-year-old Arthur had fought desperately before he died, evidently accounting for the single Indian casualty. His rifle was still locked in his hands, and his arms and head were crushed and broken.

Little Loren lived on for three days, and Hannar survived in her torment for five days before she also died. The five bodies were buried in old St. James and the mother, now on the brink of insanity, was taken by friends first to Yankton, and then on to Sioux City.

It took several weeks for the news to reach Henson Wiseman in Dakota Territory. He immediately left his unit without permission, and the army never pressed the issue. After a marathon ride, he arrived back in St. James twenty-five days after the murders. Everything was peaceful and still as he approached the comfortable little cabin which he had built with his own hands in the pleasant hilltop clearing to stand, staring mutely through the silent doorway at the floor, varnished black with the blood of his children.[25]

As word of the outrage spread, drivers of mail coaches between Sioux City and Fort Randall refused to make their runs, and on September 18, a passenger coach running between the two terminals was attacked by the Sioux and one passenger killed.[26]

The trouble was not confined to the northern territories. Telegraphic dispatches reported that the Cheyennes had raided Fort Craig in New Mexico Territory, making off with a large herd of mules which were only recovered after a sharp fight with troops from the garrison.[27] Hit-and-run raids on the Pawnee Agency continued, and freighters returning to Omaha from late season runs to Denver brought news of minor depredations all along the Denver Road.

The resulting clamor of the frontier people for military protection was answered by the recruitment of the Seventh Iowa Veteran Volunteer Cavalry. The Seventh was a hard hitting outfit, many of its members having served terms of enlistment with the federal armies fighting in Missouri and Arkansas. The first six companies arrived in Omaha by July 27, 1863, and were posted to various stations along the overland route. Companies I, K, L, and M were formed from troops already on duty around Fort Randall. Company B was sent north to the Niobrara River, and Captain James B. David's Company E was ordered to the Pawnee Agency to replace Captain Edwards and his men who were due to be mustered out. Companies F and G were detailed for duty at a new post to be constructed near Cottonwood Springs. Even though the arrival of the Seventh Iowa gave the frontier people reason to breathe a bit easier, they continued to call for the return of their First Nebraska Cavalry, which had by this time become a tough, battle-seasoned fighting force.

As fall slipped into winter, the Sioux retired to their lodges and the Seventh Iowa troopers rushed to complete their log barracks at Fort Cottonwood. Travel along the Platte route slackened, but enough business remained on the trail to keep the ranchers happy. There were still a considerable number of freight outfits and, of course, stagecoaches on the trail when winter leveled its first blow at the High Plains.

On December 1, a gigantic snowstorm swept the Platte Valley, causing chaos among the stages and late-season freighters. Frank Root's coach was caught by the blizzard in the Little Blue Valley, causing it to lay over for repairs. By the time the coach reached Cottonwood Springs, freezing rain had so iced the trail that the passengers were forced to get out and help the horses power the vehicle up slippery inclines. Then, after leaving American Ranch on the Denver Road, the stage was hit by yet a third storm, reaching a place of safety only through the instincts of the horses.[28]

The first blizzard of 1864 struck in January, catching a Denver-bound train in the open near Fort Cottonwood. The wagons were wrecked and the draft animals so used up that the train was unable to proceed when the weather finally cleared. Army officers at the fort bought up the cargo of flour and shelled corn.[29] Another succession of storms blasted the trail in February, and snow in late March prevented the grass from greening up. Many ox-powered trains sat idle, waiting for grazing conditions to improve, rather than pay high prices for forage at the road ranches.

Over the bitter winter of 1863-1864, refugee Santees and Yanktonnaise found their ways to the camps of their Lakota brothers. Many had been entirely innocent in the original uprising, but General Sully was hunting Indians with a very large net which did not distinguish between the innocent and the guilty. In Minnesota, the settlers became so hostile to all Indians that they drove even the docile Winnebagoes from their state.[30] As the snow drifted deep among the Sioux lodges, the talk inside was of arrogant traders, corrupt agents, broken promises, failed annuities, and hunger. The anger, humiliation, and frustration mounted with each retelling of the old stories of hardship and betrayal, and the sense of hopelessness hardened the resolution of the young warriors to die fighting.

The intense cold and slashing snowstorms also kept the white people inside their dwellings—except they were telling tales of massacre, trading gossip with travelers and neighbors, and pondering what lay in store for the plains and for the country at large in the new year. Settlers in Dakota were agitated at being caught between the warring Santees and Yanktonnaise from the east, and the potentially explosive Lakotas from the west—and then the exiles from Minnesota had been dumped right into their midst.

Road ranchers along the Oregon-California route were also discussing the coming trail season. All agreed that travel during 1864 would likely be the heaviest ever seen along the Platte. The Missouri River towns were filling up with miners, homesteaders, and former Confederates who had read the unmistakable signs of collapse in the rebel government. The crush of emigrants and freighters could hardly do other than incite the Indians to strike with increased hostility and in greater numbers. They knew also that General Sully would be ascending the Missouri once again with a force large enough to sweep the country clean all the way to the Yellowstone. The government sorely needed the gold which was flowing from the Idaho and Montana mines, and Sully was determined to keep open the vital water route up the Missouri. All the factors were falling into place which could make the summer of 1864 a season of violence from the Platte to the upper Missouri. Yet, for all the troubles with the Sioux, it would be events in rapidly maturing Colorado Territory which would determine the chances for peace on the plains, particularly between the Platte and the Arkansas—the rapidly shrinking hunting grounds of the Cheyennes and Arapahoes.

Chapter Seven notes

1 Catton, *The Coming Fury*, 121.

2 Utley, *Frontiersmen in Blue*, 212.

3 Hyde, *A Life of George Bent*, 115.

4 Details of the attacks on the Pawnee Reservation are taken from "Letters Received–Pawnee Agency."

5 Stolley, *History of the First Settlement*, 46.

6 Wilson, *Fort Kearny on the Platte*, 104.

7 Stolley, *History of the First Settlement*, 47.

8 The story of the Smith - Anderson murders is synthesized from the following sources:
Andreas, *History of Nebraska*, Vol. 2, 933.
Ball, *Lake County, Indiana.*
The Crown Point (Indiana) Register, October 31, 1861; February 23, 1862.
Federal Census, Lake County, Indiana, 1850; 1860.
Grand Island (Nebraska) Daily Independent (2 articles), July 2, 1932.
Stolley, *History of the First Settlement*, 47-48.

9 More detailed accounts of the Sioux troubles of these years may be found in Nadeau, *Fort Laramie*, and Utley, *Frontiersmen in Blue.*

10 Danker, *Man of the Plains*, 9-10; Lushbaugh to Indian Superintendent, July 8, 1862, in "Letters Received–Pawnee Agency;" Grinnell, *The Fighting Cheyennes*, 64 (Grinnell gives the wrong year).

11 Wellman, *Death on the Prairie*, 8.

12 Athern, *Forts on the Upper Missouri*, 93.

13 O. R. Series I, Vol. 3, 578-579.

14 Britton, *The Union Indian Brigade.*

15 Halsey, *Who Fired the First Shot?*, 86-87.

16 Ibid., 34; see also *War on the Frontier* (Time - Life History of the Civil War).

17 Hyde, *A Life of George Bent*, 373.

18 Grinnell, *The Fighting Cheyennes*, 128; Ware, *The Indian War of 1864*, 140.

19 Halsey, *Who Fired the First Shot?*, 89-90.

20 Grinnell, *The Fighting Cheyennes*, 128.

21 *Biographical and Historical Memoirs*, 345.

22 Root and Connelley, *Overland Stage*, 24-25.

23 Ware describes Lushbaugh as having a bunched growth of brilliant red whiskers under each ear, a practice soon copied by some of the men of the Seventh Iowa regiment. He also states that the agent was very fond of "ardent spirits" and intensely proud of the work being done at the agency.

Hyde (*The Pawnees*) however, is very severe toward the agent, and accuses him of mishandling funds and misleading his superiors. Hyde also states that, during the Sioux raid of June 23, the agent and cavalry officers made no attempt to defend the Pawnees. Grinnell (*Two Great Scouts*) is more truthful, but accuses Captain Edwards of turning back with a "trifling wound."

From Frank North's description of the raid, Lushbaugh and Edwards were apparently far out in front of the pursuit, placing themselves in great danger. Edwards' facial wound was such that he was blinded by the great amount of blood pouring from beneath the flap of flesh which hung down over his eye—not exactly a trifling wound.

Hyde offers no proof that the agent misused government funds, and it seems unjust to fault the agent for viewing his Pawnees and their acculturation through rose-colored glasses. The position of agent to the Pawnees was anything but a sinecure—sometimes dangerous and always frustrating. Lushbaugh's attempts to encourage large-scale farming among the Pawnees were defeated by drought, grasshoppers, and rampaging Sioux and Cheyennes. His major fault appears to have been a penchant for overlooking evidence that his Indian charges were a good deal less civilized and acculturated than he wanted to believe they were. After all, it had been little more than twenty years since the Pawnees had offered up their last human sacrifice to the Morning Star. (See Father De Smet's account of the 1837 sacrifice of a fifteen-year-old girl in "Narrative of a Year's Residence Among the Indian Tribes of the Rocky Mountains" in NSHS, *Transactions and Reports*, Vol. 2 [1887]).

24 *The Omaha Nebraskian*, July 17, 1863.

25 After leaving his company, Wiseman stopped in Yankton to report to Captain Tripp, whose wife visited Omaha shortly thereafter and gave an account of the affair to the *Omaha Nebraskian* of August 7, 1863. Information on the Wiseman tragedy is found in Frerichs, *Cedar County Gleanings*.

26 *The Omaha Nebraskian*, September 18, 1863.

27 *The Omaha Nebraskian*, August 14, 1863.

28 Root and Connelley, *Overland Stage*, 318-319.

29 Ware, *The Indian War of 1864*, 73.

30 Sully's punishment of the Sioux did not prevent them from harassing the Winnebagoes, whom they hated equally with the Pawnees. Over the winter of 1863-1864, the Winnebagoes fled south into Nebraska Territory where they were sheltered by the Omaha tribe.

Part I
Chapter Eight

"The shortest road to the people's hearts"

When William Gilpin arrived in Denver City on the stagecoach that May 27, 1861, to take up his duties as first governor of Colorado Territory, there were said to be at least 10,000 citizens of that territory eager and willing to bear arms for the Confederacy "as soon as an opportunity is presented."[1] A staunch Unionist, seasoned Westerner (he had been with Fremont's 1843 expedition), military man and lawyer, Gilpin seemed to be the ideal person to guide the raw territory toward eventual statehood. But, beset by strong Confederate sentiment within Denver City and by danger from disaffected Cheyennes without, Gilpin began to assert his independence, appointing a military staff and raising an unauthorized regiment of volunteers to meet the twin threats. When he issued $375,000 worth of unapproved drafts on the U. S. Treasury, President Lincoln had no choice but to remove him from office in April, 1862.[2]

His replacement was John Evans, a doctor and Republican politician from Chicago, who had worked actively for Lincoln's election in 1860. In addition to being a member of the faculty of Rush Medical College, Evans was instrumental in founding Northwestern University and the city of Evanston, and he made a fortune in real estate. As he understood things, a major part of his executive duties concerned the settlement of nagging Indian problems on the Colorado frontier.

Upon his arrival in Denver City, Evans moved immediately to bring a halt to the continuing raids between Utes and the Cheyennes and Arapahoes. His actions were universally resented by the tribes.

He also determined to begin immediate implementation of the Treaty of Fort Wise.

Even though only isolated bands of Cheyennes and Arapahoes had been parties to the treaty, Evans began working to consolidate all members of the wild tribes on the Arkansas reserve. Until the Indians' title to lands on the South Platte was effectively extinguished, there could be no legal settlement and administration of the country they had occupied under the Treaty of 1851. Though nearly all the chiefs were opposed to war with the white people, there was such general dissatisfaction with the new reservation and with the treaty as a whole that small groups of young warriors began to slip away from the camps to commit minor depredations. They were also hungry.

On December 5, 1862, a party of young Cheyennes attacked the stage station fifty-five miles east of Fort Lyon (formerly Fort Wise). They stole some food and provisions and burned some hay, but otherwise harmed no one. Agent Samuel Colley investigated, but was unable to identify the guilty parties. In March 1863, some young braves raided ranches near the mouth of the Cache la Poudre River, stealing food but doing no other damage. Governor Evans warned the military authorities that a pattern of depredations was commencing and that more troops would be needed to meet the growing Indian threat in Colorado Territory.

It was about this time that a soldier at Fort Lyon committed a depredation of his own when he paid an Arapaho in whiskey to procure an Indian bedmate for him. When the Arapaho failed to return, the soldier went looking for him, found him in one of the lodges, and shot him in the arm. Officers at the fort were able to settle the matter without a fight, but the unsuccessful solicitation did nothing to promote harmony between the races.

Early in 1863, a party of Utes did some petty thievery around Camp Collins. Major Edward Wynkoop of the First Colorado Cavalry took off in pursuit but was unable to catch up with the raiders. Also in March, a war party of Cheyennes set off on a return raid on the Utes. On their way, they looted more ranches on the Poudre River. Lieutenant Hawkins of the First Colorado gave chase and soon caught up with a party of Cheyennes that turned out to be entirely innocent. The Indians complained bitterly to Hawkins about all the provocations they had endured in recent years, and dejectedly said they expected to be forced into fighting the whites eventually.

During the Poudre raids, a few Arapahoes stole some cattle belonging to the Van Wormer Ranch about thirty-five miles east of Denver City. Van Wormer himself caught up with them, and they frankly admitted butchering and eating some of his cattle. During the talks,

Van Wormer noted the presence of the notorious squawman, Robert North, in the Indian camp. It was a sinister omen of things to come.[3]

As these minor depredations were taking place in Colorado, the Lincoln administration was at last becoming aware of Confederate attempts to recruit the plains tribes for the rebel cause. The government determined to beat General Albert Pike to the punch, and arranged for a delegation of Cheyenne, Arapaho, Comanche, Kiowa, and Caddo chiefs to leave the frontier on March 27, 1863, for Washington, D. C. There the chiefs were shown the power of (northern) white civilization, had their photographs taken, met the Great Father, and apparently had a wonderful time. Lean Bear (Grinnell claims his name was more accurately Starving Bear) was among the group, and he returned home to his people proudly wearing a medallion around his neck and clutching a large flag.[4]

Governor Evans also wished to meet with the chiefs, but he had less success than President Lincoln, probably because he had less to offer. In May 1863, he learned that a grand council of Cheyennes, Sioux, and Arapahoes was being held one hundred miles north of Denver City. Sensing that this could be an opportunity to begin his program of consolidating and confining the tribes to the Arkansas River reserve, Evans sent a message to the council asking the Indians to meet him in Denver. The chiefs begged off, sending back word that their ponies were still too weak after the long winter to travel so far.

Already trouble was brewing along the Arkansas where Mexican traders were providing a fountain of liquor for a large camp of Cheyennes, Arapahoes, and other bands gathered in the vicinity of Fort Larned. On July 9, a drunken Cheyenne named Little Heart rode to the fort, looking for more whiskey so he could get really drunk. In attempting to ride over the sentry, Little Heart was shot dead. Colonel Jesse Leavenworth, commanding the post, counciled with tribal leaders, and hostilities were averted, though the incident was far from forgotten. Leavenworth strongly urged that additional troops be posted along the Santa Fe route, and questioned why Colonel Chivington, the district commander, kept the bulk of the First Colorado Regiment close to Denver City. There followed an acrimonious three-way debate among Leavenworth at Fort Larned, Lieutenant Colonel Tappan at Fort Lyon, and Chivington in Denver. This, along with other factors, led to Leavenworth's dismissal from the service on October 9, 1863. He was replaced at Larned by the alcohol-benumbed Captain James W. Parmetar, of the Twelfth Kansas Infantry.

It must be said that, despite the alcohol, hunger, and provocations, the Cheyennes and Arapahoes remained unusually peaceful during 1863. In his report of August 14, Governor Evans expressed his confidence that the Cheyennes, Arapahoes, and Platte River Sioux were still friendly, and emphasized that he had worked hard to bring an end to the raids between the Utes and Cheyennes.[5] He was still determined to have his council with the tribes, however, and sent runners to summon them to a talk on the Arickaree Fork of the Republican River, to be held on September 1.

The Indians knew very well what it was he wanted to council about, and they refused to meet him for reasons of scanty food supplies, hunting, lodge-making, health of their ponies—any convenient excuse. Attempting to force a breakthrough, Evans asked squawman-trader Elbridge Gerry to go among the tribes to implore them to attend the talk on the Arickaree. Gerry owned a ranch on the South Platte, had married a Cheyenne woman, and was well-liked and trusted by the Indians—but they still refused to talk with Evans. They did, however, consent to gather for a council with Gerry during which they repudiated the Treaty of Fort Wise, refused to have anything to do with the Arkansas reserve, and voiced their continuing bitterness over the killing of Little Heart.[6]

On the appointed date, Evans showed up at the council site. The Indians did not, and the governor was forced to return empty-handed to Denver City where he received Gerry's report of his own council. Thus far, all the governor's efforts to pacify and clear Colorado Territory of Indians had been for naught. The tribes had steadfastly refused him the opportunity to plead his case with them. Neither could he force the issue militarily. There were not sufficient troops available. Besides, the Cheyennes and Arapahoes were behaving much too circumspectly to justify the use of military force, as opposed to the action on the upper Platte and in the Dakotas, where the Sioux were giving the government all the drama it could handle. What Evans did not know was that those Sioux had offered the warpipe to the Cheyennes, who had declined to join the fight.[7]

What was the governor to do? The Indians refused to recognize the treaty. They refused to move to the reservation. They refused to even talk about it. And they refused to give reason for military action against them. Evans was certain that trouble lay ahead, but as long as the tribes remained peaceable, his warnings sounded like the clucking of a nervous old hen.

His apprehension was not entirely baseless. Agent Colley was of the opinion that the Sioux were creating enough dissatisfaction among the Cheyennes to induce them to attack settlers along the South Platte and the Arkansas. Interpreter John Smith at Fort Lyon confirmed the disruptive influence of large bands of Sioux prowling along the Smoky Hill River. But it was the letter from the squawman,

Robert North, that really turned up the fire under the governor. On November 10, 1863, North wrote to Evans that all the plains tribes were preparing for a huge, concerted offensive against the whites during the coming spring. The Indians, said North, were only pretending to be friendly in order to stockpile arms and ammunition for their war. North claimed that his special position among the plains tribes allowed him to be entrusted with this information.[8] Without questioning the accuracy of the report or the reputation of its author, Evans wrote in early December to Secretary of War Stanton, asking for an increase in military forces stationed on the Colorado frontier, as well as authority to call out the Colorado militia to be posted along the Smoky Hill River and the Denver Road.

The truthfulness of North's report has always been denied by the Cheyennes. George Bent, the half-breed son of the "Little Whiteman," William Bent, described North as a "miserable white man who had been loafing around the Arapaho camp and keeping an Arapaho wife . . ."[9] Bent was staying in the camp of the Cheyennes, his mother's people, during the time they were supposedly planning this spring war, and he flatly declared that North's story "was a lie from beginning to end." It might be safest to say that North's motives in writing to Evans were understood by no one but himself.

The motives of Governor Evans, too, have been the subject of much debate. His actions during his time in office were sometimes confusing and contradictory. His efforts to defend himself in later years appeared disingenuous and hollow. It may be too much to say that he deliberately fomented a war with the plains tribes, but there is little doubt that he, like most citizens of the territory, believed that such a war was inevitable. Perhaps Grinnell put the best construction on the governor's actions when he wrote that "The work he (Evans) had to do was so much and so varied that little of it was done well."[10]

Convinced by the reports he had received from Smith, Colley, Gerry, and North, Governor Evans did not content himself with merely writing letters, but journeyed personally to Washington to plead his case. Receiving but little for his efforts, he returned to spend the remainder of the winter of 1863-1864 preparing for the worst. He would not be disappointed.

The severity of the winter of 1863-64 cost the Cheyennes a number of ponies and greatly weakened the rest, keeping the Indians close to their camps in the spring. On March 16, Governor Evans wrote to Colonel Chivington that the Indians were all quiet and friendly, but there were persistent reports that the northern Sioux were still bent on a major war effort in the spring.[11] However, when General Robert Mitchell, now commanding the District of Nebraska, interviewed interpreter John Hunter at Fort Cottonwood, he was told that the upper Platte tribes were friendly and satisfied.[12] Obviously someone was wrong.

On the positive side, the District of Nebraska, at least, was better prepared to counter potential hostilities than it had been a year before. The Seventh Iowa Cavalry was on station along the Platte, and in January 1864, General Samuel Ryan Curtis had taken command of the Department of Kansas, with headquarters at Fort Leavenworth. The department included all the present states of Kansas, Nebraska, and Colorado plus half of Wyoming—over 2,300 miles of major trails to be guarded, and twenty-nine military posts to be garrisoned. The demands of his new position were as awesome as its geographical area, for General Curtis unknowingly came to a department which was, in effect, a powder keg with lighted fuse—and, ironically, Indian troubles were about the last things on his mind.

Curtis was not a "difficult" commander. He was, rather, an amiable gentleman and a graduate of West Point; civil engineer with experience on every kind of project from river dams to the old Cumberland Road; a lawyer, former mayor of Keokuk, Iowa, and former member of the U.S. Congress.[13] As head of the Department of the Southwest and later, the Department of Missouri, he had labored valiantly to keep Missouri loyal to the union in those first, hectic days of the Civil War. The Battle of Pea Ridge had thus far been the climax of his military career, and his federal forces had persevered until they had pushed Confederate General Sterling Price and his army completely out of the state and into Arkansas. But Curtis had become so unfortunately tangled up in radical Missouri politics that Lincoln had removed him from his post. Due to his friendly relations with Lincoln and with radical Kansas Senator James Lane, Curtis was transferred to the command of the Department of Kansas. Some may have considered the fifty-eight-year-old general to be a bit long in the tooth for a frontier command (after all, his father had fought in the Revolution), but he was nevertheless energetic and conscientious. General Curtis' two major concerns were the guerilla war being fought out by bushwhackers and Jayhawkers along the Kansas-Missouri border, and the likely possibility of a renewed effort by General Price to recapture Missouri. These two concerns were directly linked.

Ever since the Wakarusa War, large gangs of heavily armed bushwhackers had roamed over northwest Missouri crushing Unionist sentiment and generally killing anybody they felt needed killing. Led by men such as William Quantrill and John C. Calhoun (Coon) Thornton, these were formidable forces, each containing as many as

400 to 500 men, having great popular support, needing no supply lines or permanent camps, and able to strike quickly and brutally before melting away into the rugged river bluffs. As opportunities arose, they made short, frightful forays into eastern Kansas, Quantrill's massacre at Lawrence being one of the worst of these. The war against the bushwhackers had become personal for General Curtis several months before he came to Fort Leavenworth. On October 4, 1863, his eldest son, Henry Z. Curtis, an aide on the staff of General Blunt, was ambushed with his unit by the guerrillas at Baxter Springs, Kansas. Wounded in the hip and thrown from his disabled mount, Henry Curtis was executed with a shot to the head.[14]

Shortly after the general took command at Fort Leavenworth, it became known that General Price was gathering forces in Arkansas for another invasion of Missouri in the summer of 1864. If Price was successful in pushing into the western part of the state, thousands of guerilla bushwhackers would attach themselves to his army, enabling it to cross the border and create havoc among the Kansas settlements, possibly threatening Fort Leavenworth itself. For General Curtis, Price and the bushwhackers had become the personification of all the evil which had plagued the border country for nearly a decade.

Southern Kansas also faced the threat of invasion by forces moving up out of Indian Territory or even from Texas. In this case, the Santa Fe Trail would be cut and southern California and all of New Mexico lost to the Union cause. In addition to these threats, it was necessary to protect the routes to the gold fields, namely the Oregon-California Trail, the Denver Road, and the steamboat route up the Missouri River.

It all made a very full plate, and General Curtis would need all his political skills to coordinate the efforts of some very strong personalities: General Rosecrans, his superior in St. Louis; Generals Pope and Sully in the Dakotas; General Clinton Fisk of the District of Northern Missouri; Colonel George Wright of the Department of the Pacific; Nebraska Territorial Governor Alvin Saunders; Colorado Territorial Governor John Evans; and Kansas Governor Thomas Carney, who hated James Lane and had scant use for Curtis himself.

In his far-flung command, Curtis was forced to rely heavily upon his subordinates. In charge of the District of Kansas, with headquarters at Paola, was Brigadier General Thomas J. McKean, who had formerly commanded the District of Nebraska.

The District of Colorado was in the hands of Colonel John Chivington, the former Methodist preacher whose aggressiveness earlier in the war had been largely responsible for turning back the Confederate invasion of New Mexico. On March 28, 1861, then-Major

Chivington became a hero of the First Colorado Regiment when he led his brigade on a flanking maneuver around the rebel forces of General H.H. Sibley, completely destroying Sibley's supply train. Upon the resignation of Colonel John Slough, Chivington was promoted to the command of the regiment.

Heading up the District of Nebraska was Brigadier General Robert B. Mitchell. Like Curtis, Mitchell was a veteran of the Mexican War. As colonel of the Second Kansas Regiment in the Civil War, he was severely wounded at the Battle of Wilson's Creek. Upon his recovery, he rose to command the cavalry of the Army of the Cumberland. He appeared to be ideal for the command of what was essentially a cavalry district.

With the exception of the Wiseman murders and the severe raids on the Pawnee Reservation, the summer of 1863 had been calm on the plains. If Chivington and Mitchell could simply maintain the status quo, Curtis would find it possible to devote most of his energies to the invasion threats in Kansas. This was evidently what he had in mind when, on March 26, 1864, he dropped a political bombshell on Governor Evans: All available troops in Colorado Territory (presumably meaning the First Regiment) would soon be withdrawn to the southern border of Kansas.[15]

Evans and Chivington had been expecting trouble all winter, but not from Fort Leavenworth. Less than two weeks after Curtis' notification of the troop withdrawal, there began a series of events which completed the destruction of the peace along the Platte River trails. It is impossible to establish the actual truth in regard to many of these encounters between the Indians and Colorado military forces, since their respective accounts are so completely at odds. It is clear, however, that as a result of command policies and military actions, the Cheyennes and Arapahoes were maneuvered into a position from which they could not escape, and forced to fight a war they knew they could not win. The first incident of the summer began on Bijou Creek, about forty miles from Denver City.

The financial losses incurred by the Pony Express left the great freighting firm of Russell, Majors, and Waddell overextended and undercapitalized. Fearing that the company might default on army freighting contracts, the government increasingly turned to Irwin, Jackman and Company to deliver vital stores to the posts on the frontier. In fact, throughout most of the Civil War, Irwin and Jackman held a virtual monopoly on army freighting in the West.[16] Over the winter of 1863-1864, the company sent many of its draft cattle to pasture on Bijou Creek. On April 5, some of the herders came in to Denver City to report that many of the animals were missing—no doubt stolen by the Cheyennes. It was not unknown for negligent herders to allow the stock in their charge to stray, as the loss could always be credibly blamed on the Indians. George Bent later wrote that the Cheyennes had no reason to run off the stock, as their winter hunt had been passably good, and the Cheyennes would never eat "tame meat" if buffalo was available.[17] Nevertheless, Colonel Chivington ordered Lieutenant George Eayre and McLain's Independent Battery to recover the cattle and punish the Indians.

After battling through a late spring snowstorm, Eayre came upon the Cheyenne villages of Crow Chief and Coon near the head of the Republican River. The Indians had ample warning of his approach (McLain's Battery not being a particularly speedy outfit) and had fled their villages. Eayre entered the deserted camps and did, in fact, find a few of the missing animals. The Cheyennes always maintained that they had found the cattle wandering loose on the prairie, but Eayre was determined to punish them. But his forage was running low, and the wagons were proving too heavy for their teams, so the lieutenant could only burn the camps and return to Denver City.[18] There he replenished his supplies and commandeered fifteen light vehicles off the streets of the town. On April 24, Eayre left Denver City on the second round of his Indian hunt, and nothing more was heard from his expedition for several weeks.

As McLain's Battery took the field against the Cheyennes, Colonel Chivington ordered his cavalry patrols to disarm any Cheyennes they encountered. On April 12, a detachment of the First Colorado under Lieutenant Clark Dunn met up with a Cheyenne war party headed north to fight the Crows. The soldiers were searching for some stolen stock, but the Indians were unaware of any trouble and they certainly had not heard of Chivington's order. As the two parties met, the Cheyennes rode up to the soldiers and began to shake hands with them. Without explanation, the troopers began grappling for the braves' weapons and a running fight developed. Three warriors and two soldiers were killed in this action which occurred three miles below Fremont's Orchard (present Orchard, Colorado) on the South Platte. The Cheyennes always considered this affair to be an act of treachery which ignited the Indian War of 1864.[19]

Even now, the damage was not irreparable. No serious incidents had occurred along the Arkansas, and the troubles on the Platte and Republican had involved only a small number of the Cheyennes and none of the Sioux. But the curious embassy of Captain Logan was an indication that the Colorado authorities had already reached a decision on the future of the Indians in the territory.

While Eayre and Dunn were out hunting Cheyennes, Captain Logan of the First Colorado was traveling down the South Platte, talking to the ranchmen and gathering information on the disposition of the tribes for peace or war. On April 9 he arrived at Fort Cottonwood.[20] Military officers along the trail were aware that General Mitchell was coming out from Omaha to council with the Sioux in an attempt to persuade them to remain peaceable and to remove themselves from the Platte Valley. Captain Logan stressed to the officers at Cottonwood that, unless Mitchell was successful in winning the cooperation of the Sioux, there would probably be a general Indian war all along the Platte. His statements give the impression that the Colorado authorities were depending on Mitchell's talks to enable them to fight a limited war involving only the Cheyennes and Arapahoes. Given the closeness of the Sioux and Cheyenne peoples (and particularly the intermarriage which was so prevalent among the Dog Soldiers), this was asking poor Mitchell to do the impossible.

At any rate, the general carried off his mission badly. On April 17, Mitchell and the officers at Fort Cottonwood met with a number of Brule and Ogalala Sioux chiefs.[21] In their warmup speeches, the Indians expressed their anger over the flow of "drunk water" into their camps, and the party of surveyors which was mapping out a new road along the Niobrara River. General Mitchell listened to their complaints and was doing fairly well—until he ordered them to stay out of the Platte Valley. This high-handed demand shredded their pride, and Spotted Tail rose to threaten that the Indians were willing and able to give the white men all the war they wanted.

The conference was clearly over. Mitchell succeeded only in securing the Indians' promise to meet him for a second talk in fifty days. After tempers had cooled, chiefs and officers entertained each other at a pair of feasts, but there was no denying that the first council had been an abysmal failure. So much for Captain Logan's warning.

In the meantime, the Colorado volunteers kept the heat on the Cheyennes. On April 16, the day before Mitchell's conference, Major Downing and Lieutenant Dunn attacked an encampment at Cedar Canyon on the South Platte. Twenty-five Indians were killed, including the usual toll of women and children, and a large number of ponies were captured and distributed "among the boys." Finding himself short of rations, Lieutenant Dunn took his men back to Denver City to resupply. Then, a week later, he hit the Cedar Canyon camp a second time. The Cheyenne camp was burned and the Indians fled for their lives.[22]

Up until this time, all the fighting had taken place on the South Platte, and in early May, Major Wynkoop reported to Colonel

Chivington that all was peaceful along the Santa Fe Road. Lieutenant Eayre was still missing on his Indian hunt, however, and on May 16, he located the villages of Lean Bear, Wolf Chief, and Black Kettle. This time there was no question about who started the fight, as Cheyenne accounts were later corroborated by testimony from Eayre's soldiers.

Accompanied by Star, Lean Bear rode out to meet Eayre's troopers, proudly wearing his medal from Washington and clutching his reference papers. The two Cheyennes had advanced to within forty feet of the soldiers when Eayre called out the order to fire. Both Cheyennes fell into the prairie grass, and the troopers advanced and shot them again where they lay. The outraged warriors immediately attacked the Colorado troops, and Eayre began a disorganized withdrawal in the direction of Fort Larned.[23]

The Cheyennes would have ended the service of McLain's Battery then and there except that Black Kettle rode out among the young warriors and cried out for them to stop fighting. A number of them refused to listen and forced Eayre to fight a rear guard action all the way to Larned. Upon reaching that post the next day, Eayre reported to Captain Parmetar on his "victory." Parmetar just happened to be sober enough to realize the serious consequences of Eayre's actions, and telegraphed to Fort Riley a warning that the Cheyennes would undoubtedly begin retaliatory action all along the Santa Fe Trail, and he had not enough troops to keep the road open.

Thus it appeared that the deliberate persecution of the Cheyennes was having the desired effect. The actions of McLain's Battery and units of the First Colorado Cavalry were indeed so flagrantly provocative that they would later become a focal point of the investigations into the massacre at Sand Creek. At that time, William Bent would tell the committee: "Since I have been there (living along the Arkansas) nearly every instance of difficulties between the Indians and the whites arose from aggressions on the Indians by the whites."[24] Kit Carson, who had enhanced his reputation by polishing off the Navajo people, would tell investigators, "And in relation to the war with the Cheyennes, I have heard it publicly stated that the authorities in Colorado, expecting that their troops would be sent to the Potomac, determined to get up an Indian war, so that the troops would be compelled to remain. I know of no acts of hostility on the part of the Cheyennes and Arapahoes committed previous to the attacks made upon them."[25]

Jesse Leavenworth, by that time Agent for the Kiowas, Comanches, and Apaches, would agree:

> *Knowing their disposition (the Cheyennes), and knowing Lieutenant Ayers* (sic), *having appointed him myself as lieutenant, I stated to the Indian department that if he (Colonel Chivington) was not stopped in his course of sending Lieutenant Ayers after the Indians we should get into a general Indian war on the frontier . . . There never were two bands of Indians more friendly to the whites than Black Kettle's band, and One Eye, who was killed in this massacre (Sand Creek).*[26]

John Smith, interpreter and special Indian agent for the Upper Arkansas would testify,

> *I have heard this whole Indian war has been brought on for selfish purposes. Colonel Chivington was running for Congress in Colorado . . . and last spring a year ago he was looking for an order to go to the front, and I understand he had this Indian war in view to retain himself and his troops in that country, to carry out his electioneering purposes.*[27]

George Bent, who spent much of that summer living with his mother's people, later wrote:

> *I could never understand why the soldiers made these attacks on the Cheyennes in April, 1864. There was no reason for it. One of Colonel Chivington's political enemies once hinted that there was politics back of the whole business, and that is the only possible explanation I can see. Chivington and the clique of officers he had gathered about him were all in politics. These Colorado volunteers had just been ordered to go to Kansas, to fight the Confederates, and the attacks on the Cheyennes began immediately after this order was received. The attacks were evidently planned at headquarters, for the troops went after our people at about the same time at widely separated points. If Colonel Chivington did not want to obey the order to go east, the easiest way out of his difficulty was to attack the Indians and stir them up. The troops would then be needed in Colorado, and the officers would have a splendid chance to make reputations as Indian fighters. On the frontier, this was the shortest road to the people's hearts.*[28]

All of this is hearsay, of course, but if it is true, there is no indication that General Curtis was ever apprised of the undocumented decision to harry the Cheyennes, or that he was kept abreast of developments in Colorado Territory in any but the sketchiest manner. At any rate, questions of why and how had now become academic along the Arkansas. On the day after Lieutenant Eayre was chased into Fort Larned, the Cheyennes began raiding with a vengeance. Convinced that the white soldiers' only purpose in attacking them had been to start a war, they opened their side of it by driving off all the stagecoach mules and other stock from the Rath Ranch, thirty-two miles east of Larned.

On May 18, reports began to reach the fort of other attacks up and down the trail, including raids on the Walnut and Cow Creek ranches. Because the ranchman at Walnut had married a Cheyenne woman, the raiders spared his life. During their unwelcome visit, they told the man of their fight with Eayre on the Smoky Hill and the killing of Lean Bear. Now, they said, they intended to kill every white man they could find. They would not kill him for the sake of his wife, but they warned him to leave the place and carry their words of grievance among the white people.[29]

All along the Santa Fe Trail now, ranchers were deserting their homes, fleeing for safety to the military posts or even as far as Denver City. Stagecoach and freighting operations were severely damaged, and the Colorado authorities began once again to clamor for assistance.

It was in this manner that war with the Cheyennes had come to the Colorado frontier—and no one could forecast with any degree of certainty what the Sioux might be up to.

The disposition of the Sioux would depend in part on the results of their second conference with General Mitchell, who rode into Cottonwood on May 26. The signs were not positive. Since his last visit, the Cheyennes had gone to war, and a party of young Sioux hotheads had killed two travelers on the north side of the Platte in plain view of Fort Cottonwood. Waving the bloody scalps in triumph, the warriors had taunted the soldiers, who were unable to render any aid, since the river was running too high and too cold to be forded.[30] Mitchell was aware how closely the Cheyennes were bound to the Sioux, and felt it necessary to have some up-to-date intelligence of the former tribe. Accordingly, the post commander, Major George O'Brien, sent two white squawmen to invite the Sioux bands to a council and to obtain as much fresh news of the Cheyennes as they could get. With fresh mounts, ample provisions, and O'Brien's instructions in mind,

Alfred Gay and John Smith rode south from Cottonwood to a small Sioux village, where three warriors agreed to take them on to the main encampment. Hostile Cheyennes surrounded the five men, harassing them all the way to the large camp, which was located near present Oxford, Nebraska. The Sioux were indignant with the Cheyennes for treating their guests so rudely, and they willingly gave the scouts what information they could. However, it was simply not possible for white men, even white squawmen, to go among the Cheyennes at this time. One week after their departure, Gay and Smith returned to Cottonwood and wrote a report on their harrowing journey. It was the clearest possible warning of the impending war:

> *It is the impression of the Sioux generally that the Cheyennes and their allies will attack the settlements on the Platte at an early date, destroying all who may come within their reach, and at the same time supply themselves with horses, arms, and ammunition in order to prosecute the war more vigorously . . . The hostile Indians are camped on Indian Creek, about 50 miles north of Fort Larned, and are supposed to number 1200 lodges . . . They design to divide, half going to the Platte River to destroy ranches, murder immigrants (sic), and take horses and mules; the other half of them doing the same on the Arkansas River.*[31]

The intentions of the Cheyennes were certainly unambiguous. What about those of the Sioux?

On June 8, Major O'Brien held a preliminary talk with the assembled chiefs. They steadfastly maintained that they were abiding by the treaty and would not fight on either side. They were also fearful, they said, of being mistaken for hostiles by the whites, and attacked through error. They asked O'Brien to send a white representative to live in their camps, to show them what they were to do, and to interfere if they were mistakenly attacked. Major O'Brien had not been allowed to speak at Mitchell's first conference, and his talk with the chiefs, while firm, was more tolerant than that of his commander. The Sioux were much relieved.[32]

With this intelligence in hand, General Mitchell was ready for his second talk with the chiefs. It began on a positive note. The surveying expedition on the Niobrara had been recalled, and the general had ordered rations of bacon, molasses, and hard bread to be added to the tribe's annuities.

But from there, the council went downhill. The Indians still demanded that the white people leave the hunting grounds between the Arkansas and the upper Missouri. Mitchell still demanded that the chiefs exert a greater control over their young braves and keep their bands out of the Platte Valley. Nothing of substance had changed since the first council, and the chiefs went glumly back to their camps on the Republican. Once again the white man had called and they had come running. Once again they looked like fools.

Mitchell had offered the Sioux no incentive to remain peaceful, other than threats, and it would probably be only a matter of time until at least some of the Sioux joined the Cheyennes and Arapahoes in prosecuting the war. Bad Wound and Spotted Tail discussed the situation with their people, then began moving their camps far to the north to avoid getting mixed up in the hostilities. Some of Bad Wound's young Ogalalas found his report of Mitchell's conference more than they could stomach. Before the camp began to move, they slipped away, more than a dozen of them, to raid up and down the Platte Valley. Upon discovering their absence, the chiefs were enraged and "soldiered' the young warriors—destroyed all the personal possessions they had left behind.

But the little party was gone beyond the chiefs' recall. It is probably safe to assume that these young Ogalalas were responsible for the attack on Looking Glass Creek—an affair which cast the first, long shadows of war over the white homesteads between the Pawnee Reservation and Omaha.[33]

Since the Military District of Nebraska was committed to maintaining a military garrison at the Pawnee Agency, it was necessary to provide for the subsistence of men and animals. In the spring of 1864, the contract for supplying hay to the cavalry was awarded to a Columbus, Nebraska, farmer named Patrick Murray. The young Irish immigrant had come to the area in 1857 and settled a claim about three miles northwest of the young town. With never a day of schooling in his life, Murray was quite unable to read and write, but his business sense was first rate. His sister, Margaret, had married Adam Smith, a young German immigrant who engaged in freighting with a friend, Luther North. In fact, it was Smith who had seen North's hat atop the warrior's head at Fort Kearny the previous summer.

Murray and Smith had no trouble gathering a work crew to cut hay for the cavalry mounts. Itinerant workers were plentiful along the trails. Everyone seemed to be moving to or from somewhere else, and everyone needed money. Such was the case with Reason Grimes, a thirty-nine-year-old farmer who had recently come to Columbus from Morrison, Illinois, with his wife and young daughter.[34] Grimes was recruited for the haying crew along with four others: a local man and a teenage boy; an old frontiersman who had lived for many years with the Sioux; and nine-year-old Stephen Hendricks.[35] Murray's wife, Bridget, agreed to stay with the men in camp and cook their meals. With his crew complete, Murray took them west to begin cutting hay in the broad meadows east of Looking Glass Creek near the Pawnee Agency.[36] When the work was well underway, he left them to journey to Omaha. Murray had heard that the army was about to award a contract for the supply of beef to the troopers of Company E, which was stationed at the agency, and he intended to win that, also.

Looking Glass Creek descends southward through the bluffs, passing about a mile and a half east of the Pawnee Agency, to empty into the Loup River. Its winsome name is a free translation of the Indian words which meant "water in which one can see his reflection." Most of the land on either side of the little stream remained unclaimed in 1864, and Charles Whaley, the farm supervisor for the Pawnees, had previously cut hay from the flat meadows there. It was a pleasant place in which to work, and there was fresh, clean water available from the creek. As Pat Murray's men began the work of mowing, raking, and stacking the sweet-smelling hay, the full heat of summer had not yet arrived; the drought was not yet severe; and the Sioux had not yet attacked the Pawnees.

On Friday evening, June 24, the haycutters were relaxing in their camp beside Looking Glass Creek, resting tired muscles and savoring the supper which they had just finished. Murray's horses and Adam Smith's mules were securely tied to a picket line for the night, and Bridget Murray was bustling about the camp, finishing the last of her supper chores. It was past seven o'clock when the men saw the Indians riding over the brow of the bluffs less than a mile to the northwest. Supposing them to be Pawnees, no one felt any alarm as the file of more than a dozen braves walked their horses into the camp.

The old man on the crew immediately recognized them as Sioux, and began speaking to them in their own language. The presence of Sioux so near the Pawnee Reservation was not a good sign, although up to this time they had not harmed any white people in the area, at least until pressed by Captain Edwards the previous summer.

The demeanor of these Sioux, however, was sinister and surly, and bows and arrows were much in evidence. Some of them wanted something to drink. Others wanted food. As the old man continued his dialogue with them, several braves walked over to the picket line where they began to slowly untie the animals. The whites cautioned them sharply to leave the horses and mules alone, and the smirking braves retied them. The conversation continued, unintelligible to all except for the old man, and soon the Indians began once again to deliberately untie the draft animals. The whites knew now that they were being bullied and were indeed in a tight fix. They were isolated from the agency by the bluffs, outnumbered and unarmed, and the young Sioux were merely toying with them. At last the old man had had enough, and walking over to some camp equipment, he reached into his valise, possibly to get a handgun.

Instantly the camp erupted in fury. One warrior crushed the old man's skull with a war club and neatly stripped off the scalp. War cries shattered the stillness and arrows flew everywhere. Reason Grimes was pierced through the midsection; Adam Smith received numerous arrows through the body; the other two men were wounded painfully, if less seriously. Bridget Murray at first attempted to defend the camp with a pitchfork, then ran to Adam Smith in her hysteria and attempted to pull the arrows from his body. She also was shot down, receiving arrows through her arms and legs. During the yelling and confusion, Stephen Hendricks scurried undetected to one of the haystacks and dug in, covering himself with the loose prairie grass. Grimes, Smith, Bridget Murray, and the other two men were still alive, though immobilized and in great pain. The Sioux allowed them to live and unhurriedly ransacked the camp. As the sun sank below the northwestern bluffs, the warriors departed, taking the horses and mules with them. Dusk fell on the ruined camp, quiet now except for the groans of the wounded.

The little boy remained hidden in his stifling hot haystack long after the Sioux had gone. At last he could stand it no longer, and crawled out to find all the horses gone and all the adults too badly wounded to walk. He alone was able to go for help. It would be a terrifying walk in the dark, for the Sioux might be lying in wait for him anywhere between the Looking Glass and the agency.

Slowly and cautiously, Stephen picked his way along the creek bank. A friendly, three-quarter moon arose making the dark journey only a little less scary. At last he reached the familiar trail and followed it up into the bluffs to the Pawnee Agency. When he arrived, he was taken to Captain James B. David, and soon the story of the Looking Glass raid was on its way to the outside world.

It was still very early morning when the troopers of Company E reached the scene. All except the old man were still alive, but Bridget Murray was nowhere to be found. In her pain and delirium, she had crawled all night over the prairie, calling out for help. Even as the troopers arrived at the ruined camp, her cries were heard by a Mormon family named Saunders, who took her into their cabin and dressed her wounds as well as possible.

Hostilities in Eastern Nebraska Territory prior to Aug. 7, 1864

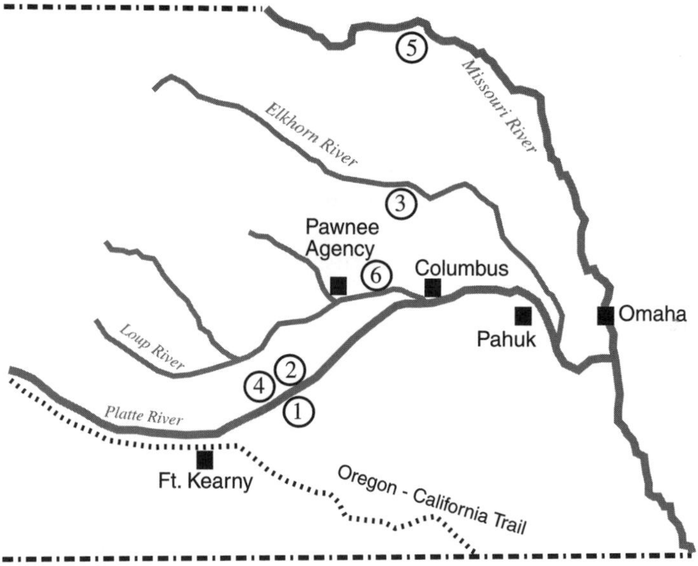

1. Captain Stewart, First Cavalry, attacks Cheyenne war party, Aug. 25, 1856.

2. Cheyennes attack four Mormon wagons, Aug 26, 1856.

3. General Thayer catches up with Pawnees, July 12, 1859.

4. Smith-Anderson murders, February 5, 1862.

5. Wiseman children murdered, July 23, 1863.

6. Pat Murray's haycutters attacked by Sioux, June 24, 1864.

Captain David and his soldiers took the wounded men to the nearby cabin of two traders, the Bowman brothers, where Adam Smith soon died. It proved nearly impossible to extract the arrow from Reason Grimes, and when at last it was pulled free, a portion of his liver came with it. All the wounded were taken by wagon the twelve miles back to Murray's farm. John Peter Becker, who had settled a claim farther up the Looking Glass, sent an urgent telegram to Murray in Omaha. After giving the news to the press, Pat Murray hurried back home to look after his family and count up his losses.

Reason Grimes lived on several weeks in his agony. By the latter part of July, he also was dead. The others recovered, although Bridget Murray was painfully crippled for a year afterward. Captain David sent a brief dispatch over the wire to General Mitchell's headquarters in Omaha, and from there the word was flashed to Fort Leavenworth and along the line to Fort Kearny. But the Sioux raiders had melted away, and Captain David's pursuit was no more than a token effort. Pat Murray could do nothing more than bury his brother-in-law and Reason Grimes and the old man in the small pioneer burying ground near his farm.[37]

There would be no more hay cut along Looking Glass Creek in the summer of 1864. The cost had already been unacceptable: three dead, three wounded; two women widowed and at least four children made fatherless; $2,500 worth of horses and mules stolen, and the sense of security among the settlers north of the Platte severely breached. It seemed clear, to these homesteaders at least, that the Sioux had abandoned their "hands off" policy toward the white people for good. After June 24, men would go out to cut their hay or tend their corn cautiously, apprehensively studying bluffs and hillocks and the banks of small streams for telltale signs of danger. And their families could never again be quite so sure that their husbands and fathers would be returning safely home by sunset.[38]

The immediate reaction to the Looking Glass raid was curious. Unlike the Wood River incident over two years before, no angry citizen posse formed to chase down the marauders. The Pawnees could have wiped them out easily, of course, but most of the tribe was apparently off on the hunt. Captain David, for whatever reason, was unwilling or unable to venture too far from his camp at the agency. Pat Murray was inclined to blame the northern Sioux, while the army cautioned Fort Kearny to be on the lookout for Sioux moving southward. Very likely the raid was carried out by a party of young warriors who had lost all patience with the Sioux chiefs and, as such, did not represent the policy of any band or tribe in general. But this was small comfort to the citizens of Nebraska Territory; nor were they much reassured by a letter from John Smith at Fort Cottonwood to the *Nebraskian* of June 28, which informed readers that, while the Cheyennes were intent on prosecuting the war which had already begun in Colorado Territory, the majority of the Sioux remained peaceably disposed.

If Smith was correct, this peaceful disposition would be the only reserve of goodwill General Mitchell could count on as he rode westward for his third conference with whatever Sioux still remained in the vicinity of Cottonwood. The general was already convinced that he was on a fool's errand, but there was still the slimmest of chances that something positive might be salvaged from the stalemate. In an attempt to bring some peaceful resolution to the ancient enmity between the Sioux and Pawnees, the general had brought along a group of Pawnee warriors under the leadership of Frank North, an employee and interpreter at the agency, and older brother of Luther. It was not a good move.

On the afternoon of July 19, separated by a line of Seventh Iowa troopers, the Pawnees and Sioux harangued each other until they lost control of their tempers, and Mitchell's final conference blew up in his face. The exasperated general ordered the Sioux to be gone, and they splashed across the Platte, howling and shouting imprecations upon the white people as they disappeared northward. Even though the sun had set, General Mitchell left at once on the march to reinforce Fort Laramie, taking along troops F and D of the Seventh Iowa, as well as his Pawnees. After camping for the night at Jack Morrow's ranch, the troops continued up the North Platte. The Pawnees were keenly aware of the strength of the invisible Sioux who were watching the march, and the nervous, frenetic behavior of the scouts en route so irritated the men of the Seventh Iowa that they finally sent their Indian auxiliaries home.[39]

General Mitchell had tried, however clumsily, to ensure a summer of peace along the Platte route, albeit at terms unacceptable to the Sioux. Instead of securing peace, he had only pushed them further into the embrace of the Cheyennes, who were by this time irrevocably committed to war. On July 27, Mitchell's troopers reached Fort Laramie. As the general sent them into camp north of the parade ground, he remained quite unaware of how badly they would soon be needed back at Cottonwood.

Chapter Eight notes

1 So wrote Francis Marshall to Jefferson Davis. O. R. Series I, Vol. 3, 578.

2 Monahan, *Destination: Denver City*, 107.

3 Hoig, *The Sand Creek Massacre*, 21-24; Grinnell, *The Fighting Cheyennes*, 130-136.

4 Hoig, *The Sand Creek Massacre*, 25.

5 Grinnell, *The Fighting Cheyennes*, 134.

6 Ibid., 132-133; also Ball, *Go West, Young Man*, 61.

7 Grinnell, *The Fighting Cheyennes*, 131.

8 Ibid., 135; U. S. Congress, "Massacre of Cheyenne Indians," 81.

9 Hyde, *A Life of George Bent*, 120-121.

10 Grinnell, *The Fighting Cheyennes*, 136.

11 Ibid., 137.

12 Ibid.

13 Biographical information on General Curtis is from:
Castel, "War and Politics."
Dictionary of American Biography
The National Cyclopedia of American Biography
Stuart, *Iowa Colonels and Regiments.*

14 Britton, *The Union Indian Brigade*, 314-316.

15 Grinnell, *The Fighting Cheyennes*, 137.

16 Walker, *The Wagonmasters*, 241.

17 Hyde, *A Life of George Bent*, 124.

18 Grinnell, *The Fighting Cheyennes*, 137-139; Hyde, *A Life of George Bent*, 126.

19 Grinnell, *The Fighting Cheyennes*, 141-142.

20 Ware, *The Indian War of 1864*, 100.

21 Ibid., 105-108.

22 Grinnell, *The Fighting Cheyennes*, 143-144.

23 Ibid., 145.

24 U. S. Congress, "Massacre of Cheyenne Indians," 93.

25 Ibid., 96.

26 U. S. Congress, "Sand Creek Massacre," 4.

27 Ibid., 6.

28 Hyde, *A Life of George Bent*, 127.

29 Grinnell, *The Fighting Cheyennes*, 146; O. R. Vol. 34, Part 3, 661; Vol. 34, Part 4, 150.

30 Ware, *The Indian War of 1864*, 142.

31 Ibid., 143; O. R. Vol. 34, Part 4, 460-461.

32 O. R. Vol. 34, Part 4, 459-460. Ware (*The Indian War of 1864*, 144) recorded that Mitchell arrived at Cottonwood on May 26, took an escort up the road a little ways, and then returned. On May 31, an invitation to the council was sent out to the Brule and Ogalala chiefs. When the Sioux came in to camp near the post, "Captain O'Brien went up to see them upon some order, I don't know what." Evidently Major O'Brien (and possibly his brother, Captain Nicholas O'Brien) held his own preliminary council with the Sioux in their camp, after which the Indians came in to Cottonwood to talk with Mitchell.

33 Ware, *The Indian War of 1864*, 146; Hyde, *Spotted Tail's Folk*, 100-101; Hyde, *Life of George Bent*, 138-139.

34 No record of the Grimes family in Columbus has been located. It is presumed here that the wife and daughter were still living in 1864 and accompanied Grimes to Columbus.

35 Who was Stephen Hendricks, and what was a nine-year-old boy doing with the haycutters? His name occurs only in Curry's *History of Platte County*. Curry most likely heard the story from Adam Smith, Jr., whom she knew quite well. He, in turn, would have gotten his information from his uncle, Patrick Murray.

It seems that Bridget Murray never bore Patrick any children, so the couple took in a number of "unattached" or dependent youngsters. Stephen was born in Iowa about 1855, probably to parents of Irish birth. After his frightening experience on the Looking Glass, he did not remain long with the Murrays. At the age of fifteen he was living by himself in a boarding house in Lincoln, working as a day laborer. Nothing further has been learned of his life prior to 1864 or after 1870. He probably had a younger brother, as the census for 1870 shows a David Hinrix, age eleven, living with the Murrays. By that year, the couple had also taken in three young Sullivan children. For whatever reason, Pat Murray's foster sons left the farm as soon as they were able. By 1880, both David and the seventeen-year-old Sullivan boy were gone.

36 Hyde (*The Pawnee Indians*, 267) states that the whites were illegally cutting hay on the Pawnee Reservation. But Looking Glass Creek lies three quarters of a mile east of the reservation boundary. Moreover, a letter to the *Omaha Nebraskian* of July 8, 1864, states that the men were cutting hay on the *east* side of the creek, well off the reservation.

37 When the City Cemetery and Catholic Cemetery were laid out in the 1870s, some of the graves in the old pioneer burial ground (the exact location of which is unknown) were relocated. Adam Smith's remains were removed to a family plot in the Catholic Cemetery, where the date of death on his tombstone is incorrect. The burial places of Reason Grimes and the old man remain unknown.

38 The story of the Looking Glass raid is compiled from :

Andreas, *History of Nebraska*.
Lushbaugh to Superintendent Albin, September 30, 1864.
Charles Whaley to Agent Lushbaugh, September 26, 1864.
Curry, *History of Platte County*.
Federal Census, 1860, Illinois, Whiteside County, Morrison P. O.
Federal Census, 1860, 1870, 1880, Nebraska, Platte County, Columbus and Monroe Townships.
Land Records, Office of the Recorder, Platte County, Nebraska.
Lizzy Ricketts Whaley to Mrs. Charlotte Ricketts, August 1, 1864; August 9, 1864 (Platt Family Papers).
The Omaha Nebraskian, July 1, 1864; July 8, 1864.
The Omaha Republican, July 1, 1864.
Phillips, *Past and Present of Platte County*.

39 Ware (*The Indian War of 1864*, 176-195) states that General Mitchell was angry and humiliated over the failure of his third conference with the Sioux, and his mood was not improved by the antics of his Pawnee scouts. Frank North was probably just as humiliated over the fiasco. In the copious writings of the North brothers, there is no reference to this first, experimental company of scouts. If it were not for Ware's account, the episode would have been lost to history.

Part I
Chapter Nine

"An expensive Indian war is about to take place"

How quickly things change. In March 1864, the Sioux and Cheyenne were at peace with the whites, if not with the Pawnees. The pent-up traffic from the river ports flowed unrestricted, except for the weather, along the Santa Fe, Oregon-California, and Denver roads. Then April arrived and the Colorado volunteers had attacked the Cheyennes and Arapahoes. By the latter part of May, the Indians had driven the settlers from the mid section of the Santa Fe Trail; General Mitchell had alienated the Sioux; and Confederate General Price had begun his invasion of Missouri, sending the 6,000 men in the van of his force northward under General Marmaduke in the direction of St. Louis.[1]

On the last day of May, Deputy Marshal H. L. Jones reported from Salina that the Arkansas route was deserted and that the Indians were planning a general plains war to be led by white renegades and coordinated with guerilla activities in western Missouri.[2] On June 3, Postal Agent Charles Ingersoll complained to General Curtis that the Indians were disrupting the mail service, and asked for military escorts to accompany the mail coaches. The general immediately sent orders for such escorts to Forts Riley and Larned.[3] On June 4, Curtis received a wire from his superior in St. Louis, General Rosecrans, warning that several hundred guerrillas were concentrated along the Kansas-Missouri border.[4] Just where along the border Rosecrans didn't know—somewhere between St. Joseph and Fort Scott, which is a long border indeed. That same day, the Adjutant General of Colorado received a warning from Major Wynkoop at Fort Lyon: The major had received intelligence that indicated without a doubt that a large body of Texans was approaching his post, and he was feverishly preparing to block their invasion.[5] It seemed that every day brought some new and ominous development to headquarters at Fort Leavenworth. And, like a befuddled grandparent in a room full of unruly toddlers, Curtis had barely time to focus his attention on one misbehavior before he was distracted by another. The Department of Kansas was beginning to shake itself apart, and the attentions of its commander bounced helter skelter from Governor Evans to guerrillas to Cheyennes to Texans to General Price.

Next it was Governor Carney's turn to scold. Topeka, he said, was in need of military protection, and he reminded Curtis that it was, after all, the capital of the state and the repository of all state documents. Curtis replied on June 6 that he had sent a force to garrison the capital, but that it had been detoured by Indian depredations. His dispatch went on to say, "It is my duty to repeat to you, however, that my force is very small, and that I am constantly informed of danger from accumulating bushwhackers, who are said to be gathering in Missouri."[6]

Not one to give up easily, Carney wired back the next day, this time asking Curtis to send troops to guard the settlers in the Emporia area. Again the general declined, reminding the governor that his "slender resources" did not permit, and suggesting that Carney call out units of short-term militia.[7]

But it was the Colorado situation that was the most puzzling. Somehow the reports of Indian outrages and Lieutenant Eayre's glorious victory seemed out of joint. There was something not quite right in the District of Colorado and Curtis was unable to divine just exactly what it was. On June 3, he sent his Inspector General, Major T. I. McKenny, on a fact-finding mission to Fort Larned, where things appeared most in disarray. As he waited for McKenny's report, Curtis received word of a serious attack on June 9, committed against three families of emigrants along Bijou Creek about sixty-five miles from Denver City. There had been no injuries or deaths, but the Indians had stampeded all their draft animals and the emigrants were left stranded.[8] Then on June 11 occurred the atrocity which electrified the Colorado frontier.

The Van Wormer Ranch southeast of Denver City had been hit hard by the Indians in the past weeks, and much of its stock had been scattered. Ranch manager Ward Hungate had ridden out in search of strays when he saw smoke rising from the direction of the ranch house. Racing back to protect his wife and daughters, he found the buildings in flames and his family dead. The attackers had not yet finished their work when he arrived, and Hungate himself was killed before he could escape.

A search party found the bodies of the Hungates later that day.[9] The woman had been stabbed and scalped, while the little girls had their throats slashed so violently that their heads were barely still attached. On the opposite side of a small creek lay the body of Ward Hungate, terribly mutilated and its scalp torn off. With a singular lack of respect for the dead, the searchers took the tortured bodies into Denver City and placed them on display in the window of an unused building. Bypassing General Curtis completely, Governor Evans wired directly to Secretary of War Stanton on June 14 that "murdered, scalped bodies were brought in," and begged authority to raise a regiment of volunteers for one hundred days' service.[10]

On June 15, four days after the Hungate murders, Major McKenny wrote a report of his investigation into affairs at Fort Larned, including recommendations for action. It was a sobering document which drew a grim picture of the atmosphere of incompetence and demoralization which infected the post:

> *Arrived at Fort Larned on the evening of the 14th, during a very heavy thunderstorm, and found the commander of the post with about half the garrison on a scout after Indians, but they got no Indians but plenty of buffalo. Captain Parmetar, of the Twelfth Kansas Infantry, in command here, is reported by every officer and man that I have heard speak of him as a confirmed drunkard. Fort Larned is only a fort in name . . . the sight presented in the huts occupied for quartermaster and commissary stores was awful. The water had been streaming down amongst the corn, flour, beans, and everything else, and by this rain alone over 100 sacks of flour were ruined; besides, I saw over 1000 bushels of corn, according to Lieutenant Crocker's (the assistant quartermaster) estimate, which was ruined . . . I think this loss might have been materially lessened by proper attention of officers responsible . . .*

McKenny had also uncovered some unpleasant truths about Lieutenant Eayre's fight with the Cheyennes:

> *Lieutenant Eayre, with two mountain howitzers and 84 men, all told, went in search of Indians with instructions to burn (his) bridges and kill Cheyennes whenever and wherever found. With his 84 men and only fifteen wagons he wandered off out of his district, within fifty miles of this place.*

> *The Indians, finding his command well scattered, his wagons behind without any rear guard, artillery in the center 1-1/2 miles from them, and the cavalry 1 mile in advance, made an attack, killing three instantly and wounding three others . . . In regard to these Indian difficulties, I think if great caution is not exercised on our part there will be a bloody war. It should be our policy to try and conciliate them, guard our mails and trains well to prevent theft, and stop these scouting parties that are roaming over the country who do not know one tribe from another, and who will kill anything in the shape of an Indian. It will require but few murders on the part of our troops to unite all these warlike tribes of the plains, who have been at peace for years and are intermarried amongst one another.*[11]

On June 20, there came an unsolicited confirmation of McKenny's analysis. On that day, Major H. D. Wallen, of the Seventh Infantry, wrote to the Adjutant General:

> *I have just crossed the plains and am sure, from authentic information, that an expensive Indian war is about to take place between the whites and the Cheyennes, Kiowas, and a band of Arapahoes. It can be prevented by prompt management.*[12]

But on the very day McKenny wrote his report to Curtis, Governor Evans had received a very different report from the tattletale squawman, Robert North. The murderer of the Hungates was an Arapaho named John Notanee, wrote North. The Cheyennes had been along on the raid, and were doing their level best to form a confederation of plains tribes, confident that such a combination would be strong enough to drive the white people completely out of the territory.[13] Once again Evans took North's statements as gospel truth, and fired off an ill-tempered dispatch to General Curtis, accusing him of refusing to believe the many warnings which the governor had sent him. He had proof, said Evans in barely civil terms, that all his reports of Indian atrocities had been true, and he challenged Curtis to prove otherwise.[14]

Then it was the guerrillas again. On June 23, Curtis received a dispatch from the Department of Missouri, warning him that guerrillas were gathering around the little town of Parkville, Missouri, making preparations to attack the town of Leavenworth itself.[15] The message went on to say that this information had been obtained from Negro slaves who had overheard their secessionist masters plotting to aid the bushwhackers, and included the caution that the guerrillas might dress in Union uniforms to carry out their raid. This was followed three days later by a dispatch from General Mitchell telling of the Sioux attack on the haycutters' camp on Looking Glass Creek.[16]

On June 27, Curtis wired to General McKean at Paola the news of McKenny's fact-finding mission and alerted him to the fact that Colonel Chivington was supposed to be bringing some Colorado troops eastward along the Arkansas route. The message concluded: "A good commander of that region must be arranged. Captain Parmetar, at Larned, must be immediately disposed of."[17] But McKean could spare no competent officers to take command at Larned.

Finally, on June 29, Curtis composed a lengthy dispatch to Colonel Chivington, which he hoped would reach the Colorado commander somewhere between Forts Lyon and Larned. He began by stating flatly that Lieutenant Eayre's battle with the Cheyennes had been "not so well reported," and that his staff officer had been highly critical of the lieutenant's tactics. He then proceeded to issue Chivington three directives:

1. The troops were to be forbidden to go out on fruitless Indian chases or buffalo hunts, in order to spare their horses.

2. "If, when you reach Larned, you find the drunken captain still in command, see that he is immediately relieved, superceded, or arrested."

3. Make certain that any reports of Indian depredations are well authenticated.

The letter also included the incredible suggestion that "a good company or two, with two howitzers well attended, is no doubt sufficient to pursue and destroy any band of Indians likely to congregate anywhere on the plains . . ."[18] Such a statement regarding the warlike capacities of the High Plains tribes was worthy of the most ignorant greenhorn along the trails and hardly equated with that "prompt management" urged by Major Wallen.

Following his message to Chivington, Curtis dashed off another testy dispatch, this one to Governor Evans, sharply rebuking him for his attitude:

> *I may not have all you have seen and heard, but I am sure I have a great deal more on the subject which you have not seen nor heard . . . I am scarce of horses everywhere . . . It would take a great deal more force than we now have to insure our wide scattered settlements in Colorado, Nebraska, New Mexico, and Kansas . . . however much we may have rea-*

son to apprehend a general Indian war we should not conclude them as such a thing in actual existence before doing all in our power to prevent such a disaster.[19]

Having cut down the Colorado officials a notch or two, General Curtis next turned his full attention to the potential disaster in his own backyard. On July 7, a gang of bushwhackers captured the little town of Parkville, Missouri, only seventeen miles southeast of Fort Leavenworth.[20] After properly looting and terrorizing the place, they continued their march northward. On July 10 they captured Platte City, only nine miles from the fort. Weston, Missouri, looked to be next in line and its mayor began frantically calling on Curtis for help.

These affairs were all on the Missouri side of the river in General Fisk's department, and thus technically none of Curtis' business. But there was a sort of gentleman's agreement between the two officers by which Curtis would offer such assistance as he could, and at the time, Fisk had every man of his command deployed to other hot spots throughout Platte and Clay counties with none to spare for the defense of the small river towns.[21] The bold successes of the bushwhacker gangs had authorities in Kansas understandably nervous, and General Deitzler, of the Kansas Militia, wired directly to President Lincoln that "Missouri is alive with bushwhackers, but it is believed that 2,000 can be concentrated on the border within two days. That they are proposing to overrun Kansas this summer there is no doubt."[22]

Curtis moved decisively to neutralize the gathering peril, dispatching a force to guard Weston, which was little more than five straight-line miles north of the fort. On Monday, July 11, scouts came in to Leavenworth with news that at least 200 guerrillas were gathered in Platte City, recruiting forces which they promised would link up with Quantrill. Their leader, a misfit named Coon Thornton, held a public meeting in the center of the town, threatening destruction upon any federal forces, and death to any loyal citizens foolish enough to oppose his prosouthern irregulars.[23]

General Curtis was holding a meeting, too, but he was doing it by military telegraph. Together with McKean in Paola, Fisk in Missouri, and Colonel Ford of the Second Colorado Cavalry in Kansas City, the general laid plans for an assault to break up Coon Thornton's party.

The warlike Lieutenant Eayre and McLain's Battery were called over from their station in Lawrence. Colonel Ford brought his regiment up the Missouri by steamboat, and General McKean sent up two companies of the Sixteenth Kansas Cavalry from Olathe and Shawneetown. The strike force gathered at Fort Leavenworth before crossing the river at Weston to march down on the unsuspecting guerrillas, whose intelligence happened to be faulty just then.

On July 13, Colonel Ford's troops assaulted Platte City. The battle, in spite of Coon Thornton's bluster, was quick and one-sided. Faced at last with an enemy that knew something about the business of fighting, Thornton's bushwhackers were driven in disorder into west central Missouri. Behind them they left their stores of guns and ammunition, and fifteen of their dead. By eight o'clock that evening, Ford reported that all was quiet on his front.[24] With the guerrillas routed and Colonel Ford in pursuit, there was no time lost in congratulations as General Curtis diverted his attention once again to the Indian situation on his western frontier. While he had been preoccupied with bushwhackers, Governor Evans had had a brainstorm.

On June 27, the governor published his circular "to the friendly Indians of the plains." The proclamation instructed those Cheyennes and Arapahoes who were friendly to the whites to assemble themselves near Fort Lyon, while friendly Kiowas and Comanches were to gather near Fort Larned.[25] The object of this sorting out, said the governor, was "to prevent friendly Indians from being killed through mistake." Lean Bear's band must have been incredulous when they heard these words.

William Bent was given the task of delivering Evans' proclamation to the Cheyennes and Arapahoes in the vicinity of Fort Larned. There were some Comanches there also, and Satanta's Kiowas were casting covetous eyes on the military horse herd. Satanta was even bold enough to invite the Arapahoes to join him in a raid on the corrals, but Chief Left Hand declined the generous gesture, and warned Captain Parmetar of the Kiowas' intentions. The warning went unheeded, and soon after, the Kiowas staged a dance. While the soldiers were distracted by the entertainment, the Kiowa warriors made off with a large number of army mounts, including most of the horses originally brought in by Lieutenant Eayre's battery.[26] Captain Parmetar was in a vile temper, and issued orders to shoot any Indian who even attempted to approach the fort. Of course, he neglected to inform the Indians.

Left Hand had tried to be a friend to the whites, but they had failed to do their part. Now he decided to try once again, and taking with him twenty-five of his young men, he approached Fort Larned to offer his services in recapturing the stolen horses. Without warning, the Arapahoes found themselves under fire from the guard and were forced to flee for their lives. Left Hand remained unruffled and philosophical over this latest act of idiocy, but his braves were in a white-hot rage and began slipping away from camp to join the implacable

Dog Soldiers. Too little too late, Colonel Chivington arrived and replaced the "drunken captain" with Captain William Backus of the First Colorado.[27]

To the disarray in western Kansas, General Mitchell added some bad tidings from Nebraska Territory. On July 19 he reported that there had been serious Indian raids above (north of) Julesburg and he himself was headed into the field with two companies of cavalry and a section of a battery.[28] (He did not mention his Pawnee scouts.) To meet the growing threat in the west, Mitchell was shuffling field officers and troops all over the District of Nebraska. Lieutenant Ware was relieved of his court martial duties at Fort Kearny and sent back to Cottonwood to prepare his Company F for the march to Fort Laramie. Major John Wood was relieved of the command of Fort Kearny to take over as post commander at Fort Laramie. To replace him at Kearny, Colonel Samuel Summers was ordered out from regimental headquarters in Omaha. Upon his arrival, Summers became so alarmed at the shortage of manpower he immediately called back to Omaha for reinforcements.[29] The shortage of horses had also become acute throughout the district, and two dismounted companies were ordered to march to Fort Kearny. In addition, Captain Edward Murphy and Company A of the Seventh Iowa were ordered to leave Dakota City immediately and ride to Fort Kearny (they still had horses) via Omaha.[30]

Meanwhile in Missouri, Colonel Ford had temporarily forgotten that he was a military officer instead of a politician, and had allowed the guerrillas to dribble away from him. Now they were collecting once more at Plattsburg, just twenty miles east of Platte City. In Paola General McKean wanted his troopers of the Sixteenth Kansas back on station. The Kansas militia was calling on Curtis to furnish arms and ammunition. General Fisk in Missouri was calling for arms and ammunition. Harassed and fed up with the whole situation, Curtis wired back to his nervous colleagues that he would loan them federal arms in a real emergency, but he really felt that the border area was in no immediate danger. He himself was going west to take the field against the Cheyennes in person, explaining briefly to Fisk, "I am troubled with Indians."[31]

On July 21, General Curtis set off on his Indian campaign. The line of march was designed to reassure the frontier settlements and to intimidate the Cheyennes and Arapahoes. Just possibly it might also serve to demonstrate that the elderly commander was still capable of leading his troops in the field, the same as Mitchell and Chivington were doing. The troops he led were little more than a scratch force—396 men, mostly unreliable militia, some U. S. Volunteers, and a section of the Ninth Wisconsin Battery. The wild tribes could have chewed up his ragtag army with ease. Instead, they chose to let the whites tire of chasing them and return to the east again, and indeed that is pretty much what happened.

Curtis intended to push all the way through to Denver City and had ordered four troops of the First Colorado to meet him en route for support. His order to Major Wynkoop had been peremptory, of course, but Wynkoop had been warned to clear all troop movements with Chivington, and dutifully forwarded Curtis' order to Denver City for approval. Consequently the troops were delayed, and Curtis got all the way to Fort Larned before meeting up with Wynkoop's companies, greatly angering the department commander for whom very little seemed to be going right these days.

On July 30, General Curtis wrote a stinging rebuke to Colonel Chivington, directly laying the blame for depredations along the Arkansas on the tardy troops. Mindful of Chivington's crass politicking in the face of approaching territorial elections, Curtis wrote:

> *I fear your attention is too much attracted by other matters than your command, and hope you will feel the importance of concluding a good record which you commenced in the line of your present duties, whatever turn other matters of public interest may take in Colorado.*[32]

In a letter to Governor Evans, Curtis was more conciliatory. He praised Colonel Ford and the Second Colorado Regiment and asked for fresh news of Indian troubles on the South Platte. He could get no intelligence from the Indians around Larned, the general explained, because his militiamen were so ferociously worked up over the present state of hostilities that even the friendly Indians were shying away from them. In fact, his militiamen were unwilling to go any farther west, so Curtis proposed to turn south and scout along the Arkansas before heading back to Leavenworth, where he was needed at headquarters.[33]

He was indeed. Coon Thornton had been murdered by his own men, but now Quantrill was reported to be east of Independence with a large force of guerrillas.[34] And things were heating up along the upper Platte where General Mitchell had reached Fort Laramie with his Seventh Iowa companies.

"I find the difficulties much more than I anticipated," wired the general. "From present appearances you may expect an Indian outbreak in all this western country."[35]

So General Curtis ended his Indian campaign, returning by way of Council Grove and Lawrence, which he reached on August 6. Though he had fought no Indians, he consoled himself with the belief that he had scared them away from the Arkansas route, and his efforts were highly commended by newspapers in both Lawrence and Leavenworth. But in actuality, little of substance had been accomplished. The general had established two small military posts between Salina and Fort Larned (one of them, Fort Zarah, he named for his fallen son), but none in that dreadful stretch between Larned and Fort Lyon.

Of more significance was his creation of the new District of the Upper Arkansas, command of which was given to the ill-tempered political general from Kansas, James Blunt.[36] Blunt was indeed a fighter, but the existing hatred between him and Governor Carney probably made his appointment a poor choice. The new district included both Forts Lyon and Larned, however, removing them from Chivington's command and effectively confining that officer's influence to the area between the headwaters of the Smoky Hill and the South Platte.

Other than this, Curtis' campaign was notable for the endurance of its commanding officer. In eighteen days, the general had ridden over 500 miles, and must have been exceedingly weary as he returned to his headquarters. But he would get no rest anytime soon. The worst was just around the corner.

Chapter Nine notes

Notes 1 -18 are from Official Records, Vol. 34, Part 4.

[1] 149.

[2] 149-150.

[3] 205.

[4] 227.

[5] 208.

[6] 250.

[7] 287-288.

[8] 405.

[9] 354-355.

[10] 381.

[11] 402-405.

[12] 476. The word *expensive* may be an error. *Extensive* makes more sense.

[13] 422-423.

[14] 512-513.

[15] 526.

[16] 567.

[17] 575.

[18] 595-596.

[19] O. R. Vol. 41, Part 2, 53.

[20] Ibid., 92.

[21] Ibid.

[22] O. R. Vol. 34, Part 4, 476.

[23] A synopsis of Coon Thornton's address to the citizens of Platte City appeared in the *Omaha Republican* of July 22, 1864.

[24] O. R. Vol. 41, Part 2, 92-191.

[25] Lavender, *Bent's Fort*, 380.

[26] Hoig, *The Sand Creek Massacre*, 81.

[27] Ibid.

[28] O. R. Vol. 41, Part 2, 276.

[29] Ibid., 277.

[30] Ibid., 276-277.

[31] Ibid., 314.

[32] Ibid., 483-484.

[33] Ibid., 484-485.

[34] Ibid., 476, 483.

[35] Ibid., 428-429.

[36] Garfield, *Defense of the Kansas Frontier*, 140-142; "General Blunt's Account of his Civil War Experiences," 251-252; Hoig, *The Sand Creek Massacre*, 91-92.

Nebraska State Historical Society

A bull train of freight wagons belonging to the firm of Hawks and Nuckolls leaves Nebraska City.

Nebraska State Historical Society
Maj. Gen. Samuel Ryan Curtis

Courtesy Colorado Historical Society (F22-BPF)
Colonel John Milton Chivington

Kansas Historical Society
Brigadier General
Robert Byington Mitchell

Nebraska State Historical Society

Henson Wiseman

Part I
Chapter Ten

"All quiet on the Platte"

It hardly seemed possible in the summer of 1864 that, only a scant twenty-one years before, the number of people going over the Oregon Trail had totaled about a thousand for the entire season. From the trail's head at Westport, Missouri, the over-burdened farm wagons of the Great Migration had creaked and groaned all the way to the Columbia River on a pathway so faint it had required a tag team of guides—John Gantt and Marcus Whitman—to keep everybody on the trail. For those daring emigrants of '43, there had been no military posts, no road ranches, no rapid communication with loved ones back in "the states," and no hostile Indians.

In the summer of 1864, those brave, perilous days were but a dim memory. The country was in the midst of a cataclysmic internal war which was, in turn, fueling an industrial boom. The Atlantic and Pacific coasts were linked by the electric telegraph. No longer was the Independence-Westport area the undisputed head of the trail. Most westbound traffic now originated at the river ports of St. Joseph, Nebraska City, Brownville, and Bellevue. The routes from those towns joined the Omaha-Fort Kearny Military Road just east of the fort to form a broad, dirt superhighway up the Platte Valley, a road which historian Merrill Mattes has called the Great Platte River Road.[1] That road still went all the way to Oregon and California, but in 1864 it also branched off to follow the South Platte to Denver City. Although there was another trail between Denver and Leavenworth via the Smoky Hill River through Kansas, the majority of Colorado-bound traffic followed the lead of Ben Holladay's stagecoaches and stuck to the Platte Valley route where there was always an abundance of water.

Since the valley was broad and flat, there was no reason for the trail to confine itself to a single, narrow track. As eastbound trains passed westbound trains, and as mule outfits overtook bull trains, the trail grew continually wider, garlanded with innumerable cutoffs, turnouts, and campsites, all beaten into the earth by the sheer crush of ironshod traffic.

The physical appearance of the trail made a deep impression upon many of the travelers. Louisa Cook described the road through present Jefferson County, Nebraska as "smooth as a house floor and as wide as a street in a city for the last day or two."[2] Along the Little Blue River, the road was more than 100 yards wide in most places, allowing two or three wagons to travel abreast. Freighter Frank Helvey noted that this stretch of the trail "used about all the ground between Tom Helvey's Ranch, Big Sandy Creek, and the Little Blue River for the roadway and camping places, or a strip of country about two miles wide and six or eight miles long. So they patronized all the ranches and ran over about all the territory, till it is hard to tell the exact course of the trail."[3] Lieutenant Ware described the Military Road west of Omaha as "a well-beaten track, four or five hundred yards wide . . . hard and smooth as a floor, for the dust and gravel had been blown off from it by the violence of the wind."[4]

But it was the spectacular amount of traffic on the trail which the ranchers and travelers found most awesome. Mattes has estimated the number of emigrants over the trail in 1864 at 20,000, and this does not include military or commercial traffic, which was the greatest portion of the travel.[5] Even though March was exceptionally stormy with snowfall late in the month, the traffic from January through April was the heaviest ever witnessed for that season.[6] The *Omaha Nebraskian* for May 6 reported:

> *Our streets are jammed every day with the rolling tide of the emigration. Though only beginning, the like has not been seen since the great California mania. A gentleman who has just arrived from eastern Iowa informs us that the road is lined for a space of fifty miles with wagons—the great majority making a bee line for the central Platte Valley route.*

Along the old Oregon Trail, James Bainter guessed that, during the height of the travel season, an average 300 teams per day passed his ranch on the Little Blue River, all coming from Westport, St.

Joseph, and Brownville.[7] A single encampment of 400 wagons in the Little Blue Valley formed a corral a mile long and a half mile wide.[8] Some forty miles farther up the trail, thirteen-year-old Harriet Hitchcock noted in her diary for May 13:

> *This afternoon we reached the great thoroughfare from Nebraska City to Denver. The road is filled with emigrants and my eyes ache with looking at the long trains of wagons which we can see for miles ahead some of them drawn by six and eight yoke of oxen.*[9]

Three days later, she wrote that her train had overtaken 200 ox teams and had met fifty headed east.

Along the Platte, Lieutenant Ware climbed a high bluff known as Sioux Lookout and trained his glass on a passing line of wagons which was so long that it became indistinguishable in the distance.[10] A few miles from Sioux Lookout, the people at the McDonald Ranch counted 900 wagons passing in a single day.[11] Atop his stagecoach, messenger Frank Root tallied 600 freight wagons alone during a single day's run.[12] Numerous small outfits were compressed to form aggregations ten to fifteen miles long, shaking the ground and assaulting the senses with an indescribable atmosphere of noise, dust, and odors.

In moments of reflection, a few of the travelers recalled that once, the trail corridor had been carpeted with bluestem and buffalo grass, visited only by Indian tribes on the hunt. In a letter of June 1864, George Blanchard wrote:

> *So the poor Indian must fade and disappear before this human avalanche . . . If the Indians had the capacity to understand this invasion of their last retreat on earth: or if they could unite to defend it in any considerable numbers, hundreds of trains, cattle, provisions, and all would be their easy prey.*[13]

It was just this possibility that was causing nightmares for the military commanders in the District of Nebraska. The treaties had failed. General Mitchell's talks with the Sioux had failed. The officers could do little more than shuffle their meager resources and prepare for the emergency they all hoped would never come.

Amid the throng of freighters and prospective homesteaders jostling over the hard-packed Military Road, Colonel Samuel

Summers rode westward through the dust and heat of mid July toward Fort Kearny. Though the Seventh Iowa Cavalry had been in the field for nearly a year, its commanding officer remained most of the time in Omaha. Because the various companies of the Seventh were scattered from the Dakotas to Kansas, General McKean had assigned the regimental headquarters to Omaha. The city was also the territorial capital, a center for communication both by telegraph and by river steamer, and the headquarters of the Military District of Nebraska, the offices of which were located in the Herndon House Hotel.

Colonel Summers was not a physically imposing man, like Colonel Chivington or General Mitchell.[14] At a skinny 140 pounds, he often gave new acquaintances the impression of having a rather unhealthy constitution. His bright, black eyes and caustic smile also gave the impression, correctly, of a person of great energy, a man who was shrewd in financial matters, who clung to his worldly treasure. The forty-three-year-old officer had not been overly bothered by the fact that his superior, General Mitchell, was constantly in the field, traveling hundreds of miles up and down the trails in Nebraska Territory. It was more comfortable in Omaha. Besides, the regimental majors were running the day-to-day affairs of their battalions efficiently and professionally. Colonel Summers had not really been needed along the line, nor was he much wanted there, either. It seems the Seventh Iowa was not terribly fond of its commanding officer.[15]

But as peaceful relations with the Sioux, Cheyennes, and Arapahoes had crumbled, Major John Wood, commandant at Fort Kearny, was needed at Fort Laramie. There was no assistance to be had from the deputy commander of the Seventh Iowa: Lieutenant Colonel John Pattee and several companies were away with General Sully in the Dakotas. So, at last, on July 14, General Mitchell had ordered Summers to take command at Fort Kearny.

The old post wasn't really a fort at all in the usual sense of the word—only an unenclosed collection of buildings set around a four-acre parade ground. The construction materials of the "little old rusty frontier cantonment," as Ware called it, were heavy on adobe and cottonwood logs.[16] Larger buildings such as barracks, officers' quarters, and commanding officer's residence were built from dressed lumber hauled out from the East. The fort had a few amenities: numerous wells, some large cottonwood trees for shade, a telegraph office, and even an ice house. The ammunition magazine, like the ice house, was built entirely above ground, because first water lay only about four or five feet below the surface. The commanding officer's quarters was a house containing six rooms in a story and a half, with large porches front and rear.

As the colonel took up his duties at Fort Kearny, Indian hostilities along the western trails were boiling up like thunderheads on a hot, muggy day. On July 17, General Mitchell was on his way west with a hastily recruited company of Pawnees, headed for his third, final, and most disastrous council with the Sioux. It was on that same day that the pattern of Cheyenne depredations along the South Platte reached its zenith. On that single day, the Cheyennes attacked freighters at Fremont's Orchard, driving off eight horses. They also attacked Junction Ranch, Junction Station, and Murray's Station, stealing horses and shooting the cattle full of arrows. At Bijou Ranch, two seventeen-year-old wagoners were killed, scalped, and mutilated. Minor thievery was done at Beaver Creek Ranch, Beaver Creek Station, and Godfrey's Ranch, while at Moore's Washington Ranch, twenty-eight horses were stolen. To punctuate the day's activities, two emigrants were killed and cut into pieces.[17]

On July 19, Colonel Summers received word from General Mitchell at Cottonwood that the Indians were "cleaning out the country above Julesburg," and that the general was headed west with Major Wood and two companies. There was also news of a large concentration of Cheyennes along the Republican, and the Sioux depredations between Fort Laramie and Deer Creek Station had reached alarming proportions.[18] Any day, another wire might come from the west, demanding more of Fort Kearny's garrison, and the colonel had scarcely enough men now to defend the post if those Cheyennes on the Republican decided to strike northward. Captain Murphy's Company A would not arrive from Sioux City for another week or so. Until then, Summers and his officers could only advise the constant stream of emigrant and freight outfits to combine into large trains for mutual protection. Providing escort service with his handful of troopers was beyond the colonel's power.

Some of the emigrants chafed at the delay and at the inconvenience of having to travel with a cumbersome, noisy, dirty aggregation of wagons. As a freighter, James Green had been over the trail to Colorado and back many times. He knew the country and, he thought, the Indians. Green and his bride of two months reached Fort Kearny late in July and decided to continue westward on their own, in spite of the danger which was said to await travelers west of Fort Cottonwood. Upon reaching that post, however, the news of recent depredations along the South Platte was much worse than they had expected. The Greens thought it over and decided the risk was unacceptable, even if traveling in a large company. Their decision made, they reluctantly turned their ox teams back toward Fort Kearny.[19] Unwittingly, the Greens had placed themselves in the very path of the approaching storm.

The first hint that the Indian unrest was moving eastward came on July 22, when General Mitchell ordered Colonel Summers to send an officer with a detachment of twenty troopers to garrison Plum Creek Station only thirty-five miles west of Kearny. The colonel also needed some intelligence of that supposedly hostile Cheyenne camp along the Republican, and on July 23, he ordered Captain Wilcox and Company B to scout for the rumored camp. His naive order directed Wilcox to locate the Indians and ascertain the "cause for their disaffection," and concluded with this confusing mandate:

> *You will act on the defensive, but if attacked, exterminate them . . . Owing to the disturbing state of feeling among the Indians you will be careful not to attack them and bring on difficulty.*[20]

The colonel would understand before he got very much older that the Cheyennes were indeed along the Republican; that they had good cause for their disaffection; and that the only people in danger of extermination were the men of Company B.[21]

Oddly enough, all the military maneuvering appeared to be having the desired effect. The raids along the South Platte began mysteriously to diminish, and the obnoxious hit-and-run scares west of Plum Creek ceased. The reinforcement of Fort Kearny, the military scouting parties, and General Mitchell's expedition to Julesburg and on to Laramie had evidently scared the savages away from the Platte River Road. Within a few days, the deluge of reports of murder and mayhem had slowed to a trickle, and the *Omaha Nebraskian* of July 29 printed a small paragraph proclaiming,:

> *All quiet on the Platte. A dispatch from Julesburg this morning informs us that the aborigines have changed their base, and that the property taken by them from the emigrants and freighters has all been retaken.*

At Fort Kearny, everyone began to relax. The cautions previously issued to the emigrants were diluted. Toward the end of the first week in August, the outfit of Thomas Morton, out of Sidney, Iowa, pulled into the fort. The Mortons had heard the stories of the depredations taking place farther west, and they anxiously inquired of the officers the latest conditions of the trail.

There was no longer so much danger, they were informed. Military scouting parties had been moving constantly up and down the road, and the Indians had been cleared away. The Mortons might proceed with safety and, of course, reasonable caution.[22]

Thus reassured, Thomas Morton, his wife and in-laws, hitched up their mules that August 7 and headed their wagons westward along the old Oregon-California Trail toward their place in history. And Colonel Summers' response to their tragic fate would mark the close of his military career, not with acclaim or commendation, but with acrimony and criticism in the frontier press.

Chapter Ten notes

[1] Mattes, *The Great Platte River Road.*

[2] Holmes, Ed., *Covered Wagon Women*, Vol. 8, 32.

[3] Dawson, *Pioneer Tales*, 55.

[4] Ware, *The Indian War of 1864*, 12-13.

[5] Mattes, *The Great Platte River Road*, 23.

[6] Ware, *The Indian War of 1864*, 98.

[7] *Biographical and Historical Memoirs*, 345.

[8] "Early Days on the Little Blue," 128.

[9] Holmes, Ed., *Covered Wagon Women*, Vol. 8, 237-238.

[10] Ware, *The Indian War of 1864*, 101.

[11] Ibid.

[12] Root and Connelley, *Overland Stage*, 609.

[13] Blanchard, "The Overland Trail," 78.

[14] Biographical information on Colonel Summers is taken from:
Stiles, *Recollections and Sketches*, 614-617.
Stuart, *Iowa Colonels and Regiments*, 633-638.

[15] Ware, *The Indian War of 1864*, 85, 445.

[16] Lieutenant Ware wrote an interesting description of Fort Kearny to his parents in a letter of July 11, 1864, during the time he was on court martial duty at the post:

> *Fort Kearny is an old government post dating back many a year. It is built on a plain in the shape of a quadrangle, surrounded by large well finished buildings(.) innumerable wells are dug and an immense quantity of supplies are at the post. The buildings are large and old fashioned frame buildings 2 stories with an attic and gable windows in the roof and immense brick fireplaces in each room. The wall(s) are all bricked in and the plastering and finishing is of the finest quality(.) The buildings (are) surrounded with 2 rows of porches and the windows covered with nice green blinds(.) Porches and walks shaded by planted trees now 18 inches in diameter make everything pleasant and cool. It is a government post whose history belongs to the old regime.* (Papers of Eugene F. Ware)

[17] Monahan, *Destination: Denver City*, 155-156; O. R. Vol. 41, Part 2, 92-191 various places.

[18] Unrau, Ed., *Tending the Talking Wire*, 146-150.

[19] Green, "Freighting on the Plains," 1-6.

[20] Fort Kearny Letterbook; *Report of the Adjutant General (Iowa), 1865*, 1013.

[21] Fortunately, Company B found no Indians. Obviously the soldiers didn't look in the right place. *Report of the Adjutant General (Iowa), 1865*, 1013.

[22] Stevens, "Affidavit."

Part I
Chapter Eleven

"Ash Hollow will be nowhere"

The last paltry rains fell around the middle of July and their moisture quickly evaporated. Under a searing sun, the people and animals of the plains clustered close to the rivers which were the lifeblood of the country.[1] As the month ran out day-by-day, the chances for peace on the plains dribbled away. With each passing day, the wild tribes became more irrevocably committed to total warfare.

The warnings of the impending conflict had been numerous over an ample period of time. The first had come from William Bent in 1859. Successive cautions came from Robert North in November 1863 (a spurious one, but nobody really knew that at the time); from Deputy Marshal Jones in Salina on May 31, 1864; from Bad Wound and Spotted Tail at Cottonwood on June 8; from Al Gay and John Smith at Cottonwood on June 10; from Major McKenny at Fort Larned on June 15; from Major Wallen at St. Louis on June 20; from General Mitchell at Fort Laramie on July 27; and most recently, from a flinty rancher named James Bainter, who lived along the Little Blue. Events would show that these alarms forecast with uncanny precision exactly what the Cheyennes and Arapahoes were going to do. It would appear that all went unheeded, but perhaps it is more fair to say that the people who were aware of these warnings simply did not know what to do about them.

As military commander of the Department of Kansas, General Curtis proved to be the individual in the hottest seat. To maintain the peace in his sprawling domain, he had available (as of May 1864) only one complete volunteer regiment (the First Colorado), portions of nine others, and two batteries of artillery. These fifty-eight companies totted up to 185 officers and 4,161 enlisted men, divided among twenty-nine posts. Chivington's District of Colorado counted only the 660 men of the First Regiment, while Mitchell's District of Nebraska (stretching 782 miles from Omaha to South Pass) mustered only 1,483 men present for duty—and the chronic shortage of horses had converted many of Mitchell's cavalrymen into walk-a-heaps.[2]

Curiously, however, when Mitchell, Evans, Carney, and Fisk bombarded Curtis with requests for reinforcements, he continually put them off with references to his shortage of troops. Yet, when Secretary Stanton telegraphed him on June 28 to ask if he had sufficient forces for the work at hand, Curtis answered that his total forces (evidently including active militia) numbered 6,562 men, and that he was "all right," although he could use an infantry regiment of 100-day volunteers and a Negro battery, as his troubles with Indians and bushwhackers were increasing.[3] The following day he received authorization from Stanton to call upon Governor Carney for the hundred-day regiment.[4]

In retrospect, it is apparent that the situation in the Department of Kansas demanded a hard, even a ruthless military leader who was able to enforce discipline among his subordinates while conciliating the Indians. Curtis' personality, style of management, and written communications portray a man who was polished and civil, accustomed to settling differences by reasoned debate and compromise—a man too amiable and too polite to deal effectively with the aggressive personalities that confronted him in his command. Under the blizzard of demands that fell upon his desk at Fort Leavenworth, his engineer's mind became distracted and inconsistent. He allowed the deteriorating military situation in Colorado to continue far too long and demonstrated almost total ignorance of the Indians' grievances. And, if he did not understand how to treat them, he understood even less how to fight them when war became a reality.

General Curtis did the best he could with what he had. Like so many other military leaders during those frantic years of the Civil War, his best proved not nearly good enough. One can only speculate on how many other officers, given the conditions under which he labored, could have done a better job.[5]

By the latter part of July, the situation had slipped beyond the control of General Curtis or anyone else on the plains, for that matter. In their camps along the Solomon River, the Cheyennes and Arapahoes, some of the hardline Brule, Ogalala, and Minneconjou Sioux, and a healthy representation of Kiowas and Comanches, were united as never before, arguing around the council fires a new and diabolical strategy.[6] For two months the wild tribes had been giving the white people a real headache along the upper Platte and the Arkansas. Their horse herds were swollen with captured stock, while many of the white soldiers had to walk. There were many scalps in the lodges and some white men had even been scared away from the hunting grounds, turning their big wagons back down the Platte toward safety in the country of the Pawnees. But still other white men had continued to come by the hundreds, finding food and forage and protection at the little ranches along the trails. Now some of those little ranches had soldiers in them, too. The raiding along the Arkansas had been a good thing at first, but that trail did not have the importance or the opportunities of the white man's Medicine Road. Below Cottonwood, the white-topped wagons crawled along, sometimes two or three side-by-side, all heavy with good things.

Below Fort Kearny the whites felt safe, and they were numerous there. If the raiding was carried east to Kearny and beyond, the whites would be taken by complete surprise. Their ranches and coaches and freight wagons would fall like so many ripe plums. And, if enough of them fell, the white people might decide to give up on the land—to take their Medicine Road somewhere else.

From an advance base on the hunting grounds along the Republican, the tribes could easily send small groups of warriors north to the Platte. They would walk their ponies along the trail in plain sight. Most whites were accustomed to seeing Indians coming and going and couldn't tell a Cheyenne from a Pawnee, anyway. The red men may have even prepared a cover story: If questioned, those who could speak a little English could simply reply that they were going to St. Joe. Then, by August 7, the warriors would be in place, and attacks on targets of opportunity could commence at their pleasure. White women and children could be captured, if they didn't cause too much trouble, to be sold back to the whites when they decided to bargain for peace, as they always did sooner or later. There would be scalps and mountains of plunder in the camps, and along the white man's trail there would be blood in the dirt and the smoke of destruction. White families would mourn for their dead the way the families of Lean Bear and Star and the refugees of Cedar Canyon had mourned for theirs.

Thus resolved, the Cheyennes and their allies rode north to wage war along the Oregon-California and Denver trails.

In this way, the month of July slipped into August, with its lengthening shadows falling across the wide plains country between the

Arkansas and the upper Missouri—a vast theater of disparate peoples and cultures playing out diverging roles in the deepening crisis.

The aboriginal peoples were overwhelmed with dismay at the uncountable numbers of whites swarming over their prairie home. For years they had been badgered by this alien culture that was bent on making them live and work and worship like the whites, and killing them if they would not. It was a strange culture, one in which men worshiped gold which could not be eaten and wasted the buffalo which could—which made many promises and broke them all sooner or later. The red people had been cheated by unscrupulous traders and agents; decimated by disease; demoralized by liquor and prostitution; coerced time and again into renegotiating treaties that forced them onto smaller and less hospitable reserves. They had been beguiled by white squawmen and renegades who were traitors to their own race; propositioned by two separate white governments whose quarrel they only dimly understood; forced to watch helplessly as a wild and free way of life slipped farther away with each white wagon that violated their homeland.

The Sioux were still smarting from the injustice of their punishment for the Grattan Affair only ten years earlier; for the violent and indiscriminate reprisals visited upon them following the Santee uprising in Minnesota; for the new roads that the whites were forever pushing through their sacred haunts; and for the arrogance with which the whites demeaned their great chiefs in ordering them to stay out of the Platte Valley.

The Cheyennes felt themselves ill repaid for their mighty efforts to remain on good terms with the whites. They had endured the wanton vandalism of the gold seekers; the establishment of Denver City in violation of the Treaty of 1851; and finally, the treachery of the Colorado volunteers who seemed bent on exterminating them altogether.

To be sure, most of the white people of the plains did not have extermination in mind. Whether or not they were invaders was not even relevant. They had a divine mandate to settle the land, and the cost of their achievements had been high. They were scarred and coarsened by the rigors of homesteading in a bountiful but unforgiving land; tired of having their windows darkened and their homes invaded by grunting, begging, unwashed natives; unsettled by the gruesome memories of the Spirit Lake Massacre and the Minnesota Uprising and by the unrelenting raids upon the Pawnees; fearful of rampaging guerrillas from the border counties to the south—beasts in the form of men whose savagery surpassed even that of the aroused red man. They were angered over the suspected influence of

Confederate organizers sent north to stir the plains tribes into rebellion; weary of civil war and its hideous casualty lists; frustrated over a magnificent Union army which could never quite bring the rebel forces to bay.

The homesteaders were a resilient, private, and in some ways, a coarse people, but they were not unemotional. And it is not difficult for us to imagine them resting their aching bodies in the dooryards of their cabins or sod houses at the close of the day, watching their children playing noisy games in the prairie grass, and feeling the sudden, hot stab of fear as they remembered:

The Wiseman children had played like that before their blood splattered the floor of their cabin home. They remembered the Smith boys lying crushed and bleeding on the snowy bank of the North Channel, Willie's mouth sliced from jaw to ear. Perhaps they thought about the two little Hungate girls, their heads nearly cut from their bodies. Or the haycutters along the Looking Glass and Reason Grimes with a shaft through his liver. They realized this could happen to their children, and to them.

When a man returns home to find the bodies of his children bleeding in the dooryard, he cares little about the forces which drove his enemies to rob him of his life's treasure and purpose. He becomes enraged and filled with hatred, and he yearns for those savages to be whipped like old Harney had done on Bluewater Creek back in '55. He could shout to the heavens his agreement with the *Nebraskian* when it trumpeted:

> *We apprehend that General Mitchell has been after the red devils as he used to be after the rebs. If he once gets a chance at them, they will long remember the lesson . . . Ash Hollow (Bluewater Creek) will be nowhere.* [7]

In the years following the Treaty of 1851, it had taken a great deal of "bad management or some untoward misfortune" to bring about the impending disaster. Those who were doomed to suffer were quite unaware of the details, lacking the perspective to understand how a complex system of events, conditions, and personalities had been working over the years, like the grinding of an infernal mill, to bring about the approaching catastrophe.

The Indian War of 1864 was quite unlike the Civil War as it was being fought out east of the Mississippi. It was guerrilla warfare at its most classic, pitting small bodies of men against each other in a vast theater of featureless prairie. And, because the opposing forces could not, or dared not come to grips with one another, they turned their fury on the noncombatant population. The war would eventually be ended, not so much by military action, as by the telegraph, the steam engine, the plow, the small town, and the disappearance of the buffalo. The decisive action would not be a thunderous artillery barrage followed by a headlong charge, but an osmotic filling up of the disputed country by common people and their families.

In time the war would give way to peace and tranquillity. But, while it lasted, it unleashed some of the worst demons to be found in the human heart.

Chapter Eleven notes

[1] The intense heat and drought of July and August were well documented by a number of sources including George Comstock, John Gilbert, Nancy Stevens, Charles Whaley, Lizzie Ricketts Whaley, Frank Nicholas, J. K. P. Miller, and the *Nebraska Advertiser* of August 11. All the rivers were reported to be very shallow and steamboat traffic on the Missouri was hampered as well. The grasshopper plague of late July and August is further testimony to the severe drought which extended from the Missouri to the Rockies, though curiously, not far below the Kansas-Nebraska border.

[2] O. R. Vol. 34, Part 2, 156, 620-621.

[3] O. R. Vol. 34, Part 4, 585, 594.

[4] Ibid., 604.

[5] The extraordinary demands of the Department of Kansas were acknowledged by *The Council Bluffs Weekly Nonpareil* of December 17, 1864, which commented that "The Missouri (Kansas) Department has generally provided a sepulcher for its commanding officers . . ."

[6] This description of the Indian war councils is based on Grinnell, *The Fighting Cheyennes*, 153-155. Unfortunately, George Bent, who could have left us an eyewitness account of these days, was at his father's trading post on the Arkansas and did not rejoin the Cheyennes until the raiding in Nebraska was well underway.

[7] *The Omaha Nebraskian*, July 29, August 17, 1864.

Part I
Chapter Twelve

August 6, 1864

Early that Saturday morning, a disappointed James Green and his wife, Elizabeth, yoked up their oxen and turned their heads eastward from Cottonwood Springs. Their dream of a new home in the foothills around Denver City would remain just that—a dream. The Indian depredations occurring along the South Platte west of Julesburg made the journey too risky, and the Greens were reluctantly returning to their home at Shinn's Ferry east of Columbus.

After nooning on the banks of the Platte near Gilman's Ranch, Green was preparing to yoke up again when he was startled by the sudden appearance of "nine of the biggest, blackest war painted Indians" he had ever seen.[1] Some of them spoke enough English that they proceeded to bargain for his "squaw." The one-way negotiations had reached the price of four ponies when the entire party suddenly bolted out of the camp, kicking their ponies into a dead run for the southern bluffs. The shaken Greens looked up to see a detachment of the Seventh Iowa Cavalry approaching from the direction of Fort Kearny.[2] Never had the U. S. Army staged a more timely arrival.

At about this same time, on the north bank of the Platte and a few miles farther upstream, young Luther North stopped to rest his team. He had delivered a load of grain upriver and was also heading back to his home near Columbus. Since North had lived and worked among the Pawnees for several years, the appearance of small parties of Indians camped along the river did not seem unusual to him. As he sat on his motionless wagon, a noisy group of about thirty warriors came splashing across the river to circle around his outfit. This was not a social call. The Indians were obviously quite agitated, and North began to realize that he was in a very tight fix. It may have crossed his mind that, only six weeks earlier, his friend and freighting partner, Adam Smith, had been cut down by Sioux arrows on Looking Glass Creek. As the braves milled around his wagon, one of them confronted North directly, stringing an arrow and pointing it at the young man's chest. North was only a fraction of a second from sharing Adam Smith's fate when another warrior rode up and knocked the arrow aside. The two Indians engaged in a heated debate, none of which North could understand. Finally, the whole party whipped their ponies away from the wagon and plunged back into the river. North was unable to identify the tribe to which they belonged (they definitely were not Pawnees), and he was only too happy to start his team back down river where he camped for the night with a westbound freight outfit.[3]

For most people of the plains, however, life that Saturday moved onward less dramatically. At about ten o'clock that morning, Horace Smith halted his westbound train of six wagons at Charles Emery's Liberty Farm to purchase four sacks of feed grain for his horses and mules. As Emery threw the sacks up into one of the wagons, his attention was drawn by its cargo: a bright, red threshing separator, the first ever seen along the Little Blue River. The threshing machine and its horsepower drive were being freighted, along with a large lot of hardware, to Denver City. Emery stood in his yard and watched as the train pulled away and trundled up the trail toward Pawnee Ranch.[4]

Northwest of Columbus, Bridget Murray lay in her house, sick and exhausted after her ordeal on the Looking Glass. And at Fort Kearny, Colonel Summers was pondering why the Cheyennes were so "disaffected." He was also considering some strange warnings sent down by James Bainter, a rancher along the Little Blue. The Indians weren't acting right, claimed Bainter. They had suddenly become sullen and secretive. Indeed, Bainter and his neighbors were puzzled at the large number of Indians which had been passing down the trail in recent days, all of them claiming to be headed for St. Joe.[5]

The day wore on, hot and cloudless. Evening fell on an encampment of twelve wagons west of Fort Kearny. Three of the wagons belonged to Frank Morton and his wife, Nancy Jane, making their third freighting run to Denver City. The Mortons had been joined by two other freighting outfits that were hauling grain and machinery to the Rockies. There were sixteen people in the combined trains, including nine-year-old Danny Marble, who was accompanying his father's three-wagon caravan. Everyone bedded down early, hoping to get off to an early start on Sunday. The next night would find them near Plum Creek, one day closer to their destination.

A day's ride east of Fort Kearny on the Nebraska City Road, twelve-year-old Robert Martin and his fifteen-year-old brother, Nathaniel, lay on their hot bunks, wearily facing the prospect of another day working with their father in the dusty, dry hayfields near their sod home.

Along the Little Blue River, sixteen-year-old Laura Roper also went to bed in the family's log house, pleased at the thought of visiting her neighbor friend down the trail on the morrow. Laura always liked to be on the go. It was more pleasant than working around the homestead. And, since tomorrow was Sunday, it would be a good time to hike to the Eubanks' place near The Narrows for some neighborly conversation.

In Lawrence, Kansas, a weary General Curtis stopped for the night, nearing the end of his 500-mile ride. The morrow would find him back at his headquarters at Fort Leavenworth where, once again, he could turn his attention to matters of guerrillas and General Price. The people of Kansas had been reassured and highly pleased with his efforts to pacify the western trails, and Curtis was confident that his campaign had cowed the truculent Cheyennes. They would give no more trouble for quite some time.

Chapter Twelve notes

1 Green, "Freighting on the Plains," 2-3.

2 This may have been Captain Wilcox's Company B, which left the fort on July 31 to escort a train of forage and supplies to Camp Rankin near Julesburg. *Report of the Adjutant General (Iowa), 1865*, 1013.

3 Grinnell, *Two Great Scouts*, 69.

4 Charles Emery's testimony in Thomas Simonton and George Tritch, Indian Depredation Cases #1174 and #3102.

5 *Biographical and Historical Memoirs*, 345; Ellenbecker, *Indian Raid on the Upper Little Blue*, 10.

PART II

Day of wrath, O day of mourning.
See fulfilled the prophet's warning.
Heaven and earth in ashes burning.

Thomas de Celano, c. 1250 (translated)

Part II
Chapter One
The Little Blue River

The Little Blue River is not long, as rivers go—something more than 150 miles from its source south of Fort Kearny to its junction with the Big Blue south of Marysville, Kansas. Though quite narrow in places, the valley of the Little Blue ran in exactly the right direction to accommodate the Oregon Trail, and many thousands of emigrants followed its friendly course northwestward toward the Platte.

Many of those emigrants were impressed, as people still are, with the pastoral beauty of the valley. In 1850, Dr. Charles Clark found the Little Blue to be "a very pretty stream" running within a deep, narrow, and serpentine channel. He noted that its banks were skirted with cottonwood, willow, and ash trees undergrown with dense thickets of wild plum bushes whose fruits had a sweet, delicious pulp and thick, astringent skin. Woven among the trees and plum bushes were networks of wild grapevines which formed secluded arbors and retreats. The surrounding prairie was richly ornamented by a profusion of wildflowers and studded with patches of prickly pear cactus. Already at that time, the tide of emigration had greatly thinned the population of rattlesnakes, but Dr. Clark found bullsnakes and garden snakes in abundance. Wolves and coyotes were large and numerous, and packs of the predators had been known to attack draft animals picketed for the night.[1]

In the early summer of 1864, Maurice Morris traveled up the valley, and he also pronounced the Little Blue a "very pretty stream." Morris commented at length on the riverside growth of "cotton-trees" (cottonwoods), oak, scrub, walnut, and sumach (sumac). From the waters of the river, his company pulled chub and "horndace" which they fried and declared excellent. The party also dined on buffalo steaks and on rabbits, which they found numerous and tasty in spite of the season.[2]

Despite its aesthetic beauty, settlement of the valley did not begin until Dan Patterson located his homestead at the Oregon Trail crossing of Big Sandy Creek in 1856.[3] At that time, the road ranch phenomenon had not yet been born, and the trains of Russell, Majors, and Waddell accounted for nearly all the commercial traffic on the trail, as they shuttled back and forth from Leavenworth carrying supplies to Forts Kearny and Laramie.

When the Colorado gold rush began in 1858, William Russell lobbied his partners for an express route between the Missouri River and the infant Denver City. Majors and Waddell were unwilling to risk the venture at that time, so Russell formed a second partnership with a John Jones to launch the Leavenworth and Pike's Peak Express, which began service to Denver City via the Kaw and Smoky Hill River valleys in 1859. The new business quickly ran into debt, and its interests were taken over by Russell, Majors, and Waddell.

Alexander Majors had always favored the firm's freighting route along the Oregon Trail. Thus, in 1860, the L&PPE was reborn as the Central Overland California and Pike's Peak Express, with passenger and mail service via the valley of the Little Blue. By this time, settlement had advanced, allowing the newly established road ranches to double as stagecoach stations along the line. But Russell's thoughts were again moving far ahead of his partners', and he began to pressure them to act on his newest brainstorm–mail service to the west coast by fast horse relay. His persuasion paid off, and when the Pony Express began service on April 3, 1860, more than half the required relay stations were already in existence as road ranch or stagecoach stations. Even so, it cost the firm $100,000 to get the Pony Express up and running.

On October 4, 1861, the transcontinental telegraph was also up and running, and the Pony Express soon faded into history. Its eighteen-month run to glory had yielded Russell, Majors, and Waddell a net loss of $500,000, putting the firm on such precarious financial footing that the initials COC&PP came to stand for "clean out of cash and poor pay" among its employees.[4] In order to remain solvent and to replace its worn-out rolling stock, the company began to negotiate private loans with Ben Holladay, a highly successful freighting contractor from Weston, Missouri. Holladay took mortgages on the rights and equipment of the Central Overland, which never did earn enough to pay its bills. By March 1862, the firm of Russell, Majors, and Waddell was broke, and Holladay bought the line at public auction.

Beginning with its name, the Overland Stage Line was rebuilt from the ground up. Holladay surrounded himself with men of great managerial ability and financial acumen. He equipped his line with 110 coaches costing as much as $1,500 apiece; seventy-five drivers, well paid, handsomely outfitted, and subject to rigid discipline; and 1,700 of the fastest horses and mules that could be found. The result was a level of service unique for its time. Overland Stage Lines offered daily coaches both east and westbound. In the fall of 1863, one of Holladay's coaches actually made the run from Denver City to Atchison in five days and eight hours. Another coach running through the Little Blue Valley carrying fourteen passengers and a half ton of express, traveled fourteen miles in fifty-two minutes, a fraction better than sixteen miles per hour.[5]

Those who rode the stages found the valley of the Little Blue to be the most pleasant part of the trip. At strategically located stations, the ranch families worked as stock tenders, agents, and cooks. Meals served at the eating stations in the valley invariably included eggs, chicken, coffee with cream, butter, and vegetables from the ranch gardens. At Liberty Farm, roast turkey was a frequent entree, while fried bacon and ham were menu staples both along the Little Blue and the Platte.[6]

The freedom to homestead their own ranches while being on the Holladay payroll was a golden opportunity for settlers in the Little Blue Valley. Whole families established themselves along the trail, drawing hired help from Beatrice, Marysville, and the Missouri River towns. Thanks in great part to the Central Overland California and Pike's Peak Express and, later, the Overland Stage Line, the valley had become, by 1864, a settled and industrious place, seemingly far removed from the growing troubles of the Indian frontier.[7]

As the promise of free land had drawn great numbers of emigrants westward to Oregon in the 1840s, so the Kansas-Nebraska Act paved the way for the settlement of Nebraska Territory in the 1850s. Many of these settlers emigrated from New York, Massachusetts, Connecticut, Illinois, and Ohio, while a number of them came all the way from England, Ireland, Germany, and Bohemia. At strategic locations the people gathered themselves into settlements which grew into towns—Topeka and Marysville, for example. Along the Missouri River, St. Joseph, Brownville, Plattsmouth, Bellevue, and Omaha sprang up almost overnight. In the latter half of the 1850s, pioneers pushed westward from the Missouri River towns into the area along the Big Blue River between present Crete and Beatrice, Nebraska, founding such short-lived settlements as Blue Island, Swan Creek, and Stevens Creek. The rivers were the lifeblood of the prairie, and none of the early settlers thought of locating their homes anyplace but along the banks of the streams.

Up the Oregon-California Trail from Marysville and over the divide from the Big Blue the settlers pushed north and westward along the valley of the Little Blue River, providing support services for the trains of Russell, Majors, and Waddell, the COC&PP coaches, the Pony Express, and the Overland stages. By 1864, there were more than fifteen homesteads along the Little Blue west of Dan Patterson's place, some of them doubling as stage or mail stations. One of the first and best known was Oak Grove

The Comstocks and Oak Grove

In 1859, Russell, Majors, and Waddell sent out a crew of workmen to construct a trailside store building some thirty miles upriver from Patterson's. The finished store was about sixteen by twenty feet in size, constructed of native logs with a shingled roof. Its windows and doors were shipped up from Leavenworth.[8] The building was situated between the trail and the Little Blue River, which was behaving itself just then. Within a short time, the company sold the store to two of its bookkeepers, Charles and Preston Butler, brothers from Atchison. When the Butlers took possession of the store in the spring of 1861, the river was out of its banks and the log building was a soggy mess. The brothers moved the store across the trail to higher ground and added on a room, doubling its size. When Charles Butler became seriously ill, the brothers leased the store to Erastus Comstock and his sons, who purchased it outright after Charles died in 1863.

Erastus Comstock was fifty-three years old when he brought his seven children to Oak Grove. Born in Connecticut, he had moved with his parents to New York at an early age, and was educated in the common schools there. In the years following his marriage, he took his growing family first to Wisconsin, then on to Ohio, Michigan, Texas, Illinois, and then to Johnson County, Nebraska. After the death of his wife in childbirth, the aging widower moved to the valley of the Little Blue with his children, all of whom (except for little Sarah) were grown or in their teens.

By 1864, Oak Grove was one of the more impressive establishments along the trail. The house itself had two large rooms on the lower level, with the west room serving as kitchen and dining room. The first floor was furnished with both a cookstove and a large fireplace, while stairways at both east and west ends of the building led up to two large bedrooms above. The rear of the house was sheltered by looming river bluffs some fifty feet high. Backed up against those bluffs about sixty feet behind the house was a bank barn 160 feet long, having room to stable 100 animals. Between the house and the barn stood a small smokehouse, while a few yards east of the buildings was a grove of native oak trees from which the ranch took its name.

George Comstock, the eldest son, was about twenty-eight years old when the family came to the valley. In early 1864, George moved with his wife and four children and his eighteen-year-old brother, Ansel, nearly forty miles up the trail to take over the operation of Thirty-two Mile Creek Stage Station, so named because it was just that distance from Fort Kearny. James Comstock, the next oldest son, also left Oak Grove, taking his wife and two young sons about five miles up the trail to Little Blue Station. The departure of his sons left Father Comstock short handed. So during the summer he hired three helpers from the Big Blue settlements: John Barratt, who had immigrated from England;[9] Tobias Castor, who had come from Ohio; and Castor's seventeen-year-old brother-in-law, George Hunt, whose family had come to the Big Blue from central Iowa.[10]

George Comstock's establishment at Thirty-two Mile Creek was equal in size to that of his father. The house there was not so commodious as the one at Oak Grove, being merely a long, one-story building. But Thirty-two Mile Station was a dinner stop on the Overland Stage Line, and extra hands were required to maintain the level of service which Ben Holladay demanded of his people. During the summer of 1864, the station housed a complement of eleven: George and his wife, Hannah; four children—John, Mary, Charles, and Mack; two hired girls from the Big Blue settlements—Elizabeth and Jane Artist; Mike Connelley and Frank Baker, both employees of Overland Stage Lines.[11] The temperamental Baker was a good friend of John Barratt, who was working at Oak Grove. The large staff must have eased the sense of isolation which lay about the station, situated as it was at the extreme western end of the string of ranches that lined the Little Blue Valley.

Kiowa Station

Six miles east of Oak Grove, on the benchland of the river, stood Kiowa Station, a swing station (place where teams were changed) on the Overland Stage Line. An impressive story-and-a-half log building with an L shape, Kiowa Station was managed in the summer of 1864 by an oldtimer in the valley, James Douglas, who lived at the place with his wife, Harriet, and three-year-old daughter, Ada. Several other

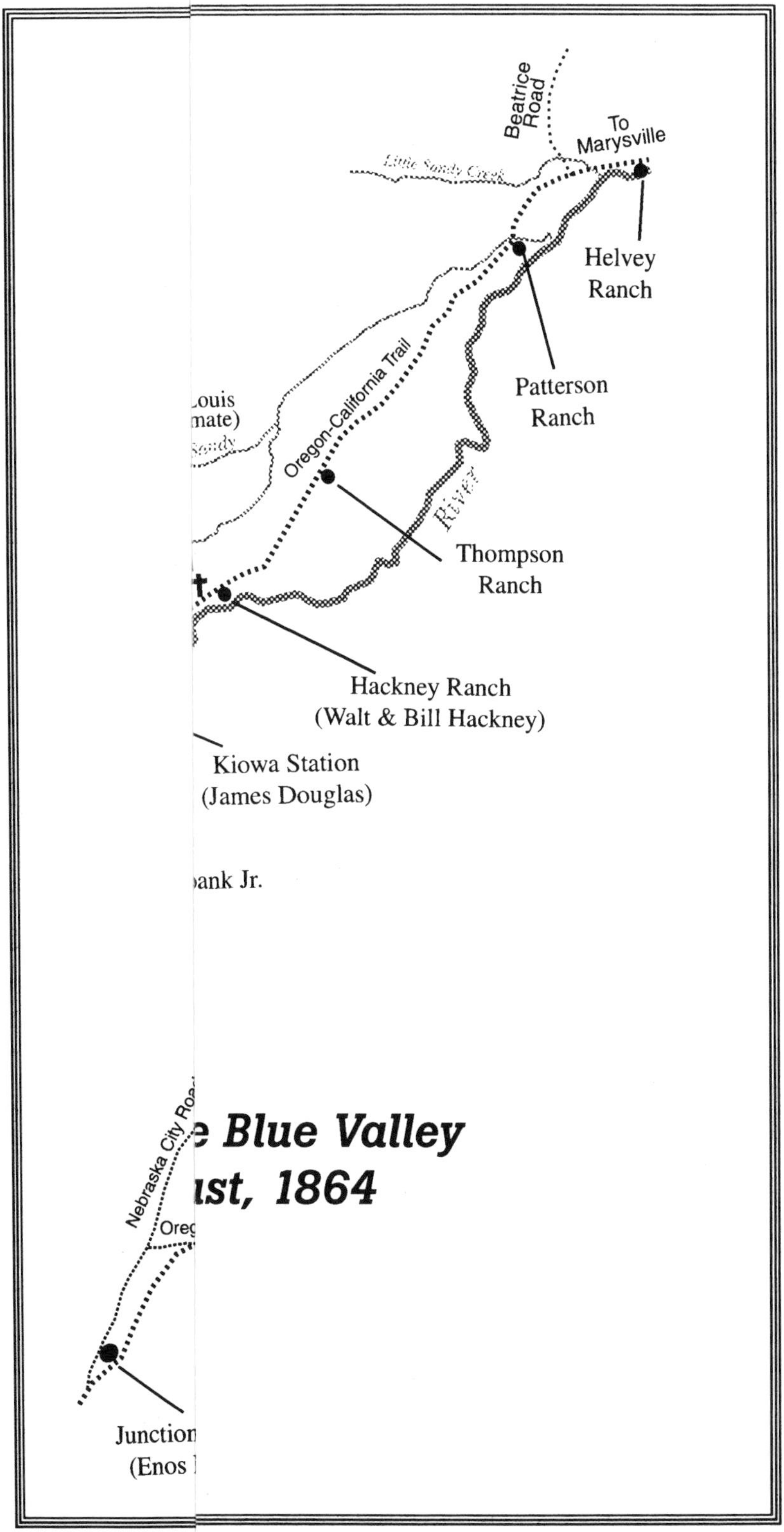
Beatrice Road
To Marysville
Little Sandy Creek
Helvey Ranch
Patterson Ranch
Oregon-California Trail
.ouis
mate)
Sandy
River
Thompson Ranch
Hackney Ranch
(Walt & Bill Hackney)
Kiowa Station
(James Douglas)
bank Jr.
Nebraska City Road
Oreg
e Blue Valley
ust, 1864
Junction
(Enos

employees of the stage company also lived at the station, including John Gilbert.

Tough, self-reliant, and painfully honest, Gilbert was the quintessential frontiersman. From his birthplace in New York state, he moved to Wisconsin and Missouri, before heading for Pike's Peak with the gold rush of 1859. Like thousands of other would-be miners, he returned east a short time later, broke and disillusioned, to become an employee of Russell, Majors, and Waddell. Initially, he did some construction work for the company, building several stations in the Little Blue Valley. But most of his career with the firm, and later with Ben Holladay, was spent as a stage driver. In his spare time, he slipped over to the Big Blue settlements to court Elizabeth Artist, the young girl who was working at Thirty-two Mile Station during the summer of '64. An incident which occurred during his courtship made Gilbert a local hero.

For some weeks, a stranger on a large, black horse had been visiting the settlers' homes, demanding damages from them because they had supposedly jumped his claim. He was so bold and so intimidating that a number of families actually gave him a horse or mule to forestall trouble. The stranger also accosted the Artist family, and by an unfortunate bit of timing, showed up on a day when Gilbert had come to call. The suitor buckled on his gunbelt and stepped outside to confront the big man on the black horse.

The conversation was brief. Gilbert informed the man that he really ought to be someplace else; that the settlers were much aroused over his false claims; that if he bothered one more family he would be hanged from the nearest convenient tree. The stranger left without his "damages" and was never seen again.[12] Shortly after, Gilbert had left the employ of the stage line, but not the valley. His work at Kiowa during the summer of '64 would keep him reasonably close to Libby Artist.

The Eubank Family

About three-eights-mile west of Kiowa Station was the ranch of Joseph Eubank, who had been the station keeper at Kiowa before Douglas. Born into a family of Kentucky "mountain folk," young Eubank had moved with his people to Adams County, Illinois, and on to a farm southeast of Kirksville, Missouri.[13] About 1860, he left his kinfolk to find employment as a driver with the Central Overland Lines.[14] His normal run was through the Little Blue Valley, and he was apparently stationed at Kiowa part of the time. Soon after coming to Nebraska Territory, he met and fell in love with Harriet (Hattie) Palmer, whose family had settled on the Big Blue. The two were married when Hattie was sixteen or seventeen (she was never quite able to remember the exact year) and began making plans for a ranch of their own. Joe left the stage line in early 1864 and moved with his wife into a new log home west of the station. Evidently, he was a sharp horse trader, one of those rancheros who "make their pile pretty quickly," according to Maurice Morris; for by late summer, Joe Eubank's ranch was well stocked with draft animals rehabilitated from passing trains. To help with the work on the still unfinished homestead, Joe had the assistance of his brother, Fred Eubank, and Hattie's brother, John Palmer, with whom he was in partnership.

The rest of the Eubank family had not prospered. They somehow never made a living on their Missouri farm, and were subject to several court actions brought against them by their debtors. When at last the Adair County Sheriff rode out to the farm to seize their belongings to sell at auction, he was forced to return to the court, declaring that the Eubanks had absolutely nothing worth confiscating. The family was entirely destitute.

To make matters even worse, the Civil War had laid a hard hand on Adair County, along with most of northern Missouri. In August 1862, the Battle of Kirksville had been fought out between secessionist militia and loyal state militia backed up by some Third Iowa Volunteers. It had developed into a vicious fight involving over 4,000 men, and when it was all over, the secessionist forces had been routed with the loss of 150 killed. One noncombatant was killed in her own home, and fifteen rebels found to be in violation of their paroles were executed. Increasing guerrilla activity and an expected invasion by General Price promised more violence for 1864. It was a good time for the Eubanks to leave Missouri, particularly since the county sheriff had seized the family farm and advertised it for public auction. The Missouri Eubanks were now homeless as well as destitute.

Joe Eubank's father brought the rest of the family to homestead along the Little Blue at a point known as The Narrows, about nine miles upstream from his son's ranch. The rest of the family was a fair-sized group: Besides Fred, who lived with Joe and Hattie, Joe Sr. had brought along his wife, Ruth; daughters Hannah and Dora; sons George, William, James, and Henry; and grandson, Ambrose Asher. George went to work as a drover with a freight train, and William had a family of his own: wife, Lucinda; three-year-old daughter, Isabelle; and six-month-old son, Willie. Hannah found employment with the stage line, and Dora, who was mentally handicapped, worked around the family homestead.[15] Their first summer on the Little Blue was a tough time for the Eubanks. Their house at The Narrows was poorly built of logs with a dirt roof and dreadfully small to house so many people. It would be much worse during the approaching winter. While Joseph Sr. had acquired two wagons and two yoke of oxen and several horses, the family had virtually no furnishings with which to make their rude cabin a comfortable home. If Joseph Jr.'s ranch was growing prosperous, the hovel occupied by his parents and siblings was known by neighbors as "the poorest place on the road."

The Uhlig Family

About three-fourths-mile west of Joe Eubank Jr.'s ranch was the homestead of the Uhlig family.[16] Joanna (Johannen) Uhlig had immigrated with her husband and five children from Saxony (Germany) in 1847. Following the death of her husband, Karl, Joanna moved her family to Wisconsin for a time, coming to Brownville, Nebraska, in 1857. The two eldest children, Charles and Ida, both married. Sometime around 1861, Joanna Uhlig came to the Little Blue Valley with her three remaining children: Edmund Hugo, Otto, and Theodore, who was nineteen years old in the summer of '64. Since no one was quite sure how to pronounce, let alone spell their name, the Uhligs were generally referred to along the trail as "The Germans."

The Roper Family

The trail at The Narrows runs for a short distance at the river's edge, crowded against the low bank by the encroaching bluffs. Once through The Narrows, it was slightly less than a mile upstream to the ranch of Joseph Roper and family.[17]

There were actually three Roper brothers who came to Nebraska Territory at different times. Fordyce Roper brought his family to the Big Blue settlement along Stevens Creek (later Indian Creek) in 1857, and was one of the original founders of the town of Beatrice. Younger brother, Fred, made a respectable amount of money in the gold fields of California, and arrived on the Big Blue very early in 1860. Joseph was the oldest of the three, and he brought his family to a new homestead on Cub Creek west of the Big Blue in February 1860.

Ford Roper was by nature a dynamic builder and promoter. In partnership with another founder of Beatrice, Mr. J.B. Weston, Ford built Pawnee Ranch trading post on the Little Blue at the mouth of Pawnee Creek, living there with his family for a short time before returning to Beatrice in 1859. There he joined in partnership with a young Ohio man, Marshall Clarence Kelley, to build a bridge, dam, and gristmill on the Big Blue. There was always a good living to be made as a miller in any growing community, as nearly all the settlers raised corn, buckwheat, and rye for their own needs. Roper and Kelley had their mill nearly ready to operate when an unseasonable rain and thaw pushed the Big Blue out of its banks in February, 1861. Bridge, dam, and mill were swept into Kansas, and Ford Roper was left to start over from scratch.

Shortly after the flood, Kelley entered a partnership with Joseph Roper, whom he had probably come to know while he was working on the mill with brother Fordyce. Joe Roper certainly needed a partner, since he was the head of a very feminine household. Joe and his wife, Paulina, were raising four girls: Clarisa and Laura were teenagers, while Francis and Kate were "little girls."

The details of what followed were not a source of pride to the family, and are lost to our knowing. We might surmise that, as Kelley became more intimately acquainted with his new partner's family, he became unaccountably smitten by Laura Roper, who had turned fourteen in June 1862. And Laura, for her part, must have been a precocious girl who enjoyed the attentions of her father's partner, who was probably more than ten years her senior. By the time summer was out, Laura found herself pregnant with Marshall Kelley's child.

The pioneer homesteaders were certainly not saints. But out-of-wedlock pregnancies were threats to the family and contrary to community standards of morality. Though marriage of young girls was commonplace, fourteen was just a little too young for Joe Roper. Laura's pregnancy must certainly have been awkward for all involved.

In some fashion, an agreement was worked out. Apparently Kelley and Laura were to be considered engaged until such time as her parents felt she was mature enough to marry. The child would be raised by the Ropers until its parents were legally married and financially secure.

On May 16, 1863, just a month short of Laura's fifteenth birthday, she gave birth to a little boy who was named Clarence Marshall Kelley—"Marsh," for short.[18] The following February, Kelley and the Roper family left the Big Blue settlements for the Little Blue Valley. Kelley had purchased the preemption rights to the abandoned Ewing Ranch (Jesse Ewing, having killed a woman and wounded her husband from ambush, had left the country very suddenly). Roper and Kelley worked hard to turn the small building into a respectable-sized log cabin and storehouse, while Laura was kept out of mischief by sending her to work as a combination nanny and housemaid for the Lemmon family at Liberty Farm. When she returned to the family at the end of March, she found them comfortably situated in a double log cabin containing three rooms, each about seventeen feet square. Near one corner of the house was a large smokehouse about ten feet square, and a log stable and grain bin stood a little farther off. The middle room of the house was packed with supplies for sale to passing trains.

A well had been dug in the yard and a large field of potatoes had been planted on the sandy bottoms closer to the river. Joe Roper always had a flair for doing things with style, and word passed along the trail that the Roper-Kelley Ranch was one of the two or three best places along the way between Atchison and Fort Kearny.

Mudge and Milligan's Buffalo Ranch

Two hundred yards past the Roper-Kelley place, the trail swung away from the Little Blue to ascend Nine Mile Ridge, forced out of the valley by the rugged bluffs which piled down to the water's edge. Within a half mile, the road climbed eighty feet. About 400 yards to the west, between the trail and the river, was Little Blue Station, a mail station originally established by Russell, Majors, and Waddell as an outfitting store for the drovers who traveled with their freight trains. The log store building was roofed over with dirt and sod, and was now home to the James Comstock family.

Passing Little Blue Station, the trail continued to climb another thirty feet for its run across the gently undulating and unpopulated landscape of Nine Mile Ridge. At the western end of the "ridge," the road descended sharply to once again approach the Little Blue River. On the eastern slope of a nearby ridge, a short distance north of the trail, was Buffalo Ranch.

In late 1859, Russell, Majors, and Waddell had sent John Gilbert to the site with a work crew to erect buildings for a stagecoach relay station. Gilbert's men put up a stable, quarters for stock tenders, and a log building of one and a half stories for a store. For a brief time, this new station (which apparently was never named) served as an outfitting post for travelers on the trail. When the Pony Express came into being, the company combined its stage and pony operations at Liberty Farm, about three miles farther west, and the buildings which Gilbert and his crew had built were allowed to go to ruin. The site remained abandoned until the arrival of the Mudge and Milligan families in the summer of 1863.[19]

In 1855, William and Elizabeth Mudge set sail from Liverpool, England, for the United States. Three days out on the Atlantic, Elizabeth gave birth to their first child whom they christened William Jr. After farming for a time near Chillicothe, Missouri, the Mudge family, which now included two sons, came to settle on Mud Creek near the Big Blue River. Their immediate neighbors were Joe and Sally Milligan, immigrants from the "old sod" of Ireland. Joe and Sally were a bright and jovial pair and, since they were childless, they came to adore the Mudge boys. So congenial was the association of these two family units that Mudge and Milligan formed an unofficial partnership. In the spring of 1863, they moved their families to new homesteads on Elk Creek, southwest of the Little Blue Valley.

All would have been well had not a party of wandering Sioux visited the homestead one day when the men were gone. The Indians meant no harm but rather enjoyed frightening the women. At last the Indians rode away and the women took the boys and fled for the safety of the trail, where their husbands found them. Elizabeth and Sally emphatically refused to spend one more day alone on Elk Creek. The men had no choice but to move again.

Joe Milligan wanted to locate along the busy Oregon-California Trail, but Will Mudge objected, explaining to his partner, "I don't think I would like to have my boys be among all kinds of men as stop at these stations." But summer was slipping away and the women were adamant about moving, so necessity forced the decision. From past trips up the trail, the men knew of the abandoned stage line property at the west end of Nine Mile Ridge So, in late July, the families made their move. The log cabins were dismantled and hauled to the new homesite. A few architectural improvements were made, and by September they were comfortable in their relocated cabins, now roofed over with heavy layers of slough grass and sod.

Mudge and Milligan raised a stable and several three-sided log sheds, and hired several hunters to harvest the plentiful buffalo that still roamed the surrounding prairie. The slaughtered animals were partially dressed, quartered, and hung to cure in the "cold storage" sheds, from which meat was sold to passing trains. Hides and tallow were hauled to Brownville to be traded for food staples. Word of the availability of buffalo meat spread along the trail, and the Mudge and Milligan homestead became known as Buffalo Ranch. As winter descended on the Little Blue Valley, the families were secure physically and financially—and just in time. In September, Elizabeth gave birth to a third son, christened Samuel.

The Lemmon Family and Liberty Farm

Several miles past Buffalo Ranch and out of sight around the end of a small ridge, was Liberty Farm, built by James Lemmon in 1860.[20] Like many of his neighbors, Lemmon had been a rover. From his birthplace in Ohio he had journeyed to Oregon where he took part in the Indian war of 1847. Then he trekked southward to the gold fields of California where he made a small fortune, not by mining gold, but by mining the pockets of the miners through his retail business. In 1850, Lemmon returned east to marry Lucy Whittemore of Marengo, Illinois. Having sold his bride on the delights of frontier life, Lemmon took her westward by covered wagon in 1853. A few miles east of the forks of the Platte, Lucy gave birth to their first child, a son whom they named Hervey. By this time the season was growing late, and the family continued westward at considerable risk.

They got as far as Bountiful, Utah, when winter caught them at last. By the time spring arrived, the Lemmons had grown fond of the region around Bountiful and decided to remain there. James Lemmon became friends with the Mormon leader, Brigham Young, and when Lucy gave birth to a second son in 1855, they named the boy Moroni, after the Mormon angel. A third son, George Edward, was born in 1857. But this was also the year of the Mormon War, and the situation began to grow uncomfortable for the Lemmons. By 1859, James Lemmon was convinced that Bountiful was no longer a safe place for "us Gentiles," so the family of six, which now included an infant daughter named Alpharetta, loaded their belongings in a wagon and turned eastward, stopping in the valley of the Little Blue River a third of a mile upstream from the mouth of Liberty Creek. Here they built Liberty Farm, probably the neatest and best of all the ranches along the Little Blue.

In 1860, the Lemmon homestead became a stage and Pony Express station, and a base of operations for drivers, stock tenders, and hunters—those types of men whom Will Mudge did not want to be around his boys. The three young Lemmon boys, however, found life among these roughnecks always exciting. The hard-drinking Frank Baker was stationed at Liberty Farm for a time, and when Wild Bill Hickok stopped there overnight shortly after he had shot down the McCanles men at Rock Creek Station, the Lemmon boys followed their gun slinging hero around all evening like puppies.

The Emery Family

James and Lucy Lemmon were conscious of the need to educate their brood in something other than gun fighting and stagecoach driving, so in March 1864, they sold Liberty Farm to Charles Emery for $3,000.[21] With Emery's down payment in his pocket, James Lemmon took his family to Marysville where he enrolled his boisterous sons in the common school.

Charles Emery was born in Maine.[22] An avid freesoiler, he had moved with a company of like-minded individuals to the abolitionist town of Lawrence, Kansas, in early 1856 at the height of the Wakarusa War. Being a part of the antislavery movement paid no bills, however, so Emery began driving stages between Leavenworth and Topeka. In 1858, he married Mary Benson of Lawrence, an Irish immigrant. Their first son, George, was born in 1860.

Charles Emery was hard working and reliable, an excellent driver and horseman—just the type of individual that Ben Holladay wanted in his organization. When Emery was offered the charge of the Overland Stage Line eating station at Thirty-two Mile Creek, he brought his family up the trail to Nebraska Territory. Mary Emery soon established a reputation along the route as a neat housekeeper and an extremely good cook. On one of his flying inspection trips along the line, Ben Holladay had taken a meal at Thirty-two Mile Station. He found the fried bacon and corn dodger which Mary served him to be so excellent that he gave her a $20 gold piece as a bonus.

The Emerys found life along the trail very agreeable. The only disadvantage was that Thirty-two Mile Station belonged to the stage company. When the Lemmons decided to sell Liberty Farm, Charles Emery jumped at the chance to have a homestead of his own, and eagerly gave James Lemmon a down payment. So the Lemmons moved to Marysville; the Emery family, which now included two sons, moved down to Liberty Farm; and the Comstocks came up from Oak Grove to manage Thirty-two Mile Station.

Pawnee Ranch

About three and one-half miles west of Liberty Farm, the Fort Riley Road joined the Oregon-California Trail Another mile and a half beyond that was Pawnee Ranch, the trading post originally built by Fordyce Roper and J. B. Weston.[23] Standing solidly between the trail and the river at the mouth of Pawnee Creek, the ranch in its early years looked more like a fort than even Fort Kearny did. Its cabin, sheds, chicken house, smoke house, corn crib, and large barn were surrounded by a stockade complete with rifle ports. The main house had a large upper room in which Ford Roper once fed a delegation of Pawnee chiefs on panfuls of boiled potatoes. By the summer of '64, much of the stockade had been removed, and the ranch was under the management of Newton Metcalf and his wife, who were expecting their first child. Living with the couple was Newton's brother, George—a large, bluff fellow who was somewhat of a bully.

The Bainters of Spring Ranch

After leaving Pawnee Ranch, the westbound traffic crossed the creek and ran a little more than a mile to Spring Ranch, owned by James Bainter and his family.[24] Bainter and his wife, Elizabeth, were born and raised in Ohio, married and started their family there. About 1859, they came west to Bethany, Missouri, where James worked for a time as a farm laborer. Sometime in the early 1860s, the Bainters moved to the valley of the Little Blue near the mouth of Spring Creek, and there Spring Ranch came into being. By the summer of 1864, James and Elizabeth and their three young children were comfortably quartered in a snug cabin measuring about twenty by thirty-six feet, which also contained the usual pilgrim room and store for paying customers. Bainter also built a large storage shed, a stable with space for ninety animals, two corrals, and fenced off a garden area of twenty-five acres with posts and rails. On June 22 of that year, he paid fees totaling $25 to the Internal Revenue Service for liquor and hotel licenses, and Spring Ranch became a legal and thriving commercial operation.[25]

West of Spring Ranch the homesteads became sparse. For about a dozen miles the route of the trail lay between the Little Blue and Spring Creek, passing Lone Tree Stage Station, managed by James Billingsley. After another four miles the trail crossed Elm Creek, where the station on the west bank of the stream was operated by Andrew Hammond. Yet another four miles brought the trail to Thirty-two Mile Creek and the station managed by George Comstock. Then there was a long, desolate run of twenty-two miles, broken only by a stop at Summit Station, before the westbound traffic descended into the Platte River Valley to join the Nebraska City Road at Hook's Junction Ranch.

These, then, were some of the people of the Little Blue Valley—a restless, highly mobile lot hailing from many diverse places. Mostly young, energetic, self confident, and opportunistic, they were also loving and devoted to their families, and built neat cabins for them which, by the standards of the country, were quite comfortable. They were people who liked their space, yet considered anyone living within ten or fifteen miles as "near neighbors whom we could drop in and see at most any time." [26] They went to each other's aid, socialized as much as distance and labors would allow, and built up bonds of comradeship which were firmly cemented by the great tribulation which visited the Little Blue Valley during that August 1864.

Chapter One notes

[1] Clark, *A Trip to Pike's Peak*, 29 ff.

[2] Morris, *Rambles in the Rocky Mountains*, 49-51.

[3] DAR, *Nebraska Pioneer Reminiscences*, 139.

[4] Frederick, *Ben Holladay*, 62.

[5] Root and Connelley, *Overland Stage*, 71-72.

[6] Ibid., 95.

[7] Many accounts left by survivors of the Indian raids confirm this statement, and stress the treachery of the Indians and the complete surprise which they achieved. Typical is Paulina Roper's testimony, given on November 1, 1892: "The Indians became hostile very suddenly, and without cause or provocation, as far as Mr. Roper or I myself, knew." (Heirs of Joseph Roper, Indian Depredation Case #7007)

[8] John Gilbert to George Follmer, August 29, 1911; George Comstock to George Follmer, July, 1911. (Papers of George Follmer)

[9] *Portrait and Biographical Album of Gage County*, 208.

[10] Gregory, *Pioneer Days in Crete*, 19.

[11] Comstock family genealogy; George Edward Lemmon to John Comstock, printed in *The De Witt Times-News*, August 18, 1927. Frank Baker's personality is recalled in Yost, *Boss Cowman*, 23, 58.

[12] *De-Witt Times-News*, August 25, 1927.

[13] Information on the Eubank family was obtained from land records of Adair County, Missouri; testimony in the Eubank/Walton Indian Depredation Claims; and from an interview with Mr. and Mrs. Dewey Ellis.

[14] Root and Connelley list Joe Eubank as a stage driver in the early 1860s, along with John Gilbert, James Douglas, Carl (Charles) and Bob Emery, James Hickok, and Bill Cody.

[15] James Bainter (*Biographical and Historical Memoirs*, 347) states that Dora was "feeble-minded." In her testimony to support her father's depredation claim, Laura Roper recalled that she and Lucinda looked back and "saw a lot of Indians chasing a half-foolish girl that had been left there (at Eubanks')." (Heirs of Joseph Roper, Depredation Case #7007)

[16] The spelling and pronunciation of the name baffled their neighbors. Various sources give it as Ulig, Uligh, Ulich or Yulick. The depredation claims, Otto's newspaper advertisements, and the family tombstone all spell it as Uhlig. Being German, they would have pronounced it with a final sound something like a soft "k".

[17] Information on the Roper family was taken from:

DAR, *Nebraska Pioneer Reminiscences.*
Ellenbecker, *Indian Raids of 1860-1869.*
Federal Census, 1860, 1870, 1880, Gage County, Nebraska.
Joseph Roper Heirs, Indian Depredation Claim #7007.
Landers, *Nebraska Stories.*
Leasure, Personal communications with the author.
Brownville Nebraska Advertiser, March 4, 1861.
Nebraska State Agricultural Census, 1885, Gage County.
Vance, Manuscript materials

[18] Information on Laura Roper's son, Clarence, was taken from:

The Beatrice Express, September 26, 1872.
Virginia Leasure to the author, July 5, 1995.

Tombstone of C. M. Roper, Rosehill Cemetery, Grant Precinct, Gage County, Nebraska.

[19] Ellenbecker, *Indian Raids on the Upper Little Blue*, 6-10.

[20] Yost, *Boss Cowman*; *Trail of Memories*, 259-260.

[21] This is the figure given by Will Mudge (Ellenbecker, op. cit.). But in his testimony of February 12, 1887, Lemmon claimed that the sale price was $1,600. And Emery, testifying in July 1891, claimed that the farm belonged to him at the time, which, of course was false, or Lemmon could not have repossessed it.

[22] Dobbs, *History of Gage County*, 155; Federal Census for Nebraska, 1870, Gage County, Beatrice P. O.

[23] Yost, *Boss Cowman;* Landers, *Nebraska Stories.*

[24] *Biographical and Historical Memoirs*, 345-346; Federal Census for Missouri, 1860, Harrison County, Bethany P. O.; Federal Census for Nebraska, 1870, Jefferson County, Big Sandy P. O.

[25] Bainter Depredations Claim (Papers of John Rodgers Maltby).

[26] *Oak—The Way it Was*, 2.

Part II
Chapter Two

The Raid on the Little Blue

Sunday, August 7, 1864

The first rays of the morning sun reached the valley of the Little Blue River shortly after 5:30 a.m. Those settlers who were up with the sun (and that was just about all of them) recognized the dawning of another hot and cloudless day with little breeze and not the faintest sign of rain. It had come to be the pattern of the past several weeks, and the torrid dry spell had taken a toll on men and animals as well as on the crops. While some of the ranchmen planned to cut and haul hay, many others had decided to rest. No one would be going to church this Sunday—the nearest houses of worship were at Beatrice, Brownville, or Nebraska City.

Erastus Comstock was visiting at Thirty-two Mile Station, and was up early to take breakfast with his sons, their family, and hired help. He faced a long ride back to Oak Grove and knew he would have to stop frequently at ranches along the way to water and rest his old white horse. Son George, Mike Connelley, and the Artist sisters decided to ride part way with Father Comstock, just for recreation. The sun would be up in full strength well before noon, and riding would be quite uncomfortable by then.

A short distance west of Lone Tree, Horace Smith and his five teamsters harnessed up to make a late start. Their six wagons with their cargoes of hardware and stoves, crockery, and the threshing machine could, with good fortune, spend the next night in the Platte Valley. At Lone Tree Station, Frank Baker was also up early to begin his eight-mile ride back to his home base at Thirty-two Mile Creek, his fishing trip of the past several days now only a pleasant memory.

At Spring Ranch, the Bainter family took breakfast with the Reverend Charles Wesley Wells and his brother, Richard. The Wells brothers had recently purchased a mowing machine and had contracted to cut forty tons of prairie hay for James Bainter, but the good parson took a dim view of working on Sunday. Visiting was permissible, however, and at midmorning, the brothers, accompanied by eleven-year-old Jacob Bainter, drove their wagon over to Pawnee Ranch to spend the day with the Metcalfs, where the early melons would be ripe in the garden.

Close by Buffalo Ranch, the William Wilder train yoked up to resume its empty run to Atchison. At the south end of Nine Mile Ridge, Patrick Burke hitched up to continue his solitary drive to Fort Kearny. He had a wagonload of shelled corn to sell to the military officers there, to supplement what he earned in his blacksmith shop in Beatrice. The load was heavy, and Burke planned to spare his team in the heat, driving only the seventeen miles to Pawnee Ranch where he would lay over for the night.

Nearby, at Little Blue Station, Jim Comstock prepared to take his visiting sister back to her home at Oak Grove. His wife, Perlina, and little son would go along to visit with all the brothers and sisters. They would remain until late afternoon. If Erastus had not returned by then, perhaps they would meet him on their way home.

A half mile south of the station, the Roper family planned nothing more than a day of rest. Their lives had been disrupted back on July 27 when a few Indians had raided their livestock. Joe had lost his only two horses—a pair of roan ponies—in the affair, and he had taken his family to Beatrice until the seriousness of the threat could be determined. Dan Freeman, who had a little store just east of Oak Grove, chased the raiders that day, but the Indians escaped with one of his horses, too. All told, Joe Roper and his neighbors lost ten horses. They knew that the valley had long been a haven for Indians, but since the coming of the road ranches, there had been no real trouble. Nothing more had been seen of the raiders, and the Ropers had returned to their home the previous Thursday. They were low on certain supplies, however, and Joe Roper scraped together what money there was and gave it to his partner. Marshall Kelley promised to arrange for the purchase of the necessary items at the Missouri River.[1]

Laura Roper had her heart set on a visit to the Eubank family a mile away. She had been to their homestead only once during the five months her family had lived in the valley because part of that time she had spent riding herd on the wild Lemmon boys, and the rest of the time she was kept busy around home. Today she would renew her budding friendship with Lucinda Eubank.

Joe Roper had no objections to his daughter's visit, but events of the previous two weeks had him very much on edge. Not only had the Indians escaped the valley with $2,000 worth of the settlers' horses, but in recent days there had been many more Indians than usual passing along the trail. There had also been warnings of their intentions from Jim Bainter up at Spring Ranch and reports of increasing troubles along the Santa Fe route and the upper Platte. The situation called for increased caution.

Joe's horses were gone, of course, so Laura would have to walk to the Eubank place. Perhaps she might fall in with some travelers, just to be safe. It would be well if the Eubanks would see her home again. In any case, she was to be back well before dusk. At that point Marshall Kelley intervened. He and a visiting friend, Jonathan Butler, were preparing to start for the river for supplies. Laura could ride along with them in Butler's wagon as far as the Eubank place.

The Eubank families were operating short-handed this day. Ruth Eubank had become so disheartened by her grubby life along the trail, so homesick for her former home and relation, that she and daughter Hannah had gone back to Kirksville for an extended visit. Joe Sr. planned to take his wagon south to help sons Joe and Fred haul in their hay. Thirteen-year-old James and seven-year-old Ambrose Asher would go along. The youngest boy, Henry, was ill and would be best off resting at home through the heat of the day.

The people at Oak Grove had also planned to rest for the day. In addition to the family and hired hands, there were two travelers, Nelson and Lewis Ostrander, who were there purely by necessity. A few weeks before, the Ostrander brothers had left their homes in New York for the gold mines of Colorado, in company with a friend, John Bare. While the men were camped along the Little Blue, a deer appeared suddenly from the river and someone carelessly pulled a rifle from the wagon for a quick kill. The gun discharged, wounding Lewis severely. He was brought to Oak Grove to recover, but the outlook was not positive. Bare returned to the East and Nelson Ostrander went to work with the haying crew as his brother struggled to survive. But no hay was to be made this Sunday. The only significant activity around Oak Grove was to be a large dinner in the early afternoon.

West of Kiowa Station, Joe and Fred Eubank planned to rake and haul hay. With the aid of John Palmer and Joe Sr.'s wagon, they could have several good sized haystacks built by nightfall.

At Kiowa, Jim Douglas planned to begin cutting hay on the following day, with the help of John Gilbert and several other hired hands. Camped on either side of Kiowa Station, three freight trains combined under the leadership of wagon master George Constable planned to lay over for the day. They would resume their westward trek on Monday after their day of rest.

So the sun continued its climb into a hazy sky and the shadows shortened, while the heat of mid day settled down over the valley. In a score of homes scattered along the trail, the chores and meals, the idle conversation and minutia of family life began to give form to the day of which John Barratt later wrote, "There is so much to tell of that seventh of August, 1864, that I cannot put it all down on paper, but I shall always recollect it."[2]

Frank Baker had not ridden far when he caught up to Horace Smith's freight wagons.[3] The dust kicked up by the animals' hooves was hanging in the air and he hurried to get ahead of them, exchanging greetings with the teamsters as he rode by. Soon he was a good half-mile in front of the wagons and descended into a shallow ravine known locally as Indian Hollow. On either side of the trail were great fields of six-foot-tall prairie sunflowers, their broad leaves showing a soft grayish-green under their dusty coatings. Erastus Comstock and his party had come through the hollow a few minutes before, and all was peaceful and still as Baker continued through the draw and up the other side. Within ten minutes or so, the freight wagons came rolling down into Indian Hollow behind him. It was not even mid morning yet and the drivers were drowsy and relaxed on their bouncing seats.

Without warning, the air was filled with the rustle of feathered arrows flying from ambush. Before they could reach for their guns, all six men were shot off their wagons. With shouts and war cries the Indians sprang from cover to chase the terrified horses and mules which stampeded out of the draw and off the road in all directions. The actual attack lasted only a few seconds, after which the warriors ransacked the wagons, throwing much of their contents out on the ground. After cutting the draft animals from their harness and setting some of the wagons ablaze, the Indians departed the opening scenes of the day's tragedies. On the ground in the hollow, Horace Smith and four of his drivers lay dead—scalped, bloody, and bristling with arrows. The sixth teamster, a young, redheaded Irishman, had managed to crawl into the protection of the sunflowers. He was horribly wounded with an arrow in his back and another embedded in his skull above one eye. In his shock and agony, he dragged himself among the thick stalks to lie helpless under the hot, August sun—knowing he must die, yet terrified of the return of the savage attackers.

As Erastus Comstock approached the vicinity of Lone Tree Station, his companions bade him goodbye and turned their horses back the way they had come. Within a few minutes they were riding down into Indian Hollow, coming within sight of the burning wagons on the far side. As they rode gingerly through the scene of destruction, they saw that the drivers had been scalped. One of the bodies bristled with thirty-six arrows, and the amount of blood was incredible. The gruesome sight sickened the Artist sisters, and the party hurriedly left the hollow and galloped back to Thirty-two Mile Station.

At midmorning, Reverend Wells and his brother hitched up their team and set off with Jacob Bainter for Pawnee Ranch. The Metcalfs were pleased to have company, and the morning passed in sampling the melon crop and in general conversation. It was about noon when Erastus Comstock rode in on his white horse, and the Metcalfs invited him to stay for dinner. While the meal was being prepared, the men exchanged views on the Indian situation and thoroughly discussed the latest rumors. It was apparently a topic which was much on the minds of everyone, and the discussion continued through dinner.

By early afternoon, the people at Pawnee Ranch finished their dinner and Erastus Comstock left for home, having stayed longer than he had intended. It would likely be after dark now before he reached Oak Grove. He jogged past the junction of the Fort Riley Road and soon met Patrick Burke, trundling along with his load of shelled corn.

Shortly after four o'clock, the people at Pawnee Ranch saw Burke's wagon approaching from the east. At the same time, several mounted Indians rode past the ranch from the west, their behavior strangely excited. As the Metcalfs and their guests watched in curious disbelief, the warriors headed straight toward Pat Burke and gathered round his wagon. The Wells brothers had seen enough. Running to their team, which they had left in harness, they worked frantically to mount and ride out to Burke's assistance.

There were no arrows this time. One of the Indians shot the outnumbered man through the back of the neck, and his team bolted. Pat Burke fell from the wagon seat to be scalped in a moment and left bleeding in the dirt of the trail. By the time the Wells brothers reached him, the Indians had disappeared. Burke was still alive, for the bullet had gone completely through his neck, coming out his mouth. In great agony, he nevertheless recognized his rescuers and made them understand that he did not want to be moved until he was dead. Returning to Pawnee Ranch, the brothers found the load of corn standing in the front yard. They unhitched Burke's horses, hooked them to their own wagon, and raced back down the trail. On the way, they met Charles Emery, who had ridden up from Liberty Farm with his hired man. Everyone helped place Burke in the wagon as gently as possible. Then Emery and his helper galloped back to Liberty Farm where they arrived just in time to see nine warriors emerge from the bluffs to butcher one of Emery's cattle and stampede the rest.

The Wells brothers brought Burke back to Pawnee Ranch where they attempted to make his last hours as comfortable as possible. By sundown he was dead and the men wrapped him in his blankets and buried him behind the ranch buildings.

The Indian scare talk of the afternoon and the murder of Pat Burke aroused the people at Pawnee Ranch to a frenzy of activity. Everyone began cleaning guns and distributing ammunition, preparing the stout cabin for defense. Jacob Bainter must have been terribly worried about his family, but nobody had either the courage or foolhardiness to ride back and warn the Bainters. As their fright began to wear away, everyone settled down for a hot, sleepless night—concerned, yet entirely ignorant of the fate suffered by neighbors up and down the valley.

It was about one o'clock when Laura Roper climbed aboard Jonathan Butler's wagon for the ride to the Eubank place. Upon reaching their dirt-roofed hut, she alighted and bade the men goodbye, and they continued on to Oak Grove. Laura spent the next several hours with Lucinda Eubank, visiting and helping with things around the place. Possibly they walked over to the river to pick wild grapes and plums which were just then coming ripe. Laura told the family of her father's concern over the Indians and asked if they could see her home. Although the Eubanks had several horses and a wagon in the yard, they opted to walk the mile home with Laura, while Dora stayed behind with Henry. Soon Laura and her companions set off for the Roper Ranch, with Lucinda carrying the infant Willie, and Isabelle toddling along, holding her father's hand. It was four o'clock.

As at Pawnee Ranch, the main event of the day at Oak Grove was a sumptuous dinner. It would have to be sumptuous, for the assembly of diners was the size of a small church picnic. Most of Erastus Comstock's children were there, of course. They and their in-laws, hired help, and neighbors made a grand total of seventeen hungry people.[4] By three o'clock the meal was finished, and many of the folks

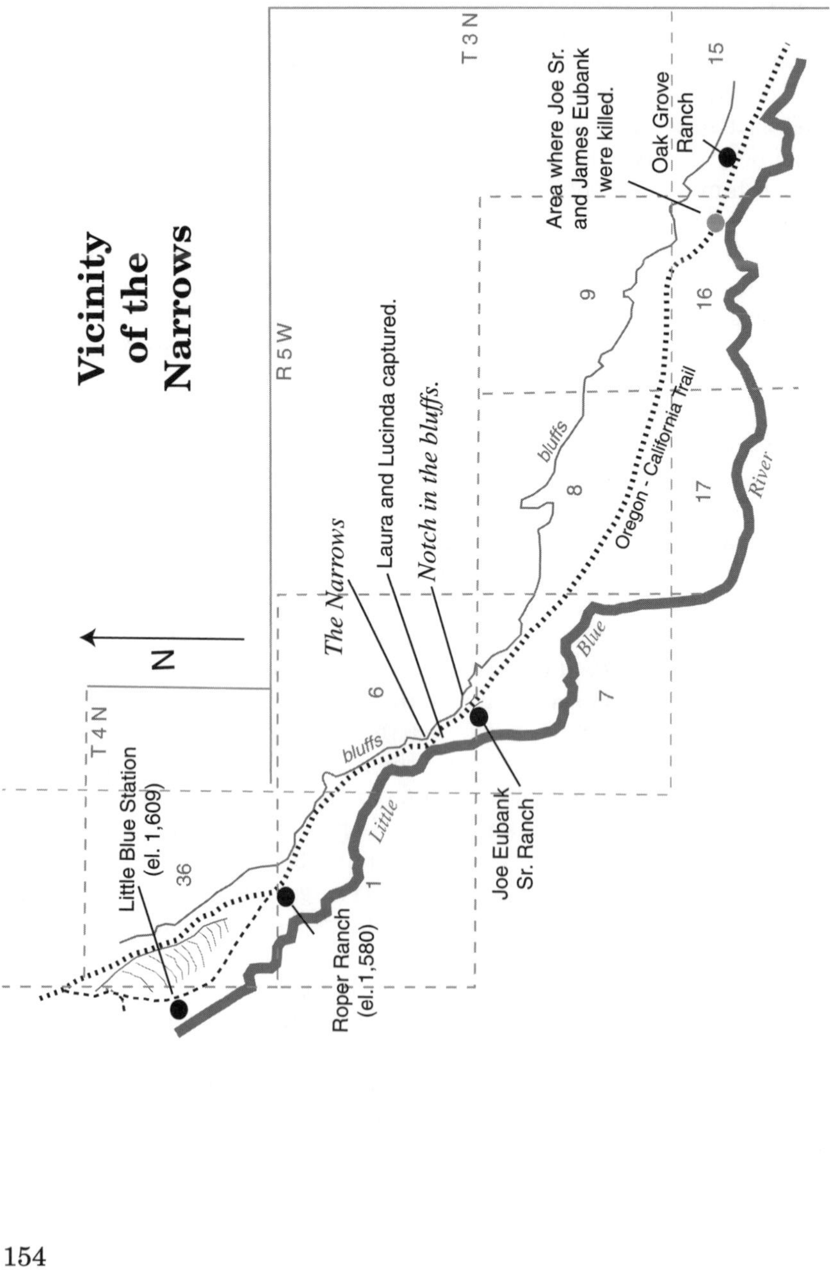
Vicinity of the Narrows
N
T 4 N
T 3 N
R 5 W
Little Blue Station (el. 1,609)
36
Roper Ranch (el. 1,580)
1
Little
bluffs
6
The Narrows
Laura and Lucinda captured.
Notch in the bluffs.
Joe Eubank Sr. Ranch
Blue
7
8
bluffs
Oregon - California Trail
17
River
9
16
Area where Joe Sr. and James Eubank were killed.
Oak Grove Ranch
15

wandered outside into the shade to spend the rest of the afternoon in relaxation and idle conversation.

A farm wagon lumbered past, drawn by two yoke of oxen. Old Joe Eubank was driving, plainly recognizable by his long, gray beard and the fringe of hair around his bald head. Slowly the wagon and its three occupants continued up the trail, disappearing around a bend.

The three Eubanks reached a point little more than half a mile above Oak Grove where the river looped northward to come within a couple hundred yards of the road. From the tall grasses along the riverbank, a single Indian warrior emerged, riding casually up to the wagon to ask for a plug of tobacco. The oxen came to a halt and old man Eubank reached into his pocket for a twist of tobacco, cut it in half, and gave part to the Indian, who took a chew and put the rest into a little pouch. There was nothing unusual about the transaction. Indians always begged tobacco when they felt the need.

But this Indian wasn't finished. Fitting an arrow to his bow, he began making threatening motions toward the oxen. Old Joe Eubank warned him by signs and sharp words to leave the animals alone. Slowly the arrow came around to point at young James, then moved sideways toward Ambrose. The boys were motionless, paralyzed by fright as the arrow moved again to point at the old man. Then it was gone, buried in his side. As old Joe Eubank faltered, the warrior drove several more arrows into his body. James leaped from the wagon in mindless terror and began to run in the direction of home. It was the signal for the rest of the Indians, nearly fifty of them, to charge howling from the concealing tallgrass. James was killed in the road.[5]

One of the warriors dismounted and wrestled Ambrose from the wagon. The Indians boosted the little boy onto the back of a pony, tied his legs underneath and his hands together under the horse's neck. Others stripped the clothes from the bodies of James and old Joseph, leaving them lying in the dirt of the trail, all smeared with bloody mud. Then they stampeded the oxen toward the Eubank place in a shower of arrows, leisurely following after with their frightened, young captive.

Though his father had departed for home, young Joe Eubank was not quite ready to quit for the day. On the opposite side of the river east of Kiowa Station there were several acres of uncut bluestem grass which he wanted to survey for possible cutting, so he rode downstream to take a look. John Palmer departed the hayfield on an errand of mercy. His sister, Hattie, was pregnant and not feeling at all well. She craved the strong water from a mineral spring that bubbled out of the bluffs about a mile from her home. Leaving Fred Eubank to rake the last of the cut hay, Palmer rode to the spring to get the water for his sister.

When he returned to the hayfield, he could see no signs of activity. At last he spied the wooden hayrake standing alone without its team. Riding closer to investigate, Palmer found the body of Fred Eubank stretched across the machine. There was an arrow in his back, and his head was bloody where the scalp had been. There was no need to look further. Palmer wheeled his horse and raced back to the cabin to warn Hattie.

Five hundred yards below Joe Eubank's ranch, Kiowa Station sweltered in the afternoon sun. John Gilbert and James Douglas were taking their ease with other employees of the stage line when a youngster rode up on an Otoe Indian pony. Nineteen-year-old Theodore Uhlig had been sent by his mother to get some eggs from Douglas. He even had a little tin bucket to put them in. Theodore's older brother, Otto, had been to Brownville several days before to pick up some sections of steel teeth for Douglas' horse-drawn mowing machine. Douglas asked Gilbert to ride back home with Theodore and bring back some of those teeth to repair his mower.

Gilbert teased Theodore, betting him that his Cheyenne pony could outrun the youngster's Otoe pony back to the Uhlig place. Theodore took the challenge but, to stack the deck in his favor, he left on a run before Gilbert could get his own horse saddled. By the time John Gilbert could get mounted, Theodore had a quarter-mile head start.

Gilbert's horse was a fast runner, but he couldn't see that he was gaining on Theodore, so he reined in near Joe Eubank's place to let his horse cool down. As he walked his mount closer to the cabin, he heard the sound of anguished crying from inside and turned toward the house to see what was the trouble. As he did so, he caught momentary sight of four Indians ahead, riding atop the bluffs in the direction of the Uhlig place.

Gilbert soon learned from John Palmer that Fred Eubank had been killed and that Joe was likely dead as well. A large group of about sixty warriors had been sighted riding downstream on the south side of the river in the direction that Joe had taken earlier. Sensing now that danger lay all around, Gilbert forgot that he was chasing Theodore, and he and Palmer coaxed Hattie onto a horse for the short ride down to Kiowa where the parked trains would afford some protection.

Theodore Uhlig raced around a bend in the trail and looked back. He had pulled a neat trick on Gilbert, who was nowhere in sight.

Having outrun his pursuer, Theodore reined his horse to a walk to allow it to cool down before reaching home. When he was only two hundred yards from the cabin, the boy was met by four warriors who came down from the bluffs. The Indians surrounded him and caught hold of his horse's bridle, possibly waiting for Gilbert to catch up. But John Gilbert did not appear, and Theodore soon panicked and attempted to break free. Within sight of his home and family, he, too, was cut down by arrows and left to die in the dust of the trail. Now Joanna Uhlig had lost not only her husband, but her youngest son as well.

The carnage continued a mile and a half east of Oak Grove where William Bowie and his wife were murdered in their dugout. Closer to Kiowa Station, Bill Canada (or Kennedy) was shot down outside his small cabin.

Being torn through with arrows is, when one dwells upon it, a terrible and excruciatingly painful way to meet death. But what made these attacks even more frightening, if that is possible, was that they occurred so totally without warning, at the hands of a people the homesteaders had come to believe were friendly, or at least benignly pesky. But the game had begun in earnest now, and the Cheyennes, Arapahoes, and Sioux intended to sweep the table clean.

The maddened oxen pulled the empty Eubank wagon into the riverbottom close by their home, stopping only when a rear wheel caught on a tree trunk. By this time, Laura and her companions were beyond a notch in the bluffs and some 500 yards up the trail. The surface of the road had been ground to a fine powder by thousands of wheels and hooves, and Will Eubank was barefooted. When he ran a sliver into his foot and began limping, he told the women to continue up the trail. He would take care of the sliver and catch up, since Isabelle's short legs were slowing them up, anyway. So Laura took Isabelle's hand and the women continued their idle walk up the road, passing around the sharp projection of the bluffs from which The Narrows takes its name.

They had advanced about fifty yards past The Narrows when they heard frantic screaming coming from the Eubank home behind them. There was no doubt that Dora was in a desperate situation. Carrying both children, Laura and Lucinda ran back around the projection of the bluffs where they could see Will Eubank sprinting back down the road toward the sound of his sister's cries.

Dora was outside now, battling her way toward the river, kicking and clawing at her attackers. If she was slow-witted, she was at least putting up the fight of her life. As the women rushed to the shelter of some underbrush on the riverbank, Laura caught a glimpse of the Indians grabbing for Dora, swinging her around, trying to get close enough to immobilize the frantic girl. And then they came for Will Eubank—several warriors on horseback. Unarmed, with nowhere to hide, his only chance of escape was toward the river. The Indians pursued leisurely enough and could have caught him easily. But the Cheyennes did not take adult male prisoners, certainly not this day. From a hiding place in the bushes along the riverbank, Laura and the family watched as Will Eubank splashed desperately across the Little Blue, lunging for the relative safety of the far side. He had just reached a sandbar against the opposite bank when the arrows struck him, and he dropped, dying, in the sand.

The Indians turned away from the river and continued their ride up the trail in the direction of the Roper cabin. As they passed the brushy hollow where the women had taken refuge, little Isabelle loosed a childish scream of fright. Instantly, the warriors whirled their ponies and flushed the whites from cover. There was no use trying to resist or escape, and the women probably saved their lives by their peaceable surrender. The Indians took Laura's shoes and pulled Marshall Kelley's signet ring from her finger. Then they lifted their captives onto the ponies and started back down the trail toward the Eubank place.

The screaming had ended now. Beside a path leading to the river, about two hundred feet from the cabin lay the body of Dora Eubank. The girl was still alive, but she had been mortally stabbed and was threshing around in the grass in her last agony. Henry had also been stabbed and clubbed, and sometime during the attack, had managed to crawl out of the house to hide in a brushy ravine leading to the river. There he collapsed to lie for hours, sick and abandoned, tormented by thirst and flies, waiting for his life to leave him.

The Indians were in no hurry. They made thorough work of their destruction, smashing crockery and dishes, trashing the small house and grabbing such loot as pleased their fancy. During this time they allowed Laura and Lucinda to wander at will. Laura sidled over to a cut in the bluffs where, unobserved, she removed a locket and chain from around her neck and dropped them into her underwear. Lucinda searched in a daze through the wreckage of her home and managed to find two small dresses for Isabelle and a sunbonnet for herself. After a while, Ambrose was led up on his pony to where he could watch the destruction of his home. While most of the warriors occupied themselves in looting, another came riding up to the wrecked house, howling and swinging Dora's scalp from which blood was still dripping.[6]

The work of destruction lasted about an hour. Then the Indians were ready to depart. It was after six o'clock when they boosted the captive whites up onto ponies, grabbed the Eubanks' small dog, and set fire to the little house. As flames sputtered uncertainly inside the walls of the shoddy structure, the Indians splashed across the Little Blue and rode southward with their five captives. In a space of two hours, the Joseph Eubank family was all but wiped out. The father, five sons, and a daughter had come to a gruesome end. Only the absent mother, daughter, son, two daughters-in-law, and three grandchildren survived the massacre. None would ever return to live in the valley again.

In the dappled shade of the friendly elms and cottonwoods, the people at Oak Grove passed the time after dinner in conversation. The heat of the day had reached its peak and travel on the road was minimal, as most freight outfits were stopped for "nooning." Before anyone was quite aware of what was happening, the dooryard silently began to fill with mounted warriors. There were nearly twenty of them, walking their horses in a deliberate and sinister manner. The alarmed whites began to move into the house, but one of the Cheyennes called out in English to Marshall Kelley to stay outside. There was nothing to fear.

Kelley faced the spokesman, who was mounted on a white pony, and told him that their appearance indicated that they were on the warpath. What was it they wanted?

"Oh," came the reply, "we friendly. We no hurt white man."[7] So saying, the leader dismounted and approached Kelley to shake hands. They had just come from a big battle with the Pawnees, he explained. Of course, the Cheyennes had whipped them good, but had unfortunately lost all their provisions—so they had come to see the white man to get a cold drink from the well and beg some food.

Most of the Indians were walking around in the yard now, and the whites began to relax a bit. Little Ella Butler came shyly out of the cabin to get a closer look. Although the Cheyennes were doing their best to appear cordial, Tobias Castor could not help worrying about his horses pastured across the river. The friendly talk might be only a ruse to occupy the whites' attention while the herd was stampeded. Wishing he had put them up in the stable with Jim Comstock's team, Castor began to move toward the river to keep an eye on his animals.

One of the braves had noticed a fine, new lever action rifle in Butler's wagon, and he wanted to see how it worked. Jonathan Butler obligingly began to explain the action when there were sounds of a commotion across the river. The horse herd was being raided. As

Butler and Kelley became aroused to the trick, the Indian grabbed the rifle, levered a shell into the chamber, and shot Butler at point blank range.

The ranchyard exploded in pandemonium. War cries and arrows filled the air. The rifleman whirled and snapped off another shot at George Hunt, hitting the youth in the thigh and knocking him down. An arrow struck Marshall Kelley in the chest, passing completely through his body. He was dead within seconds. Nelson Ostrander tried to run, but arrows struck him in both arms and he was stabbed in the back by a warrior who caught him from behind. Little Ella Butler reached the front door of the house just as an arrow ripped her dress. Tobias Castor ran for his life as, across the river, his fine team of horses was being driven down the valley. Hotly pursued by several Cheyennes, Castor reached cover in the oak grove where he proved very difficult to catch. His pursuers soon gave up, leaving him shaken and very angry.

The attack lasted only a matter of seconds. As suddenly as they had appeared, the Cheyennes disappeared. In the yard the air was filled with fine dust stirred up by the ponies, and the bleeding bodies of Marsh Kelley and his friend lay crumpled in the dirt, while George Hunt and Nelson Ostrander attempted to drag themselves painfully toward the house. Except for the marvelously sudden departure of the Indians, they also would have been as dead as Kelley and Butler. Inside the house, Ella Butler was hiding in an empty flour bin while John Barratt and the Comstocks feverishly loaded guns and prepared for the next assault, which they feared would come at any second.

But the Cheyennes were gone, and the reason for their hasty disappearance soon became apparent as the lead wagons of William Wilder's bull train came rumbling at top oxen speed into the corral near the house. Tobias Castor emerged from the timber, and the stunned survivors of Oak Grove spilled from the house to begin caring for the wounded.

Wilder's men brought shocking news: Just a half mile up the trail, an old man and a boy were lying dead by the roadside, all naked and bloody. Why, that could only be old man Eubank. But he had two boys with him. One of them must have been killed somewhere else or taken captive. The Eubanks must have been killed by the same bunch that attacked Oak Grove. If there was a Cheyenne war party on the loose, Erastus Comstock could be in great danger out on the trail.

As the day neared seven o'clock, there came a rattle and shouting in the yard as the stage from Atchison pulled up on the run. Out tumbled the passengers with more dreadful news: Two men had been killed close to Kiowa, and the widow of one of them was at the station in a sorry state of shock and grief. Providentially, one of the passengers was a Dr. Hickman, who was returning to his home in Colorado. He promptly set about giving professional care to the wounded Hunt and the Ostrander brothers. The coach would remain at Oak Grove overnight as the people struggled to make sense of this triple tragedy and figured out what to do next.

It was nearly dark as Erastus Comstock came upon the tortured body of Dora Eubank and the wreckage of her home. The fire had gone out before the walls and roof were consumed, and Erastus poked around inside, not really knowing what he was looking for. His attention was caught by the wounded oxen in the trees near the river. The forward yoke seemed to be in fairly good shape, so he turned them loose. The wheel oxen he thought would die. He had no doubts that the trail might now be a very dangerous place for a lone rider, so Erastus urged his white horse up through the bluffs to the rim of the valley. Cautiously he rode along the open ground to a point near Oak Grove. It had grown completely dark before he eased his tired mount down through the bluffs to approach his ranch from the back side.

Those who were on watch noticed the shape of the white pony approaching. It wasn't much more than a lightening of the darkness against the bluffs. Hadn't the leader of the Cheyennes ridden a white pony? Hearts beat faster, guns were readied, and a challenge rang out. Back came the familiar voice of Father Comstock, and inside the house the tension broke and there was joy and relief in the midst of sorrow.

No one understood just yet how fortunate Erastus Comstock had been. Like a man dodging lightning bolts, he had ridden blithely along, completely untouched by the murder and destruction that the Indians were visiting upon the valley that day. He was too early for the attack at Indian Hollow, too early at Pawnee Ranch, too late at The Narrows, and too late at Oak Grove. The entire Comstock family had more than its share of good fortune that day. And now, standing in his own front yard, amid the dim shapes of Butler's wagon, the Atchison coach, and the white tops of the bull train corralled nearby, Erastus Comstock was safely home at last, his lucky ride at an end.

When the people at Oak Grove added up the pieces of information brought by Erastus, by the Atchison coach, and by Wilder's train, the picture which came together was shocking. The old Oregon-California Trail had been devastated from The Narrows to Kiowa. The Eubanks were all gone, and maybe Laura Roper with them, since Kelley had said she stopped off there. Nobody knew anything about the Uhligs or Bowies or Bill Canada, but everyone imagined the worst. There had been so many Indians going back and forth all day that every homestead along the road was probably gone. The Cheyennes would certainly return with the dawn to finish what they had begun, and Oak Grove had neither the guns nor the defensive works to fight it out with them. There was really nothing left to do but to get away as far and as fast as possible. The Comstocks were resigned to the loss of their homes, and resolved to take with them to safety only their most important belongings. Wilder would take the refugees in his empty wagons, since most of the Comstock's horses, like Tobias Castor's team, were gone.

No one really expected the Indians to attack during the night, and James Comstock and his wife wanted to return to their home at Little Blue Station to gather up a few valuables. On their way, they would check up on the Roper family. Nobody knew if they were alive. As the folks at Oak Grove rested and planned for the morrow, Jim Comstock brought his team of Overland Stage horses up from the stable, hitched up, and drove away with Perlina into the darkness.

Southwestward over the darkened prairie, Laura Roper rode behind one of her captors. She was no longer fearful of being killed because, she reasoned, if the Indians had wanted to kill her, they would have done so immediately. About midnight a shadowy rider closed in abreast of her and asked in good English if she was afraid. He turned out to be a young half-breed named Joe Barroldo, and he expressed the opinion that she would probably be set free before too long. Then he rode away, leaving Laura somewhat comforted and very weary.

The Roper family spent the evening hours in a terrible state of apprehension. As sunset neared and Laura failed to return, Paulina Roper told her husband she was going to walk down the trail and look for her daughter. But Joseph knew instinctively that his worst anxieties had come to pass and that there was danger lurking all around. Laura would not have stayed away this long unless she had met with some misfortune. Their wisest course now was to remain in the cabin and protect the other three children. Joe Roper firmly forbade his wife to leave. Back in July, when the Indians had stolen his roan ponies, Joe decided that, if the situation ever grew really threatening, he would bury a box of the family's clothing and some valuables in the smokehouse, which had a packed earth floor. Now the time had come. Gathering the children together in the hot cabin, he and Paulina filled a box with clothing and supplies, carried it to the nearby smokehouse, and buried it. As if to confirm his fears, a few Indians appeared to

a box with clothing and supplies, carried it to the nearby smokehouse, and buried it. As if to confirm his fears, a few Indians appeared to scatter his hogs and run off with Marshall Kelley's horse. The Ropers retreated to their stout cabin, secured the doors as well as possible, and huddled together in an agony of worry.

Near midnight, there were noises outside, and then a pounding at the door. Upon recognizing the voice of Jim Comstock, the Ropers opened the door and the Comstocks hurried inside. Where, they wanted to know, was Laura?

She had gone to the Eubanks and never returned, they were told.

"Then she is killed," came the reply, "for all the Eubanks have been killed."[8]

There was no time for shock to set in and no time for grieving. The Ropers must prepare to flee their home. Comstocks would pick them up on the way back from Little Blue Station, and all would go with the empty train at Oak Grove. Grimly the Ropers prepared Francis and Kate and little Clarence for the flight to safety. They had lived in the valley barely six months. Now their home was to be destroyed; the daughter who had caused them so much worry was probably dead; her fiancé—Joe's partner and the father of Clarence—was dead of an arrow. They had little time for reflection, for within a few minutes, they heard the rattle of Jim Comstock's wagon approaching down the cutoff road from Little Blue Station.

The sliver of a waxing moon had set before the family shut up their cabin for the last time and climbed aboard the wagon. Joseph pleaded with his wife to lie down flat in the wagon bed in case they were attacked going through The Narrows, but she steadfastly refused. "I do not care whether they kill me or not," she responded. "I will never lie down when we are liable to run over Laura's body at any minute."[9] Mercifully the bodies of the Eubanks were hidden by the darkness as the wagon rolled past their ruined homestead and past the scene of the attack on old Joe's wagon.

They arrived without incident at Oak Grove where the excitement was still intense. The ox train would not be moving until first light, but nobody seems to have gotten much rest. The early morning hours passed fitfully for the survivors, torn between fleeing and staying, alternating between hope and fear. But August 7 had ended. Its date would be forever fixed in the hearts and minds of the people of the Little Blue Valley—those who survived the events of that day, and by the generations that followed.

Monday, August 8

As dawn began to creep into the eastern sky, the trail near Buffalo Ranch came alive. With a drumming of hoofbeats and rattle of wheels, the eastbound stage out of Denver and Fort Kearny pounded past to begin its climb onto Nine Mile Ridge. In the nearby camps of two freight trains, the teamsters and bullwhackers yawned and grumbled their way through their morning routines. By sunup they had completed their breakfast, hitched and yoked their stock, broken camp, and begun their day's drive to the west. At Buffalo Ranch, Will Mudge and his family were about their morning chores. Their work this day included caring for the Milligan's stock as well as their own, for Joe and Sally had gone to Nebraska City for a load of supplies.

Sometime around seven o'clock, the stillness around Buffalo Ranch was broken by shouts and clatter as both the eastbound and Dr. Hickman's westbound stages skidded down off Nine Mile Ridge and braked to a stop in the yard. Drivers and passengers were nervous and excited as they clamored to tell the Mudge family of the Indian attacks that had occurred from Indian Hollow all the way to Kiowa. The Mudges had seen extraordinary numbers of Indians passing along the trail in recent days, and they knew now that their lives were in jeopardy. Hurriedly they gathered up personal papers and valuables—citizenship papers, marriage and baptism certificates—and climbed aboard the stage.

The coach raced the three miles to Liberty Farm, where the refugees told their neighbors about the spreading destruction. The Emerys loaded what few items they could into the coaches. Mary boarded with her two little sons, and the cavalcade set off for Pawnee Ranch, the only really defensible homestead along this part of the trail. Charles Emery and his hired man followed, driving some of the stage line horses.

In their haste to get away, the Emerys threw a mound of loose bedding into one of the coaches. Buried within the bedclothes was a box of wooden matches that somehow caught fire from the violent motion of the bouncing stage. Before anyone noticed what was happening, the bedding and interior of the coach were on fire. There was nothing to do but to cut the leather springs, topple the body of the coach off its running gear, and let it burn. With all their bedding going up in smoke, the unfortunate Emerys and their fellow passengers crowded aboard the second coach and continued on to Pawnee.

Barely a mile short of their destination, they came upon the charred hulk of a queer-looking wagon. They felt close enough to safety now to allow a little time for investigation, and soon found the body of a man lying off to the side of the road. The passengers of the westbound stage had seen ever so many bodies the day before, but this was only one. It seemed indecent to leave him lying where he was, so they stopped and hurriedly buried him. It was hard to be certain, but the unfortunate man was apparently Red Cloud Tom, a peddler who traveled up and down the road selling notions and trinkets to the ranchers and, some suspected, guns and whiskey to the Indians. If indeed it was old Tom, there was a general feeling that his demise was no great loss.[10]

After the hasty interment, the coach rolled on the last mile to Pawnee Ranch where the passengers found the ox and mule trains which had camped near Buffalo Ranch the previous night corralled for defense. Everyone climbed down from the vehicle to hear the details of how Indians had cruelly murdered Patrick Burke the day before and how he had been buried in his blankets behind the corral. The warriors had also run off nine horses from Lone Tree Station. The people at Pawnee were preparing for an attack they feared could come at any moment. Nearby settlers were coming in for protection, and Jim Bainter's hired men had returned to Spring Ranch to bring the Bainter family back to Pawnee. Already there were enough people gathered there to make a pretty decent defense of the place.

A Mormon couple had been traveling with the freighters for protection, and the lady was already in action. She organized the women to mold bullets and sent the few children present on a hunt for tubs and containers to fill with water. Meanwhile the men began pulling apart the smokehouse, chickenhouse, and corn crib, ricking up the logs between the freight wagons to form breastworks. If and when the Cheyennes decided to attack, they would find Pawnee Ranch a very tough nut to crack.

James Bainter was out early this morning, searching for additional hayfields for his hired men to cut. They should already have been at work, having taken yesterday off. Perhaps he would find them back at Spring Ranch when he returned.

About a mile and a half north of the ranch, Pawnee Creek ran in a crooked cut across the prairie. As Bainter rode slowly toward the creek, he saw a lone Indian approaching. This was hardly unusual, for there were always Omahas, Otoes, Pawnees, or Sioux moving here and there across the countryside. What was unusual on this particular morning was the Indian's behavior: Upon catching sight of Bainter, he ducked into a nearby ravine leading down to the creek. Bainter had become suspicious of the Indians' activities during the past few days and was on his guard. Dismounting from his mule, he drew his revolver and cautiously approached the ravine. Several times he saw the Indian's head peeking over the edge, but he held his fire. As long as he had lived on the Little Blue, Bainter had never had any trouble with the Indians, and he wasn't about to start any now. At length the warrior saw that his hiding place had been discovered, sprang onto his pony, and rode down to Pawnee Creek to join two of his comrades. Bainter was certain now that the attacks which he had feared would soon come to pass. Hurrying back to his mule, he rode at top speed back to his ranch where he set Elizabeth to work molding bullets.

Within a few minutes there came a great clatter of hoofbeats in the yard as Jacob and the Wells brothers returned from their dreadful night at Pawnee Ranch. The trio came bursting into the house with the dreadful news of Patrick Burke's murder and the preparations for an attack on Pawnee. Bainter knew there was no way that Spring Ranch could be defended, so he set his hired men to work hitching up the family wagon for the flight to Pawnee. After starting his family off toward relative safety, he mounted a race mare and headed west up the trail to warn the station keeper at Lone Tree, and to obtain some news of what was happening to the west. With his pistols and fast mare, Bainter would not be an easy mark for an attacker along the road.[11]

Following a restless night, the people at Thirty-two Mile Station had also risen early this Monday morning. After a quick breakfast, they loaded food, tools, guns, and a keg of water into the wagon for the return to Indian Hollow. Frank Baker and the Comstocks had briefly revisited the scene the previous evening and found some of the wagons of the Smith train still smoking. They had carried the bodies of the five teamsters up out of the ravine and laid them in a row alongside the trail, but darkness came before there was time to do any more. Finding no survivors, they returned to the station, deciding to revisit the scene the following morning to give the dead men a decent burial.

Everyone went along. The women and children stayed close to the wagon while several men stood guard. The rest went to work digging a common grave. After a time, they were joined by Jim Bainter, who had ridden up past Lone Tree.

It was odd that, while there were six wagons, only five of the drivers were accounted for. Carefully the men began searching through the tall sunflowers back in the hollow. Before long, they came upon the sixth teamster. Incredibly, he was still alive. The young Irishman had lain among the sunflowers all through that long, hot Sunday and through the night. He had heard the Comstock's voices when they returned to the scene the evening before, but he had remained hidden, fearing in his terror and delirium, that the Indians had returned. The men found him now, lying in the weeds, begging for water, the arrows still protruding from his head and body. His face had turned completely black and was swollen to grotesque proportions. George Comstock later recalled that "He was the most awful looking human being that can be imagined."[12]

After being given some water, the man was able to relate to his rescuers a few details of the attack, and he begged them to take him someplace where he could die without seeing the bodies of his fellow drivers. The men picked him up gently, intending to take him back to the station. Before reaching the top of the hollow, he died in their arms. It proved impossible to remove the arrow from his forehead, so it was simply broken off and his body was carried to the common grave. The Comstocks wrapped all the bodies in some unburned blankets and laid them in the ground. No one knew their names, and the experience of that lonely burial at the top of Indian Hollow left George Comstock with a lingering feeling of melancholy.

The burial party was just beginning to fill in the grave when it was joined by George Lloyd, the division agent for the Overland Stage Line at Kearny City. The atmosphere of foreboding that had hung over the trail for the recent day or two had made the agent jumpy, and when the stage from Atchison failed to arrive that morning, Lloyd had feared the worst. Taking a spare coach, driver, and an escort of two soldiers from the fort, the agent set off down the trail to find out what had gone wrong. Though the day was growing unbearably hot, the stage team had been driven hard for forty-one miles. The sight of the bloody bodies in the trench confirmed Lloyd's worst fears, and he was distressed to recognize one of the teamsters as Henry Sullings, a citizen of St. Joseph, and a man whom Lloyd knew quite well.

When the burial was completed, the Comstocks gave Bainter all the information they had. The Atchison coach had failed to reach Thirty-two Mile Creek, or even Spring Ranch, for that matter. The theft of the horses from Lone Tree, the destruction of Horace Smith's train, and the murder of Patrick Burke were pretty fair indications that a major attack was in progress along the trail and probably involved more than merely an isolated war party. All things considered, it seemed prudent to abandon the search for the missing coach and get everybody to Fort Kearny as quickly as the horses could run.

Bainter mounted his race mare for the ride back to join the defense of Pawnee Ranch. George Lloyd's coach swung around for the drive back to Thirty-two Mile Station. Once there, the men tied the jaded horses behind the coach and put a fresh team into harness. With the

Comstocks and their employees trailing behind in a wagon, the coach took off for a high speed run to Fort Kearny. Indians could be seen at a distance, moving in and out of the draws, and Lloyd's party was thoroughly frightened. The stage horses were driven unmercifully, and before reaching the Platte, two of the fatigued animals collapsed and died in the road. Not far behind them came the people from Lone Tree, who had also abandoned their post and were in panicky flight to the fort. Their mad dash to safety killed five more of Ben Holladay's horses.

With the morning light, the ox train that had corralled at Oak Grove began yoking up. Now that the time of departure was at hand, the people were in a rush to get under way—but what should they do with the bodies of Marshall Kelley and Jon Butler? The day promised to be hot, as usual, and it would be most unpleasant to carry them along. Neither did anyone want to take the time to dig a grave. Someone suggested putting them in the little smokehouse until soldiers might come along in a day or two and give them a decent burial. This was done hurriedly, and the train, with its freight of exhausted and heartsick people, pulled away from Oak Grove and stretched eastward along the trail. The valley was quiet and there was no sign of Indians anywhere about.

The train had traveled little more than a mile and was nearing a long bend in the road when little Sarah Comstock looked back toward her former home. Already a column of grayish smoke was billowing up into the morning sky. The Cheyennes had been close all the time, and they had not waited long before closing in on the abandoned ranch. The oxen were urged onward and the train rounded the bend and passed by the William Bowie homestead. No one had any ideas of stopping to bury the couple, and the bodies of Bowie and his wife were left where they lay.

After two hours of steady running, the train approached the vicinity of Kiowa Station. Fifty yards off the road was Joe Eubank's Ranch. It was a heap of smoking ruins. In the dead of night, the Cheyennes (presumably—no one actually saw them) had come upon the empty cabin and put it to the torch. Passing the Eubanks' former home, the train rolled by George Constable's ox train and up to Kiowa where it halted for a rest. It is possible that some of the men helped to lay Theodore Uhlig's body in its lonely grave north of the station.[13] Then the refugees, now including John Palmer, Hattie Eubank, Harriet Douglas and little Adah, climbed aboard the wagons and the train took its way eastward once again. Every mile traveled was one mile closer to safety in Marysville. If all went well, they might reach the

Hackney Ranch in early afternoon and spend the evening six miles farther on at Thompson's. If so, Joe Roper would not be along.

Early that morning, the fleeing ox train met an outfit of nine mule wagons, determined to go west through the valley in spite of the Indians. Feeling that Paulina and the children would probably reach Marysville in safety now, Joe Roper hitched a ride with the mule train. He was desperately tired and probably not thinking very rationally. He knew only that, somewhere back to the west, was his daughter. He simply had to find her, and he couldn't very well do that in Marysville.

On either side of Kiowa Station, George Constable's westbound freight trains remained in camp. After the firing of Joe Eubank's cabin, the drovers had spent a sleepless night, guarding their animals closely. If Joe Roper and the mule outfit wanted to go back up the valley, that was fine. Constable's people were staying put. They were all tired, and none were looking forward to what awaited them along the trail ahead. Once upon Nine Mile Ridge, the wagons could travel two or three abreast for better protection. But to reach the ridge, they would have to be strung out in single file to get through The Narrows, where they would be sitting ducks. No, they would wait another day to make sure the Indians had left the valley.

John Gilbert and James Douglas were waiting, too, hoping for the stage to bring them news of what was happening up the line. They had no way of knowing that the eastbound stage had burned up in the mad dash back to Pawnee Ranch. This Monday there would be no eastbound stage past Kiowa.

Joe Roper and the mule train passed the smoking ruins of Oak Grove in the heat of mid day. Not an Indian was to be seen, and the valley was much too quiet. West of Oak Grove, the caravan came upon the darkening corpses of old Joe Eubank and young James, lying as the Indians had left them by the side of the trail. Joe and the muleskinners carefully lifted the bodies into one of the freight wagons and took them up to the ruins of their home, intending to bury them there. No sooner had they removed the bodies from the wagon, when a few Indians made their appearance on the nearby bluffs. The burial was forgotten as the spooked drivers jumped back onto their seats. The mules strained in their harnesses as they drew the heavy wagons past the Roper place and up onto Nine Mile Ridge, leaving behind them the bodies of the Eubank family, still unburied, but at least together at the place they had called home.

In the evening, the westbound stage overtook the mule train, and Joe Roper was happy to forsake the jarring wagons for the relatively greater comfort of the coach. The caravan continued on its way, unmolested by marauding warriors. It was well after dark when the exhausted mules pulled into Liberty Farm. The Emerys were gone and had taken all the stage stock with them. Sheer fatigue demanded an end to the day's hard journey. Joe Roper himself had been more than forty hours without sleep. Stage passengers and freighters settled their aching bodies around the abandoned stage station for a night's rest, unaware that, by the following night, Liberty Farm would also be a heap of ashes.

Near the Big Blue River, the Robert Nicholas family heard the approaching hoofbeats and gathered in front of their home to see who might be pushing a horse so fast on this hot evening. As the lone rider galloped into their yard, they recognized him as a settler named Thomas Freeman. He looked half wild and his horse was white with foam and sweat.

The Indians were coming, he croaked. Massacre on the Little Blue. Get the women and children to safety immediately. He had ridden so far and yelled so much that his voice was nearly gone.

The Nicholas family panicked, as much from the condition of the messenger as from the content of his message. Robert Nicholas yoked the oxen to his wagon, loaded up his family, and started down the Big Blue for the hamlet of Beatrice, twelve miles to the southeast. Little Frank Nicholas was only a few months past three years old, but he never forgot the atmosphere of desperate fear which hung over the family as they bumped along over the darkened prairie in their lumbering wagon.

The Nicholas family finally reached Beatrice to join a crowd of displaced settlers that was growing by the hour. People were coming in on horseback, by carriage, by mule and ox wagon, even on foot. All night long, refugees from the west splashed across the ford of the Big Blue. One wagon upset in the river, spilling its occupants into the water which, due to the drought, was fortunately quite shallow.

Some of the men gathered around the ford to repel a possible attack from the direction of Big Sandy. In the excitement, it apparently never occurred to anyone that attacking Indians would hardly need a ford to cross the Big Blue. Some of the women made plans to take their children to safety in the Missouri River towns if an attack developed. Nobody had any concrete information except that there had been disastrous raids along the Little Blue. To be sure, not all the settlers had come in from the endangered areas to the north and west. Some had refused to leave their claims, treating the warnings, if indeed they had heard them, with a healthy skepticism. But in

Beatrice it was a night of fear—a night during which people huddled together and counseled with one another, and took a measure of comfort in their enforced closeness.

All day long, in his office at Fort Leavenworth, General Curtis was hard at work, catching up on situations which had developed in the Department of Kansas during his absence along the Arkansas. He read a dispatch from Colonel Chivington in Colorado—a very conciliatory message assuring the general that his subordinate was devoting himself wholeheartedly to his military duties.

Before turning his attention once again to the problem of guerrillas, most of whom had moved eastward away from the Missouri, Curtis composed a dispatch to Chief of Staff General Halleck in Washington. On paper, at least, it was an impressive list of accomplishments, although the general had to admit that his forces had been unable to overtake the Indians. Still, Curtis had energetically discharged his obligations. And, although Mitchell was having his hands very full up around Laramie, it appeared that the overall situation in the Department of Kansas was coming under control at last.

Through the hours of darkness, Laura Roper clung in exhaustion to her pony. The seven Indians had kept their captives constantly on the move since the raid, riding ever southward and west. They had been joined that afternoon by five more Cheyennes with extra horses, making it possible for Laura to have a mount to herself. The party was descending into a deep ravine when Laura's saddle broke loose, throwing her to the ground and tripping her pony. In his wild scramble to regain his feet, the horse kicked her in the face, breaking her nose. The Cheyennes whipped the pony hard and wiped the blood from Laura's face with a sheet which they had looted from the Eubank cabin. Then they remounted her behind one of the warriors, and the procession continued on its way through the darkness, ever farther from the Little Blue Valley.

Tuesday, August 9

The sun was well above the horizon as George Constable's freight trains prepared to move. There was no further sign of Indians in the valley, and every day the wagons sat idle was costing the owners money. If all went well, Constable's outfits could be past The Narrows by noon, the most dangerous part of the day's drive behind them.

There were now four separate trains in the group. Niles' mule train, loaded with liquor, had been several miles ahead of the others and had turned back for fear of the Indians. It was now encamped with Varney's mule train a hundred yards east of Kiowa Station. About 200 yards west of Kiowa Station was the camp of Young's ox train, loaded with $12,000 worth of shelled corn, and Constable's ox train with its cargo of iron hardware. When these sixty-nine wagons stretched out in single file, as they would need to in order to traverse The Narrows, they would form a line over a mile long, making the train extremely vulnerable to the hit and run tactics of the Indians.

Before the freighters got under way, a coach came charging up the trail from Big Sandy, bearing five brave, if foolhardy, passengers.[14] Driving the coach was Robert Emery, whose brother Charles had fled with his family from Liberty Farm the day before. Bob Emery had received no news on the fate of his brother's family and, even though unfamiliar with the route, he volunteered to make the run through the valley so he might find out for himself whether Charles and Mary and their two boys were still alive.

The men at Kiowa made sure that Emery and his passengers understood the danger, but no one seems to have tried to talk them out of the journey. Certainly John Gilbert did not, for he was no doubt anxious to find out whether Libby Artist was safe up at Thirty-two Mile Station. So Gilbert, Lan Hoffman, and James Douglas grabbed rifles and ammunition and climbed to the top of the coach. On the box with Emery was messenger (guard) John Ames, while inside rode three men—John Rollins, E. Umphrey, and G. C. Randolph—all of them armed with revolvers. Mrs. Hattie Randolph and an unidentified young lady rounded out the complement of passengers. With a fresh team in harness and ten souls on board, the coach pulled away from Kiowa Station for its trip into the unknown.

Emery drove slowly to spare the team, knowing they might have to travel the entire seventy miles or more to the Platte. As the big wheels mushed through dirt so recently churned up by William Wilder's refugee train, the men on the coach, alert and vigilant, scanned the valley ahead. The dusty, dry landscape was cloaked in an eerie silence.

Far away to the northwest, atop the bluffs, there appeared, just for an instant, a human figure on horseback. Most of the people on the coach thought it must be a white man. Indians rarely pressed an attack for more than a few hours, and nobody wanted to believe they might still be in the valley two days after their deadly raids. The figure disappeared and the coach rolled on to the Uhlig place, now forlorn and silent.

Nearby, about two and three-fourths miles west of Kiowa, the trail divided. The original road swung to the northwest here, climbing up close to the foot of the bluffs. With drier conditions in recent years, the travel had cut off toward the river bottom in order to spare the draft animals. This cutoff road ran little more than a mile to the crossing of a tiny spring branch. Five hundred yards past the spring it forded a small stream and immediately began a sharp ascent back onto the tableland north of the Little Blue. The spring branch was no more than 400 yards in length, and where it turned eastward to empty into the Little Blue, it was lined with young ash, willow, and cottonwood trees. On this bright, August morning, it was also lined with Indian warriors, waiting in the shade of the timber for Bob Emery's coach.

But Emery's coach didn't take the cutoff road this morning. He may not have known this section of the trail very well, but John Gilbert did. For seven months, Gilbert had driven the coaches over the route—had, in fact, even driven the very horses that were pulling the coach this morning. He knew everything there was to know about the road. Along the cutoff road there was ample cover for an ambush. And, if attacked, the coach would have to climb a grade to escape no matter which direction it went. If an attack came as the stage crossed the stream at the foot of the ascent, there would not be room between the stream bank and the sharp climb to turn around without upsetting. If that figure seen on horseback atop the bluffs was an Indian scout, then the cutoff road could easily become a trap. It would be much safer to climb to the high road along the bluffs, even though it had not been much used for several years.

Bob Emery knew Gilbert's advice was good, and guided his team onto the ascent toward the bluffs. Steadily the horses pulled the coach over the neglected trail to a point just north of the little spring. Almost everyone saw the danger at the same time.

In the dappled shade of the trees along the lower turn of the spring branch sat the Indians—a heart-stopping sight if ever there was one. Gilbert later recalled, "They looked awful naked sitting there on their ponies, their lances glistening in the sun."[15] The warriors were so intent on watching the cutoff road that they remained oblivious to the coach on the shoulder of the bluff just 600 yards to the north.

Emery stopped his team. What to do now? If they continued, they were sure to be noticed sooner or later, and would probably have to race the Indians through The Narrows, beyond which they could expect no help. The route was deserted. Gilbert thought it wise to turn back. One of the passengers proposed that they take a vote. The decision was unanimously in favor of turning back toward Constable's freight trains which would surely be underway by this time.

Emery clucked to his team and began the wide, sweeping turn toward the river. As the leaders came full circle, he started them into

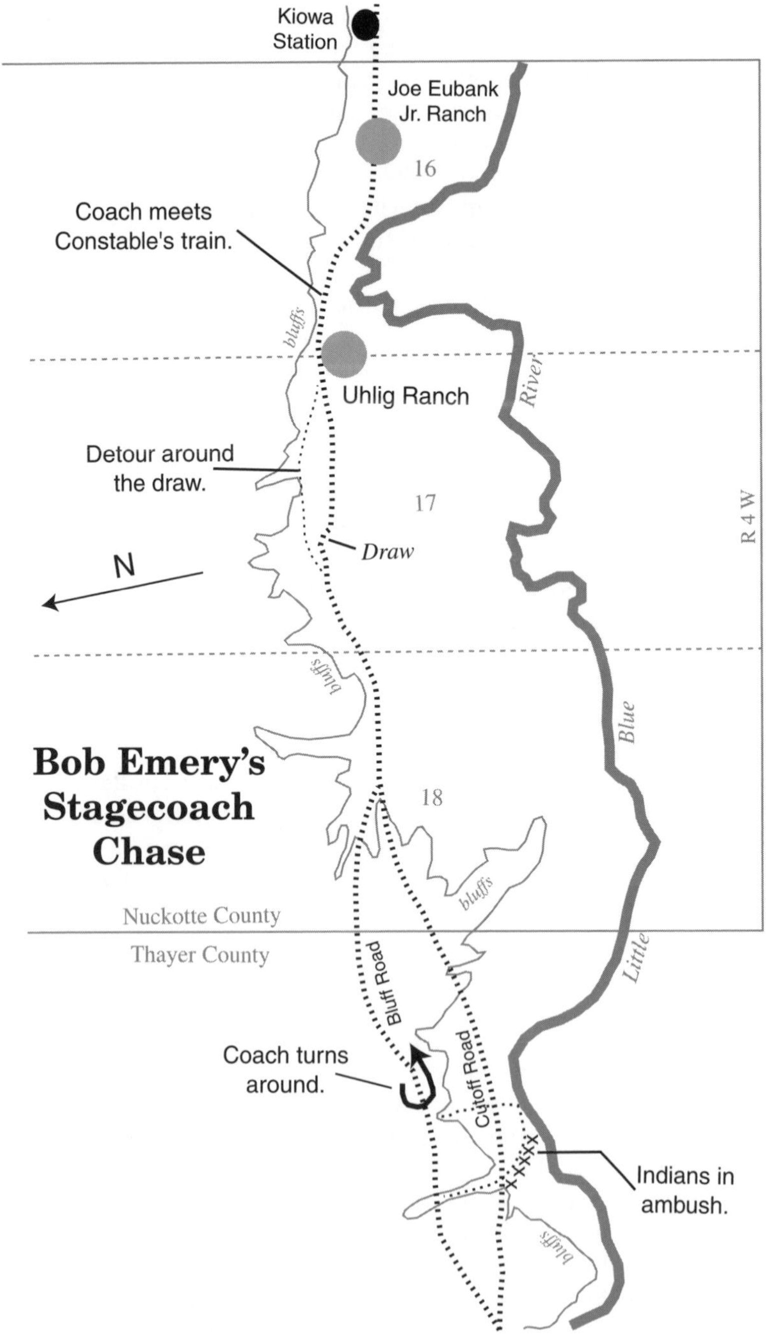
Kiowa Station
Joe Eubank Jr. Ranch
16
Coach meets Constable's train.
bluffs
Uhlig Ranch
River
Detour around the draw.
17
R 4 W
Draw
N
bluffs
Blue
Bob Emery's Stagecoach Chase
18
bluffs
Nuckotte County
Thayer County
Little
Bluff Road
Cutoff Road
Coach turns around.
Indians in ambush.
bluffs

a trot, and the rattle of the coach caught the attention of the mounted warriors at last. With unearthly yells, they exploded out of the timber and galloped eastward along the cutoff road, intent on intercepting the coach at the junction. John Gilbert's fears had been well founded. Had Emery taken the cutoff road this morning, the number of victims of the raids would probably have been increased by ten.

Though their lives were certainly in peril, the people on the stage had several factors in their favor. They were well armed, of course. The horses were some of Holladay's best, and they were rested and eager to run. Best of all, they would be running downhill, dropping more than thirty feet within the first mile and a half, while the Indian ponies would be forced to climb thirty feet out of the river bottomland within the first half mile of the chase. Also, due to their relative positions, the Indians would have slightly farther to travel to reach the junction. Nevertheless, they made it uncomfortably close. After a run of a mile and a quarter, the careening coach thundered back onto the main road, a good fifty yards ahead of the leading warriors.

The chase that followed was the classic race-for-life later to be immortalized in so many Hollywood western movies. Everything depended on the horses maintaining their stride while running flat out. Emery showed no excitement during the race, calling out to the magnificent animals, driving with a cool, steady hand. There was no whipping or yelling or histrionics. None were necessary. The three men inside the coach leaned out the windows and blazed away with their pistols, while from the top came the deeper bark of the four rifles. Of course nobody could hit anything from their swaying, bouncing perch, but the gunfire forced those few Indians who could keep up to maintain a respectful distance. The people on the coach noted that, in addition to bows and arrows, some of the warriors carried pistols and lances, but they never came close enough to do any damage with either.

At one point in the chase, the trail dropped into a shallow draw, made a right turn toward the river, and then swung back toward the east. Normally those turns posed no hazard, even to a coach being pulled at a brisk trot. But to take them at full speed would be certain to overturn the fleeing stage. And, if Emery were to slow his team to a safe speed, the flanks of the turning horses would be exposed to the bullets and arrows of the pursuers. Once again, John Gilbert had the solution.

During wet years, the bottom of the draw was naturally soggy, and much of the travel curved northward along an old track which crossed a series of draws near their heads where they were shallow. This track, like the bluff road, had not been used for a long time. Now

Gilbert shouted to Emery, pointing out the alternate route, and the driver guided his streaking team slightly toward the left. Up and down rolled the coach, over the heads of the shallow draws, and now they were nearly home free.

Little more than a quarter mile ahead lay the abandoned Uhlig homestead and, on the trail, the lead wagons of Constable's bull train came into view. Behind them the line of canvas-topped freight wagons was winding its way up from the river bottom to the bench land. None of the freighters had expected Emery's coach to come flying back down the trail, but the shooting had been heard, and the bull train had stopped squarely in the middle of the road. There was no time to prepare a defense. The drovers could only scramble for their weapons and stand by their wagons, watching in amazement as the coach came bucketing toward them under a boiling cloud of dust.

As the stage drew to within about 400 yards of the lead wagon, the Indians called it quits and trailed off south into the timber along the Little Blue. Bob Emery slowed the team to a walk and braked to a stop facing the lead oxen of the train. George Constable came riding up to the head of his outfit as, inside the coach, five very relieved passengers sank back into their seats and struggled to contain their nervous excitement. It had been a wonderful race—something over two and three-quarters miles in seven or eight minutes—but the Indians probably enjoyed it a lot more than had the white people.

As the horses regained their wind, the bullwhackers kept a wary eye on the Indians milling about in the timber. John Gilbert had gotten used to bossing the movements of the coach, and now he decided on his own that Emery should return to Kiowa Station. In a loud voice, he ordered the leading bullwhackers to crowd their animals over to one side of the road so the coach could get past. Constable shouted back at Gilbert that he, George Constable, was running this train, and the two fell into a heated argument. Inside the coach, the two ladies began to understand that Gilbert intended to leave the protection of the train and return to Kiowa, and they settled the matter promptly with some vehemence. The coach would stay with the freighters, they decreed, and John Gilbert realized that, with the crisis past, he was no longer boss.

Once again the oxen swayed ponderously into motion. Once again Bob Emery swung the coach around to join the freighters, traversing for the third time that morning the trail between Uhlig's Ranch and the bluffs.

After passing the ruins of Oak Grove, the train approached the area of The Narrows where the bodies of the Eubank family still lay in the open some forty hours after they had been killed. Gilbert noticed that someone had taken up the remains of James and old Joseph and had laid them in front of their burned out home. The sight and smell must have been nauseous, and the people on the coach felt their sense of decency so offended that they begged Constable to stop the train long enough to bury the Eubanks. But the wagonmaster wanted nothing so much as to get his outfits safely up onto Nine Mile Ridge before lunch, and he emphatically refused. The wagons rolled on, leaving the flycovered bodies of the Eubanks where they lay.

After squeezing through The Narrows, the combined ox and mule trains passed the remains of the Roper-Kelley Ranch to climb out of the valley. There, close by the wreckage of Little Blue Station, the trains corralled, and Emery halted the coach. Constable's mules were unharnessed within the circle and fed, while dinner was prepared for the men. The work cattle were unyoked and led down across the river where there was better pasturage.

It was a bad decision and the Indians made the most of it. Swooping down the river bottom, they stampeded the oxen back down the valley, leaving the wagons stranded with their heavy cargoes. George Constable was seething in impotent fury. It was now very clear that the Indians were still in the valley in considerable force. True to their goal, they were rolling back the years to the time when the valley had been peopled only by the red man, completely free of the white man and all his works—and they meant to keep it that way, at least for a while.

The night had passed uneventfully at fortified Pawnee Ranch. Well, almost uneventfully. One of the guards had heard a crackling noise in the brush and had fired off a shot in that direction. But no attack came, and after awhile the men lowered their guns and the women put down their pitchforks and axes, and the defenders of Pawnee lay back down on the floor for a fitful sleep.

At last the morning sun rose, brilliantly illuminating the surrounding landscape. Not an Indian was to be seen. The mood at breakfast was cautiously positive. Perhaps a scouting party should ride out to see if the danger was really past. After the morning meal was finished, the Wells brothers and several others mounted their horses and set out to reconnoiter the countryside. The party had gone barely a mile when Richard Wells' horse became unmanageable, reared up, and fell over backwards. As Richard hit the ground, his gun discharged, severely wounding his leg. Jim Bainter pulled a silk handkerchief through the bullet hole and poured cold water on the wound. The scouting party returned to the ranch in a dejected mood.

The defenders of Pawnee were momentarily cheered by the arrival of the coach from Atchison. Refreshed by his short night of rest, Joe Roper emerged with more details about the burning of Oak Grove and the murders of the Eubanks. Although Buffalo Ranch and Liberty Farm had not yet been damaged, the raids were indeed widespread and the valley between Kiowa and Pawnee was deserted, except for the mule train, which was still on its way. Meanwhile, the passengers had experienced a harrowing journey and the stage team was nearly used up. The coach would remain at Pawnee for a while.

There were by this time some sixty people gathered at Pawnee Ranch, but no Indians had been sighted. By mid afternoon, the long-delayed Dr. Hickman and his fellow passengers from Atchison were eager to leave. The team was brought up from the barn, the passengers loaded, and the coach which had remained at Pawnee overnight departed for the west. There were still plenty of men left to defend the ranch, but not all of them had guns.

The stage was not long down the road when the lookout at Pawnee saw the smoke—a thin, gauzy veil giving way to darker puffs and billows high above Liberty Farm. So, the Indians were not gone. They were only five miles away, and Charles Emery's home was going up in flames. A new sense of crisis seized the assembly and a messenger galloped after the coach to bring it back. Every man and every gun would be needed now. (The coach prudently decided to keep going.)

At four o'clock, the lookout reported activity down the trail toward Liberty Farm—men on horseback. They appeared to be riding in some sort of military rank and file formation, but they had halted on the trail too far away for the defenders of Pawnee to discern whether they were Indians or a column of militia. Surely there were militia units in the field by now. The people waited anxiously, but the distant horsemen remained halted in the road. Behind the log breastworks, the tension mounted. Was Pawnee Ranch saved or was it about to be attacked?

Arriving on the crowded coach with the Emerys and Mudges were six passengers from California. One of them, an intrepid young man by the name of Joe Markham, volunteered to ride down the trail to see if he could identify the mystery riders. Picking out one of the stage horses, "California Joe," as he had been nicknamed, rode south from the ranch on his risky mission. Charles Emery and several other men rode out behind him in support. Jim Bainter placed a ladder against one side of the cabin and climbed to the roof where he could signal the daring scout if danger suddenly developed.

Bainter watched intently as California Joe rode down the trail, saw some of the distant horsemen peeling off to flank him on either side, and began frantically signaling the young man to turn back. From a quarter mile away, Joe Markham saw Bainter's signals, saw the flanking movement, and turned his horse back in a run for the ranch. He delayed a few seconds too long, and some of the riders were already slightly ahead of him. Galloping at full speed, he snapped off some shots at them, wounding one. Just as the race appeared to be won, some of the pursuers fired back, and a bullet slammed into Joe's upper arm, shattering the bone. In intense pain, he reached the log breastwork and announced, as if there was any doubt, that the distant riders certainly were Indians. Some of the men helped him inside the cabin and laid him on a cot. Every few minutes, his arm, like Richard Wells' leg, was bathed with cold water from the well.

Now the battle was joined. The Indians enveloped the ranch, poking gingerly at its defenses with some long range arrows and bullets. But a frontal assault on a prepared position was not their style of warfare. The men behind the log ramparts were greatly excited, but they fired back coolly and effectively, conserving their ammunition as best they could.

Some of the warriors dismounted to creep closer to the defenses. One brave on a white pony (the whites thought that any Indian on a white horse must be a chief) circled round the ranch to put the barn between himself and the cabin. The defenders were watching, however, and a rifleman sprinted out to the barn. As the Indian approached to within very close range, the guard pulled the trigger—and the gun misfired. The Indian ran like the wind, while the man inside the barn broke into the loudest and most prolonged cursing the Reverend Wells had ever heard.

For more than an hour the battle continued in a desultory fashion, with Indians and white defenders exchanging scattered shots. Joe Roper had been nipping steadily from a bottle of whiskey to steady his nerves, and was by this time really too excited and inebriated to be of much use. At what seemed to be a lull in the action, Joe concluded to climb the ladder to the roof to survey the battlefield.

""I'm going up to see the posish (position)," he announced to Jim Bainter.[16]

"You'd better stay down here or you'll get a posish," Bainter warned, but Joe was on his way. Up he went, hand over hand. He had nearly reached the edge of the roof when the Indians loosed a volley, and an arrow grazed the side of his head, gently parting his hair. Joe let go all holds and dropped to the ground. Everyone thought he was dead and the Indians raised a great chorus of war cries. But Joe Roper picked himself up and soberly marched away to reflect on his narrow escape.

The assault was not going well for the Indians. Unless they could induce the whites to leave their fortifications, Pawnee Ranch was going to remain very much in business. It was time to play the old game of stampeding the cattle, but with a slight variation. The freighters' cattle were pastured with Metcalf's herd across the Little Blue, so the Indians began rounding them up and driving them back across the river toward the ranch. On the way, they shot some of the unfortunate beasts full of arrows, though not to kill. The cattle went wild, bawling and jumping around from the pain and the smell of blood. It was a diabolical strategy designed to draw the defenders out to save their cattle, but the men stayed put behind their log defenses.

During the mad confusion of the "cattle drive," someone noticed one of the warriors crawling up a swale leading to the corral. Jim Bainter took his rifle up into the second story room where he pried out some of the chinking between the logs of the outer wall. Sure enough. From his vantage point he could see the Indian slithering along the bottom of the swale, pausing now and then to raise up for a look. Bainter took steady aim through the space between the logs. The Indian crawled still closer, stopped, and raised his head and upper body for a peek. Bainter's shot hit him square in the breast, killing him instantly. Inside the cabin, Elizabeth Bainter called out gleefully to the people below, "Jim has killed one!" That crack shot marked the end of the Battle of Pawnee Ranch. Within thirty minutes the remainder of the cattle had been driven down river and the Indians were gone.

Everyone believed the Indians would try another assault, but for the present, the defenders of Pawnee could breathe a little easier. As their frenzied excitement wore down, the psychological effects of fear and tension began to work on the people, leaving them dazed and tired. It worked on Newton Metcalf's wife, too. She went into labor and gave birth to a healthy baby boy.

In the freighters' camp near Little Blue Station, the people spent the waning afternoon hours pondering their dilemma. No one wanted to go any farther. So far the Indians had been merely toying with them. There were surely enough Cheyennes and Sioux still in the valley to destroy the train, if they were of a mind to do so. All there was left to do now was to sacrifice the ox train to the Indians and get everybody back to Big Sandy alive. After nightfall most of the Indians would probably withdraw to their camps, and the mules would be rested enough to pull the Niles and Varney wagons back through The Narrows and eastward to safety—but not with the heavy barrels of liquor aboard. The wagons must be made as light as possible.

Everyone went to work removing the liquor barrels and lining them up on the ground.

At last darkness came to the valley, and the men hitched up the mules. The bullwhackers, with nothing to whack anymore, climbed into the empty wagons. Then stagecoach and freight wagons dashed back down off Nine Mile Ridge, through The Narrows, and eastward to Big Sandy.

John Gilbert and James Douglas both realized at last that Kiowa Station was indefensible, in view of the great number of Indians still roaming the valley. When the mule trains reached Kiowa, they loaded aboard a few personal effects, rounded up the stage animals, and drove them eastward to Big Sandy. Mile after mile, the white man was abandoning the Oregon-California Trail to the Cheyennes and their allies.

The refugees aboard Wilder's ox train arrived at Big Sandy, thirty miles from Oak Grove, worn out and desperately hungry. They had eaten nothing since the previous noon. The word went out among the neighboring ranches, and soon homesteaders began to arrive bringing food and drink to their unfortunate neighbors. They stayed to listen to the bloodcurdling tales of the Sunday raids, to see the arrows that Paulina Roper had brought from Oak Grove. With every retelling, the number of Cheyennes multiplied, their treachery became more odious, the flames over the Eubank ranch more lurid. There seemed little doubt that the Indians intended to sweep all the whites from the Little Blue Valley. Perhaps within a matter of hours they would make their appearance in the hills around Big Sandy.

The refugee train would lay over a day as people and animals regained their strength. But the alarm spread, and the ranchers around Big Sandy returned to their homesteads to gather up their children and spend a sleepless night shut up in their cabins before they, too, took flight from the wrath of the Cheyennes and their cohorts.

Laura Roper was now in great pain, her face badly swollen from the kick of the stumbling pony. Still the Cheyennes rode westward with their captives. At last they stopped in the early afternoon and spread buffalo robes in the grass for a rest. They painted Laura's face with a red concoction and allowed her to sleep for a while. One of the warriors killed a wild turkey which the women roasted and fed to the white captives. Thus refreshed, the party prepared to move again in the early evening.

One of the Cheyennes picked up little Isabelle to place her on a pony, but the little girl wanted to go to her mother instead, and began to kick and scream with all her might. Having little patience with this behavior, the warrior drew his knife and grabbed her by the hair.

Laura was horrified and raced over to clutch the Indian's arm, imploring him not to hurt the child. All the Cheyennes began laughing, the knife disappeared, and Isabelle was safe for the moment.[17] Soon captives and captors were on their way, resuming their plodding march under the stars.

Wednesday, August 10

The coach carrying Dr. Hickman and his fellow passengers reached Fort Kearny at one o'clock in the morning. Possibly no other group of travelers in the history of American transportation has endured a more harrowing journey. Since leaving Atchison the previous Saturday, they had ridden 253 miles, narrowly missing the attacks at Kiowa, Oak Grove, and Pawnee Ranch. They had seen seventeen mangled bodies and had buried one of them. From the time they departed Pawnee until they reached Hook's Junction Ranch on the Platte, they had been the only living white people on the trail, and their lives had been in danger every mile of the way. Even at Hook's the Indians had made a raid on Monday, driving off some horses and killing three men who had foolishly given chase.[18]

There were at Hook's a number of refugees who had already brought word of the disaster which had befallen the Horace Smith train at Indian Hollow. But the passengers of the westbound coach brought the first news of the murderous rampage which had taken place south of Lone Tree. And the news they heard at Hook's was equally grim.

The day before, in plain sight of a military detachment at Plum Creek, the Indians had wiped out a train of wagons and killed thirteen men. They also attacked every road ranch between Fort Kearny and Cottonwood Springs and had killed a number of the ranchers, nobody knew how many for sure. As they pooled their information from east and west, the people at Hook's must have been chilled to realize that they were the first to know the true immensity of this Indian war. The overland route was besieged from Kiowa Station to Denver City, a distance of some 400 miles, and there was no safety anywhere.

Shortly before midnight the coach had pulled away from Junction Ranch for the ten-mile run to Fort Kearny, where at last the sufferings of the people of the Little Blue Valley were put on the telegraph wires and flashed to the nation. Throughout the day, the weary passengers recounted their experiences for the military authorities, including Lieutenant Charles Porter, who assembled a garbled dispatch which he forwarded by coach to Omaha.

The night had passed quietly at Pawnee Ranch. The people awoke with the dawn and their eyes searched the surrounding landscape for some sign of the Indians, but there was none. The valley was still and peaceful. Perhaps the time had come to leave their improvised fortress. Joe Markham's wounded arm had grown much worse overnight, and it was now feared that his life was in danger. The defenders agreed that the remaining coach should take him, as well as Mrs. Metcalf, her baby, and several other women to Fort Kearny.[19] Of course there would be no fresh teams available until they reached Hook's, but if driven carefully, the horses should have no trouble completing the run to the Platte. With a rested team in harness and passengers aboard, the stage took the trail to Fort Kearny and safety.

The remaining people began making preparations to leave. There was not enough food at Pawnee for them to stay any longer. Men brought horses and mules from the corral and stable and hitched them to farm and freight wagons. No one doubted that Pawnee Ranch would be burned as soon as its defenders had gone, and the people worked to save some of Metcalf's household goods. Now that the time of departure was at hand, everyone was in a mad scramble. Men who had coolly exchanged fire with the Indians during the heat of battle now gave way to intense excitement, getting in each other's way and working at cross purposes. Reverend Wells was trying to get his wounded brother into their wagon but he was unable to slow anyone down long enough to help him. It promised to be a bumpy trip, the wagons being springless. Some of the men forked some hay into the wagon beds for the people to sit on, but it would prove to be not nearly enough.

James Bainter, ever afterwards known as "the old Indian fighter," (he was only about thirty-four) was elected wagon boss, and the train stretched out for its run to safety. Richard Wells was in agony from the jarring ride, and his brother drove slowly, stopping every few minutes to bathe the swollen, fevered leg. Bainter's wagon train was in no mood to wait, and the Wells brothers soon fell far behind, left to themselves on the empty trail. The reverend tried not to be bitter, but he was mightily disappointed in his fellow man.

The train passed the blackened ruins of Spring Ranch, and everybody felt sympathy for their wagon boss, whose family had lost everything they owned. Onward they drove, most of the time at a fast trot, fearfully watching the swales and hollows for signs of Indians. The wagons rolled past the abandoned Lone Tree Station and down through Indian Hollow without incident. They had come eleven miles, and everyone was hungry. Bainter called a halt near one of the unburned Smith wagons, and several men climbed up to examine its contents. To the great joy of everyone, they found a supply of smoked hams which the people sliced and ate between chunks of bread brought along from Pawnee. Their hunger appeased and their animals slightly rested, the people drove on to the first crossing of Thirty-two Mile Creek. There was danger at the ford. The sunken creek bed in its narrow, twisting defile fringed with woods was an ideal place for Indians to lie in ambush. But the wagons made the crossing hurriedly and without incident.

Another four miles brought the refugees to the second crossing and the abandoned Thirty-two Mile Station. By this time the salty ham had made everyone terribly thirsty but Bainter was in such a hurry to cross that he refused to stop for water. At the third and last crossing, the little children were crying piteously for a drink, but the wagons rolled onward to the wreckage of Summit Station at the peak of the divide between the Little Blue and the Platte. People and animals were suffering severely by this time. For the rest of his life, young Willie Mudge would remember the monotonous clucking rumble of the wagons, the atmosphere of fear and tension, the heat and sun and raging thirst. And he would vividly recall the "awful feeling" of traveling a deserted trail through "a weird and forsaken land."

It was after dark when James Bainter's refugee train rattled down from the bluffs and into the Platte Valley. Everyone stared at the spectacle before them. On all sides of Junction Ranch, the trail side and riverbanks were a vast field of twinkling campfires marking the temporary dwelling places of people whose lives had been turned upside down by the Indian raids. Fort Kearny was still another ten miles to the west, but nobody in Bainter's train had any desire to ride another foot. The Mudge family and the Bainters, the Emerys, Metcalfs, and their neighbors could stop running now, look after their young, and prepare for the night. The desperate fear which had driven them for the past several days began to melt away, leaving tiredness and fatigue in its place.

The day began badly for General Curtis at Fort Leavenworth. The first three dispatches of the morning had been unaccountably delayed for some thirty-six hours, and now they brought the first word that the Overland Road from Fort Kearny to Denver City was in bloody chaos. Two of the telegrams were from General Mitchell at Julesburg. His tone of desperation was unmistakable:

The Indians are infesting my lines for 500 miles. Have just learned a train was burned at Plum Creek this morning between Cottonwood and Kearny. I must have at least 800 horses or abandon this line of communication, and if possible, I want the First Nebraska veterans (cavalry) *ordered in the field, now at home on furlough. Can I depend on horses? Please reply immediately . . . Since my dispatch to Maj. S.S. Curtis (Adjutant) this morning there have been two additional attacks on this route. One at Dogtown, east of Kearny ten miles . . . Half the troops in this district on foot.*[20]

There was also a petulant message from Governor Evans:

Of course you have news of outrages near Plum Creek. We are in a desperate condition on account of our communications being cut off by Indians.[21]

From Nebraska Territorial Governor Alvin Saunders came a calmer dispatch, repeating news of the Plum Creek attack and urging rapid action. Colonel Robert Livingston had offered the services of his First Nebraska Cavalry veterans, said the governor, except they weren't really cavalry right now because they had no horses. Would Curtis authorize his quartermaster to purchase sufficient mounts for two companies?

To General Curtis, the developing situation was beginning to resemble the recent Indian troubles along the Arkansas, except the troops there had horses. Why, the federal government probably had 6,000 horses standing around its huge Giesboro depot outside Washington, and there weren't any hostile Indians back there. With the pleas of Mitchell and Evans ringing through his mind, the general set out to convince his superiors that he needed money for horses.

More telegrams came to the general's desk, and the day which had started out so badly now caved in completely. There was shocking news from Agent Gillespie of the Overland Stage Lines in Atchison:

One coach arrived from west. No mail or passengers through. Indians have murdered all families on Little Blue. One entire family, eight in number. Fifteen are known to be killed. All families are moving in for safety.[22]

Curtis wired back immediately:

When were Indians last seen? How far from Kearny or Atchison? What militia could be called out nearest to the scene of slaughter?[23]

Gillespie shot back:

One hundred and eighty miles from Atchison; seventy this side of Kearny. Two men killed ten miles this side Kearny and train burned thirty-five above yesterday.[24]

Curtis launched into a flurry of activity. He wired a request to Kansas Governor Carney for militia. He wired Colonel Summers at Fort Kearny to pursue the Little Blue raiders "if your force is sufficient." Another message went to General Mitchell, now at Laramie, instructing him to order troops from Fort Kearny to march south to the Little Blue. And finally, to Chief of Staff Halleck in Washington, went an admission that the situation in the Department of Kansas was far from being under control:

Indians have attacked and killed inhabitants on Little Blue this side of Fort Kearny on the Overland Stage route. Stage just arrived at Atchison without passengers. Cannot some of General Sully's command move down to Nebraska?"[25]

Curtis was grasping at straws. Even if Sully could spare some of his troops (which he could not), they could not possibly arrive on the Platte for many days. The fortunes of war had turned quickly, and General Curtis was running out of answers.

Not so Governor Evans. He spent a busy day firing off I-told-you-so telegrams to Secretary of War Stanton and Indian Commissioner Dole, trumpeting his estimate that it would now require 10,000 troops to crush the hostile Indians, and demanding authority to raise a 100-day regiment of volunteers as the first installment of that force.[26]

Laura Roper and the Eubanks rode most of the day with their captors across the arid High Plains. It was mid afternoon when the Indians became excited and began to speed up the pace. They were approaching the main village now, and they expected a warm welcome.

It was warm indeed. Upon their arrival in the immense camp, Laura was pulled off her pony and turned over to the squaws for a good beating. After a few minutes of this unpleasantness, she was rescued by an Indian woman named Yellow Squaw and led away to a tepee where the Indians allowed her to sleep. The squaws had done her no real damage, other than unbraiding her long hair. Except for being fatigued from riding and terribly hungry, Laura concluded that she had not been badly treated. As she lay down on her buffalo robe bed, she made up her mind to be as pleasant with the Indians as possible. They seemed to respond to that, and it would make her captivity easier to bear.

Thursday, August 11

Once again the ox train carrying the refugees from Oak Grove took the trail for Marysville, joined by a flock of homesteaders from Big Sandy, fleeing from the painted hordes of Cheyennes whom they feared were sweeping down the Little Blue Valley. Within a mile or two of Patterson's Ranch were sixteen homesteads, almost all of which were left abandoned. The Biktolds, Farrells, Jenkins, Slaughters, Weisels, Blairs, Shumways, Powells, and Helveys all sent their women and children ahead with the family treasures, while the older boys and men followed behind driving the stock. As the flood of humanity rumbled southward, settlers along the route added their families to its wash, leaving in their wake the abandoned crops and deserted cabins of a people driven by unreasoning terror.

About seven miles from Patterson's was Shumway's Ranch at the crossing of Little Sandy Creek, and nearby was the junction of the Nebraska City-Beatrice Road. Some of the refugees probably left the ox train here, traveling in private wagons eastward to Beatrice. John Palmer and Hattie Eubank followed this road to their father's homestead southeast of Beatrice, while the Uhligs planned to drive through to their former home at Brownville, where they could share their grief with daughter Ida and her husband. Tobias Castor had probably come this way already the day before, transporting his badly wounded brother-in-law back to the Hunt homestead on the Big Blue.[27]

John Gilbert had remained with several other men back at Big Sandy. It was the fourth day after the raids had begun, and there would surely be militia units coming up the trail from the river towns. There had been no news from the upper valley, and of course, no news from Libby Artist. George Constable had also remained at Big Sandy, still in a fury over the wrecking of his freight trains. For both men, this Indian war had become very personal.

It was indeed the fourth day after the deadly raids of Sunday, and the U.S. Army had so far done nothing except to fire telegrams back and forth. Help was on the way, however; for it was on this Thursday morning that a group of men assembled in Beatrice to go over the divide and up the Little Blue Valley. They knew that a few hardy souls had remained at Big Sandy. Perhaps they could all go up the road together to rescue stranded homesteaders and gather fresh information. They would fight Indians, if necessary, but no one was really planning for a battle.

The party which left Beatrice included many pioneer settlers of Gage County. Hugh Dobbs, Horace Wickham, several of the Wells family, several of the Pethouds, and Daniel Freeman all went. Sheriff Joe Clyne was along and, since Beatrice had no jail as yet, he brought along his only prisoner.[28] Altogether there were about thirty men who arrived at Jenkins' Ranch on the Big Sandy. There they found Gilbert and Constable, along with Albert Howe and Dave Kneeland. Together they talked things over and decided to form an ad-hoc militia company. In true democratic fashion, they held an election of officers. A loud talker named Stoner beat out John Gilbert for captain by two votes, so Gilbert became lieutenant. Their organization complete, the company of thirty-four made plans to leave Jenkins' Ranch the following morning.

The first official responses to the Indian raid came Thursday. In his office atop Omaha's Capitol Hill, Governor Alvin Saunders issued orders for the activation of twelve militia companies to augment and cooperate with federal volunteer troops. Borrowing an idea from the Massachusetts Provincial Assembly of 1774, the governor called for the formation of groups of "minute men" within each company—that is,

> *men who can and will, if necessary, move at a moment's warning to the scene of these depredations, and assist in punishing these murderers and robbers, and driving them from our country.*[29]

In his capitol in Denver City, Governor Evans also issued a proclamation. Forty-five days had passed since he had issued his "circular" to the plains tribes, warning friendly Indians to dissociate themselves from their warlike brethren and congregate around Forts Lyon and Larned. As far as Evans could see, very few had responded to his warning. If the government would not authorize him to form a 100-day regiment, he would do an end run and obtain his volunteers another way. Governor Evans was tired of waiting for Washington to respond to the emergency on the Colorado frontier.

Stripped to its essentials, the proclamation which he issued on this day was a license for citizens of Colorado Territory to hunt and kill Indians and appropriate their possessions. Of course the proclamation intended that only hostile Indians should be killed, so the hunters should stay away from Lyon and Larned. But it included no sanctions against whites who killed peaceable Indians, nor did the proclamation suggest methods by which citizens might discern peaceable Indians from hostiles. Those citizens who recovered property stolen by the Indians would be rewarded in an equitable fashion. Of course, forty-five days was not quite enough time for the separating out process to be completed, regardless of the Indians' intentions. And, knowing the feelings of the gentle folk of Colorado Territory toward Indians, it was inevitable that mistakes would be made. Evans' proclamation removed the restraints now, and the citizens of Colorado Territory were to be unleashed to embark upon a de facto war of extermination coupled with a macabre souvenir hunt.

Surprisingly, Governor Evans received, on this very same day, authorization from the War Department for the recruitment of a regiment of 100-day volunteers under the militia laws, the men to be paid as regulars and reimbursed for the subsistence and use of their personal mounts. The governor also received a wire from General Curtis at Fort Leavenworth. The general was coming to Omaha to take the field in person against the Cheyennes and Sioux. Curtis also notified Agent Gillespie at Atchison that Captain S.P. Thompson and a company of sixteenth Kansas Calvary with one mountain howitzer had left Leavenworth for the Little Blue Valley.

It was like closing the barn door after the horses were gone; and the horses were gone—literally. That very day, with schedules in shambles, passengers nonexistent, and stations abandoned, Superintendent George Otis gave the order to shut down operations of the Overland Stage Line. By August 15, all stock was to be removed from the route and the coaches returned to their terminals.

The army was having horse problems of its own. In the afternoon, General Curtis wired Mitchell the authority to begin buying up horses wherever they could be found for a maximum $150 per animal. It seemed to be the only way to solve the shortage of cavalry mounts for, as Curtis complained in his telegram, "I get no action by Cavalry Bureau."[30] No one foresaw on that Thursday that the general's solution would be received with a most grudging compliance.

For days, Jacob Hunt and his wife, Susan, had been worrying about their son. Rumors of Indian depredations to the west were too persistent to be ignored, and even the friendly Otoes had been pestering the settlers, being unwilling to do their usual hunting along the Republican River. Mrs. Hunt wished her son had not gone off to work along the Little Blue. But he was, after all, just about eighteen, a nearly grown man who was very much like his father. She had worried, too, when Captain Hunt had gone off to fight in the Mexican War. George had been born during his father's absence—a splendid present for Jacob upon his return.

The Hunt's youngest daughter, Alicia, was playing a solitary childish game behind the family's cabin when a light wagon drove up to the front door. Jacob walked to the wagon, greeted the driver, and looked inside. Then he turned and called Alicia, grasping the little girl by the shoulders.

"Run in and quiet your mother," Jacob said. "George has been wounded."[31] He returned to the wagon, lifted out his son, and carried the feverish teenager into the cabin to lay in his own bed. Four days after the massacre on the Little Blue, George Hunt had come home from his own war.

The word spread quickly through the morning streets of Marysville: Governor Carney had ordered out the militia, and Colonel Edwin Manning had alerted the local company of the 17th Kansas Militia to be ready to march at noon. Riders had come in the previous evening with particulars of the massacre on the Little Blue and appeals for help. Throughout the morning, additional messengers arrived with news that the Indians were coming down the trail in huge numbers, burning the ranches and murdering all who fell within their grasp.

It took time to assemble the militia, and not until after dark did the fifty men of the Marysville Company sally forth to the aid of their neighbors in Nebraska Territory. Colonel Manning intended to travel all night at a walk to keep his horses fresh. The militia would reach Rock Creek Station early the next morning, one of the first military units to respond to the emergency.

Friday, August 12

In the morning, the Beatrice and Big Sandy citizen company left Jenkins' Ranch for its reconnaissance through the devastated valley of the Little Blue. Like the refugees from Pawnee Ranch, they found the country desolate, its population vanished. There was no sign that Indians were anywhere near. There were plenty of signs that they had been there, however. Hackney Ranch, until just recently owned by Fred Roper, had been burned to the ground and its charred timbers dumped into the well, clogging it so the whites might not draw water from it. The company marched cautiously on to find that Kiowa Station was also in ruins. It was well that Gilbert and Douglas had left when they did. The company made camp for the night on the bluffs north of Kiowa and prepared for the grisly tasks of the morrow.

The people of Beatrice felt vulnerable. Even with thirty men gone to Big Sandy, there were still a good many men remaining to defend the town. But the Big Sandy company included many of the leading citizens, including the sheriff; and Mr. J.B. Weston had gone to Nebraska City to bring back additional arms and ammunition. The emotional climate in Beatrice was unstable and primed for a burst of hysteria, needing only a spark to set it off.

The spark was supplied by "a half idiotic individual named King Fisher" and several confederates who, having nothing better to do with their time, set fire to the dry prairie and came racing into town with the dreaded cry: The Indians were coming![32] To people who were already scared, the rolling clouds of smoke looked very convincing. In no time at all, a regular stampede was under way—out of Beatrice to the Missouri in whatever had wheels.

Despite the panic, Beatrice was not depopulated. From an ever widening territory people continued to flock into the little town—men with families who saw nothing humorous about King Fisher's twisted joke. The mood of the people began to swing from unreasoning fear to anger. The stampedes to safety came to an end. In place of hysteria there was a grim determination to fight. Everyone was tired of retreating from shadows and gossip. If the savage hordes continued to roll eastward, sooner or later there would have to be a big fight. Beatrice might as well be the place.

Northeastern Kansas was rippling with intense excitement. The citizens of Marysville placed an armed guard at the crossing of the Big Blue River, and people from outlying homesteads began to move in around the town for mutual protection. Those who stayed on their farms lived in constant fear, and many spent the nights sleeping in the woods or on the surrounding prairie. The Shroyer brothers, only twelve and fourteen years old, carried a basket of rocks up the stairs to their bedroom in the loft of their cabin for the purpose of bashing the heads of any savages who might attack them in the night. Thomas Hynes and his wife loaded family and household goods into their wagon and left their home on a frantic drive to Marysville. Halfway there, they realized that they had forgotten one little boy in their haste, and drove all the way back to get him.

As the excitement spread eastward to Seneca, the tales of horror grew with every retelling. Sioux and Cheyennes were said to be murdering unarmed men and defenseless women and children. Women were being captured and forced to yield their persons to savage lusts (everyone knew what *that* meant). General Byron Sherry, a prominent Seneca attorney, called out all the militia companies from Washington, Marshall, Brown, and Nemaha Counties. Colonel Manning's company was already on the march, and other units were to assemble on the following morning. The Kansas militia would move first to secure the Oregon-California Trail and rescue any survivors of the raids. Then they would scour the country for the raiders, resolved to administer a punishment not soon to be forgotten.

Nearly sixty hours after the first news of the murders in the Little Blue Valley arrived with the westbound coach, the army at Fort Kearny began to move. On this morning, Colonel Samuel Summers ordered Captain Edward Murphy to take his Company A of the Seventh Iowa and any other troops he could scrape together and march southward to the Little Blue. Murphy's expedition was not necessarily to force a fight with the Indians (the odds being somewhere on the order of ten to one), but was more of a reconnaissance in force. And a small force it was. When Murphy swung eastward out of the post around noon, he had 125 men, only fifty of them mounted, and rations for ten days. Everything at Kearny that even looked like a horse had been pressed into service.

Somewhere along the line of march, Murphy's troops encountered James Bainter's wagons from Pawnee Ranch, now on the last leg of their journey to the fort. The officers stopped to talk with Bainter while the troops marching past the wagons raised a great cheer for the refugee people. Nine-year-old Willie Mudge looked with dismay at the soldiers hoofing it along on foot, and thought to himself that, without horses, they would not be likely to catch any mounted Indians.[33]

Apparently, Captain Murphy was thinking the same thing. He had the reputation of being a splendid officer, aggressive and fearless, one who kept his command well under control. When Company A was ordered to leave Dakota City and march to the reinforcement of Fort Kearny, the citizens of that town sent a letter of commendation in Murphy's behalf to the Omaha newspapers. But those personal qualities which make for strong leadership also have a way of nettling those who are in authority, and Captain Murphy had been in the regimental doghouse earlier that year, being under arrest at Fort Kearny for nearly two months. Now the aggressive captain was to prove once again that he could be a pragmatic cutter of red tape.

When his unit reached Hook's Junction Ranch, Murphy discovered that a number of horses belonging to the stage line were still in the corral, the Indians having failed to carry out their mission completely. Every man who was mounted made his force more effective, the captain reasoned, so he simply "borrowed" Ben Holladay's horses. Complaints about Murphy's impressment reached Fort Kearny later that afternoon, and an exasperated Colonel Summers sent a messenger after him, bearing an order for him to march his force back to the post the following morning, returning the borrowed animals to their corral at Junction Ranch.[34]

Murphy never received the order. As he later remembered it, some citizens at the fort, anxious for the latest word from the Little Blue, bribed the messenger to return without delivering the order, saying he had been forced back by hostile Indians. There is probably some truth to his explanation. Certainly, the people from Pawnee Ranch must have been very anxious for the troops to march down the valley, saving what little was left to save. At any rate, Murphy and his men continued on their way, climbing up out of the Platte Valley under the heat of a late afternoon sun.

Murphy now had at least 126 men. Joe Roper was not interested in going to the fort. Every mile up the trail took him one mile farther from his daughter. His chances of finding her, or at least finding out about her, were far greater with the troops than at the fort. So Joe bade goodbye to the people of Bainter's wagon train and tagged along with Murphy's command, gamely retracing his path back into the desolate valley.

At the headquarters of the District of Nebraska, Assistant Adjutant General John Pratt found himself very much the man in the middle. Like his boss, General Mitchell, the Boston-born Pratt was a lawyer of considerable ability and, while the general was in the field, Captain Pratt had been left in Omaha to mind the store.

No sooner had his quartermaster received orders to begin purchasing horses, when someone remembered that cavalry horses also require equipment—saddles, bridles, picket pins and ropes and the like—and there was none of this to be had in the District of Nebraska. Captain Pratt wired Major Charlot, Assistant Adjutant General at Fort Leavenworth who, like Pratt, was running the department in the absence of General Curtis. Charlot doubted he could find anything like the 800 sets of horse equipments needed at Omaha. Colonel Robert Livingston, commander of the First Nebraska (horseless) Cavalry, then suggested that Pratt send a requisition downriver to General Curtis en route, requesting that the general endorse it and forward it to St. Louis, along with an explanation of the emergency. But Captain Pratt did not feel that he had the authority to make such a request. That was the prerogative of General Mitchell.

Other knotty problems were dumped on his desk. Governor Saunders asked the army to issue arms and ammunition to the militia companies which were being mustered for service. (Despite our modern idea of the frontier population as a ferocious, gun-toting people, nobody seems to have had any weapons when they were really needed.) Saunders also wanted the army to furnish transportation for weapons from the territorial armory to Columbus and Grand Island City. But in so doing, the army would be liable for any loss incurred, and Captain Pratt simply did not have the troops available to escort the arms along the Military Road. In addition, the militia companies gathering around Nebraska City had demanded that army rations be sent to sustain them in their campaign against the marauding Indians.

At last, the frustrated adjutant sent a wire to General Mitchell, who he thought might be at Cottonwood Springs, asking for some official guidance:

> *I will endeavor to push things along and do the best I can, but like as frequent and full direction from you as possible, so that I may work understandingly and carry out your views. General Curtis was at St. Joseph yesterday on his way here.*[35]

General Curtis was indeed on his way, but it was beginning to appear that he might not get a whole lot farther than St. Joseph. Figuring to make the journey to Omaha in the least possible time, the general had opted to go by river steamer, a trip normally made in about four days. But nothing was normal this summer. The severe drought had so lowered the level of the river that the general's steamer *Colorado* found itself bumping against mudbars, dodging all over the Missouri in a continuous search for the elusive navigation channel. It was an inauspicious beginning for the general's personal campaign against the raiders of the overland route. Even the Missouri River seemed to have taken sides with the Indians.

Saturday, August 13

After camping overnight on the bluff, the citizen company from Big Sandy continued its cautious march up the deserted trail. All the men remembered the road as it had been—long lines of freight wagons, riders on horseback, families working around their cabins, the clattering of Buckeye mowers—all the sights and sounds of industry and tranquility. But this morning there was only a haunting, empty stillness.

The men found the body of Bill Canada and buried it near the remains of his cabin. They examined the blackened embers of Oak Grove. The smokehouse also had been burned, and all that remained of the bodies of Kelley and Butler were their lower legs. For some reason, the charred bones were apparently left in the ashes.

Then they came to the Eubank place. Someone noticed oxen in the trees, still attached to the stalled wagon. They were very hungry and weak, but still alive after six days. The men removed the arrows from the wounded beasts and cared for them as best they could. Then they began the revolting task of burying the bodies of the Eubank family.

Some of the men began digging graves while others examined the remains. There was not a great deal left to examine. For six days the bodies had lain exposed to the sun and flies and heat. They had burst open and had been torn by scavengers. Hair had fallen out and the eyes were gone. The bodies of James and Dora and their elderly father were naked and blackened. It would be difficult to even move them.

When the work of digging was completed, John Gilbert and several others gathered up the remains and lowered them into the ground. One grave held the bodies of old Joseph, James, and Dora. Another grave was dug for eleven-year-old Henry (the "little boy," as Gilbert later referred to him) whose body was found in the ravine where he had crawled in his misery. Advancing up the trail, the men found the body of Will Eubank still lying on the sandbar in the river. They simply scooped out a hole in the sand, rolled in the remains, and piled the wet sand back on top.

These grisly tasks consumed a large part of the day, and it was late afternoon before the company went into camp near what was left of Little Blue Station. The buildings had not been burned, but all the windows and doors had been ripped away. Even a portion of the board floor had been torn up, and the grain sacks emptied to the four winds. The abandoned wagons from George Constable's ox train were still there, although many had been burned by the Indians and their cargoes of hardware and machinery were strewn about the ground. Some of the liquor barrels had been broken open and a fair amount was missing. But there was still an enormous quantity left, and after what they had seen that day, the men of the citizen company needed nothing so much as a few stiff drinks. Technically, the liquor was still the property of George Constable, but he was not of a mind to object. No one seemed to worry about danger from the Indians as the liquor flowed freely, dulling memories of the sights and sounds and smells of the day's ghastly work.

Captain Murphy's command broke camp early in the morning and moved on to the site of Summit Station. There they prepared their breakfast and examined the ruined buildings. One end of the house had been torn out. Windows and doors were ripped off and furniture was smashed to kindling. Apparently, the station people had been sitting down to breakfast when the warning came to leave. Ham and bread and coffee had been left on the table as the station was hurriedly abandoned.

Their morning meal finished, the troops continued their march toward the Little Blue, making a total of twenty-five miles for the day. Passing the graves of the six wagoners at Indian Hollow, they made evening camp near the abandoned Lone Tree Station. Exactly a week before, Frank Baker had laid over there for the night, and Erastus Comstock had been visiting his sons at Thirty-two Mile Station and all the Eubanks had still been alive. It had been a tumultuous week in Nebraska Territory and, although it was ended, the killing and destruction would go on yet a while longer. The issue had not yet been decided.

The men of the Seneca, Kansas, militia company gathered at 8 o'clock in the morning. The Reverend J.S. Griffing had been away from home until the previous day and he was quite weary from traveling, but he loyally reported for duty. The men had provisions enough for five or six days in the field, but privately, Reverend Griffing believed the whole expedition to be a waste of time. He doubted they would be gone for very long and he doubted they would even see an Indian. He did not even bother to take along a coat or blanket. Those men who had horses rode, and those who had none were taken in wagons. Thus organized, the men of the Seneca company ventured forth to battle.

They ventured exactly two miles when everyone was suddenly hungry. The command stopped on the spot to prepare dinner: bacon, fried dough, and coffee. Refreshed, the company pushed on another fifteen miles to camp for the night. All day there had been definite signs of a break in the weather—an end to the furnace-like heat, and possibly even some rain. After sunset the earth cooled rapidly, the wind began to turn, and Reverend Griffing began to wish that he had brought more clothing. Borrowing a blanket, he was soon fast asleep in the bed of one of the wagons.

Sunday, August 14

The last bodies had been returned to the earth. Now, as if a sorrowing Nature was determined to cleanse their blood from the trail, the skies grew heavy and a cold, drizzling rain commenced to fall on the parched, stained ground. Throughout the day, it pattered down on those stately, green sunflowers at Indian Hollow. It fell on the dried hay that Fred Eubank never got the chance to rake, and it compacted the loose dirt that the citizen company had mounded over the Eubanks' graves. The rain also soaked the men from Beatrice and Big Sandy, dissolving their purposeful sense of comradeship into a prickly irascibility.

After two days in the field, the company's *esprit de corps* was melting away in the drizzle. Of course the previous day's work and the liquor helped that along. But, though the men's martial spirits were flagging, other spirits were plentiful in their canteens as they went slogging up the gloomy trail. Over the tableland of Nine Mile Ridge they went, dropping back down into the valley, coming at last to Liberty Farm. Not quite everything had been burned. The large corncrib had been built of thick logs which had failed to catch fire, and as many men as possibly crowded under its roof.

A number of the men were tipsy, and all were highly uncomfortable. Nerves were taut and personalities grated against one another. At last, the irritations boiled over. Sheriff Joe Clyne had heard about all of Captain Stoner's bluster he could take, and the two fell to fighting. The other men separated them and no harm was done, except to Stoner's pride. His embarrassment was such that, from then on, he gave his orders only through John Gilbert. Soon the excitement died away and the company resumed its soggy march toward Pawnee Ranch.

Captain Murphy's troops had arrived at Pawnee that morning to wander around, gawking in amazement at the arrows and bullet holes in the stout log walls. It was plain that a desperate fight had taken place here, as Joe Roper must surely have told them. The soldiers straightened things up a bit, hauled in some hay for their animals, and set up camp in the house and stable.

Around three o'clock that afternoon, Murphy's guards detected a party of men approaching from the east. Suspecting that it might be a company of militia, the captain sent out a rider to display the company guidon. Through the gloom and drizzle, the men from Big Sandy recognized the swallowtail shape of the flag and came racing in to Pawnee in giddy joy. They had much to tell.

George Constable was practically wild by this time. He told Murphy of the destruction of his ox train at Little Blue Station, stressing the great financial loss incurred by its owners, of which he was one. He hoped that the troops might yet catch up with the Indians and recover some of his lost work cattle. Murphy told the men of his resolution to continue down the trail. He intended to find the Indians and punish them, recovering such stolen property and stock as was possible. Though the danger was great, he hoped the citizen company would go with him.

The combined companies spent the remainder of the day preparing arms and ammunition for the potential battle. Everyone was overjoyed when the boxes labeled "glass" in one of the abandoned freight wagons proved to contain a number of long-barreled .36 caliber pistols. With this addition to their firepower, the troops and citizen volunteers might give a decent account of themselves, at least in short range combat. For longer range work, Murphy had brought along a howitzer. They would all start south in the morning. George Constable was sure he knew just about where the Indian camp was located.

Just about everyone in eastern Kansas and Nebraska knew by now where the Indian camp was located. The Cheyennes and their allies were making no attempt at secrecy. Why should they? The warriors were numerous and united as never before, hunting at will over the grounds of their ancient enemies, the Otoes and Pawnees, and daring them to do anything about it. Their herds were swollen with captured horses and mules. The camps were filled with plunder, and many of the women were busy making shirts for the men from calico and silk yard goods brought back from raids on the Oregon-California Trail. It was just like the old days, only better.

The people in Marysville knew about where the Indians were, and they were happy to share their information with Captain S.P. Thompson, who arrived that afternoon out of Fort Leavenworth with seventy-five men of the Sixteenth Kansas Cavalry. The captain paused here to send an express back to General Blunt at Fort Riley, informing him that the Indians had moved to the Republican "with from 800-1,000 head of oxen and a large number of horses and mules." Captain Thompson planned to scout up the trail a ways before swinging around toward the Republican. He closed his dispatch to Blunt by saying

> *It is eight days since we have had any communication farther than fourteen miles above Little Blue. In that fourteen miles they have murdered sixteen men, women, and children, and burned all the ranches. The people were flying from their*

homes all over the country yesterday, as I came along, but I have steadied them down, and the men are all going out after the Indians.[36]

General Sherry and the Seneca militia knew about where the Indian camp was located. They passed through Marysville about nine o'clock that morning, a few hours ahead of Captain Thompson. Reverend Griffing marveled at finding "every house overflowing with men women and children, who had fled from their homes in the frontier counties and sought an asylum here."[37] Like Thompson, General Sherry planned to take his militia up the Oregon-California Trail a ways to make sure the route was clear of Indians, before striking south toward their camps which were said to be on the Republican near the mouth of White Rock Creek.

Among those people who were overflowing the houses of Marysville were the refugees from Oak Grove. Destitute and worn to a frazzle after their flight by ox train, they now found themselves dependent upon the hospitality of the good people of the town. With Kate, Francis, and little Marsh in tow, Paulina Roper sought out the Lemmon family and was welcomed into their home. The tiny boy reduced all the adults to teary-eyed pity. Poor little Marsh—his father horribly killed by arrows and the body left to the savages, his mother either dead or carried away to who knows what horrible fate. Nobody could find it in their hearts to restrain the little guy in any way, and the fourteen-month-old toddler made the most of his freedom, tearing about the house and running roughshod over the bewildered Lemmon boys. (The unfairness really rankled, and many years later, Ed Lemmon recalled how much Marsh upset the brothers: "O, how that kid's privileges cling to my memory."[38])

The Comstock family remained with the ox train until it reached Seneca. There it was that the wounded Ostrander brothers were taken from the wagons and left to local medical care. Theirs was a melancholy saga. They had come so far, with such high hopes, only to be struck down by a cruel twist of fate and some uncommonly bad luck. Before the week was out, both brothers were dead.[39]

There was no room in Marysville for the refugees from Big Sandy. Messengers informed them that the place was jammed and there was no feed available for the stock they were driving. Joel Helvey's boys decided to camp with their animals near G.H. Hollenberg's Ranch fifteen miles north of the town. Other ranchers camped nearby, grazing their stock and foraging for food in the gardens of local settlers. After a time, Captain Hollenberg rode out at the head of the local militia, warning the people to move in to Marysville. The Indians would surely get them if they stayed near his ranch.

But the Indian scare was wearing thin, and the Big Sandy people were beginning to suspect that they were running from a threat that had been badly overstated. They informed the captain they would stay right where they were and take their chances. Hollenberg went on up the trail with his company, worried more about the depredations of the refugees than those of the Indians. Within a few days, many of the people would drive their stock back to their homes along Big and Little Sandy Creeks. They would sleep out among the cattle at night, relying on the animals to give the alarm in case Indians approached. It would be worth the risk just to be home again. And as the fire of fear continued to cool and the refugees returned to their homesteads, they would discover the cost of their panic.

A few of the Indians ventured as far as Big Sandy where they burned Biktold's Ranch before pushing on to the Little Sandy, where Nelson's Ranch was put to the torch.[40] But most of the people would return to find their homes intact, though plundered, more by Captain Hollenberg's militia than by the Indians. They would also find their crops damaged, their gardens choked by weeds, poultry and livestock missing. The fever of fear would pass; but on August 14, it was doing just what the Indians wanted it to: The fear was clearing the whites out of the river valleys and driving them back down their Great Medicine Road.

If General Curtis didn't know where the Indians were, he would on the morrow when he received Henry Atkinson's dispatch. Even now, Atkinson, who was assistant provost marshal for the District of Nebraska, was interviewing Otto Uhlig. Like many other refugees from the raids of a week past, the sorrowing survivors of the Uhlig family longed to return to a familiar place, a place they had once called home, to share their grief with friends and kinfolk. After reaching Big Sandy, they left the ox train to stop briefly in Beatrice. From there they traveled over Saturday night, reaching Brownville late this Sunday afternoon. Now Otto Uhlig was giving Atkinson a remarkably clear and accurate account of the tragedies of the week just ended, and Atkinson was preparing a dispatch for General Curtis, who was expected to reach Brownville early the following morning:

> *A reliable citizen of this place has just arrived from Beatrice. He left there at 6:30 last evening. He says the Indians have committed no depredations except on the stage road on the Little Blue, and only in small parties on the road. Main force of the enemy, about 2000 strong, are*

on the Republican, southwest of Fort Kearny. Informant had a brother killed on Little Blue. Small parties first attack trains, and if repulsed return in greater force. A citizen company of fifty men, commanded by Captain Gilbert, are on the Little Blue. Several ranches have been burned. There are 200 families at Beatrice and about 200 men, but have few arms and little ammunition. People are a good deal excited and reports are exaggerated ... It is believed there are rebels leading the Indians as they talk good English.[41]

By this Sunday eve the militia response to the raids was well under way. Early in the morning, a company had left Nebraska City for the relief of Beatrice, where they found the citizens organizing a home guard and making preparations for an attack. A second unit of militia was organizing at Nebraska City, and other companies were marshaling at Falls City, Plattsmouth, Pawnee City, and Omaha.

The Seneca militia company pushed up the trail into Nebraska Territory where they encamped for the night. General Sherry planned to go another ten miles on the morrow. If no Indians were sighted, he would turn the command south toward the Republican. Exactly what he planned to do with his handful of men against more than 2,000 well armed Sioux, Cheyennes, and Arapaho warriors is hard to figure. Apparently the prospect did not bother his men as they bedded down for the last comfortable night they were to experience on the campaign.

Monday, August 15

Back down the trail went the citizen company, bolstered by the soldiers from Fort Kearny. The combined units stopped at Little Blue Station where Murphy could see once again the destruction wrought by the Indians. The citizen company took note of the liquor barrels, their mobile supply having been long since exhausted. Soon another drunken row was under way. This time, Sheriff Clyne and George Constable went after each other and several more men became involved. Captain Murphy, thoroughly disgusted, asked John Gilbert to help quiet the men.

There was really only one good way to quiet the men and that was to get rid of the liquor. Constable recognized the threat and asked Murphy to destroy it, but the officer was too cagey for that. He did not intend to give the owners of the train any excuse to file a claim for damages against the government. At last Constable agreed to dump the liquor himself. With several helpers, he went about smashing bottles and kegs, and thousands of dollars worth of alcohol ran across the sodden ground making a terrible stench.

Having disposed of this problem, Murphy detailed Captain Henry Kuhl, of the First Nebraska Veteran Cavalry (formed from the old Second Nebraska), to take a party south to bury the Eubanks. Gilbert and several of the more sober citizens went along, knowing that the work had already been done. At least they could show Kuhl where the graves were located. Once at the site, the captain never even dismounted, but rode across the river and poked around in the underbrush looking for more bodies. Finding nothing of importance, all returned to camp.

The dismal day dragged to a close. Murphy wanted to campaign one more day, he told the citizen volunteers, and he hoped they would go south with him on the morrow to find the Indian encampment. Several of the Beatrice men asked to leave the following morning and permission was granted. Not Joe Roper, though. Anything going south was going his way. Murphy recalled later that, by this time, Joe was nearly crazed with worry about his missing daughter.

The rains came again, and clouds blanketed the friendly moon. The night was as black as pitch, with no whiskey to warm the men's spirits or prop up their courage for the action which they all expected on the morrow.

The Seneca militiamen had seen no Indians along the trail, so they crossed the Little Blue and headed off to the southwest toward White Rock Creek and its confluence with the Republican. All day they jogged and rumbled across the prairie, covering some thirty miles. They halted to make camp, and soon the rains came down once more. At eleven o'clock that night it came Reverend Griffing's turn to stand watch, and he soon decided that this was the most miserable night of his life. Everyone in the company was soaked to the skin for lack of shelter, and already some of the men were very sick. This soldiering had long since ceased being glamorous.

It was contrary to General Blunt's aggressive nature to sit idly at Fort Riley. He was itching to get a crack at those Indians who had so bumfuzzled Mitchell up in Nebraska. But General Blunt didn't have enough soldiers available to mount much more than a short hike across the Flint Hills, so he consoled himself by sending dispatches to Captain Backus at Fort Larned and Lieutenant Ellsworth at the crossing of the Smoky Hill, warning them that Indians might be headed in their direction, driving large herds of captured animals with them. It proved fortunate for those officers that the Indians had other plans.

Unlike Blunt, General Curtis was on the move, if slowly. The low water in the Missouri slowed the *Colorado* to a crawl at times, but by evening on this Monday, he had reached Nebraska City. There he received word that Captain Palmer had left Fort Leavenworth with a company of sixty recruits. Well, they weren't exactly recruits. They had already been through several hard years of soldiering, albeit with the Confederate Army. Lately they had accompanied General Morgan across the Ohio River and had been captured. The Yankee government, in a moment of high inspiration, had given them a choice: They could continue their military careers on the western frontier or go to prison camp. Since the first option was much the better of the two, these "galvanized Yankees" were now on their way north to ease Curtis' manpower shortage. It appeared that the local militia units were also responding well. With these twin bits of good news, the general retired to his cabin for some rest. Tomorrow he would arrive in Omaha.

Tuesday, August 16

No sunshine greeted the men of Captain Murphy's command as they roused themselves from sleep and prepared to move south. The rain had ended but the atmosphere was very thick and dim and heavy, and a clammy fog enveloped the Little Blue country in gloom.

The combined companies marched down from Nine Mile Ridge and forded the river, continuing southward for about two miles. In the distance they observed a large number of moving objects on the south side of Elk Creek. Murphy stopped the command and asked John Gilbert to send two of his people in advance to identify the moving objects. Joe Clyne and George Constable rode forward a half mile and returned. It was much too foggy, they said, to tell what lay ahead. Not satisfied, Murphy ordered another reconnaissance. This time, four men rode out with orders from the captain not to return until they had positively identified whatever it was they had seen. Again the men went as far as Elk Creek, where Joe Clyne crossed and continued on alone. It was still impossible to tell whether those objects moving in the distance were Indians or buffalo.

Recognition came suddenly as the phantom figures moved swiftly in his direction. Soundlessly, like wraiths in the fog, they approached on both sides, attempting to surround Joe Clyne. The Sioux were out hunting buffalo this morning, and the chance to hunt a lone white man was too good to be true. Clyne suddenly noticed the Indians moving along on either side of him and wheeled his horse back toward Elk Creek. In his mad dash for life, the sheriff lost both his hat and his gun, but he and his comrades regained Murphy's position, their mission fulfilled.

Captain Murphy gave the order to advance across Elk Creek, but the sharp banks presented a problem for the three wagons and the howitzer. John Gilbert guided the command several miles west to the Fort Riley Road where there was a decent ford. Murphy had little faith in the military prowess of the citizen company, so he strung them out in a long skirmish line in front of his troopers. Then the men began to advance, driving the Sioux buffalo hunters ahead of them.

After pushing forward several miles, the skirmishers began to notice reinforcements streaming up to join the retreating warriors. The news had reached the camp on the Republican, and hundreds of Sioux and Cheyenne braves were coming to the aid of their kinsmen. The Indians fell back some ten miles. Then they stopped retreating.

The citizens' skirmish line had fallen apart during the advance, but Gilbert, Constable, and a teenage boy had remained together.[42] Now the three found themselves far out in front and virtually alone as the Indians began the old familiar flanking movement. The three had been firing constantly, but now Gilbert decided it was time to go. George Constable was not ready to retreat, not just yet. He was still boiling mad over the destruction of his train and, having found the Indians who supposedly were responsible, he stayed where he was to get in a few more shots—just a couple more . . .

Gilbert and the youngster galloped back north, down into a shallow draw and up the other side. Their horses were in a dead run back toward Murphy's troops when the boy shouted that they had lost Constable. Gilbert checked his mount and turned around. As he did so, he caught sight of a riderless horse dashing up and away from the draw. The boy begged Gilbert to return with him to pick up Constable. In spite of the danger, the two rode back to the edge of the draw in time to see two warriors race up the far side and away to the south. There was no need to go any farther. At the bottom of the draw lay the body of George Constable. Gilbert could plainly see the arrow buried in his side. The two turned their horses away to resume their flight, but now the race would be much closer.

The shriek and explosion of a howitzer shell and the sight of Murphy's troopers coming over the crest of a hill caused the pursuing warriors to pull away and regroup. The soldiers continued their advance down into the draw, where they loaded Constable's body into one of the wagons. But that was all the time there was. The Indians came swarming back to the attack like so many maddened hornets, hundreds of them now. Captain Murphy had seen enough and he didn't like the odds. Turning the command around, he began the retreat back to Elk Creek.

The firing was constant all the way. The howitzer was so much useless baggage, now. In an effort to get maximum range, the gun crew had elevated the muzzle too far, and its first (and last) shot had cracked the limber. During the ten-mile retreat back to Elk Creek, the citizen company pulled itself together and fought a harried rear guard action as the warriors nipped at the flanks and heels of the retiring whites. Behind them the fog boiled with shadowy figures as more and more Sioux and Cheyennes swarmed to the chase. A bullet knocked the heel from Joe Roper's boot and wounded his horse. Several other horses were wounded and one of Captain Kuhl's private soldiers was killed in the running fight which ended only after the companies had safely crossed Elk Creek once again.[43]

It was prematurely dark as the men dragged themselves back up the ridge to Little Blue Station to find a company of Kansas Militia camped there. Captain Murphy's troops prepared their supper and added up the results of the day's work. They were not impressive.

The citizen skirmish line had become badly disorganized and the men widely separated. The artillery piece was wrecked. One soldier was dead, and George Constable had become a victim of his own thirst for revenge. The two casualties were buried that night, close by the remains of the freight wagons which Constable had so foolishly pushed up the trail from Kiowa. In the final analysis, the Sioux and Cheyennes had driven the combined companies from the field, and everybody knew there was no more that could be done.

During the morning, General Curtis arrived in Omaha to find a dispatch waiting for him. General Mitchell was now at Fort Kearny, the wire informed him, after days of shoring up weak spots in the defenses along the trails. It had been like plugging holes in a sponge. Mitchell concluded:

> *My troops are just scattered enough to be cut up by detail. Captain Murphy, Seventh Iowa Cavalry, has been on the Blue since last Thursday with his company. Have heard nothing from him since he left Pawnee Ranch.*[44]

To Governor Saunders, Mitchell sent a blunt assessment of the situation:

> *If troops are not in the field this road will go back to the aborigines.*[45]

Mitchell also ordered Adjutant Pratt to urge the governor to call out all available militia companies, with the assurance that the federal government would arm and subsist them. Certainly the days were long past when General Curtis had been of the opinion that a good company or two with howitzers well attended would be enough to deal with the victorious plains tribes.

The sodden men of General Sherry's militia somehow got a fire started—a roaring, big fire. The men stood as close as they dared, toasting themselves and drying their steaming clothing. Even as they ate their breakfast, the weather showed signs of improving. Soon they were on the march once more over the broad prairies. Men and animals were understandably tired, since no one had slept very well in the pouring rain. General Sherry and his staff set a torrid pace and by afternoon, were long out of sight.

Night fell. The clouds thickened and the rain began again. The militiamen lost all sense of direction and were soon wandering about the prairie, hopelessly lost. The march ground to a halt as the men, bewildered and fatigued, sank down in the grass to sleep in spite of the rain.

About nine o'clock, the voice of General Sherry could be heard as he came splashing up with his staff. The general found a good camping place on Rose Creek, before noticing that his command was no longer with him. He turned back to look for them, searching over three hours in the rain and darkness. Now he would guide them to the campsite previously selected. Rose Creek was not far away. The weary, dispirited militiamen hitched up wagons and saddled horses, and soon the march was under way again. Would this miserable rain never end?

They marched an hour. Two hours. Then it was midnight and they were still marching. No one had the foggiest idea which direction Rose Creek was. General Sherry was lost. They were all lost—and cold and wet and sick and miserable. They could imagine the Sioux and Cheyennes, snug in their tepees, roasting sides of buffalo over crackling campfires. It was grossly unfair. Even the weather had swung to the side of the Indians.

Wednesday, August 17

Cavalry horses—We call special attention to the advertisement of Captain Moer, A. Q. M., for cavalry horses. He offers the very liberal price of $150.00 per horse. If he cannot purchase the horses, orders will be immediately issued to *press them into service. We would therefore advise all our friends to sell without further delay.*[46]

With this unsubtle threat, the *Nebraskian* lent its editorial weight to the war effort. While a few animals had been obtained, the horse purchase program was going far too slowly. Much to the frustration of the army, the citizens of Omaha and the surrounding territory seemed disinclined to part with their animals for the price of $150 which, at the time, was really not liberal at all.

The Kansas Militia wandered around, lost on the rainy, trackless prairie for most of the night. At last in the early morning hours, they stumbled upon Rose Creek and made their camp. Here they remained for the day, resting from their waterlogged ordeal. Without even having seen an Indian, the Kansas Militia was *hors de combat*.

The citizen company from Beatrice and Big Sandy was finished as well. Leaving Little Blue Station, hopefully for the last time, the men took their weary way eastward. At Jenkins' Ranch they broke up, some continuing down the trail to Marysville, most going on to Beatrice, all searching for families and loved ones scattered in the aftermath of the raids.

Joe Roper was whipped. If his daughter was still alive, she was in a place where it would be impossible to rescue her by force of arms. He had only one, small consolation: Neither Laura's body nor that of Lucinda Eubank had been discovered. Perhaps the Indians were holding them captive and would bargain for their release. With this faint hope, Joe Roper began the long ride to Marysville to find his family, to rest, and to decide how to begin all over again.

Captain Murphy marched his command back to Fort Kearny. He had told the citizen company that his rations were short; but, if he had taken ten days rations as ordered, he should have been able to stay in the field until at least August 20. The plain truth was that, given the severe disadvantages under which he worked, the officer had accomplished everything that was possible, and that was precious little. The Sioux, Cheyennes, and Arapahoes controlled the country from the Republican to the Platte, and there was nothing Murphy or anybody else could do about it right then.

This Wednesday afternoon, Lieutenant Thomas Flanagan, of the Sixteenth Kansas Cavalry, obtained his first look at the hysteria that was overspreading the territory. Early in the morning he marched from Plattsmouth with his thirty-five men and two fieldpieces, headed west for Fort Kearny. West of Saline Ford on the old Ox Bow Trail (several miles northeast of present Ceresco, Nebraska) the artillery detachment ran into a storm of people, all leaving their homes and possessions for fear of the Indians. Flanagan tried to reason with them, tried to convince them to return to their homes. There was not a hostile Indian within many miles, he argued. The trouble had all been far to the south and west. But terror was stronger than reason this summer. All afternoon and all the next day the people swept on past, rushing to the safety of the Missouri River towns. Flanagan's men continued on to Kearny, noting that, at many of the abandoned homesteads, passing emigrants and freighters had entered the houses and torn down fences to use for their campfires. It was somehow ironic that the Indians had set out to destroy the stations and ranches, and the white people were helping them do it.

Thursday, August 18

Sunrise found the men of the Kansas Militia feeling decidedly better for their day of rest. Breakfast made them feel even better, and soon they were in the saddle and in the wagons, headed for the Republican. They had not gone far when buffalo began to appear, first singly and in groups of three or four, then in large herds. The men had never seen so many of the shaggy beasts in one place, and the opportunity for a little sport was too good to pass up.

The order of march was abandoned. Some of the men circled round to drive a portion of the herd back toward their comrades, who blazed away without scoring a single kill. No one seems to have considered that the firing might attract Indians, and no one seems to have reasoned just why it was necessary to kill the animals in great numbers. They were simply there and it was all such wonderful excitement. Any lingering disenchantment over those rainy nights on the prairie faded away in the thrill of the hunt. So the herds thundered past and the guns blazed wildly and the hunters chased and hollered like madmen, and General Sherry's horse bolted with all his equipment never to be seen again.[47] The Kansas Militia had been completely undone by a herd of buffalo. Mercifully, no Indians appeared.

At last the company pulled itself together, and by mid afternoon established camp on the banks of the Republican. A superficial scout of the surrounding territory turned up no hostiles, and General Sherry concluded that there were no Indians on the Republican—at least not here. The men would stay in camp for the night and turn back north on the morrow. Perhaps they would have another chance to hunt buffalo.

John Barratt rode homeward through a deserted land. Nearly all the homesteads along the Big Blue were empty and silent, their people gone to Marysville or Beatrice. Since leaving the citizen company at Big Sandy, Barratt had had plenty of time to think. He was not exactly a stranger to war. As a member of the Second Nebraska Cavalry, he had been involved in several minor battles with the Indians and had been with Sully at White Stone Hill. But that proved to be scant preparation for what he had experienced these past twelve days. The burning of homes and freight wagons; the narrow escape at Oak Grove; the decaying bodies in the trail; the screaming of the Indians and the harrowing retreat under fire at Elk Creek—all were depressing experiences which clung like burrs to his memory. People of a later time would diagnose his melancholy as post traumatic stress syndrome. Barratt knew only that he was heartsick and anxious.

Before coming to Nebraska Territory, the young bachelor attached himself to the George Grant family, and they took him in as one of their own. Now as he approached their dugout home, he was cheered to see that they had not abandoned the place. It was late in the afternoon and supper was cooking.

After a round of fervent greetings and conversation, Barratt walked outside and climbed to the top of the dugout to be alone and out from underfoot for awhile. As he sat, off in a world of his own, there arose a low, rumbling sound, growing ever louder—a swelling avalanche of hoofbeats. Barratt looked up and froze: There were several hundred Indians seemingly headed straight for the dugout. His mind went blank, and he surrendered without moving a muscle, prepared for the inevitable shock of the arrows. He may have had a fleeting vision of Marshall Kelley.

But there were no arrows this time. The Indians were Otoes, on their way back to their reservation near Beatrice following an abortive hunt between the Little Blue and the Republican. Like Barratt, they, too, had been chased out of the country by the Sioux and Cheyennes. Without even pausing, the Indians swept past the dugout and disappeared in the distance. The badly shaken Barratt climbed slowly from his perch and walked on unsteady legs inside for supper.

The results of Captain Murphy's expedition to the Little Blue came to Omaha in the afternoon on the wire from Fort Kearny:

Major-General Curtis:

Captain Murphy has just returned from the Blue. Undertook to go from the Blue to the Republican. Got as far as Elk Creek. Met 500 well-armed Indians; had a fight; killed ten Indians and lost 2 soldiers. Was compelled to fall back after driving Indians ten miles. Indians followed him thirty miles on his retreat. Things look blue all around this morning.

Robert B. Mitchell[48]

But General Curtis was no longer in Omaha. Major Charlot had miraculously located 500 sets of horse equipments at Fort Leavenworth and shipped them upriver. The quartermaster had also been able to purchase some sixty additional horses, enabling the army to mount two companies of the First Nebraska veterans. With these troops the general had left Omaha in the morning, headed west for Fort Kearny. There he intended to organize another expedition against the treacherous Cheyennes and their allies. If he could scare them away from the Great Platte River Road as he had from the Santa Fe Trail, emigrant and commercial traffic would once again flow unmolested across the High Plains.

Friday, August 19

Following an uneventful march over the divide from the Republican River, the Seneca militiamen reached the Oregon-California Trail near Oak Grove. There they made camp and wandered around the abandoned ranch site, poking among the charred embers. Reverend Griffing searched for souvenir arrows, but there were none left. Some of the men went to examine the ruins of the little smokehouse and, to their horror, uncovered the blackened bones of Marshall Kelley and Jonathan Butler (which presumably they buried). Reverend Griffing also recorded that, in a small building some distance away, the men found a headless male body.

With their expedition at an end, the militia would return to Kansas the following day by way of Big Sandy. There they would hear eyewitness accounts of Captain Murphy's fight south of Elk Creek. From the descriptions of the battle, it would be easily reckoned that the Kansans had come within ten miles of a concentration of more than 5,000 hostile Indians. The militia was more fortunate than Murphy's troops: The Indians weren't hunting buffalo that day.

In a letter to his wife, Reverend Griffing wrote a definitive summary of the ill-conceived martial contributions of these pitiful companies which were the first to respond to the massacre on the Little Blue: "If they (the Indians) had given us fight we would probably have been cut to pieces, as we were all raw Militia with untrained horses and they must be strong or they would not be so bold. We had about consumed our rations and were glad enough to find our destination

homeward for reinforcements with whole scalps. We all thought it fortunate we did not find any Indians."[49]

Joe Roper arrived in Marysville, his life seemingly in shambles.[50] His horses were gone, pigs slaughtered, business ruined. His family's neat cabin was in ashes; his partner and almost son-in-law had died painfully; and his daughter was missing or dead. He had come within a whisker of being killed at Pawnee Ranch and again south of Elk Creek. As he arrived to hunt up his family, there was probably not a more grubby, disheartened man in all of Marysville.

The town was too crowded to be pleasant, though, and the Lemmon boys were heartily sick of little Clarence's depredations on their childhood territory. So the Ropers gathered themselves together and somehow found transportation back to Nebraska Territory. Daughter Clarisa was a schoolteacher in Nebraska City, and their only immediate source of respite.

As the Ropers passed through the reservation south of Beatrice, they showed the arrows Paulina had carried away from Oak Grove to the friendly Otoes, who merely grunted knowingly, "Ugh! Cheyenne." This was a welcome and important verdict. The Ropers, like most of the settlers, were acquainted with the salient provisions of the Indian Intercourse Act of 1834, designed to prevent treaty Indians and whites from exacting private revenge against each other to settle grievances. Under provisions of the act, whites who had been financially injured by members of tribes in amity with the United States could be indemnified by the government, which then withheld the amount of the claim from annuities issued to the offender's tribe. As things stood at the time, there was little danger of the people of the Little Blue Valley taking revenge on the Indians. George Constable had tried that and he was dead. The settlers' only hope of redress, then, was the Intercourse Act. But, in order to file a claim for damages, it was necessary to know which tribes were guilty of the depredations. The attackers at Oak Grove had readily admitted that they were Cheyennes, and now the Otoes had confirmed the fact. The participation of the Sioux and Arapahoes was less certain at this time.

By early September the Ropers had secured temporary lodging in Nebraska City. Then they went to work on their claim, drawing up affidavits to be notarized and listing their possessions lost in the raid. While the children played quietly nearby, Joseph and Paulina probed their memories of their former home on the Little Blue, calling out items as they came to mind. Clarisa sat at a table and wrote everything down. The 116 items on the completed list included a library of forty-two volumes, the cabin, smokehouse, and sets of carpenter and wagonmaker's tools. With the subjective addition of $1,000 for the loss of their road ranch business, the Ropers' claim totaled $5,158.30, and was filed with the Department of the Interior. Joe planned to go west again to search for Laura, and he may have been hoping that the government would act promptly to reimburse his losses. The family was, after all, impoverished.

But the government did not act promptly. The claim required corroborating testimony and proofs, statements from neighbors and character witnesses, etc. Little acquainted with the convolutions of government bureaucracy, Joe Roper remained in Nebraska City—desperate to support his family, and plagued with worry for his lost daughter.

In the Little Blue Valley behind the departing militia, the ashes were cold at places which had once been road ranches and stagecoach stations. The people who had made those places warm and alive were all gone. Their gardens were throttled by weeds, their chickens killed and thrown into the wells. Around the abandoned freight wagons lay the devil's own junkyard of shoes, yard goods, feedsacks, hardware, and smashed crockery. The rains had washed away the last traces of blood and spilled whiskey and the broken eggs from Theodore Uhlig's tin bucket.

The Indians would maintain their presence in the valley for weeks to come, and occasional military patrols would pass along the haunted trail. Militia units would clear away the wreckage at Little Blue Station and Pawnee Ranch to establish military outposts at those places. But the scene of major fighting would shift to the west, along the trail between Fort Kearny and Denver City. Along this section of the great road, the killing and destruction had equaled that along the Little Blue. Already military units were gathering at the fort in preparation for General Curtis' campaign to reopen the road.

At 9:00 p.m. on this Friday, the general rode into the little town of Columbus with his escort and several companies of the First Nebraska. It would be these Nebraska cavalrymen, along with those of the Seventh Iowa, who would bear the brunt of the fighting in weeks to come. They were all combat veterans, having been blooded at Pea Ridge, Wilson's Creek, Fort Donelson, and Shiloh. The militia units would be confined largely to garrison duty and escort work between the forts and their outposts.

No one really doubted that the overland road would be made safe once again, or that the wild tribes would eventually be vanquished. Colonel Edwin Manning, editor of the *Marysville Big Blue Union*, spoke for an entire frontier when he declared, ". . . twill only be a question of time as to the extermination of our intractable, dusky brethren."[51] But on August 19, 1864, the Indians were still very much the masters of the plains.

Chapter Two notes

1 This was the story Joe Roper told in Marysville on about August 18. But testimony given later by his widow and daughter (1892) claimed that the storehouse was filled with goods. James Comstock also claimed that Kelley had planned to go only as far as Oak Grove, returning later in the day with the Comstocks, while Jonathan Butler continued on with his team and wagon. The true reasons for Kelley's actions that Sunday remain uncertain.
2 John Barratt to George Follmer, January 14, 1912.
3 Most of the cargo on Smith's train was owned by George Tritch, a Denver merchant and alderman. The wagons, draft animals, and threshing machine were the property of Thomas Simonton, also of Denver. The attack on the so-called Simonton-Smith train is reconstructed from these sources:
James Bainter, in *Biographical and Historical Memoirs.*
Frank Baker to George Follmer, March 31, 1912.
George Comstock letter reprinted in *Oak - The Way it Was.*
John Comstock letter in the *De Witt Times-News*, August 18, 1927.
George Lloyd, Testimony as to the Claim of Ben Holladay.
The Nebraska City News, August 18, 1864.
Thomas Simonton and George Tritt, Depredation Claims #1174 and #3102.
4 In 1911, George Follmer began compiling a list of those who had been present at Oak Grove that Sunday. But forty-seven years had passed and memories were fuzzy. Those who were there that day were not all well acquainted with each other, and a number of folks came forward claiming to have been there who definitely were not. James Comstock remains the most authoritative source of information on the subject. In a letter of 1911 (otherwise undated), he identified those who survived the raid as "Father, Brother Harry, Mrs. Blush and 1 child Elley (Ella) and Marry(;) My wife and one child and her mother and child(;) T Caster, Hunt and a man who was with Ostrander and myself." James Comstock had two young children at the time, but according to his letter, only one was along, which seems most unlikely. Samuel Morrill also remains unidentified, but Comstock's writing suggests the possibility that he was the "child" accompanying Comstock's mother-in-law. The completed list:

Francis Comstock Butler, 29 (later married Charles Blush)
Ella Butler, 8 (Francis' daughter from her first marriage)
Harry Comstock, 17
Mary Comstock, 19 (died 2-1/2 years after the raid)
Sarah Comstock, 6
James Comstock, 24
Perlina Cartwright Comstock, 23 (wife of James)
Erastus, 8 months, or Frederick, 2, son of James and Perlina
Etta Cartwright (mother of Perlina)
Samuel Morrill
Nelson Ostrander (died later from arrow wounds)

Lewis Ostrander (mortally wounded in hunting accident)
George Hunt, 17
Tobias Castor, 23
John Barratt, 26
Marshall Clarence Kelley
Jonathan Butler

5 The details of the attack are known only from the testimony of Ambrose Asher, taken in 1894, in which he states that *two* of his uncles were on the wagon and were killed in the road. All other accounts indicate that Henry Eubank was indeed at home, and his body was found days later in a patch of corn or weeds about 100 yards from the cabin, where he had crawled to hide.

6 More lurid accounts state that Dora was staked to the ground and raped, but this is not mentioned in the accounts of those who actually saw her body—Erastus Comstock, John Gilbert, Ambrose Asher, or Laura Roper. The passengers on the westbound stage said only that Dora's body lay about 200 feet from the house, having been "horribly abused and mutilated." There is disagreement between Laura Roper and John Gilbert as to whether Dora was scalped. Gilbert says she was not, but he and his party of citizen volunteers did not see her body until it had lain exposed to sun and scavengers for six days.

7 Of all the people who were at Oak Grove that day, apparently none of them ever wrote a detailed and factual account of the attack. Gregory refers to an unidentified and undated newspaper clipping containing an account supposedly given by George Hunt which she found in the archives of the Nebraska State Historical Society, but the clipping is missing. The present account is reconstructed from interviews with eyewitnesses published in the *Brownville Nebraska Advertiser*, August 11, 1864; the *De Witt Times-News*, November 25, 1926; the *Omaha Nebraskian*, August 17, 1864; and a few cryptic notes from an interview which Gregory conducted with George Hunt in 1918.

8 Francis Roper Jewell quoted in Ellenbecker, *Indian Raids of 1860-1869.*

9 Testimony of Francis Roper Jewell, Joseph Roper (heirs) Depredation Case #7007.

10 Only Ed Lemmon (Yost, *Boss Cowman*) gives us the story of Red Cloud Tom. But an article from the *Nebraska City News* of August 18, 1864, says, "Another unknown man was found dead on the 8th inst., this side of the junction (of the Fort Riley Road)." Also, the passengers of the westbound stage told Lieutenant Porter at Fort Kearny (*Omaha Nebraskian*, August 17, 1864), "Just before we arrived at Pomme (Pawnee) Ranch, a man was killed by Indians within sight of the place—we found his body and buried it . . ." Lemmon later recalled that the body of Red Cloud Tom was never found (by any of the neighbors). An employee of James Lemmon later claimed to have recognized the slippery old man in a Wyoming Indian encampment, but got no response to his inquiries.

11 Bainter's two accounts of those August days are virtually impossible to harmonize with other stories, or even with each other. His affidavit of February 5, 1866, (Bainter Depredation Claim) states that "When he received news of the advance of the Indians, he moved his family to Pawnee Ranch and before he left the Indians were in sight and he saw them shoot a man who was passing his said Ranch, and he was compelled to leave in such haste to secure his family that he lost every article (and) thing in and about his premises, and he was left without even a coat to ware (sic) as all they saved was what he and his family had on."

12 George Comstock letter quoted in *Oak—The Way it Was.*

13 John Gilbert to Addison Sheldon, August 29, 1911 (Papers of George Follmer). Gilbert says that Theodore's body was buried north of Kiowa Station. A few days after the raid,

Otto Uhlig and his brother-in-law, Joseph Schuetz, returned to the valley and retrieved the youngster's body for burial in Walnut Grove Cemetery in Brownville, where it remains today.

14 The westbound coaches left Atchison at 8 o'clock every morning and were due at Kiowa Station about thirty-three hours later at 5:30 p.m. Bob Emery's coach was evidently an extra or a mailcoach, possibly dispatched by Sam Jerome, the division agent, who happened to be in Atchison on August 9, and had no telegraphic communication with the route along the Little Blue. Emery probably took the coach out of Big Sandy about 2 o'clock that morning. It is also possible that he was to secure information on the missing eastbound coach. Where the passengers came from is a mystery. They may have boarded in Atchison, or joined the main line from Beatrice.

15 John Gilbert to George Follmer, January 18, 1918.

16 *Biographical and Historical Memoirs*, 346. Wells does not mention Joe Roper's narrow escape at Pawnee Ranch. He may not have witnessed it. Bainter's colorful account, though, is highly credible.

17 We have only Laura Roper's account of this incident, so in spite of her habit of prevarication, we will assume it to be true.

18 Hook's Junction Ranch was also known as Valley City, Sobieski's, and Dogtown. No eyewitness accounts of the Monday attack have been located, and only sketchy information is found in the following sources:

The Council Bluffs Weekly Morning Bugle, August 11, 1864.

The Omaha Nebraskian, August 17, 1864.

O. R. Vol. 41, Part 2, 613, 642.

19 Willie Mudge and Charles Emery (Simonton and Smith Depredation Cases #1174 and #3102) both understood that California Joe's arm was amputated at Fort Kearny. Mudge heard that he later died from the effects of the operation.

20 O. R. Vol. 41, Part 2, 612-613.

21 Ibid., 613.

22 Ibid., 642.

23 Ibid.

24 Ibid.

25 Ibid., 641. It is unclear which coach Gillespie was referring to. There is no record of the eastbound schedule passing down the Little Blue Valley as scheduled early on Tuesday, August 9. The only other coach would have been the one driven by Bob Emery, which could hardly have arrived in Atchison before the late evening of August 10, the day of Gillespie's telegram. At any rate, Emery's passengers and mail certainly did not get through, as Gillespie said, but probably returned to Atchison.

26 Ibid., 644.

27 We are speculating here. George Hunt's wound was so serious that he would have been taken home as quickly as possible, most probably by his brother-in-law.

28 The prisoner was T. M. Coulter. As justice of the peace, Coulter presided over a farcical trial in which he acquitted Wild Bill Hickok of the murders of David McCanles and two others at Rock Creek Station. Shortly thereafter, Coulter was elected to the office of county treasurer, in which position he embezzled funds from Gage County. He survived the Murphy expedition and, after being returned to Beatrice, was eventually allowed to escape, much to the relief of the citizens who were tired of the whole case. (*Nebraska History* X #2, April-June, 1927, 90-92)

29 *The Omaha Republican*, August 19, 1864.

30 O. R. Vol. 41, Part 2, 659.

31 *The Lincoln Sunday Journal and Star,* May 29, 1932.
32 *The Beatrice Express*, July 20, 1876.
33 Willie Mudge remembered meeting up with Murphy near the crossing of Thirty-two Mile Creek. But all accounts say that the refugee train from Pawnee arrived at Hooks on Wednesday night, and Murphy did not leave Kearny until Friday noon. In the many years which had passed since he was a little boy, William Mudge got a few small details mixed up; yet his memory of the incident is so strong that it must have taken place. Murphy also wrote of meeting the settlers in their wagons. The only possible explanation is that Bainter's train rested all day Thursday and met Murphy as they resumed their drive from Hook's to Kearny on Friday.
34 Fort Kearny Letterbook, August 12, 1864.
35 O. R. Vol. 41, Part 2, 672.
36 O. R. Vol. 41, Part 2, 708.
37 Reverend J. S. Griffing to his wife, August 23, 1864, in "Movements of Militia Company."
38 George Edward Lemmon, letter in the *De Witt Times-News*, August 4, 1927.
39 The federal census for New York, 1860, lists numerous Ostranders living in that state, but none really fit the description of the Nelson and Lewis Ostrander wounded at Oak Grove. Likewise, there are no records in Seneca, Kansas, of their burials, and their graves are apparently unmarked. The *Nemaha Courier* for August 18 has been lost, and it probably carried the notice of Nelson Ostrander's death. The death of Lewis Ostrander, of New Hackensack, New York occurred on August 19 and was reported in the *Courier* of August 25. The funeral took place on Saturday, August 20. The newspaper also reported that he had been accidentally shot in the back, leaving the interesting speculation that either his brother or their traveling companion, John Bare, may have inadvertently fired the fatal shot.
40 As government lawyers later pointed out, nobody actually witnessed any Indians burning ranches, except for the Eubank place at The Narrows. It is only an assumption that the Indians burned the Biktold and Nelson homes.
41 O. R. Vol. 41, Part 2, 721. Atkinson did not identify his informant, but it almost certainly was one of the Uhligs, probably Otto, who seems to have been the family leader.
42 Gilbert evidently questioned the boy briefly, learning only that the teenager was not a part of Murphy's command. Wells writes that Bill Canada, who was killed at his cabin, had a fourteen-year-old son who rode on Bob Emery's coach in the famous chase of August 9, but this is clearly untrue. If indeed Canada had a son, this could have been the youth who was with Gilbert that day. On the other hand, his concern for Constable might indicate that he was one of Constable's bullwhackers. These were times of great upheaval in which people found themselves thrown together in life and death situations without ever learning each other's names.
43 Post returns from Fort Kearny list a Private John Creek as being killed in action at Elk Creek. Records of the Nebraska Adjutant General's office indicate that the thirty-five-year-old Omahan was mustered into Captain Kuhl's Company C, First Battalion, Nebraska Veteran Volunteers on June 7, 1864.
44 O. R. Vol. 41, Part 2, 734.
45 Ibid.
46 *The Omaha Nebraskian*, August 17, 1864.
47 General Byron Sherry was a financially comfortable Seneca attorney. He actually lost two horses on the expedition—a large, brown horse with a jockey saddle, and a sorrel mare. Upon of the return of the militia to Marysville, he posted a $50 reward for their

return. General Sherry had much more on his mind than horses, or Indians, for that matter. On September 15 he married Miss Mary Nelson of Seneca. (*Marysville Big Blue Union*, August 27, 1864; *Seneca Nemaha Courier*, August 25, 1864)

48 O. R. Vol. 41, Part 2, 765.

49 Rev. J. S. Griffing to his wife, August 23, 1864. The image of the citizen-soldier, that martial descendent of the grizzled farmers of Lexington and Concord, died hard. The sorry performance of the militia did not go unnoticed, either by the Indians or by the *Nemaha Courier*, which editorialized: "Our militia is not fit for the work; is not armed, officered, organized, or equipped for such duty. It will require time to place them upon such a footing, if it is done at all." (August 25, 1864)

50 It is not certain when Roper arrived in Marysville, but it must have been very close to August 19.

51 *Marysville Big Blue Union*, August 27, 1864.

Materials used in the preparation of this chapter:
Primary Sources

DAR, *Nebraska Pioneer Reminiscences.*
Ellenbecker, *Indian Raids 1860-1869.*
– *Indian Raids on the Upper Little Blue.*
– (annotated by Lyn Ryder) *Tragedy at the Little Blue.*
Follmer, Papers and Correspondence.
Griffing, "Movements of Militia Company."
Indian Depredation Claims (see Bibliography):
Adams, Bainter, Biktold, Comstock, Douglas, Emery, Eubank, Hammond, Lemmon, Roper, Simonton and Tritch, Uhlig.
Lemmon, "Early Days on the Little Blue."
Majors, Papers and Correspondence.
Oak–The Way it Was.
Official Records of Union and Confederate Armies.
Palmer, "History of the Powder River Expedition."
Root and Connelley, *Overland Stage.*
Testimony as to the Claim of Ben Holladay.
Vance, Biography and Correspondence.
Wells, *A Frontier Life.*

Secondary Sources

Biographical and Historical Memoirs.
Dawson, *Pioneer Tales.*
Dobbs, *History of Gage County.*
Follmer, "Incidents . . . Nuckolls County."
Frederick, *Ben Holladay.*
Gregory, *Pioneer Days in Crete.*

Papers and Correspondence.

Hansen, "True Story of Wild Bill - McCanles Affray."
History of Spring Ranch.

Hyde, *Life of George Bent.*
Kaura, *Saline County History.*
Landers, *Nebraska Stories.*
Leasure, "The Captivity of Laura Roper Vance."
Portrait and Biographical Album.
Trail of Memories.
Watkins, "Incidents in the Indian Outbreak of 1864."

Newspapers

The Atchison Freedom's Champion, August 25, 1864.
The Beatrice Express, August 18, 1872.
The Brownville Nemaha Advertiser, November 22, 1860; August 11, 1864.
The Council Bluffs Weekly Morning Bugle, August 11, 18, 1864.
The De Witt Times-News, November 11, 18, 25, 1926; April 14, 1927; June 23, 1927; August 4, 18, 25, 1927.
The Lincoln Sunday Journal and Star, May 29, 1932.
The Omaha Nebraskian, August 10, 17, 1864.
The Omaha Republican, August 19, 26, 1864.
The Seneca Nemaha Weekly Courier, August 25, 1864.

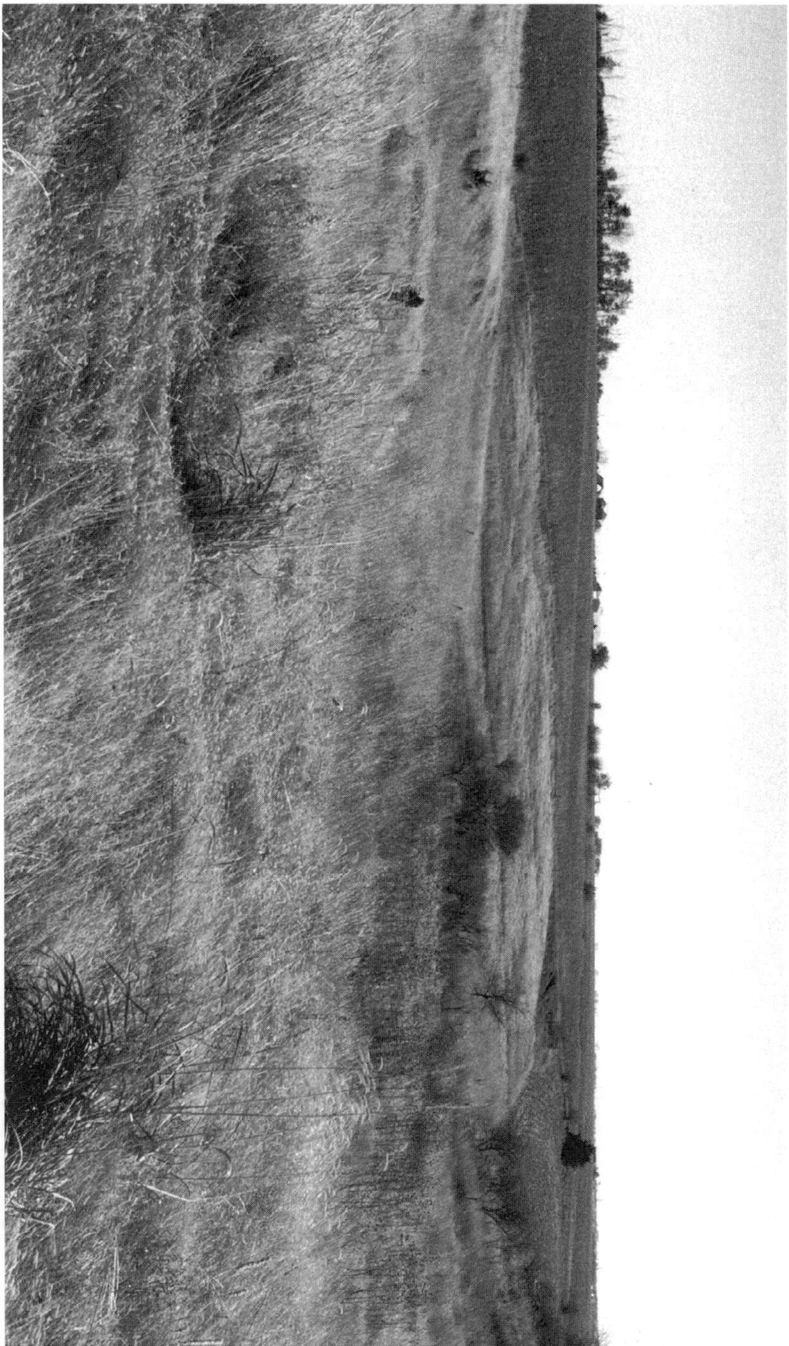

Indian Hollow

Author's photo

Nebraska State Historical Society

The Roper family cabin was a three-room structure made from cottonwood logs. Following his mother's directions, a son of Laura Roper Vance made this drawing in Frebuary, 1927.

Nebraska State Historical Society

Erastus Selden Comstock, 1858

Nebraska State Historical Society

Joseph Beach Roper c. 1866

Author's Photo

The ascent to Nine Mile Ridge as seen from the site of the Roper cabin. About 440 yards away and barely visible to the right of the dead tree on the skyline, is the trough of the Oregon-California Trail.

Author's photo

As seen from the Eubank Ranch, the Oregon-California Trail passes through a notch worn in the bluffs to approach the Narrows, which lies another 300 yards ahead.

Part II
Chapter Three

The Raid on the Martin Family

Few of those Americans who responded to Manifest Destiny via the Platte Valley could remain indifferent to the river. For the emigrants, the Platte was the first major landmark of the journey, and was totally unlike any body of water they had ever seen.

In 1832, Washington Irving pronounced the Platte "the most magnificent and most useless of streams."[1] Peter Burnett noted in 1843 that, like the Nile (which he had never seen), the Platte "runs hundreds of miles through a desert without receiving any tributaries. Its general course is almost as straight as a direct line."[2] More sophisticated mapping would later show that the river makes several reverse curves as it crosses Nebraska, and that it does indeed receive a few tributaries.

The pioneers marveled that the river's banks were almost nonexistent. The Indians' practice of burning the prairies prevented any trees or shrubs from growing along the banks, helping to give the queer impression that the river was actually higher than the valley floor. James Evans noted in 1850 that "My first impression on beholding the Platte River was, that as it looked so wide and muddy, and rolled along within three feet of the top of the bank with such majesty that it was unusually swollen and perfectly impassible. Judge my surprise when I learned that it was only three or four feet deep . . . The plains are so low and level that if Platte River could rise five feet it would cover a country at least ten miles wide."[3]

Nancy Morton described the Platte more poetically: "But this river, when in season of high water, assumes a beautiful appearance. Its broad bosom is dotted with islands of the richest verdure, and adorned with gorgeous hued flowers and delicate vining vegetation . . . The Platte is subject to great variations, however, now fearfully rapid and broad inundating the ancient valley then sinking to an insignificant stream."[4]

The drivers for the Western and Overland stage companies found the river most intriguing and developed a theory as to why it never seemed to flood. The riverbanks were quicksand, they reasoned, the same as the riverbed. When the water level rose, the banks rose right along with them.[5] And yet we have William Newby's word for it that, at least in 1843, the "River over flode."[6]

The Platte was difficult to cross in any season. The stage drivers maintained it could not be forded because of the quicksand; could not be bridged because it had no bottom; and could not be ferried because it was too shallow. Out of the combined wisdom of stage men, freighters, emigrants, and military personnel, grew the traditional descriptions of the Platte: Mile wide and inch deep; the river that flowed upside down; too thin to plow and too thick to drink. But drink it they did, and with varying results, for the Platte was virtually the water of life for 600 miles and more.

The river also worked subtle psychological changes upon the people of the trail. The barren flatness of its valley floor, its tricks of mirage and perspective generated what Merrill Mattes has called "an eerie, unearthly (or at least unfamiliar) atmosphere."[7]

Just east of Fort Kearny the north channel wandered away from the rest of the braided stream, running by itself for about forty-five miles before reentering the river southeast of the present town of Chapman. The land enclosed by these two sections of the river became known to everyone after Robert Stuart in 1813 as La Grande Ile, or the Big Island.[8] It was in the vicinity of this island that all the trails from the various river towns merged into a great Platte River Road.

As the town of Nebraska City grew to prominence, its bull trains rolled westward over the Oxbow Trail, which swung northeast to meet the Platte south of Columbus. But this route was long and arduous, and it gave Nebraska City no advantage over Omaha as a freighting terminal.

In 1858, Russell, Majors, and Waddell moved the headquarters of its freighting operation to Nebraska City. The firm purchased 138 lots in the town for an outfitting area which accommodated a warehouse, blacksmith shop, and wheelwright's shop. It planted 600 acres west of the town in corn, hired hundreds of men, assembled thousands of

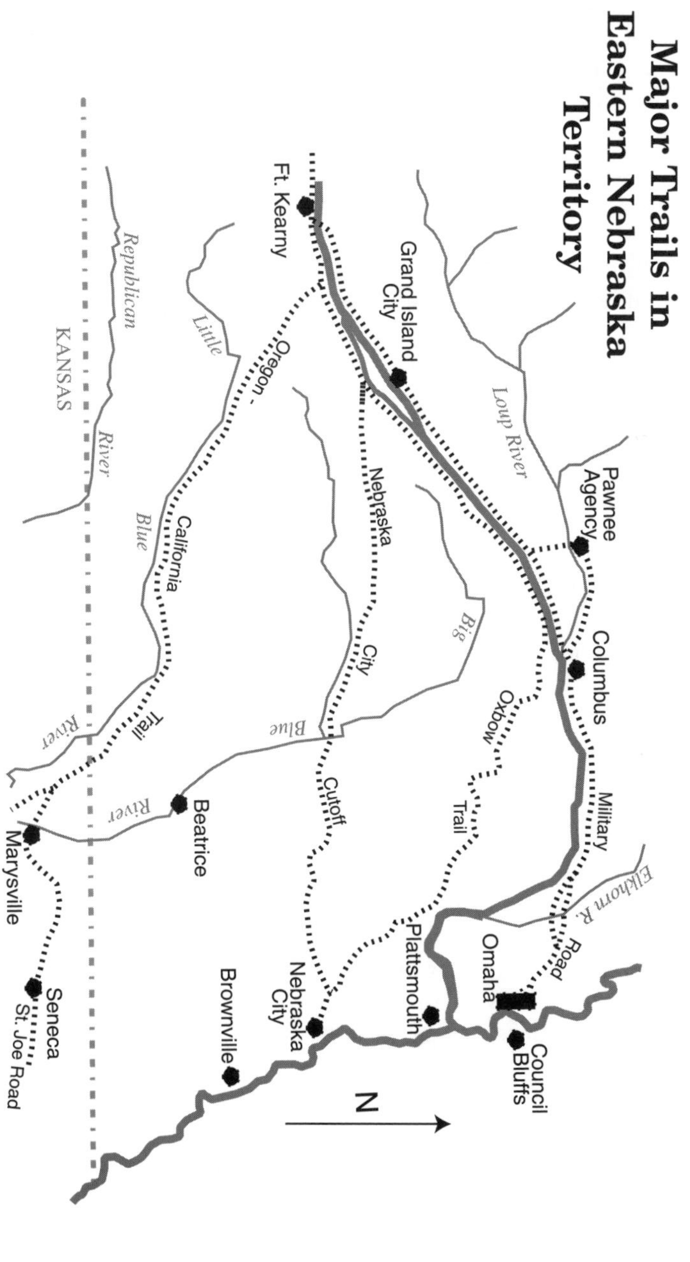
Major Trails in Eastern Nebraska Territory
Ft. Kearny
Grand Island City
Loup River
Pawnee Agency
Columbus
Military Road
Elkhorn R.
Omaha
Council Bluffs
Plattsmouth
Nebraska City
Brownville
Oxbow Trail
Nebraska City Cutoff
Oregon - California Trail
Big Blue River
Little Blue River
Republican River
KANSAS
Beatrice
Marysville
Seneca
St. Joe Road
N

oxen, and provided a dynamic kick for the local economy. From the first, Alexander Majors saw that the Oxbow Trail was too long and traversed too many wetlands to be economically viable, so he hired Augustus Harvey, the town engineer, to survey and mark a new route directly westward to Fort Kearny. In 1860, traffic began to move over the Nebraska City Cutoff, which Harvey thoughtfully blazed with a single plowed furrow. Though water was not as plentiful as along the Oxbow Trail, the cutoff was a good forty miles shorter.

The new trail was an immediate success and Nebraska City's share of the trade grew rapidly. By 1864, merchandise leaving the town was reckoned at twenty-three million pounds for the year—a volume requiring approximately 2,132 wagons and 18,720 oxen. This was truly the golden age of the High Plains freighter.[9]

The excitement intensified in July 1862 when the steamer *West Wind* docked at Nebraska City bearing the latest in transportation technology. Shortly after the boat had tied up at the wharf, the mighty Steam Wagon puffed and clanked off its deck and up the levee. The brainchild of a Minnesota promoter and inventor named Major Joseph Renshaw Brown, the Steam Wagon was designed to tow trains of wagons across the plains, replacing mules and oxen. The engine was a thrilling spectacle as it chugged around town on its ten-foot-high red driving wheels, trailing clouds of awestruck citizens and setting fire to a spectator's straw hat. Few doubted that it would revolutionize the freighting industry.

But things didn't happen quite that way. After a few kinks were ironed out of the Cutoff Road, the lordly steam wagon rumbled out of town on its maiden run to Denver City, 605 miles away. With something like 602 miles left to go, one of the crank rods snapped, leaving the run to be completed by those low technology oxen. Major Brown took the broken casting to New York where he discovered that all the foundries were working full time on war production. When at last the replacement part was forged, Brown left immediately for Nebraska City. It was mid August when he reached Chicago—to be greeted by the news that his family was caught up in the Sioux uprising in Minnesota. Brown rushed to his home and the replacement crank never did reach Nebraska City. Eventually, the Steam Wagon was dismantled.[10]

Still, it had not been all for naught. Due to the exertions of Brown and Majors, the route to Fort Kearny had been wonderfully improved. The new trail had been smoothed and straightened and several streams had been bridged. On July 1, 1862, the Western Stage Company inaugurated a thrice-weekly run via the Cutoff Road to Fort Kearny and through to Denver City. The new route lacked only a few road ranches to make it equal to the trail through the Little Blue Valley.

Anne Weavers was widowed with a young son when she married George Martin in Wallington County, England. In the next several years, the family celebrated the arrival of a daughter, Hepzibah, and a son, Henry Nathaniel. Leaving their native England for America in 1851, the Martins stopped briefly in Cleveland, where another son, Robert, was born. Then they moved on to Henry County, Illinois, where George Martin farmed for nine years. During this time, two more children, William and Annie, were born. Although Anne's son from her first marriage was now a grown man, there were five children in the Martin family, and the parents began to look westward in anticipation of a new homestead law which would open Nebraska Territory for settlement.

In 1859, the Martins sold their Henry County farm and removed to Fremont County, Iowa, just across the river from Nebraska City. The freight traffic to the Colorado mines was enormous and George Martin obtained work as a bullwhacker. It was on his trips westward along the Cutoff Road that he fell in love with the Platte River Valley. The country was wide and unsettled, its soil was fertile, and water could be found only a few feet below the surface. It seemed the ideal place for a family homestead, so he discussed his dream with his wife.

Anne Martin was a remarkable woman, as subsequent events were to show. Physically tough and with great strength of character, she governed her entire life according to the values and principles which flowed from her deep Christian convictions. She was perfectly willing to move her family to the frontier, but with one condition: Their home must not be near the trail. Like William Mudge, Anne Martin did not want her children exposed to the coarseness and cursing of the teamsters and bullwhackers who traveled with the freight outfits.

In August 1862, George Martin headed west from Nebraska City with his three sons—Nathaniel, Robert, and Willie—and a wagonload of supplies. He had decided upon settling a place by the side of the road south of the German Settlements and about thirty miles east of Fort Kearny, a place where the trail swung southwest to draw near the gentle bluffs at the edge of the valley. Upon reaching the site, he stopped the team and jumped off the wagon with a shovel, announcing to his boys, "I am going to dig a well here."

While Nat and Bob unhitched the horses, Martin hacked away at the tough sod. The digging went quickly, and the sand a few feet down began to grow moist. With the river only a mile away, the water table was correspondingly high, and soon the hole began to fill with water.

Some type of casing was necessary to prevent the inflow of water from washing sand back into the hole, so Martin got a wooden barrel off the wagon, knocked out the ends, and sank it into his well. After bailing for a few minutes with a small bucket, the water became quite clear. The first step in building a homestead had been completed.

Father and sons next turned their attention to the construction of a house with two rooms. Its architecture was predictably "Early Roadranch," with the first room being reserved for the pilgrim trade, and the back room reserved for the family's private use. When the place was liveable, the Martin men returned to Nebraska City for the rest of the family. Anne Martin's reaction when she discovered that her new home was squarely along the Cutoff Road is unrecorded. But her husband had presented her with a *fait d'accompli*, and it was too late in the season to do anything but move in.

Aside from its rustic charm, the place did have its advantages. The new homestead was well sited for a brisk trade and possibly a stagecoach station, and the surrounding acres of grass would support a worthy herd of livestock. Besides, it was simply impractical to live any distance from the rivers and trails in the new territory, so Anne Martin took up the task of making the sod house into a real home for her family. She and her husband would spend the remainder of their lives in this place.

As the fall days grew shorter, work on the ranch progressed with greater urgency. The Martins built the necessary sod barn and corral, and Nathaniel cut wood on the Platte islands to use in curbing up a deeper well. The Western Stage Company established a swing station at the ranch, reserving half the space in the barn for the company's horses. Once a month, winter and summer, Anne Martin and young William drove two wagons to Nebraska City for supplies, a round trip of 290 miles.

In the spring of 1863, the Martins planted their first crops, and the boys transplanted a row of young cottonwood trees which they brought up from the islands in the Platte. There were Indians constantly going back and forth over the white man's road, and twice a year the Pawnees left their reservation on the Loup and headed southward to hunt buffalo along the Republican. Just about the whole village went—dogs, travois ponies, children, and all. Sometimes nearly a thousand Pawnees made their evening camp near the Martin ranch. The Martin children were always welcome in the Pawnee camp, and they learned some of the language and much about the domestic affairs of these Indian people.

This broad, untamed country had many lessons to teach the neophyte road ranchers, and their education sometimes bordered on disaster. George Martin was a lover of horses, and in the spring of 1863, he somehow came into ownership of a remarkable horse trained to hunt buffalo. Upon hearing that a large herd had been sighted a day's journey to the southwest, Martin assembled a hunting outfit of two wagons, a hodgepodge of firearms, Willie and Nathaniel, and the buffalo horse. Several miles to the east of the Martin place was a one-room hotel/feedbarn/drygoods store/saloon run by a man named Mabin, and he also was invited to go along on the hunt.[11]

The hunting party drove across the prairie to the place where the buffalo herd had been reported. In due time, the hunters spotted their quarry, and George Martin climbed bareback atop his buffalo horse, armed with a double barrel rifle and a pepperbox pistol. Mabin and the boys watched as he cut a likely kill from the herd. It soon became obvious that the horse knew its business well, while the rider did not. The chosen buffalo ran a short distance before turning to face its pursuer. The horse immediately began responding to the movements of the buffalo, darting this way and that. First Martin lost his gun, then his grip. As he bounced in the grass, the horse accidentally kicked his leg, bruising it badly. Scrambling upright to face the charging buffalo, Martin dug the pepperbox pistol from his pocket and fired, wounding the beast in one eye. The enraged buffalo spun round and round in its pain, allowing the hunter time to stumble to his horse and grasp it around the neck. Then the buffalo charged again and the horse turned to kick the shaggy head with its hind legs. At last the buffalo horse turned and trotted back to the wagons with Martin still clinging under its neck.

Mabin did a most unneighborly thing, jeering at Martin and calling him a fool. Then he mounted his mule to show the proper way to hunt buffalo. Mabin's hunt was brutally short, and he soon came flying back to the wagons minus his gun, with the pursuing buffalo hooking his mule several times along the way.

The hunting party huddled for protection behind the wagons as the wounded buffalo pawed the turf and prepared for another charge. The adult hunters had been completely discomfited, so thirteen-year-old Nathaniel grabbed another rifle and dropped the beast with one lucky shot. Little William, who had stood by, helplessly watching the mad proceedings, remarked later that their evening meal was the dearest, sweetest buffalo dinner the family ever ate.

In spite of, or perhaps because of such experiences, the Martins were, by the summer of 1864, becoming seasoned plainsmen, and their roadranch quite successful. The burgeoning freight traffic created a demand for all the prairie hay the Martins could cut and stack over the summer. Like their fellow ranchmen along the Little Blue, George

Martin and his sons were spending those first, hot, dry August days putting up hay when the bitterness and wrath of the Sioux and Cheyennes overtook them and changed their lives forever.

The long, hot day was drawing to a close as George Martin started his team of stallions toward home.[12] He and his boys, Nat and Bob, had spent the entire day hauling in the valuable hay crop from the Platte bottoms. They were dirty and hungry and very tired. Now, with this last load of the day, Martin was homeward bound for supper. Nat and Bob would follow with the second wagon drawn by a yoke of oxen. The boys brought with them to the field a brown mare and now, for whatever reason, they were delayed by the intricacies of hitching her in front of the work cattle. Before they got under way, their father was three-quarters of a mile ahead of them.

From his perch atop the swaying load of hay, George Martin saw them coming down through the gentle bluffs—nine Indian warriors. For a few seconds he was unsure of their intentions as they raced toward the wagon, but the first war whoops and a scattered volley of arrows cleared up his indecision. He whipped the stallions into a run for the soddy nearly a half-mile away, and fell on his stomach into the trench-like depression caused by the binding pole which passed over the top of the load. Unlike his neighbors on the Little Blue, Martin carried his seven-shot Spencer rifle with him to the field. Over the edge of his breastwork of hay, he squeezed off his first shot, wounding one of the attackers. His second shot crippled one of their ponies, and his third shot alerted the Indians to the fact that he had a repeating rifle, and they began to fall back—all except one. That brave ran his pony close up behind the wagon and loosed an arrow which hit Martin at the base of the neck, slicing a large artery and lodging in his collarbone.

As the spooked stallions raced at full speed past the front of the soddy, Martin slid down from the load and rolled along the ground as his attacker turned back for a killing shot. Alerted by the rifle fire and war cries, Anne Martin dashed outside to drag her husband to safety while Hepzibah leveled an old shotgun at the warrior, who ducked and raced away. Martin was bleeding profusely, and his wife applied crude but effective first aid. With a horsehair and a long pin, she knitted the edges of the wound together enough that the blood began to clot.

Having discovered that the family was well armed, most of the Indians retreated back up into the bluffs. It was really the horses they wanted, but the two stallions had pulled the haywagon up onto a large pile of firewood near the soddy. There they stalled, horses on one side and wagon on the other, and altogether too close to the house for the warriors to approach safely. But several ponies and the stage horses were in the barn, as well as a pair of colts belonging to the boys' brown mare. The warrior who had wounded George Martin made one fast swing around the barn and managed to drive away a pony belonging to Bob.

The two boys had watched their father's race for life from their wagon in the hayfield a mile away and were uncertain as to its outcome. They knew only that the attack had ceased and that one of the Indians was coming up the trail in their direction. After unhooking the cattle from the loaded wagon, Nat boosted Bob onto the mare's back and jumped up behind him. Turning their mount toward the river, they attempted to disappear behind a rise of ground which cut off their view from the road.

It might have worked except that the Indian near the barn drove Bob's pony to the river, and in so doing, caught sight of the boys on their mare. That brave turned and signaled to the others, who came galloping down from the bluffs toward the youngsters. They could do nothing now but retreat back down river, farther away from home.

The old, brown mare ran only a short distance before she sensed trouble back at the barn. One of the colts there was hers, and the other she had "adopted" when its mother died. Now she did what any good mother would do: She ran to protect her young. Nat and Bob could only hang on for dear life.

Straight through the Indians she ran on a bee line for the barn. One of them tried to frighten her and turn her around. Yelling like a demon, he closed in and came alongside—but he got too close. In a blind fury the mare bared her teeth and bit his pony on the neck, nearly throwing horse and rider to the ground.

The Indian pony recovered its stride and the rider made a second attempt to head off the flying mare and her passengers. As he came alongside, the mare grabbed at his saddle blanket while Nat reached for his bow. Three times the boy lunged for the weapon, but he and his horse both missed their opportunities and the warrior, tired of the game now, loosed his first arrow. From short range it drove into Nat's elbow, the four inch head wedging itself solidly into the joint. In fear and pain the boy broke off the arrow and flung it back into the Indian's face.

The mare was running with everything she had, and home was only a quarter mile away. George and Anne were worried frantic about their sons and ran outside to climb to the top of the root cellar to see what had become of them. There they were, both hanging on to the brown mare, galloping furiously for home with an Indian brave close behind. It was then that the pursuer loosed his second arrow.

This one went true. With terrific velocity it tore through Nat's back beneath the shoulder blade, pierced his liver, came out through his lower chest, and lodged in Bob's backbone. A third arrow sliced through Nat's thigh and lodged in Bob's left hip. Thus pinned together, the boys struggled to stay atop their plunging horse, while the violent motion caused Nat excruciating pain as the feathered shaft worked back and forth in his wound. Desperately they looked toward their home. Over a swell in the ground they could see their parents standing atop the root cellar, and Nat knew he wasn't going to make it. As his world began to spin and grow dark, he had just strength enough to hook his hands inside the waist of his brother's pants. Both boys slid from the back of the rampaging mare and crashed to the ground. Their horse soon became entangled in the loose reins and was captured.

The force of the fall tore the arrow completely through Nat's body and dislodged it from Bob's spine. Several warriors rode up and dismounted, walking around the two and wrestling with a problem of procedure: Should they scalp the boys or not? Nat and Bob did not look like very big boys as they lay crumpled in the grass, and both had recently had their hair cut short. At last one of the attackers said in plain English, "Leave the boys alone." The rest agreed, grunting that "Papoose scalp no good—no honor kill papoose." Nat, they knew by the fountain of blood pouring from his chest, would soon die. Bob was still moving, so they knocked him unconscious with a war axe. Then they rode away.[13]

From the top of the cave, George and Anne Martin had witnessed, as they believed, the death of their sons, whose bodies now lay out of sight behind the gentle swell of the prairie. Inside the soddy, supper was cooling on the table, although hunger had been forgotten. Fearing that the Indians would attack again, the Martins' only thought was to get the rest of the children away to safety as quickly as possible. Anne threw some food into a sack and rushed Annie, Willie, and Hepzibah outside to where their father had cut the stallions out of their harness. The family mounted bareback and left their home on a run for Fort Kearny. Several of the Indians followed behind at a discreet distance. After all, George Martin still had that rifle.

The family had ridden about a mile when one of the stallions began to stumble. An examination disclosed that an arrow was buried in its vitals. The three children were mounted on the remaining horse while the parents walked alongside, and the wounded stallion was left in the road where the pursuing Indians found it and cut its throat. The warriors who remained behind entered the house and gobbled up the untouched supper. Something must have been wrong with the coffee, because they kicked the coffeepot out the door. Then they went to work on the supplies, slitting open the bags of sugar, flour, beans, and grain, pouring everything on the floor and dancing around in it to mix it up good and proper. They also sliced open the feather beds and smashed the dishes. At last the Indians gathered up their horses and departed the scene of their destruction, melting away into the southern bluffs.

By 7:15 the sun was hanging just above the western horizon, and the earth was beginning to cool. The two boys had lain for nearly an hour in the grass. The fountain of blood which had poured from Nat's chest had shut itself off, forming a huge clot under his shirt. As consciousness returned slowly, he called weakly to his brother, "Are you alive?"

Bob responded by whispering, "Are you alive?"

They were both alive, but grievously hurt. They tried to stand but were too weak to gain their feet. Slowly they crawled up the little rise of ground, raised up on their arms, and looked toward home. It was very dark and quiet. Perhaps the rest of the family were all dead. They continued the pitiful crawl on hands and knees, finally reaching the horse trough, where they cupped their hands and drank until the raging thirst of injury was satisfied. Nat was at the end of his strength, so he dragged himself into the barn and collapsed on the hay. Bob crawled to the house to see what had become of the rest of the family. He found the soddy forlorn and still. Feathers from the slashed bedding had blown everywhere, and the floor was covered with the spilled provisions. The family was gone.

Bob crawled back to the barn to tell his brother what he had found. Night was now upon the prairie and the two youngsters, weak with pain, heartsick and abandoned, lay side-by-side in the empty barn. Soon they were asleep.

As George and Anne plodded nervously onward with the children and the remaining stallion, their panic began to give way to anguish at the thought of their sons' bodies lying exposed on the open prairie. They were nearly halfway to Hook's Junction Ranch when they came upon the camp of a westbound freight train. Rushing into the circle of wagons, they excitedly recounted their misfortunes to the drovers, begging them to accompany the family back to their home to retrieve the bodies of their boys from being ravaged by the night scavengers. The wagon master refused, however, and the force of logic was on his side. If the boys were dead, he reasoned, there was no use traveling back in the dark and risking an attack. They would be just as dead in the morning. Presumably, the Martins would also be calmer and more rational by then. With his answer, the family had to be content, so they bedded down with the freighters to wait anxiously for the morning light.

Weariness and excitement from the past night kept the train in camp later than usual the next morning. Naturally the freighters did not want to backtrack a half day's run to the east. In puzzling out what to do with the distraught family, the men sighted an approaching eastbound train, and thereby the problem was solved.

Traveling with the empty train was a young man named Beck Martin. Although he was no relation to the family, he had spent some time at their ranch as a stocktender for Western Stage Lines. Taking leave of their hosts of the past evening, the Martin family joined Beck and his train for the return trip to their home.

As they rolled eastward along the Nebraska City Road, the drovers became emotionally caught up in the family's plight. It was nearly two o'clock in the afternoon when they came in sight of the Martin homestead, and Beck Martin ran ahead of the slow moving train to see whether any of the stage horses might have been left in the barn. Peering cautiously inside, he spied the two boys sleeping side by side on the hay.

Beck Martin bolted from the barn and gestured wildly to the approaching wagons, yelling at the top of his voice, "Here's the boys! Here's the boys!" The entire company broke into a run for the barn and the bullwhackers crowded inside to see the miracle. Their happy surprise suffered a severe jolt when they caught sight of the bloody mess. When Anne Martin reached the barn, they cleared a path for her. Nat was awake by this time, but so weak he was unable to raise his arm. The rest of the family brought water and some clean cloths, and Anne Martin set to work cleaning away the caked blood and dirt. As Nat's shirt was cut away, the enormous gout of blood on his chest was exposed. "Here is his wound," Anne said.

The boy whispered weakly, "That is where it came out."

"Where it came out? Where did it go in?"

The boy mentioned his back and the men turned him over gently to reveal another large clot of dried blood.

Anne Martin had kept a tight rein on her emotions thus far. But as she realized that an arrow had passed completely through her son's body, her instincts told her there was no way he could survive such a wound and its ensuing infection. Defeated at last, she began sobbing to her son, "Boy, you will die."

Nat would have agreed with her the evening before, but now he whispered to his mother that he thought there was still hope.

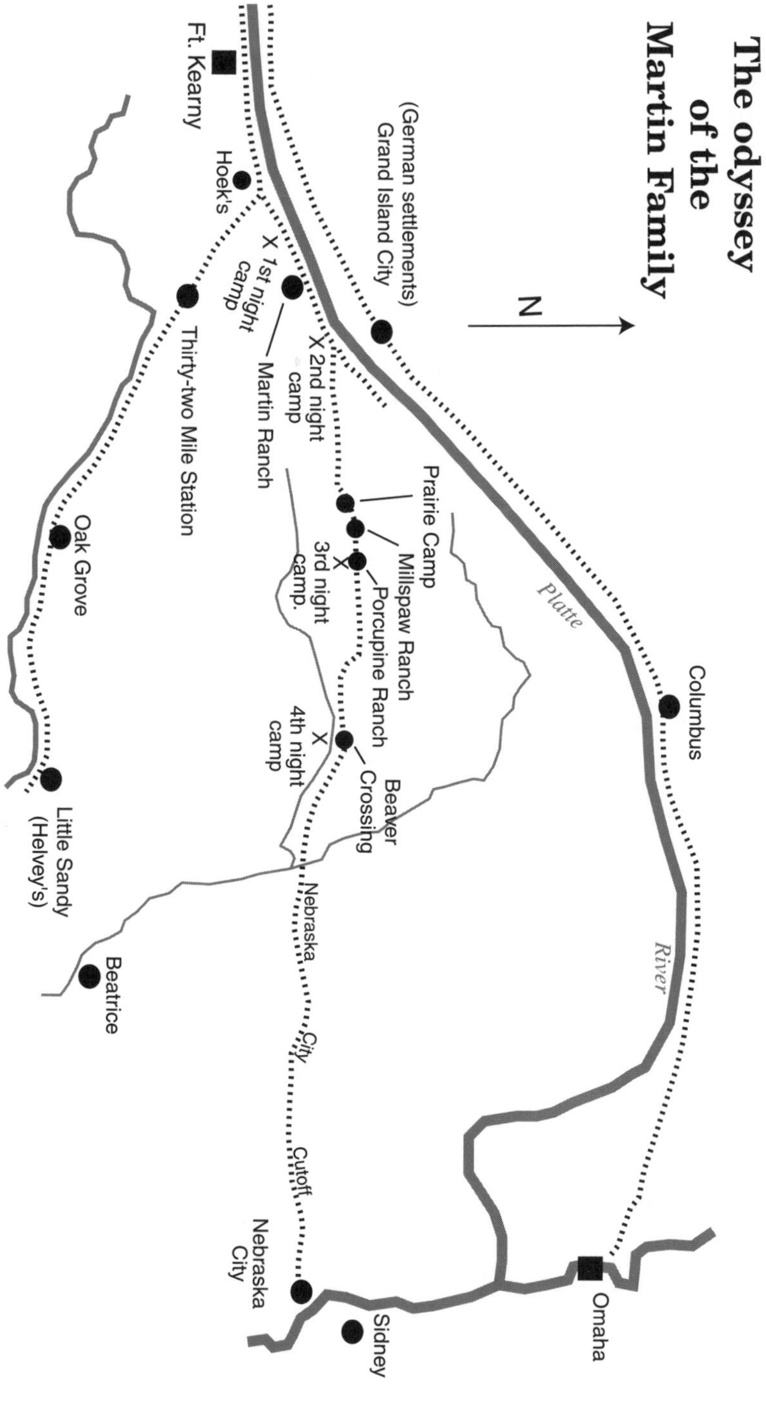
The odyssey of the Martin Family
N
Ft. Kearny
Hoek's
(German settlements)
Grand Island City
X 1st night camp
Thirty-two Mile Station
Martin Ranch
X 2nd night camp
Prairie Camp
Millspaw Ranch
Porcupine Ranch
X 3rd night camp.
Oak Grove
Platte
Columbus
X 4th night camp
Beaver Crossing
Little Sandy (Helvey's)
Nebraska City Cutoff
River
Beatrice
Nebraska City
Omaha
Sidney

In turning the boy over, George Martin had noticed his grossly swollen elbow with a string hanging out. The arrowhead was still lodged in the joint. Quietly, Anne told her son it would have to come out. His father got a grip on the arrowhead with shoeing pincers and tugged. The tool slipped off and Nat fainted away. When he came to a moment later, his father had once again locked the pincers on the arrowhead and two bullwhackers were holding the arm rigid. With a quick tug, the arrowhead came free, and Nat lost consciousness once again. He would not awaken for eighteen hours.

The boys' wounds were washed and dressed as well as circumstances permitted, but they desperately needed the best medical care available. The Martins abandoned their plans to go to Fort Kearny and prepared for a trip in the opposite direction—to Nebraska City, 180 miles away. It was an interesting decision, since there was a doctor at the fort only twenty-nine miles to the west. Perhaps the bull train had brought news of the recent attacks at Hook's and Plum Creek. Perhaps the Martins chose to go to Nebraska City because it was a familiar, friendly place. They had traded there for several years. They knew the town and they were known there. At Nebraska City they would find a doctor and friends to share their misery. Maybe it was the place they wanted to be when Nathaniel died, because they knew he had only the slimmest chance of reaching the Missouri alive.

The bullwhackers were anxious to be gone, but they must have pitched in to unload the haywagon and pull it down off the woodpile. Once again George Martin hitched the versatile stallion to the wagon and laid his wounded sons on a thick bed of hay. The bull train pulled away and the Martin family trailed eastward after the departing freighters.

It was dark when they made camp for the night, having come an agonizing ten miles. Their campsite was exactly six miles south of the German Settlements, where there was also a doctor, but they may not have known that. In any case, their hearts were set on reaching "home" in Nebraska City.

Everyone was so exhausted that they slept late the following morning. Nat had not regained consciousness since the arrowhead had been removed from his elbow, but he awoke as his parents were lifting him into the wagon. He ached terribly and did not want to be moved, but his mother and father said it must be done. All day they drove, past the junction of the Oxbow Trail, past Prairie Camp and Millspaw's Ranch to Porcupine Ranch, where at last they made camp for the night.

Early the following morning the journey resumed—hours and endlessly slow miles of jostling and agony for Nat and Bob. By nightfall they had reached the crossing of Beaver Creek, where they made camp in an abandoned log shack on the east bank. There were still 120 miles to go.

When Nat awoke in the morning, his entire body was sickened with pain. The excruciating wagon ride had broken his will to live, and now he begged his parents to leave him to die while they continued on to Nebraska City with Bob. George Martin knew his oldest son pretty well, and he realized now that the journey was over. Leaving Anne to set up housekeeping in the old shack and care for the invalids, George Martin mounted the trusty stallion and started off for help—but not to Nebraska City. For whatever reason, he turned back the way they had come and headed for Fort Kearny.

His excitement had not diminished by the time he reached the post. Reverend Wells was there, caring for the wounded Richard, and the good parson was so impressed by Martin's excited narrative that he later wrote it down, getting most of the facts wrong.

Martin begged help from the officers at the fort. Whether he spoke with Colonel Summers or a subordinate, he was told that the army could do nothing for him. He got the impression that the Civil War was winding down to a conclusion and that the officers intended to do as little as possible until they were mustered out. For many years after, he carried bitterness and resentment over their refusal to help. But in truth, the officers at Fort Kearny had more than they could handle. The military reservation was swamped with distraught settlers and emigrants looking to them for protection and subsistence. Captain Wilcox had taken most of his company to Julesburg, and Captains Murphy and Kuhl had taken all the serviceable horses and most of the garrison down on the Little Blue. It is uncertain just exactly what kind of help George Martin was looking for, but he would not find it at Fort Kearny. After several days, he mounted his horse in disgust and rode back toward Nebraska City.

Nearly two weeks had elapsed from the time of his departure until he arrived back at the shack on Beaver Creek. There, to his great delight, he found both his sons up and around. Nat was still very weak, of course, and both boys were in constant pain, but they were very definitely on the mend.

The Martin family took a sober look at their situation. On the down side, their provisions were destroyed. Except for the faithful stallion, their livestock was all gone. Both George and Anne were near forty-five years old—maybe too old to start over one more time.

On the positive side, they would not be starting from scratch. Their sod house was unharmed. Barn and corrals and haystacks were intact. The land was as good as ever and the garden would still yield something. They still had their wagons and their good name in Nebraska City. Best of all, their two sons, whom they had given up for dead, were still very much alive. Militia and federal volunteer forces were mobilizing, forcing the theater of operations against the Indians far to the west. The decision was not really difficult: The Martins would return to their ranch and pick up where they left off.

Once again the family boarded the wagon for the trip home. Nat and Bob were well enough to ride on the spring seat, although both had to be lifted in and out of the wagon. Back across Beaver Creek they went; past Prairie Camp and down into the Platte Valley; past Mabin's old ranch, and back to the place they called home.

Chapter Three notes

1 Root and Connelley, *Overland Stage*, 245.

2 Burnett, "Recollections and Opinions," 70-71.

3 James Evans quoted in Mattes, *The Great Platte River Road*, 162-163.

4 Czaplewski (*Captive of the Cheyenne*) discovered that this and other passages from Nancy Morton's manuscript are nearly identical to passages from the account of Sarah Larimer, *Capture and Escape, or Life Among the Sioux*, (1870).

5 Root and Connelley, *Overland Stage*, 246.

6 Newby, "Diary of the Emigration," 223.

7 Mattes, *The Great Platte River Road*, 161.

8 The Wood River originally flowed into the north channel southeast of the present village of Alda. In an attempt to keep the annual June rise of the river from inundating nearby cultivated fields, the Nebraska Legislature, in 1869, approved a plan to dam the north channel. After the dam was in place, the western section of the north channel dried up, and what had formerly been called the north channel became known as the Wood River. It was not until 1963 that the name change was made official by the U.S. Board of Geographic Names. (Anderson, "Old North Channel," 1, 3.)

9 Noble, *Historically Eventful Nebraska City*, 25.

10 Sheldon, *Nebraska*, 218; Noble, *Historically Eventful Nebraska City*, 27-28.

11 Gilman, *Pump on the Prairie*, 97-98; *History of Hall County*, 149-150.

12 On what date did the attack on the Martin family occur? There is nothing to show that Nathaniel ever gave the exact date. Probably he did not know. After all, one day making hay on the prairie is about like every other day. The Martins' actions suggest that they had not yet heard of the attacks on Plum Creek or along the Little Blue. A careful reading of J. K. P. Miller's journal indicates that he had the impression the Plum Creek Massacre and the Martin raid occurred nearly simultaneously, or on August 8. Analysis of William Stolley's letter to his brother and his *History* shows that the attack on Plum Creek and the raid on Boyd's Ranch on the Wood River (also on August 8) caused the Grand Island settlers to leave their homes for one night. It was news of the *second* attack, or the Martin raid, which caused the Wood River settlers to abandon their homes, passing the German Settlements on August 13 and 14. Comparison of these and other sources indicate that the most probable date for the attack on the Martins was August 9, or possibly the eighth.

13 The arrows which the Martins saved from the attack were Pawnee arrows, yet the boys knew the Pawnee people well enough to know that their attackers were not Pawnees. It is possible that they were some of the same Sioux who had attacked the haycutters near the Pawnee Reserve just forty-seven days before. One must also question why the Sioux would speak English among themselves. Again, it is very possible that there were one or more white renegades among them. Such men would have been more likely to speak English and would have had less stomach for killing young white boys. Certainly there were white renegades or half-breeds involved in the raids at Plum Creek and on the Little Blue, as we know from Laura Roper and Nancy Morton.

Nebraska State Historical Society
The Martin Ranch in 1866. From left: Unidentified, Hepzibah Martin (on horseback), George Masterson, unidentified, Annie Martin, Eliza Weavers, Robert Martin, Ann (Mrs. George) Martin and George Martin.

Nebraska State Historical Society
George Martin

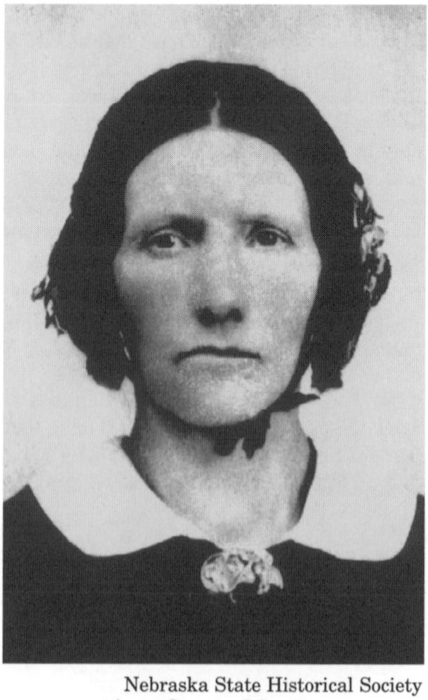

Nebraska State Historical Society
Ann Owers Martin

Stuhr Museum of the Prairie Pioneer

The Martin brothers - Henry Nathaniel (left) and Robert Owers.

Nebraska State Historical Society

Nathaniel Martin and the arrows that wounded him.

Part II
Chapter Four

The Great Platte River Road and its People

West of Fort Kearny the Platte River Road stretched out flat and level through a landscape which was at once mystically beautiful, yet somnolent and boring. To the north of the road lay the raveling channels of the Platte, over a mile in width, with little towheads and shifting sandbars curbed between low banks. South of the road lay the bluffs and canyons of the "Coast of Nebraska," cloaked in dusty green grasses which shimmered in the summer heat, closing around the darkly threatening arroyos with their stands of sober, green cedars.

Westbound travelers found the trail along the Platte to be a hard pull. The soil was sandy and the road itself was climbing toward the Rockies, more than seven and a half feet for every mile. It was hard work for the draft animals. Even though the road itself was deceptively level, veteran freighters and stage drivers noticed the effects of the climb on their teams.

The road ranches had come to this section of the trail earlier and in greater numbers than they had come to the valley of the Little Blue. In fact, everything about the Platte road ranches was different from those east of Kearny. The first of them had appeared along the middle Platte even before the Colorado gold rush began. They were more trading posts than road ranches, and they carried on a brisk business with the tribes of the High Plains as well as with the emigrants. With the discovery of gold and the establishment of Denver City, the road ranches multiplied along the trail like toads after a spring downpour. Many were built near some useful natural feature—a wooded island in the Platte or a spring of good water. Other ranches grew up where they did simply because their proprietors had broken down there. Unable to move any farther for the time being, these people set up shop right where they crashed. Along both sides of the trail there popped up a string of wretched little houses built of mud and sod. Their architects were Necessity and Practicality, and their *raison d'etre* was profit—all-in-all, a typically American combination.

Some of the owners gave up after a short time and either moved on to a better site or left the country entirely. Behind them squatted the empty sod hovels, sometimes sheltering a sick emigrant, always in the process of decay. The mud plastering soon cracked and fell from the inner walls as the new tenants—mice, fleas, and snakes—took over. The violent summer rains soaked the jerry-built sod walls which began to bow and sag. Soon the poles and branches that supported the roof gave up the fight, and the entire building collapsed in a heap of mud and dead grass, somehow symbolic of the builder's perseverance.

Other ranchers stayed on to improve their claims, sinking shallow wells, fashioning corrals and outbuildings from sod or from the thousands of cedar trees that clogged the ravines in the southern bluffs. Oddly enough, even where the clean, aromatic cedar was available, the ranchmen generally continued to live in sod dwellings simply because they were snug and warm in the winter and surprisingly cool in summer. For this, they were willing to put up with occasional visits of bugs and snakes.

Due to the extreme privations of living on the High Plains, the early ranches along the middle Platte tended to be masculine affairs. Of course, members of the fairer sex had been trudging along the trail to Oregon and California for more than twenty years, but it was not until January 1860 that Charles McDonald brought his wife, Orra, to his ranch at Cottonwood Springs, making her the first white woman to reside in Shorter (now Lincoln) County, Nebraska Territory.[1] Women's domestic skills were particularly in demand at the Pony Express and stagecoach stations, and several more ladies followed Orra McDonald to a life along the Platte later that same year. In fact, by June 1860, there was a grand total of sixty-two people living along the thirteen-mile stretch between Gilman's Ranch and Cottonwood Springs.[2]

The business carried on at the ranches that summer was varied and spectacular. The little sodhouse stores dispensed everything from goggles to oysters in tins, and served meals besides. There were Pony Express animals to be cared for, hay to be cut and cured and sold to passing trains. Cedar wood was cut and sold to the emigrants for their cookfires, and fresh supplies had to be continually freighted out from the Missouri River ports. Jaded draft animals were taken in trade to be rehabilitated in the ranch corrals. There was bread to be baked, buffalo to be killed and dressed, and even cheese to be made. There was so much work to be done that any transient amenable to hard labor could be hired on the spot.

But, other than making hay and doing a little dairying, there was almost no farming done. Very few of these ranchers had any faith that corn and vegetables could be successfully grown on the High Plains. Even when Moses Sydenham near Fort Kearny, and Washington Hinman near Cottonwood raised excellent gardens, the idea was never really popular with ranchmen along the Platte. Their main cash crop continued to be prairie hay which, of course, needed neither planting nor tending.

The road ranches along the Platte flourished for less than a decade. Then they were gone. Like the big white-topped wagon caravans, the ranches fell victim to progress in the form of the Union Pacific Railroad. But during their short heyday, they succored untold thousands of hungry, weary humans and animals, and they became unfortunate ingredients in the violent reaction which occurred between the stream of white civilization and the volatile tribes of the High Plains.

By the summer of 1864, the trail between Fort Kearny and Julesburg was thickly settled by frontier standards, with road ranches every several miles along the way. Some of the proprietors were shadowy figures who appeared from somewhere in the East, built their shanties and corrals, did their trading for a time, and then disappeared from the scene—all without leaving behind the barest information regarding their lives. They were like so many voiceless bit players in the tumultuous drama of the westward course of empire. Hardly more than scenery, they moved briefly across the stage, barely seen and never heard. Others managed to build businesses and reputations which have endured, growing into near legendary figures in the great Westering adventure. They need to be known, if only casually.

The station for the Overland Stage Lines at Fort Kearny was situated about a mile west of the parade ground. About a mile west of the station, the westbound stages came to Dobytown—a motley collection of sod buildings housing a crude store, hotel, saloon, and eatery. The real name of the place was Kearny City, but somehow Dobytown seemed more descriptive, and the name stuck. An earlier attempt at townbuilding just to the north of Dobytown had been boldly named Central City, but by 1864, its only surviving establishment was Dirty Woman Ranch, a most appropriately named brothel.

About sixteen miles west of the fort was Hopeville, the ranch of an interesting character named Moses Sydenham, who was also the postmaster at the fort.[3] Sydenham was born in the Jewish section of London and spent most of his childhood and teen years working at a variety of labor intensive jobs. After sailing the high seas for several years, he immigrated to Georgia and from thence to Kansas City. In 1856 he signed on with a Russell, Majors, and Waddell train carrying supplies to Fort Laramie. Trapped by a blizzard at Ash Hollow, Sydenham and his fellow drovers were fed and sheltered by a band of Ogalala Sioux.

Returning as far as Fort Kearny, the freighters found themselves stopped by another blizzard. By that time, the young teamster had had enough of life on the trail, and he took a job in the sutler's store. Within a short time, he acquired his own ranch which he named Hopeville. Sydenham was a curious and energetic person who kept detailed records of the weather and planted an extensive garden for economic and experimental purposes.

After Hopeville, the coaches passed Fred Smith's Twenty-five Mile Ranch and the Shakespear Station to run on to the area of Plum Creek. Near Plum Creek Station were two stores—that of the Thomas Ranch, and another three hundred yards to the east, operated by Louis Wiscamb and Bernard Blondeau.

Crossing Plum Creek, the coaches continued another six miles to the ranch of Daniel Freeman (not the same Freeman who lived at Beatrice), who had gotten his start in Kansas.[4] Maybe there was money to be made in freighting between Leavenworth and Pike's Peak, but Freeman hadn't seen any of it. After one disastrous run which nearly wiped him out financially, he came to Nebraska Territory in 1861 and established a little trading post near Plum Creek. In the spring of 1862, he was joined by his wife, who drove all the way from Leavenworth with their three children in a wagon.

Fortune smiled on the Freeman family in Nebraska. Dan trapped furs in the winter, traded with the Indians for buffalo robes, hauled freight, and killed buffalo for meat. He also kept a herd of cattle which included twenty-five milk cows. Mrs. Freeman made butter and cheese from the milk, cooked meals for travelers (at $2 apiece), and reportedly baked 100 pounds of flour into bread every day. A large sign on their sod house proclaimed simply "BREAD" to passing trains, and the fifty-cent loaves were snapped up eagerly by emigrants and freighters. Mrs. Freeman estimated that, during the peak of the travel season, she made $30 a day in bread sales alone.

Eight miles past Freeman's and forty-seven miles from Fort Kearny was the Willow Island Ranch of Pat Mullaly, who had worked

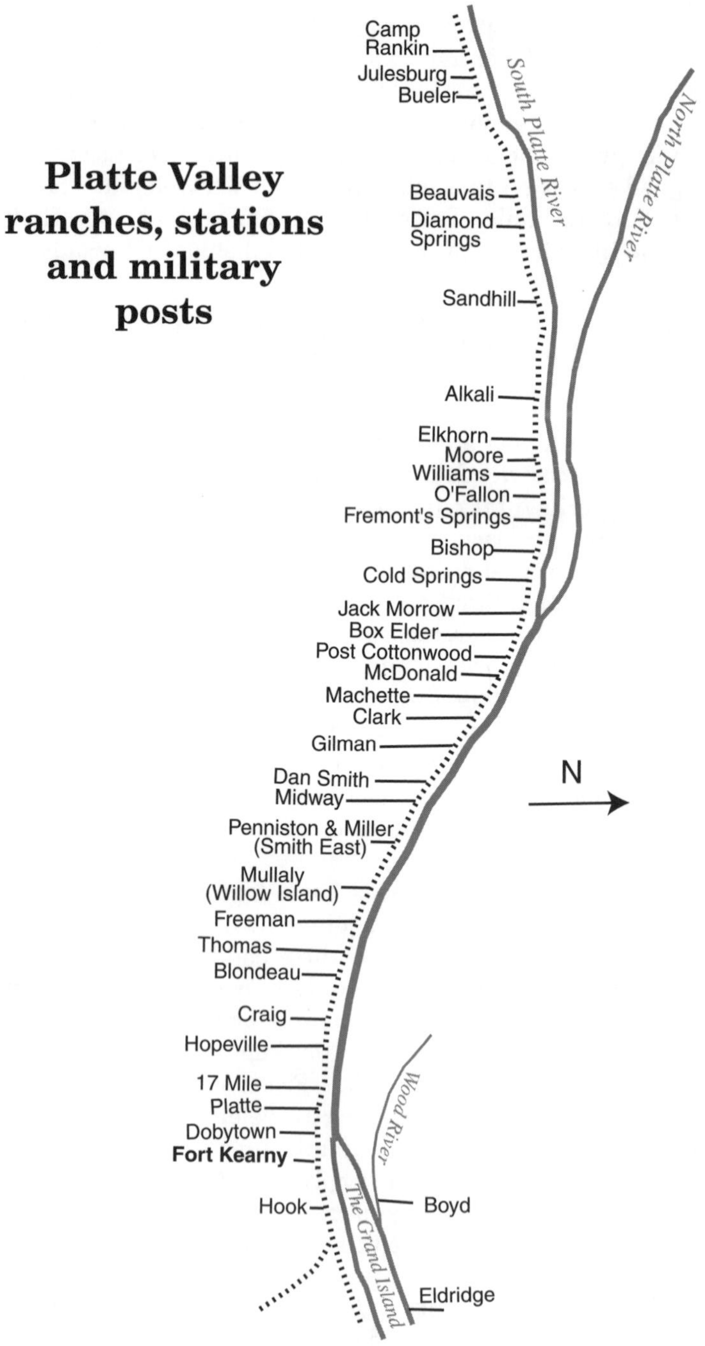
Platte Valley ranches, stations and military posts
Camp Rankin
Julesburg
Bueler
South Platte River
North Platte River
Beauvais
Diamond Springs
Sandhill
Alkali
Elkhorn
Moore
Williams
O'Fallon
Fremont's Springs
Bishop
Cold Springs
Jack Morrow
Box Elder
Post Cottonwood
McDonald
Machette
Clark
Gilman
Dan Smith
Midway
N
Penniston & Miller (Smith East)
Mullaly (Willow Island)
Freeman
Thomas
Blondeau
Craig
Hopeville
17 Mile
Platte
Dobytown
Fort Kearny
Wood River
Hook
Boyd
The Grand Island
Eldridge

as a laborer at the fort until 1861. Another eight miles brought the coaches to Dan Smith's East Ranch, operated in 1864 by the partnership of Miller and Peniston. Then came Midway Station, Dan Smith's West Ranch and, some seventy-two miles west of Kearny, Gilman's Ranch and Station.

The Gilman Ranch was the Platte Valley counterpart of Oak Grove—a bustling place crowded with family, friends, traders, layover travelers, and hired help. It was where it was because the Gilmans' wheels had literally fallen off at that place.[5]

Like Erastus Comstock, John and Jeremiah Gilman had come from the east coast states, New Hampshire, to be exact. Moving first to Iowa and then on to Nebraska City, the brothers and some friends attempted to set up a courier service to Colorado in 1858. Finding very little demand for couriers and a large demand for freighters, the Gilmans contracted with Hawke and Nuckolls of Nebraska City to deliver a load of goods to Denver City in the spring of 1859. Prices in Denver were naturally high and the freighters' profits were large. One trip convinced the Gilman brothers that those profits were not so much in the hauling of goods as in the buying and selling. In July they headed back for Denver City with two wagons loaded with merchandise which they had purchased on their own.

The Gilmans' wagons were not the large, rugged vehicles normally used by commercial freighting firms, and they were grossly overloaded with food, tools, trade goods, even a large, iron water pump. As they rolled up the Platte Valley, the dry heat of summer and the sandy soil began to tell on the overburdened wheels, loosening spokes and tires. The brothers attempted to keep the wheels together by soaking them with water, and progress slowed to a crawl. Then, some thirteen miles east of Cottonwood Springs, an axle snapped. There was no replacement, so a new axle would have to be crafted on the spot—an arduous job. It appeared that the Gilman's late season run to Denver City had ended far short of its destination.

Reluctantly, the brothers set up their camp. However, they found very little time to work on their wagon because every train going up or down the trail stopped to trade. Everybody seemed to need supplies, and it began to dawn upon the Gilman brothers that they really had no need to go to Denver City. The rainbow ended here, thirteen miles below Cottonwood, and there was a pot of gold to be made along the Platte.

By the spring of 1860, Gilmans' Ranch was in business. It consisted of two sod houses, a corral, and a stable. The storehouse boasted a hewn log counter with stools and a table of cedar wood, a cast iron cookstove, and a fireplace in one end. It was during the heat of that first summer that a sick and wounded Indian stumbled into the store one day. The Gilman brothers cared for him and in so doing, earned themselves the friendship and considerable trading prowess of Two Face, a mixed Sioux and Cheyenne Indian who was to gain a prominent, if somewhat checkered reputation along the trail between Forts Kearny and Laramie.

The ranch continued to prosper, due to the heavy trail traffic and the brothers' unofficial partnership with Two Face, who brought in rare goods from distant Indian camps for trading. In 1861, John Gilman married Martha Fitchie, of Nebraska City, who came west to share his life and lighten the burdens of the business. In 1862, Ben Holladay established at Gilmans' a stagecoach station, housed in a new building of cedar logs.

In late summer of 1863, Company F of the Seventh Iowa Cavalry came up the trail from Fort Kearny to construct a new military post at Cottonwood Springs. The Gilman brothers, along with other nearby ranchers, obtained a government contract to supply cedar logs for the new post, and there was a potential market for cut hay as well.

The new army post was situated near a popular camping ground which had developed around natural springs flowing from the bluffs. As early as 1858, Isidor Boyer and Joseph Robideau built a crude sod shanty on the site, from which they dispensed canned goods, ammunition, and whiskey to travelers. In 1859, Richard Darling began building a storehouse on the south side of the road near the springs, but soon sold out his interest to Charles McDonald. When the troopers of the Seventh Iowa came to the vicinity, they used the McDonald ranch house as their headquarters until the cedar buildings of the post were completed.

Several miles west of McDonald's was the ranch of Washington Hinman, a former government employee at Fort Laramie who brought his Indian wife, Clara, to the Platte road in 1860.[6] Hinman was, like Moses Sydenham, a person of great curiosity and industry. He set up a small sawmill and fenced off 250 acres of pasture and garden land. The vegetables and melons which he raised proved extremely popular with travelers, both white and Indian, and his produce brought high prices. Hinman was fluent in the Sioux and Cheyenne tongues, and served the army as interpreter at the new Camp McKean, which everyone insisted on calling Fort Cottonwood.

After passing Hinman's and Box Elder Ranch, the stages came to the super ranch of Jack Morrow, the gentleman thief, gambler, badman, and businessman. From Morrow's, the string of ranches and stations marched steadily westward along the South Platte to Diamond

Springs Station and Beauvais Ranch, after which the route divided, running south to Denver City or north to Fort Laramie.

As the Cheyennes and Arapahoes had observed, the route along the Platte was thickly populated, compared to the Santa Fe Trail, and they understood the important role played by the road ranches in the conquest of what had been their country. Their raids along the south Platte in July 1864 had heightened fears among the ranchers west of Kearny. Even the Gilman brothers, who had traded on friendly terms with the tribes for several years, built a cedar stockade around their ranch. During those July raids along the Denver Road, the hostile tribes took the measure of the military forces protecting the road ranches and had found them ineffective. Now, in early August, they were prepared to devastate the road west of Kearny as they had laid waste to the valley of the Little Blue—but it would be done differently.

The trail along the Little Blue was terrorized by small groups of warriors moving slowly and openly among the whites, their murderous intentions not betrayed by their ominous behavior until it was too late. Between Kearny and Cottonwood, where the valley floor was wide and flat, the white ranches and trains would be struck by great, howling war parties stretched across the prairie in long battle lines, thundering toward their ill-prepared quarry at frightening speed. And, if the tactics were to be different, the results would be the same: White people lying dead or in flight for their lives, abandoned ranches, wrecked trains, hundreds of lost draft animals, and economic disaster for those who survived. For the Platte River Road, August 8, 1864, was the day appointed for the explosion.

Chapter Four notes

1 Gilman, *Pump on the Prairie*, 57.

2 Federal Census, 1860, Nebraska Territory, Shorter County.

3 Wilson, *Fort Kearny on the Platte*, 183-188; Sydenham, "Freighting Across the Plains in 1856 . . ."

4 DAR, *Nebraska Pioneer Reminiscences*, 64-66.

5 Gilman, *Pump on the Prairie.*

6 Ibid., 57. Ware, *The Indian War of 1864*, 46.

Sources

DAR, *Nebraska Pioneer Reminiscences.*
Dawson County Historical Society, "Exploring the Great Platte."
Federal Census, 1860, Nebraska, Shorter County.
Federal Census, 1880, Nebraska, Lincoln County, North Platte.
Franzwa, *Maps of the Oregon Trail.*
Gilman, *Pump on the Prairie.*
Hutton, *Early History of North Platte.*
Miller, *The Road to Virginia City.*
Wallace, Plum Creek File.
Ware, *The Indian War of 1864.*
Wilson, *Fort Kearny on the Platte.*

Part II
Chapter Five

The war along the Platte

Monday, August 8

As the eastern edge of the night began to melt into a pale glow spreading upward from the horizon, the Platte River Road west of Fort Kearny began to stir into life. At the road ranches, the people left their beds to perform morning chores. Within the parked trains, the teamsters and bullwhackers began the ritual of breaking camp—yoking up, hitching up, greasing wheels, and a thousand other tasks performed a thousand other times. They knew these hours before dawn would be the coolest part of the day and that the first half of the day's run would be finished by ten o'clock. Then many of the trains would go into camp once again, laying over until late afternoon when they would commence their journey, not to halt again until eight or nine o'clock that night. It was a schedule decreed by sun and heat and dryness, and it conserved the strength of animals and men.

At the Thomas Ranch near Plum Creek Station, Lieutenant Joseph Bone was preparing for another day in the saddle. Three months before, his Company G, Seventh Iowa Cavalry, had left the Platte for its new station at Council Grove, Kansas. The red-haired, fiddling lieutenant had been left behind because of a chronic disability which caused him to be unfit for rigorous duty.[1] Now he was on his way home and out of the army. Lieutenant Bone had spent the night at the Thomas Ranch with his small escort. Soon they would resume their journey directly into the burning face of the August sun.

About four miles west of Plum Creek lay the camp of Mart Bowler's bull train. The twenty-six wagons were the property of Byram and Howe, freight contractors out of Atchison, and were returning from a run to Fort Laramie. Two hundred yards west of Bowler's camp was the corral of another eastbound train that had arrived late the previous evening.

East of the Thomas Ranch three and three-fourths miles was the solitary wagon camp of James Green and his wife—the same Green who had decided to turn back at Cottonwood, only to be badly shaken when those "biggest, blackest Indians" had tried to buy his wife. The Greens intended to make a "breakfast drive" to beat the heat, that is, they hoped to travel as far as Sydenham's Ranch at Hopeville before stopping for breakfast. With good fortune, they could be there around nine o'clock.

A hundred yards east and on the opposite side of the trail from the Green's wagon was the sleeping camp of the composite Kelly-Morton-Marble party, all bound for Denver City. Six of the wagons belonged to Michael Kelly of St. Joseph, who was freighting a load of shelled corn and farming implements west. Three wagons belonged to Thomas Frank Morton, of Sidney, Iowa. He and his wife, Nancy Jane, along with her brother, William Fletcher, and a cousin, John Fletcher, were taking a load of provisions and domestic articles to the Rockies. The trip was intended to be a tonic for Nancy, who was still deeply depressed following the recent deaths of the couple's two small children. For a change of pace from the bouncing wagon, she had even brought along her little saddle horse to ride.

The remaining three wagons in the camp belonged to William Marble, of Council Bluffs. He had been over the road several times before as an employee of several Council Bluffs businessmen. On July 23, Marble loaded his wagons at the warehouse of J.D. Lockwood and pulled out for the west with 9,200 pounds of hardware and provisions.[2] Sharing the driving duties were James Smith and his wife, Charles Iliff, and a Mr. St. Clair. William Marble evidently had little concern for danger from the Indians, as he had taken along two of his sons, nine-year-old Danny and twelve-year-old Joel. What was to have been a memorable adventure for the boys began to go wrong when, on the road east of Fort Kearny, Joel became very ill and had to be sent back to the care of his mother, Ann, in Council Bluffs.

These three parties, representing, as they did, the three most heavily used jumping-off places—Omaha, Nebraska City, and St. Joseph—had gathered quite by happenstance the previous day at a campground west of Kearny. To their anxious inquiries, the officers at the fort replied that the army was patrolling the trail and the Indians had quieted down. They would have little cause for alarm, at least as far as Cottonwood. The three groups evidently made no plans to travel together, as the Mortons had left early to make the drive to Plum Creek alone. They had been rejoined in their camp the previous evening by the Kelly and Marble wagons, and the men agreed among themselves to take turns standing watch through the night. They worried more about lawless whites than about marauding Indians.

As James Green and his wife began their drive that Monday morning, they passed the sleeping Kelly-Morton-Marble camp. Only Frank Morton and one other man were awake as the Greens' wagon rolled past, heading toward the lightening eastern sky and away from the deadly peril which was even then gathering silently in the southern bluffs and along the low banks of the Platte.

Although he was only fourteen years old, Will Gay was a large, strong boy capable of doing a man's work. With his father's consent, he had found his way into a man's world along the trail. His first trip from Atchison to Laramie with Mart Bowler's bull train was the hardest experience of his young life, but he also tasted a freedom which he found wild and intoxicating. It had been an interesting and, in some ways, an emotional experience. He formed a close friendship with Johnnie Moore, another boy drover. But Johnnie Moore carelessly pulled a loaded shotgun barrel-first from a wagon one day, and Will Gay was not ashamed to cry bitterly as he watched his friend being buried beside the Platte. Then, up near Beauvais Ranch, Bowler's train made camp near a westbound Mormon train. Lured by the promise of as many wives as a man could keep in the new Zion, three of Gay's comrades underwent a sudden conversion to Mormonism and deserted their employer to join the emigrants for Salt Lake City. Now in the faint morning grayness of August 8, Gay was herding 300 head of work cattle toward the opening in the wagon corral for the familiar routine of yoking up. As the bullwhackers sought out their animals, it became apparent that some were missing. In the dim light of predawn, Gay could see several of the cattle standing forlornly on an island in the river. Mounting Bowler's mule, he headed north toward the Platte to retrieve the strayed animals.

The boy bullwhacker had gone about 200 yards from camp when the mule began to act oddly nervous. The river was still a hundred yards away, but the mule was clearly unhappy about something. With every step it snorted, flattened its ears, and thrust them forward again. Gay was puzzling over the animal's balky behavior when, from the low riverbanks, came a chorus of war cries and a flurry of arrows. It was still too dark for accurate shooting, but one of the arrows slammed into the thick, buckskin pleat on the front of the boy's jacket and pierced his chest.

The mule needed no urging. It whirled around and raced back toward the wagon corral, while the frightened young rider drew his revolver and fired off all five shots in the general direction of the charging Indians. The attack came so suddenly that the bullwhackers were still running for their pistols as Gay thundered into the corral, slid off his mule, and grabbed frantically in the wagon for his rifle. Close on his heels came a score of mounted warriors who charged right into the circle of wagons, yelling like demons and creating an uproar among the yoked cattle. Some of the drovers located their weapons and opened fire on the invaders.

Will Gay pulled his rifle from under the wagon cover, whirled in the direction of a warrior, and snapped off a shot. The Indian pitched from his black pony, rolled, and lay dead near the wagon. All around the circle of wagons the men were banging away with their pistols, and another warrior fell wounded from his pony. The dust and screaming and exploding cartridges, the bawling cattle and the mounted terror which could be seen but dimly in the faint light, all drove the bullwhackers frantic. But their flurry of ill-aimed shots had an effect: The Indians broke back out of the wagon corral to join others in riding circles around the wagoners' chaotic camp. By this time, the bullwhackers in the second train had also opened fire with their pistols on the circling Indians.

Suddenly it was all over. The attackers whirled away, back to the bluffs and the riverbank, leaving two of their number behind. Through the dust and early morning haze, a third train could be seen approaching from the west. The men of Mart Bowler's outfit had been saved by sheer numbers and by Will Gay's untimely ride toward the Platte. The desperate battle probably consumed all of ninety seconds, but it left Gay and three other drovers wounded, and the rest shaking too badly to reload.

As the dust settled out of the air, there was a little talk about killing the wounded Indian who still lay inside the corral, but nobody really had much stomach for that sort of thing. Eventually, the men calmed their cattle and hooked them to the wagons, and the trains went on their way to the east, traveling three abreast to mass their firepower; for, even though the Indians had gone, they had not gone very far. As the sun arose, they could be seen shadowing the trains from the river and along the foot of the bluffs.

Will Gay had pulled the arrow from his chest during the chase back to the corral, but it was not until the attack had ended that he became conscious of the pain. The wound was not serious, thanks to his buckskin jacket, and none of the other drovers had been badly injured. All were happy to be on the move toward the safety of Fort Kearny. Behind them in the abandoned camp, they left the wounded Indian to the care of his fellows, and the strayed oxen remained standing on their river island. For the men of Mart Bowler's train it had been a very close call. Unfortunately, the day's tragedies were still to come.

It was about six o'clock when the Mortons and their companions broke camp.[3] James Smith rode out on a mule several hundred yards in advance of St. Clair and Mrs. Smith in their horse-drawn wagon. Several hundred yards behind them came the two mule wagons driven by William Marble and Charles Iliff. A short interval behind the Council Bluffs party came the three Morton wagons and, alongside them, the Kelly freighters. Thus strung out over a half mile of road, the wagons could better stay clear of each other's dust. Frank Morton had been on watch the latter half of the night, and he asked Nancy to drive while he slept in a small bed behind the wagon seat.

Bumping along behind her two span of mules, her husband asleep in the wagon behind her, Nancy Morton became lost in reverie. Deeply religious, sensitive to beauty, and something of a romantic mystic, she had, in her first nineteen years, lived an eventful life.

Born in 1845 to Samuel and Charlotte Fletcher of Clarke County, Indiana, Nancy came with her family to Sidney, Iowa, at the age of four. At fifteen, she became the bride of Thomas Frank Morton. She and Frank, as she called him, had then gone west to Denver City and beyond to the western slope, where Nancy was nearly widowed by a mine cave-in. The couple returned to Sidney that fall, where Nancy gave birth to a daughter, Charlotte Ann. On a second trip west in the spring of 1862, the Mortons purchased a small farm south of Pike's Peak, and Frank did some freighting between Pueblo and Denver City. During that happy summer, Nancy gave birth to a boy. But happiness stood in the shade of sorrow when her mother, Charlotte, died on August 7. The Mortons returned to Sidney in the spring of 1863, but a short time after they arrived, Nancy and both children contracted measles. Within a few days, the little ones were dead. Not only was Nancy emotionally prostrated by her grief, but her physical health was broken as well. During her convalescence, Frank and her brother, William, made a freighting run to Denver City and returned to find Nancy's health much improved. Frank planned to make at least one more trip to Denver before winter, and Nancy felt well enough to accompany him. The rigors of life along the trail, she felt, would complete the process of healing both mind and body.

On July 31, Frank and Nancy, cousin John and brother William, had left Sidney with three wagons loaded with goods they purchased in St. Joseph. They crossed the Missouri and spent the night in Nebraska City, where they met Nancy's younger brother, John. The teenager was concerned that the hot weather might adversely affect Nancy's health, and argued that she should stay behind. After doing her best to quiet his fears, Nancy and Frank and the Fletcher boys were guests at a dinner given in the Morton House Hotel, which was operated by Frank's relatives. The evening passed pleasantly, and the memory of that night would remain with Nancy for the rest of her days.

On August 1, the Morton wagons took the Steam Wagon Road to the Platte, camping on August 6 several miles west of Fort Kearny. Now, guiding her mules westward toward the crossing of Plum Creek, Nancy became acutely aware of the serene beauty of the river and the grayish-green bluffs of the "Coast of Nebraska." With the sun still low in the eastern sky, every detail of the landscape was etched in sharp relief. The long shadows cast by the mules and wagons crawled ahead of them, and distant landmarks appeared blurred and hazy, their colors muted to earthy pastels. All was calm, and Nancy felt her heart thrilling with a peace she had not known since the loss of her little ones. It was about seven o'clock.

Lieutenant Bone and the people at the Thomas Ranch were feeling anything but peaceful. Indians were milling around everywhere and they had not come to trade. A few braves were riding around Blondeau's store, aimless and agitated. Others were prowling the riverbank far to the west, shadowing the three trains which were approaching abreast. Indians were gathering at the mouth of Plum Creek while, a mile and a half to the east, the widely spaced column of Morton/Marble/Kelly wagons were advancing beneath the morning sun. If the wagons approaching from east and west maintained their rate of travel, they would pass each other a short distance east of the ranch. Everyone was tense with uncertainty. What were the Indians waiting for?

Then they came down out of the bluffs southeast of the Thomas Ranch—a group of more than 100 warriors, purposefully descending to the valley floor in almost military fashion. Lieutenant Bone counted five platoons of about twenty warriors each, and he watched in fascination as the Indians strung themselves out in a long, crescent-shaped battle line. Then war cries screamed from a hundred throats, and the entire line charged in the direction of the trail, straight toward the wagons approaching from the east.

Vicinity of the Plum Creek Massacre

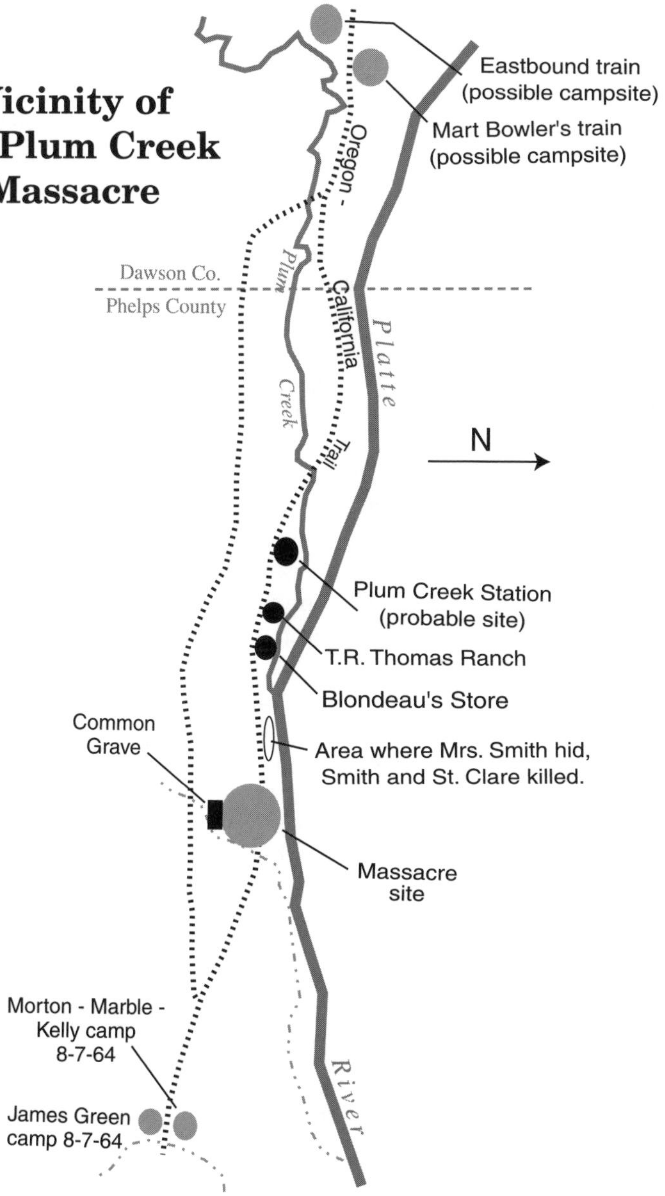
Eastbound train
(possible campsite)
Mart Bowler's train
(possible campsite)
Oregon - California Trail
Plum Creek
Platte River
Dawson Co.
Phelps County
N
Plum Creek Station
(probable site)
T.R. Thomas Ranch
Blondeau's Store
Common Grave
Area where Mrs. Smith hid,
Smith and St. Clare killed.
Massacre
site
Morton - Marble -
Kelly camp
8-7-64
James Green
camp 8-7-64

From the spring seat atop her wagon, Nancy saw, far ahead and to the left, distant objects moving through the thin haze. They seemed to be approaching rapidly, and she called her husband to take a look. Frank Morton roused himself briefly and said there was no cause for worry. Some of the road ranchers were probably out running ponies or cattle this morning. He was very drowsy and lay back down to sleep. But the galloping figures were nearer, closing quickly now. Far in the lead, James Smith wheeled his mule to ride back and warn his wife and St. Clair in the lead wagon. The Indians were upon them at once. Several warriors peeled off the end of the charging line to cut down Smith and St. Clair as the horses bolted down the trail. Terrified, Mrs. Smith leaped from the racing wagon and hid herself among the cattails in a low marshy area north of the road. She was within a half mile of Blondeau's store, and the Indians made no attempt to find her. They were intent on bigger game.

Nancy could see now that the approaching riders were Indians, and the urgency in her voice brought Frank quickly to her side. Yes, he agreed now, they were Indians.

"They are for battle!" Nancy cried.

"I think so," Frank replied, adding: "They won't kill you." He probably already knew that his own chances of survival were nil.

Nancy could hear the war whoops now, see the teams and wagons scattering ahead of them. Frank knew the mules would be crazed, and he climbed onto the seat, grabbing the reins and telling his wife sharply, "You can't handle the mules!"

Already the animals were veering off the trail toward the southern bluffs when Nancy swung over the side of the wagon and dropped to the ground. The last words she heard from her husband were, "O my dear, where are you going?" Then she hit and rolled on the ground, scrambled up quickly, and was struck a glancing blow by the wheel of a careening wagon, breaking several of her ribs. Painfully she picked herself up and began running back toward the trail. Ahead she saw her brother and cousin. They also had abandoned their wagons and were standing in the grass, firing pistols at the encircling horde of warriors. Nancy ran to join them, nursing a faint hope that they might all reach the river together. John Fletcher spied her coming and yelled, "We're all going to be killed!" Then an arrow sank deep into his side and he fell at Nancy's feet, a great river of blood welling from his body. In his last seconds of life, he pleaded, "If you get away, take care of my little children." Then he was still.

Nancy turned to her brother, who was still firing. William Fletcher glanced at her quickly and commanded, "Nan, go to the wagon." Then three arrows found him simultaneously, and he sprawled in a bloody heap. As Nancy leaned over him, he begged her to "Tell Susan (his wife) I am killed. Good-bye, my dear sister." Soon his body also was quiet.

Nancy looked about her. The pistols were all silent, now. The maddened mules galloped erratically, overturning some of the wagons. Several teams turned so sharply they broke off the wagon tongues. Mules were kicking and plunging in every state of distress, some wounded, some entangled in their harnesses. Nancy's little saddle horse broke free to go racing across the prairie with Indians in hot pursuit. The screaming, swirling mass of warriors was milling about the wrecked wagons and clustered around the fallen bodies, running the points of knives around the sides of heads and peeling off scalps. The war whoops were still sounding, and over the trail hung a pall of dust through which galloped painted warriors, maddened with the excitement of battle and blood lust. In the midst of this seething commotion, Nancy stood utterly alone and helpless. Her only dazed thought was to sit down by the side of her dead brother, keeping a sort of vigil.

An Indian rode up and demanded that she mount his pony. "I won't!" she yelled vehemently. "I'm going to hunt Frank!" Then Nancy began to run aimlessly, and several more braves rode up and warned her to stop or she would be killed. "Go ahead and kill me!" she screamed. "I'd rather die than go with you!"

But the Indians had no interest in killing the white squaw. Several braves grabbed her and thrust her bodily up onto the pony behind its painted rider. As he took her slowly through the scene of disaster, Nancy caught sight of the wagon in which she and Frank had been riding. The Indians had already ripped off the top and were ransacking the cargo. A blizzard of feathers erupted as they slit open her bed. She watched them smash open her personal trunk and scatter its contents across the prairie. Then they were beyond the destruction, riding toward the southern bluffs.

To leave a trail for the rescuers she was sure would be following, Nancy began dropping bits of clothing behind—first the collar of her dress; then a handkerchief, a shoe, a stocking, then pieces of a small apron she was wearing.

Her captor took her up into the bluffs and onto the divide for nine or ten miles before stopping near a small lake. Other warriors were already there, and a white renegade among them approached and asked her if she had noticed the arrows. Nancy looked at him blankly and asked what he meant. He showed her an arrow lodged under the skin of her left side and another dangling from her thigh. Her shock and grief had been so great that she had not even felt the pain. The white man produced a knife and helped her cut the skin so the arrows could be removed.

More Indians approached the lake, and Nancy could see that there was one other survivor from the wrecked train. Little Danny Marble had also been captured, and now he came running to her for comfort.

"What will we do?" he asked plaintively. "They have killed my father."

Nancy had no words of comfort, no solutions. So Danny supplied his own. "Let's do what they want and then they won't kill us." He also had a lot of questions: "What will my mother do when she hears that Father is killed and I am with the Indians? What will we do when we get to where the squaws are and what do they look like?"

Again Nancy had no answers. Finally, the two just sat in the grass and cried together. Danny was quite thirsty, and Nancy asked the warriors for some water which they brought from the lake in a coffeepot. Then it was back onto the ponies again for the ride south. Nancy was out of markers to leave on the trail behind the war party, but it didn't matter. Nobody was following as the Indians took the white woman and the little boy farther from the Platte River Road and into captivity.

Lieutenant Bone watched in agony as the wagons scattered under the attack. Some turned off toward the bluffs, while others veered toward the Platte where they bogged down in the sandy soil. He saw a few men trying to fight back with revolvers. Apparently, nobody in that outfit had a rifle. The Indians seemed to care little for the handguns, and rode right up to the wagons without fear. It was frustrating to see how those people were putting up so little resistance.

While the attack was in progress, the eastbound bull trains pulled a short distance past the Thomas Ranch and stopped. The drovers could plainly see the action taking place a little more than a mile ahead, and Will Gay thought that, if the men left the wagons, they might have time to run to the rescue. But Mart Bowler was befuddled and exerted no leadership, and many of the bullwhackers were still emotionally undone by the terror of the attack a couple of hours earlier, so everyone just stood around watching. Someone from Bowler's train carried the news of their early morning fight to Lieutenant Bone, who confused the two attacks in a frantic telegram to Colonel Summers at Fort Kearny: "Send company of men here as quick as God can send them. One hundred 100 Indians in sight firing on ox train."

One hundred Indians. Against them the ailing officer had only a handful of soldiers and maybe sixty drovers, none of whom were of a mind to attack the howling warriors with only their pistols. It seemed that Will Gay had the only rifle in the combined outfits. It was bitterly cruel, but the lieutenant could do nothing but watch through his glass as, one by one, the pistols stopped firing and then there were no longer any white men in sight. The decision had been made for him: There would be no heroic rescue. In truth, the attack had come so swiftly that it was over before any horses could have been saddled.

The bullwhackers watched as Nancy Morton was slung up onto a pony and taken south to the bluffs. They saw clouds of flour in the breeze as the sacks were spilled into the grass—saw the feathers flying and the mules captured, and Blondeau and his people come running from their store as fast as their legs could carry them.

The Indians were in no hurry. They brought some of the captured draft animals alongside the wagons and loaded sacks of coffee and sugar and all sorts of other plunder on their backs. It required a great amount of time to sort everything all out and properly mutilate the dead. By late morning, some of the warriors began trailing away to the bluffs with their captured booty. Others paid a return visit to Blondeau's abandoned store, ransacked the place, and thoughtfully left a drink for their white enemies: a bucket of whiskey with a strychnine mixer. Then the people at the Thomas Ranch saw the smoke and knew that the wagons were burning.

By early afternoon the day's work was done. The last ponies walked southward into the gentle bluffs and the dust settled around the burning wagons. Throughout the bluestem grass were scattered blotches of white—mounds of flour and naked bodies whose blood was blackening in the afternoon sun. And still there was no sign of Colonel Summers.

Where could he be? The operator at the Thomas Ranch had sent the wire at seven o'clock that morning. Given an hour to mount the company and six hours to ride to the site of the massacre, the colonel should have arrived no later than two o'clock. But as the sun slipped below the horizon in a puddle of fire, more than twelve hours had gone by and there was still no sign of the troops from Fort Kearny. Until they arrived, nobody at the Thomas Ranch was going anywhere. The bull trains remained parked squarely in the road while the drovers wrestled with their emotions. A mile down the trail, there were smudges of smoke rising into the darkening eastern sky, blowing across the Platte in the hot breeze.

The relief column was indeed on its way, if not quite as fast as God could send them. Not until eleven o'clock that morning did Colonel Summers leave Fort Kearny at the head of a force of civilian volunteers, Captain Murphy's Company A, and a few men from Company B whom Wilcox had left behind. Near Hopeville, they encountered James Green, inquiring where he had camped the night before. As they compared notes, Green realized that the outfit which had been so peacefully camped a hundred yards east of his wagon that morning had been wiped out, and that he and his wife had been within a few miles of being wiped out with them. The Greens decided this was one narrow escape too many, and would remain to make their home in Nebraska.

The relief column plodded on and stopped two hours for dinner. Through the hot afternoon the civilians chafed and muttered their displeasure at the colonel's dawdling march, and Captain Murphy came close to mutiny. Summers was worried about the condition of his horses, he said, and at one point ordered everyone to dismount and lead their animals for several miles. As the sun set over the trail ahead, the command was still a good distance from Plum Creek. By this time, none of the men had any illusions as to what they would find when they got there.

The column stopped briefly at Fred Smith's Ranch, or rather, at what was left of Smith's Ranch. Fred Smith and his wife had fortunately left for Dobytown that morning. As a matter of fact, James Green had seen the Smiths arguing as his wagon passed their place. Green got the impression that Smith wanted his wife to stay behind and help the hired man mind the ranch while he was gone, but Mrs. Smith wanted to visit Dobytown, too. Perhaps she did not altogether trust her husband away from home. Luckily for her, she prevailed, and only the hired man was on the ranch when the Indians arrived. Colonel Summers looked around the burned out place as his men hurriedly buried the body of the hired man near the front of the house. Then it was on to Plum Creek.

At ten o'clock that night, the troops arrived at the scene of the massacre. The heavy plank bodies of the wagons were still smoldering. Scattered in the trail and through the trampled grass, the ghostly bodies of the victims glowed faintly under a lowering, crescent moon.

In the marsh reeds north of the road they found Mrs. Smith, disoriented and incoherent, totally out of contact with the realities of the day past. Since it was too dark to accomplish much, they took Mrs. Smith in to the Thomas Ranch where the colonel's men set up their camp and went moodily to bed. No one was looking forward to the tasks of the coming day, and Mrs. Smith made the night miserable with her wailing and sobbing. As the men from the bull trains settled down for a night of disturbed rest, the scenes of the day played through their minds over and over again. Will Gay was still so shaken by what he had seen that he questioned how God could even exist.

At this time, none of the people at the Thomas Ranch knew of the devastation which had occurred the previous day along the Little Blue River; nor did they know that the Sioux and Cheyennes had appointed a further visitation of death and destruction on the morrow—this time to the ranches around Fort Cottonwood.

Tuesday, August 9

A fiery sun rose over the Oregon-California Trail, rousing the people at Gilmans' Ranch to their duties. Martha Gilman busied herself preparing breakfast for six, two more than the usual complement of hungry diners. Herman Angell, a friend from Nebraska City, had recently arrived for a visit, as had Martha's sister, Jennie, who was feeling much more chipper than when she had arrived the previous morning.

Jennie's coach ride from Nebraska City, with its layover at Fort Kearny, left her buffeted and battered. The trail was rough, of course, and everybody on board seemed to be expecting trouble from the Indians. The men riding inside all were armed and alert, but nothing happened. By the time the coach reached Midway, the passengers had relaxed their vigil and drifted off to sleep. Jennie arrived at Gilmans' Station in the wee hours of the morning and slept a good part of the day.[4]

John Gilman had been at Fort Cottonwood the previous afternoon—had heard the details of the Plum Creek attack, and realized that his sister-in-law had come within hours of being part of the massacre. The Indians may have already been in the bluffs as her coach passed through. It wasn't until this morning that the family told Jennie the sad news.

Gilmans' Ranch and Station now harbored sixteen people.[5] In addition to John and Jeremiah, Martha and Little George and their two guests, there was an agent and three stock tenders at the station, two hired men, and the Gillett family, who were living temporarily in one of the small sod houses. Mr. Gillett, his son, and a partner were building their own ranch several miles east of Gilmans'. While the men worked, their wives cared for an infant and kept house in the little soddy. Despite growing apprehension of trouble from the Indians, the men had continued to drive down the trail to work each day, sometimes not returning till late at night.

The Gilman brothers had traded amicably with the wild tribes for several years, and always attempted to treat them fairly. Consequently, they had never been troubled. In fact, Indians often camped close by the ranch, as they had the previous night. Even so, since all the trouble had begun along the Denver Road, the Gilman brothers thought it risky for three men to be working at an isolated place down the trail. They knew that this morning the men had gone to work as usual. They heard Gillett's horse leaving the ranch before sunup.

The family was still idling around the breakfast table when they heard galloping hoofbeats. Outside, Mr. Gillett's riderless horse dashed past the stockade with an Indian in pursuit. At the same time, the yard west of the ranch erupted in a flurry of shots and a chorus of war whoops.

There had been times in the past when young braves coming in to trade would announce their arrival by yelling and shooting into the air. But the news of Plum Creek and the sight of the riderless horse had made the Gilmans anxious and alert, and they were of a mind to take no chances. The noise and commotion near the corrals were not the behaviors of young braves who were merely feeling their oats. The Gilmans hurried back into the house and armed themselves for trouble.

The cacophony outside continued for several minutes before it moved eastward down the trail. Cautiously, John Gilman peered out the door to see Indians stampeding the bulk of his horses and mules into the morning sun.

As the family emerged from the house, the eastbound stage rattled into the station, and out stepped George Carlyle, agent and freight contractor for Holladay's Overland Stage Lines. Carlyle's coach had been within a half mile of Gilmans' when Indians had suddenly appeared everywhere ahead. As the stage had braked to a stop, the passengers watched, horrified, as warriors rode down into the breakfast camp of two men and killed them instantly. Other Indians went after a man named Robert Corriston, who was cutting hay along the river, and shot him off his mower. As the raiders whipped the Gilmans' stock away down river, the coach raced into the station to see whether anyone there was still alive.

The Gilmans were indeed all alive, but they held little hope for the safety of the Gillett men, who were working directly in the path of the raiders. The riderless horse was pretty convincing evidence that something had already gone wrong.

After exchanging information and calming their nerves, Carlyle and the other passengers climbed back aboard the coach to resume the perilous run to Fort Kearny. John Gilman went to the barn to saddle one of his few remaining horses. He would tag along with the coach to see what had become of the Gilletts, whose terrified women had since come running to the shelter of the main house.

They had gone only a short distance when they came upon the body of the elder Gillett, lying in the road, bristling with arrows. Continuing on to the site of the new ranch, John Gilman could see immediately that it would never be finished. The bodies of young Gillett and his father's partner lay in front of the house. They were cut up and spiked with arrows.

Looking toward the river, the people on the coach could see a few Indians moving eastward along the bank, apparently shadowing the whites. John Gilman was not particularly worried for himself. He was mounted on a big roan which was exceptionally fast and had the endurance to run full speed all the way back to the station, if necessary. But the coach could be an inviting target.

In spite of their hostile escort, Carlyle and the other passengers decided to continue on to Kearny, so Gilman turned his horse around for the ride back to his ranch, trying to figure out some gentle way to tell the three Gillett women that they were now widows.

At the ranch, the Gilmans hitched up the lumber wagon to retrieve the three bodies, which they would cover with some of Martha's good white sheets. The women hurriedly packed some food, water, clothing, and a few personal treasures. When the lumber wagon returned with its sad freight, the family boarded and turned west toward the safety of Fort Cottonwood. John Gilman rode out in front on his big roan. One of the hired men drove the wagon with Jennie on the seat beside him, holding Martha's good silverware and the Gilmans' family treasure box. In a seat behind, close to the bodies of their loved ones, rode the three sobbing women, young Gillett's wife cradling her baby in her arms. The other hired man drove the buggy with Martha and Little George, and the short procession set off at a trot for Fort Cottonwood.

The thirteen miles had never seemed so long, but they reached the post without incident. From their place of refuge, the family turned anxious thoughts to the safety of Jeremiah and Herman Angell, who had remained behind to defend the ranch. Too much hard work and sweat had gone into the place to give it up so easily.

The stage line animals were gone, and the three stock tenders had been killed in the morning raid. The agent, however, was determined to stay at his post. The three men were fairly sure they could hold the stockade against one or two dozen raiders. Grimly, they set about pumping pails of water and distributing loaded guns at strategic points. South of the road in front of the stage station sat two wagons loaded with shelled corn, waiting to be unloaded. Jeremiah decided against trying to move the wagons into the stockade. The Indians might return at any time and catch the men preoccupied with the task, so the wagons were left to their fate. The men closed up the stockade and took up their lonely vigil along a trail which had become unusually silent and empty.

With the dawn, Colonel Summers' men moved out to perform the post mortem of the Plum Creek raid. The freighters went along to help and to gawk at the incredible destruction. One of Mart Bowler's men picked up a scalp which the Indians had dropped. It had closely cropped red hair, and probably was not much to brag about.

The troopers and civilian volunteers spread out to search the area thoroughly. Three wagons and a light buggy were unburned. The rest were no more than smoldering heaps of black cinders. Thousands of articles from the wagons were strewn haphazardly over the prairie as if by a tornado. Someone found a silver-headed cane inscribed, "To D. C. James, by a friend, Council Bluffs, Iowa, 1856." There was also a Bible belonging to the Baker family and some school receipts made out to children of the same name. Everything not burned or destroyed by the Indians was gathered up, along with the remaining Marble wagons, and placed in the custody of Lieutenant Bone.

Then there were the bodies, thirteen, in all. One of the dead was a tall, strikingly handsome young man of about twenty-three. A gold ring still remained on the fifth finger of one hand. Nearby was the body of an older man, stout and well built, who apparently had fought a desperate battle for his life. The searchers found eight bodies lying in or close to the wide trail. Three others were found in the grass south of the road. Young Will Gay walked through the field of wreckage, physically sickened by what he saw. Most of the bodies had been scalped, their clothing stripped off, and shot full of arrows. Some had their eyes pried out. Others had their tongues cut out, or private parts cut off and stuffed into their gaping mouths.

On a little bench of land south of the trail, the men began digging a common grave. Then they laid eleven of the bodies side-by-side in the trench.[6] While they were working, Mrs. Dan Freeman and her children came hurrying by the scene of the massacre. The news of the raid had terrified them, and early in the morning, they abandoned their homestead to flee to Fort Kearny. Mrs. Freeman looked briefly at the remains of the men lying in the trench, and was struck by the enormous amount of blood smeared over the bodies. She also found it incongruous that some of them still had their boots on.

George Carlyle's coach came rattling down the trail, and he jumped out to watch the men fill in the trench. Lieutenant Comstock had already left the scene with some of the men to escort the distraught Mrs. Smith back to Fort Kearny. Though she appeared to understand that her husband was dead, she was unable to give any particulars of the attack or of the people who were killed.

The men of the burial party finished their grisly work and took their way sadly to the east. Back at Fort Kearny, Lieutenant Charles Porter assembled a dispatch giving particulars of the affair which he termed the "Plum Creek Massacre," and as such it has remained known down through the generations.

The freighters resumed their run to Atchison, and the prairie east of the mouth of Plum Creek fell silent once again. There remained only the charred timbers and scorched iron hardware of the wagons to mark the place where thirteen lives had come to an end. For a time, the trampled and littered grass would remain blotched by puffs of white flour and gouts of dried blood. And, of course, there remained the long mound of bare earth marked only by a stick—a common grave that was thoughtfully examined by nearly everyone who passed by. For more than twenty years, the ugly scar remained visible on its low bench of land south of the trail, until at last the wild prairie grasses reclaimed it under a shroud of dusty green.

The main events of August 9 had ended. All that remained for the Sioux and Cheyennes was a little mopping up here and there. They ran off the stock from Dan Smith's Ranch that afternoon, and even took a few animals from Fort Cottonwood itself. That evening, at Fort Kearny, one of the pickets drew some long range rifle fire from a passing warrior.

There was also a second raid on Gilmans' Ranch that afternoon. With preparations as complete as they could be, Jeremiah Gilman climbed up onto the roof, partly to keep watch, partly to escape the heat inside the enclosed stockade. Sweeping the river bottom with his telescope, he could see nothing moving anywhere. The trail and the river bottom were quiet.

The afternoon wore on. The sun burned down through a cloudless sky. The sweat dripped and the flies buzzed around. Perhaps the raids were ended. He would take another look. Jeremiah raised his glass to scan the riverbank to the northwest, and what he saw would have chilled the stoutest heart. A huge band of primarily Sioux warriors was crossing the Platte. There were hundreds of them, and soon they came racing down the trail and riverbanks toward Gilmans' Station. Jeremiah's yells alerted the other two men, and Herman Angell climbed up to join him on the rooftop. There was no way they were going to save the ranch. Nothing less than half a regiment could stop this raid.

The Indians surrounded the stockade, whooping, yelling, shooting, and raising an infernal racket. Smoke, then flames appeared from the grain wagons in front of the stage station. Fighting back was out of the question—and then Jeremiah Gilman got lucky. Some of the young braves milling about in front of the stockade looked familiar. They had probably come in to trade there at one time or another. Calling out to one of them, Gilman threw down his rifle and began shouting to him in the Sioux tongue as he had learned it from Two Face and some of the squawmen. The warrior stopped to listen. Then he raised his hand in greeting and began shouting to the others. Suddenly, the whole band took flight like a flock of blackbirds, thundering down the valley, until the drumming of hooves and the yipping and yelling died away in the distance.

By a turn of luck and some quick thinking, the men were still alive and the buildings intact. Only the burning freight wagons were lost that day (along with 3,360 pounds of shelled corn worth $672). The ranch and station were saved, not by a defensive stand, but by an appeal to the sense of justice within the enemy. Herman and Jeremiah climbed down off the roof. For a long time, the air inside the stockade was heavy and thick with fine dust and the odor of smoldering, popping corn.

By sundown on August 9, the initial fury of the Cheyennes, Arapahoes, and Sioux had spent itself. The war was not over by any means. Gilmans' Station would survive, although Martha, Jennie, and Little George were sent to safety in Nebraska City. In weeks to come there would be a few more deaths along the trail, mostly the result of random strikes for which it was impossible to prepare. But the worst of the killing was over. The South Platte Trail and the Overland Road from Julesburg to Big Sandy had been immobilized, seasoned with grief, and peppered with heaps of ashes, animal carcasses, and graves. The summer of 1864 was fast slipping away, but between Omaha and Denver City, the season of fear was still young.

Chapter Five notes

1 When Company G was ordered to Fort Riley on May 2, 1864, Lieutenant Bone remained at Cottonwood on detached duty as Acting Assistant Quartermaster. Family history has always maintained that his disability was the result of an arrow wound which became infected, but post returns from Cottonwood Springs prior to June 30 record no Indian skirmishes. Ware describes Bone as a redheaded farmer of no military capacity whatsoever. He did, however, play a good fiddle for the dance at McDonald's Ranch on April 24. Following his frightening experience at Plum Creek, Lieutenant Bone resigned his commission and was mustered out at Omaha on September 28, 1864, due to his disability.

Czaplewski, *Captive of the Cheyenne*, 56-58, 136.
Post Returns, Fort Cottonwood, 1864.
Roster and Record of Iowa Soldiers, Vol. 4.
Ware, *The Indian War of 1864*, 120.

2 Apparently, the goods on board William Marble's wagons were still the property of Lockwood. Marble likely was going to sell them in Denver as Lockwood's agent, receiving a commission. His gross profit from freight charges alone on this trip would have been about $1,012. He may also have been transporting some household goods for a family emigrating to Denver, possibly even towing their buggy and family carriage behind his freight wagons. Soldiers later found the buggy unharmed and the carriage burned at the scene of the attack. They also recovered a family Bible and school receipts belonging to the Baker family. If Marble planned to follow the pattern of the Gilmans and other independent freighters, he was probably saving money from his trips in 1864 to purchase his own stock of goods to sell in Denver the following year, which would have greatly enhanced his profits.

3 Of the many eyewitnesses to the attack at Plum Creek, only Will Gay and Nancy Morton wrote about their experiences. If Colonel Summers, Captain Murphy, or Lieutenant Comstock ever wrote an official report, such has never been found. Comstock, however, did interview witnesses at the Thomas Ranch and shared his information with Moses Sydenham and Lieutenant Porter at Fort Kearny. These second and third hand accounts fit quite nicely with that of Will Gay, even though Gay wrote his memoir later in life and was wrong on the date and some of the geographic details. The present reconstruction of the event is synthesized from the accounts of Gay, Nancy Morton, the report of Lieutenant Porter, and Indian depredation claims filed by Nancy Morton Stevens and Ann Marble. Also useful were the records written by people who subsequently traveled past the scene of the attack, USGS maps, interviews, known astronomical and meteorological conditions, and personal examination of the site as it exists today. There is simply no way to conclusively prove the truth of all the statements in the text. It is merely the best possible interpretation of what few facts are available.

4 Musetta Gilman states that Jennie's coach changed teams at Plum Creek just hours before the attack. But if the coach was anywhere close to being on schedule, it would have passed through Plum Creek somewhere between four and six o'clock on Sunday afternoon, arriving at Gilmans' Station before sunrise, about sixty-six hours after leaving Atchison. There was no through coach from Nebraska City, that section of the trail being served by the Western Stage Company. (Frederick, *Ben Holladay,* 113-114, 289-290; Gilman, *Pump on the Prairie.*)

5 There may have been more. Ware counted 150 men fit for military duty among the ranches from Gilmans' to Morrow's inclusive, and stated that "the largest number was probably at Gilman's Ranch." (*The Indian War of 1864*, 60.)

6 Eyewitness accounts agree that eleven bodies were buried in the common grave; yet Lieutenant Comstock, who was there, told Lieutenant Porter back at Fort Kearny that *thirteen* bodies were found. It must be remembered that James Smith, his partner (probably

St. Clair), and Mrs. Smith were far in front of the rest of the train. Thus Smith and his partner were killed about a half-mile west of the common grave, probably between the trail and the river, and would have been buried right where they fell, somewhere in the vicinity of Blondeau's store. Clyde Wallace related that, many years ago, a crew digging holes for fenceposts east of the Thomas Ranch uncovered some human remains, which may or may not have been those of Smith and his partner.

How many people, then, were with the combined outfits? Nancy Morton claimed there were thirteen, but she was barely acquainted with the St. Joe teamsters or the Council Bluffs party. No other information has been uncovered in regard to the loss of a family named Baker, so this is a possibility:

St. Joe (6 wagons)	Nebr. City (3)	Council Bluffs (3)
6 teamsters	Nancy Morton	James Smith
	Frank Morton	Mrs. Smith
	Wm. Fletcher	Mr. St. Clair
	John Fletcher	Charles Iliff
		William Marble
		Danny Marble

This makes a grand total of sixteen people. Nancy, Danny, and Mrs. Smith were not killed, which leaves thirteen male bodies to be buried, just as Lieutenant Porter and Moses Sydenham wrote to the *Nebraskian.*

Sources

Adjutant General's Report, Iowa, 1865, 1866.
Czaplewski, *Captive of the Cheyenne.*
DAR, *Nebraska Pioneer Reminiscences.*
Frederick, *Ben Holladay.*
Gay, "An Extract from the Life."
Gilman, *Pump on the Prairie.*
Marble, Indian Depredation Case #892.
Morton, Indian Depredation Case #332.
Official Records, Vol. 41, Part 2.
The Omaha Nebraskian, August 17, 1864.
Roster and Record of Iowa Soldiers.
Stevens, Affidavit.
Testimony as to the Claim of Ben Holladay.
Wallace, Plum Creek File.
Ware, *The Indian War of 1864.*
Watkins, "Incidents in the Indian Outbreak of 1864."

Nebraska State Historical Society
Nancy Fletcher Morton, age fifteen

Lyn Ryder, personal collection
Thomas Frank Morton

Courtesy State Historical Society of Iowa - Des Moines
Colonel Samuel Summers

Author's photo

The Plum Creek Massacre site. The common grave lies hidden in the prairie grass in the center foreground. The Indians rode down to attack from the bluffs at the extreme right of the picture.

PART III

The great errors of the age are very useful. One cannot remind oneself too often of crimes and disasters. These, no matter what people say, can be forestalled.

Voltaire

Part III
Chapter One
The defense of Grand Island

To Americans living in 1830, the concept of a transcontinental railroad seemed fantastic beyond belief. The very thought of spanning thousands of miles of wasteland with iron rails had an aura of insanity about it. Even if such a project could be completed (and this was by no means certain), it would be a monumental waste of resources. The lands between the Missouri River and the west coast were fit only for the aboriginal tribes that roamed aimlessly over its barren features.

But by the mid 1860s, the idea of a transcontinental railroad had matured greatly in the minds of the American public. Many now saw the project as desirable, even inevitable. It was also acknowledged that such an undertaking would be so mammoth that only one such line would ever be built. The important question was—along which route should it be built?

For a number of years, people from Ohio and Indiana, Iowa, Illinois, and other eastern states had been following the course of empire westward across the desolate region via the Platte Valley. Their descriptions of the route in letters sent to family and friends had so educated public opinion that, by 1857, it was a foregone conclusion that the proposed coast-to-coast railway would follow the route of the great overland trails up the valley of the Platte. And, if the line went by way of Council Bluffs, it would certainly stay north of the river, following in the track of the pioneering Mormon companies. Any towns located along its route could be expected to grow explosively, and in that growth, there were profits to be made.

Thus it was that, in the spring of 1857, a private investment firm in Davenport, Iowa, formed a company for the express purpose of locating a town along the projected route of the transcontinental railroad opposite the Grande Ile of the Platte. The firm of Chubb Brothers and Barrows quietly assembled a town company of five Americans and thirty-two Germans, recent arrivals in Davenport who had fled the "Prussianization" of their homeland. It was an excellent mix of people, embodying both vision and perseverance.

With ox teams and overloaded wagons, the company plodded across Iowa, crossed the Missouri River at Council Bluffs and the Loup at Columbus, and followed the Military Road until it reached a point near the mouth of the Wood River (approximately two miles southeast of the present village of Alda). As the surveyor began laying out the site of Grande Island City, the other members of the company made preparations for the harsh winter that they knew would soon come.

The Davenport Company (as it is usually known) proved to be as hardheaded and contentious as had the Separatists who had come to Cape Cod 230 years before. They bickered and quarreled among themselves, and one of their early town meetings adjourned with a fistfight. Just as Grande Island City was taking root, Chubb Brothers and Barrows went bankrupt. Without financial backing from Davenport, some of the Americans left, and the infant town died aborning. The Germans spread themselves out on squatters' claims along the Military Road, mutating from town builders into road ranchers. They could hardly have timed it better.

As travel roared up the trails to the gold fields in 1858 and 1859, the Germans were ready with abundant supplies of cut hay, corn, and vegetables, and Major Charles Augusta May awarded them a generous contract for the supply of shelled corn to Fort Kearny. By late 1859, the stoutly-defended claims north of the Grande Ile had become known along the trail as Grand Island City, or The German Settlements.

Those early years were marked by troubles with hunger, with the whistling blizzards of winter, and with lawless white men, one of whom burned down a portion of the settlement. But the Germans were bothered not at all by Indians. They pursued their "live and let live" policy with strangers, both red and white, if not with each other, and were quite accustomed to seeing large bands of Sioux, Cheyennes, or Pawnees roaming nearby. But the murders of the Smith and Anderson people in early 1862 began to alter the Germans' benign attitude toward the Sioux and Cheyennes.

Like most of his neighbors, William Stolley was a refugee from his native Schleswig-Holstein, and had been a sharpshooter in the uprising against the Prussian invaders. Unlike most of his neighbors, Stolley foresaw a time when the settlers would be compelled to organize a defense of their claims against those Indians whose hostilities were, for the time being, confined to the country along the North Platte River.

The year following the Smith and Anderson killings, Stolley began the construction of a fortified blockhouse on his claim. The building was twenty-four feet square, and built entirely of cottonwood logs. He also stockpiled powder, surplus arms, and food. The work progressed slowly, since he was acting virtually alone. Indeed, Stolley had to endure the derisive comments of his neighbors who considered his actions cowardly. But Stolley was never very good at being intimidated, and kept doggedly on with his work until, by August 1864, the blockhouse was complete, except for its roof.

Early on August 8, the news of the Plum Creek Massacre came over the telegraph wire. That same day, Indians drove off some stock from James Boyd's ranch on the Wood River, and for the first time, the Germans became frightened. Many gathered around Stolley's farm, looking for leadership and mutual reassurance. There they spent the night, talking together and laying plans for action in case the raids moved nearer. By the following morning, the sense of crisis had evaporated, and most of the people returned to their homes, though a number of Stolley's closer neighbors remained to help him complete his blockhouse.

The construction progressed rapidly. The workers soon finished the roof and began building an earth-sheltered stable eighty feet long, connected to the blockhouse by a tunnel. They also dug a well in one corner of the little fort, and moved in forty pounds of powder and a two-month supply of food. Stolley had planned his blockhouse to shelter only his family and a few close neighbors, and he figured its maximum occupancy at thirty-five. Since there were over 200 people in the settlement by this time, there was an obvious need for another fortification, unless the Germans intended to leave their homes and flee down the trail to Columbus. Nothing could have been farther from their minds.

A mile and a half east of Stolley' claim, two Germans named Koenig and Wiebe operated a general store which they called the O.K. Store. Lieutenant Ware had stopped there the previous summer on his way to Cottonwood Springs, and noted that it contained a large variety of goods for sale. It also contained a telegraph office. Now it was to become a fortress as well.

A number of men began work on sod ramparts enclosing the store and its adjoining stable. There had come to the community a man named Wilhelm Thavenet—reportedly a descendant of the Marquis de LaFayette—who was knowledgeable about military engineering, and he was placed in charge of the construction. The Germans also organized a home guard and elected Dr. Wilhelm Thorspeken captain.

It was the news of the attack on George Martin's ranch that drove the Germans into their defenses. Beginning on August 13, a horde of panicked homesteaders from along the Wood River came pouring down the Military Road, leaving homes and crops behind them in their wild flight to safety. In heavily loaded wagons they came, on foot and by horseback, crowding the trail for a distance of twenty miles back, raising a mighty cloud of dust to mark the path of their exodus.

Stolley, Heinrich Egge, and other leaders of the German community went out to the trail to meet the Wood River refugees, pointing out to them the dangers of being all spread out and disorganized along the road, remonstrating and pleading with them to stand their ground and fight for their homes.

"As far as I'm concerned, let the red devils come," said Stolley. "We will take scalps instead of giving them up." His pugnacious stand should have been infectious—but it had no effect at all. Throughout that hot Saturday and Sunday, the road remained crowded with fleeing families. A few of the Germans sent wives or personal treasures down the trail to safety, but only a few. The rest gathered in Fort O.K. and in Stolley's Fort Independence to prepare a warm welcome for the red invaders.

The defenders of Grand Island City sent patrols out into the nearby countryside and piled stacks of hay and brush in strategic locations. In case of attack, these would be fired to warn all those outside the protective works, much as signal fires had been used 276 years earlier to alert the English defenses to the approach of the Spanish Armada.

Probably no one thought about it at the time, but the defense of the German settlements was a surrealistic melding of the modern with the medieval. Inside the prairie castles with their sod ramparts and log watchtowers, the defenders cared for their children and animals, ate their stockpiled food, drew water from protected wells, and prepared to light signal fires at the approach of a foe who fought with bows and arrows, lances and clubs. Yet in the midst of this mobilization from the Dark Ages, the electric telegraph clicked away merrily, bringing news of troop movements and events hundreds of miles away. The Germans were at once physically isolated from, yet technologically connected to their countrymen all across their adopted land. And they were united with each other.

Stolley later wrote, "What foresight and reason could not do, fear soon did, and almost all the Germans in this region became united. Isn't it a wonder that Germans actually became united for once? Surely the club lay with the dog."[1] Surely, too, the Sioux and Cheyennes would find the Germans' fortifications an even greater test than Pawnee Ranch.

But they did not. They never even tried. There was no reason for the Indians to attack the Germans since the focus of their anger was along the Oregon-California-Denver Road south of the Platte. By the time the wagons dispatched by Adjutant Pratt arrived with the requested arms and ammunition, the threat had about worn itself out. Not that the arms would have done much for the people in the forts, anyway. According to Stolley, they consisted of sixteen old, bent blunderbusses on some of which the screws and locks were missing. (Surely he exaggerated. Pratt would have never wasted the effort to transport such a ridiculous load.)

The Germans were justifiably proud of their courageous stand. They had withstood challenges to their claims from red men and white. The panic which had swirled around them for two days had been mainly generated by the newcomers along the Wood River. But if the Germans had not allowed themselves to be caught up in the growing hysteria, there were other settlements north of the Platte which now found themselves in the path of a retreat which had developed far beyond the fondest imaginings of the Sioux and Cheyenne warriors.

Chapter One notes

1 Stolley, "The Defense of Grand Island," 225. The English equivalent for Stolley's German idiom would be "the lion lay down with the lamb."

Sources

Anderson, "Old North Channel."
Egge, "Diary."
Manley, *The Town Builders.*
Stolley, "The Defense of Grand Island."
– *History of the First Settlement.*
Ware, *The Indian War of 1864.*

Part III
Chapter Two

The fortification of Columbus

The prairie hay was growing dusty and withered in the heat of the August sun. But no hay was being cut at the Pawnee Agency this summer—not since June 24, anyway. The Sioux attack on Pat Murray's crew so frightened whites and Pawnees alike that Charles Whaley, the government-employed farmer to the Pawnees, found it impossible to induce hired help to cut hay in the meadows along Looking Glass Creek. With the hay unharvested and the gardens shriveling in the drought or being chewed up by grasshoppers, the approaching winter promised to be a very lean time for the Pawnee tribe.

The incident on the Looking Glass had badly shaken the citizens of Columbus as well. The Smiths were some of their own. Adam Smith, whose body now rested in the little pioneer cemetery, had, with his brother. Michael, been one of the earliest settlers of the young town.

Michael Smith had been part of a Columbus, Ohio, town company with a knack for harmony in design, if not in its interpersonal relationships. The original townsite, laid out in 1856, measured fourteen blocks by eighteen. Four public squares were set near the four corners and a large public square of ten acres was reserved near the center. There were a few lots missing where the Loup River chewed its way through the southwest corner of the townsite, but on the whole, the plat was orderly and regular. The company's pride and joy was the American Hotel, located just south of the main square. A pine building of two and one-half stories, measuring forty by sixty feet, the hotel boasted its own well and privy. Six blocks south of the hotel was the ferry across the Loup River. Though its toll was considered high, the ferry was popular because it saved travelers the inconvenience of having to follow the historic Mormon Road twenty miles up the Loup to a safe ford near the Pawnee Reserve.[1]

On August 8, the news of the Plum Creek Massacre came to Columbus over the telegraph wire. As in Beatrice and along the Wood River, the virus of fear had been incubating in the town, and now the fever began to manifest itself. The citizens called a town meeting and organized a home guard. But, as in so many other places that summer, the home guard was sorely in need of weapons and ammunition. On August 10, the town dispatched a man named Hays to Omaha to beg the release of some territorial arms from Governor Saunders. No sooner had the man departed on his mission when word of the killings on the Little Blue began to arrive on the wire from Fort Kearny.

As bad as the situation sounded, it rapidly got worse. Over the Loup ferry came a stranger who claimed to be an independent freighter. He had been resting his oxen in the angle between the Platte and Loup Rivers, he said, when a war party of forty Sioux braves surrounded his camp. Of course he feared for his life, but as luck would have it, he recognized some of the Indians from past encounters, and they recognized him as a friend. Because of this, they not only spared his life, but took him into their confidence.

They were only a scouting party, they told him, for a huge force of warriors—several thousand of them, actually—which was making its way down the Platte, mopping up all the white people in its path. The Indians allowed him to leave (presumably with his oxen) and solemnly enjoined him to keep the big raid a secret. Of course he did no such thing, but crossed the Loup and spread the alarm with all possible speed.

Columbus exploded in a frenzy of preparation. The news went out on the telegraph along the Military Road, and riders dashed north to warn the German and Irish settlers along Shell Creek. Soon there were knots of refugees streaming southward toward the town. Pat Gleason and Tom Lynch, friends of Pat Murray, brought in their families. On their heels came the Carrigs, Lusches, Reinkes, Ahrens, and Losekes—all coming in by wagon and on horseback, and bringing their livestock with them. Not only did they bring their cattle, but also their hogs, sheep, even their chickens. Best of all, many of these people brought in wagon loads of cedar poles and fencing from their farms. Soon 300 men were busily erecting fortifications around more than a half dozen blocks in the center of town. The stockade enclosed Buffalo Square on the east and the American Hotel on the west, and the hotel became headquarters for the home guard as well as for the town government.

A number of settlers living along extreme upper Shell Creek fled to the Pawnee Agency. Before Captain David quite knew what was happening, he was beset by throngs of frightened homesteaders, looking to his cavalry for protection. But David was finding himself short of serviceable horses, and could do little more than position his men for defense and wire Omaha (via Columbus) for instructions. No guns and no horses. It was the litany of frustration throughout the District of Nebraska that summer.

Mr. Hays arrived in Omaha for an audience with Governor Saunders which proved fruitful, in a limited way. The governor agreed to release fifty outdated muskets and 2,000 rounds of ammunition for the use of the hardy settlers of Columbus. Mr. Hays' next task was to get the arms back to the town.

To the Herndon House he went, to appeal to Adjutant John Pratt for a federal wagon. Pratt was unwilling to furnish a wagon to carry the arms without an escort, and there were simply not enough mounted troops available at district headquarters for escort duty. He would wire General Mitchell for instructions, but in the meantime, Mr. Hays would do well to beg a wagon from Governor Saunders.

Somehow the scare which sent Mr. Hays to Omaha was not as intense in Columbus as it was in Beatrice. Possibly that was because the attacks, while horrible indeed, were farther away. Then too, the citizens of Columbus were old hands at dealing with Indian troubles. They recalled with pride and self confidence how their town company of militia had participated in the Pawnee War only five years earlier. For whatever reason, the rush to Columbus was more rational and better prepared than the rush to Beatrice. During the daylight hours, many of the refugees returned to work on their farms. At night, though, everybody crowded into the stockade. Of course, the animals were as much dismayed by their strange environment as the people were, and with their bawling and grunting, screeching and cackling, nobody got very much sleep.

Even though the people were excited and apprehensive, there was also a general conviction not far under the surface that the threat of danger from Indians was greatly overblown. A posse of citizens rode out to the place between the rivers where the freighter claimed to have been surrounded by Indians. They searched the ground thoroughly but found no corroborating hoofprints, no sign that Indians had been anywhere nearby. The story was beginning to smell very much like a hoax.

Luther North had recently returned from his frightening encounter with the hostiles along the Platte, and the home guard detailed him, along with two other men, for guard duty one evening. The three took their blankets and rode out toward Pat Murray's farm to keep watch.

Herschel Needham was one of the more excitable settlers. He brought his wife and four-year-old daughter in to the safety of the stockade, though he returned to work on his farm which was located a mile north of Pat Murray's place. North and his companions knew that Needham would be returning after dark, and concocted a little practical joke to play on the unfortunate man.

As Needham came driving down the darkened road back toward Columbus, the three "guards" wrapped themselves in their blankets and rushed at his wagon from ambush, giving the war whoop with all their might. The terrified settler whipped up his team and raced back to the stockade, witless with fright. His vivid description of the attack so alarmed everybody that sleep was impossible for the night. Needham was so sure the defenses would be overrun that he cautioned his wife, "Now Christina, if the Indians come, it is everybody for himself, and you will have to skulk."

But for the citizens of Columbus, help was on the way. Adjutant Pratt had finally scared up a wagon and escort to transport Mr. Hays and his arsenal back to the town. By the time the weapons arrived, the big scare was winding down. Everybody was cross and fatigued from lack of sleep, and the Indian menace seemed to be moving westward, anyway. The people remained forted up a while longer—— better to be safe than sorry—but their fears of an attack were dwindling day-by-day. By the last week in August, the stockade began to come down and the settlers returned to their homes for good. By that time, the tide of fear had swept down the north side of the Platte and across the Elkhorn, all the way to Omaha.

Chapter Two notes

1 A measure of the importance of the Loup Ferry can be found in the records kept by the Columbus town company for the first six months of 1859. In that period of time, the ferry transported 1,807 wagons, 5,401 men, 424 women, 480 children, 1,610 horses, 6,010 oxen, 406 mules, and 6,000 sheep. (Danker, "Columbus," 283.)

Sources

Andreas, *History of Nebraska.*
Bureau of Indian Affairs, Letters Received, Pawnee Agency.
Danker, "Columbus"
DAR, *Nebraska Pioneer Reminiscences.*
Federal Census, 1860, Nebraska Territory, Platte County.
Land Records, Platte County Recorder; Columbus, Nebraska.
Lizzy Ricketts Whaley, Letters; Platt Family Papers.
The Omaha Republican, August 19, 1864.
Official Records, Vol. 41, Part 2,693.
Phillips, *Past and Present of Platte County.*
Taylor, *History of Platte County.*

Part III
Chapter Three
Panic in Omaha

Omaha was a tough town, no question about that. From its waterfront westward to the brave, new territorial capitol building perched atop Capitol Hill, the city lay in a regular pattern of dirt streets lined with mercantile and outfitting houses, grog houses, and less reputable houses. Lieutenant Ware found the place unsurpassed in the adhesive qualities of its mud, the steadiness of its winds, and the vileness of its whiskey. The brawling streets were jammed with a seething swirl of freighters' outfits, riverboat crews, military and government personnel, and, of course local citizens. Children escaping the rush of the streets ran off to play by the river. Already during the summer of '64, several had drowned in its muddy currents. Fires and shootings were frequent, and it seemed to Ware that someone was killed every day.

A large part of the local economy was driven by the business of the trails, particularly the transshipment of goods from river boats to points along the Platte Valley and to Denver City. To support this activity, the markets for produce and forage were booming, and numerous blacksmith shops added their acrid charcoal smoke to the atmosphere that overhung the pungently perfumed streets. The community was informed of all the latest local and national news by two newspapers—one Republican and one Democratic in philosophy—whose editors consistently took nasty swipes at each other, while saving their best editorial shots for either Lincoln or McClellan; for 1864 was, after all, an election year of unsurpassed importance.

The days of the High Plains freighter were numbered. The end of the war would certainly bring a resumption of work on the transcontinental railroad. Already a few miles of roadbed had been graded westward from the city, and speculation in land was running wild. Of course this twin transportation boom—wagon freight and railroad construction—and its attendant speculation, resulted in a robust banking system in Omaha, and vaults were bulging, not only with the cash flow of the local economy, but also with gold and valuables transferred up from southern parts of the territory where the danger of guerrilla raids was much greater. By the summer of '64, the contents of those vaults was pretty much an open secret, one which was giving Omaha a bad case of the jitters.

Only eleven months before, the town of Lawrence, Kansas, had been ravaged by William Quantrill's gang of bushwhackers. Operating in the Kansas-Missouri border region, Quantrill had for two years presided over an orgy of barbarism that rivaled that experienced on the Pennsylvania frontier in the closing years of the French and Indian War. His savage revenge on Lawrence had revolted the stomachs of hardened frontiersmen, and all efforts to hunt him down brought nothing but disaster to his pursuers.

In the months following the Lawrence raid, a number of prominent citizens in Omaha received anonymous letters threatening similar attacks on the river town. Indeed, three outlaws believed to be members of Quantrill's legion were seen boldly strolling the streets of Omaha, recognized by local citizens who had known them in the border country years before. It seemed reasonable that they must be studying the layout of the streets and the locations of the various banking houses.

It was incredible to think that a city of such size and vitality, bristling with armed men, would be considered by the bushwhackers to be an inviting target. Yet, only forty-five miles to the south, a guerrilla band had for some time been quartered in Nebraska City. Though the gang had been routed from town by the guns of its citizens, and further weakened by attacks of citizen posses from Brownville and Sidney, Iowa, nobody was quite sure where the survivors might turn up next. The banks of Omaha could be a powerful drawing card for such undesirables.

To be sure, the city had long felt itself safe from the type of raid that brutalized Lawrence. With the Missouri River at its back, Omaha was further buffered by friendly Indian tribes and outlying settlements along the Military Road on the north and west. However, the southwest approaches to the city remained unguarded. From that direction, a gang of guerrillas might approach the city over miles of open prairie, virtually unpopulated as yet by white settlers. Such a gang might even disguise itself as a band of Indians (which were in such abundance in the area) and in so doing, ride undetected right into the outskirts of the city.

On August 8 began the first trickle in the flood of reports of Indian raids along the trail between Fort Kearny and Julesburg. This was quickly followed by news of the butchery along the Little Blue. On Friday, August 12, Mr. Hays arrived from Columbus with news that the settlers were fortifying the center of town, and requesting donations of firearms and ammunition for its defense. It took him only a day to gather a stock of muskets and shot, which left Omaha on a military wagon that Saturday evening.

On August 11, Governor Saunders issued his appeal for the formation of select groups of minutemen willing to march to the scene of Indian depredations at a moment's notice. All available military personnel had long since been sent westward to stations along the Military Road and the Oregon-California Trail. Omaha quickly began to jam up with freight outfits and travelers who were waiting for the army to put a lid on the Indian troubles before they would venture west.

All the pieces of a dangerous situation had fallen into place: the anonymous letters; the sighting of known border ruffians boldly walking the streets; the bank vaults stuffed with valuables; the removal of the military; the general uprising of Indians and depopulation of the Little Blue Valley; rumors of huge war parties sweeping down the Platte Valley and the fortification of settlements only eighty-five miles to the west; pro-Confederate guerrillas active around Nebraska City; unnumbered Confederate deserters and bushwhackers infiltrating the burgeoning throng in the streets; and all that barren, lonely prairie stretching away to the southwest and across the Platte. The threat of violence had moved uncomfortably close, and Omahans were not feeling so secure anymore. The town was primed for a panic which needed only a single incident to set it off.

Such an incident was not long in coming. At two o'clock in the morning of Tuesday, August 23, a disorganized group of twenty families came rushing headlong into town. They were refugees from homesteads along the Elkhorn River directly west of the city, and they had been frightened away from their farms by large bands of Indians hanging around in a threatening manner. No, there had been no warlike acts or injuries done, and no one really knew which tribe they represented, but with the terrible uprising raging along the Oregon-California Trail, could there really be much doubt? The settlers' nerves had finally gotten the best of them, and they had joined together for protection and run for the cover of Omaha as fast as their animals could carry them.

Before the city had fairly digested this ominous news, a number of frightened men came flocking in from the southwest. They had been herding several hundred work cattle down along the Platte—animals which belonged to Ed Creighton, the contractor who built the transcontinental telegraph line. Now the cattle were gone, stampeded the previous night by a large band of Indians who had crossed the Platte and driven them off. The herders ran for their lives, straight to Omaha to give the warning. No, they did not know which tribe the Indians belonged to, but with the bloody work being done by the Sioux and Cheyennes to the west, could there really be much doubt?

Omaha was in an uproar. Hostile Indians had crossed to the north side of the Platte! For some citizens it seemed a good time to head for safer places. All day long, the Missouri River ferries carried load after load of people across to the security of Council Bluffs and there was talk of passing an emergency ordinance to prevent their defection. Most Omahans, however, reacted more with anger and determination than with fright. Local authorities ordered all businesses closed until further notice, and convened a meeting at the courthouse at two o'clock that afternoon to lay plans for the defense of the city. The meeting also organized a home guard, and by sunset Tuesday, companies were dispatched to protect all approaches to the city. Up on Capitol Hill, Governor Saunders issued an executive order for the enrollment of every able-bodied male in the territory between the ages of eighteen and forty-five into four-month militia companies. Seven such companies were immediately formed, four of them in Omaha itself. For some reason, Company D was composed of older men, and naturally dubbed the "Graybeard Company."

There were in the city, a number of men who had military experience, having served with the former Second Nebraska Cavalry. Captain Roger Beall's company of the old Second had been assigned to garrison duty at Fort Kearny, and he now took command of militia Company A. Former Major John Taffe, originally from Dakota City, assumed command of Company B. Taffe, an imposing man with a full, bushy beard, and his second lieutenant, Abraham Deyo, had both seen action with Sully in Dakota Territory the previous year. In fact, it had been Taffe's original Company I to which the tragic Henson Wiseman had been assigned. On Wednesday, August 24, he set his unit of fifty mounted men in motion southward toward the Platte and the scene of the stampeding of Ed Creighton's cattle.

The expedition proved to be anticlimactic. Upon reaching the Platte, Taffe discovered a few of the herders had stayed nearby and had already recovered most of the cattle. The stampede turned out to be an ill-timed prank of the friendly Omaha tribe, returning from an abortive hunt on the Republican. There were no hostile Indians anywhere in the vicinity.

Perhaps there were none along the lower Platte, but they were in abundance sixty miles north of Council Bluffs. For, as Taffe was scouting the scene of the cattle stampede, a band of hostile Santee Sioux crossed the Missouri River near Decatur, Nebraska, and attacked some friendly Winnebagoes near Onawa, Iowa, killing eleven of them. Citizens of Omaha who had fled to Council Bluffs must have wondered if their hasty exodus had been such a good idea after all.

Captain Taffe turned his men north toward the deserted homesteads on the Elkhorn, scouting the area thoroughly. There were no hostiles to be found, but the meddlesome Omahas had helped themselves to goodies left behind by the fleeing whites. Taffe continued his scout northward along the Elkhorn nearly to the crossing of the Military Road, but turned up no traces of Sioux or Cheyennes. The entire scare had been perpetrated, wittingly or not, by the Omahas. With rations exhausted, Company B returned to the city on September 2 where Taffe's report quickly calmed the remaining anxieties of the citizens. The outlying sentinel duty soon ended and businesses were reopened, except from four to six p.m. daily when the home guard was drilled; for, if the threat from hostile Indians had evaporated, the danger from guerrillas was still very real.

To their credit, the citizens of Omaha had not panicked, at least most of them had not. They had kept their heads, organized, and taken stern measures for their defense. The *Omaha Republican* of Friday, September 3, published a calming and common sense summary of the whole affair:

> *With so much trouble on the Atchison route, it is not to be wondered at that a feverish excitement prevails in the Valley, and that a very slender story will soon assume alarming proportions. Here in Omaha, we have at no time apprehended danger from the Indians. It is the fear that there is working, at some point not remote from us, a more dastardly foe in the shape of* guerillas *that has caused our people to suspend business and organize and arm themselves for any emergency. Let that organization be perfected, and let us not relax one iota of our vigilance—for the danger from the last named source is as imminent as at any previous moment.*

Chapter 3 Sources

DAR, *Nebraska Pioneer Reminiscences.*
Noble, *Historically Eventful Nebraska City.*
    –Frontier Steamboat Town.
Official Records, Vol. 41, Part 2, 828.
The Omaha Republican, August 19, 26, September 3, 1864.
Sorenson, *History of Omaha.*
Ware, *The Indian War of 1864.*

Part III
Chapter Four

The Denver Road

The last stagecoach from the east rolled into Latham Station, Colorado Territory, on August 15. A few large freight trains continued to make the harrowing run from Fort Kearny, but by the third week in August, even the most daring had corralled to wait for more peaceful conditions. For all practical purposes, the Oregon-California-Denver Road was closed.

The effects were immediate. Prices in Denver City leaped upward. Flour, nearly all of which had to be imported, jumped from its normal cost of $9 per cwt. to $16, then shot up to $25, when it could be had at all. The *Rocky Mountain News* ran out of newsprint and only maintained publication with colored tissue paper, printed on one side only.

Along with the shortages, the people of Denver lived in constant dread of an Indian attack. Mollie Sanford recorded in her diary that for weeks she slept at night with her clothes on, ready to flee at a moment's notice. A scare earlier that summer sent women and children jamming into the fortress-like U. S. Mint building. What with the threat of attack, the fiery destruction of the commissary warehouse at Camp Weld, and the late May flood on Cherry Creek which swept a large part of the town down the South Platte, the people of Denver City were feeling hexed. Now, as food prices climbed dizzily, the few crops that had been grown on ranches outside the town had either been eaten up by grasshoppers or remained unharvested for fear of the Cheyennes.

With the Overland Stage Lines at a standstill, mail service ceased between Denver City and the East. Essential mail from eastern cities was taken by steamship to the Isthmus of Panama, carried overland, reloaded on northbound ships for San Francisco, and there placed aboard stagecoaches for shipment to Denver City. Of course, mail already en route had to be put somewhere. Westbound mail piled up at Fort Kearny, while eastbound mail collected at Latham Station—some two to three tons of it.

Passengers collected, too. Due to its location at the junction of the main line to Salt Lake City and the branch line to Denver City (located about three miles east of present Greeley, Colorado), Latham Station continued to accumulate travelers from the West until there were seventy-five people gathered there. Latham was also a storage depot for three of Ben Holladay's divisions, and consisted of a one and one-half story log building with a single story addition which housed a kitchen, dining room, and warehouse—but it was not large enough to accommodate several tons of mail and seventy-five passengers with anything approaching comfort. The sleeping arrangements were primitive, at best. Everyone had to lay down on the floor facing in the same direction, stacked together something like Dixie cups. Periodically, a leader would call out, "Turn over!" and the whole mass of sleepers would bump and grind until all were facing the opposite direction. It was togetherness of the first order.

Just as the unwilling detainees at Latham Station thought things could hardly get any worse, they did. On August 20 there came word that a force of 900 Indians was on its way down the South Platte, cleaning the whites out of the valley ahead of them. Those few hardy ranchers who had remained on their claims now came rushing in to seek safety at the stage station, much as their countrymen on the Wood River had fled to Columbus and beyond. In a short time, there were 150 people gathered at Latham—enough to organize a "home guard" and a night watch. Of course the usual wandering cattle soon had the night guards shouting the alarm and working everyone up into a panic. Very quickly the food supply began to shrink toward the critical level, and the pitiful ranch gardens had all been devoured by grasshoppers. In fact, the insects even chewed all the leaves from the cottonwood trees. If Latham Station wasn't the end of the world, it was beginning to look like a very close second.

There was indeed a major Indian raid in the offing. Several miles to the east of Latham was the ranch of squawman Elbridge Gerry, the same Gerry who had counciled with the Cheyennes the past spring. On the night of August 18, two elderly Cheyenne warriors—Long Chin and Man-Shot-By-A-Ree—stole up to Gerry's cabin and awakened his wife, who was Long Chin's sister. They warned her that a great war camp of Apaches, Comanches, and Arapahoes was located on Beaver Creek, about 120 miles east of Denver City; that the warriors were planning a coordinated attack on the line of the Platte as far down as the mouth of Bijou Creek; and that she should warn her husband to take their stock and flee to a place of safety.

Leaving his wife at the ranch, Gerry, accompanied by a Cheyenne named Spotted Horse, rode to Denver City, warning all the ranches and stations along the Denver Road. It took him four horses and two days, but at last Gerry and his companion arrived at Governor Evans' house shortly before midnight on August 20. Orders for defense went out immediately to the military, and feverish preparations to counter the raid were soon under way all along the threatened section of the trail. As a result of Gerry's ride, the upper South Platte did not become a second Little Blue Valley. Soldiers and citizens were well forted up and prepared as war parties began poking gingerly at the trail. After a few desultory attacks, the great raid was called off. Ironically, a party of ten Cheyennes visited Gerry's ranch on the night of August 21, running off 150 head of horses belonging to Gerry and his partner, Antoine Reynal.

So the war which had begun in eastern Colorado continued to plague the Rocky Mountain frontier, and Governor Evans continued to bombard Secretary of War Stanton with hyperventilated telegrams. On August 22 he wired: "No government saddles within 700 miles of here. No government horses to mount 100-days' regiments of cavalry, nearly full. Unlimited information of contemplated attack by a large body of Indians in a few days along the entire line of our settlements."[1]

But even as the "contemplated attack" fizzled, General Curtis was assembling an expedition of his own, a sortie to sweep the entire Platte Valley clean of hostiles and reopen the trail. It was high time the army went into action. Nebraska Territory had been stung badly by the hostile warriors, and its newspapers were not inclined to be so complimentary as those in Kansas.

Chapter Four notes

1 O. R. Vol. 41, Part 2, 809.

Sources

Ball, *Go West, Young Man.*
Grinnell, *The Fighting Cheyennes.*
Mattes, "The South Platte Trail."
Monahan, *Destination: Denver City.*
Official Records, Vol. 41, Part 2.
Root and Connelley, *Overland Stage.*
Sanford, *Mollie.*

Part III
Chapter Five
The press covers the war

In his office at district headquarters, Captain John Pratt was indignant over what he had just read in the *Omaha Republican*—so indignant, in fact, that he dashed off a wire of complaint to General Mitchell at Fort Kearny. What the *Republican* had printed was a crude form of investigative journalism, alerting the public to the fact of Colonel Summers' lackadaisical march to the scene of the Plum Creek Massacre:

> *We are informed that the Indians attacked the train at Plum Creek at an early hour in the morning, in full view of the telegraph station at that point. The operator, who witnessed the massacre, telegraphed Colonel Summers at Fort Kearny, giving the particulars, and calling for help. The dispatch was sent at 7 o'clock in the morning. Col. S., as we are informed, got ready to move, with one company of his command, at 11 o'clock—four hours after the dispatch was received, and arrived at Plum Creek, 32 miles distant, at 10 o'clock at night, occupying* eleven hours *in the march. This was less than* three miles an hour*, and for a cavalry force with fresh horses, is* too slow *for the Indian service! We are informed that Colonel Summers halted his command* two hours *for dinner, and at one point compelled his men and the citizens who were with him, to* lead their *horses for* five miles! *Some of the Indians, we are told, remained in the vicinity of Plum Creek well after sundown; so that if the military had marched there by one or two o'clock P. M., as they*

> *clearly should have done, the outrage could have been avenged, and the women and children whom they captured, might have been rescued.*
>
> *We repeat the expression of the hope that there may be some satisfactory explanation of this most extraordinary charge. If it shall prove untrue, we shall take the earliest opportunity to correct it. If, on the contrary, it is in all respects reliable, then we have no fears that General Mitchell will permit such a commander to repeat the disgraceful performance.*[1]

It wasn't that Captain Pratt found the article incredible. He knew Colonel Summers fairly well. The foundation for his offended sense of propriety was that "The publication of this report, even if all its allegations are correct, was premature and unjustifiable."[2]

If Captain Pratt seemed more concerned for the image of the military than for the freedom of the press, his outrage at the criticism of Colonel Summers nevertheless illustrates the important role played by the frontier press in reporting the events of the Indian War of 1864.

In the first frantic days of the raids in Nebraska Territory, the newspapers struggled to give their readers factual accounts of the devastation which was occurring along the overland trails. To do this, they relied solely on letters, telegrams, and the oral contributions of people who were, or who had been close to the action. As additional information came to their offices, the papers clarified and corrected their original reports. Without so much as sending a single reporter into the troubled area, they printed names, details, body counts, and numbers of burned ranches and trains. Amazingly, they did a fairly accurate job.

But the reliance on opinion, hearsay, and undocumented sources also tended to propagate a number of falsehoods among the frontier population, one of which was the wholesale murder of white women and children by the Cheyennes. In his dispatch to the *Omaha Nebraskian*, Lieutenant Porter invented heartrending scenes of the,

> *poor, helpless wife and mother, carried away captive, to suffer in mental anguish more than a thousand deaths . . . the baby horribly butchered, its brains dashed out upon the wagon wheel, the body cut open and the entrails torn out and scattered over the ground . . .*[3]

At a later time, this revolting theme would be expanded by senile, ersatz Indian fighters and by erroneous state and county histories into even more bloodcurdling myths in which scores of helpless women were always tortured and gang-raped, and scores of babies were always butchered. Certainly such incidents did occur in the 230-odd years during which Americans had been fighting Indians. Yet, in the raids of August, the only women known killed were Mrs. Bowie and Dora Eubank, the latter probably because of the vicious fight which she put up. Laura Roper, Nancy Morton, Lucinda Eubank, and Mrs. Snyder (taken in western Kansas) were all captured alive. Far from being weak and helpless, they proved fairly tough and resourceful in their efforts to survive. Willie and Isabelle Eubank were not butchered, but survived their captivity, as did Danny Marble and Ambrose Asher. Henry Eubank could not have been a very large boy, and the reason for his killing is not known, while the Martin brothers were wounded by the Sioux only after they had frustrated attempts to capture their horse. In the first phase of the war, contrary to Lieutenant Porter's agonizing, the Cheyennes, generally speaking, lived up to their reputation for killing adult males and preserving the lives of captured women and children.

A second distortion propagated by the press revolved around the important role played by guerrillas and Confederate organizers in the attacks. Of course, the involvement of the rebel government in the troubles on the plains had long been suspected, and evidence of white involvement in the August raids was too weighty to be ignored. Laura Roper encountered Joe Barroldo among her captors, and a white man helped Nancy Morton to remove the arrows from her wounds. Such involvement was apparently common knowledge among emigrant trains as well, as Harriet Laughery recorded that she had seen a number of white squawmen who were "a great menace to the emmigrant (sic) trains, since it is doubtless true that they plot and plan the most of the terrible massacres committed by the Indians."[4] And only a week after the Plum Creek Massacre, General Mitchell reported that "From the best information I have, I believe every party of Indians on this line has been led by white men."[5]

Not only the squawmen, whom Harriet Laughery believed to be fugitives from justice or from the war, but guerrillas were widely reported to be orchestrating the Indian attacks. Deputy Marshal Jones said as much in his May 31 report from Salina, over two months before the raids began along the Oregon-California Trail. The *Nebraska Advertiser* of August 11 stated flatly that,

> *These Indians are accompanied in their hellish work by white men, supposed to be Quantrill's guerillas—incarnate*

fiends.

The *Daily Rocky Mountain News* of the same date reported that,

> *It is well known that renegade whites, supposed to be from Quantrell's* (sic) *old party, are associated with the Indians in their depredations.*

Since the guerrillas piously proclaimed themselves to be irregulars of the Confederate Army, it required no great logic to assume that the prime source of incitement had been the rebel government in Richmond. Writing from Brownville, Lt. Henry Atkinson reported to General Curtis that there were "rebels leading the Indians."[6] Along the trail, the boss of Philura Clark's wagon train had learned "that a bunch of whites, evidently rebels, are hanging around them (the Indians). They are stirring them up."[7] Governor Saunders lent official sanction to the theme of Confederate instigation in his message to the Nebraska Territorial Legislature, January 7, 1865:

> *From facts which have come to the knowledge of this department, it is deemed certain that these Indian depredations and disturbances were the result of combined action between several tribes, aided and counseled by lawless white men, who hoped to share in the plunder which would result from their robberies and massacres. It is by no means certain that these coadjutors of the savages were not the emissaries of the rebel government, prompted to their inhuman work by the hope of creating a diversion in favor of their waning cause in the South.*[8]

It was a conviction which lived on with the survivors of the great raids. As late as 1907, James Lemmon recalled that "we lived here on the Little Blue River for four years in perfect peace with them (the Indians) . . . There were among the Indians, some of the rebels who put them up to go on the warpath."[9] Thus the theme of Confederate liability was so universal that, lacking any means of investigation, the newspapers printed as truth what was only a fiction, albeit a very popular fiction.

But, not long after reporting the events of the raids along the trails, the metropolitan newspapers began to hedge. General Curtis had barely stepped off the *Colorado* when the *Council Bluffs Weekly Bugle* of August 18 opined: "We do not believe as some do that it is the intention of the Indians to make war upon the emigrants." Then, despite the fact that there had never been a direct coach between Council Bluffs and Denver, and despite the fact that the Overland Stage Line had ceased all operation two days before, the *Bugle* carried on:

> *The stage between this city and Denver City makes regular trips and the last report is that no Indians were seen on the route.*

The article concluded with a swipe at the departmental commander:

> *General Curtis has arrived in Omaha with 400 regular troops—some say as his bodyguard, others say to be sent upon the plains; we presume, however, that it is the general's intention to proceed at once to the scene of the disturbance and ascertain 'what's the matter' . . . When we can obtain correct information as to who has been killed and what damage has been done, we will publish it for the benefit of all concerned . . . All we know is that somebody has been killed and from appearances Indians killed them.*

Such "correct information" was coming in daily. In fact, for the next two months the newspapers were well supplied with letters and eyewitness accounts to the destruction wrought by the Indians. As late as October 28, the *Omaha Nebraskian* printed this letter from a traveler recently through from Denver City:

> *The trip was mostly a pleasant one as far as to the weather, but I was shocked and saddened by the scene of desolation and ruin witnessed for a distance of nearly three hundred miles, above and below Fort Kearny. Deserted ranches mark almost the whole of that distance, mostly the work of warlike bands of Sioux and Cheyennes who have burned and destroyed everything they could lay their ruthless hands on . . .*

In the face of the detailed and voluminous testimony from those who knew best, could there really be any doubt that a tragic upheaval had taken place along the Oregon-California Trail?

Well, it seems that there could. In that same October 28 issue of the *Nebraskian*, the editor sarcastically minimized the horrors of the past ten weeks:

> *It affords us great pleasure to announce "to all whom it may concern," that the Indian troubles on the road from Omaha to Denver have been surpressed (sic). Numerous reports have been heralded abroad which did Omaha great injustice by making the impression that it was in danger of an attack. Now we declare there never was the least particle of danger. Refugees are perfectly safe in "returning to their respective places of abode," and in staying there until another scare which will take place just before the 'next draft'.*

Not to be outdone, the *Bugle* set a new standard for revisionism in its paper of September 15 in which it editorialized:

> *The fact is that upon the Platte route but one train has been attacked this side of the mountains this season, and that attack was provoked by the whites who followed after the Indians, and as some say fired the first gun, and in return were attacked and eight or ten,* not more *of them were killed. Since that time there has been no trouble on the Platte route and teams single and in trains are arriving in this city daily from Denver City, Salt Lake City, and the Gold mines of Idaho.*

What was happening here? How and why had the catastrophic events of August '64 become a nonevent?

Perhaps the cause was money, or more precisely, the lack of it. A significant portion of the economy, both in Omaha and in Council Bluffs was derived from or related to the business of the western trails—transshipping, merchandising, outfitting, etc. With the overland road virtually closed and prospective homesteaders frightened away, there was precious little of that going on. No longer were waves of settlers funneling through Omaha, bound for claims in the Platte Valley—people to be outfitted for the frontier, who would continue to purchase their staples through Omaha.

No peace along the Platte meant no settlement; no outfitting; no freighting; no profits. Very simple from a businessman's point of view. To restart this river of travel, the eastern states had to be reassured that things had never really been all that bad in the first place. The Omaha and Council Bluffs press would take the lead in spreading a layer of cheer over the grim realities of the past month. But, if the raids of August and the continuing chaos in Nebraska and Colorado Territories were to be sold to the eastern public as overblown hyste-

who, then was to blame?

The *Council Bluffs Bugle* had cooked up some answers to this question, too—neat, slippery answers which laid the blame for the river ports' economic constipation at the feet of those dastardly predators known as "speculators," who had, in fact, played a double game. First, there were those who had shipped great surpluses of goods to the Rocky Mountain region. They had then managed to foment an Indian war to squeeze off the flow of supplies in order to drive up prices, at which point they sold off their stockpiled supplies at huge profits. Other speculators (or could it be those same, unprincipled individuals?) had instigated an Indian war in order to obtain freighting and commissary contracts for the large military forces which would be sent to the frontier. Just how all these speculators managed to drive into open rebellion the Apaches, Comanches, Kiowas, Cheyennes, Arapahoes, and Sioux, the *Bugle* never explained. Perhaps nobody asked.

There was yet a third possible explanation for the high profile which the Indian difficulties had attained. The government had scheduled a draft of 500,000 men for the Union armies, to commence September 1, 1864. However, the War Department would exempt all those who were serving in the 100-day militia forces of the territories.[10] Although this made service in the 100-day regiments extremely attractive, they could hardly be called to duty without a good reason. Therefore, it was in the interests of the frontier people to stir up a little Indian trouble and embroider the accounts of the difficulties. It is a plausible explanation, and perhaps not entirely without some foundation. But what the *Bugle* called "a false cry of 'Indian War in the West'" hardly begins to explain the dead bodies at Indian Hollow, Kiowa Station, Oak Grove, The Narrows, Pawnee Ranch, Junction Ranch, Looking Glass Creek, Gilmans', Smith's, Gilletts', and Plum Creek.

Perhaps, too, the frontier was beginning to feel a mite shame-faced for its season of panic. In fact, for someone who had not been right in the middle of it all, the stampeding of several thousand people to Marysville, Seneca, Beatrice, Omaha, Council Bluffs, and Columbus seemed a little ludicrous. Perhaps it was time that Nebraska Territory took a deep breath and snickered at its own jumpy nerves.

In that vein, a remarkable piece of satire appeared in the *Nebraskian* of September 1, the work of a Mr. Brewer, whose ranch lay a dozen miles east of the German Settlements at Grand Island City. The author advanced the shocking premise that the rush of people from Wood River was caused by nothing more than a herd of buffalo:

> *What is very singular in connection with this whole affair is, the most experienced Indian traders were unable to make out to what tribe the invaders belonged. They were remarkably stout built, had split hoofs, bushy tails, and—from signs it was judged—they were particularly given to ruminating. A complete description of them has been sent to the Indian Bureau in Washington, in hope that that piece of furniture may be able to throw some light on the vexed question.*
>
> *Notwithstanding their victory, the people of Wood River deemed it "strategy" to fall back for reinforcements. Accordingly they fled triumphantly down the valley. Before it was discovered that the Germans at Grand Island City were braver than other people . . . the inhabitants of that enterprising colony had laid the foundation and reared the superstructure of Fort Nicht-kom-heraus . . . its very name is a tower of strength; by interpretation it signifies the unwillingness of its defenders to come out and surrender in the absence of the enemy . . . Major General Curtis (may his weight be a thousand pounds,) presented this Teutonic temple of Mars with a piece of artillery. Some fellow . . . has circulated the story that it was, on the first half day, charged to the muzzle with sour krout (sic) and sausages.*

The author next turned his sarcasm to the stockade at Columbus, bestowing upon it a name which reflected the sharp and sometimes questionable business practices of the local merchants:

> *In an incredibly short space of time, one half of the population had run away, and the other half had reared that prodigy of military architecture, Ft. Sockittoem (how appropriate and euphonious are Indian names.) Ft. Sockittoem is still plainly visible to the passer by.*

Yes, perhaps it was time for renewed resolution, a time for the territory to take a fresh look at its troubles and smile at itself—or at least that part of the territory which had not recently buried loved ones alongside the trail or seen everything it owned going up in flames.

Chapter Five notes

[1] *The Omaha Republican*, August 19, 1864.

[2] O. R. Vol. 41, Part 2, 722.

[3] *The Omaha Nebraskian*, August 17, 1864.

[4] Holmes, Ed., *Covered Wagon Women*, Vol. 8, 132.

[5] O. R. Vol. 41, Part 2, 722.

[6] O. R. Vol. 34, Part 4, 721.

[7] Clinkinbeard, "Across the Plains in '64," 44-45.

[8] *The Omaha Republican*, January 13, 1865.

[9] *Proceedings and Collections*, NSHS, Vol. 15 (1907), 128.

[10] The federal draft was headline news in most frontier newspapers. The information in the text was taken from the *Daily Rocky Mountain News* of August 9, 1864. The War Department exemption was headlined in the *Seneca Nemaha Courier*, August 25, 1864.

Sources

Andreas, *History of Nebraska*, Vol. 1.
The Brownville Nebraska Advertiser, August 11, 1864.
Clinkinbeard, "Across the Plains in '64."
The Council Bluffs Weekly Morning Bugle, August 18, September 15, 1864.
The Daily Rocky Mountain News, August 9, 11, 1864.
Holmes, Ed., *Covered Wagon Women*, Vol. 8.
Laura Roper Vance, Autobiography and Letters.
Nancy Jane Morton Stevens, Manuscripts "Plum Creek Massacre."
The Omaha Nebraskian, August 17, September 3, October 28, 1864.
Official Records, Vol. 34, Part 4; Vol. 41, Part 2.
Proceedings and Collections, NSHS, Vol. 15 (1907).
The Seneca Nemaha Courier, August 25, 1864.

Part III
Chapter Six
General Curtis' second campaign

By the third week in August, mobilization of federal and territorial forces was well under way in Nebraska Territory. Militia units were organizing and drawing provisions; several companies of Colonel Livingston's First Nebraska veterans left Omaha and rode west on the Military Road; and Fort Kearny was preparing to host a delegation of high ranking brass such as was rarely seen in this backwater of the Civil War. Generals Curtis and Mitchell, Colonels Livingston and Summers would soon be counseling together to send the great Indian hunting expedition on its way.

At Columbus, General Curtis decided that the Loup Ferry was of sufficient strategic importance that it should be guarded by troops. There were, of course, some three hundred men at "Fort Sockittoem" just a quarter mile from the ferry, men who should have been enrolled in militia companies, but for some reason they were not, and would soon return to their scattered farms for good. The big scare was blowing over. Thus the only force available for guard duty were the men of Company E, Seventh Iowa. So the order went out: Captain David was to move his soldiers to Columbus—lock, stock, and even barracks.

The decision left everyone on the Pawnee Reservation stunned with disbelief. Agent Lushbaugh protested strenuously (to no avail) and the indignation of the civilian employees was fierce. Lizzy Whaley wrote to her mother:

> *We are left here now to protect ourselves(.) all the soldiers have gone to Kearny. I think it is too bad that they should have to leave here just when there is so much danger. The*

Pawnees are in from their hunt now and perhaps they would fight the Sioux as they are at war with each other.[1]

J. B. Maxfield, teacher to the Pawnees, was even more vehement in his September report to Lushbaugh:

No blame whatever can be attached to any person for their leaving for a place of greater safety when we remember that in the hour when danger seemed the most imminent the troops stationed here for our protection were withdrawn by order of the military authorities. If troops were necessary for our defense in times of peace, was it wise, was it humane to remove them and leave us entirely defenseless in time of war when carnage was raging all about us?[2]

But the troops must guard the ferry. And the Pawnees—their fall hunt stymied by hostiles along the Republican, their gardens gobbled by waves of grasshoppers that had stripped the countryside all the way to Latham Station and beyond—they would just have to protect themselves and get along as best they could. It was a time of emergency, and the white man's treaty obligations would just have to be waived for the time being.

General Curtis was a very weary man as he left Columbus that Saturday, August 20. He had thus far scratched together a force which included a company of the Eleventh Kansas Cavalry (his headquarters guard), several companies of the First Nebraska Veteran Volunteer Cavalry, and some of the First Battalion, Nebraska Cavalry (the old Second Regiment). At Columbus he was joined by Frank North, older brother of the practical joking freighter, Luther. Curtis took an instant liking to young North, and was particularly impressed by his experiences with the Pawnees.

Twenty-four-year-old Frank North came with his parents and siblings to Omaha from New York, in 1856. His work as a trapper and trader in the country around Omaha brought him into contact with bands of Pawnees that wandered out from their village of Pahuk on the Platte. Shortly after Frank and his brothers moved on to Columbus, the Pawnees left Pahuk to go onto their new reserve at the Mormon settlement of Genoa. Frank and Luther soon obtained employment at the agency, hauling logs for the government sawmill. Frank's continued association with the tribe and his interest in their culture and welfare earned him a position of great respect among the Pawnees, and his command of their language became quite fluent.

If General Curtis had been unacquainted with the tribulations visited upon the Genoa reserve by the Sioux and Cheyennes, Frank North probably gave him all the particulars. The tribe had been continually thwarted in its attempts to make peace with its enemies, partly because the government never seriously attempted to mediate, and partly because the young Pawnees themselves refused to obey their chiefs and forego the joys of stealing horses from their ancient foes. In spite of their comic opera showing with General Mitchell's expedition to Laramie the past July, the Pawnees were superb scouts and ferocious warriors, and they were tired of being picked on.

The exact origin of the Pawnee Scouts is somewhat hazy. Long before Mitchell had taken his Pawnees up the North Platte, Colonel Edwin Vose Sumner had utilized five warriors during his 1857 campaign against the Cheyennes. As both Sumner and Mitchell had discovered to their chagrin, the results were disappointing. Credit for organizing the Pawnee Scouts is usually given to General Curtis, even though he had no control over the Pawnees, whose welfare rested in the hands of Agent Lushbaugh. Already in 1862, Lushbaugh had gone personally to Washington to request that a regiment of volunteers be recruited from among the Pawnee warriors. The request was turned down on the advice of General Halleck.[3]

On September 30, 1864, the agent wrote again to the Indian Bureau:

> *Upon the arrival of General Curtis to this locality last August, some eighty Pawnees volunteered to accompany him upon an expedition against the hostile tribes, on the plains, and from two to three hundred more of the best warriors in the tribe expressed an anxiety to join the expedition, but inasmuch as we had been deprived of the meager military protection which had been provisionally accorded, I did not deem it judicious to permit them to go, and thus leave the agency wholly undefended. I did propose, however, to General Curtis, if he was to station a company of cavalry at the Agency, that I would give him all the warriors in the tribe for service west. This proposition was declined by the general, and there matters stand at the present.*[4]

Lushbaugh continued his letter urging the Indian Bureau to consider creating a legitimate military organization of the Pawnees for use against the hostile tribes.

Whether the origin of the Pawnee Scouts came from Sumner, Mitchell, Curtis, North, Lushbaugh, or from the Pawnees themselves, the fact is that Curtis asked Frank North to return to the reservation and organize a company of scouts to accompany the expedition. It took only a short time to enroll seventy-seven warriors. Post interpreter James McFadden, who had seen service with Harney on Bluewater Creek in '55, was appointed captain, with Frank North as his lieutenant.

The organization of the scout company gave Curtis additional grounds for optimism. He had not had any Indian scouts with his expedition along the Arkansas (the Indians had all been too afraid of his ferocious militiamen), and he had not found any hostiles, either. This time he would be fighting the wild tribes with their own worst enemies.

During the next dozen years, the Pawnee Scouts (with a changing cast of characters) would gallop to fame and glory against the tribes of the High Plains. But as McFadden's Pawnees prepared to join the white soldiers at Fort Kearny, the concept was still in the teething stage. That would soon become evident to the assembled military brass.

From Columbus, General Curtis plodded onward with his troops, down the Military Road to the German Settlements which he reached on Monday, August 22. The general could hardly believe his tired eyes. There alongside the trail stood the sod ramparts of Fort O.K., and some 2,000 yards to the west were the thick log walls of Fort Independence, with the first United States flag in Hall County curling in the breeze. The astonished Curtis inspected both forts and pronounced them excellent (he was, after all, a military engineer), and he thanked the settlers for their firmness and bravery. Stolley later wrote: "General Curtis is on the whole a good natured man who easily wins the liking of everyone. He gave us the assurance that the Indians would be thoroughly disciplined for he said 'I have had enough of this war.'"[5]

As the satirist in the *Nebraskian* had duly reported, the general left one of his fieldpieces—a six-pounder smoothbore—for the defenders of Fort O.K., to show his appreciation for their fortitude. It was an obsolete piece of artillery and an encumbrance to the expedition, which would rely on the twelve-pounder Napoleons, the workhorse artillery piece of the frontier army. Nevertheless, the people at Fort O.K. were grateful. Stolley was so miffed that his fort did not also receive a cannon that he renamed it "Castle de Dependence."

After completing his tour of inspection, General Curtis mounted his command and once again took the Military Road west to halt beyond the Wood River. During the night, a terrific thunderstorm battered the encampment. None the worse for their soaking, the general and his men trooped into Fort Kearny the following day, where they could see that Colonel Summers had already begun work on several stockades to protect vital portions of the old post.[6] To the accompaniment of axes and saws, the commanders began planning their campaign to "discipline" the recalcitrant Cheyennes and Sioux.

The month of August was drawing to a close and no one at Fort Kearny was sorry to see it end. "Bad management" and "untoward misfortune" had resulted in an unrelenting stream of disasters in Nebraska Territory—but there was hope on the horizon. General Curtis was marshaling forces for an extended sortie into the lair of the hostile savages responsible for all this misfortune. As a first step, he sent Colonel Livingston ahead to Plum Creek to prepare his Nebraska veterans for the coming campaign.

There was no way Colonel Summers was going to be left behind. Certainly there was little glory to be won in fighting aborigines on a trackless frontier, but what little was to be had would most likely come during the Curtis expedition. It was also a chance for the colonel to remove some of the tarnish which clouded his reputation as a result of the dawdling march to Plum Creek on the day of the massacre. Besides, General Curtis was taking some of his Seventh Iowa troopers, and the colonel ought to make at least one campaign with his regiment. Upon his request to General Mitchell, Colonel Summers was relieved from the command of Fort Kearny to lead his troops in the field.

The new version of the Pawnee Scouts also arrived from the reservation—seventy-seven warriors under the leadership of Captain McFadden, who was a sight to behold. The captain had long been a squawman, had taken up living in an earthen lodge, allowed his hair to grow long and greasy, and wore little more than a breech clout. It was to prove fortunate that Frank North was along as "vice commander" of the Pawnees.

Taking his Kansas escort under Captain Gove, General Curtis moved on ahead to Plum Creek. At six a.m. on September 1, the remainder of the Fort Kearny contingent formed up in the road west of the parade ground and began the march to the rendezvous. Leading the procession was Colonel Summers with his Seventh Iowa companies under Captains Murphy and Wilcox. Next came Lieutenant Humphreyville and his detachment of the Eleventh Ohio Cavalry; Lieutenant Flanagan and his Sixteenth Kansas battery; Captain Tom Stevenson and the four companies of Nebraska Militia; and the Pawnee Scouts, this time wearing their native dress (or undress) and riding their own ponies. A supply train brought up the rear.

One day was occupied in attending to last minute details at Plum Creek. Then on Saturday, September 3, the column of 628 men left the Great Platte River Road and turned southwest toward the Republican. On the following day the command crossed the river and pressed on to Crooked Nose Creek, where the Pawnees proved their worth by killing some buffalo for supper.

On they went, across Beaver Creek, across Prairie Dog Creek, finally reaching the Solomon River on Wednesday, September 7. Curtis sent Captain Wilcox on a short scout to the south fork of the Solomon, a dangerous mission for a single company if it should happen to stumble upon a large camp of hostile Sioux or Cheyennes. But so far, nobody had seen any sign of hostile Indians. There were supposedly thousands of them passing back and forth between the Solomon and the Republican. Where were they?

In order to find out, General Curtis split his command. General Mitchell took the Seventh Iowa companies, Lieutenant Flanagan's artillery, and half the Pawnees under McFadden—some 340 men—westward toward the head of the Solomon. Curtis took his Kansas troops, Colonel Livingston's First Nebraska companies, Stevenson's militia, and the remainder of the Pawnees—some 285 men—and headed eastward down the Solomon. That night in camp he sent a messenger on ahead to Fort Riley with a dispatch to his headquarters. It was an oddly worded message which badly misrepresented the situation along the Platte:

> *Trains are passing through from Leavenworth from Kearny to Denver and Salt Lake. Escorts are not needed. Have explored up Beaver and Republican to a point on Cottonwood. No buffalo here and very few Indians. Am moving eastward.*[7]

But the Indians were very much there, whether Curtis had seen them or not. Two days after he wrote his rosy dispatch, a large force of warriors attacked the twenty-one men of a surveying party on the Republican very close to where the expedition had crossed on September 4. The men escaped in a running fight, but lost five oxen.

General Mitchell scouted westward about thirty miles finding nothing, so he turned back northwest toward Cottonwood Springs. By the time he made camp on the evening of September 12, his horses were becoming badly jaded. He would have to slow the pace.

On the following day, his scouts sounded the alarm. A body of horsemen were approaching in the distance. Mitchell swung his tired men and animals into line for a charge and waited. The strangers proved to be a posse of Colorado citizens, dutifully following Governor Evans' directive to hunt down and kill Indians and confiscate their property. So intent were they on their mission that they had passed out of Colorado Territory by a good sixty miles.

After the false alarm, the Colorado citizens turned back and Mitchell brought his troops back by easy stages to Cottonwood, arriving there at ten p. m. on September 15. Lieutenant Flanagan was so ill that he was immediately confined to the post hospital.

Two days later, using such horses as were fit to travel, the general took a force up the North Platte to deal with a band of hostile Sioux reported near Ash Hollow. The troops arrived at the old campground to find the area deserted. The aggressive Captain Murphy took his company up Bluewater Creek a short distance, but found no sign that hostiles had been there, either. Even if they had, the Indians would have been in little danger, since Murphy's horses could no longer run.

With his latest sortie a failure, General Mitchell turned back down the North Platte, arriving at Cottonwood on September 24. While he had found no hostile Indians around Ash Hollow, they had certainly been in the broken country south of the fort. On September 20, a party of eight soldiers from the Seventh Iowa were sent out to pick wild plums for Lieutenant Flanagan and the other patients in the post hospital. The Cheyennes were waiting among the cedars of the canyon, and two of the men were killed.

Meanwhile, Curtis had seen no more hostiles than had Mitchell. Tired of what was turning out to be a wild goose chase, he was pushing hard to get back to his headquarters. Not that there hadn't been some excitement on the campaign. A party of his men rode off one afternoon to kill buffalo for supper. They should have let the Pawnees do the hunting for, while they did manage to make a kill, it proved to be an old bull whose meat was so tough it was practically inedible. It was a costly hunt, too, for in the heat of the chase, several of the men had shot their horses in the heads, killing them. At least they had saved their saddles and equipment.

Frank North then volunteered to kill something a little more palatable. Sighting a young calf, North gave chase, only to find that he had forgotten his gun in the wagon. Undaunted, he lassoed the buffalo and attacked it with a butcher knife which he always carried concealed in his boot. After a comical chase, he succeeded in dispatching the animal, but in the process, he slashed his right hand so badly that, when he arrived back at camp, he fainted dead away. No wonder Curtis was anxious to end this hapless expedition.

On or about September 15, Curtis and Livingston led their weary men into Fort Riley. General Blunt was not there, having gone west on an Indian campaign of his own. What Curtis found waiting for him was more important than General Blunt. It was a telegram from his headquarters, bearing the very news he had been dreading ever since last January: Confederate General Sterling Price was coming! Every available soldier in Kansas was needed along the border. Curtis forgot how tired he was. After a forced march, he and his escort arrived back at Fort Leavenworth late on September 16 to prepare for the battle to save Kansas.

Colonel Livingston and his Nebraska troops rested for several days, finally departing Fort Riley on September 19. Captain Stevenson's Nebraska City militia company was in a foul mood as the command marched north to the old Oregon-California Trail. Their humor did not improve when they learned of their new assignment: fortifying and garrisoning the abandoned Pawnee Ranch and Little Blue Station. Livingston marched on, seeing no recent signs of hostile Indians, and finally arrived back at Fort Kearny at one o'clock on the afternoon of September 28. There he ordered rations to be given to the Pawnees and sent them home to their reservation. Despite the promises made to them when they enrolled, none ever received a cent for his services.

Both Curtis and Mitchell were greatly displeased with Captain McFadden's manifest inability to command his scouts. There was really no reason for them to obey him. He was practically one of them and his instructions meant little more than if they had been given by another Pawnee. On the way to the Solomon, Curtis had begun giving his instructions directly to Frank North, who then gave the orders to the Pawnees and saw that they were carried out. The general was not about to give up on the idea of utilizing the Pawnees as scouts. The concept was a good one. It only needed a little fine tuning to make it successful.

During the campaign, General Mitchell had come to the opinion that a subdivision of his elongated district would simplify the making of logistical and command decisions. Therefore, on the day following his arrival at Kearny, Colonel Livingston took command of the Eastern Subdistrict of Nebraska. The Western Subdistrict would be commanded by Colonel William O. Collins at Fort Laramie.

The Nebraska City militia cared little about command arrangements, and proved their mettle by staging a mutiny.[8] Forty of the men took off for home, defying their officers to do anything about it. By some process which remains unknown, Colonel O. P. Mason, commanding the militia brigade, induced the men to return to their duties. But the work of fortifying Pawnee Ranch had been seriously delayed. It was vital work because great pressure was being brought to bear on the military commanders to guarantee the safety of Ben Holladay's coaches, and there was intense pressure on Holladay to get the stage and mail service back into operation very soon.

Thus the great Indian campaign sputtered to an indefinite conclusion. Its only results appeared to be frustrated men, used up horses, and mutinous militia (although in his official report, Colonel Livingston praised the conduct of his four militia companies). But good conduct and fortitude could not hide the fact that the expedition had found no hostile Indians. It was clear that white soldiers, mounted on heavy, grain-fed horses and trailing a long tail of heavy wagons and artillery, were never going to bring a halt to this Indian war. Lieutenant Flanagan said as much in his report, recommending that wagons and artillery be left behind in favor of pack mules. But he was just a junior officer whose advice was little heeded.

But even as Curtis and Mitchell were plodding upriver and down, a cessation of hostilities was beginning to materialize. Though the officers were unaware of it, a tentative prospect for peace was taking shape, not because of the military maneuvering, but because Black Kettle and White Antelope and a few other Cheyenne and Arapaho chiefs were heartsick over the killing and plundering. They foresaw, as most of their people did not, that eventual retribution would surely come. They had never wanted to make war against the whites, but it had come anyway, and it had been terrible. Perhaps, for the sake of the captives, the white people would be willing to listen to the grievances of their red brothers. With so much to gain and so little to lose, the peace chiefs decided to make an attempt to bring the Indian War of 1864 to an end.

Chapter Six notes

[1] Lizzy Ricketts Whaley to Mrs. Charlotte Ricketts, August 29, 1864.

[2] J. B. Maxfield to Lushbaugh, September 1864. Pawnee Agency Letterbook.

[3] Ware, *The Indian War of 1864* (note by Clyde Walton,) 437; O. R. Series I, Vol. 13, 645.

[4] Lushbaugh to Superintendent William Albin, September 30, 1864. Pawnee Agency Letterbook.

[5] Stolley, "The Defense of Grand Island," 226.

[6] On July 31, 1864, General Curtis had issued Field Order #2, which mandated stockades at all military posts "west of the Kansas and Nebraska settlements." This was a week before the raids began in Nebraska, and the main object of the order appears to have been the protection of the valuable horses, rather than the soldiers.

[7] O.R. Vol. 41, Part 3, 112.

[8] Captain Stevenson's rowdy militia company finished its term of service with a desertion rate of 15.5 percent, not including one man who was AWOL for a month, and another who spent almost his entire enlistment locked in the guardhouse at Fort Kearny. By way of comparison, Captain Kuhl's Company C, First Battalion Nebraska Volunteers, had a desertion rate of 22.9 percent. Captain White's Company C of the Nebraska Militia had a desertion rate of only 5.7 percent. Captain White's men were all from Gage and Pawnee Counties, and many of their families had been at risk during the initial raids. In this instance, at least, it appears that the men primarily concerned for their homes and families showed the greatest devotion to duty.

Sources

Anderson, "Ownership of Cannon."
The Columbus Daily Telegram, June 15, 1986.
Dudley, *Roster of Nebraska Volunteers.*
Frank North, Papers and Correspondence.
Grinnell, *Two Great Scouts.*
Lizzy Ricketts Whaley, Letters. Platt Family Papers.
Official Records, Vol. 41, Parts 1, 2, 3.
Pawnee Agency Letterbook.
Stolley, "The Defense of Grand Island."
—*History of the First Settlement.*

Part III
Chapter Seven

The odyssey of the captives

Following their deadly raids of the first week in August, the small groups of warriors filtered back across the treeless plains, some driving stolen stock, others carrying mountains of plunder, and trailing white captives. Though the long trek back to the Indian villages was uneventful enough, it nevertheless exacted a toll, both physical and mental, upon the white women and children as they rode with their captors mile after endless mile across the arid land.

There was very little in the way of deliberately cruel treatment. The Indians rode day and night, stopping when they felt the need for a snooze or a quick meal, adhering to no recognizable routine. The whites, whose hours for meals and sleep had been fairly regular, were soon exhausted.

Food was nearly as scarce as sleep. Many of the Indians carried little in the way of staple provisions, having taken mostly coffee, sugar, and clothing from the road ranches. Their major source of food was the land itself. They obtained fresh meat by killing buffalo, antelope, jackrabbits, or even land terrapin. Wild plums and grapes, as well as various roots and herbs, eked out the sparse fare. The Indians really made no attempt to withhold food from their captives. When Nancy Morton asked a warrior to pick some cherries for herself and for Danny, he willingly obliged. When she and Danny were hungry, their captors offered them a piece of raw ox liver, which they refused to eat. Later they were given meat which had been roasted. Likewise, Laura Roper's captors gave her roasted buffalo meat for her breakfast and supper. On occasion, the captives also dined on crackers, coffee, and tea. At best, the meals were spartan and irregular by virtue of a lack of victuals and the indifference of the captors, and the alien diet soon had all the whites quite ill.

After his first, sleepless night in captivity, Danny confided to Nancy Morton that he had been very sick all night and expected to die soon. But a squaw brought him some roasted meat which he devoured, and soon he began to feel better. Nancy also had fallen ill, and the Indians doctored her with roots and herbs. Her arrow wounds and broken ribs, however, continued to cause her great pain, aggravated as they were by the motion of her horse.

Even after reaching the main encampment, the white people continued to be plagued by illness. The Indians cured Laura of some unspecified complaint by pouring hot herb water over her head. When the camp moved on, they allowed her to ride in a travois. When Nancy Morton became ill, she received a house call from the medicine man. He treated her by filling her tepee with the smoke of burning green grass and then brushing her with sagebrush. Curiously, the whites responded to these ministrations by recovering their health.

Perhaps more insidious than the physical ordeal was the mental trauma which was inflicted upon the white captives. Each of the six (Willie excepted, because of his age) had witnessed violence unlike anything he or she had previously experienced. Lucinda, Nancy, Danny, and Isabelle had lost the human beings whom they loved most deeply—had, in fact, witnessed their final degrading moments of helpless agony. Nancy believed she could actually hear the blood pouring in a stream "as thick as my arm" from her cousin's side after the arrows ripped into his chest. Over the weeks following the raids, the whites found their normal and necessary grieving processes fettered by their alien environment and by their desperate fears for their own survival.

The children's ordeal was mitigated, to a small degree, by the nearness of the adults. Though Laura Roper cared for her after a fashion, Isabelle Eubank was still too young to comprehend the idea of death. But she had seen the gruesome end of her father and had absorbed much of the horror of his suffering. And, if the warriors were frightening to the adults, to a three-year-old girl they must have inspired a terror inexpressible in words and, as it turned out, beyond her coping capability. It is uncertain whether Danny actually witnessed the bloody death of his father, but he certainly understood that his parent and protector was dead, and he cried incessantly from his loss and homesickness. In his need for security and affection, he attached himself to Nancy Morton, whom he had known barely forty-eight hours. Converting her into a surrogate parent, he talked with her about his mother back in Council Bluffs and about their chances for eventual freedom. He put his arms about her and gave her a kiss. She in turn held his head, combed his hair, dried his tears, and sometimes cried right along with him. When, in a moment of black despair, she said she wanted to die, he was terribly alarmed and protested, "Then I will be left all alone!" Nancy felt a great tenderness toward him and, when several drunken braves tormented him by chucking arrows and spears in his direction, she warned the Indians sharply to leave him alone because "He is my papoose." Throughout the first harrowing days of captivity, a bond of necessity grew between the two, and the Indians seem to have allowed them a great deal of time together.

Ambrose Asher also was greatly affected by witnessing the death of his grandfather and young uncle. As the individual groups of raiders began to combine, the white captives were also brought together. When Nancy was able to visit Laura and Ambrose, the boy told her in detail how the Indians had shot the old man, pulled him off the wagon by his arms and stripped off his clothing.

The captives also became disoriented both in time and in space. As they rode with the Cheyennes day and night across the barren prairie in a seemingly never ending search for water holes and campsites, they quickly lost their sense of direction. As one day melded into the next in a mind numbing odyssey through shortgrass and sage and prickly pear, across tiny creeks and around the dusty gray-green bluffs, they lost track of time as well. It was a child's haunting nightmare of unending, wandering abandonment spilled over into waking reality.

All this would have been severe enough had they been with people of their own kind. But none of the captives had ever had much contact with the red people before. They had heard, of course, all the "bloodthirsty Indian" stories and had seen many Indians moving up and down the trail past their homes. But they were not at home, now. They were alone, surrounded by and dependent upon people of a foreign culture—people who spoke an unintelligible language, whose appearance was frightening and grotesque, and whose predilections and whims were unfathomable and highly suspect. Individual chieftains and braves treated them with kindness and solicitude, while others were heartless and cruel. Even the half-breeds whom they encountered followed this pattern.

Shortly after her arrival in the main camp, Nancy was visited by a "Frenchman" whom she remembered had called himself John Brown.

After asking, "Where in the hell are you going?" and "Where in the hell do you come from?", he laughed and proclaimed his joy over the killing of her family. This cheery encounter was followed by a visit from George Bent, who was exceptionally polite and concerned about her welfare. He also expressed the opinion that she would be given up when peace was made.

With their lives seemingly in deadly peril, the captives suffered the torment of the "emotional roller coaster." Hypersensitive to every word and look and action of their captors, the whites found their emotions racketed between hope and despair. One minute they were to be killed. The next they were saved by the interference of a chieftain. One day the soldiers were coming to rescue them. The next day they were not.

The captives also learned something of what it is like to be property instead of independent human beings. During the first weeks of their ordeal, they were traded from one chief to another, even from one tribe to another. Laura's Cheyenne captor sold her to an Arapaho, then decided he had made a bad deal and bought her back again. Eventually, she was sold to Arapaho Chief Neva.

The extreme stress naturally called forth adaptive behaviors, some healthy, others not. Nancy and Laura earned something of the Indians' respect by acquiescing in their uncomfortable situations as gracefully as possible. Laura accompanied the young maidens to pick wild fruit and allowed them to comb her hair, which delighted them to no end. Nancy shot at targets and even killed an antelope. She rode a horse around inside a circle of chanting braves and gamely gave the war whoop. They applauded her with delight and called her "We-Ho" (White Person).

Lucinda did not take her captivity so graciously. She was in constant fear of losing her two children, and for a time believed that Isabelle was dead. Since Laura had been holding the little girl at the time of her capture, the Indians were convinced that she was Isabelle's mother, and nothing could shake them from that notion. Not until they arrived at the main village did the Indians allow Lucinda to see her little girl for a short time. She continued to breast-feed Willie throughout her captivity, afraid that if he were weaned, the Indians would take him away from her. Lucinda also spurned offers of marriage from the son of a chief, who had hit upon that particular method of winning her away from the abusive chieftain who was her "owner."

Dealing with their frightening environment demanded all the wits, determination, and strength the captives possessed. Laura fared quite well, and seems to have been little concerned over the fate of the Eubank children. Nancy managed to put the best possible face on the situation and protected young Danny in the process. Lucinda was never a gracious prisoner, and her treatment was correspondingly harsh.

George Bent had left his father's trading post on the Arkansas that fall to live with his mother's people. He found their main camp along the Solomon River in western Kansas—Cheyennes, Arapahoes, Dog Soldiers, and Sioux—the largest village he had ever seen.

Bent rode in amazed wonder through the individual camp circles, all of them choked with the spoils of war. Everywhere there were bolts of silk and fine clothing, bags of coffee and sugar, cured bacon and hams, crackers, shoes, and everything imaginable—all looted from freight trains bound for Denver City. The villages throbbed with war dances, and many of the young men strutted about proudly wearing fine shirts and women's bonnets and veils. War parties were in constant motion, leaving for the advance camps, or returning from the action along the Platte Road, their ponies laden with edible goods and fine apparel that would never see the shelves of businesses in Denver City.

Black Kettle and some of the other head men were worried. The raiding was going well—too well, in fact. These chiefs knew that, sooner or later, there would be a terrible price to pay. The whites were unbeatable. Those Indians who had been to Washington could testify to that. They would probably not be fighting each other in the south much longer, and when they stopped fighting, then they would all join together to descend on the Cheyennes in a plague worse than the grasshopper hordes that had swept across the plains this summer. They knew that William Bent was worried, too. They had received a message from the "Little Whiteman" urging them to make an attempt to start peace talks with the white people.

At last, some of the chiefs met in council and came to an agreement. The war had to stop now, while there was still a small chance of short circuiting the inevitable white backlash. Apparently, this council was mainly an affair of the Cheyenne and Arapaho peace chiefs, as there were many other tribes and bands that were enjoying the war just wonderfully. But to whom should the overture be made? Obviously they should make contact with their agent, Samuel Colley. But he had long been funneling money from their annuities into his own pockets and could not be trusted entirely.

To ensure some type of check on their suspected agent, the chiefs determined to write two identical letters—one to Colley, and the other to the commanding officer at Fort Lyon. The letters would have to be written in the best possible English if they were to sound convincing.

Fortunately, George Bent and his cousin, Edmond Guerrier were in attendance at the council. Bent in particular was well educated by the standards of the day, having been schooled at Westport and St. Louis. He and Guerrier sat down to write, and the chiefs began dictating what they wanted to say. Bent must certainly have made some suggestions during the dictation, and phrase by phrase, the letters took form:

Cheyenne Village, August 29, 1864
Major Colley
Sir

We received a letter from Bent wishing us to make peace We held a consel in regard to it & all came to the conclusion to make peace with you providing you make peace with the Kiowas, Commenches, Arrapahoes, Apaches and Siouxs. We are going to send a messenger to the Kiowas and to the other nations about our going to make (peace) with you. We heard that you (have) some (Indian) prisoners in Denver. We have seven prisoners of you which we are willing to give up providing you give up yours. There are three war parties out yet and two of the Arrapahoes. They have been out some time and expect now soon. When we held this counsel there were few Arrapahoes and Siouxs present. we want true news from you in return, that is a letter

Black Kettle and other Chieves[1]

When the writing was finished, two Cheyenne chiefs—One Eye and Eagle Head—took the letters and bravely set out for Fort Lyon, while Black Kettle and "other Chieves" moved their camps southward along Hackberry Creek. Their desire for peace was far from universal as the village was accompanied by elements of Dog Soldiers and Sioux who still wanted no part of peace with the white man. Now the peace faction could do no more than wait for a return letter bearing "true news."

The two emissaries were understandably cautious as they reached the road west of Fort Lyon. One Eye had brought his wife along on the perilous journey, and the three Indians soon encountered Lieutenant Dawkins and several troopers of the First Colorado, who were on their way to Denver City. The soldiers wisely held their fire and escorted the Indians back to Fort Lyon. At last Major Wynkoop had in his hands some representatives of a race which he had long considered to be cruel and devoid of all feeling and affection. Gruffly he ordered them to dismount, and took the letter written by Guerrier into his headquarters. The Indians he clapped in the guardhouse until he could confer with his officers.

For all his expressed animosity toward the Indians, Wynkoop was not a man with a closed mind. Rather, the major was at heart a compassionate person, something of a romantic idealist. As he read the letter, he realized that he was in a terrible bind. A solution to the plains war had dropped into his hands like a bolt from the blue. The Cheyennes had offered him the key to the emancipation of the captive white women and children. But there were problems: Wynkoop had no power to make peace with the Cheyennes, let alone the other hostile tribes; there were no Indian prisoners in Denver to exchange; and the whole thing could be a setup to lure him and his soldiers into a repeat of the Grattan fight (although Black Kettle's letter did not ask him to make an expedition from the fort—only for a return letter). Neither were his officers unanimous in their willingness to venture out among the hostile tribesmen, for, if he left the recently arrived company of the First New Mexico Volunteers back to garrison the post, Wynkoop could mount at most an expeditionary force of 130 men. One hundred and thirty against more than 3,000 well-armed and highly-successful warriors. If things went bad, the fight might last a half hour at best.

There was a further complication: Permission for such a movement would have to be obtained from the district commander at Fort Riley, who was General Blunt. This could take time and might even be refused. The opportunity offered by the peace chiefs had to be seized quickly.

After some lively discussion, the major and his officers decided to take the risk and march to Black Kettle's camp. Possibly, their decision was influenced, not only by the plight of the captives, but by the language of the letter itself, which asked for "true news." They could hardly ignore, either, the deportment of the messengers who pledged that the Cheyennes would keep their word, and were willing to forfeit their lives if that word was broken.

Leaving Agent Colley to notify Governor Evans, Wynkoop took his First Colorado companies and two mountain howitzers and set out on September 6 for the Indian encampment at Bunch of Timbers. On the way, he sent Eagle Head in advance with a message to the chiefs, advising them that the expedition was approaching. On the afternoon of September 9, the troops found themselves confronted by a battle line of 800 hostile warriors. Wynkoop massed his few wagons and strung out his men in a company front. It was a situation that called for nerves of steel. The chiefs saved the day, holding the young warriors in check while the cavalry fell back several miles and went into camp.

On the morning of September 10, the council got under way. In their opening gambits, each side maneuvered to find common grounds for trust. The white soldiers had given telling evidence of their trust in the chiefs by virtue of merely being there. Wynkoop further disarmed them by being bluntly honest about his position. He did not want to fight, he said, but would if it were forced upon him. He could not offer an end to the hostilities, could not even guarantee anything more than his personal willingness to expedite the peace process. If the Indians were sincere, they would release the white prisoners, after which the major would personally conduct their representatives to meet with the Indian superintendent in Denver. Wynkoop promised them safe passage, going and returning. Beyond that he could offer them nothing.

One-by-one, beginning with Bull Bear of the Dog Soldiers, the Cheyenne head men poured out their catalogue of woes—the whole, sad story of how their relations with the white people had come to such a low estate. They, too, were honest in confessing that there were a great many warriors and chiefs who did not want this war to end and were in favor of holding the captives yet a while longer to force the white man to cut a better deal. Black Kettle had purchased as many of them as he could, but it might not be possible to bring in all the white captives immediately.

In the course of the dialogue, the deal clarified: If the chiefs gave up the prisoners in their immediate possession, Major Wynkoop would conduct their representatives safely to Denver and back, the object being to meet with Governor Evans, who was ex-officio Indian Superintendent, to agree upon terms for ending the conflict.

The council was much divided, and it was clear that the Indians had some internal wrangling to do before a deal could be finalized. Undeniably, Wynkoop had asked the Indians to give up a great deal without any guarantee of receiving something in return, and he thought it best to let them argue the matter among themselves privately. He would move his camp to a better location twelve miles away and wait there two days for the chiefs to reach a decision.

Laura Roper had become a valuable commodity, as evidenced by the amount of trading which centered around her. It was Arapaho Chief Neva who told her that a letter proposing a peace settlement had been sent to Fort Lyon. Though Laura had never really doubted her eventual freedom, the news boosted her morale.

It turned out to be true. Several days later, Neva came to Laura with the good news that soldiers were in camp just a few miles away and she was to be turned over to them. A pony was led to her lodge, and with a wonderfully light heart, Laura mounted to ride with Neva to the soldiers' camp.

Perhaps Neva had left the council early and did not realize that Wynkoop had moved his encampment. When they reached the place where the soldiers had been, it was deserted. The disappointment was crushing. Neva did not quite know what to do, so they turned around and rode back to the village. On the following day, Neva came again to her lodge to explain what had happened. The soldiers had not followed Black Kettle's advice about where they should make their camp, and had located themselves on a dry creek. It had not been a good choice, and they had marched off to camp beside a lake a few miles away. The Arapahoes would take her there, but no further.

Once again Laura mounted her pony and set off in search of the soldiers, hardly daring to hope that today they would be successful. Chief Left Hand joined them, possibly with better knowledge of Wynkoop's location. It was early in the afternoon when Laura got her first welcome sight of the First Colorado Cavalry encampment. The Arapahoes set the ponies to running and the little party galloped right into the midst of Wynkoop's troopers. After thirty-seven days in captivity, Laura Roper was free.

The following day, a lone Cheyenne brought word that Black Kettle himself was approaching with the captive children. With a "wildly throbbing heart," the major mounted and rode out with the messenger to meet them. After riding briskly for most of an hour, Wynkoop saw the group approaching in the distance. It was, as he wrote later, the happiest moment in his entire lifetime.

Some distance in advance of the rest, the major met a little boy riding an Indian pony. Wynkoop thought him a handsome fellow and, shaking his hand, inquired, "Well, my boy, who are you?"

"My name's Dan and I have been a prisoner with the Indians. Are you the soldier man who has come to get me?"

"I am."

"Well, bully for you."

"Are you glad to get away from these Indians?"

"You bet. But say, will they let me keep this pony?"

"No, but you shall have a better one."

"All right."[2] And so saying, Danny Marble rode off in the direction of the soldiers' camp. He had obviously made some adjustment since those first days when he and Nancy Morton cried together.

Wynkoop next greeted Ambrose Asher, but the boy had very little to say. There were a number of Cheyenne head men riding behind Ambrose, but the major's attention was caught by the small, blonde head of Isabelle Eubank, peeping out from within an Indian blanket.

Wynkoop rode closer, and the little girl held out her arms to him. As he placed her on the saddle in front of him, Isabelle wrapped her arms around his waist and murmured, "I want to see my momma." The major trotted his horse a few yards away from the Cheyennes so that, in case he lost control of his emotions, the Indians would not see him weeping.

As the children approached the camp, the Colorado soldiers turned out to welcome them with shouts and cheers. These men had been badly frightened, mistrustful of the Cheyennes, and nearly to the point of mutiny. Now, as they reached up to help these littlest captives off their ponies, more than one grimy, bewhiskered face was streaked with tears. Black Kettle had kept his word, and Wynkoop and his officers were beginning to look very much like heroes.

There still remained four other captives. One of them would not be coming in at all. Mrs. Snyder had attempted to escape, had been caught and returned to the village. With her husband dead and escape seemingly impossible, her will to live had been extinguished. Tearing her calico skirt into strips, she wove them into a rope. The Indians found her hanging from a lodge pole.

That left Nancy Morton, Lucinda Eubank, and little Willie. Black Kettle had sent traders to purchase them from the Sioux, but their captors were unwilling to free them at any price—had, in fact, staked them to the ground and covered them with buffalo robes to prevent their discovery. Already they were on their way north with the hostile Sioux. Black Kettle had done his best. He had given Laura, Danny, Ambrose, and Isabelle their freedom. He, like Wynkoop, was very limited in what he could accomplish among his own people.

Major Wynkoop accepted the situation as the best that could be gotten, and turned his column back toward Fort Lyon. Accompanying him were the emissaries to the governor: Black Kettle, First Chief of the Cheyennes; White Antelope, Chief of the Central Band; Bull Bear, Chief of the Dog Soldiers; Neva, Arapaho Subchief; Bosse, Arapaho Subchief; Heap-Of-Buffalo, Arapaho Chief; and Na-ta-ne, Arapaho Chief. These Indians were now matching Wynkoop's display of trust and courage with one of their own. They had agreed to go with him to

Denver City, where the overwhelming majority of whites would love to see them hang.

On September 18, the column arrived back at Fort Lyon. Private William F. Smith, of Company D, took charge of Danny Marble, who soon charmed his way into the hearts of the company and received their donations of $72.50. Private Smith became very attached to the boy and scoured the post for some suitable clothing for him. He found little, as there was no one at Fort Lyon near Danny's size.

Major Wynkoop ordered rations to be sent along with the annuities to the Cheyennes camped on Hackberry Creek. The chiefs also sent word back to their people that everything was alright so far, and that they were still going to Denver to make peace. Wynkoop drafted a report to General Blunt at Fort Riley, presenting him with the accomplished fact that the expedition had taken place and had, by any measure, been extremely successful. He reminded Blunt that there were still more whites in captivity, and argued that he would be in a better position to secure their release from Denver than from Fort Lyon.

The major was playing fast and loose with army procedure. Not only had he undertaken the march to Bunch of Timbers on his own initiative, but he now proposed to leave his district, conveying emissaries of the enemy to the District of Colorado for a peace conference which had yet to be arranged—all without asking permission from the volatile and unpredictable district commander at Fort Riley or from departmental headquarters at Fort Leavenworth.

Wynkoop, however, saw extenuating circumstances that approved his actions. He was, after all, stationed in Colorado Territory. The governor and ex-officio Indian Superintendent for that territory was in Denver City. Furthermore, the governor's circular of June 27 was still in effect and the Indians were responding to it, albeit somewhat tardily. As the highest ranking officer in the area encompassed by the circular's promise of sanctuary, Wynkoop would rightly be expected to make every effort to implement the governor's wishes. Finally, he, and no one else, was in a unique position to effect at least a partial cessation to this Indian war which was costing the government so much money. The fact that he had already won the release of four white captives (those "women and children" which the press made so much fuss about) should do much to mollify the commanding general. Had that general been anything but an unstable martinet, Wynkoop's assumption would have been a solid one.

By September 19, Major Wynkoop's column was in motion for Denver City. Escorting the seven chiefs were officers of the First

Colorado Cavalry—Major Wynkoop, Captain Silas Soule, and Lieutenant Cramer of Company C, commanding the escort of forty troopers. Agent Colley's son, Dexter, was along, as was interpreter John Smith. Private William Smith had asked to care for Danny Marble at Fort Lyon until passage to Council Bluffs could be arranged, but Wynkoop wanted all the children to appear in Denver City. Before leaving the fort, the major had sent a message ahead to Governor Evans, advising him of the impending visit. Evans promptly communicated this surprising information to Colonel Chivington, who wired General Curtis on September 26: "I have just been informed by E.W. Wynkoop, commanding at Fort Lyon, that he is on his way here with Cheyenne and Arapaho chiefs and four white prisoners they gave up. Winter approaches. Third Regiment is full, and they know they will be chastised for their outrages and now want peace. I hope the major-general will direct that they make full restitution and then go on their reservation and stay there."[3]

It was about September 22 when the column reached Boonville (present Boone, Colorado). Wynkoop took the four ex-captives and Dexter Colley and rode ahead to Denver City, arriving there on Sunday evening, September 25. Citizens of Denver greeted the white youngsters with curiosity and sympathy, and a prominent citizen established a subscription fund to provide for their physical needs. Wynkoop arranged temporary lodging for them at the Planters House, and engaged his father-in-law to take a formal group photograph of them in their donated clothing.

Laura enjoyed the attention at first, and repeated her story of captivity time-after-time. Soon it all grew monotonous and she went on a shopping spree, armed with vouchers drawn on the subscription fund. She engaged a seamstress to fabricate a new dress, and added a cloak, hat, gloves, and fur trimmings, all of which amounted to over $134. Only $18 remained for the use of the three smaller youngsters, and this money was turned over to the Colorado Relief Association, which now assumed responsibility for the welfare of the former captives.

Ambrose and Isabelle were uncommunicative and gave no information about their homes or families, so calls went out soliciting families to adopt them. Even though some additional contributions were received, the money in the subscription fund was far short of what was needed to feed, house, and provide medical care for the children, all of whom were suffering a variety of illnesses. Laura rightly guessed that her parents would be in Nebraska City, and persuaded the Relief Association to send a 25-cent telegram there, informing Joe and Paulina that their daughter was free and would be sent home as soon as the trail was safe.

Major Wynkoop went to see Governor Evans at his home. The governor was sick in bed, however, and would not receive him, so the army officer returned to his quarters and retired for the night. The following morning, Evans called for Wynkoop at the hotel. The major found him chatting in the parlor with Dexter Colley—the young trader who, it will be recalled, had bragged about the fortune he had made in his shady dealings with the Indians. Wynkoop told the governor of his mission, explaining that the chiefs would be arriving soon for the council which had been promised them. Evans' reply had more the tone of a spurned suitor than a high official. Certainly his attitude was a baleful portent of what was to occur over the next sixty-two days.

The governor was sorry Wynkoop had gone to all this trouble because he would have nothing to do with these Indians. They had declared war and would just have to take their punishment. Making peace now would give the impression that the United States had been whipped.

Strange, the major replied, that the United States should consider itself whipped by a few Indians. As an officer, he had given a pledge to these people and had brought them 400 miles for a conference with their superintendent. If Evans refused the Indians an audience, it would place the major in a very dishonorable position. The governor would please honor the pledge of his officer.

Evans stood firm. He was due to leave the next day for the Ute Agency on business. More to the point, he did not want to see the Cheyennes anyhow. Wynkoop continued to remonstrate with the governor, begging him to delay his trip to council with the chiefs and thereby maintain the integrity of the United States and its officer.

By this time Evans was clearly angry and frustrated, resentful that he had been manipulated and his authority compromised. At last he exposed the real reason for his reluctance to meet with the chiefs: Third Regiment was in camp and ready to campaign. The governor had belabored the War Department loudly and long for the authority to recruit that regiment. He strenuously represented to Secretary Stanton the necessity of raising and equipping the hundred-day men. If they did not fight Indians, it would all look like a useless exercise and a needless expense. The governor would have cried wolf too often. His enemies might even accuse him of malfeasance in office, and the non-use of the regiment could have severe repercussions at home, where residents of Denver City were already poking fun at the idle force, dubbing it the "Bloodless Third." That regiment, said Evans, "had been raised to kill Indians and they must kill Indians."

The emotions of both men were now running high. Apparently, they had both forgotten, for the moment, that any agreement made with the seven chiefs would be limited in effect to the bands they represented. Others may in time follow their lead, but for the time being, only the adherents of Black Kettle and the peace chiefs would be affected. There were still plenty of hostile Sioux, Cheyennes, and Arapahoes to worry about. But the governor was being boxed in. Events in Colorado Territory were nudging him into a crisis of decision for which none of his previous experience had prepared him. In his frustration, he repeated to Wynkoop over and over again, "What shall I do with third regiment if I make peace?"[4]

It was an eerie reprise of that distant day in 1818 when Tum-A-Tap-Um had asked the fur traders, "If we make peace, how shall I employ my young men?" Except that the wheel had spun halfway round. Now it was the young white men who "delight in nothing but war." The governor's anguished query was at once ironic and prophetic–and it was an admission that events in Colorado Territory had slipped out from under the control of men.

Governor Evans remained in Denver City. On September 28, he granted the chiefs an interview at Camp Weld, the headquarters of the First Colorado Cavalry (and the Third) south of the city. After allowing the chiefs a brief time to speak of their grievances, the governor berated them for their failure to attend the councils he had previously called. He accused them of making alliances with the Sioux and causing great destruction. He chided them for their ingratitude for all the money and goods which the government had lavished upon their people. He pumped them for information regarding depredations committed by hostile bands. He threatened them that his time to make war was in the winter, and that was fast approaching. And he would promise them absolutely nothing.

The chiefs corrected the governor on several points, but they admitted that the actions of their people had given cause for retribution. Several times they even made offers to fight alongside the whites against the unrepentant hostiles, but their overtures were ignored.

The chiefs summoned all the eloquence at their command to convince the governor of their sincerity. It is impossible to read their impassioned speeches without a feeling of pity that such proud men were willing to humiliate themselves, to beg for basic human rights in the name of a people over whom they had so little control.

The conference appeared to be going nowhere when Bull Bear rose to speak: "I am not yet old. I am young. I have never hurt a white man. I am always going to be friends with the whites; they can do me good . . . I have given my word to fight with the whites. My brother (Lean Bear) died in trying to keep peace with the whites. I am willing to die in the same way and expect to do so."[5]

Colonel Chivington then stated that it was his practice to fight his enemies until they laid down their arms and submitted to the military authorities. If the Indians were willing to do that, they could report to Major Wynkoop at Fort Lyon, since they were closest to that post. Final peace terms could only come from the big white war chief at Fort Leavenworth. On this inconclusive note, the conference at Camp Weld adjourned.

Photographer Wakely took a group portrait of Wynkoop, Soule, the chiefs, and several other participants. In the photograph, the chiefs appear tense and ill at ease, all except Black Kettle. He sits immediately behind Wynkoop, a bemused half smile on his face. Whatever his thoughts and feelings at the moment, his enigmatic expression appears to be that of a man who has done his utmost for his cause, a man apparently at peace with himself and with his fate.

Major Wynkoop stayed on in Denver City for several days, spreading the word that it was now safe for ranchers to return to their homes along the Arkansas. Then he accompanied the chiefs back to Fort Lyon, from whence they returned to their villages to begin the process of bringing their people nearer to the fort. On October 8, Wynkoop sent a dispatch rider to General Curtis at Fort Leavenworth, bearing a complete account of all that had transpired, and asking for the general's explicit instructions for obtaining peace with the tribes.

Meanwhile in Denver City, the Relief Association was struggling to care for the three children Wynkoop had redeemed, all of whom were suffering from illness and general poor health. The little information which exists on Danny Marble gives the impression that he was a resourceful, intelligent, and highly verbal little boy who had seemingly come through his ordeal in good shape. But only a week after his arrival in Denver City, Danny became fevered. Contributions to the subscription fund had dried up and nearly all the money had gone to Laura, leaving virtually nothing to pay for his care. Though Doctor W. F. McClelland offered to treat him for free, Danny was moved to the Camp Weld military hospital on Ferry Street. There, in the care of Dr. A.A. Smith, Assistant Surgeon for the First Colorado Cavalry, Danny's illness was diagnosed as typhoid fever.

He appeared to be on the mend when Laura Roper came to see him about the first of November. The Relief Association had paid for her passage home with a wagon train and she was to leave the next day. Danny begged her to stay a little longer. Then he would be well and they could go back together. But, if Laura was to remain in Denver City, she would have to pay her own way. The Association had done all for her it was willing to do, and she would just have to leave with the train.

On a bitterly cold November 9, Danny Marble died. Dr. McClelland had not been allowed to see him in the hospital, nor did the military make an attempt to contact his mother, who learned of his death only through a letter from McClelland. The abbreviated edition of the *Daily Rocky Mountain News* did not even report on his passing or burial, which occurred November 14.

The Relief Association was still searching for a family to adopt Ambrose Asher when it received word from the boy's mother, who was living at the old family home in Kentucky. She was coming to Atchison to meet her son, and the Association agreed to send him there as soon as comfortable transportation could be arranged.

Laura's train stopped overnight at Sam Fitchie's Ranch near Cottonwood Springs, where she complained at length about her poor treatment by the Relief Association. They had collected a lot of money, as she told it, but she and the children had seen precious little of it. The few clothes they had given her had gotten lost somehow, and they had paid her fare only as far as Fort Kearny. How was she to get to Nebraska City from there? Her tale of woe aroused her listeners to indignation and they collected $80 for her on the spot.[6]

Laura left her train at Fort Kearny, boarding a coach for Nebraska City, which she reached without incident. Upon receipt of her telegram, Joe Roper took the children back to the family's former home in Pennsylvania while Paulina remained behind with Clarisa to await Laura's arrival.

The reunion must surely have been a happy occasion, though Laura's joy was tempered somewhat by news of Danny's death. On November 28, shortly before leaving for Sullivan County, Pennsylvania, Laura wrote to Ann Marble extending her sympathy and promising to send her a copy of the photograph of the children which had been taken in Denver. Then, bidding Clarisa goodbye, Laura and Paulina embarked on their long journey to the east. By the end of 1864, the Joseph Roper family was reunited among friends and relation they had left nearly five years before.

There remained only little Isabelle. During her first days in Denver City, she had been entrusted to the care of Mollie Sanford, who had thoughts of adopting her. But Isabelle was a badly damaged little girl. Her behavior was bizarre, and nearly every night, she awakened with eyes wide and staring to recount in detail the murder of her father on the sandbar in the river. Her emotional disturbance was more intense than Mollie could bear, and she was given to the care of Dr. Caleb Burdsal, Surgeon for the Third Regiment. But Dr. Burdsal and the Third were preparing for a campaign against the Cheyennes, and Isabelle was apparently passed among several other families. In the process, someone changed her name to Mary. It all proved too much for the four-year-old to tolerate. Whether from disease, general weakness, or emotional trauma which remained untreated, the little girl gave up the fight without ever getting to see her "momma." Isabelle Eubank died on March 18, 1865.[7] With her death, Denver City's involvement with the Cheyenne captives came to an end.

Chapter Seven notes

[1] Grinnell, *The Fighting Cheyennes*, 158. A photograph of one of the letters appears in *The Indians* (Time-Life Series of the Old West), 182.

[2] Wynkoop, *The Tall Chief*, 94-96.

[3] O. R. Vol. 41, Part 3, 399.

[4] U.S. Congress, "Massacre of Cheyenne Indians," 77.

[5] Ibid., 90.

[6] It was common for trains traveling empty to the east to carry paying passengers. The cost was much less than traveling by coach. Exactly why the Relief Association paid Laura's passage to Omaha instead of Nebraska City is unknown. Probably, they wanted to get her out of Denver on the first train going east. At any rate, they paid her fare of $25, whereas the cost of a coach from Denver to Fort Kearny alone was $108 (see Frederick, *Ben Holladay*, 112). Laura evidently concocted her story at Cottonwood hoping to raise money to get her where she wanted to go in better style. After hearing her tale of woe, Sam Fitchie wrote the *Rocky Mountain News* for an accounting, which was published in the edition of November 19, 1864. The citizens of Denver had contributed $247.75 for the relief of the four children. All but $8.36 had gone to Laura, most of it before the money was turned over to the Relief Association, which no doubt used a small amount of its own treasury to cover expenses for the three younger children. The chairman of the association expressed his opinion that the shortage of funds and resultant neglect was responsible for Danny Marble's death. Judging by a short item which appeared in the *Rocky Mountain News* on November 28, Laura's selfish spending spree and subsequent criticism left a very sour taste among the citizens of Denver City, and the care given the three children does not reflect creditably on any of those involved.

[7] Mollie Sanford believed the Cheyennes tortured Isabelle by cutting her with arrowheads. The *Daily Rocky Mountain News* of March 21, 1865, reported that her death was caused by "inflammation of the brain," but that an indirect cause was three arrow wounds in different parts of her body. No doubt there had been some physical damage done to the girl, but it must be noted that Isabelle died during the time Colonel Chivington was being examined by a military court of inquiry for his role in the Sand Creek Massacre. The *Rocky Mountain News* would not have passed up anything to create sympathy for him. Isabelle's wounds were a reminder of the brutality of the Indians which supposedly justified Chivington's actions.

Sources

Ann Marble, Indian Depredation Case #892.
Craig, *The Fighting Parson.*
Czaplewski, *Captive of the Cheyenne.*
Daily Rocky Mountain News, September 24, October 13, November 16, 19, 28, 1864; March 21, 1865.
Editors of Time-Life, *The Indians.*
Grinnell, *The Fighting Cheyennes.*
Hyde, *Life of George Bent.*
Laura Roper Vance, Autobiography and letters.
Lavender, *Bent's Fort.*
Official Records, Vol. 41, Part 3.
Nancy Jane Morton Stevens, Affidavit and manuscripts.
U. S. Congress, "Massacre of Cheyenne Indians."
Wynkoop, *The Tall Chief.*

Author's photo

The six-pounder cannon "donated" by General Curtis to the defenders of Fort O.K. now rests on the lawn of the Hall County Courthouse.

Nebraska State Historical Society

Luther North

Nebraska State Historical Society
Major Frank North, organizer of the Pawnee Scouts.

Kansas State Historical Society
Colonel Thomas Moonlight

Nebraska State Historical Society
Colonel Robert Ramsey Livingston

Nebraska State Historical Society

The released captives in Denver. Laura Roper holds Isabelle Eubank. The boy on the left is probably Ambrose Asher. The youth on the right is Danny Marble. This photo appeared on the front page of the June 8, 1930, *Denver Post*. It identified Ambrose Asher as Connie Eubank.

Courtesy Mrs. Dorothy Ellis Lingelbach

Lucinda Eubank

Courtesy Colorado Historical Society

Participants in the Camp Weld Council: Kneeling in front are Major Edward Wynkoop (left) and Captain Silas Soule. Although Indian identities are not certain, those seated in the first row are probably (from left) White Antelope, Bull Bear, Black Kettle, Neva and No-Ta-Nee. Back row (from left) unidentified man, Dexter Colley, interpreter John Smith, Heap-of-Buffalo, Bosse, Samuel Elbert, and an unidentified soldier.

Part III
Chapter Eight

The trail laid waste —by the White Man

For General Curtis to proclaim that the Platte route was safe for trains without escorts was either a giant stretch of his imagination or some very wishful thinking. It is true that, during the marshaling of his expeditionary force at Plum Creek, at least one large train out of Virginia City passed by the station. There may have been others as well, but they were traveling without escorts, not because the route was safe, but because the general had all the troops with him. The military had been refusing to escort emigrants and freighters most of the summer because of a lack of men and horses. The trains continued to travel at their own risk only because they had no alternative.

When the raids began on August 7-9, many trains were caught in transit between Fort Kearny and Julesburg. Others were en route from mining camps in the west or from the Missouri River ports. Those already on the Platte had little choice but to corral near a military post and combine forces before continuing onward. Those en route from the Missouri could hardly turn back and unload, although several Mormon trains did retreat from the Little Blue to wait out the raids in Kansas. In one way or another, the wagons continued to roll, although the volume of traffic was greatly diminished and even came to a virtual stop for a time. The few outfits that did reach the Missouri from the west were probably the inspiration for the *Bugle*'s rosy statement that trains were reaching Council Bluffs from Denver daily. They did arrive, if not daily, then every few days, and in much smaller numbers than was normal for the season.

At least one train was completely abandoned along the South Platte road. Having sold Liberty Farm and moved his family to Marysville, James Lemmon contracted to haul a load of castings and heavy equipment to the Colorado mines. When the raids erupted, his train was near Julesburg. The terrified bullwhackers deserted the outfit, stranding the heavy wagons, two of which contained a large boiler assembly. Before Lemmon could return with help and retrieve his outfit, some other enterprising freighter hooked on, delivered the equipment, and collected the charges.

Those who were desperate or foolhardy enough to make the journey along the Great Platte River Road found it bathed in an aura of unreality. The valley appeared drowsy and serene in the late summer sunlight, outwardly as pacific as the Garden of Eden—until the random fields of littered cargoes, the burned out skeletons of heavy wagons, and the wreckage of abandoned homesteads shocked the mind into believing what it already knew was true. The desolate wrecks and new graves that dotted the landscape infused the awareness of the more sensitive pilgrims with an unearthly sense of calamity.

The coarser element was unfazed by evidence of human and material destruction. As they saw it, abandoned property was up for grabs, empty homes were for looting, and the pitiful pole fences around weedy gardens or small corrals made wonderful campfires. Not only travelers, but military patrols also, as a matter of privilege, "appropriated" chickens and hogs for their camp kettles and helped themselves to Ben Holladay's hay and corn as it pleased their fancy. Where an agent remained at the stage station to protest the pillage of company stores, the officers flippantly promised him they would "chalk out a receipt," meaning that the stage line was simply out so much food and forage.[1] At last, the Overland agent at Fort Kearny appealed to General Mitchell, who ordered all troops along the line to stay clear of the stage stations.

Not only stage agents, but homesteaders along the trail angrily protested the highhanded thievery of their possessions, though with little hope of redress. Of their home and trading post at Plum Creek, Mrs. Dan Freeman later recalled: "The Indians never troubled us except to take one team during the war, but I was always afraid when I saw the soldiers coming. They would come in the store and help themselves to tobacco, cookies, or anything. Then the teamsters would swing their long, black-snake whips and bring them down across my chicken's (sic) heads, then pick them up and carry them away to camp."[2]

A letter from John Nye to the *Daily Rocky Mountain News* (October 6, 1864) bitterly assailed the thievery of the Kansas Militia,

> *who came up the road as far as there was no danger, ostensibly to fight the Indians and protect the road, developed their real purpose, and showed out their real nature, by making a regular raid, as though they were in an enemy's country, by carrying off all they could pack on their horses . . . I have seen horses loaded down with sacks of monkey wrenches and ladies fine shoes; strings of boots and dry goods, enough to make one endorse a possible assertion that such men are not even the peers of those who sacked Lawrence . . . Most of the ranchers who fled with their families, returned to find their effects taken away or destroyed by those from whom they had reason to expect protection.*[3]

A similar letter to the *Omaha Nebraskian* of October 28, 1864, eloquently expressed the effects of the widespread bullying and looting on the morale of the homesteaders:

> *. . .a large amount of destruction, I am sorry to say has been caused by soldiers and emigrants who do not hesitate to take what little has been left by the Indians. We saw in several instances squads of soldiers under the direction of petty officers, tearing down and carrying away by the wagon load the timber and material from partly destroyed houses and barns.*
>
> *I also heard of several instances of freighters and emigrants taking and carrying off in their wagons, cooking stoves, and in fact everything that could be made useful or profitable in the mountains. In civilized communities we call such acts by the name of theft or robbery, but those who commit the acts seem to consider everything lawful plunder, which the Indians have not destroyed.*
>
> *We met a number of families returning to what were their homes, and which they will find completely desolate. In conversation with some of them, they expressed much feeling, and some of them went so far as to say that as between Indians, soldiers, and emigrants they had but little to choose.*[4]

Very little difference indeed, but with one distinction: The Indians could be expected to pillage and burn, for they were at war to the knife. But to be looted and robbed by one's own people was a source of bitter disillusionment to those who had chosen to make their homes along the White Man's Medicine Road.

Chapter Eight notes

1 According to Ware, the officers of Company F issued vouchers for any supplies they procured from civilians, but this was not always the case with other units. The term "chalking out a receipt" emerged in testimony given by employees of Overland Stage Lines in support of Ben Holladay's claim for damages.

2 DAR, *Nebraska Pioneer Reminiscences.*

3 The text of Nye's letter reached Colonel Edwin Manning of the Seventeenth Kansas Militia, who was then under criticism by the Overland Stage Line for borrowing seven of its horses at Rock Creek Station. Manning published an angry rebuttal in his *Big Blue Union* (August 27, 1864), concluding that, in the future, "The Indians may commit as many depredations as they please up the road, may burn every station down to the state line, may steal every horse and burn every coach belonging to the Overland Company, and, it being out of the state, I will not march one mile nor send one man to their relief." Nye answered in a letter to the *Marysville Enterpriser* (December 9, 1864), clarifying his remarks and absolving Manning's militia of the blame for thievery of abandoned goods, and blaming instead the people of Beatrice and Captain Murphy's troops.

4 There are numerous accounts of damage done to settlers' homes and property by the cavalry, the militia, and by travelers on the road. J.K.P. Miller recounted how his party pulled apart an abandoned stagecoach station for firewood. The widespread vandalism became a point of contention in the settlers' prosecution of depredation claims against the Indians in later years. In his report of February 23, 1887, Special Investigator Leonard Poole wrote, ". . . testimony shows that the whites did much damage and took whatever the Indians left." (Heirs of Joseph Eubank, Indian Depredation Case #2504)

Sources

DAR, *Nebraska Pioneer Reminiscences.*
Dawson, *Pioneer Tales.*
Daily Rocky Mountain News, October 6, 1864.
Joseph Eubank Heirs, Depredation Case #2504.
Lyon, "Freighting in the '60s."
Miller, *The Road to Virginia City.*
Official Records, Vol. 41, Part 1.
The Omaha Nebraskian, October 28, 1864.
Stolley, "The Defense of Grand Island."
–*History of the First Settlement.*
Testimony as to the Claim of Ben Holladay.
Yost, *Boss Cowman.*

Part III
Chapter Nine

The stages roll again

Fortunately for the United States Postal Service, Ben Holladay was independently wealthy. The money lost by his Overland Stage Lines in the summer of 1864 was enormous and as yet unreckoned and uncompensated. Despite the severe financial reverse, he was hard at work to restore his operations along the overland route. Not a single piece of mail would be carried across the plains until the stage line was running again, and that was not going to happen without military protection.

Toward the end of September, Holladay hired a number of daring men (Charles Emery was among them) and organized them into labor parties that went along the line, rebuilding stations and corrals and cutting hay. On October 1, he sent a blunt dispatch to General Curtis, informing him that Indians had been sniping at his hay cutters and ferry coaches along the Little Blue. Holladay presented the general with his conditions for the resumption of service: The army must post a minimum of four or five soldiers at each station, and four troopers must escort every coach which passed along the line between Big Sandy and Latham Station.[1]

Despite cost and danger, the work advanced. At last, on October 3, the word went out on the wire from Atchison to Leavenworth, on to Omaha and farther on to Fort Kearny: The westbound mail coach was leaving Atchison that morning bound for Denver City. After forty-nine days without service, Ben Holladay had the Overland Stage Line back in operation.[2]

Colonel Livingston was as ready as he could be. He had dealt out his troopers at outposts roughly every fifteen miles along the trail.

Their mission was simple enough: Escort the stages and patrol the vicinity for hostile warriors. It all proved rather too much for the Nebraska City militia company, which had been divided in order to garrison both Pawnee Ranch and the restored Little Blue Station. On October 7, Captain Stevenson took out a detachment of his men to scout for a band of hostiles that had been reported north of Elk Creek the previous night. Joined by Lieutenant Bremer and a detachment from Little Blue Station, Stevenson explored slowly and cautiously down Liberty Creek and across to Elk Creek. With dusk fast approaching and a good deal of territory left to scout, the captain called a halt to make camp for the night. Lieutenant Bremer refused to obey the order to stop, evidently figuring to finish the reconnaissance and return to his station. He had been over much of this country the previous day and he already knew there were no hostile Indians anywhere near.

But they were there now, in the cover of a thicket along Elk Creek. No sooner had the lieutenant crossed the creek with four of his men when a bullet dropped him dead in the grass. Arrows flew, cutting one of the soldiers. The survivors fled in terror back across the creek, while the Indians burst from the thicket and dashed away to the south.[3]

Nevertheless, it was due in large part to the exertions of the militia that the Atchison coach rolled smartly up the Little Blue Valley, arriving at Fort Kearny on that same October 7. Everyone was much relieved. Colonel Livingston was so relieved that he dashed off an immediate wire to General Curtis, informing him that there had been no trouble on the road. So far the army was looking good.

It looked good for exactly five days. Then the Indians struck again. West of Plum Creek stood the abandoned Freeman Ranch, one of the many empty homesteads along the trail. Except on the night of October 12, Freeman's Ranch wasn't exactly deserted. A band of hostile warriors had moved in to lie in wait for the westbound coach.

The attack was a complete surprise. The first shots killed one of the lead horses, bringing the coach to a halt directly in front of the ranch house. Passengers and soldier escorts tumbled out and opened a hot fire. One of the passengers was slightly wounded and a soldier suffered a severe head wound, but the whites blasted shots into the house for fifteen minutes until the Indians made a dash for freedom. Inside the riddled building, two of their number had made their last raid.[4]

Lieutenant Flanagan met the coach the next morning. He had been ordered to turn over his artillery and equipment (after all, the trail was safe again) to Colonel Summers, now commanding at Fort

Cottonwood, and return with his detachment to Fort Leavenworth. After talking with the people on the coach, the officer and his men continued down the trail. The lieutenant had good reason for his anxiety: As a result of Colonel Livingston's order, his nineteen men were armed only with seven revolvers.

Lieutenant Flanagan had sailed up the Missouri from Leavenworth to Plattsmouth. He marched hundreds of miles to Cottonwood, to the Solomon, and back to Cottonwood, all without even seeing a hostile Indian. This was about to be corrected. Somewhere between Smith's Ranch and Mullaly's Willow Island Ranch, a large war party slipped out of the southern bluffs, heading for the Kansans on a dead run. Flanagan ordered his several wagons stopped in the road and strung out his men in a long, naked skirmish line. For a few breathless seconds they stood there waiting—nineteen men with seven handguns, facing the charge of fifty or more mounted warriors.

The bluff paid off. The Indians halted well out of range for a short council. Then they turned around and melted back into the bluffs. Flanagan's party continued a short distance farther and forted up in an abandoned stable for the night.

During the evening, several men from the First Nebraska galloped past. Their detachment had been scouting the bluffs when it was attacked, possibly by the same war party. The men were hurrying to Plum Creek for reinforcements, and they advised Flanagan to remain on the alert.

The lieutenant finally reached Fort Kearny on October 15, where he succeeded in having muskets issued to his command.[5] Leaving Kearny on October 20, Flanagan and his men returned to Fort Leavenworth via the Little Blue Valley. On the very day they rode through, marveling at the destruction in the valley, their comrades of the Sixteenth Kansas were at Westport, fighting the battle which drove General Price and his Confederate army southward in defeat, and away from Union soil forever.[6]

Chapter Nine notes

All notes are from *Official Records.*

1 Vol. 41, Part 3, 549-550.

2 Ibid., 596.

3 Vol. 41, Part 1, 843.

4 Ibid., 246, 830.

5 Ibid., 246.

6 Major R.H. Hunt, Chief of General Curtis' artillery, was expecting Flanagan's return to Fort Leavenworth already on October 16. At that time, Price already had captured Lexington and Warrensburg, Missouri, some forty miles east of Westport (Kansas City). Vol. 41, Part 4, 15.

Part III
Chapter Ten

The close of 1864

With the stages running again and many of the freight outfits back on the road, the Indians settled into a pattern of resistance which was highly effective and increasingly bold. Small war parties hid in the bluffs overlooking the Platte Valley, watching the movements of the soldiers, waiting for targets of opportunity. Then a lightning strike—a few arrows, a few bullets—and the warriors departed as swiftly as they had come, vanishing into the cedar-choked canyons of the "Coast of Nebraska."[1] It was maddening and impossible to prevent. Colonel Livingston could do nothing more than build his defenses and organize his escorts.

The colonel began to operate under an unofficial martial law, impressing empty freight trains to haul his logs and fuel and impressing civilian mowing machines to cut the badly needed supply of hay for the winter. By the end of October, his string of makeshift forts and stockades was complete.

On October 17, Livingston received orders from an exasperated General Mitchell to burn the prairie from the south edge of the Platte Valley to the Republican.[2] On October 22, with a stiff north wind at their backs, Colonel Livingston's post commanders fired the dry grass on the divide, from twenty miles west of Julesburg all the way to Hook's. Thus deprived of game, forage, and cover, perhaps the hostile Indians would find war making more difficult.

But the Indians refused to let up the pressure. On October 18, they crossed the Platte near Alkali Station and killed an emigrant on the north side. Captain Murphy rode out in pursuit, but again, his horses were not in condition to catch up with the raiders, and the Indians turned the trick by following Murphy back to Alkali and attacking his post.

On October 22, hostiles attacked woodcutters near Midway Station. On October 28 they attacked haycutters near Sandhill Station. On November 19 they attacked a train three miles west of Plum Creek Station. Major Tom Majors and a detachment of the First Nebraska galloped to the rescue but the Indians attacked them, too. Captain Weatherwax and Company G of the First Nebraska finally rescued everybody.

Of all the senior officers on the plains in 1864, Colonel Livingston appears to have had the most profound grasp of the course which the war was taking. The continuing spate of hit and run raids was frustrating to him, but not unexpected. Neither was he inclined to credit the Confederate government with inciting the Cheyennes, Arapahoes, and Sioux into rebellion. In a lengthy report of November 1 to the Adjutant General in Washington, he thoughtfully explained:

> *I discard the opinion which has been freely advanced by so many that this Indian war has been instigated and aided by whites. Its origin is in the natural antipathy between the Indian and Anglo-Saxon races. The rapid strides of civilization toward and over the Rocky Mountains foreshadow to the Indian a future so abhorrent to all his natural instincts that he cannot help turning upon the white man and attempt in his savage way to check this annually increasing current of white emigration toward his once quiet and bountifully supplied hunting grounds.*

Looking to the future, the colonel offered a gloomy prediction for the year 1865:

> *I confidently look for a renewal of hostilities on a much larger scale in the spring, for the reason that the war this past summer has been a success for the Indians . . .*

He then concluded with ominous prescience:

> *I firmly believe that unless a terrible example is made of them—for instance, the total annihilation of some of their winter encampments, . . . they will from their past successes be encouraged to a more vigorous and audacious warfare as soon as the grass is green next spring.*[3]

At dawn on November 29, 1864, Colonel Livingston's prediction became reality as troops of the District of Colorado attacked the Cheyenne and Arapaho villages on Sand Creek, about forty miles northeast of Fort Lyon. The number of Indians killed is variously given between 137 and 148. Two thirds of the slain were women and children. Cheyenne chiefs lost in the attack included White Antelope, Standing-In-Water, One Eye, War Bonnet, Spotted Crow, Two Thighs, Bear Man, Yellow Shield, and Yellow Wolf. These men, along with Black Kettle, who escaped with his badly wounded wife, had formed the very heart and core of the peace movement among the High Plains tribes. In the years since the massacre, Sand Creek has become a synonym for the grossest kind of perfidy and subhuman barbarity.

A critical discussion of the affair on Sand Creek is beyond the scope of this work. At the same time, the Sand Creek Massacre is considered to be the logical climax to the series of events which had its beginning with the August 7 butchery on the Little Blue. Having traced the whole sorry business this far, it is in order to set down some of the salient facts surrounding the climactic events which ended the year 1864 on the High Plains.

On the day of the council at Camp Weld, General Curtis wired his requirements for peace with the tribes to Colonel Chivington. He demanded that (1) those guilty of depredations be surrendered; (2) all stolen stock be replaced; (3) and Indian hostages be taken to ensure compliance. His telegram also instructed, "I want no peace till the Indians suffer more . . . No peace must be made without my directions."[4] The subsequent behaviors of Major Wynkoop and the Cheyenne chiefs do not indicate that they were aware of this stern communication.

While the chiefs were still away in Denver City, the bands broke up their camps on Hackberry Creek and began moving southward toward Fort Larned. On their way down Pawnee Fork, they had the bad luck to stumble upon an expedition out of the fort under the command of General Blunt. After a brief and confusing firefight with Blunt's advance guard, the Indians retreated back northward to the Smoky Hill where Black Kettle and the other chiefs found them.

The chiefs were puzzled over their inconclusive hearing with Governor Evans. Had they made peace or not? No one really knew. They had done everything they knew how to do to end the hostilities, and they trusted Wynkoop enough to move their people closer to Fort Lyon while they awaited peace terms sent down by the big white war chief. They apparently did not know that the white war chief had already decreed that the Cheyennes must suffer more before he would consider offering them peace.

They did not know, either, that the white war chief had other problems, for Confederate General Price had been turned away from St. Louis and was at that time marching westward. His orders required him to create a diversion in the West by marching across Missouri and down through Indian Territory, raising as much hell as possible and sweeping the country clean of cattle, draft animals, and militarily useful supplies as he went.[5] General Curtis was scraping together all the soldiers and militia he could find to stop Price and the gaggle of bushwhackers who were daily attaching themselves to his lumbering command. For the time being, the problems of the Cheyennes and Arapahoes would be on the general's back burner.

Curtis withdrew General Blunt from the frontier and placed him in field command of the army along the border. But, before knocking heads with Price, he found time to settle accounts with Wynkoop. Unknown parties had been making serious accusations against the major: He had left his district without permission, and he was even making unauthorized peace conventions with the Indians around Fort Lyon, in direct defiance of Curtis' orders. On October 17, Major Scott Anthony of the First Colorado was ordered to relieve Wynkoop at Fort Lyon, and on November 2, the major left for Fort Leavenworth to explain himself to General Curtis, who by this time was the victor of the Battle of Westport.

Under Major Wynkoop, Fort Lyon had become a friendly place for the Cheyennes and Arapahoes, and the Indians felt comfortable in visiting the post at their leisure. With Wynkoop gone, the social atmosphere around Lyon became decidedly chilly, and the word spread that Anthony did not like Indians and was not to be trusted.

Nearly two months had passed since their meeting with the governor at Camp Weld, and the chiefs were wondering why there had been no final peace terms proposed. About November 25, Black Kettle and fifty of his braves rode down to Fort Lyon to talk with Anthony. The major told them that he had not received any peace proposals from Curtis as yet, but when he did, he would immediately notify the Cheyennes.

Three days after the chiefs left the fort, Colonel Chivington rode in with the Third Regiment. Taking Anthony, several companies of the First Colorado, and a detachment from the First New Mexico, he attacked Black Kettle's camp on Sand Creek in the gray light of a bitterly cold November morning. General Curtis had his wish. The Cheyennes certainly suffered more. Rarely, if ever, since the 1637 slaughter of the Pequots in Connecticut had murder and human agony been visited in such proportions on an aboriginal village.

Those Cheyennes and Arapahoes who managed to escape Chivington's troops found their ways to the camps of their kinsmen on the Smoky Hill, from whence war pipes were sent to the Brule Sioux and to the Arapaho camps along the Solomon. Within several weeks, a huge encampment had formed on the Cherry Creek fork of the Republican in extreme northwestern Kansas. Here it was that, over the white man's Christmas holidays, the Northern Arapahoes, Southern Cheyennes, Dog Soldiers, Pawnee Killer's Ogalalas, and Spotted Tail's Brules smoked together and planned a winter campaign—a thing almost unheard of on the plains.

Colonel Livingston, who had been so realistic about so many aspects of the recent war, had badly underestimated the Indians. Sand Creek had not cowed or demoralized the tribes. The Cheyennes in particular were wholly and fanatically dedicated to revenge for the suffering of their people at Sand Creek. Throughout the encampment of 800 to 900 lodges, women and children contributed their efforts toward the preparation of their men for total war. It would be the bloodiest and most gigantic effort of which they were capable. And it would begin in the dead of winter, the very time when Governor Evans said he could make war the best.

Following the attack, Colonel Chivington led his victorious troops back to Denver City, where the men were hailed as heroes by an ecstatic population. Indian scalps and relics were given as gifts. For three nights running, scalps and Indian body parts were exhibited during a hastily written melodrama staged at the Denver Theater, beginning ironically on December 28—the Feast of the Holy Innocents. Colonel Chivington's popularity had now reached its zenith. His military career, which had begun so brightly in the Glorieta Pass campaign, was now invested with an aura of brilliance. The Omaha newspapers had draped the mantle of Harney on the wrong man–for Chivington, not Mitchell, was the new Harney. And Sand Creek, not Ash Hollow, would henceforth stand as an unfading reminder to the Indians of the far reaching power of the white man. Another such campaign or two would write a finish to the Indian wars on the plains, and it was widely believed that the chastisement of Sand Creek had broken the power and will of the Cheyenne and Arapaho people.

Widely believed, but not universally by any means. In Denver City itself there was a minority of citizens who were aghast at the barbarity of the Colorado troops. They could hardly help but wonder that, with Third Regiment discharged and much of First Regiment coming due for muster out of the service, what would happen to Colorado Territory if the power of the Cheyennes and Arapahoes was not as broken as was generally believed? If the High Plains tribes refused to wait until next summer to renew hostilities, who would protect Denver City? It was an anxiety which extended far beyond the Colorado frontier—in fact, all the way into eastern Kansas.

Colonel Ford of the Second Colorado Cavalry was now in command of the District of the Upper Arkansas at Fort Riley. Even before the year was out, he had begun to receive letters from settlers to the north and west of the fort, begging protection from the wrath they were sure would follow Sand Creek. On January 3, 1865, he wrote to Fort Leavenworth:

> *I forward you (a) petition of settlers living in and about Clifton, a settlement northeast (northwest) about sixty miles, praying for protection. Heretofore they have been unmolested, but the late operations in the western part of this district against the Indians have awakened their fears . . . Colonel Chivington's attack upon the tribe of Indians near Fort Lyon has precluded all possibility of a peace. . .*[6]

Immediately after writing this communication, Colonel Ford left Riley on a tour of his new district. Five days later he sent an even stronger message from western Kansas:

> *The people here, and, in fact, all the citizens of the border, are very much enraged at the course taken by Colonel Chivington and his troops. By the accounts of some of his own regiment stationed at Fort Lyon who were present it was a horrible affair; but whether he was right or wrong, it has precluded all possibilities of peace, and it is now war to the knife.*[7]

It would be all that and more, but Colonel Chivington would have no further part in it. On December 21, 1864, he received orders from General Curtis to relinquish command of the District of Colorado.

Throughout his Civil War service, Curtis had grown increasingly disgusted with the corrosive effect of local and factional politics upon his best efforts to maintain loyalty in Missouri and peace in Kansas and Colorado. In a letter of December 30, he complained to General Halleck,

I may do something if I can get men disconnected with Kansas affairs and worthy of credence. There is so much political and personal strife in our service, it is impossible to get an honest, impartial determination of facts.[8]

To break up this parochial chicanery, Curtis hit upon the idea of sending Kansas regiments to duty in Colorado and Idaho Territories, replacing them with men drawn from Wisconsin and other eastern states. Getting rid of Chivington would kill two ducks with the same shell. It would help to defuse any recriminations coming out of the Sand Creek affair, (which Curtis sensed would be forthcoming), and it would open the command position in the District of Colorado for a disinterested officer. And General Curtis knew exactly whom he wanted to succeed Chivington: Colonel Thomas Moonlight of the Eleventh Kansas Cavalry.

Moonlight was headstrong and impetuous, something of a martinet. But he had proven himself to be a loyal subordinate and a tenacious fighter. It was Colonel Moonlight who had commanded Curtis' advance force against the army of General Price, fighting stubborn delaying actions as the rest of the federal army coalesced around the doomed Confederates. Now Moonlight would go to Denver City, and Chivington, whose commission had long since expired, would be out of the volunteer forces of the United States.[9]

Colonel Moonlight had barely unpacked his bags in Denver City when the Indians struck. On January 7, 1865, they attacked Julesburg, sacking the stagecoach offices and warehouse, and ambushing Colonel Summers and a detachment of Company F, Seventh Iowa Cavalry. Subsequent attacks on ranches along the South Platte line confirmed fears that, far from being broken, the power of the Cheyennes and Arapahoes (joined by even more of the Sioux) was about to descend on Colorado Territory with greater ferocity than ever. Even though the troubles at Julesburg were not in his district, Moonlight soon found that his battle against Price had been a Quaker picnic compared to the demands of his new position. In fact, he was close to resigning his commission when he wrote angrily to Curtis on January 11:

The Indians have attacked Julesburg, Valley Station, and several other points on the Overland route . . . the Overland line is now in their hands, and all mail communication by that route is shut off . . . All this I have to contend with and submit to the howl and sneer of parties who cannot believe but that I ought to start after the savages with nothing more

> *than my headquarters force . . . Of the 1000 horses purchased for the 100-days' regiment, only about 400 have been turned in to the quartermaster, and they are all unserviceable for the present. Out of the 600 ponies reported captured at Sand Creek by Colonel Chivington, only about 100 have been turned in to the government, and not one of them is fit, or will be, to ride."*[10]

On his way out of office, Colonel Chivington had left the affairs of his district in a monumental mess. Not only was there a total lack of continuity in administrative matters, but Moonlight was finding that he had no troops, no arms, no method of raising another volunteer regiment, no control over the militia, and no effective command over several companies of "irregulars" that had been formed. There were no serviceable horses, the governor was politicking in Washington, and the Indians were everywhere. Poor Moonlight had inherited a district in a complete shambles.

Unknown to Colonel Moonlight, affairs in Colorado Territory were becoming very much the talk of official circles in Washington. The reports of Colonel Ford, letters to eastern newspapers, and telegrams to congressional delegates, all on the subject of Sand Creek, had set the poisonous stew of Colorado politics to steaming. Not everyone in the territory was sleeping better since Chivington "broke" the power of the Cheyennes, and some of those people were writing some very disturbing letters.

One of the first to scramble for cover was Agent Samuel Colley. On December 20, he wrote a self-serving letter to the *Missouri Intelligencer*, complaining,

> *I was in hopes our Indian troubles were over. I had 250 lodges near this place under my protection and that of Fort Lyon. All the chiefs and their families were in camp and doing all they could to protect the whites and keep the peace, when Colonel Chivington marched from Denver, surprised the village, killed one-half of them, all the women and children, and then returned to Denver. Few if any white men can now live if the Indians can kill them.*[11]

On January 10, as the first news of the attack on Julesburg was spreading through Denver City, Judge H.P. Bennet, Congressional Delegate from Colorado Territory, received a wire from one J.B. Chaffee, calling for prompt action at the national level:

You can hardly be too urgent with the Secretary of War, or the President, about our Indian troubles. Unless something is done to settle this trouble, we are virtually killed as a territory . . . I am inclined to believe that our administration, both civil and military, have failed to comprehend the situation. I mean Evans and Chivington. I think this whole difficulty could have been arrested; but this is nothing to the case now . . . There is no use to depend on General Curtis, Evans, Chivington, or any other politician.[12]

With the sour odor of Sand Creek stealing through the halls of Congress, the pressure began to build in army headquarters as embarrassing questions were raised about the past conduct of affairs in the Military Department of Kansas. A major political storm was in the wind, and General Halleck, who happened to be a very good political weather forecaster, began to chart a safe course for the army. On January 11, he wired General Curtis:

Statements from respectable sources have been received here that the conduct of Colonel Chivington's command toward the friendly Indians has been a series of outrages calculated to make them all hostile. You will inquire into and report on this matter, and will take measures to have preserved and accounted for all plunder taken from the Indians at Fort Lyons (sic) and other places.[13]

It is interesting to note that the order did not direct Curtis to investigate outrages of the Indians' human rights. Rather, the chief concern was the series of events which led to the closing of the routes of communication and commerce, placing in financial jeopardy the interests of important investors from the east. It would require more time and more revelations to stoke the slow fire under the country's sense of moral outrage.

Now at last, General Curtis was beginning to appreciate just how hot his seat was getting, and he began an immediate campaign to clear his skirts. On January 13, he sent a copy of Colley's letter to Colonel Moonlight, explaining,

I clip a scrap from the Intelligencer of the 7th, which is probably a part of the occasion of General Halleck's order concerning an investigation of the conduct of Colonel Chivington. I suppose a commission of officers better be ordered and have so telegraphed you. I have also attached

> *Fort Lyon to your command, so as to accommodate the matter. If the colonel did attack that camp, knowing it to be under the instructions of the commander at Lyon, or the Indian agent, he committed a grave error, and may have very much embarrassed our Indian affairs.*[14]

Curtis also sent Halleck a curious wire, his growing anxiety clearly evident in its waffling logic. He admitted that Chivington may have departed from Curtis' field orders, but he might be out of the service by now. Even if he was not, it would be next to impossible to assemble enough high ranking officers to conduct a court martial. The officers were all scattered hither and yon fighting Indians. The massacre at Sand Creek was abhorrent, but the settlers were at least partially to blame because it was hard for the military to resist their clamor for indiscriminate slaughter. Besides, some of those Indians at Sand Creek were probably guilty of depredations, and Wynkoop was wrong for allowing them to camp there. Curtis was also forced to admit that the Indians were raising havoc with the overland route again, but that, he claimed, was only because the severity of the winter weather was driving them to desperate measures to obtain subsistence. Then, in a final burst of uncomprehending analysis, the general stated:

> *It is not true, as Indian agents and Indian traders are representing, that such extra severity (as at Sand Creek) is increasing Indian war. On the contrary, it tends to reduce their numbers and bring them to terms.*[15]

Curtis may have also sensed (not without satisfaction) that, for Governor Evans, there was political trouble in the wind. His letter to Evans was accordingly blunt and severe, if not entirely candid:

> *I feel your Interior Department will make me trouble, by proposing military evolutions which conflict with my own . . . I cannot carry on war on other people's plans. I want no fancy movements, such as occurred last summer, when one of your Militia companies marched down the line, passing my troops, and claiming to have "opened the overland route," as though others had not been over most of the places on the Blue, and on Plum Creek and elsewhere, where most of the losses had transpired. This move of Chivington's against the bands that had congregated on Sand Creek, at the instance of Major Wynkoop, was also an inspiration of over-zeal which did not emanate from my headquarters.*[16]

General Halleck was surely no Indian fighter. He was, however, the quintessential political bureaucrat, and a master at detecting an officer's attempts to shift blame.[17] This had been going on for over a year now—the depredations, the brave excuses, the show of great exertions, the hollow results, then more and worse depredations—and Halleck had finally had enough. Nothing more than a monumental shuffle and a few rolling heads could clean up the disarray in the Department of Kansas. Primly, Halleck sat at his big desk, stroked his elbows, and began maneuvering for the big shakeup.

On the last day of January, 1865, General Order #11 reorganized the Military Division of the Missouri.[18] General Rosecrans was out. His failure to support Curtis in the pursuit of Price's army was one of several failings which cost him his job. His place was taken by the pompous Major General John Pope, who had done a surprisingly effective and creditable job heading up the Department of the Northwest in Milwaukee.

The Department of Kansas was merged with the Department of Missouri, although headquarters would remain at Fort Leavenworth. It would not be easy to replace General Curtis. His congressional record, his support for the transcontinental railroad, and his political connections with the Lincoln administration made it necessary to treat him very carefully. Halleck consulted with General Grant who, while he knew next to nothing about fighting Indians, had an excellent grasp of the political situation. What with General Butler's pathetic showing and the Army of the Potomac being stalled in the trenches before Petersburg, Grant was a little frustrated just then and, like his chief of staff, was heartily tired of the numerous entreaties and excuses coming from Fort Leavenworth. With Grant's approval, General Curtis was ordered to replace Pope in Milwaukee. The command of the combined departments of Kansas and Missouri would go to General Grenville Dodge, a born fighter who was guaranteed to get results along the overland route. Pope was immediately ordered to St. Louis to speed Dodge on his way to replace Curtis as soon as humanly possible. As Halleck stated testily, "The Overland Mail Route requires efficient protection from Indian hostilities."[19]

The change of command on such short notice could not be a smooth one.[20] General Dodge had not the slightest familiarity with the posts and problems of his new department, nor was his task much clarified by a warning he received from the gossipy Halleck:

> *It is proper to state in this connection that others report these stories of Indian hostilities as greatly exaggerated, if not gotten up merely for the purpose of speculation, and respectable authorities assert that they are encouraged by agents of the Overland Mail Company in order to cover their frequent failures to transport the mails according to contract.*[21]

The ignorance of this statement did little to affirm the reputation of the Chief of Staff as "Old Brains." Certainly a tour of the Great Platte River Road would have educated the man, but he was too valuable to be spared from Washington. So as General Halleck sat at his desk shuffling commanders and regiments and papers, the Indian War of 1865 flamed brightly amid the snow and sub-zero cold of the High Plains.

The war this year would be different. It would be even more vicious. It would include the destruction of the telegraph lines, the Indians having only lately come to appreciate their importance. Neither would the wild tribes be so much concerned about capturing white women and children. The Indians had little use for them in their camps. Moreover, the massacre at Sand Creek can hardly have had a positive effect upon the continued captivity of Nancy Jane Morton and Lucinda Eubank, whose ordeals now remain to be told.

Chapter Ten notes

[1] Hyde, *Life of George Bent*, 142.

[2] O.R. Vol. 41, Part 4, 62.

[3] O.R. Vol. 41, Part 1, 825-832. Colonel Livingston's report also gives a detailed summary of his preparations along the road as well as the numerous attacks made upon military and civilian parties.

[4] O.R. Vol. 41, Part 3, 462. According to testimony in the Sand Creek investigations, Major Wynkoop's courier had not yet returned with the long awaited comprehensive peace terms prior to the attack on the Indians' camp.

[5] According to Britton (*The Union Indian Brigade*, 447), Price's orders came directly from General Kirby Smith, commander of the Trans Mississippi Department.

[6] O.R. Vol. 48, Part 1, 407-408.

[7] Ibid., 462.

[8]. O.R. Vol. 41, Part 4, 970-971.

[9] Colonel Chivington's commission expired on September 23, 1864. Technically, he was no longer an officer of the United States Volunteer Army when he led the attack on Black Kettle's camp at Sand Creek. (*Official Army Register of the Volunteer Forces of the United States Army*, Vol. 8, 22.)

[10] O.R. Vol. 48, Part 1, 491.

[11] Ibid., 511.

[12] U. S. Congress, Senate, Report of the Secretary of War, 79-80.

[13] O.R. Vol. 48, Part 1, 489.

[14] Ibid., 511.

[15] Ibid., 502-503.

[16] Ibid., 503-504.

[17] Historian Bruce Catton offers some wry insights into the character and personality of General Halleck in *This Hallowed Ground*, 87, 270.

[18] O.R. Vol. 48, Part 1, 686.

[19] Ibid., 694.

[20] Ibid., 849. The shuffling of commands was done so precipitously that it bordered on comic opera. On February 14, Pope telegraphed Dodge, "What is General Mitchell doing at Omaha City while the Indians are overrunning his district? Please order him to his proper station and duty forthwith." Dodge wired back, "General Mitchell's district headquarters are at Omaha. He has been on the plains all winter."

[21] Ibid., 714

Part III
Chapter Eleven
The ordeal of Nancy Morton

Nancy Morton and Lucinda Eubank could only watch in despair as Black Kettle's people disappeared in the distance with Danny, Isabelle, and Ambrose. The two women's hopes of being ransomed and going home had become barren. Soon their camp was on the move again, resuming what to the women seemed to be a pointless, eternal wandering through a purgatory of hunger and scalp dances.

Several days after the children left, the Indians planted a tall stake in the ground and surrounded it with piles of wood. Nancy concluded that she and Lucinda were to be burned, an idea which the Indians seized upon to torment the two.

They were not to be burned, however. The pole was to be the centerpiece of a religious ceremony which included the burning of several buffalo heads and much dancing. During the dance, one of the gyrating warriors snatched little Willie from his mother's arms and pretended to throw him into the blaze, but Lucinda's captor grabbed the child and handed him back to her.

The camp moved again, stopping near a spring that bubbled from the ground in such volume it appeared to be boiling. Nancy was so hungry that she used every opportunity to scour the prairie for prickly pear and wild rosebuds to eat. Fortunately, there was an abundant supply. But if Nancy was getting her vitamins, she wasn't getting much else, and she became weaker by the day, exhausted by hunger and depression. She received a little meat when the Indians killed a buffalo, and the camp moved on to another spring around which grew a supply of wild grapes and plums. In this encampment Nancy grew delirious, a condition that persisted for several days. The Indians ministered to her in their own ways and slowly her reason returned.

A war party came into camp bringing a collection of medicine bottles looted from a train. One of the warriors approached Nancy with a small, plain bottle in his hand. He wanted to know what it contained, and produced a small label that had been attached. Nancy took the paper and saw the word *strychnine*. While she was pondering just how to explain this substance, the brave took a pinch from the bottle and tasted it. Licking his lips, he pronounced it good—and seconds later he pitched over dead. The Indians compelled Nancy to bury the evil bottle, after which they held a dance of grief over the departed warrior.

The band crossed to the south side of Beaver Creek and welcomed a wagon into their camp. The cargo consisted of firearms and ammunition which the Indians told Nancy had been procured for them by some friendly white men. Other warriors returning from a raid brought in what appeared to be a woman's hands and feet, which they burned in a special ceremony. As the Indians prepared to move again, Nancy became quite ill with a malady which she identified as "mountain fever." She was unable to remain on a pony in her weakened condition, so the Indians placed her in a travois. During the march they killed an antelope and gave her some of the meat, but her illness only grew worse.

Her captors decided that Nancy's illness (was it dysentery?) would never improve if she continued to eat, so they withheld all food from her, which only caused her to grow still weaker. One of the squaws, a woman oddly named "Happy," had a professional disagreement with this treatment. Placing some cooked corn and meat in a small pan, she smuggled it into Nancy's lodge under her blankets. Nancy was extremely grateful, and in several days, her condition began to improve.

The Indians allowed Nancy and Lucinda to be together often, and during their conversations, they came to the conclusion that, if they were ever going to get free, they would have to do it all by themselves. There were, of course, soldiers and bands of Colorado citizens prowling the country, a fact which kept the Indian camps constantly on the move. If the women could escape the camp, there was a fair chance they might meet up with one of these patrols. The thing had to be tried.

The two managed to secure and clean a buffalo paunch to use for a canteen. One routine day in camp, they informed the squaws that they were going off to hunt for wild grapes, and began a slow search of the banks of a nearby stream. Soon the women were out of sight of the lodges and making top speed in their bid for freedom. They stayed close to the stream where the thickets and low bushes provided the only cover to be had. They had gone about two miles and were beginning to feel the thrill of escape when the squaws caught up to them. Nancy and Lucinda were marched back to camp, their great escape a failure. They hadn't even found any grapes.

Shortly after their return to camp, a war party came in bearing, in addition to the usual plunder, a tiny baby girl. They also had a ring which they had taken from the girl's mother, and a photograph of the parents. The little girl had very beautiful black hair, and Nancy noticed that the army officer in the photo had black hair, also. The Indians brought the baby girl to Nancy and asked her to give it a name. All her feelings of tenderness, so long inhibited, came bubbling to the surface. Overcome with emotion, and perhaps remembering her own lost babes, Nancy named the little girl Francis Jane Morton. Now she, like Lucinda, would have someone to care for, and a reason to survive whatever might lie ahead. Nancy, of course, had no milk to give the baby, so the Indians took it away. She never saw the child again.

The incident had a dismal effect on Lucinda as well as on Nancy. When another war party left the camp for a raid, it proved to be too much for her nervous temperament. Screaming, "O, they are going to kill more whites!" Lucinda groveled on the ground, babbling incoherently, taking bites from the sod. When the Indians lifted her up, she bit her own arm. Her captor immediately picked up Willie to prevent him from being harmed. By the time the camp moved again, she had calmed somewhat, and the Indians allowed her to ride with Willie in a travois.

As the procession was crossing a stream, one pole of the travois slipped into a deep hole, tilting the whole outfit precariously. Lucinda became startled, threw Willie into the water, and jumped in after him. Again the Indians recovered both mother and son, repacking them in the travois so the march could resume.

Lucinda's behavior was becoming intolerable to the Indians. On the evening after the travois incident, Nancy's captor confided that Lucinda's chief was thinking of killing her just to be rid of the nuisance. Nancy implored him to intercede for her life because, after all, she did have a papoose and he needed his mother. By the following day Lucinda was more rational and Nancy felt greatly relieved. She even argued the Indians into giving her friend something to eat.

Food continued to be an obsession with the women, and often there simply was none to be had. The wild tribes' complaints of starvation had not been groundless. Hunting was poor, winter was approaching, and the Indians were determined to hold out as long as possible before trading their captives for provisions. And, if the tribesmen were finding the dining fare sparse, the white captives would find it even worse.

Small war parties continued to enter and leave the camp, but they brought in more scalps than food. With game scarce and the military so active, the Indians decided somewhere along the upper Republican to split up their camp. The decision came so quickly that the two white women had no time for farewells. As the lodges of Lucinda's band moved south toward the Arkansas, Nancy's band turned back northward. Her captors explained to her that Lucinda was to be taken towards Denver City and released, while she would accompany them to Fort Laramie to be exchanged for food.

The sudden departure of her comrade in misery left Nancy with a feeling of desolation. She had borne her trials with fortitude as long as there had been someone to live for, but one by one they had all been taken from her—first Danny, then the black haired infant, and now Lucinda. Her captor's daughter, Mitimonie, was kind and solicitous, but the cultural chasm was wide and not easily bridged. Feeling sure that she was the last of the white captives to remain unransomed, Nancy fell into a black depression. She had one goal in mind, now: to end her ordeal.

Left alone in her lodge, she scrounged up a length of rope which she tied as high up as possible around one of the lodgepoles. It was not an ideal situation for a hanging, so Nancy devised a backup plan. Gathering armfuls of dried grass, she piled it under the rope and prepared to set it ablaze. If the hanging failed she would at least burn to death, or such was the hope in her tormented mind. But again the meddlesome squaws interrupted her plans, and the chief learned of her attempt at suicide. She began to receive larger portions of meat, and she was watched very closely.

The camp was moving north now, towards the Platte, dodging numerous alarms of soldier patrols, most of which turned out to be false. For a time, the meat supply gave out entirely, and Nancy fell back on her rosebud and cactus diet until the chief ordered a pony slaughtered for food.

The weather was growing noticeably colder, too. In the mornings there was thin ice over the surface of the ponds and sluggish streams. The Indians crossed the South Platte at night while pinpoints of light flickered in the distance, supposedly the campfires of soldiers. During the Platte crossing, Nancy deliberately fell from her pony into the water and attempted to swim away under cover of darkness, but the Indians fished her out of the frigid water and the northward trek continued.

Then the village crossed the North Platte and fortune smiled briefly. An antelope made its appearance, and Nancy, whose marksmanship the Indians admired, scored a clean kill at long range. The Indians were elated, and her chief declared that he would not sell her now even for 500 ponies. She was too valuable as a hunter. After this the young maidens gathered round her, washed her face, and affectionately combed her hair.

Still they continued northward, drifting over the endless, bleak landscape with hunger their constant companion. At length they were in the vicinity of Fort Laramie, and Nancy's chief decided it was time to open the trading game. Selecting two trustworthy braves, he sent them to the fort to announce that he had a captive to trade. With their arrival at Fort Laramie, the army, for the first time since the council at Camp Weld, knew what had become of Nancy Jane Morton.

Major John Wood, post commander at Fort Laramie, had been hoping for the news brought in by the two braves. Back in August, he had received an alert from General Mitchell that Cheyennes might be traveling north with some white captives. The summer was gone, now, and the major was anxious to secure their release before the harsh winter came to the Bighorn country. With the knowledge that the captives were nearby, he played his first card in the game of redemption.

Major Wood fitted out two friendly Cheyennes—Spotted Horse and Little Horse—with several ponies laden with foodstuffs and presents. Trailing their pack animals, the two rode north out of Fort Laramie.[1]

Seated on a fallen log, Nancy cried from hunger and frustration as she attempted to make some sense out of the Indians' behavior. Some squaws had coaxed her into a bullboat and had taken her to the center of a small lake. There, for some unfathomable reason, they pushed her out of the boat into the frigid water. Nancy survived her painful dunking, but her health, both mental and physical, continued to deteriorate. As she sat on her log absorbed in tears, she looked up to see two small Indian boys standing before her, quietly waiting to be noticed. Through signs, they made Nancy understand that she was to follow them, and they led her directly to one of the lodges. Inside, she found a young squaw who spoke excellent English. The woman's husband was a trader named Williams who worked as a scout at Fort Laramie. He had recently sent her word that soldiers were dispatching several wagons loaded with supplies to buy Nancy's freedom. Mrs. Williams then seated her at a wonderful meal of buffalo steak, bread, and coffee, and her spirits were immensely lightened.

Shortly after, Spotted Horse and Little Horse arrived in the village—if not with wagons, at least with pack animals loaded with goods for the trade. The chief convened a council at which the two Cheyennes distributed presents and made their sales pitch. Loud arguments resounded among the lodges, and the talks collapsed. Nancy was simply too valuable to be given away for so little. Trailing their pack horses, the two emissaries returned to Laramie, their mission a failure.

Nancy's hopes of a rescue disappeared with the Cheyenne traders. Soon her band moved farther north to camp near the Powder River. The snows came in earnest now, drifting in deep banks before the bone chilling winds. The cold had become as much an enemy as starvation.

Incredibly, there continued to come through the icy white wilderness several more mountain men and traders, intent on winning Nancy's freedom. Louis Richard (or Reshaw, from the French pronunciation of his name) and a companion came from Platte Bridge Station, but once again Nancy's captor was unwilling to deal. A short time later, Williams himself, along with Joe Bissonette, came trudging all the way from Laramie in an attempt to unsnarl the negotiations. The unhappy effect of all this activity was to convince Nancy's chief that she must be a great deal more valuable to the whites than he had realized. She might even be the wife of some great white chief. His price continued to climb. Bissonette became angry and threatening, but there was no way to force a deal. The traders all left the village, and once again Nancy's fragile hopes for rescue came to naught.

Shortly after Williams, Bissonette, and Richard had gone, Nancy's captor, along with five other lodges, moved farther up the north fork of the Powder into the Big Horn Mountains. They made their new camp on the shore of a small lake, which was by this time solidly frozen over. It was here that Nancy was to experience three beautiful, but deeply disturbing apparitions.

On a day when the skies had cleared and the weather moderated, she went to sit by the side of the frozen lake to escape the gloomy confines of the lodge. She was startled when, from nowhere, a snow white cat leaped from the ground into her lap. She put out her hand to touch the strange creature, and the cat vaulted away and vanished.

Food supplies were growing short again, and Nancy's chief sent a brave named Gray Head slogging south through the snow to Platte Bridge to inform the white soldiers that the Indians were ready to trade for the white woman. While he was gone, Nancy went again to the frozen lake, cleared the snow away from a patch of ice, and skated on her moccasins until she was tired. Retreating to her fallen log for a rest, she witnessed the second apparition—a snow white dove which fluttered noiselessly down to perch atop the walking stick she was holding. As before, she put out her hand to the ghostly creature, and it flitted away into nothingness.

A third and more puzzling incident took place not long after. Mitimonie had begged Nancy to sew a dress for her from some material obtained, either from the traders or from the raids on freighters along the Platte. On a sunny day, Nancy carried her sewing work to her favorite spot beside the lake. After working for a time, she paused to look out toward the center of the ice, and slowly a vision began to materialize. It gathered size and substance as it moved toward her—a baby in a long, white dressing gown, all more brilliant than the purest snow. The babe had wings on its back and, as it hovered near, Nancy thought she recognized her own tiny daughter, gone nearly two years now. Wistfully she called out, "Anna? O, if only I had wings that I might fly away . . ."

Slowly the apparition began to dissolve, and a spiritual voice infused her consciousness with a message: "You are not alone." Then Nancy emerged from her reverie, and the ghostly babe was gone, and there was only the snow and the gloomy green of the pines. Shaking and weeping, she returned to the lodge where Mitimonie met her. The Indian girl seemed to understand that something out of the ordinary had taken place, for Nancy's face was drawn and colorless, her eyes wide and staring. But the voice had told her she was no longer alone and, although she did not know it, the time of her rescue was at hand. Already the traders sent by Major Wood had reached a friendly Arapaho village a few miles to the south. It was to be the third and final expedition to rescue the white woman who had grown to be of such great value to two antagonistic cultures.

Major John Wood was frustrated but not beaten. His last attempt to free Nancy had failed, said the trader John Rousseau, because the Indians believed she was the wife of a very important white man. Therefore the price of her ransom ought to be higher. If anything could pry her loose from her captors, it would be a certain gray mare which the major owned, and which the Indians much coveted.

In the latter part of December, Major Wood decided to play his expensive trump card. He summoned squawman Jules Ecoffey, gave him the gray mare and a brown saddle horse—both the major's personal mounts—and sent him north to the camps in the Powder River country. In addition to the horses, Ecoffey also took a pack train laden with food, tobacco, lead, powder, knives, and trinkets. Ecoffey persuaded the more experienced Joseph Bissonette to accompany him, and the two traders set off on a long, bitter march through the snow and crackling cold over two hundred miles northwest to the Sioux camps. By mid January, they had arrived at a village of friendly Arapahoes. Thus far, their mere survival in the bleak, wintry Powder River country had been a feat of wonderful skill. For their next trick they must win Nancy Morton's freedom. It was an undertaking that required everything they had ever learned through long years of experience among the wild tribes of the plains.

Nancy was making a batch of bread inside her lodge when the word came that traders had arrived in the village. They must certainly be serious to have come so far in the dead of winter. But she had been so often disappointed in the past, that she allowed no room for hope that this time the results would be favorable. But things went well. Ecoffey and Bissonette argued and dealt, appealing to the chief's vanities as well as his fears. The negotiations went on a good part of the night, and at last the old chief gave in. The traders had brought along a buffalo robe and some heavy winter wear for Nancy, but the old chief demanded that as well. She would be badly underdressed for her ride through the brutal weather.

Early the next morning, the party prepared to leave the camp. Mitimonie and some of the squaws were anguished over Nancy's departure, and their tears flowed freely. Then the men turned the horses south and the party began its frozen, desperate ride for Fort Laramie. Ecoffey and Bissonette had brought along an escort of a dozen Arapaho braves because, as they explained to Nancy, the old chief might prove treacherous and change his mind at any time, leading a war party to recapture his lost "daughter." They kept the horses on the run most of the way to the Arapaho village where the traders planned to spend the night. Here they would also be able to procure heavy robes and clothing necessary for Nancy to survive the icy journey. Upon their arrival, Nancy ate a good supper and went to bed in one of the lodges, sleeping soundly under a pile of blankets and buffalo robes.

Morning brought bad news. The run to the village had been hard on the horses. Nancy's mount had been run nearly to death and was unfit to continue. While Ecoffey and Bissonette pondered a solution, a visiting Sioux brave came to the rescue. He had been touched by the white woman's suffering, and offered his own animal so she could continue her journey. Just as the voice had told her, she truly was not alone. Deliverance was coming from the most unlikely places.

In the morning they were off again, bucking through the deep, powdery snow. The cold was so intense that every few miles they halted while Ecoffey dug sagebrush from the snow to make a quick, warming fire. Every frozen mile Nancy lived in dread of being recaptured again. She even imagined hearing the old, familiar war whoop in the empty snowfields behind.

One of the pack horses gave out and was left floundering in the snow. Everybody was numb and exhausted from the piercing cold. Night camps were sleepless as the men fought to keep the pitiful sage-brush fires from dying out. The final night of the desperate journey they spent in an Arapaho village.

Morning found them back on the trail once again. They traveled slowly now, the horses weakening with every mile. The afternoon had begun to grow dark when the party arrived at the top of the gentle slope leading down to the North Platte River. Nancy was thrilled to see, in the fading light, the rude buildings of the military outpost at Platte Bridge Station, huddled bravely in the snowy wilderness along-side the frozen river.

After an overnight stay, the party resumed its journey eastward down the Oregon-California Trail. It had been a week since Nancy had left the village of her captivity, and the most brutal part of the trek was past. From Platte Bridge Station she rode in an army ambulance, somewhat protected from the hostile elements.

All day, ambulance and escort mushed through the snow to Deer Creek Station, where the party remained over Saturday to rest. On Sunday morning the journey resumed, ending at La Bonte Station late that afternoon. Monday evening they arrived at Horseshoe Station where the operator sent a wire to Fort Laramie advising the post of the imminent arrival of the former captive and her escort.

Every mile of the way, Nancy had lived in fear of hearing the old war whoop. At one of the stations, she thought she recognized Big Crow, one of the Cheyenne chiefs who had captured her at Plum Creek and had made her life miserable during the early part of her captivity. The suspect was living in a tepee close to the soldiers' quar-ters, and behaving like the best Indian in the whole world. Nancy decided to inform the commander at Laramie of her suspicion and allow the military authorities to deal with Big Crow, if that in fact was who he was, but the sighting was a chilling reminder that, until she was safely at the fort, it was still possible for something to go wrong. Then her fear gave way to relief when a military patrol met the ambu-lance a few miles west of Laramie. So, she was to be safe after all. She had survived some 176 days of grief, depression, sickness, starvation, cold, and exhaustion.[2] It would require time for Nancy to readjust herself to her own society again, to accept emotionally the reality of her freedom.

Fort Laramie was ready to do its part. Her ambulance pulled up in front of the residence of sutler's agent William Bullock and his wife. It seemed to Nancy that all the comforts of the civilized world were to be found in the Bullock's home, and she was unable to resist dissolving into tears and offering prayers of thanks to God for her deliverance.

The Bullocks had planned a big evening to celebrate her arrival. The festivities began with a grand dinner which was probably a little rigorous for her deprived stomach. The regimental band played "some of the most melodious selections," and a continual stream of guests came through the house to offer their congratulations. As had happened to Laura Roper, so the guests called upon Nancy to relate bits and pieces of her experiences during the past, long months, and several times she burst into tears in front of her admirers. But that was acceptable to the guests, perhaps even expected. It was, after all, a sentimental age.

Although Nancy was anxious to return to her father's home in Iowa, the trails east of Laramie were too dangerous for travel just then. The wild tribes were fully engaged in their reprisals for Sand Creek. Communications along the route were at a standstill and, only two days after Nancy reached Laramie, the Indians burned Julesburg to the ground and headed northward for the Powder River country. On February 4, Colonel Collins left the fort with every available trooper for the relief of the beleaguered telegraph station at Mud Springs. Nancy would have to wait several weeks for the situation to improve. Meanwhile, the ladies at the fort would make her stay as interesting as possible.

She was profoundly grateful to Major Wood for the personal sacrifice that was responsible for her freedom. But the major was no longer at Fort Laramie. Elements of the Seventh Iowa were approaching the end of their service on the plains, and Major Wood had returned to Omaha to be mustered out of the army. Major Thomas Mackay of the Eleventh Ohio Cavalry was now commanding at Fort Laramie, and it was to him that Nancy related her sighting of Big Crow. The major wasted no time in acting on her suspicions, and an investigation indicated that the Cheyenne in question was indeed Big Crow (also known as Two Crows, and Old Crow). His presence so close to the soldiers was highly suspicious, and Mackay had him arrested as a spy and brought to Fort Laramie in chains.

Nancy had long been troubled at the thought of the bodies of her loved ones being left on the prairie to be torn by scavengers. There were men of the Seventh Iowa at the post who assured her that Colonel Summers had buried all the victims of the Plum Creek

Massacre before they had been disturbed. Nancy was grateful for their information. Now she had one less burden to carry with her.

During her stay, she also met Sarah Larimer, herself an escaped captive of the Indians. Her tales of endurance were similar to Nancy's except that Mrs. Larimer had been more fortunate: Her husband had survived the Indians' attack.

The tight little frontier society at the fort kept Nancy and Mrs. Larimer from being bored by offering a ceaseless round of entertainments and dinners, organized, of course, by the energetic Mrs. Bullock. But eventually, there came the time for departure, and once again Nancy found herself struggling with her emotions, as feelings of joyful anticipation mingled with sadness at leaving her newfound friends who had shown her such kindness during her stay at Laramie.

On Monday morning, February 26, the train which would take Nancy through to Fort Kearny formed up near the parade ground. Friends came to bid her farewell, and she was presented with a purse of $1,400 which had been collected for her at the post. The regimental band played "Home Sweet Home," and some of the crowd joined in singing the words. Then the command to mount rang out along the column, the draft animals leaned into their harnesses, and Nancy was on her way home with a joy in her soul which "was almost indescribable."

The wagons rumbled past Camp Shuman and the battlefields of Mud Springs and Rush Creek. Nancy saw, for the first time, Scotts Bluff, Chimney Rock, and Courthouse Rock, and she thought the scenery spectacular.

The journey continued down Lodgepole Creek to cross the Platte near the blackened ruins of Julesburg. At Beauvais Station, the soldiers rushed out to present her with a gift of $10, and at O'Fallon's Station, Captain Wilcox did his best to entertain the travelers overnight.

Then the wagons reached Cottonwood, and Nancy discovered a cousin stationed there with the troops. He showed her a letter recently received from her father in Sidney, plaintively asking for any news of Nancy. Was she still a captive or had she been found dead anywhere? She read and reread the letter, treasuring her father's handwriting.

Then the train rolled on toward Fort Kearny. The wagons crossed Plum Creek and halted near the place from whence Nancy (and Danny) had been taken so many months before. The rest of the party remained at a respectful distance as she picked her way past the scorched tire irons and axle thimbles and charred hunks of wood, over the ground which had received the blood of her loved ones, to the site of the common grave which contained their bodies. Nancy was entering a world now where none could follow, where none could console, and for the first time since her captivity had ended, she became filled with black grief as she knelt upon the scarred earth of the long mound beside the trail:

> *Terrible were the scenes that passed through my mind, as the sight of the savages as they came upon us that morning, came fresh to my memory and were truly appalling. No one only those who have had a personal experience can realize the thoughts that fired my brain, and oppressed my heart, as my memory led back to the sight of the ghastly corpses about me, and the savages with blackened faces, and fierce and uncouth gestures, which seemed to me is to be a never-to-be-forgotten scene. As I now look back upon that horrifying morn, I wonder that I ever survived, and as I turned to leave the graves of those so dear to me the picture of that fatal morning came repeatedly before me not as a picture in memory but as a present reality.*

From Plum Creek, the wagons continued on to Fort Kearny, where Nancy bade farewell to the faithful escort which had brought her the many miles from Laramie. Soon she was aboard the eastbound coach for Nebraska City, with the long miles unrolling behind. Past Hook's Junction Ranch, past the Martin Ranch, Porcupine Ranch and Beaver Crossing; over the bridges spanning the Big Blue and Salt Creek and the forks of the Little Nemaha the coach rolled onward, following the Steamwagon Road to the Missouri.

Nancy was very weary by the time she arrived in Nebraska City. Like Laura Roper, she was tired of telling her stories of captivity over and over again. Her emotional control was eggshell thin, and she was embarrassed about breaking into tears in front of total strangers. From the stage depot she walked to the Morton Hotel, the place where she and Frank and John and William had been so gaily entertained that last, hot day in July. No one recognized her as she checked in (probably under an assumed name) and went exhausted to her room. She found the hotel supper quite good, but the bed was terrible. In fact, it hardly compared to the cozy bed of blankets and robes in the village of the friendly Arapahoes.

In the morning she boarded the stage which was to take her across the river to Sidney, Iowa. But the stage was not going anywhere this day. The Missouri was choked with ice floes large enough to punch a hole in the side of the flimsy ferryboat. The stage got no farther than the waterfront.

This was a disappointment not to be taken meekly. The passengers walked to the edge of the turbulent river, and somehow, Nancy didn't think it looked all that dangerous—not after all she had been through. She and several others hunted up the owner of a stout skiff who agreed to take them across the icy channel. It was a hair raising adventure. The jagged ice cakes banged and ground against the sides of the little boat, pushing it more than a mile downstream before it gained the eastern bank. There the passengers climbed out and somehow managed to scare up another coach for the continuation of their journey.

At three o'clock on the afternoon of March 19, 1865, the rattling coach drew up in front of the Fletcher home in Sidney, the driver shouting at the top of his lungs, "Hey, Fletcher, I have Nan in here!" Samuel Fletcher exploded through the door yelling, "My God, you have not!" But Nan really was in there, and soon her family—all eight of them—were propelling her into the house amid a storm of hugs and kisses. Her homecoming, she wrote later, was the nearest possible thing to being resurrected from the dead and finding herself in paradise. Word of her arrival spread quickly, and by evening, the house and yard were crowded with hundreds of people come to pay their respects of sympathy and congratulations.

As it turned out, there was one other survivor of the raid at Plum Creek. Several days after her arrival, Nancy's younger brother, Sam Jr., came up from the barn leading her saddle horse. The plucky animal had been wounded by arrows, and the scars were still plainly visible, but he had escaped the Indians' efforts to capture him and had made his way back to Nebraska City, from where he had been returned to Iowa. Until March 9, that horse had been the last living link between the Fletcher family and their lost daughter and sister, and had been lovingly nursed back to health.

Now spring was coming into the land. Tenderly cared for by her family, Nancy recovered rapidly. She was, after all, only twenty years old, and at that age, all the world seems to be at one's feet. But it would never be the same world she had known before August 8, 1864. It had grown somehow more beautiful and rich. In the comfort of her family, and through her naturally optimistic and buoyant spirit, Nancy came to understand her ordeal as a lesson learned, a fire in which she had been refined and even strengthened: "The darkest cloud has its silver lining, if not its golden border. Till I had known sorrow, I had not known sympathy."

Chapter Eleven notes

1 This was not the first such mission for the two Cheyennes. Several women had been taken along the South Platte during the terrible raids of July 17, and on September 4 Major Wood had sent them north to attempt a rescue, the success of which is unknown.

2 Nancy Morton would have lost track of time while in the Indian camp, thus the days and dates given in her manuscript do not always agree. Once at Platte Bridge, however, she certainly would have become aware of the days of the week, and she is quite certain that she reached La Bonte on Sunday, and Fort Laramie on Tuesday. This would have to have been Tuesday, January 30, as Colonel Collins left for the relief of Mud Springs on February 4, and thus was not at the fort on the following Tuesday. From such internal evidence, we can construct a timetable showing that Nancy and her escort probably left the village of her captivity about Thursday, January 18; arrived at Platte Bridge Station on Thursday, January 25; and reached Fort Laramie on Tuesday, January 30.

Sources

The incidents in Nancy Morton's captivity are condensed from her two manuscript accounts. Other sources include:

Czaplewski, *Captive of the Cheyenne.*
Daily Rocky Mountain News, February 21, 1865: letter from "One of the Boys."
Federal Census, 1860, Iowa, Fremont County, Sidney Post Office.
Spring, "Old Letterbook."
Stevens, Affidavit. (also contains affidavit of John Wood)

Part III
Chapter Twelve
The ordeal of Lucinda Eubank

Lucinda Eubank never did reach Denver City. "Married" as she was to her captor, albeit unwillingly, she remained with the Cheyennes as the autumn days grew shorter and the winds increasingly chill.

As the village turned back toward the north, it came into contact with a mixed band of mainly Ogalala Sioux headed by the ubiquitous trader, Two Face. He had for several years been associated with the Gilmans, and was recognized by General Mitchell as a friend of the white soldiers. But, even though he was a familiar figure along the trail between Kearny and Laramie, his whereabouts were often unknown, his actions enigmatic. His chance meeting with Lucinda might have been a stroke of good fortune for both of them, but things did not quite turn out that way.

At considerable expense, Two Face purchased Lucinda from the Cheyennes, and the bands went their separate ways. Life with Two Face was better in some respects. Since his band was friendly with the whites, they were never afraid to visit ranches or military posts for a handout. Thus, Lucinda (and Willie, too, who "celebrated" his first birthday on October 1) had more to eat than she had with the Cheyennes. Also, Two Face did not buy her to be his wife. Perhaps he just needed another domestic around the lodge. At any rate, Lucinda was not required to yield sexually to her new owner.

But she still was not free. Like Nancy, she endured occasional whippings, torments, and teasing from the squaws. And, as the snow drifted among the lodges and the temperatures sank far below zero, she was miserable with hunger and cold. Through her loneliness and privation, she somehow managed to feed Willie so that he remained healthy.

During that long winter, a minor chief named Blackfoot purchased Lucinda from Two Face, and she was forced to give up her body to a new owner. Of all her captors, it was Blackfoot that Lucinda came to loathe the most, and the squaws in his lodge treated her unmercifully.

Quite a number of peaceful bands weren't involved in the hostilities over the winter, but with the warming days of spring and the increased military activity, there was always danger that the camps might come into harm's way by the soldiers. The villages were now about a hundred miles north of Fort Laramie, and Two Face was beginning to have troubling thoughts about keeping a white captive in a camp which was supposed to be friendly.

Much worried, he went to Blackfoot with an offer to buy Lucinda back again. He planned to take her in to Laramie as proof of his continued usefulness to the white people. There was also a chance that he might be rewarded for his faithfulness. But Blackfoot was not tempted by the offer. The white woman was his squaw and would remain in his lodge. There would be no deal.

Unable to purchase Lucinda at any price, Two Face hit upon a more devious solution. Catching her at a solitary moment, he arranged a time for her to steal away from Blackfoot's lodge in the dead of night. Two Face would be waiting outside the village with the horses, and together they would ride to Fort Laramie. Lucinda was both desperate and trusting enough to follow his instructions.

On the appointed night in mid May, when all were asleep, she gathered up Willie and quietly stole out of the lodge, through the silent camp, and out onto the black prairie. Two Face was as good as his word. He lifted Lucinda and little Willie onto a pony and the three of them struck out for Laramie. Once away from the village, they rode swiftly, arriving days later opposite a large encampment of friendly Sioux some ten miles down river from the fort.

All winter long these Indians had camped here, near to James Bordeaux's trading post, in a desperate attempt to stay clear of the war which was raging along the Platte. Many of the Indians were the so-called Laramie Loafers who had hung around the post for years, living on handouts and annuities. But in March the village was joined by 150 more lodges of "wild" Sioux and ninety of Northern Arapaho. There seemed to be no way for the army to feed so many mouths, and General Mitchell had wired General Dodge on March 6: "A large number of friendly Indians at Fort Laramie are in a starving condition. What shall I do with them? They say they dare not leave their camps to hunt or provide for themselves in consequence of the threats of hostile Indians."[1]

General Dodge instructed Mitchell to feed the Indians on condemned and spoiled army rations, but it was a drop in the bucket. The food situation remained desperate. To make things worse, shortly before Two Face arrived with Lucinda and Willie, Chief Little Thunder added sixty lodges of Brule Sioux to the village. The task of keeping order had been turned over to squawman-scout Charley Elston, who had raised a squad of Indian police.

Such was the situation on May 18 when Two Face arrived opposite this sprawling camp with his white captives. He could see at once that crossing the North Platte was going to be a challenge. The river was running high and very cold, and the current was too much for the ponies to manage with riders on their backs.

Two Face proved to be as creative as he was sly. With lariats, he tied little Willie on the back of one of the ponies. Then he instructed Lucinda to lie flat along her animal's back. If he foundered in the swift water, she was to slide off his rump and hold on to his tail, that he might tow her across. Leading the ponies, Two Face waded into the chilly, turbulent river. The crossing was an ordeal. The chances of something going wrong were dreadfully great. But the river was forded and the trio came at last into the friendly camp unscathed.

Word of their arrival spread quickly, and before long, Charley Elston appeared with his Indian police, placed the unlucky Two Face under arrest, and escorted Lucinda and her son back to the fort. Only three months before, Mrs. Bullock had welcomed Nancy Morton back into her own world and among her own people. Lucinda was given to the tender care of the wife of Captain Fouts, of the Seventh Iowa Cavalry. Certainly she needed some tender care, for her condition was appalling.

Her beautiful reddish hair had grown long and was knotted and tangled, dull and lifeless from lack of care. Her slim body was scarred and bony and beaten, and what little clothing she had was tattered and filthy. But she had lived through nine long months of sickness and privation, and it was going to require a very long time for Lucinda Eubank to fully comprehend that she was a free woman once again. She had never been a robust person, but the ordeal had toughened her. She had survived and preserved the life of her baby boy.

The social atmosphere around Fort Laramie had changed greatly since Nancy Morton left there. Colonel Collins was gone, back to Ohio and out of the volunteer army. His humanity and common sense had done much to keep a large number of the Sioux friendly, and his influence would be sorely missed along the North Platte. Collins' successor as commander of the reorganized North Subdistrict of the Plains was none other than Colonel Thomas Moonlight, recently transferred from his unenviable position in Denver City. From the standpoint of maintaining peaceful relations with the Sioux, it had not been a good move; for, although Moonlight was certainly no Chivington, he nevertheless had little patience with the Indians.

Lieutenant Colonel William Baumer, of the First Nebraska Cavalry, was now commanding the post at Laramie. As he and Moonlight listened to Lucinda Eubank's story, they became incensed at the outrages perpetrated upon this tattered woman. Lucinda's hatred of Blackfoot figured prominently in her accusations, and soon Charley Elston and his Indian police were on their way north to arrest him as well.

Lucinda recounted graphically how Blackfoot had abused her so terribly, had forced her to yield to his sexual advances. Her Cheyenne captor had abused her sexually too, and had starved her, and Two Face, well, he held her captive—not once, but twice. He had bought her from the Cheyennes and sold her to Blackfoot who had whipped her and threatened her and his squaws had tormented her and Two Face stole her back again and he tied Willie on the pony's back with a rope . . .

But Lucinda was confused, now, and her story came out in disconnected bits and pieces. Nine months of places and events and Indians swirled around in her jumbled memory to emerge, shaped and colored by the corrosive hatred with which she had sustained herself in her long battle for life. After a long period of rest and loving attention, she might be able to recount her terrible odyssey in a way that made sense.

Baumer and Moonlight were in no mood to wait for her thoughts to rearrange themselves. It hardly seems probable that Colonel Moonlight spent much time listening to her anyway, since his official report speaks of Willie as "her little daughter." His immediate goal was to make a terrible example of the Indians who had treated a white woman so maliciously. Her original Cheyenne captors were somewhere out on a million square miles of prairie, but Two Face and Blackfoot were very accessible—and they would hang.[2]

William Bullock had heard terrible things from Nancy Morton, but he was also aware that the Indians in the large camp near Bordeaux's were becoming very restive. Not long before Lucinda had come in, Big Crow, Nancy Morton's tormenter, had been hanged on a gallows erected on a slope of ground west of the fort. The Indian had had one of his legs shackled to a heavy weight and, as the body hung there decaying in the warm spring sun, the weight had pulled the leg off. The disrespect shown to the Indian body had roused the friendly tribesmen to a high pitch of indignation, and Bullock feared that the impending execution of the two Sioux might fire a revolt. Given the size of the camp down river, the trouble might prove more than Fort Laramie could handle. The courtly Bullock hastened to Colonel Moonlight's office to remonstrate with him in the most forcible terms.

The colonel was all business, and his business was retribution. "Well, Colonel Bullock," he snorted, "you think there will be a massacre? Let me tell you that there will be two Indians who will not take part in it."[3] And with that, Bullock was curtly dismissed.

On May 24, Two Face and Blackfoot were taken out to the gallows to hang alongside the one-legged corpse. Two Face's worst crimes were arguably naivete and stupidity. Those who could have spoken in his defense—Colonel Collins, General Mitchell, or the Gilman brothers–were far away. Sadly, his redemption of the white woman counted for nothing. At the place of execution, the trace chains from an artillery caisson were wrapped around their necks. For a time, their death songs could be plainly heard on the parade ground. Then there was only silence and three bodies swaying slowly in the spring breeze—left hanging as an example to other "bad Indians."[4]

Colonel Moonlight's action virtually guaranteed a final chapter in the ordeal of Lucinda Eubank. As Bullock had feared, the execution fanned the smoldering fire of indignation in the friendly camp to a white heat. Once again it had been demonstrated to the red people that the path of peace with the white people, like the path of war, ended in death. It would require little provocation for their repressed fury to explode into a wildfire of hostility and murder. It certainly did not require the string of stupidities which followed the hanging of Two Face and Blackfoot.

Events were set in motion by General Dodge, who had little more patience with Indians than had Moonlight. "The military have no authority to treat with Indians," he wired to Colonel Ford at Fort Riley. "Our duty is to make them keep the peace by punishing them for their hostility."[5] The general had his suspicions about those Indians in the friendly camp. Summer was approaching, the ponies were gaining strength, the hunting would improve, and hostile Indians would be influencing many of those friendlies to return to the warpath. It was an expensive drag and certainly no business of the army to have to feed them. If they truly intended to remain peaceable, they should have no objection to being moved far back of the war zone, say to Fort Kearny. It would also be much less expensive to feed them there, if that continued to be necessary.

The removal of the huge camp to Fort Kearny would be a massive and misguided undertaking. Only one who was ignorant of affairs among the plains tribes could have imagined that the Sioux would be willing to have their families moved so close to the lair of their hated enemies, the Pawnees. If the white soldiers had been unable to protect the Pawnees who were their friends, they would certainly have no interest in protecting the Sioux. The order for the removal of the village turned out to be a blunder of enormous proportions.

It is probable that a revolt was in the works even before the forced migration began on June 11. On that day, troopers of the Seventh Iowa came down from Laramie and took up position in the van of the march—Company D and detachments from companies A and B, with Captain Fouts in command. Behind the troops came the supply wagons and ambulances in which rode Lucinda and Willie, as well as the families of Captain Fouts and Lieutenant Triggs. When the cavalcade began its march on Monday, June 12, it was joined by a number of empty wagons owned by traders James Bordeaux and George Beauvais, who were taking advantage of the military escort to return east to resupply their posts. Shuffling along in the dust behind everyone else came the 1,500 Sioux, shepherded by Charley Elston's Indian police. Even discounting the provocations of weeks past; beyond the unwisdom of the relocation itself; and beyond the indignity of the Indians being forced to eat dust in the rear of the column, the conduct of the march defies logic.

The Sioux were all well armed with bows and arrows as well as rifles. Since the army had supplied them no rations, it would be necessary for them to hunt on the march. The soldiers of the escort were also armed, of course, except that their guns were empty. Whether to forestall a spontaneous act of aggression on the part of the troops, or to discourage unauthorized hunting forays, Fouts had issued no cartridges to the men of the escort.

While encamped for the night, some of the soldiers engaged in unauthorized hunting trips of a different sort. Fouts seems to have taken no measures to prevent his men from going into the Indian camp and choosing bedmates from among the young squaws. While liaisons between soldiers and women from the Laramie Loafer band were not at all uncommon, this tawdry behavior exacerbated the ill feeling which already existed, especially among the wild Sioux, and angered them beyond all endurance.[6]

The Indians took it for three days. Every night, warriors from the hostile bands stole in and out of the camp, and plans were laid for the great escape. By June 13, the assembly was encamped on Horse Creek, site of the Treaty of 1851 (which could only be broken by bad management or untoward misfortune).

On the morning of the fourteenth, Captain Wilcox moved out several miles in advance with the detachments from Companies A and B. The Indian camp seemed to be uncommonly slow in packing up this morning, and Captain Fouts rode back across Horse Creek to hurry them up. Approaching a group of warriors, he demanded that they get moving promptly. Blankets opened, rifles swung up, and Fouts was dead when he hit the ground.

The supply wagons had caught up with the advance guard when Captain Wilcox heard the shots. He ordered the wagons corralled at once, and sent a messenger galloping east to Fort Mitchell (formerly Camp Shuman) for reinforcements. He was already fearing the worst as Company D, now under the command of Captain Haywood, galloped into the corral. Wilcox issued cartridges to Haywood's men, and with their sabers, they began digging shelter pits for the women and children. Presently the Indians charged, but they were only covering the retreat of their own women and children who were streaming across the North Platte to be met by hostile tribesmen on the other side.

Several volleys from the soldiers prevented the now-hostile "friendlies" from coming too near the wagon fort, and before long, the remaining warriors had crossed the dangerous river and climbed into the northern hills. The troopers returned to the site of the abandoned camp and recovered the body of Captain Fouts, which had been stripped and mutilated as usual. His widow, unable to control her anguish, screamed for revenge—a feeling which Lucinda knew only too well.

Captain Wilcox reorganized the column for the march to Fort Mitchell. The following day, reinforced by some of Captain Shuman's men, he returned to Horse Creek and attempted a crossing of the North Platte. All thoughts of pursuit were given up after Captain Shuman nearly drowned and had to be hauled from the river by his men.

So the abbreviated column pulled itself together and trudged on to camp in the shadow of Chimney Rock. There were only a handful of Indians along now, mainly orphans and the very old. At last the sad procession arrived at Fort Sedgwick (formerly Camp Rankin) near the ruins of Julesburg. There the troopers of the Seventh Iowa met Colonel Herman Heath, who had taken over command of the regiment from Colonel Summers the previous February.

There was only one other woman at Sedgwick, a laundress, Mrs. Noble Wade. She invited Lucinda to stay with her until the eastbound coach arrived to take her on to Fort Kearny. After the tension of the march, the desperation of the short battle, and the anguished crying of Mrs. Fouts, Lucinda sorely needed some rest and someone to talk with. She found Mrs. Wade to be congenial, a willing and sympathetic listener. As she began to relax, Lucinda felt free to confide in Mrs. Wade her terrible secret: She was pregnant with Blackfoot's child—and she had no intention of bringing it into the world alive.

At one point during their conversation, a stranger came to the door and asked to see Lucinda. He was from Denver City, and, having heard that she was traveling down the trail, he had come on a pathetic mission. Gently he placed into her hands a small bundle of torn and terribly dirty cloth. She knew, even before he told her, that it was Isabelle's dress—a sad reminder of that day over ten months before when the sweetness and comfort of family life had ended with an afternoon walk through the deep dust of the trail.

The man was Mr. Davenport. He had received Isabelle from a Mr. Smith, and had cared for her until she died. Lucinda was deeply shaken by the experience, but had so hardened herself by this time that grieving was well nigh impossible. Mrs. Wade's abiding memory of Lucinda Eubank was that of a woman completely possessed by profound resentment. Shortly before leaving her hostess, Lucinda promised again that the thing which was growing inside her would never be born alive.

While at Julesburg, Lucinda also swore out a deposition regarding her time in captivity. The document was written and witnessed by Lieutenant Triggs (Lucinda was illiterate) and Captain Zabriskie, District Judge Advocate. Then on June 22, she boarded the eastbound coach with Willie, who was, after all, the only thing she had salvaged from her first twenty-four years of life. She had survived for him and she would live for him. Ten and a half months after her ordeal began in the valley of the Little Blue, the last of the captives was really free.

Chapter Twelve notes

1 O.R. Vol. 48, Part 1, 1105.

2 Author George Hyde denounces Moonlight and Baumer as incompetent drunks who were forced out of the army soon after their execution of Two Face and Blackfoot. But Hyde gives no sources for his information, and the careers of the two men hardly bear out his allegations. They deserve to be better known.

William Baumer, post commander at Fort Laramie, was thirty-nine years old when Lucinda was brought in. Born in Muenster, Westphalia, he had become an architect before immigrating to America at age twenty-four. After working at his profession in Cincinnati, Dubuque, and St. Joseph, he came to Omaha in 1861, where he was commissioned captain of Company B, First Nebraska Volunteers. He was shortly advanced to major, and on October 4, 1862, was promoted to lieutenant colonel, becoming vice commander of the regiment under Colonel Livingston.

Following the battles around Cape Girardeau, Missouri, Baumer was tendered the thanks of the community and given a ceremonial sword "for his brave and gallant defense of our city." Toward the end of his frontier service, Baumer was breveted colonel and brigadier general before being mustered out on July 1, 1866.

Baumer and his wife continued to make Omaha their home, and remained childless. In July 1869, Mrs. Baumer embarked alone for a visit to her native Prussia. During her absence, William Baumer died suddenly of apoplexy at his home around August 25. He was forty-three years old.

Thomas Moonlight had immigrated alone from his native Scotland at age thirteen. Arriving penniless in Philadelphia, he spent his teen years as a laborer before enlisting in the army in 1853. Following service against the Seminole Indians, he married a New York girl and began work in the commissary at Fort Leavenworth. At the outbreak of the Civil War, he was commissioned a captain, and attained the rank of colonel in April, 1864. At the time of his duty at Fort Laramie he was thirty-one years old.

After his muster out of the army, Moonlight became prominent in Kansas politics, winning elective office as secretary of state and state senator. From there he grew into national politics, and was appointed sixth territorial governor of Wyoming by President Cleveland in 1886. After serving as U.S. Minister to Bolivia from 1894-1898, Thomas Moonlight returned to Leavenworth where he died the following year at age sixty-five.

(*The Omaha Weekly Herald*, October 27, 1869; *The National Cyclopedia of American Biography*, Vol. 12.)

3 Spring, "Old Letterbook," 244.

4 In his journal for May 25, 1865, Will Young describes his arrival at Fort Laramie at two o'clock in the morning, passing by the bodies of Two Face and Blackfoot "dangling in the air." He does not mention Big Crow.

Hervey Johnson reported that, on April 23, an old Indian chief was hanged at Fort Laramie after being recognized by Nancy Morton as one of her captors. Czaplewski (*Captive of the Cheyenne*) gives additional accounts of the execution of Big Crow, or Old Crow, a Sioux (Cheyenne) chief.

Susan Bordeaux Bettelyoun witnessed the sight of Big Crow's body hanging legless on the gallows, although it seems strange that the leg would give way before the neck. She further states that it was still hanging there when Two Face and Black Foot were executed.

James Lemmon was also at Fort Laramie during this time, and he later told his son, George Edward, that there were four bodies hanging from the gallows. (Yost, *Boss Cowman*)

5 O.R. Vol. 48, Part 1, 961.

6 Such sexual liaisons between soldiers and women from the loafer camp had been troublesome since the early 1860s. But the squaws from the wild bands were not so debauched. Charley Elston told Lieutenant Ware that the Sioux squaws were the most virtuous women on earth. (Ware, *The Indian War of 1864*, 214.)

Sources

Alexander, Correspondence.
Burnett, "History of the Western Division."
Czaplewski, *Captive of the Cheyenne.*
Grinnell, *The Fighting Cheyennes.*
Hyde, *Life of George Bent.*
The Omaha Nebraskian, July 18, 1864.
Official Records, Vol. 48, Part 1 (Captain Wilcox's report)
Pattison, "With the U.S. Army."
Spring, "Old Letterbook."
Susan Bordeaux Bettelyoun, Papers.
Unrau, *Tending the Talking Wire.*
Wade, "New Light."
Young, Journal.

PART IV

To everything there is a season,
and a time to every purpose under the heaven...
A time to kill, and a time to heal...
A time to weep and a time to laugh...
A time to love and a time to hate;
A time of war, and a time of peace.

Ecclesiastes 3

Part IV
Chapter One

"Reflect on times that are past"

The war that exploded in 1864 blazed on through the bitter winter and into 1865—the Bloody Year on the Plains[1]—with Lucinda Eubank an unfortunate eyewitness to some of its deadly drama.

At the Camp Weld conference, Governor Evans had threatened the chiefs that the approaching winter was his time to make war. But just about all the war that was made that winter was made by the hostile tribes. Beginning with the two attacks on Julesburg, continuing with Colonel Collins' desperate fights at Mud Springs and Rush Creek, and through the Sioux revolt on Horse Creek, the Indians controlled every engagement fought. And when Colonel Moonlight sallied forth from Fort Laramie to punish them for their Horse Creek breakout, they caught him unprepared, stampeded his horses, and, as it turned out, cost him his job.

The Horse Creek escapees headed north toward the Black Hills and thence westward to the Powder River, where a huge confederation of tribes was forming. There they found Northern and Southern Cheyennes and Arapahoes, and numerous bands of Lakotas—Ogalalas, Brules, Minneconjous, and Sans Arcs. The mood of the camps was triumphant and warlike. Chiefs such as Spotted Tail and Man Afraid, who continued to argue for peace, were shouted down in the councils.

Determined to sever the Oregon-California Trail at a vulnerable point, a large war party of Sioux and Cheyennes attacked Platte Bridge Station on July 26, 1865. They succeeded in wiping out a small supply train and in killing a few soldiers (including Colonel Collins' son, Caspar), but when the dust settled, the army still held the bridge.

In the spring, General Patrick Connor was placed in command of the newly-formed District of the Plains. Connor immediately issued orders for three strong columns of troops to march from Omaha and Fort Laramie to trap and destroy the hostile tribes. A combination of Cheyenne resistance, incompetent civilian supply contractors, mutinous troops, and an untimely blizzard wrecked the expedition. One of the columns lost virtually all its horses and was rescued by Captain Frank North's Pawnee Scouts. Though he could hardly be blamed for the many factors which were beyond his control, Connor had no more been able to whip the wild tribes than Curtis or Mitchell, and he lost considerably more horses in proving it.

Though the tribes were victorious on the warpath throughout 1865, they did not take time to do their normal hunting. The brutal winter of 1865-1866 caught them desperately short of robes and meat, and their taste for war became tempered by their need to survive. Many of the hostiles trekked southward to Fort Laramie to beg for rations. Spotted Tail lost his beloved daughter to pneumonia and brought her body to Laramie, where the new commander, Colonel Henry Maynadier, arranged an impressive burial ceremony.

The years of bickering between army and Indian Bureau, as well as Connor's expensive disaster in the Powder River country, inspired the government to press for a policy of cooperation between officers and Indian agents. It was a propitious time. The winter had devastated the wild tribes, and the volunteer soldiers were rapidly being mustered out of the service. Both sides were ready, if not for a lasting peace, at least for a healthy breathing spell, and Colonel Maynadier was the ideal officer to make the most of the opportunity.

The inevitable peace commission formed, headed by E. B. Taylor, Indian Superintendent in Omaha, and journeyed to Fort Laramie to meet with the wild tribes which had been gathering there under Maynadier's wing. Aside from halting the hostilities, the chief aim of the commission was the securing of the Indians' consent to allow travel on the Bozeman Trail, which connected the Oregon-California Trail to the gold diggings at Virginia City, Montana. The more militant Sioux and Cheyennes refused to attend the council, and many of those who did were noncommittal.

As things turned out, the new spirit of cooperation had somehow stripped its gears in General Dodge's headquarters. His order to fortify the Bozeman Road resulted in the dispatch of Colonel Henry B. Carrington's column to duty in the new Mountain District north of Fort Laramie. Carrington's untimely arrival at the fort torpedoed the peace talks and laid the foundation for two years of bitter warfare with the Sioux and Northern Cheyennes, a series of events popularly known as Red Cloud's War, which would include the second instance of a battle between United States troops and Indians in which there were no white survivors.

During December 1865, most of the Southern Cheyennes returned to their old haunts in western Kansas and eastern Colorado. Their resentment over Sand Creek remained high, although some of the white heat of their anger had burned down. While they had been away on the Powder River, a commission which included old General Harney and William Bent met with some of the more peaceful elements that had remained on the southern plains. The usual treaty was signed, this one ceding the hunting grounds along the Republican and Smoky Hill Rivers. The returning Cheyennes would have none of it, and even Edward Wynkoop, newly appointed as their agent, was unable to obtain their consent.

Despite the fact that the summer of 1866 remained relatively quiet on the Kansas frontier, the belligerence of the Dog Soldiers and the fears of the settlers were sufficient to induce Congress to appropriate funds for a military show of force in western Kansas in the year 1867.

Leading the expedition out of Fort Riley was Major General Winfield Scott Hancock. The general was a national hero, best known for his superb combat record with the Army of the Potomac. The handsome, decisive Hancock was accompanied by the flamboyant Lieutenant Colonel George A. Custer and eleven troops of the newly formed Seventh Cavalry Regiment. Neither Hancock nor Custer had any experience in dealing with the plains Indians, nor were they much given to taking advice from those who had. The avowed purpose of the expedition was to show the Indians that the army could catch them and whip them at will. But, as he blundered about the High Plains, Hancock succeeded only in driving the Cheyennes back to the warpath, from whence they proved that neither Hancock nor Custer could catch them if they didn't want to be caught.

The trouble began in mid April when Hancock advanced too aggressively upon a Cheyenne camp on Pawnee Creek in western Kansas. The Indians, with bad memories of Sand Creek, predictably abandoned their village and fled. Disappointed over their lack of trust, Hancock ordered the village burned with all its provisions and equipment, and the Cheyennes renewed the war with a vengeance.

The Little Blue Valley had known precious little security since the bloody days of August 1864. There were a few nuisance raids in 1865, including a July 4 incident in which sixteen warriors attacked field hands working at Liberty Farm. Everyone was armed, though, and

James Lemmon stationed guards at each end of the cornfield. After losing one of their number, the Indians withdrew.

Again in 1866, Liberty Farm was attacked by a few wandering Sioux who were out looking for Pawnees to kill. This time the ranch was defended only by five boys, which was actually quite a lot, the Lemmon boys being a rough bunch. Besides Hervey, Moroni, and Edward, there were at the ranch two thirteen-year-old neighbor boys, as well as Mrs. Lemmon, Alpharetta, and Clarisa Roper, who was working for the Lemmons that summer. The youths defended the ranch nobly and no harm was done during the raid, which ended when James Lemmon returned with a squad of soldiers.[2] But after the burning of their village on Pawnee Creek on April 19, 1867, the Cheyennes fanned out once again over the old battlegrounds of 1864, from the Smoky Hill north to the Platte and down the Little Blue Valley.

On June 9, the Indians drove off sixteen horses from James Douglas' rebuilt Kiowa Station, and seven more from Hackney Ranch. Continuing down the valley, they shot to death a widower named Haney, leaving his three daughters orphaned. Once again the people of the lower valley began leaving their homes.

On June 10, S.J. Alexander left his ranch on the Big Sandy to retrieve some personal belongings for the Thompson family, who had sought safety at his ranch the night before. Indians met Alexander in the road and chased him back to his homestead, where by now another crowd of refugees was gathering.

Toward the end of July, and into August, the Indians returned to kill at least six more men in the vicinity of Hackney Ranch, several of them recent immigrants from Poland who had absolutely no idea what they were getting into when they brought their families to the valley that summer.[3]

Again, as in 1864, the Indians raided east of Fort Kearny along the Nebraska City Road, and for the second time in three years, George Martin's children were attacked, though with different results. It happened that Hepzibah and Annie Martin had walked to the home of a neighbor to visit, much as Laura Roper had done that August 7, 1864. Shortly after the girls left Jerome's to return to their home, several Cheyenne warriors swooped down from the bluffs and caught them out on the trail. Hepzibah did not have her shotgun this time, but Mr. Jerome was watching, and he easily shot one of the attackers off his pony. The others turned to assist their comrade and the Martin girls scampered to safety.[4]

More tragically reminiscent of the 1864 raids was the attack on the Campbell family just five miles east of the Martin Ranch.[5] Peter

Campbell brought his family from Scotland to Nebraska Territory in 1865. His wife had long been in frail health and, when she died the following January, Campbell was left to care for the six children by himself. On July 24, 1867, Campbell, his son, and a few neighbors were harvesting wheat about six miles east of their home when a rider brought warning that Cheyennes were raiding in the neighborhood. The Campbells immediately mounted their horses and started for home. On the homestead of Thurston Warren, a quarter mile east of the Campbell farm, they found Mrs. Warren shot to death in her doorway, holding the body of her infant son, who had been pierced by an arrow. Her fourteen-year-old son was still alive, but his thigh had been shattered by a bullet.

The Campbells reached their home to find their house ransacked and the children gone. A nine-year-old daughter had escaped the Indians by crawling away through a corn field, and she was presently brought home safely. But the Cheyennes had taken captive two teenage daughters and twin four-year-old boys.

Early that following August, a war party of Turkey Leg's Northern Cheyennes derailed a handcar and train on the Union Pacific line west of Plum Creek Station. For several days, the Cheyennes continued to make periodic visits to the wrecked train to loot the broken cars. A company of Pawnee Scouts was dispatched to the scene of the wreck and caught up with the Cheyennes south of the Platte River, almost exactly on the same ground over which the captive Nancy Morton and Danny Marble had been taken three years before. In the course of the disorganized battle, Cheyenne women and children were captured, one of whom was Turkey Leg's nephew.

By the time of the raid on the railroad, the government had decided upon yet another attempt to remove the Cheyennes and their allies from the area between the Platte and the Arkansas. A short time after the fight between the Cheyennes and the Pawnee Scouts, a commission rode hopefully westward, arriving the first week of October at end-of-tracks, which was the developing town of North Platte, Nebraska. There, Turkey Leg sent them a proposal:[6] If the white people would return his nephew and an Indian girl (later named Island Woman), he would give up the Campbell children. The exchange of captives took place at the railroad eating house in North Platte, and the Campbell family was reunited once again—a far happier outcome than that which befell the children captured in 1864.

So far, so good. The commission continued on to Medicine Lodge Creek in Kansas where it negotiated a treaty with the Cheyennes, Arapahoes, Kiowas, Apaches, and Comanches. this treaty reflected the latest government brainstorm, namely the concentration of all the warlike tribes of the southern plains on two great reservations. There the Indians could finally complete their metamorphosis from nomadic warriors to sedentary agriculturists and, not incidentally, they would be far removed from areas of white expansion between the Platte and the Arkansas.

The treaty held for about seven months, until a war party of Cheyennes rode to eastern Kansas to attack the Kaws over some past indiscretion. As a consequence, the arms and ammunition allotted to them by treaty for hunting purposes were withheld from their annuities. In retaliation for this perceived breach of the treaty, a large war part headed north to attack a favorite target—the Pawnee Reservation. On the way, some combination of arguments and incidents caused most of the disgruntled Cheyennes to turn aside and attack white settlers along the Saline and Solomon Rivers in northwestern Kansas, burning cabins and killing fifteen men. Maybe Black Kettle was still wholeheartedly for peace, but the majority of his people, their passions aroused by the events of 1864, felt little inclination to abide by the provisions of a treaty they barely understood anyhow. Fueled by the blandishments of large numbers of warlike Ogalalas, Brules, and Northern Cheyennes who had slipped south to join this latest phase of the war, the agitated Southern Cheyennes and Dog Soldiers unleashed a new reign of terror on the Kansas frontier, killing seventy-nine settlers.

The raids drew a quick response from the new commander of the Department of the Missouri, General Philip Henry Sheridan, who was even more aggressive than Hancock and every bit as untutored in the ways of the plains. Throughout 1868, Sheridan dispatched the Seventh and Tenth Cavalry Regiments, elements of the Fifth, the Nineteenth Kansas Volunteers, and a company of special frontier scouts to trouble spots between the Republican and Smoky Hill Rivers. Sheridan and his superior, General Sherman, were in agreement that the Indians could be whipped only by carrying on a total war effort during the coming winter.

While Sheridan had been sent to fight the hostiles, General William B. Hazen had been dispatched to Fort Cobb on the new Kiowa-Comanche Reservation to establish a haven for those southern bands that wished to keep out of the war. In mid November, Black Kettle and Little Robe took their people to Hazen to ask for asylum. Unfortunately, many of Black Kettle's young men had been involved in the depredations in western Kansas, and he frankly admitted to Hazen that, although he had tried his best to keep them off the warpath, he was utterly unable to control them. General Hazen was frank, too. Since it was impossible to keep the warmongers from slipping in and out of the friendly villages, it would not do for Hazen to offer sanctuary to some of the very Indians whom Sheridan was trying to punish. Since some of Black Kettle's men were guilty, he would have to make his peace with General Sheridan first.

For Black Kettle, Hazen's reply must have seemed like a recurring bad dream. Four years before, Governor Evans had declared a sanctuary for peaceable Cheyennes at Fort Lyon; yet, when Black Kettle had expressed his desire to lead his people there, he was told that he must first make peace with the white war chief. He had led his people into camp on Sand Creek to wait for an answer to his plea for peace.

Now it was 1868, and Black Kettle and Little Robe could do nothing but return to their bands camped along the Washita River and wait for the nightmare to play itself out. In the gray dawn of another bitterly cold November morning, a force of blue coated soldiers once again attacked the sleeping village. They were not hundred-days men under Colonel Chivington this time, but regulars of the Seventh Cavalry under Custer, who had followed the trail of a war party straight to the slumbering camp. Once again, sleepy Cheyennes bolted from their lodges to flee down the bed of another stream. Custer later claimed 103 Indians killed.[7] The Cheyennes claimed they lost about thirty-eight, including the inevitable women and children.

One might surmise that Black Kettle knew it would end this way. The attack came just two days short of the fourth anniversary date of Sand Creek, and the circumstances were nearly identical, except this time the camp was in Indian Territory instead of Colorado Territory; the camp contained white prisoners and ample evidence of raids on the Kansas frontier; and this time there would be no escape for Black Kettle. Both he and his wife, mounted on a single pony, were shot down as they attempted to cross the river. After Custer's troops departed, returning warriors found the body of the peace chief, face down in the icy water.[8] It was a bitter end for the man who was one of the most astute and visionary chiefs of the High Plains tribes. Grinnell wrote of him: "Black Kettle was a striking example of a consistently friendly Indian, who, because he was friendly and so because his whereabouts were usually known, was punished for the acts of people whom it was supposed he could control."[9]

The Battle of the Washita, the harsh winter, and Major Carr's defeat of Tall Bull's Dog Soldiers at Summit Springs in July 1869, all broke the fighting spirit of the Southern Cheyennes at last. But life on the reservation proved to be everything they had feared. There the Cheyennes found themselves continually plagued by white outlaws who stole their horses, while they were forbidden to retaliate. Other white trash plied them with poisonous whiskey in trade for buffalo robes until the problem of drunkenness within the tribe regained its former levels of the 1830s and 1840s. And, completely ignoring the Treaty of Medicine Lodge, white buffalo hunters streamed across the Arkansas to chase down the dwindling herds.

The provocations mounted up, and in 1874 the Southern Cheyennes and some allies struck back, attacking a group of illegal hunters at an old ruin known as Adobe Walls. The attack was not well coordinated, the element of surprise was lost, the hunters were naturally well armed, and the Indians broke off the action after several fruitless charges. Some of them rode north to take out their anger in a revenge raid on the Smoky Hill. There, ten years after their bloody attacks on the Overland route, they killed several members of the John German family and abducted four children, all of them girls.

But this hostage taking had gotten to be a bad business. General Sheridan soon had the High Plains swarming with troops, and as these columns crisscrossed the plains throughout the harsh winter months, the revolt was doomed. The hostile bands soon wearied of the relentless pursuit, and they worried about their treatment when, inevitably, they would be returned to the reservation. On November 8, 1874, a detail under Lieutenant Frank Baldwin found the two youngest German girls abandoned by the Cheyennes in Gray Beard's village. The two older sisters were surrendered at the agency on March 1, 1875. Aided by their testimony, the agent and military commanders began a roundup of those Cheyennes who had committed crimes during their season of raiding. Eventually, thirty-one braves and one squaw were shipped off to a federal prison at Fort Marion, Florida.

Roughly 220 of the hostile Cheyennes did not surrender at the agency, but broke away in an attempt to join their kinsmen in the north country. A detachment of the Sixth Cavalry caught them on Sappa Creek in northern Kansas and whipped them severely.

For the Southern Cheyennes, the days of war and hunting and horse stealing were in the past. The future held little but sickness, despair, and an unrelenting campaign to educate and Christianize them—to remake a warlike, nomadic people into a reincarnation of the docile, agricultural Cheyennes who had lived in the upper Mississippi Valley so many long years before.

With the hostile tribes occupied in the Powder River country, 1865 was a quiet year on the Pawnee Reservation. Troops returned to guard the agency again in 1866 as the old pattern of hit-and-run raiding resumed.

Eighteen sixty-seven proved to be a proud year for the Pawnees. The techniques of railroad construction had been refined until the Union Pacific tracks were probing the flat plains west of Grand Island City, and hostile Sioux and Cheyennes were fighting the construction gangs every mile of the way. At last, General Christopher C. Augur assigned Frank North to recruit four companies of Pawnee Scouts to protect the railroad workers, and once again the Pawnees rode forth to give battle to their ancient enemies. They even had the honor of escorting General Sherman from end-of-tracks to Fort Laramie. At home on the reservation, favorable weather blessed the tribe with bountiful crops. The years 1867 through the early seventies were good years on the Pawnee Reservation and, had they continued free of interference, the latter history of the Pawnee people might have been far different.

In 1869, the Quakers took over the agency and the superintendency in Omaha, determined to make the Pawnees live and work as Christians ought. There would be no more tribal wars, no more wandering all over the plains, and no more horse stealing. The children were enrolled in the agency school where the boys had their treasured scalplocks cut away and were forced to wear hats and work in the gardens as a part of their education. It is easy to understand the confusion that reined at the agency when Frank and Luther North returned with their Pawnee Scouts, waving scalps and trailing strings of captured ponies. Suddenly, war and horse stealing looked pretty respectable again, and the North brothers were heroes who never had trouble filling the ranks of their scout companies.

But by 1870, the buffalo were nearly gone. Even the Pawnees could see that, in a few short years, the hunt would be a thing of the past. That summer, even the chiefs and leading warriors went into the fields to work, as examples to their people. And, even though their crops were excellent, the Quaker agents came up with a new program: From henceforth, the tribe would farm on a commercial scale, raising only wheat, staking its future on a single cash crop. This would require more and different machinery, of course, and since the money was not to be had from Washington, the reservation lands south of the Loup River were sold off to raise money for the necessary seed and implements. The experiment was an abject failure, and a few of the more disgruntled Pawnees jumped the reservation to visit their cousins, the Wichitas, down in Indian Territory.

In August, 1873, nearly 400 Pawnees headed south to begin what was to be their last winter hunt. They found the buffalo very scarce in the country north of the Republican, and on two occasions, parties of white men warned them that a large body of Spotted Tail's Sioux was nearby. Angry and frustrated, the Pawnees refused to believe the warnings, thinking them a trick of the whites to keep them away from the few buffalo left on the divide.

In a shallow canyon leading south to the Republican, the Sioux caught the Pawnees. By the time a company of U. S. cavalry from Fort McPherson galloped to the rescue, at least sixty-nine Pawnees were dead, including thirty-nine women and ten children. The soldiers transported the wounded survivors to Plum Creek for medical care. Then all were put aboard Union Pacific cars and taken east to Silver Creek, the nearest station to the reservation. Of all the events which contributed to the subsequent misery of the Pawnee people, the affair at Massacre Canyon was certainly the most traumatic.

The malcontents who had been visiting the Wichitas now returned and began agitating for a removal to Indian Territory. Although the agent and the chiefs opposed such a move, the rabble rousers succeeded in stirring up strong factional unrest within the grieving tribe, and with a small contingent of followers, they departed once again for the south. The Bureau of Indian Affairs gave in to frustration, deciding that maybe removal of the reservation would be for the best. Besides, white settlers were coveting the reservation lands along the Loup.

In 1874, the agent declared that there would be no more buffalo hunts. The tribe would depend solely on its wheat crop and gardens for economic and physical survival. But 1874 was the first year of the great grasshopper plagues which swept across Nebraska, and the Pawnees lost all. Again came an invitation from the Wichitas to come south among friends, where the old wandering life still existed and the buffalo were still plenty. The Pawnee chiefs knew better, of course, but the superintendent came out from Omaha and put the question of removal to a crude plebiscite. The votes were tallied and the agent announced that the majority were in favor of the move. The chiefs and head men, tired and beaten, gave up the fight.

The new reservation which the government selected for the Pawnees was slightly larger than the Genoa reserve, and was located in territory where the Pawnees had lived back in the 1600s when they had still been a numerous and nomadic people. The first group moved to Indian Territory already in the fall of 1874. Head chief Peta-Neh-Sah-Doh (Man Chief) was fording the Loup River when he shot himself in the leg.[10] He was taken back to the village on Beaver Creek where he died a few days later of blood poisoning. Some of his people considered him fortunate, while it was also whispered that the fatal shot had come in retaliation for his strenuous opposition to the removal.

In the spring of 1875 there were only 500 Pawnees left at Genoa. They put in crops as usual, but they were too few, too dispirited, and too unprotected to enjoy their last months on the reservation. Hit-and-run raids by hostile Indians and white lowlifes resulted in the deaths of a woman and a boy, killed while working in the fields. These were the last attacks made on the Genoa reservation, for in November of that year, the remnant moved south to the new agency on Black Bear Creek (Pawnee, Oklahoma). There the tribe was plagued by fever and sickness, and the Osages stole all their horses and mules. When it became necessary to build a hospital, the government withheld the money from the tribe's annuities. In every respect, the tribe which had long been the friendliest toward the white man received a worse deal than did those tribes which remained hostile.

But the white man still needed the Pawnees, or at least enough of them to make up a company of scouts. When Frank North went to the new reservation in 1876 to recruit, he was mobbed by warriors and even little boys, all pleading for him to lead them against the hostile Sioux and Cheyennes. Once again the Pawnee Scouts went to war, fighting with Generals McKenzie and Crook against Dull Knife and the Northern Cheyennes.

In April, 1877, General Sheridan ordered the scouts mustered out for the last time. General Crook's final order to Frank North read: "I think it only just and appropriate to thank you for your excellent behavior during the time of your stay in the military service under my command, and to say that the soldier-like discipline and conduct of the Pawnee scouts is the most eloquent testimony that could be adduced to prove your fitness for the position you have held as their commanding officer."[11] Then the scouts rode away to their reserve, back down Cottonwood Canyon and across the Republican—the last organized Pawnees to leave Nebraska.

The scouts returned to a tribe that had become completely demoralized. Idleness, sickness, lack of clothing, poverty, and government handouts had taken a dreadful toll on the Pawnees' health and self respect. The school had ceased to function, and there remained only about 1,440 members of a tribe that once numbered many thousands. In 1889, the government opened Oklahoma Territory for settlement, and four years later, it resettled the Pawnees on selected farm sites, thus breaking up the reservation. Many of the Pawnees rented out their farms to whites, but they soon found that the rent monies were barely enough to keep them alive.

It was in 1822 that the Pawnee Chief Sharitarish had presented to President James Monroe some Pawnee artifacts to be placed into a museum. He had done this, said the chief, so that when the old way of life had passed, "and the sod (is) turned over our bones, if our children should visit this place, as we do now, they may see and recognize with pleasure the deposits of their fathers, and reflect on the times that are past."[12] Only some eighty years later, it appeared that the record of the Pawnee people might survive only in a museum; for in 1905, there were just 646 Pawnees left. Their school building had burned down the year before, and the federal government refused to rebuild it, on the theory that it would be better for the Pawnee children to attend the public schools in Pawnee, Oklahoma, anyway.

Happily, when the Roosevelt administration came to power in 1933, the government began to increase financial and humanitarian support of the long neglected tribe, and the lot of the people began to improve. By 1940, their numbers had risen to 1,017.[13]

In the second half of the Twentieth Century, the Pawnee tribe has found new life and renewed pride in its legacy as a warrior people. The first annual Pawnee Homecoming was held in July 1946 as a sort of Pawnee Veterans' Day to honor members of the tribe which have fought in all America's wars since 1864, and particularly those who had been killed in action in the world war just ended. The spirit of the Pawnee Scouts was very much present in the person of Chief Latagotskalahar, also known as Rush Roberts, who lived until March of 1959. He was the last of the men who had served under Frank and Luther North.[14]

On July 6, 1982, Pawnees and local ranchers gathered north of Trenton, Nebraska, for the First Massacre Canyon Celebration. The activities included a guided tour of the battlefield which has come to be the Pawnee equivalent of Arlington National Cemetery, the same field where the Sioux ended the Pawnees' last buffalo hunt in a welter of blood. The resurgent tribe, now recognized by the government as an Indian nation of 2,500 people, was gratified when, in 1983, Nebraska Governor Robert Kerry proclaimed that henceforth, August 5 would be celebrated in the state as Pawnee Day.[15]

Tribal activism and resurgent social consciousness on the part of the American people became evident when the Nebraska Legislature passed LB 340 in May 1989. A year earlier, the Pawnees had learned to their horror that the Nebraska State Historical Society Museum was holding the remains of about 1,000 Pawnee bodies which had been exhumed from their graves over a period of years by amateur and professional anthropologists. Rebuffed by the historical society, the Pawnees turned to the Legislature to force the return of those remains for reburial. Passed with broad popular support, LB 340 required all museums within the state to return Indian remains to requesting tribes. On September 10, 1990, the Pawnee tribe conducted reburial rites for more than 400 of its people in the city cemetery at Genoa, on the site of the old reservation village. Future burials were assured when, the following November, President George Bush signed into law the Native American Graves Protection and Repatriation Act.[16]

Chapter One notes

[1] The term comes from Remi Nadeau, *Fort Laramie and the Sioux.*

[2] Yost, *Boss Cowman*, 41.

[3] This capsule account of the 1867 raids is taken from information in the *Thayer County Museum Muse*, Fall-Winter, 1976.

[4] *History of Hall County*, 148.

[5] Information on the Campbell attack is taken from:
Creigh, *Tales from the Prairie.*
The Grand Island Daily Independent, July 2, 1932.
Grinnell, *Two Great Scouts.*
WPA, *Nebraska–A Guide.*

[6] Hyde (*Spotted Tail's Folk,* 139) claims that Spotted Tail ransomed three white women and three children from the Cheyennes and turned them over to the peace commission in North Platte.

[7] Grinnell, *The Fighting Cheyennes*, 300.

[8] Hoig, *The Battle of the Washita*, 130.

[9] Grinnell, *The Fighting Cheyennes*, 309.

[11] Echo-Hawk (*Battlefields and Burial Grounds*) spells the name Pitaresaru. Hyde (*The Pawnee Indians*) claimed it was Pitalesharo.

[11] Frank North, Papers and Correspondence.

[12] Buchanan, *Sketches of the History,* etc., 42.

[13] Hyde, *The Pawnee Indians*, 188.

[14] "Aboriginal Claims to Land Established . . .", *The Pawnee (Oklahoma) Chief*, August 20, 1959.

[15] An account of the celebration, written by a Pawnee woman, Mary Maytubby, is in the vertical file of the Nebraska State Historical Society archives.

[16] Echo-Hawk and Echo-Hawk, *Battlefields and Burial Grounds.*

Sources

Creigh, *Tales from the Prairie.*
Echo-Hawk and Echo-Hawk, *Battlefields and Burial Grounds.*
Frank North, Papers and Correspondence.
Grinnell, *The Fighting Cheyennes.*
–Two Great Scouts.
History of Hall County, Nebraska.
Hoig, *The Battle of the Washita.*
Hyde, *The Pawnee Indians.*
Lemmon, *Early Days on the Little Blue*
Nadeau, *Fort Laramie and the Sioux.*
The Pawnee (Oklahoma) Chief, August 20, 1959.
"Pawnee Indians," vertical file in NSHS archives.
Thayer County Museum Muse.
Utley, *Frontier Regulars.*
WPA, *Nebraska–A Guide.*
Yost, *Boss Cowman.*

Part IV
Chapter Two

"Well, what more could we do?"

A day or so after New Year, 1865, while Lucinda Eubank and Nancy Morton were enduring their icy captivity north of Fort Laramie, Colonel Samuel Summers was on his way west, accompanied by Captain Murphy, who was taking a detail of men to reinforce Captain Wilcox at Beauvais Ranch. After leaving the troopers with Wilcox, the two officers continued on to Julesburg. The colonel may have told Murphy the latest news from Cottonwood: Scouts had sighted a war party of fifty Cheyennes some 125 miles south of Cottonwood Springs, heading north toward the Platte Valley. They were not expected to cause any trouble, since Indians were loathe to fight in the winter time. But if they did, the boys of the Seventh Iowa might have the opportunity for a tidy victory.

It was ironic that, while Colonel Summers had seen no hostiles during the Curtis campaign last summer, a group of them were now headed in his direction. Neither Summers nor Murphy had any inkling of the massive red storm which was rolling up from the camps along Cherry Creek to gather in the bluffs south of the Platte Valley.

When the two officers reached Julesburg, they found Jack Morrow there. During the previous months, the Indians had stampeded countless head of livestock, and there were loose cattle wandering all over the valley. Morrow was out gathering up strays for his herd. Of course, it didn't matter whose strays they were.

In the early morning hours of Saturday, January 7, a few young braves slipped away from the main party to attack the westbound stagecoach four miles east of Julesburg Station. Other than putting a few bullet holes in the coach, they did little harm, and the driver continued on the run to Bueler's Ranch a mile east of the station, where he laid over for a few minutes.[1] Then, with no Indians in sight, the coach continued to Julesburg. Sometime after five o'clock in the morning, it stopped at Camp Rankin, a mile west of the station, to report the attack.

Captain O'Brien mounted thirty-seven men of Company F—all he felt he could spare from the post—and shortly after dawn, the troopers went jogging eastward to chase down the marauding Indians. The column paused for a time at Julesburg, where they were joined by a number of ranchmen, including Jack Morrow and a telegrapher from the station. Then, led by Colonel Summers, Captain Murphy, Captain O'Brien, and Lieutenant Brewer, the reinforced company continued eastward down the trail. Seldom have so few been commanded by so many.

The troops had barely left Julesburg when the sounds of war cries and gunfire came floating across the frosty air. A civilian rider came pounding up to inform the officers that Keith and Cook's mule train was under attack close to Bueler's Ranch.[2] This would be no Plum Creek affair. The soldiers were practically on top of the action. Colonel Summers informed O'Brien that he was now officially taking command.

At the approach of the troopers, the Indians broke off the attack and drifted southward toward the rolling bluffs. There appeared to be about forty of them, so the colonel divided his force into three platoons. Lieutenant Brewer and ten men formed the left wing, while Murphy and another ten men formed the right wing. Summers, O'Brien, and the rest made up the center, and so the pursuit began.

The Indians were playing the old decoy game now, but their weakened ponies were not up to speed. The troopers overtook and killed seven of the warriors, and the charge broke apart as the men of the center platoon stopped to scalp the bodies and strip them of trophies. With the three sections now widely separated from each other, the disjointed pursuit continued southward out of the valley, into the frozen and desolate moonscape of the bluffs, straight into the center of the ambush.

Warriors boiled out of canyons and arroyos and over the crowns of the bluffs. Murphy found his platoon nearly surrounded before he could even get his men turned around. It was a second Grattan affair in the making.

Somehow the troopers got reorganized and began the flying six-mile retreat to Bueler's Ranch. O'Brien managed to form Lieutenant Brewer and his men into a rear guard to protect those troopers whose horses had been killed and were riding double. There seemed to be well over a thousand Indians in the chase now, and Jack Morrow said later that even he had never seen so many Indians in one place. Warriors continued to pour from the gentle bluffs, while the fleeing whites could see behind them, on the crowns of the hills, groups of several hundred more who simply watched the mad chase in the valley below.

None of the men panicked. They were all seasoned frontiersmen and they knew better. Colonel Summers must have known, too, that his chances for a tidy victory had gone up in smoke. It would be blind luck now if any of his force even survived. He galloped close to Captain O'Brien and ordered him to take some of the men and ride to Camp Rankin for the artillery.

The desperate retreat continued all the way to Bueler's Ranch, where the troopers returned just in time to rescue three drovers whom the Cheyennes had separated from the mule train. As the survivors gained the ranch buildings, Colonel Summers turned about and shot one of the boldest warriors dead off his horse. Then the Indians broke off the chase and began riding for the stage and telegraph station at Julesburg. There were so many of them in the valley now that they completely filled the entire area between Bueler's Ranch and Camp Rankin.

Captain O'Brien's men reached Julesburg, where they paused just long enough to pack the telegraph instruments, before cutting their way through the milling warriors the last mile to the post. Miraculously, they arrived at Camp Rankin without losing another man. Hurriedly they rolled out the howitzers and dropped some explosive shells into Julesburg. After a few rounds, O'Brien pulled his artillery down the trail and began firing canister into the mob. But the Indians were finished with Julesburg for the time being, and they began drifting slowly back toward the bluffs. Captain O'Brien continued on to Bueler's Ranch, where Summers, Murphy, and Brewer were quite glad to see him. The short winter day was already coming to a close as the survivors trudged exhausted into Camp Rankin with scalps firmly in place, Colonel Summers carrying his trophies of war taken from the brave he had dispatched.

The colonel, indeed all the officers, had displayed great coolness and bravery during the desperate six-hour fight, as had Jack Morrow and the men of Company F. But the battle had been a fiasco from the start. Under a divided authority, with no reconnaissance, a tiny command had ventured too far from its defensive works, had lost discipline and become disorganized. Company F had paid a terrible price as a result, losing fifteen men killed and one severely wounded. Five of the dead were from Lieutenant Brewer's rear guard platoon. Five civilians had also been killed along the trail, the mule train wrecked, and the stage and telegraph offices trashed. The disaster served notice that the payback for Sand Creek had begun in earnest.

News of the fight reached Omaha on Sunday evening, January 8. Although O'Brien's report didn't exactly read like a defeat, the evidences of mismanagement were plain to those who could read between the lines, and the loss of twenty men in one action sent shivers up and down the Platte Valley. General Mitchell was so disturbed that he boarded a westbound stage that same evening to investigate the disaster in person. It was just one week later that the general left Cottonwood with 640 men, embarking on what was to be his last and most disappointing Indian campaign. Colonel Summers was not along.

The order came down by telegraph: The colonel was to turn over command of Post Cottonwood to Captain Kuhl and report to Omaha to be mustered out. There, on the last day of January 1865, Samuel Summers became a civilian again.[3]

He took his Indian trophies back to Ottumwa, Iowa, the town he had adopted for his home back in 1846. His first wife was buried there, and his second wife, Marion, was waiting for her husband to come home from the war.

Though he had never felt a great desire for elective office, Summers allowed himself to be nominated for state senator in the summer of 1865. The campaign against his opponent, a former law student and partner, turned bitter, both candidates saying things which they would later regret. After his loss in the election, Summers returned to his law practice and began investing heavily in real estate around Ottumwa. Though he had never been a warm personality or a good mixer, his experiences seemed to have mellowed him, and a growing circle of friends came to appreciate him as a refined, polite gentleman with a good stock of stories and a lively sense of humor. His energetic devotion to his work and a keen business acumen provided comfortably for his wife and four children—two sons and two daughters.

He celebrated his seventieth birthday on March 8, 1890. Little more than a month later, as he was driving downtown in a light carriage, an electric streetcar approached with its usual clatter. The colonel's horse became frightened and backed away from the advancing metal monster. As it did so, it pushed the carriage backward across the rails and into the path of the car. In the resulting collision, Summers was thrown to the ground, slamming his head on the pavement. Passers by were at his side at once, and the unconscious man was carried into a nearby home where a doctor soon arrived. But the bleeding from his ears told the story: The back of his skull had been badly fractured and the brain had hemorrhaged. By 4:45 p.m. on April 16, 1890, Samuel Summers was dead.

The Indian War of 1864 bore down cruelly on General Robert Mitchell. From the moment he had replaced General McKean as commander of the District of Nebraska, he was almost constantly in the saddle, jogging up and down the trails between Omaha, Julesburg, and Laramie. He had been forced to defend a road which really could not be defended against a foe neither he nor anyone else had been trained to fight, and he had been expected to do miracles without the necessary manpower, horsepower, or equipment.

Following the Julesburg debacle of January 7, Mitchell mounted his last Indian campaign. He led it himself, since the severe climate, both political and meteorological, made it necessary for Curtis to remain in Leavenworth. To assemble a maximum force, the general denuded the Platte line of soldiers, leaving Camp Rankin in charge of invalids and protesting civilians.

From January 15 through January 26, Mitchell's strike force of 640 cavalrymen, six fieldpieces, and 100 wagons rumbled around in Nebraska and northwestern Kansas, finding nothing of the hostile Indians except their abandoned campsites. The return to Cottonwood was made into the teeth of a whistling wind, showers of snow pellets, and temperatures that dipped to twenty-three degrees below zero. Every member of the expedition suffered frostbite. Fifty men were so disabled as to require their discharge. One hundred horses were ruined, six wagons had to be junked, and General Mitchell froze his ears badly. Yet, for all this winter martyrdom, not a single hostile Indian was removed from the High Plains.

"Well, what more could we do? What more could we do?" the general asked his aide de camp, Lieutenant Ware, over and over again. Ware had never seen anyone quite so despondent, and he was deeply grieved for his gallant superior.

Four days after the frozen column staggered into Cottonwood, Mitchell received a nasty rebuke from General Curtis for leaving Julesburg undefended. Although Mitchell had already made his decision on the return march from Kansas, this wire must have been the last straw. He fired a message back to Leavenworth: The army could either arrange for his transfer to a southern command or accept his resignation.

On March 28, 1865, General Mitchell was relieved of his duties in Nebraska Territory and sent south—all the way to Leavenworth, where he assumed command of the District of North Kansas. There he served out the remaining weeks of the Civil War, after which President Johnson appointed him Governor of New Mexico Territory.

Ware describes Mitchell as a strict, stern, even a severe man. Those qualities did not endear him to his subordinates in the government of New Mexico, and they were soon clamoring for his removal. Mitchell stayed with the job until 1869, when he resigned and returned to Kansas. Even though his experience in politics had been singularly distasteful, he agreed to be nominated for a congressional seat by a coalition of Democrats and liberal Republicans. The election of 1872 went badly for him, and shortly after his defeat, Robert Mitchell moved to Washington, D. C. Following his death on January 26, 1882, he was buried in Arlington National Cemetery.

On the day after Christmas, 1866, a small group of men picked their way carefully down the bank of the Missouri River at Omaha. Leading the party was United States Railroad Commissioner Samuel Ryan Curtis. Only thirty months before, Curtis had landed on this same riverbank as commander of the Department of Kansas, on his way west to hunt down hostile Indians who had killed at least forty-eight citizens in three days.

That August had been a time of severe physical and emotional stress for the general. For two years he had been contending with the caustic political situation in Missouri and Kansas, and with the effrontery of Governor Evans and Colonel Chivington in Colorado. He had been worn out from his 500-mile campaign to clear the Cheyennes away from the Santa Fe Trail, and he had been grieving for his murdered son, Henry. Those had indeed been dark days.

But Samuel Curtis had known his triumphs, too. Had not General Dodge ascribed to him full credit for the splendid victory which shattered Van Dorn's army at Pea Ridge?[4] Moreover, he had been in command of the forces which had defeated Sterling Price at Westport, pushing the remnants of the Confederate army across the Arkansas and virtually ending the reign of guerrilla terror in western Missouri. He had served creditably in Milwaukee until the Department of the Northwest was dissolved in July 1865. His record in Congress as a powerful supporter of the transcontinental railroad, as well as his solid engineering background, made him a natural choice for the commission charged with inspecting the construction of the railroad. In recent days, Curtis and his fellow commissioners had inspected the last thirty-five miles of the road, after which they returned to Omaha for Christmas. After signing their report earlier that morning, the men set out to cross the frozen Missouri on foot.

During the rocky walk across the river ice, Curtis engaged in jovial conversation with Colonel Hunt, a member of his former military staff, and with Colonel H. C. Nutt, a close Iowa friend. A carriage was waiting on the Iowa side of the river, and the men climbed in for the ride into Council Bluffs. As the driver urged his team up the sloping riverbank, someone addressed a question to General Curtis. There was no reply.

Colonel Nutt turned to see Curtis slumped back in his seat in an apparent faint. The driver whipped the team into a run and the carriage raced the three miles to Colonel Nutt's house on Broadway. There, Curtis was lifted from the vehicle and taken inside to a bed. Doctors arrived quickly and made heroic attempts to revive him. But the old soldier had suffered a massive stroke, and the physicians were powerless. By ten o'clock that morning, the stout old heart which had chased Sioux, Cheyennes, and Arapahoes all over the Kansas and Nebraska plains was stilled.

News of his death shocked Omaha and Council Bluffs. On December 27, a large funeral service was held in Council Bluffs, after which the body was placed aboard a Chicago and North Western train for the trip to Chicago, and thence home to Keokuk, Iowa, where the family awaited his return.[5]

As the former general was laid to rest, Iowans mourned his passing and celebrated the memory of his service to the nation so recently torn asunder. And, if his efforts on the High Plains had been frustrated and impotent, there would soon be other commanders, some of them famous war heroes—Crook, Sheridan, Forsythe, Hancock, Custer—who would learn to their sorrow the very same lessons which the wild tribes had taught to General Curtis. In fact, they would learn those lessons at far greater cost.

It was shortly after the murder of his eldest son that the harassed, disillusioned commander confided to a close friend: "I feel there is nothing in the world worth the toil, care, and fighting which we have to pass through; still I will go on, trying to do my duty, hoping ultimately to reach a place where 'the wicked cease from troubling and the weary are at rest'. . ."[6] At the end of 1866, the war was over; the transcontinental railroad was well on its way to becoming a reality; and a weary Samuel Curtis was finally at rest.

From his birthplace in Montreal, through his medical education in New York and early work around Lake Superior, to a medical practice in Nebraska Territory, the career of Colonel Robert Livingston seemed destined for success. He had begun the Civil War as a captain of volunteers and was mustered out of the service in July, 1865 as a brevet brigadier general. Along the way, he had ably commanded the First Nebraska regiment in engagements along the Tennessee River and in northern Mississippi, and had for a time been in command of the District of St. Louis. Quite by happenstance, the Cheyennes and their allies attacked the trail as Livingston and his veterans of the First Nebraska were home on furlough. As a result, the veteran portion of the regiment served out its enlistment fighting Indians rather than Confederates.

Following his separation from the army, Dr. Livingston returned to practice medicine in Plattsmouth, Nebraska, becoming one of the town's leading citizens. His distinguished public career continued in 1868 with his appointment as Surveyor General for Iowa and Nebraska. He was instrumental in the construction of the Burlington and Missouri Railroad and in the location of its repair shops in Plattsmouth. In 1870, the railroad appointed Dr. Livingston Chief Surgeon, a position he held for the remainder of his life.

Dr. Livingston also served as lecturer and president of the faculty of Omaha Medical College, and was a founder of the Nebraska State Medical Society, which he served as president and corresponding secretary. He served the Masonic Order as Master of the Plattsmouth Lodge and Grand High Priest of the Royal Arch Masons of Nebraska. Somehow in the midst of all these duties, he even found time to serve on the state Board of Fish Commissioners.

All in all, Robert Ramsey Livingston was a gifted leader of men who put his life and his talents to good use. When he died on September 28, 1888, the community of Plattsmouth and the State of Nebraska lost a dedicated public servant, scholar, and humanitarian–that rare individual who is successful both in war and in peace.

For John Evans, the fallout from Sand Creek proved no more than a temporary embarrassment. The Joint Committee on the Conduct of the War criticized him severely for the "prevarication and shuffling" displayed in his testimony before them, but beyond that, no sanctions were brought against him.

Elected to Congress, Evans resigned the governorship of Colorado Territory in early 1865. But the vote for statehood failed, leaving him a senator without a constituency. He never occupied a seat in the United States Senate.

But John Evans was not one to sit and lick his wounds. He turned his boundless energies to his beloved Methodist Church, engaging in philanthropic support of many new and struggling congregations throughout Colorado Territory. In the late 1860s, he founded Colorado Seminary, which later became the University of Denver.

When it became disappointingly clear that the route of the Union Pacific Railroad would pass far to the north of Denver, Evans led the movement to organize the Denver Pacific Railroad and Telegraph Company, which in 1870 connected that city with the Union Pacific tracks at Cheyenne. He then expanded his efforts to link Denver with the country to the south and west by incorporating the South Park Railroad and the Denver and New Orleans Railroad. Reprising his earlier activities in Illinois, the Governor (as he was always referred to) made heavy investments in buildings and land in downtown Denver. In 1895, the state Legislature honored his many contributions to Colorado by naming the lofty mountain peak west of Denver, Mount Evans.

When John Evans died on July 3, 1897, the people of the Queen City and of the entire state honored the memory of the dynamic politician-philanthropist with a ceremony which virtually amounted to a state funeral.

Perhaps, with diligent effort, modern psychology might construct an explanation for John Milton Chivington. Undeniably he was an individual possessing great native talent and a coarse charisma, yet his quest for respectability was continually subverted by his personal crudeness and pathology of character. In the chaotic milieu of the Civil War frontier, the man of God who labored for the advancement of his church and faith became the sadistic militarist who longed "to be wading in gore."[7] The man who could well have become a dynamic builder of the Rocky Mountain region became instead the awful antihero of Sand Creek, living out the balance of his life in a morally shabby and pointless existence.

The early years of John Chivington's life were hard. The boy was only five years old when his father died, leaving the widow alone to raise the six children.[8] As a young man, Chivington was too impoverished to attend the regular seminary, so he studied independently for the ministry of the Methodist Episcopal Church, beginning his preaching career in Illinois in 1848. By that time, the civil war within the church had been raging for three years, the proslavery southern section having seceded from the northern districts already in 1845. Nowhere was the battle among the brethren more bitter or more physical than in the Kansas-Missouri border region. In 1852, Chivington was assigned to the strife-torn Wyandotte Indian Mission, located in the heart of present Kansas City, Kansas. During the four years in which he labored to restore the authority of the northern church among the Wyandottes, Chivington became such a vociferous and uncompromising foe of slavery that colleagues urged him to flee for fear of his life.

In 1856 he brought his wife and three children to a new assignment in Omaha. In addition to organizing the Methodist Episcopal churches within the district, Reverend Chivington also served the Fourth Territorial Legislature as Chaplain of the House.

It was in Omaha that his personal instability became more publicly manifest. For undisclosed reasons, he was not given the usual vote of thanks at the conclusion of the legislative session. His service to his church was likewise troubled. According to the Reverend James Haynes, "Mr. Chivington was not as steady in his demeanor as becomes a man called of God to the work of the ministry, giving his ministerial friends regret and even trouble in their efforts to sustain his reputation. His suavity and ambition secured for him a great influence over men, both strangers and friends, and if his life had with constancy been that of an exemplary man, his usefulness might have been unlimited."[9]

Despite his unsteady demeanor, he was appointed presiding elder for the Nebraska City District in 1859, joining his brother, Isaac, who also became a preacher in the town.[10] In April 1860, Chivington took his wife and two daughters to a new assignment in the Rocky Mountain District. Upon the outbreak of the Civil War, he spurned the offer of a chaplain's position with the First Colorado Volunteers, insisting instead on a major's commission. Thus began the brief military career which was to flower in the Glorieta Pass campaign and climax at Sand Creek.

Following his separation from the volunteer army, the former colonel entered into a partnership with the Reverend O.A. Willard, a Denver friend. Willard borrowed $10,000 from bankers in Omaha to set up a freighting business, purchasing 100 wagons and teams from the Atchison firm of Stebbins and Porter. Left to manage the nuts and bolts of the enterprise, Chivington blatantly ignored the provisions of his contracts, eventually involving Wells, Fargo and his own son-in-law, Thomas Pollock, in an elaborate scheme to defraud Willard and the Atchison firm. Willard and Pollock lost heavily in the outcome.[11]

As these machinations were being untangled, Chivington, unwilling to return to Atchison, instead took a mule train on to Fort Laramie where he laid over for the winter. There he abused the hospitality of the U.S. Army by writing to Denver and Omaha newspapers false accusations of improper relations between officers and Indian women. Finally, the post commander, General Innis Palmer, ordered him off the military reservation.

In the meantime, the first of a series of tragedies had struck the Chivington family. In June 1866, Thomas Chivington drowned in the North Platte River. Casting a covetous eye on his son's modest estate, and no longer welcome at Laramie, the elder Chivington returned to Nebraska City, his freighting misadventures apparently behind him. In the summer of 1867, Martha Chivington died suddenly while attending a camp meeting in Cass County. Only two weeks later, Thomas Chivington's daughter, Lulu, fell from the deck of the steamboat *Gallatin* and drowned in the Missouri River.[12]

These tragedies apparently did not awaken the former colonel's sympathies. Claiming that he had been a partner in his son's successful freighting operation, he demanded a large share of the estate. However, lacking legal proof of such a relationship, it was necessary to devise some scheme whereby he might collect. Soon he began paying other than fatherly attentions to his son's widow, the former Sarah Lull, who had remained living in her husband's brick house in Nebraska City.

In May 1868, Chivington took Sarah to Chicago to attend the Republican Convention. On May 18, the citizens of Nebraska City learned that their former minister and colonel had married his daughter-in-law. The union was generally considered to be highly immoral. Sarah's parents published a personal card in the *Nebraska City News* (June 6, 1868) calling the marriage a "criminal act" and "so vile an outrage," and hinted that, if they had been forewarned, they would have killed Chivington to prevent it.

The marriage estranged Sarah from her parents. Even on her deathbed, Almira Lull refused to acknowledge her own daughter. It also turned public sentiment against Chivington, and even his staunch friend and supporter, William Byers, editorialized in his *Daily Rocky Mountain News* (June 10, 1868): "What he (Chivington) will do next to outrage the moral sense and feeling of his day and generation remains to be seen; but be sure it will be something, if there is anything left for him to do."

Chivington probably cared nothing about this adverse reaction, and in June, Sarah accompanied him to Omaha where he was supposedly offered a position on the editorial staff of the *Omaha Republican*.[13] Nothing materialized, and the couple returned to Nebraska City where, in March, 1869, the Chivington house mysteriously caught fire in the predawn hours of the morning. Just as mysteriously, Chivington, who had been away at the time, arrived to put out the flames, limiting the interior damage to $200.[14]

The final settlement of Thomas Chivington's estate netted his father a paltry sum, so he had himself appointed special administrator. In the summer of 1870, Chivington and Sarah went to Washington, D.C. to prosecute a depredation claim in behalf of Thomas' estate against the Indians. Within a short time, he was hailed into police court on charges of verbally abusing and intimidating a local woman.

The depredation claim also turned out to be vintage Chivington. He managed to produce the required legal documents by forging the signature of a Nebraska senator and notarizing the forgery with a stolen seal. Facing a federal indictment for fraud, he abandoned Sarah and fled to Canada, leaving his penniless wife to work out a settlement for their unpaid hotel bill. Somehow Sarah made her way back to Nebraska City where, in October, 1871, she obtained a divorce.[15]

Chivington's exact whereabouts remain unknown until 1873, when he returned to his old home in Warren County, Ohio, on the occasion of his mother's death. According to neighbors, he absconded with the $80 she had set aside to pay for her burial, leaving his departed mother to be interred by the county in the potter's field.

Continuing on to Cincinnati, Chivington met Isabella Arnsen, a widow who owned a great deal of real estate. Within a year they were married. It was not long until the groom stole a promissory note made out to his wife, forged her endorsement, and cashed it. Belle accused Chivington of the theft and forgery, inciting him to a furious tirade during which he struck her savagely across the face, knocking her to the floor. She swore out a complaint, but later allowed the matter to drop, and the mismatched couple remained together.

For a time, the Chivingtons lived in Warren County, later moving across the line to neighboring Clinton County where the former colonel reportedly edited the *Blanchester Press* and became active once again in the Grand Army of the Republic, the Masonic Lodge, and the Odd Fellows.[16] In 1883, the county central committee of the Republican Party offered to support him for a seat in the Ohio legislature. Under the heat of a campaign, the pot of Sand Creek came once more to a boil, and the editor of his hometown *Lebanon Patriot* wrote such hostile editorials that the committee asked their embattled candidate to withdraw from the race.

Several months later, Chivington received an invitation to address the first annual meeting of the Pioneer Society of Colorado. It seemed to offer a welcome opportunity to appear before a friendly audience in the city where he had celebrated the greatest triumphs of his life, and the unsuccessful politician gladly accepted.

On September 13, 1883, John Chivington received a hero's welcome at Denver's Jewell Park. In a long, rambling speech, perfected over the years, he once again presented his case against those Indians whom he had made "peaceable for almost nineteen years." There was also some revisionist history about the causes of the Indian War of 1864, and the number of Colorado victims was pegged at 208. Then, basking in the approbation and good will of the assembly, the "fighting parson" wound up his peroration with the emphatic statement, "I stand by Sand Creek."

The enthusiastic reception accorded him convinced John Chivington that his true home was in Colorado. After returning to Ohio to sell off their property, he and Belle moved to Denver where he continued his association with the Methodist Episcopal Church, the Masons, and the GAR. Soon he was elected undersheriff of Arapaho County.

One might expect that the hospitality and trust of his Colorado neighbors would have awakened in Chivington a sense of gratitude and moral obligation. Apparently it did not. In 1887, he was brought to trial on perjury charges stemming from his filing of false reports and expense accounts. He was acquitted on a technicality, having been improperly sworn when he had submitted the reports. Later in the year he improved his reputation somewhat when he captured a local badman named Newt Vorse by threatening to blow the man's hideout to atoms with a stick of dynamite.

In 1891, Chivington was elected coroner of Arapaho County, and the following year he was accused of stealing $800 from the pockets of a dead man. Again he escaped indictment by turning over to the court all his cash on hand. Not long after this latest brush with the law he was supposed to represent, Chivington's house again caught fire. The feeling among citizens of Denver was that he had torched his own residence to collect the insurance money.

In 1892, Chivington retired from public service to purchase a dealership in hay, grain, wood, and coal. He also found time to file suit against land developers in Colorado Springs over property he allegedly owned, and he filed a new (and totally fraudulent) claim for Indian depredations upon his freight train in 1867.

On balance, it is difficult to appraise the life of John Chivington in other than negative terms. Certainly he did much to save Colorado and New Mexico for the Union cause in 1861, and the three children he fathered were generally acknowledged to be wonderful people. But beyond that, he managed to do a great deal of harm in his seventy-three years, and many who came within his orbit suffered unduly—none more than the Cheyenne and Arapaho people. Within weeks of his "victory" at Sand Creek he had been widely labeled as a murderer. Even Governor Evans and Major Anthony took pains to distance themselves from their former military commander. Major

Wynkoop referred to him as an "inhuman monster," while to General Palmer, he was one of the "greatest scoundrels in this or any other country." The sorry catalogue of his life included forgery, lying, deceit, thievery, wife battering, bullying, and probably arson and insurance fraud, and as early as 1867, the editor of the *Omaha Daily Herald* denounced him as a "rotten, clerical hypocrite."[17]

But for all this, it remains impossible for any mortal to know what was truly in his heart during the summer months of 1894 as the cancer slowly devoured his gigantic frame. Though he reaffirmed his faith in Christ before his friend, Reverend Isaac Beardsley, it is not recorded that he ever repented of his many transgressions.

After lying in a semi-conscious state for several weeks, John Milton Chivington died on October 4, 1894. The funeral, held at Trinity Methodist Church, was a vast gathering of members from the Masonic Grand Lodge of Colorado, the Grand Army of the Republic, and the Colorado Pioneers Association.[18] Here and there throughout the congregation could be seen a few old men sporting yellow ribbons–survivors of the First Colorado Cavalry, come to pay their respects to the man who had been their comrade and commander in a long ago time when his star of valor had shown so brightly at Pigeon's Ranch–when the name of Sand Creek meant no more than a trickle of water meandering across the High Plains.

Chapter Two notes

1 The name of the ranch appears variously as Bueler (Captain Murphy), Buell (Jack Morrow), Bulen (C. B. Hadley), and Bullin (Captain O'Brien). Bueler is used here for no other reason than that a choice was necessary.

2 *The Daily Rocky Mountain News*, January 10, 1865. This account of the first battle at Julesburg is written from Captain O'Brien's official report (*Omaha Republican*, January 13, 1865) as well as from Jack Morrow's dispatch, and is completely at odds with George Bent's version of the battle.

3 Any criticism of Colonel Summers was kept very quiet by the army; but a former freighter, Mr. T. K. Tyson, delivered a wry comment on the colonel's military career. In an address to the Nebraska State Historical Society, Tyson referred to the war of 1864 as the "Cheyenne War, in which Colonel S. distinguished or extinguished himself . . ." (*Proceedings and Collections,* NSHS, Series 2, Vol. 5 [1902]).

4 The eminent historian, Henry Steele Commager, goes so far as to state that "Curtis was one of the ablest—and most neglected—officers in the Union Army." (*The Blue and the Gray*, Vol. 1, 385)

[5] Samuel Curtis was a loving and devoted father who found his enforced absences from his family a great hardship. In addition to his wife, Belinda, the family included four children: Henry Z., was about forty-three years old when he was murdered by bushwhackers in 1863; Samuel S., a year younger than Henry, was a major in the Second Colorado Cavalry, and was detailed to the departmental staff at Fort Leavenworth; Sadie, twenty-two years old in 1864, had lived with her father in Washington during his congressional service; and Caddie, eleven years old, the beloved baby of the family.

[6] Curtis to General W. K. Strong, October 31, 1863. (*Annals of Iowa*, Series 3, Vol. 27 #4, April, 1946, 318)

[7] Chivington made this statement to James Combs and others at Spring Bottom Stage Station on November 25, 1864, four days before the Sand Creek Massacre. (U.S. Congress, "Sand Creek Massacre," 117.)

[8] The father, Isaac Chivington Sr., was a soldier with General William Henry Harrison at the Battle of the Thames in which the Shawnee Prophet, Tecumseh, was killed. (Dale, *Otoe County Pioneers*, 490.)

[9] Haynes, *History of the Methodist Episcopal Church*, 440.

[10] Isaac Chivington was removed from the ministry of the Methodist Episcopal Church at the Annual Conference of 1861. Among other things, he was charged with "sedition" and the misappropriation of church funds. Another brother, Lewis Chivington, joined the Confederate Army and was killed early in the war at the Battle of Wilson's Creek. (Dale, *Otoe County Pioneers*, 490.)

[11] For the accounts of this and other odious incidents in Chivington's postwar career, I have relied upon Roberts, *Sand Creek: Tragedy and Symbol*, 658-665.

[12] Dale, op. cit., 494.

[13] *Nebraska City News*, June 20, 1868.

[14] *Nebraska City News*, March 6, 1869.

[15] Sarah A. Chivington vs. John M. Chivington, Records of the District Court, Otoe County, Nebraska. Sarah remained in Nebraska City for the rest of her life, working as a seamstress and dressmaker. Her remaining child, Walter, had been named Thomas after the death of his father. In 1889, Thomas and his mother purchased several lots in the town. Five years later, he gave his mother a quitclaim deed for his share, and she sold the property in 1895. Sarah eventually developed cancer, and one arm was amputated to slow the spread of the disease. When the cancer finally claimed her life in August, 1912, she had evidently lost contact with her son, who by that time was President of the American Baseball Association. Obituaries did not mention her unfortunate second marriage. (*Nebraska City News*, August 7, 1912.)

[16] Craig, *The Fighting Parson*, 233.

[17] Anthony: *Daily Rocky Mountain News*, February 1, 1865.
Evans: Roberts, *Sand Creek*, 900, note #12.
Wynkoop: U.S. Congress, "Chivington Massacre," 63.
Palmer: Roberts, *Sand Creek*, 905, note #58.
Omaha Daily Herald, April 5, 1867.

[18] *Square and Compass*, Vol. 3, no. 8, October, 1894, 214-217;
Rocky Mountain News, October 8, 1894.

Sources for Colonel Summers

Denver Daily Rocky Mountain News, January 7, 9, 10, 1865.
Hadley, "The Plains War in 1865."
History of Wapello County, Iowa
O.R. Vol. 48, Part 1.

Omaha Weekly Republican, January 13, 1865.
Ottumwa (Iowa) Democrat, April 16, 1890.
Post Returns, Fort Cottonwood, N.T., January, 1865.
Report of the Adjutant General of Iowa, 1866.
Roster and Record of Iowa Soldiers.
Stiles, *Recollections.*
Stuart, *Iowa Colonels and Regiments.*
"Testimony as to the Claim of Ben Holladay."
Ware, *The Indian War of 1864.*

Sources for General Mitchell

Dictionary of American Biography.
Kansas Historical Collections XVI (1923-1925).
Ware, *The Indian War of 1864.*

Sources for General Curtis

Annals of Iowa, Ser. 3, Vol. 27, no. 4 (April, 1946).
Britton, *The Union Indian Brigade.*
Dictionary of American Biography.
"The Irrepressible Conflict."
"Military History of Iowa."
National Cyclopedia of American Biography.
Omaha Weekly Herald, December 28, 1866.
Stiles, *Recollections.*
Stuart, *Iowa Colonels and Regiments.*

Sources for Colonel Livingston

Andreas, *History of Nebraska.*
Morton-Watkins, *Illustrated History of Nebraska.*

Sources for Governor Evans

Dictionary of American Biography.
"Massacre of Cheyenne Indians."
"The Chivington Massacre."

Sources for Colonel Chivington

Craig, *The Fighting Parson.*
Dale, *Otoe County Pioneers*, Vols. 2 & 6.
Denver City Directory, 1888, 1892.
Denver Republican, September 15, 1887; October 7, 1894.
Denver Rocky Mountain News, February 4, 1865; June 10, 1868; October 5, 8, 1894.
Denver Times, September 13, 1887.
Haynes, *History of the Methodist Episcopal Church.*
Historical and Descriptive Review of Denver.
Land Records, County Recorder, Otoe County, Nebraska.
Morton-Watkins, *Illustrated History of Nebraska.*
Nebraska City Directory, 1881, 1891.
Nebraska City News, May 18, June 6, 20, 1868; March 6, 1869; August 7, 1912.
Roberts, *Sand Creek: Tragedy and Symbol.*
Square and Compass, October, 1894.
U.S. Congress, "Chivington Massacre."
— "Massacre of Cheyenne Indians."

Part IV
Chapter Three

"Her mind is somewhat impared"

Willie Mudge never forgot the long drive from Fort Kearny to Beatrice. His family and other refugees from the defense of Pawnee Ranch took the Nebraska City Road east to the crossing of the Big Blue, where they turned south to their former homes. Willie had the task of driving Patrick Burke's empty wagon (the corn having been sold to the quartermaster at the fort), and to keep him company, Sarah Bainter, who was several years younger, rode beside him on the seat. The small couple on their wagon must have provoked smiles from their elders, and Willie recalled later that Sadie (as she was called) was good company and chattered all the way to Beatrice.[1]

Many of the refugees continued east to Nebraska City, Brownville, or Peru. Some of those who turned south stopped off at the Big Blue settlements. At last, the half dozen remaining wagons drove down through Indian Creek and into the little town of Beatrice. There the Mudge family was warmly welcomed by Joe and Sallie Milligan, who had feared them all dead. While the families returned to their old home place about eight miles southeast of the town, Mudge and Milligan enlisted in Captain White's Militia Company C which was being formed for duty along the Little Blue. When the company was ordered to join General Mitchell's winter scout to the Republican, the families moved to Fort Kearny for several weeks. After six months the militia was mustered out and everyone returned to Beatrice.

The following summer, the Mudge family went back home to Buffalo Ranch, where Ben Holladay established a swing station to replace the burned out Liberty Farm Station. Here they remained until 1867 when the stagecoaches ceased running through the valley. Then, for the third and final time, Buffalo Ranch was abandoned, and the Mudge family took up a new homestead east of Beatrice where four more children were born. Here the parents remained, retiring to Beatrice only in their final years. Elizabeth Mudge died in 1907, and William Mudge Sr. in 1917.

Charles Emery and his family were with the Mudges all the way back to Beatrice. Even though he had given his first payment on Liberty Farm to James Lemmon, Emery took his family back to Atchison, leaving the Lemmons to repossess what was left of their ranch. Emery went back to work for Ben Holladay, rebuilding the ruined stage stations. He also did a little freighting to Denver, and in July, 1865, took over the management of the station at Fort Kearny. When the railroad passed the fort in 1867, the station was closed and the Emerys returned to the Beatrice area where they purchased a small farm. On the first day of January 1871, Charles Emery took possession of a new stone hotel at the corner of Fifth and Court Streets, naming it the Emery House. In later years he also operated a livery stable east of the hotel. Charles Emery died two days after Christmas, 1897. Mary Benson Emery survived her husband by ten years.[2] Their sons, who had been so small during the attack on Pawnee Ranch, became eminently successful men. Jack Emery spent most of his adult life in law enforcement, first as a deputy U. S. marshall, later as chief of Beatrice police and special agent for the Department of Justice. George Emery served a number of terms as Gage County Clerk and deputy clerk, eventually entering the abstract business in Lincoln.

In its burned-out condition, Liberty Farm was worth only a fraction of its original asking price, so James Lemmon decided to rebuild. In the spring of 1865, he sent his hired girl, Barbara, and her husband, Bill Ikes, to raise a new cabin on the place. Twelve-year-old Hervey Lemmon went along to help. James Lemmon himself arrived soon after with additional hands and materials to finish the construction. The family and employees were attacked again by Indians on July 4 that summer, but only the Indians suffered this time.

When the Union Pacific reached Fort Kearny, there was an immediate drop-off in freight and passenger traffic along the old trail, since it was now cheaper and faster to ship through Omaha. James Lemmon, the Comstocks, Milligan, and Newton Metcalf took their teams and families west to work as graders and tie cutters for the railroad. Before leaving for end-of-tracks, the Lemmons sealed up much of their furniture and household goods in a large root cellar.

Through the end of 1867 and much of 1868, the family lived in Cheyenne, where James Lemmon entered an ill-conceived partnership with Newton Metcalf. When their contract for railroad ties had been fulfilled at Rawlins, Wyoming Territory, Metcalf collected the full payment and skipped the country. James Lemmon trailed his former partner for a time, but turned back when told that Metcalf had been hanged for murder. (He later turned up hale and hearty in Billings.) Lemmon had no choice but to sell his teams and wagons to pay the wages due to his employees.

After the rails were joined in Utah in 1869, Lemmon tried mining for a brief time before returning to Liberty Farm. As the family and their hired men pulled into the yard of their old place that fall of 1870, they found it occupied by the Ben Royce family. After a tense confrontation, Lemmon decided to leave the Royces in peace, especially since they had not disturbed the cache of goods in the cellar. The Lemmon family continued down the trail to rent the old stage station at Big Sandy Crossing. A year later they purchased their last homestead near the site of old Kiowa Station, where Lucy died in 1873. Sadly, both the oldest Lemmon boys died young—Hervey at the age of thirty-three and Moroni at thirty-two. In 1879, Alpharetta Lemmon married John Comstock, who as a seven-year-old boy had fled with his family from Thirty-two Mile Station that August 8, 1864. The youngest boy, George Edward, who had been so upset over little Clarence Kelley's "privileges" at their Marysville home, founded the town of Lemmon, South Dakota, and lived out his remarkable life as a cowman and sheep rancher. James Lemmon outlived all except his youngest two children, passing on in 1903.[3]

Frank Baker and the Artist sisters returned with the refugees from Fort Kearny as far as the Big Blue, where they found Isaac Artist preparing to take his family back to Iowa. What with the Indian scare and the return of the badly wounded George Hunt, Isaac had had enough of Nebraska. He was so serious that Frank Baker could think of only one way to keep Jane nearby, and that was to marry her. The wedding took place on August 21, exactly two weeks after Baker had passed the ill-fated mule train at Indian Hollow. The happy couple spent their honeymoon on a wagon, driving to the Missouri for a load of lumber. As the Indian troubles receded, the Bakers returned to the Little Blue Valley to homestead the abandoned Roper place, and later the Uhlig farm. They did not remain long at either location, and soon homesteaded a farm north of Beatrice. Francis P. Baker died in June 1916, at the age of 80 years. Jane Artist Baker survived her husband by four years.[4]

After all his attempts to push up the valley to find Libby Artist, John Gilbert found her safe and sound on her father's homestead north of Beatrice. Isaac Artist (who never did return to Iowa) lost two daughters in little more than three months time that fall, as Elizabeth married John Gilbert on November 28. The couple settled on the Big Blue, close by the Hunts and Artists and Bakers. The Gilberts farmed their place for nearly thirty years, raising two sons in the process, before removing to Red Cloud on the Republican, only twenty-five miles west of the place where the Sioux and Cheyennes nearly cut to pieces the citizen company and Murphy's cavalry that foggy August morning.

After a short illness, John Gilbert died at Red Cloud exactly on his eighty-ninth birthday, February 5, 1926. He was honored by Masonic services and eulogized as one whose "whole life was characterized by strict honesty in his dealings with his fellows, and he was held in high esteem by all who knew him."[5]

Erastus Comstock and his sons also returned briefly to the valley before going on to work for the Union Pacific and later the Northern Pacific Railroad. In 1872, Father Comstock returned to the valley for good. Nuckolls County had only recently been organized, and he served several terms as county commissioner and four years as postmaster. The Comstock children also remained in the vicinity of Oak Grove, and even today the region is liberally sprinkled with their descendants. On January 29 or 30 (the record is unclear), a little more than thirty years after his lucky Sunday ride, Erastus Comstock died at the home of his son, George—a community leader and respected pioneer of the old trail.[6]

By the summer of 1865, George Hunt had recovered from his leg wound—recovered so well, in fact, that he was able to work as a bullwhacker with a train of freighters along the trail to Denver. Though the damage to his leg muscles caused him to walk with a slight limp for the rest of his life, it failed to dampen his ambition.

In 1866, he married Mary Bickle, daughter of one of the founders of Crete, in Saline County. In the early 1870s, the Hunts moved to the growing town of De Witt on the Big Blue River, where they raised nine children. George entered the mercantile business and did extremely well. The store even survived a disastrous fire which ravaged much of the business district of De Witt. But George Hunt, generous to a fault, was unable to survive the effects of the credit which he overextended to his friends. In the 1890s the store went broke, and George tried his hand at running a livery stable. The new business lasted about a year, and then it, too, was gone.

In 1899, the Hunts left De Witt to settle upriver in Crete. Mary died two years later, and in 1907, George remarried. He had always been personally popular and well respected, and after serving for a time as Saline County Commissioner, he was elected to the Nebraska State Legislature in 1917. After an illness of only several days, George Hunt died on July 6, 1919.[7]

Hunt's brother-in-law, Tobias Castor, survived the loss of his horses to go on to greater things. After several years of hard labor, he fell in with the Burlington Railroad and was charged with securing construction rights-of-way across much of southern Nebraska. The railroad town of Tobias in Saline County is named for him. Castor's four children were grown when he abandoned his wife, the former Catherine Hunt, and obtained a divorce, remarrying in 1889. Neighbors and acquaintances described Castor as a bluff, loud, even uncouth individual, and some felt that, had it not been for his lack of fidelity to his wife, his leadership abilities could have taken him to prominence in state or even national politics. As it was, he didn't do badly. After settling on a homestead near Wilbur in Saline County, he became affiliated with the state Democratic Party and was elected county clerk, treasurer, surveyor, and superintendent of schools. Following his retirement to Lincoln, Tobias Castor died in 1901. He had always been a restless and energetic man, and his wandering continued even after his death. From Lincoln, the body was taken by train for reburial on his old homestead near Wilbur. Then in 1907, it was exhumed and taken back to Lincoln for reburial in Wyuka Cemetery, where it will presumably remain.[8]

After his service with the Second Nebraska Cavalry in Dakota, and having survived the attack on Oak Grove and the Murphy expedition, one would think that John Barratt had earned a rest from the Indian fighting business. He was not ready to quit, however, and joined Mudge and Milligan in Captain White's militia company. After serving his six-month service at Fort Kearny and along the Little Blue, he was discharged and took up a homestead claim two miles southeast of De Witt.

By this time, it appeared that Barratt was a confirmed bachelor. He was, after all, twenty-seven years old. But as luck would have it, he discovered, just across the line in neighboring Saline County, a woman from his native England. On March 17, 1867, John Barratt married Ann Wheeler and took her home to live on his established farmstead. There the couple raised six children and became the eventual operators of a 200-acre grain and hog farm. Both had been well educated in their native England and were devout members of the Church of England. Thus they raised their children in the Episcopal faith and were active in the establishment and support of the public schools in Gage County. Through hard work, moral conviction, and a bit of luck along the way, the Barratts came to be financially secure, respected, and counted among the social elite of the county. Annie Wheeler Barratt died on the last day of 1914. John Barratt followed his wife in death on August 27, 1919.[9]

Like the other refugees, John Palmer and his sister, Hattie Eubank, had lost everything as they climbed aboard Wilder's empty train in the early morning hours of August 8. Several days later they arrived back on their family homestead along Plum Creek in southeastern Gage County. On March 27, 1866, John Palmer married a neighbor girl, Charlotte Cain, and moved to a homestead of his own. In time, the Palmers came to be the owners of a 236-acre farm, and the parents of seven children.[10]

Hattie Palmer Eubank stayed on at the Palmer homestead for a time before moving to Marysville, where she sought refuge with the Perry Hutchinson family, for whom she had previously worked as a hired girl. On March 15, 1865, Hattie gave birth to Joseph Eubank's child, a little girl whom she poignantly named Josephine. After several years of hard labor to support herself and her child, Hattie married Joseph Adams in 1870 and at last found financial security. The Adams family moved to Gunnison, Colorado, in 1879.[11]

Following the raids, the Bainter family moved back to their former home in Harrison County, Missouri. Several years later they returned to find Spring Ranch occupied by claim jumpers. While he carried on the legal fight to reclaim his homestead, James Bainter rented and farmed the old Hackney Ranch. His efforts were successful, and in 1871, the Bainters moved back to begin rebuilding Spring Ranch. During the years following the raids, the family had grown. James' brother, Isaac, now made his home with them, and there were seven children—the three youngest were boys bearing the martial names of Grant, Sherman, and Sheridan. In 1885, Elizabeth Bainter died and was buried at Spring Ranch. Several years later, the "old Indian fighter" moved on to South Dakota.[12]

Within a few days after the Uhligs arrived back in their former hometown, Otto and his brother-in-law, Joseph Schuetz, returned to Kiowa Station to retrieve the body of Theodore for reburial in

Brownville's Walnut Grove Cemetery. In the fall of the year, the Uhligs returned to their homestead to save what was left of their crops. Since their cabin was in ashes, they set up housekeeping in a dugout close to the riverbank. It is uncertain just how long they stayed on their claim, but we know that the family remained together in eastern Nebraska until Ida Uhlig Schuetz died in childbirth in November 1866.

After Ida's death, the family dispersed. Otto grasped the business opportunities to be found along the new railroad line, and established a general store in North Platte, Nebraska. There he advertised himself as a "dealer in Staple and Fancy groceries, Provisions, vegetables, foreign and domestic fruits, grain and feed, Ladies' and Gents' boots and shoes, Plug and Smoking tobacco, Cigars, China, Crockery." The store shared a building with the post office, and Otto shared his home with his mother, who took care of the domestic chores. After a couple years, Otto and his mother moved on to Sidney, where he operated his own stagecoach line along the Sidney-Deadwood Trail to the Black Hills. When the gold rush began, he sold his line and took his mother to live in Deadwood, then Spearfish, and finally Whitewood, South Dakota, where Joanna died in 1889. Otto Uhlig continued to operate a general store in Whitewood until his death in 1908.[13]

If Otto and Joanna adjusted to the grief over their losses, Hugo did not. After leaving Brownville, he wandered rootlessly along the route of the railroad, engaging in a personal vendetta against any Indians who happened to cross his path. He spent part of his time with the Lemmon family in Cheyenne. Ed Lemmon recalled later that the boys idolized Hugo Uhlig as a hero, despite his slow manner and odd, foreign dress. How many Indians he did away with during his campaign of hatred, nobody ever knew, and when he left the Lemmon household in the summer of 1870, he disappeared for good.[14]

With the exception of Newton Metcalf (whose legal name was apparently Merritt Metcalf), whose misadventures kept his family on the move, the people of the Little Blue Valley did fairly well for themselves in the years following their escape from the vengeance of the Cheyennes and their allies. But their suffering at the hands of the Indians was neither forgiven nor forgotten. Their thoughts on the Sand Creek Massacre are unrecorded, but presumably most of them felt it an act of justice. However, the sufferings of the Cheyennes and Arapahoes hardly compensated them for their personal losses of livelihoods, possessions, and in some cases, loved ones. Following Joe Roper's lead, many of the victims of the raids elected to invoke the

Intercourse Act to obtain at least a partial recompense for their losses.

In February, 1866, a number of men from the Little Blue, including James Douglas, James Bainter, Charles Emery, Hugo Uhlig, Andrew Hammond, and William Hess met at Fort Kearny. In the presence of a notary, they swore depositions in support of each other's claims for losses, afterward engaging legal counsel to present those claims to the Bureau of Indian Affairs. In time, nearly all the settlers who had been driven from their homes along the Little Blue and the Platte filed such claims, more than fifty of which wound up in the hands of a curious firm, Pratt and Clark.[15]

Matthew Pratt's short-lived partnership with Thomas Morton had ended, of course, on August 8, 1864, at Plum Creek. Pratt knew from personal experience that the process of filing claims against the Indians could be tortuous and unrewarding, and he had little faith that the Bureau of Indian Affairs would treat such claims fairly. In 1865, he formed a partnership with one Jeremiah Clark for the sole purpose of prosecuting depredation claims. Apparently, the partners traveled extensively along the line of the trail, actively soliciting business for which they charged a retainer and between twenty-five percent and thirty-three percent of the final settlement. But Pratt and Clark had no intention of filing these claims with the Indian Bureau. They were confident that the Congress would enact special legislation for the relief of the depredation victims, and advised their clients to "sit" on their claims, waiting for the auspicious moment. Indeed, more than thirty pieces of such legislation were proposed over the next two decades, but none were enacted into law.

Perhaps Pratt realized that he had misjudged the congressional temper. In any event, he sold out his interest in the partnership to William Fortescue in 1868. Jeremiah Clark died ten years later, and his interest in the business was assumed by his widow, Florinda. Finally, in 1882, the firm of Fortescue and Clark informed its clients that the long-awaited congressional action appeared to be doomed, and that it was retaining Washington D.C. attorney John Burch to begin active prosecution of all claims. In March 1885, Congress passed a measure referring the depredation cases to the United States Court of Claims, and Burch began filing motions requiring the Indian Bureau to release all previously submitted documents. Forced to take action at last, the bureau, in 1886, sent Special Investigator Leonard Poole along the route of the old trail to ascertain the validity of the claims. By this time there was no longer any trace of the old road ranches, and a number of claimants and deponents had simply disappeared. Nevertheless, under Poole's probing, much of the fabric of the purloined claims fell away like so much wet tissue.

In the twenty-two years since the August raids, memories had become blurred and eyewitnesses were utterly unable to agree on precisely which ranches had been burned. Relationships had become strained and distant in some cases, and a few old settlers, including Charles Emery and Erastus Comstock, recanted earlier depositions and voiced suspicions about the claims of some of their former neighbors.

Military officers of the First Nebraska Cavalry such as Colonel Livingston and Captain Lee Gillett, who in 1864 had been blamed for their ineffectiveness, were totally unsympathetic and swore that none of the ranches east of Kearny, with the exception of Spring Ranch and Liberty Farm, had been burned. Hugo Uhlig's claim for sixty acres of corn raised investigative eyebrows, as did James Douglas' claim for eighteen and one-half acres of potatoes supposedly dug up by the Indians. It was also discovered that Hugo Uhlig's claim was a duplicate of the one filed by his mother, and that the supposedly magnificent road ranch operated by the deceased family of Ruth and Hannah Eubank was nothing more than a wretched hovel, described by Frederick Roper as the "cheapest place that any family live in on the road."[16]

Reminded that the Sioux and Cheyennes would hardly have carried away grindstones, anvils, log chains, and wrenches, the settlers recalled anew the depredations of Captain Hollenberg's Kansas militia, thus reawakening old resentments between survivors and the Kansans who had rushed northward to their aid. Nearly all the claimants listed losses of many tons of hay which had, after all, been grass growing on government land. They asked several thousand dollars for their cabins which had been constructed from trees cut on that same government land. In Beatrice, Poole located William Blakely who, as assessor for the Bureau of Internal Revenue, had appraised the settlers' cabins at a fraction of what they now claimed. At every turn of the investigation there was evidence of collusion among the claimants; and, while Poole was convinced of the truth and reliability of John Gilbert's testimony (Gilbert had not filed a depredation claim), he reported that "The witness Metcalf has the worst of reputations among his old associates of any man, (unreadable) whose reputation I have ever had occasion to make inquiry."[17]

Summing up his report, the investigator concluded: "The more claims of this series that I investigate, the more evidence do I find . . . that the claimants virtually enlisted into a conspiracy to defraud the government and cheat the Indians, by one of the most corrupt jobs ever attempted to be foisted upon the office of Indian Affairs."[18]

But the Office of Indian Affairs was not yet finished. The claims were placed before the offending tribes for corroboration. It was an exercise in futility. By 1887, the various bands of Sioux, Cheyennes, and Arapahoes which had been involved in the 1864 raids were scattered on widely separated reservations, and some of the guilty were long dead. Those remaining all denied any knowledge of the Indian War of 1864, though Agent McGillicuddy reported from Pine Ridge that "The Indians have acknowledged to me freely in general and private council that they did destroy every stage and other ranch that they were able to capture . . . There is not a white man indian or half breed living and who lived at that time in the region depredated upon, but freely admit and give evidence that the depredations were committed . . ."[19] Another agent reminded the Bureau that the tribes could hardly be expected to be helpful anyway, since "The Indians get no payment for depredations committed against them."[20]

In the end, it mattered very little. There was a three-year filing deadline with the Court of Claims, and that had expired in 1867. The claimants' only recourse appeared to be congressional action for relief of their separate petitions, none of which came to fruition. The depredation cases dragged on through the legal quagmire until 1913, and in the end, the government prevailed against its own citizens. Since the Indians had been at war, reasoned the U. S. Attorney General, they logically could not have been in amity with the United States. Therefore, the Intercourse Act of 1834 did not apply. With the possible exception of Nancy Morton, none of the claimants ever received a cent for their losses.[21]

In retrospect, the business of the depredation claims left a tarnish on most of those involved. However forthright and honest they may have been in their personal dealings with one another, the settlers thought it not immoral to profit at the expense of the Indians who had caused them so much grief and, in some cases, had murdered those whom they held most dear. Though the tenacity they displayed was very much in character, their unfortunate attempts to obtain inflated compensation appear as an unworthy episode in the long record of courage and honesty which otherwise defines their lives.

In contrast, the fortunes of the road ranchers along the Platte were much less affected by the 1864 raids than they were by the railroad and the accompanying advance of civilization up the Platte Valley. During August, 1864 Jack Morrow's Junction Ranch sheltered many of his neighbors within its sod fortifications, but it was never attacked.

Perhaps Morrow's close association with squawmen and "bad Indians" over the years had given him a certain immunity. After he "went on the warpath" at Julesburg during the attack of January 7, 1865, the swaggering braggart, who gave thievery a whole new perspective, continued to build his empire and became quite a rich man. As his legitimate interests in mining and freighting began to occupy more of his attention, his depredations on the emigrants came to an end and he became almost respectable. When Lincoln County was organized in 1866, Morrow was elected a county commissioner, along with John Gilman and Washington Hinman. By 1870, he had tired of frontier life and moved to Omaha, where he occupied a luxurious house and led the life of a gentleman gambler.

No one in Omaha knew quite what to make of him. He had fought well at Julesburg and he had a reputation as a bad man with a gun, having killed a man years before in a gunfight, but he seemed more bluff than dangerous. He tried to be genteel, no longer drinking his champagne from a tin cup, frequenting only the most elegant gambling houses. But he never lost his swaggering crudeness. Over time, his gambling losses whittled away at his ill-gotten gains and his drinking sprees undermined his health. He died impoverished in 1885.[22]

Most of Morrow's neighbors did better. Washington Hinman, the progressive agriculturist, left the trail to reside in North Platte. Hinman remained young in body as well as in mind, for his second wife, Rebeka (who was seventeen years his junior), bore the first of their three children when he was forty-nine years old. At the birth of the last, he had reached the age of fifty-four.[23]

Charles McDonald also left Cottonwood Springs for North Platte, where he became a merchant and banker, eventually supplying the economic foundation for Buffalo Bill's Wild West Show. Orra McDonald, the first white woman to reside permanently in Lincoln County, bore him five children. Charles McDonald continued to manage the daily affairs of his bank until his death from pneumonia on April 22, 1919.[24]

The Gilmans saved their ranch from the raids, but their economic losses were severe. When the Union Pacific tracks advanced up the north side of the Platte, John Gilman (whose wife, Martha, remained in Nebraska City with their son) followed the rails west, doing contract work as a grader and supplier of ties. Jeremiah Gilman remained on the trail until 1868, by which time it was clear that the days of the road ranches were over. Selling out the lumber and stock from Gilmans' Station, he returned to Nebraska City where he purchased a home along the old Steam Wagon Road. In November, 1866, Jeremiah married Martha's sister, Elizabeth Fitchie, and was happy to leave the frontier for a more secure life. Their first child died in infancy, but Elizabeth bore seven more, six of them boys. The Gilmans remained on their Nebraska City farm until 1898, when they moved to a home in Lincoln. There Jeremiah Gilman died in 1904.

Brother John Gilman followed the rails all the way to Promontory Point, after which he also returned to the family in Nebraska City. But, unlike Jeremiah, John craved risk and adventure. With the irresistible lure of the gold mines in his blood, he took his family to Deadwood, South Dakota, eventually losing most of the small fortune which the brothers had accumulated through so much hard work along the Platte. John Gilman died in Deadwood in 1887.[25]

Except for the Cheyenne raids of 1867 which so nearly claimed their two daughters, the George Martin family found a peaceful and rewarding life on their homestead south of the Platte. It was over a year before Nathaniel recovered from his terrible wound enough so that he could do any physical labor. Robert appeared to heal more quickly, but was plagued by recurrent back pain for the remainder of his life. In 1866, the Martins built a fine log cabin from cottonwoods hauled up from the river islands. Although many of their neighbors left the country after the attacks on the Campbell and Warren families, the Martins remained and prospered. As Indian troubles receded and settlers began migrating to the area once again, the Martin Ranch became a post office known as Martinville.

There were hard times ahead for the people in Martin township. They endured the disastrous blizzards of 1871 and 1888 and the Easter Sunday blizzard of 1873. They weathered the financial panic of 1873-1875 and the grasshopper plagues of those same years. But the 1870s also brought the new towns of Doniphan and Hastings to the area, and a railroad connection to the Union Pacific tracks at Grand Island. During this time the story of the Martin brothers was told, retold, and embroidered a bit, becoming a permanent, if not always accurate, part of the folklore of Nebraska and of Adams and Hall Counties.

In 1875, Bob Martin left the family homestead for Ellsworth, Kansas, where he married Elizabeth Nagle. The couple remained childless. When the city of Ellsworth organized its first fire department, Bob Martin was a charter member, devoting considerable time and energy to the organization for the remainder of his life.

By 1899, his back problems had become debilitating, and he developed meningitis. Early on the morning of March 20, 1899, Robert

Martin died at his home at the age of forty-seven years. At his funeral, the floral tributes from his fellow citizens filled the area around his coffin, and the presiding minister eulogized him as "a moral, honest, just and upright man, an exemplary Christian." After the service, an escort of firefighters accompanied the body to the cemetery where his grave remains, marked by a stone on which is inscribed, "The Angels called him."

Nathaniel remained on the family homestead. In 1873, he married Letitia Donald, who bore him two children. Letitia died when the children were still quite young, and Nat then married her sister, Sarah. In 1909 the Martins moved to Minnesota, but returned after a brief time to live in Hastings. Following Sarah's death in 1926, Nat made his home with his daughter's family back on the old Martin homestead which he had grown to love so much.

On May 23, 1928, Henry Nathaniel Martin died at age seventy-nine, on the land where he had known his most severe trial and his greatest happiness. He was the last surviving member of the George Martin family.[26]

It was in the middle of the second week in August 1864, that Ann Marble's world was turned upside down. On that darkly memorable day, she received a surprise visit from Mr. N.S. Bates, Mayor of Council Bluffs. In his hand, the mayor held the telegram confirming that "Marble and boy" had been killed by Indians at Plum Creek.

The weeks that followed were cruel. Burdened with the care of her eldest son, Joel, who had returned grievously ill from his father's train in eastern Nebraska, she had also to feed and care for three younger sons, ages six, four, and two—and the death of her husband had left her virtually destitute. Then, in early October, a letter arrived from Private Smith at Fort Lyon, informing her that Danny was indeed alive and had been rescued from the Indians. Another letter followed with the news that the boy was being taken to Denver City and would soon be on his way back home. Whatever joy Ann must have felt over her son's safety was extinguished about the first of December, when a letter from Dr. McClelland informed her that Danny was dead.

On April 28, 1865, Ann Marble was appointed administrator of her husband's estate, and she promptly began work on a depredation claim against the Cheyennes. But the Council Bluffs attorneys knew that her evidence was flimsy and her chances of collecting damages were minimal, and Ann Marble had no money with which to pay for their services, so they refused to file her claim. She wrote to an acquaintance in Sidney, Iowa, asking if Nancy Morton's claim had been successful. She learned that Nancy had sold her interest in the claim to Matthew Pratt, and that Mr. Pratt might be willing to help Ann collect her own damages. Apparently, Ann Marble never sought the services of Pratt and Clark. She may have received some recompense from the remnants of her husband's train which Lieutenant Bone had conveyed to Fort Kearny, but there is no evidence of this.

So the family struggled on in their house on Oak Street. Eventually, Joel Marble took his father's place as the family breadwinner, working as a clerk in a local store. But Joel had never fully recovered from his illness, and in January 1870, Ann Marble lost her eldest son.

Finally, in February 1871, attorney John Key filed the Marble depredation claim with the Commissioner of Indian Affairs. On March 19, Ann married Horatio Strong, a single father fifteen years her senior, who had three teenage children of his own. One year later, the Marble claim was denied by the Secretary of the Interior, and Ann gave up the fight. Sometime after 1873, the amalgamated family left Council Bluffs behind them for a new life in another place which remains unknown to this time.[27]

If the experience of being a captive of the Cheyennes dramatically altered the lives of Lucinda Eubank and Nancy Morton (and, as it turned out, ended the lives of Danny and Isabelle), it proved to be a barely noticeable interruption in the chaotic childhood of Ambrose Asher. Kicked from pillar to post through no fault of his own, he seems to have been a very tough little boy from whom neither Major Wynkoop nor anyone else could obtain much information.

Ambrose had been about two years old when his father died. His mother had soon remarried and borne another son. For whatever reason, Ambrose was sent to live with the Daniel Walton family of Adams County, Illinois. The Waltons, Eubanks, and Ashers had been associated with each other for many years in Illinois and, before that, in Kentucky, and it was now decided that Ambrose's name should be changed to Connie Eubank. After a time, the boy was passed along to his Grandfather Eubank in Adair County, Missouri. But the Missouri Eubanks lost their home in early 1864, so Ambrose/Connie made the fateful move with them to the valley of the Little Blue. The boy was seven years old when the Indians captured him, and no one would argue his right to a severe identity problem.

He must have known that his name was Ambrose Asher, however, as that is how Major Wynkoop recorded it. Even so, no one in Denver could quite agree on the spelling of his name (it appears in the press variously as Asher, Ashley, or even Asholey), and Ambrose was unable to help them. In spite of the lack of information on his identity and family background, his mother, who was living back in the old Kentucky home, found out about her son's predicament and was reunited with him sometime after December 1, 1864.

The mother (who was probably Mary Eubank prior to her marriage) took her son back to Adams County, Illinois, or possibly even to Kentucky or Missouri where she died several years later. The unfortunate orphan, now approaching his teen years, went to live with his Grandmother Ruth Eubank in the boardinghouse operated by her sister-in-law, Sarah Eubank, in Quincy. It was probably during these years in Adams County that he became literate.

Of his teens we know nothing. On February 24, 1881, Ambrose married Belle Harrison, the sixteen-year-old daughter of a laborer in California, Missouri. After the wedding in the home of the bride's father, the Ashers settled down in the little town, and Ambrose found work as a teamster. Five children were born into the family, which probably existed on the edge of poverty most of the time. Sometime between 1894 and 1900, Ambrose simply disappeared. There is nothing to indicate that he died, and no reason to believe that he abandoned his family. Belle and the younger children moved with her father to Sedalia where they lived together in a hotel or boarding house. From there, the family split up as the children matured and left home, and Belle eventually moved with her daughter to Sacramento, California, where she died about 1940.

Of all the people whose wanderings led them to the valley of the Little Blue and to the country along the white man's Medicine Road, none were more ill-starred than the Asher-Eubank-Walton clan. None endured a more insecure youth than did Ambrose Asher; and none left behind a final chapter of life which is so enigmatic and so hauntingly incomplete.[28]

If the New Year is a time for beginnings, the reunited Roper family was certainly starting from scratch as they settled themselves in eastern Pennsylvania that January 1865. They found, however, that the daughter they had gotten back was not quite the same one who had left to visit the Eubanks the previous August. In a letter to the Commissioner of Indian Affairs written in November 1865, Joe Roper informed him that "My daughter has been rescued but her mind is somewhat impared (sic)."[29] Whatever the behavioral characteristics that prompted such a statement, Laura's mind was not so impaired as to prevent her from falling in love again. In February 1865, she celebrated her seventeenth birthday, and soon after married Elijah Soper, a discharged Union soldier. During 1866, the couple returned to Gage

County, Nebraska, to homestead. Their first child, Eddie, was born there on January 1, 1867.[30]

The rest of the family remained in Pennsylvania throughout 1866, working and saving to reestablish themselves in Nebraska. In early 1867, Joe Roper made a final visit to relatives in Bristol, Connecticut, where he had a formal photographic portrait made. Then, with spring upon the land, the Roper family returned to Nebraska—but not to the Little Blue Valley. Their new homestead was north of Beatrice on the east side of the Big Blue and west of the Stevens Creek settlement where brother Ford had gotten his start. They were only a mile or two from the farms of John Gilbert and John Barratt.

That previous summer, the Ropers had nearly lost their eldest daughter, Clarisa, during the defense of Liberty Farm. Now Clarisa also had had her fill of the frontier, and she returned to Beatrice to marry Allen J. Kelley, brother of the slain Marshall. Clarisa was about twenty-three years old–nearly an old maid, by Roper standards—when she married Kelley on New Years Day, 1868.

The return to Gage County was the beginning of years of back-breaking toil for Joe Roper. Besides himself and Paulina, he still had Kate, Francis, and little Clarence to feed and clothe. There was a new farm to be built up from scratch and the wasted years to be made up. By 1870, he had embarked upon a complicated series of land acquisitions and he reckoned his assets at $1,800—not really bad for someone who, only six years before, had been left with nothing. He had also acquired another grandson, a namesake. The year before, Laura had given birth to another son and had named him Joseph.

Fortune appeared to be smiling on the Roper family at last, and on November 8, 1871, daughter Francis, at the ripe old age of seventeen, married Henry Jewell of Kansas at the Episcopal church in Beatrice. It must have been especially gratifying that the *Beatrice Express*, in reporting the occasion, paid tribute to Joe Roper's industry, calling him "a fine specimen of the pluck, grit, and stamina that should enter into the composition of a pioneer farmer."[31] This was no exaggeration, for throughout 1872 he continued to acquire and plant additional land, bringing more than 100 acres under cultivation—no mean task in those days of pure horsepower.

There was also some unfinished business which needed attention. Though Laura had been giving birth regularly, she somehow never found a place in her home for her firstborn, Clarence, who was now nine years of age and attending the Roper School east of the farm. Though Joe and Paulina had raised the boy from birth, he was still legally Clarence Kelley. The country was being settled rapidly and its legal machinery firmly established, and the situation would only become more awkward for Clarence as he grew older. With Laura's consent, adoption proceedings began, and in December 1872, Clarence became a Roper in name as well as in fact.[32]

Eighteen seventy-three proved to be a banner year on the Roper farm, now solidly established and specializing in wheat and Chester White hogs. The crops matured well, and in thirteen days of furious labor, the Ropers cut and stacked 113 acres of wheat.[33]

Ever the businessman, Joe Roper spent several weeks of January 1874, at the Pacific House in Beatrice, making plans to open some sort of retail shop in town. He was quite well known by now, and nearly everything he did made news. With the energy left over from farming, he shamelessly promoted "Roperville" and found time to serve on the Roper District School Board, the county fair awards committee, the grand jury, the Gage County Board of Supervisors, and the Republican Central Committee. These were golden years for Joe Roper. Successful and respected, with his family gathered around him, he was enjoying the best times of his life. The return of daughter Kate and her husband from Kansas must surely have pleased him. It had been a mere ten years but a whole lifetime since that day at Pawnee Ranch when he had climbed up to "see the posish," and he had worked hard to earn the life which he and his family now enjoyed.

On the evening of November 2, 1875, patrons and friends—nearly 200 of them, by Joe Roper's report—jammed into the Roper School for a "literary entertainment."[34] The teacher had cast her students and a few volunteers in a series of readings, dialogues, and short plays. Of course there were quite a number of Ropers performing, and they were all terrific. Francis and her husband (some of the volunteers) did a one-act play, and twelve-year-old Clarence performed, with a friend, a happy dialogue called "The Letter." The outstanding performance of the evening came at the very end when Katie Roper and Sylvester S. Kirby were cast in a tableau entitled "Matrimony," ending when they were married—for real—by the Reverend McElwee. The surprised members of the audience whooped with delight when it dawned on them that they were unwitting guests at a wedding. It was an unorthodox evening, to be sure, and for the first time in thirty years, Joe and Paulina went home to a household without any girls. Only young Clarence was left.

After the literary entertainment, Joe Roper became less visible in the community. Eighteen seventy-four and 1875 were locust years in Nebraska. First floods, then grasshoppers wrote an end to many of the struggling farms in Gage County, impoverishing their owners and forcing many to abandon their claims. Even the brave little Methodist mission which had opened in Roperville in 1873 was terminated by the church, and Methodism reestablished itself among the influential Artist and Hunt families in nearby De Witt.[35] The land was indeed rich, but natural disaster and economic depression threatened to clean out the Ropers as neatly as the Cheyennes had done back in 1864. The proposed shop in Beatrice never got past the planning stage, and over the winter of 1876-1877, Joe Roper's health deteriorated rapidly.

He died on April 15, 1877, and was buried on an elevated plot of land north of his farm—a small area of two acres which had been donated by homesteader John Wehn for a community cemetery. Following his death, the Roper family fortunes continued their downward spiral. Clarence (who turned fifteen just a month after Joseph's death) shouldered the responsibility of managing the farm while Paulina ran the business end of things.

Laura's family meanwhile continued to expand. There were six children when, in 1883, her second son, Joseph, died at age fourteen. Then in October, 1884, came the day that would have sorely grieved Joe Roper, had he lived. With no apparent warning, Laura abruptly left Elijah and her five remaining children to run off with a newcomer to the neighborhood, James Vance, a man whom she met quite by accident in the little town of Liberty where she lived.

Over the years, Laura had become quite well-known in Gage County. But by now, the story of her capture had worn thin, and the abandonment of her family provoked a savage outburst from the *Beatrice Express*: "Mrs. Laura Soper of Liberty has departed. She isn't dead, but it were better if she were dead. Soper and five children are deserted . . . Hers has been a strangely unfortunate and eventful life. Whatever her faults, she is entitled to the pity and commisseration (sic) rather than the censure of mankind."[36]

Laura's sudden departure left Elijah in a precarious position, and he soon gave up their only daughter, Katherine, for adoption to a local druggist and his wife. About this same time, Kate returned to the farm to live with Clarence and Paulina. The marriage to Kirby which had so delighted the audience at Roper School was over (whether by death or divorce is unknown). She brought with her a seven-year-old daughter, Gertrude—not much help and another mouth to feed. Clarence was forced to hire a helper to keep up with the farm work.

The end came in 1885. In the summer of that year, Clarence Roper was reported to be one of the up and coming young farmers in Gage County. His grain and Poland China operation was touted as a model of agricultural efficiency. On August 25, he was dead.[37]

In many ways, the twenty-two-year-old was much more deserving of pity and commiseration than his mother. The product of a seduction, born out of wedlock at a time when such things carried a weighty stigma, he lost his biological father to the arrows of the Cheyennes in the raid of August 7. He survived the flight to Marysville, the return to Nebraska City, and the round trip to Pennsylvania only to be ignored and given up by his mother. He manfully worked the farm after Joseph's death, staying faithfully with Paulina and remaining in school until his late teens. His body was laid to rest beside the grave of his adoptive father in the little cemetery plot overlooking Soap Creek. The farm was dispersed, mortgages and all, among the remaining children, and Paulina went to live with Francis and Henry Jewell in Oklahoma. There she remained until her death—an impoverished, severe old woman dressed in black bombazine, sitting silently alone much of the time, nursing memories of better days, and bitter resentment over her second daughter's follies.

Laura and James Vance bounced around Kansas for a time before they also settled in Oklahoma. She bore three more children, one of which died in infancy. Despite giving birth to ten children in all, Laura's mothering instincts remained as inconsistent as her sense of commitment. She was not a loveless person, nor could it be said that she was consistently neglectful. Perhaps irresponsible is a better term. Like her own mother, Laura was never demonstrative or affectionate, and her little daughter, Nellie, assumed major responsibility for the upkeep of the Vance household as Laura flitted blithely about the community, helping this neighbor and that, minding everyone's business except her own. Happily, if oddly, she remained on good terms with the Soper boys. Charles and Eugene both lived for periods of time with the Vance family, and Edward and Winfred moved to Oklahoma where they visited their mother regularly. Even Elijah came to visit her on several occasions—the ultimate example of forgiveness.

For Laura, life's road had taken some exceedingly strange twists and turns. But the decisive event in what the *Express* termed her "strangely unfortunate and eventful life" had occurred in her seventeenth year. Forever after, she was not merely Mrs. Soper or Mrs. Vance, but always "the girl who was captured by Indians."[38] Whether or not the experience actually "impared" her mind, she seems to have enjoyed her notoriety. Perhaps, even had the Cheyennes not interfered, her life would have been very little different than it actually turned out to be. But certainly, all the actions and endeavors of her adult existence stood forever in the shadow of her remarkable experience as a captive, creating a legendary Laura more comfortable and appealing than the real one.

During the summer following her release, Nancy Morton remained at the home of her family, regaining her strength, healing in body and in mind. But however much she was resolved to resume her life unencumbered by bitterness, it remained an elusive goal.

In May, 1865, Nancy and Matthew Pratt filed their claim for reparations with the Department of the Interior. Included in their request for $9,697.05 was compensation for the loss of fourteen mules, two horses, merchandise, and damages for personal suffering. Also during that summer, Nancy met George Stevens of Sidney, only about six months her senior. The two were married on November 19, 1865, and lived close to Sidney for several years, before moving to a farm near Jefferson, Iowa. Nancy bore four more children and, although the last died in infancy, life was good for the Stevens family.

As the years passed and the children grew to adulthood, Nancy found her thoughts returning more and more to the ordeal of her captivity. During these years she wrote out at least two versions of her experience with the Indians, differing in many details as well as in general mood. Based on what she had heard from various sources, Nancy became embittered toward Colonel Summers for his failure to attempt a timely rescue (though she would probably have been killed if he had done so). His tardiness in reaching Plum Creek, she explained curtly, was due to his stopping for ice and whiskey to make himself a toddy.[39]

As middle age approached, it became apparent that Nancy's injuries were more severe than she had realized. The broken ribs, of course, had never been properly set, and the foot which had been crushed by a Cheyenne pony became a source of painful arthritis.

On April 2, 1891, she swore another affidavit summarizing her experiences as a captive and detailing her injuries.[40] Possibly she was seeking additional monetary compensation from the government for her personal suffering which was not covered under the provisions of the Intercourse Act of 1834. Witness to her testimony was John Wood, former major of the Seventh Iowa Cavalry who had sent his two horses to the Powder River country to secure her release. The document is stark and accusatory, an indication that, despite a loving marriage and secure life, the events of the Plum Creek Massacre had left Nancy with an insidious damage which never fully healed. The development of a goiter added to the discomfort of her orthopedic problems, and it became difficult for her to swallow and breathe.

Nancy Jane Fletcher Morton Stevens died from choking on August 24, 1912. She was sixty-seven years old.[41]

Unlike Nancy and Laura, Lucinda Eubank had no desire to immortalize her ordeal with the Indians on paper. Consequently, very little is known about her life even after she returned from captivity.

While at Fort Laramie, William Bullock had helped her search for her family by sending telegrams to Denver asking for information on "George Ewbanks, William Walton, and Ambrose Ewbanks," but it is doubtful that any was forthcoming.[42] From Julesburg she took Willie back down the Oregon-California Trail to Fort Kearny and on through the valley of the Little Blue, where her thoughts on passing the ruins of her former home must have been painful beyond description. At Rock Creek Station, she chanced to meet Hattie Palmer Eubank and probably saw the infant Josephine.[43] Continuing on through St. Joseph, she arrived at last at the home of her family, the Waltons, in Missouri. If indeed Lucy was pregnant by Blackfoot, the child was likely aborted, as there is no indication that she ever bore any more children.

After a time, Lucinda married a man named James Bartholomew, a miller near Moundville in the southwestern part of Missouri. For some reason, the situation was uncomfortable for Willie. During his teenage years, he left his mother for a time to live with his aunt Hannah Eubank Walton and her husband, Dan. Sometime prior to 1888, Bartholomew died, and Lucinda moved with William across the Kansas line to the little town of McCune where she married a farmer, oddly named Doctor F. Atkinson.

William married Jennie Frogue at McCune in 1895. In true Eubank fashion, he fathered a large family—three daughters and five sons. Following the death of her third husband, Lucinda made her home with her son and his family until her passing on April 4, 1913.

During her lifetime, Lucinda said very little about her captivity. At the time of her death, William knew only that he and his mother had been part of a large family which had been wiped out by Indians, and that they had been held captive for a time. For all the closeness of the Eubank/Asher/Walton clan, he seemed oddly unaware of the existence of his first cousin, Ambrose Asher. He knew, however, that he had once had an older sister named Isabelle, who also was captured. It seems that Lucinda never quite accepted the little girl's death as related by Mr. Davenport in Julesburg. There was no question that her husband was dead, of course. She had seen him killed with her own eyes. But something in her emotional makeup insisted on nursing the forlorn hope that somewhere, her little girl was still alive. William also was painfully aware of just how much of his family had been lost to him, and in his later years, he began a search for his missing sister.

Four years after Lucinda's death, William moved his family to Greeley, Colorado, then on to Kersey and finally to Pierce in 1921. It was there that he received, in the fall of 1926, a letter from John Ellenbecker, of Marysville, Kansas, who was assembling the story of the Cheyenne raids of 1864. William answered readily, begging Ellenbecker for information about the Eubank family, hoping to reconnect with any relatives that could be located. He also made contact with Martin Alexander, of Goodland, Kansas, whose brother had been chased back to his ranch on the Big Sandy by the Cheyennes in their raids of 1867. Alexander was flirting with senility by this time, and of very little help. The melancholy fact remained that the Eubanks were all gone, and neither Ellenbecker nor Alexander could bring them back again.

In 1930, William Eubank's search for his lost sister attracted the attention of Dr. Le Roy Hafen, of the Colorado Historical Society. Hafen interviewed William at his farm in Pierce and released the story to the press. The Sunday edition of the *Denver Post* (June 8, 1930) carried a front page story about the background of the 1864 raids, and told of Will Eubank's search for his lost sister. It was hoped, wrote the reporter, that someone would come forward with additional information.

Incredibly, someone did. There lived in suburban Denver a lady by the name of Mable Parriott, whose origins were hazy at best. She remembered bits and pieces of things—hiding from Indians, being captured from a wagon train and cared for by an older girl. As a child she had been passed from one family to another and finally adopted by some people named Sullivan. All her life Mable had been tormented by dreams of being cut to pieces by Indians. The lady was totally convinced she was Isabelle and so, for a time, was William Eubank. With some of his family, he paid a visit to Mable at her home in Aurora, Colorado. Shortly after, he wrote to Martin Alexander that he was certain he had found his lost sister.[44]

But the lady's age was fifty-six, while Isabelle would have been sixty-nine at the time. Since Mable had no birth records, her adoptive parents had arbitrarily assigned her an age younger than she actually was—but thirteen years was too much of a gap to be taken seriously. For this and other reasons never disclosed, William finally came to realize that Mable was not his lost sister after all. There was no way in the 1930s to scientifically prove or disprove a blood relationship, and the plaintive search came to an end when William Joseph Eubank died in 1935—the last survivor of the captives of August 1864.

Chapter Three notes

1 Ellenbecker, *Indian Raids on the Upper Little Blue*, 17.

2 *Beatrice Express*, June 17, 1871;
Dobbs, *History of Gage County.*
Charles Emery Indian Depredation Cases #1019, #1620.
Emery tombstones, Evergreen Cemetery; Beatrice, Nebraska.

3 Lemmon, "Early Days on the Little Blue."
James Lemmon Indian Depredation Case #2331.
Yost, *Boss Cowman.*

4 Baker affidavit in Joseph Roper Heirs Indian Depredation Case #7007.
Baker tombstones, Oak Grove Cemetery; De Witt, Nebraska.
De Witt Times-News, April 14, 1927.

5 *Red Cloud Webster County Argus*, February 11, 1926.

6 Comstock family genealogy; *Trail of Memories.*

7 *De Witt Times-News*, June 16, 1927.
Gregory, Papers and Correspondence.
—*Pioneer Days in Crete.*
Kaura, *Saline County History.*
Nebraska History and Record of Pioneer Days, Vol. 2 #3.

8 Gregory, Papers and Correspondence.
—*Pioneer Days in Crete.*
Kaura, *Saline County History.*

9 We have no way of knowing what, if any, psychological effect his experiences in the Indian War of 1864 had on John Barratt. It is interesting to note that the *De Witt Times-News* for December 10, 1885, reported that "John Barratt returned home from the insane hospital in Lincoln."
Barratt tombstones, Oak Grove Cemetery; De Witt, Nebraska.
Portrait and Biographical Album, 207-208.

10 Harriet Adams Indian Depredation Case #1117.
Portrait and Biographical Album, 206-207.

11 Harriet Adams Indian Depredation Case #1117.
Ellenbecker, *Tragedy at the Little Blue.*

12 Elizabeth Bainter tombstone, Spring Ranch Cemetery.
James Bainter Indian Depredation Case #1020.
Biographical and Historical Memoirs, 345-346.
Federal Census, 1870, Nebraska, Jefferson County, Big Sandy.

13 Information provided to Lyn Ryder by descendants of the Uhlig family. Also, *The North Platte Democrat*, March 28, 1872;
Edmund H. Uhlig Indian Depredation Case #2496.

14 Ed Lemmon tells the story of Hugo Uhlig (complete with German accent) in Yost, *Boss Cowman.*

15 Many, if not all, the files of cases handled by this firm contain copies of a lengthy history of Pratt and Clarke, later Fortescue and Clarke. For this chapter I have used material from the case file of John Biktold, #2505.

16 Heirs of Joseph Eubank Sr. Indian Depredations Case #2733.

17 Leonard Poole to Commissioner of Indian Affairs, September 19, 1888, in John Biktold Indian Depredation Claim #2853.

18 Ibid.

[19] Agent V. F. McGillicuddy to Secretary of the Interior, March 26, 1885, in James Douglas Indian Depredation Claim #2337 and others.

[20] Captain J. M. Lee, Acting Agent, Cheyenne and Arapaho Agency (Darlington, I. T.) to Commissioner of Indian Affairs, August 31, 1886, Heirs of Joseph Eubank Sr. Indian Depredation Case #2733.

[21] Secretary of the Interior Orville Browning, in a letter of November 20, 1868, directed the Superintendent of Indian Affairs to settle the claim in favor of Pratt and Morton, and the cover of the claim booklet is marked "Settled" and the notation "December 9, 1868." According to the summary of payments on the booklet cover, Matthew Pratt received $20,104 and Nancy Morton, $6,041. Her payment included a $5,000 indemnity for her suffering in captivity, a highly irregular settlement because such claims were not allowed under the terms of the Act of 1834. Exactly how much Nancy received is open to question, because, in a deposition of January 1871, she stated that she had sold her interest in the claim to Matthew Pratt for $1,500 (Ann Marble Indian Depredation Case #892). Perhaps the generous settlement induced Pratt to sever his connection with Jeremiah Clark, take his money, and run. Perhaps, also, Nancy's disappointment with her small recompense induced her later in life to apply for an additional settlement—hence her deposition of 1891.

[22] Miller, *Shutters West*, 104-112.

[23] Gilman, *Pump on the Prairie.*
Federal Census, 1880, Nebraska, Lincoln County, North Platte.

[24] Gilman, op. cit.; Federal Census, op. cit.
Nebraska History and Record of Pioneer Days II #2, April-June, 1919.

[25] Gilman, op. cit.

[26] *Ellsworth Reporter*, March 23, 1899.
Hastings Daily Tribune, November 15, 1926.
Hastings Democrat, May 31, 1928.
Martin file, Stuhr Museum.

[27] Mrs. Ann Marble, Indian Depredation Case #892.
Council Bluffs, Iowa City Directories, 1868-1874.
Federal Census, 1870, Iowa, Pottawattamie County, Council Bluffs.

[28] Federal Census, 1860, 1870, Illinois, Madison County.
Federal Census, 1880, 1890, Missouri, Moniteau County, Walker Township (California).
Federal Census, 1910, Missouri, Pettis County, Sedalia.
Maloney's Sedalia and Pettis County Directory, 1913.
Moniteau County, Missouri Marriage Records, Book 3, p. 127.
Other information courtesy of Mr. David J. Welch, great-grandson of Ambrose Asher.

[29] Joseph Roper to Commissioner of Indian Affairs, November 30, 1865. "Letters Received," M234, Roll 879, frames 169-170.

[30] Laura Roper Vance, Correspondence.

[31] *Beatrice Express*, November 11, 1871.

[32] The first public notice of the impending adoption was published in the *Beatrice Express* of September 26, 1872. The case was continued several times to the December session of the County Court, and no further record of the proceedings appears in the newspaper. A search for the adoption file in the summer of 1995 revealed that the records have disappeared many years ago. A clue into Clarence's feelings on the whole matter might be read from the federal census of 1880 in which he claims the origins of his parents as Pennsylvania and Ohio—obviously Laura and Marshall Kelley. In the state agricul-

tural census of 1885, taken just before his death, he gave the birthplace of his parents as New York—which could only be Paulina Roper.

33 *Beatrice Express*, August 7, 1873, and various other issues.

34 *Beatrice Express*, November 11, 1875.

35 The grim conditions around Roperville were reported to the Annual Conference of the Methodist Episcopal Church by the presiding elder for the Beatrice Circuit, Mr. J. B. Maxfield, the former Teacher to the Pawnees.

36 The article from the *Express* was reprinted in the *Lincoln Daily State Journal* of October 29, 1884. It included an inaccurate account of the 1864 raids and mentioned that Laura had once been engaged to Marshall Kelley.

37 The Roper family successfully kept secret the occasion and cause of Clarence's death. Not a clue has been found. The De Witt newspaper, which normally carried all the news of the neighborhood, does not mention him at all, and all Beatrice papers for the dates surrounding his death have been lost. Nebraska kept no birth or death records for those years, neither have any contemporaneous church records been located. None of the near neighbors—John Gilbert, John Barratt, or Frank Baker—mention his death in any of their extant letters. The family allowed Clarence a costly monument on which is inscribed simply "C. M. Roper." In a telephone interview, Virginia Leasure told the author that Francis Roper Jewell had in her possession a photograph of Clarence, dressed in white shirt and suit, which was displayed in an alcove at the Jewell home in Oklahoma.

38 James Vance soon tired of the capture story and forbade Laura to ever tell it again. Their daughter, Nellie, felt that he was jealous of the attention it brought to her mother.

39 The origins of Nancy's charge are as mysterious as they are unfounded. Any such incident would have surely appeared in the Omaha newspapers. Though Samuel Summers was not a teetotaler, he drank very sparingly and then never in the performance of his duties. It might be of interest to note that Nancy's host at Fort Laramie, William Bullock, took great pride in his creation of whiskey toddies, and that may have been her first experience with the drink. Apparently, she never sought out Colonel Summers to get his side of the story, though he lived only 120 miles from her. Of course she located Major Wood in Wapello County in 1891, but by then, Samuel Summers was dead.

40 Stevens, Affidavit.

41 Czaplewski, *Captive of the Cheyenne*, 109-110.

42 *Daily Rocky Mountain News*, May 19, June 12, 1865.

43 Harriet Adams Indian Depredation Case #1117.

44 Alexander, Correspondence. Other information furnished by courtesy of Mr. Dewey Ellis, grandson of William Eubank Jr.

Part IV
Chapter Four

"We felt very sad when we went through our old roaming place"

Two weeks after Lucinda Eubank's coach rolled eastward over the Oregon-California Trail, the first rails of the Union Pacific Railroad were laid at Omaha. The transcontinental railroad would prove to be a national project equaled only in later years by the production of the atomic bomb and manned flights to the moon. In the beginning its progress was painfully slow.

In May 1866, General Grenville Dodge resigned from fighting Indians to take command as chief engineer for the railroad, and he at last brought military organization and precision to the mammoth undertaking. Only two years after the raids along the Little Blue and the Platte, the Union Pacific had extended its iron fingers nearly to Grand Island.

Ben Holladay foresaw the rapidly approaching end of the old trail days, but the speed with which Dodge's iron road shrank his business surprised even the astute transportation king. On November 1, 1866, he sold the Holladay Overland Mail and Express Company to Wells Fargo. Once again, Holladay came out on top, receiving 1.5 million dollars in cash, $300,000 in Wells Fargo stock, and a director's seat in the company.

The last coaches trundled through the valley in 1867. Soon the gaudy stages and the great bull trains of the freighters were only a memory. The cross-country travelers were gone from the trail, having traded the jolting, dusty discomfort of the stagecoaches for the jolting, sooty discomfort of the rail coaches, although Americans continued to emigrate by covered wagon into the first decade of the Twentieth Century.[1] A few freighters continued to haul cargoes from points along the railroad by ox and mule power, and a contractor in Utah freighted with teams and wagons until 1926, when he purchased a fleet of motor trucks.[2] But for all practical purposes, the railroad had written an end to the Great Platte River Road and its long columns of wagons. One-by-one the road ranches were abandoned as new towns sprang up on the north side of the Platte. Fort Kearny was abandoned in 1871, Fort Cottonwood (Fort McPherson) in 1880, and grass returned to the old trail.

The route up the Little Blue Valley continued in use by emigrants, short haul freighters, and local farmers until around 1880. Indians continued to pass up and down the road as well, but by 1880, they no longer excited any suspicion. Not since May 1870, had a white man been killed by Indians in Nuckolls County, and the sight of a few red people plodding along the old tracks was no cause for alarm. The Indians still had not learned the finer points of the white man's civilization, however, and were given to barging into any handy residence to beg food when they were hungry.

After 1870, a new wave of settlers took up claims in the valley of the Little Blue, and it became necessary to formally incorporate a local government. On June 27, 1871, thirty-two citizens gathered under a large elm tree in what had once been the front yard of Oak Grove Ranch to elect the first officials of Nuckolls County.

In 1882, a gristmill was built on the south bank of the Little Blue, and the hamlet of Oak grew up around it. When, in 1888, the tracks of the Fremont, Elkhorn, and Missouri Valley Railroad crossed the river several miles upstream from the mill, Oak packed itself up and moved north of the river along the tracks. By 1912, the county was virtually laced together with iron rails.

Oak grew rapidly from its association with the railroad. In a short time, the bustling town had more than 200 residents. By the early 1920s there was daily passenger train service in both directions. Freight trains serviced the lumber yard and grain elevator, and the old Oregon-California Trail had been replaced by a network of county roads. A local banking family, the Scroggins, began operation of radio station KFEQ, only the second commercial transmitter in Nebraska.

It was shortly before the First World War that local citizens and officers of the state historical society began to realize that the pioneers who had survived the perilous times of the 1860s were getting on in years. These people were a largely untapped storehouse of frontier oral history, and soon they would be gone. Men like George Follmer, who had come to the county in 1871, and Benjamin Scroggin, had long been fascinated by the tales of those terrible August days in 1864. Together with Addison E. Sheldon, of the Nebraska State Historical

Society, they began a campaign to collect this history and to place monuments at the sites of some of those significant events of the 1860s.

On the afternoon of June 14, 1918, as American Marines and infantrymen were battling the Germans in the Belleau Wood, a monument to an earlier war was dedicated on the site of Oak Grove Ranch. There were patriotic songs by a church choir and speeches by local notables and stirring words of tribute to the hardy pioneers from Addison Sheldon. The monument had been George Follmer's dream, but he had passed away in 1914. James Comstock was on hand, however, along with Ella Butler (Dudley) to reminisce and pose for photographs, as was John Gilbert, immaculately attired in a starched white shirt and black vest, topped by a felt bowler. There were a few other survivors of the raid still living, such as John Barratt and George Hunt, but they were unable to attend the ceremony, mostly for reasons of poor health. So it was left to Gilbert to recall his stage driving days, and Ella Dudley told again how she had hidden in the empty flour bin.

For a decade following the unveiling of the monument at Oak Grove, a great surge of interest swirled around the people and events of the old Indian war, and efforts were redoubled to reduce the oral history of those times to writing before the remaining pioneers and their irreplaceable store of memories were gone from the earth forever.

Since those days, the changes wrought in the white man's civilization have come rapidly, and often disconcertingly. The old things have passed away leaving a crusty residue of nostalgia. As the proud little towns like Oak became more closely linked with the outside world by the automobile, the railroad service began to decay. Oak lost its passenger train service in 1935, and the rails were abandoned for good in 1971. The Scroggins' brave little radio station KFEQ was sold to a firm in St. Joseph, Missouri. One-by-one, businesses, banks, and even the school have disappeared. But pride of heritage remains strong among the sixty-eight residents. In 1964, the 100th anniversary of the great raid, a re-enactment was held at the site of Oak Grove Ranch—a practice maintained periodically down through the years. Tourists come from every direction to see the valley of the Little Blue where the Comstocks and Ropers and Eubanks suffered through the terrible events of August 1864.

The land itself has changed some since the trail days. The river has built up the valley floor a good six feet or more, and farmers still chisel up bits of broken crockery on the site of the old Roper ranch. The Little Blue has long ago covered or washed away the remains of the

Eubank family, and some years ago a human skull was observed washing down the river channel.

It was the search for older bones that led a team from the University of Nebraska State Museum to Oak in July 1994. There, within a stones throw of the place where the Cheyennes captured Laura and Lucinda and the children, the team waded into the Little Blue River to begin uncovering a treasure trove of 500,000-year-old bones from one of America's richest ice age deposits.[3]

In such surprising ways, the valley continues to give up its secrets of times historic and prehistoric. Even as the bones of animals gone for 500 millennia await discovery, groups of schoolchildren come to walk the old Oregon Trail, through The Narrows and along the Little Blue, making their first attempts to experience this place as the people of the trail must have known it, and to make the pioneer world a part of their own.

> *Hope your wish will come true that every one of the Indians will be extinguished . . . Poor little Dan wish he was alive . . . Keep up good spirits you will meet him in heaven . . .*[4]

Thus wrote Laura Roper to a grieving Ann Marble. Surely the Indian War of 1864 burned a deep and indelible bitterness into those who lost the love of their lives, and Laura's sentiments regarding the Indians could be taken as well nigh universal among the pioneers of Nebraska and Colorado Territories. Of the series of events which had pushed the wild tribes into open warfare these people cared little, and not even the horror of Sand Creek and the passing years could salve their emotional wounds. Even in the first decade of the Twentieth Century, Eugene Ware wrote of Sand Creek,

> *There never was never anything more deserved than that massacre. The only difficulty was that there were about fifteen hundred Indian warriors that didn't get killed.*[5]

And, many years after he had buried the six teamsters at Indian Hollow, George Comstock wrote:

> *One statement, however, that used frequently to be made by the early settlers and which I endorsed at that time, and as fully endorse at the present time, is 'That a dead Indian is a good Indian' and the deader he is and the longer he has been dead, the more I can Love and Respect him.*[6]

Toward the end of the 1880s, there began to appear voluminous histories of states and counties—weighty volumes which their editors filled with noble pioneers and highly exaggerated stories of bloodthirsty Indians, who carved up and burned helpless white people for the fun of it all. In the process, the events of 1864 became romanticized until they bore only the faintest resemblance to reality. The white people of the plains became beatified; the "bad management" and "untoward misfortune" which had led to the Indian wars was relegated to the status of a historical footnote; and the Indian people themselves were portrayed as savage and barely human caricatures. Even old Two Face, long dead, who had been characterized by General Mitchell as "friendly from the first," now became, (in the *Omaha Weekly Herald* of October 27, 1869) a war chief "whose treachery and bloodthirsty disposition had made him the terror of the plains."

The bitterness of the Indian people was compounded by a profound sense of sadness as they saw the old, wild freedom slipping away from tribal consciousness with the passing of every aging warrior; as they looked around the dwindling camp circles with eyes bereft of communal pride; as they remembered their great chiefs touching the pen to documents they couldn't read, and humiliating themselves behind plows that refused to go straight for them as they did for the white man. Living in the misery of the present, and with no hope for the future, they could turn only to the past for a season of joy—and those memories of better days only increased their despondency.

In 1899, a Pawnee named Harry Coons wrote poignantly to Luther North of his sentimental return to the site of the old Genoa reservation:

> *One of my objects was to visit the graves of my 2 sisters who died with measles over 30 years ago as well as to see the old Reservation where I was raised once more—although I met some kind friends there, I felt very lonesome and Sad on account of my feelings as my thoughts were full of the past. Where my sisters graves were is now cornfield(.) what few graves I did find were open and robbed of what few if any trinkets were found on the dead. Among the places I visited was the old school where I and other Pawnee children got their schooling(.) other buildings had been put on to it, but the place looked familiar to me."*[7]

Occasionally the voices of sadness and anger were muted by a fresh breath of hope. On June 21, 1933, Luther North was honored at a banquet held in Chadron, Nebraska. Also in attendance were Agent McGregor from the Pine Ridge Agency, Addison Sheldon, of the Nebraska State Historical Society, and fourteen Ogalala Sioux (former) warriors. After dinner there was time for speeches and reminiscing about the old days with all their glory and heartache. At last, Fire Thunder rose to speak. After pointedly suggesting that it was really Captain North's Pawnee Scouts who had won the plains wars, Fire Thunder expressed his gratitude that,

> *you have invited us and extended an invitation for us to come and attend this banquet tonight, and that you have taken us to the old camp ground. We felt very sad when we went through our old roaming place, but again what made us feel better is to be invited to this banquet tonight. If you could see how good we feel about it, if we could only show you, we could show you bigger than this building tonight.*[8]

It required little more than 280 years from the time the first Europeans established themselves on the coast of Virginia until the last of the Indian wars sputtered out on the Pine Ridge. From the moment of that landing at Jamestown, the destiny of the aboriginal way of life on the North American continent had been settled. The nomadic hunter-warrior societies would necessarily be forced into eclipse. The only remaining question is, could the process have occurred differently than it did?

For a time, removal of the tribes from the path of civilization seemed to be a workable solution—until that civilization pinched inward from both coasts, eventually leaving no place to which the Indians could be removed.

The government tried separating the peaceable from the hostile, but this proved utterly impossible to enforce. There was simply no way for the white man to either separate of unify the peace and war factions within individual bands.

Advocates of Indian boarding schools believed that isolation and education of the young was the best way to speed the assimilation of the Indian within white society. But this was never practiced on a sufficiently large scale, and in any case, was cruel and heartless in the extreme. The incidence of illness and death among young Indian children at these boarding schools was appalling.

Finally, the government implemented the policy of concentration and subsistence, but this quite naturally removed the Indians' control over their own destiny, robbing them of their self-respect and substituting liquor and handouts in its place.

In the end, the nomadic way of life had to be sacrificed. It was simply incompatible with the cultural imperatives of the more numerous and technologically superior white race. The task was to save the people by separating them from their way of life. It was an answer which might have worked, given two centuries. But the course of empire and of world events could not wait that long. The collision of races posed economic, cultural, and moral problems for which the American people have found no universal solutions.

Even on the threshold of the Twenty-first Century, the Indian War of 1864 refuses to go away. In June 1992, Denver's Iliff School of Theology issued a formal apology to "Native Americans" because it held commencement services in Trinity United Methodist Church, the same house of worship in which funeral services for John Chivington had been held ninety-eight years earlier[9]

The following year witnessed 150-year commemorations of the Great Migration all along the route of the old Oregon Trail. To coincide with the celebration, residents of the Little Blue Valley scheduled their re-enactment of the 1864 raids for the fall of that year. But organizers were totally unprepared for the storm of protest which broke in August of 1993 and was reported in a series of seven articles in the *Omaha World-Herald.* Indian leaders and multicultural advocates protested the re-enactments as being racist. But the Oak Village Board and the Celebration Committee stood firm. On August 22, hundreds of people jammed the tiny town to witness the controversial events described in the first chapter in this book. If the raids on Oak Grove and The Narrows were only make believe, the bewilderment of the residents was as genuine as it had been on 1864—bewilderment that a people who had previously been quiescent had suddenly become so hostile.[10]

In 1995, over 100 Pawnees, Wichitas, and Arickaras gathered for a second time at the site of the old reservation in Genoa, Nebraska, to bury remains of their people which had been held by museum researchers. Included in those remains were the bones of six members of that organization formed in 1864 at the instigation of General Curtis, the Pawnee Scouts. In a two-hour ceremony which was closed to the public, the remains of the scouts and others were laid to rest, honored by a twenty-one gun salute and the playing of taps—particularly poignant because the scouts had been killed by U.S. soldiers a month after their honorable discharge in 1869.[11]

The hand-wringing continued the following year when the United Methodist Church, unaccountably hag-ridden over its association with Colonel Chivington, adopted a resolution of apology at its General Conference. Certainly the Methodist Episcopal Church bore no responsibility for Chivington's actions (nor did the Masonic Lodge, of which he was a member), yet its descendant body appealed to the Cheyenne and Arapaho people for "forgiveness for the church's role in the 1864 Sand Creek Massacre in Colorado."[12] The drama spread from the convention floor to the television networks when a talk show scheduled a program on the apology, but canceled it when descendants of the Cheyenne and Arapaho victims of Sand Creek protested that such a show might adversely affect their unsettled claims against the U.S. government.[13]

In view of the continuing controversy over the raids and their aftermath, it seems only fitting to turn once again to the words of Chief Seattle who, in an 1854 interview with Territorial Governor Isaac Stevens, assured him that, after all the red people had perished,

> *At night when the streets of your cities and villages are all silent and you think them deserted, they will throng with the returning hosts that once filled and still love this beautiful land.*[14]

More than 130 years after the raids of August 7-9, 1864, the legacy of those events, like the spirits of Seattle's people, fills the streets of our cities and villages, refusing to allow us to forget.

Perhaps we never should.

Chapter Four notes

1 *The Beatrice Express*, May 20, 1871; See also Lyn Scott, *The Covered Wagon and Other Adventures.* Lincoln: University of Nebraska Press, 1987.

2 Walker, *The Wagonmasters*, 292.

3 *The Omaha World-Herald*, July 18, 1994.

4 Laura Roper to Ann Marble, January 7, 1865, in Ann Marble Indian Depredation Case #892.

5 Ware, *The Indian War of 1864*, 309.

6 George Comstock to his daughter, published in the *Nelson Gazette*, February 27, 1958, reprinted in *Oak–The Way it Was.*

7 Harry Coons to Luther North, September 20, 1898. Luther North, Papers and Correspondence.

8 Luther North, Papers and Correspondence.

9 *United Methodist Reporter*, June 26, 1992.

10 Author's interviews with guests at the celebration in Oak, Nebraska, August 22, 1993.

11 *The Omaha World-Herald*, June 9, 1995; author's interview with Mrs. Carol Green, Genoa, Nebraska, June 12, 1995.

12 *Lincoln Journal-Star*, February 18, 1996.

13 *United Methodist Reporter*, July 5, 1996.

14 Binns, *Northwest Gateway*, 104.

Part IV
Chapter Five

"This has been a glorious day for me"

The season was winter, but the day was bright and crisp, with gnarled clumps of ice overlaying the Little Blue River and naked trees throwing sharp shadows in the slanting sunlight. Except for the sky, the landscape was all tan and brown, splashed here and there by the blackish green of the straggling cedars. The freeze-dried bluestem grass rustled and crunched as once again, wheels rolled along the old Oregon-California Trail approaching The Narrows.

But the year was 1929, and the wheels were the narrow rubber tires belonging to a line of touring cars carrying sightseers and distinguished guests on a special excursion. At last the cars bounced to a halt and the passengers alighted. Some of the younger ones scrambled up into the bluffs to watch the proceedings in the valley below.

Slowly and heavily, an old lady dismounted from the lead auto. She was wrapped in a heavy fur coat and wore a warm, black hat against the winter chill. Carefully, deliberately, she began to study the terrain, pacing this way and that, pausing to get her bearings, then pacing some more. Satisfied at last, she stopped and announced that this was the place. After more than sixty-four years, Laura Roper had returned to stand on the ground from which she had been taken by the Cheyennes on a Sunday afternoon in 1864.

Of course the Little Blue Valley in January looks quite unlike it does in August, and the river itself had changed the landscape some; but Laura was satisfied that she was tolerably close to the fateful site, and Grover Scroggin drove an iron stake into the ground to mark the place.

Laura's return to the valley was the culmination of an exchange of letters with Addison Sheldon, of the Nebraska State Historical Society, over a period of five years. Not only did he want her personal story, but he had long planned to bring her back to address a meeting of the society. By the end of 1928, Laura's health was no longer robust, and she suffered from rheumatism in her wrists and ankles. Nevertheless the invitation was extended and she was determined to come.

It had been over ten years since George Follmer's dream—the monument at Oak Grove—was dedicated. He, of course, had not lived to see that day. But in his memory, the Follmer family invited Laura to their home near Oak for dinner and an afternoon of reminiscing, following her appearance in Lincoln. Laura accepted their invitation with pleasure.

On Sunday, January 13, 1929, some forty guests crowded around tables in the Follmer home to partake of a "pioneer dinner" of truly heroic proportions. There was roast beef and ham, chicken and noodles, mountains of mashed potatoes and gravy, baked beans, hominy, sauerkraut, cole slaw and chili sauce, four kinds of pickles, corn and wheat bread, pies (apple and pumpkin), layer and loaf cakes. There was even jelly from those wild grapes and plums that still grew along the banks of the Little Blue River.

Seated with Laura at the table of honor were a few other old pioneers. There was John Kinnison, who remembered distinctly the day when he, as a trooper of Lieutenant Cramer's Company C of the First Colorado Cavalry, had watched Neva galloping with Laura into Major Wynkoop's camp. Sarah Comstock Dudley was there also, to add her memories. Only six years old when Oak Grove was attacked, she was still able to recall clearly the terror of the raid and the column of smoke against the morning sky as the refugees looked back from the bull train to the place where Oak Grove had been.

There were lots of Comstocks there, of course. James Comstock's children and even a great-great grandson of Erastus Comstock were presented to Laura, as was a granddaughter of Charles Emery.

When they had settled accounts with the meal, the guests piled into the touring cars for the two-mile drive to The Narrows. After identifying the place of her capture, Laura was taken farther up the trail to the site of her family's cabin. A whole lifetime of events had transpired since she, as a young girl of sixteen, had last stood upon these grounds. Possibly her thoughts returned to her parents, and to Marshall Kelley and little Clarence—all long dead—and to the pleasant cabin which had been their home for a few brief months. Nothing at all remained now, except for a little debris not yet entombed by the river.

Then everyone returned to the cars for the trip back to the Follmer home, where the remainder of the day was spent in reminiscing and conversation. Banished on this day were the heartbreaks and disappointments of youthful indiscretion, the years of personal restiveness, and the angry disapproval of the Beatrice newspaper—all washed away by the respectful attention and accolades heaped upon Laura by an admiring community, all of whom had come to get a glimpse of the "wonderful old lady."

At last it was time to depart for the home of some cousins living in Hebron, before returning to her home in Oklahoma. Thanking her hosts warmly, Laura told the assembly, "This has been a glorious day for me, and I'm so glad to have met all you good folks. You have been so kind to me and I shall never forget this."[1]

The gathering in Oak on that January afternoon climaxed two decades of effort to distill and commemorate the truth of the tragic events which occurred along the Little Blue River in 1864. Moreover, the journey back to her old home brought a sense of closure to the life of Laura Roper Vance. Hers had been a long journey and strange. It came to an end on April 11, 1930, when she died peacefully in her sleep at her home in Enid, Oklahoma.

Despite the twists and turns of her long life, Laura remains, by most standards, an ordinary individual who was lifted into an extraordinary dimension by her ordeal. And yet, her captivity was only one isolated episode in a conflagration that exposed all that was good and all that was evil, all the baseness and nobility to be found in the human character–an upheaval known as the Indian War of 1864.

Chapter Five notes

1 The author has been unable to locate any record of Laura's appearance before the historical society. The account of her Sunday in Oak is taken from *The Nelson Gazette*, January 17, 1929.

Nebraska State Historical Society

Laura Roper Vance returns to the Narrows, January 13, 1929.

Author's photo

The site of Laura Roper's capture at the Narrows, 1998.

Nebraska State Historical Society

Dedication of the monument at Oak Grove, June 14, 1918. Gathered in front of the stone (from left) James Comstock, Ella Butler Dudley and John Gilbert.

Nebraska State Historical Society

William Eubank, Jr. at about age twenty.

Nebraska State Historical Society

Portrait of Laura Roper Vance, 1929

EPILOGUE

They are all gone now—the devil-may-care stagecoach drivers and cursing bullwhackers, the road ranch families, military officers and veteran volunteers, the peace chiefs, the war chiefs, Dog Soldiers and Pawnee Scouts. Gone are the leathery homesteaders with their grand dreams and rough edges. Gone are the durable women who yielded youthful beauty to the harsh climate, who fought alongside their men to domesticate the Great Plains.

They appear somehow unreal as their images stare out at us, uncomfortable and unsmiling, from their old glass plate photographs. They seem both larger than life and woefully unsophisticated as we read their sagas of bravery and bluff. And, in our tendency to focus on the suffering and deeds of daring and desperation that make for interesting reading, we neglect to remember that they also took a wonderful amount of pleasure in their existence.

They expected that life would be mostly mundane, sometimes brutal, and always imperfect. These shortcomings would be corrected in the next life. And, although we speak reverently of their sacrifices, they saw nothing sacrificial in their settlement of an untamed land. Their eyes were fixed on freedom of opportunity and the rewards which, in the economic philosophy of the day, were certain to come to those who worked hard and persevered. Neither the Eubanks nor anyone else came west intending to give up their scalps or their lives. Most of them survived quite nicely, and it is incredible to realize that many of those who waited out the dreadful isolation of that dark night of August 7, 1864, lived to enjoy a world linked by automobiles and flight, radios and telephones—a world where streets and homes were lighted by electric lights, where bodies were healed with the help of X-rays and antiseptic surgery.

The road ranches are all gone, too. They were the last word in disposable architecture anyhow, and the places where they stood have long been covered over with corn and alfalfa. The gravesite of Joseph P. Smith and his children lies unmarked at the edge of a cornfield, and Patrick Burke's remains rest next to a hog yard. A hydroelectric canal slices through the old Pawnee Reservation and—hard-to-believe—*underneath* Looking Glass Creek. The swales of the old Oregon-California Trail may still be seen at both ends of Nine Mile Ridge, and an interstate highway cuts across the old Steam Wagon Road over which the Martin brothers bounced in agony in their springless wagon. The Wood River has become a sluggish sewer of farm chemicals, and the states of Colorado, Nebraska, and Kansas are engaged in a tug of war over the precious waters of the Platte and the Republican. William Stolley's "Castle de Dependence" has given place to a community zoo, and Fort O.K. has yielded to a horse track, while the parade ground of Fort Kearny survives as a drowsy park.

In actual fact, the frontier people left us little that tells us who they really were—a few, terse journals, some faded letters and ambrotypes and relics. They left us the land, of course, perhaps not better or more beautiful than they found it, but certainly more productive and more habitable. Its grasslands and marshes, wildflowers, trees, and rivers still respond, just as they have for centuries past, to the ceaseless cycle of the seasons: seedtime, growth, maturity, decay, and dormancy. It is a cycle symbolic of the changeless decree to which every human life and every human institution is subject—a cycle acknowledged by Chief Seattle, who understood so clearly the natural order of human affairs:

> *Tribe follows tribe, and nation follows nation, like the waves of the sea. It is the order of nature, and regret is useless.*

They are words which uncompromisingly foretold the destiny which awaited the society of the American Indian. Must they not as surely apply to our own?

> *What profit hath a man of all his labor which he taketh under the sun?*
> *One generation passeth away and another generation cometh; but the earth abideth forever.*

Ecclesiastes 1: 3, 4

APPENDIX A

Known Casualties in Nebraska Territory, August 7, 1864

Killed:

Henry Sullings (at Indian Hollow)
Horace Smith
3 teamsters
Patrick Burke
William Bowie
Mrs. William Bowie
Bill Canada (Kennedy)
Theodore Uhlig
Joseph Eubank Jr.
Fred Eubank
Joseph Eubank Sr.
William Eubank
Dora Eubank
Henry Eubank
James Eubank
Marshall Clarence Kelley
Jonathan Butler
Red Cloud Tom

Mortally wounded:

1 teamster at Indian Hollow
Nelson Ostrander

Wounded:

George Hunt

Captured:

Laura Roper
Lucinda Eubank
Isabelle Eubank
Willie Eubank Jr.
Ambrose Asher

Known Casualties in Nebraska Territory, August 8, 1864

Killed:

Mr. Jones (at Hook's)
Mr. Graham
Samuel Hyde
William D. Marble
John Fletcher
William Fletcher
Thomas Frank Morton
James Smith
Charles (or W.) Iliff
Mr. St. Clair
6 teamsters of the Kelly train
Fred Smith's hired man

Wounded:

Nancy Fletcher Morton
William Gay
3 bullwhackers of Mart Bowler's train

Captured:

Nancy Fletcher Morton
Daniel Marble

Known Casualties in Nebraska Territory, August 9, 1864

Killed:

2 men in camp west of Gilmans' Ranch
2 stock tenders at Gilmans' Station
Robert Corriston
Mr. Gillette
his partner
Gillette's son

Mortally wounded:

"California Joe" Markham (at Pawnee Ranch)

Wounded:

George Martin (date uncertain)
Henry Nathaniel Martin

Robert Ower Martin
(Richard Wells and Lewis Ostrander are not included as they were not wounded by Indians.)

Known Casualties in Nebraska Territory, August 16, 1864

Killed:

George Constable (at Elk Creek)
Private John Creek
Mr. Buttery (25 miles west of Kearny)

Total Known Casualties, August 7-16, 1864

Killed:	51
Wounded:	9
Captured:	7

APPENDIX B

Disposition of Troops, Department of Kansas,
October 31, 1864

General Headquarters (Fort Leavenworth):
Major General Samuel Ryan Curtis, commanding.
1 company, 11th Kansas Cavalry
Detachment of Signal Corps

District of North Kansas (Fort Leavenworth):
Brigadier General Thomas Davies, commanding.
9 companies, 16th Kansas Cavalry
Detachment of U. S. Veteran Reserve Corps

District of South Kansas (Paola):
Major General James Blunt, commanding.

Subdistrict 1 (Fort Scott):
Colonel Charles Jennison

Ft. Scott, Kansas:
9 companies, 15th Kansas Cavalry
1 company, 16th Kansas Cavalry
2nd Bat. (pt) Kansas Light Artillery

Ft. Insley, Missouri:
4 companies, 3rd Wisconsin Cavalry

Osage Mission, Kansas:
1 company, 15th Kansas Cavalry

Mound City, Kansas:
1 company, 15th Kansas Cavalry

Pawnee Sta., Kansas:
1 company, 3rd Wisconsin Cavalry

Subdistrict 2:
Colonel Thomas Moonlight

Aubrey, Kansas:
2 companies, 11th Kansas Cavalry

Coldwater Grove, Kansas
1 company, 11th Kansas Cavalry

Lawrence, Kansas:
1 Company, 17th Kansas Cavalry

Olathe, Kansas:
1 company, 11th Kansas Cavalry
1 company, 16th Kansas Cavalry

Oxford, Kansas:
1 company, 11th Kansas Cavalry
1 company, 5th Kansas Cavalry

Paola, Kansas:
2 companies, 17th Kansas Cavalry
4 companies, 11th Kansas Cavalry
1 company, 16th Kansas Cavalry
McLain's Colorado Battery

Rockville, Kansas:
1 company, 5th Kansas Cavalry

Shawnee Mission, Kansas:
1 company, 11th Kansas Cavalry

District of the Upper Arkansas (Fort Riley):
Major Benjamin S. Henning, commanding.

Ft. Ellsworth, Kansas:
1 company, 7th Iowa Cavalry

Ft. Larned, Kansas:
1 company, 12th Kansas Cavalry
2 companies, 1st Colorado Cavalry

Ft. Lyon, Colorado Territory:
3 companies, 1st Colorado Cavalry
1 company, 1st New Mexico Cavalry

Ft. Riley, Kansas:
1 company, 17th Kansas Cavalry
1 company, 11th Kansas Cavalry
9th Bat. (pt), Wisconsin Light Artillery

Salina, Kansas,
1 company, 7th Iowa Cavalry

District of Nebraska (Omaha):
Brigadier General Robert B. Mitchell, commanding.

Eastern Subdistrict (Ft. Kearny):
Colonel Robert Livingston

Omaha City,
Nebraska Terr.: 1 company, 1st Bat. Nebraska. Cavalry

Alkali Station, Nebraska Terr.:
1 company, 7th Iowa Cavalry

Beauvais Statation, Nebraska Terr.:
1 company (pt),
1st Bat. Nebraska Cavalry.

Columbus, Nebraska Terr.:
1 company, 7th Iowa Cavalry

Ft. Cottonwood, Nebraska Territory:
1 company (pt), 7th Iowa Cavalry
1 company, 1st Battalion, Nebraska Cavalry

Dakota City, Nebraska Terr.:
1 company, 1st Bat. Nebraska Cavalry

Dan Smith Ranch, Nebraska Terr.:
1 company (pt),
7th Iowa Cavalry

Gilman's Station, Nebraska Terr.:
1 company (pt), 1st Bat., Nebraska Cavalry.

Julesburg, Colorado Terr.:
1 company, 7th Iowa Cavalry

Junction Station, Nebraska, Terr.:
1 company, 1st Nebraska Militia

Ft. Kearny, Nebraska Terr.:
4 companies, 1st Nebraska Cavalry

Little Blue, Nebraska Terr.:
1 company, 1st Nebraska Militia
Mullala's Station, Nebraska Terr.:
2 companies, 1st Neb. Cavalry

O'Fallon's, Nebraska Terr.:
1 company, 7th Iowa Cavalry

Pawnee Ranch, Nebraska Terr.:
1 company, 1st Nebraska Militia

Western Subdistrict (Ft. Laramie):
Col. William O. Collins

Camp Collins, Colorado Terr.:
2 companies, 11th Ohio Cavalry

Deer Creek, Idaho Terr.:
1 company, 11th Ohio Cavalry

Fremont Orchard,
Colorado Terr.: 1 company, 11th Ohio Cavalry

Ft. Halleck, Idaho Terr.:
1 company, 11th Ohio Cavalry

Horseshoe Station, Idaho Terr.:
1 company, 11th Ohio Cavalry

Ft. Laramie, Idaho Terr.:
1 company, 7th Iowa Cavalry

Camp Shuman, Nebraska Terr.:
1 company, 11th Ohio Cavalry

Sweetwater Bridge, Idaho Terr.:
1 company, 11th Ohio Cavalry

(More complete identification of company units and commanding officers will be found in O. R. Vol. 41, Part 4, 375-379.)

BIBLIOGRAPHY

Abbreviations Used in Sources

DAR	Daughters of the American Revolution
NARA	National Archives and Records Administration
NSHS	Nebraska State Historical Society
OR	*The War of the Rebellion: Official Records of Union and Confederate Armies.*
WPA	Works Progress Administration

SOURCES CONSULTED

Manuscript Materials

(All manuscripts are from the archives of the Nebraska State Historical Society unless otherwise noted.)

Alexander, Martin A. Letters.

Bainter, James. Claim for Indian Depredations. Papers of John Rodgers Maltby.

Bettelyoun, Susan Bordeaux. Collected Writings.

Egge, Heinrich. Diary.

Follmer, George Dallas. Papers and Correspondence.

Fort Kearny Letterbook, 1848-1871 (microfilm).

Gay, William. "An Extract from the Life and Adventures of Bill Gay." Typescript, Montana Historical Society, Helena.

Gilman, Musetta and Clyde Wallace, eds. "Nancy Morton's Own Story of the Plum Creek Massacre." (microfilm)

Gregory, Annadora Foss. Papers and Correspondence.

Griffing, Rev. J. S. "Accounts of Movements of Militia Company in Northeastern Kansas." Typescript letters.

Hutton, Mary S. *An Early History of North Platte, Nebraska.* Unpublished masters thesis, University of Nebraska, 1944.

Landers, Ella Roper. "Nebraska Stories." (microfilm)

Leasure, Virginia Naomi. "The Captivity of Laura L. Roper." Manuscript in private possession of Mrs. Virginia Leasure.

Majors, Thomas Jefferson. Papers and Correspondence.

North, Frank. Papers, including "The Adventures of Major Frank North, the White Chief of the Pawnees," told by himself and written by Alfred Sorenson.

North, Luther Heddon. Papers and Correspondence.

Office of Indian Affairs: Letters Received, 1824-1881; Pawnee Agency, 1863-1869 (microfilm).
Pawnee Agency Letterbook.
"Pawnee Indians." Vertical file in the archives, NSHS.
Post Returns of Cantonment McKean (Cottonwood). (microfilm)
Post Returns of Fort Kearny, N.T. (microfilm)
Roberts, Gary Leland. *Sand Creek: Tragedy and Symbol.* Unpublished thesis (Ph.D.), University of Oklahoma, 1984.
Special Orders, Seventh Iowa Cavalry. (microfilm)
Stevens, Nancy Jane Fletcher Morton. Affidavit. Iowa State Historical Society, Des Moines.
Vance, Laura Louise Roper. Autobiography and Correspondence.
Wallace, Clyde. Plum Creek Massacre file.
Ware, Eugene Fitch. Papers and Correspondence. (microfilm)
Whaley, Lizzie Ricketts. Correspondence. Platt family papers.

Government Publications

Iowa Adjutant General. *Reports.* Des Moines: F. W. Palmer, State Printer, 1865, 1866, 1867.
Roster and Record of Iowa Soldiers in the War of the Rebellion, Vol. 4. Des Moines: Emory English, State Printer, 1910.
United States Army, Office of the Adjutant General. *Official Army Register of the Volunteer Forces of the United States Army*, Part 8. Washington, 1867.
United States Congress, House of Representatives. "Massacre of Cheyenne Indians." Report of the Committee on the Conduct of the War, 38th Congress, 2nd Session. Washington: GPO, 1865.
United States Congress, Senate. "Sand Creek Massacre." Report of the Secretary of War, Senate Executive Document 26. 39th Congress, 2nd Session. Washington: GPO, 1867.
—"The Chivington Massacre," Reports of the Committees. 39th Congress, 2nd Session, Washington, GPO, 67.
—"Testimony as to the Claim of Ben Holladay." Report of the Committee on Claims, Misc. Document 19. 46th Congress, 2nd Session. Washington: GPO, 1879.
United States War Department. *The War of the Rebellion: A Compilation of the Official Records of Union and Confederate Armies.* Washington: GPO, 1880-1901.

Newspapers

Atchison (KS) Freedom's Champion, August 25, 1864.
Beatrice (NE) Express, May 20, 1871; November 11, 1871; August 22, October 10,1872; November 11, 1875; February 8, 1877.
Bertrand (NE) Herald, July 5-26, 1940. ("Plum Creek Massacre")
Brownville Nebraska Advertiser, August 11, 1864.
Columbus (NE) Daily Telegram, September 25, 1975; June 15, 1986.
Columbus (NE) Journal, January 7, 1892.
Council Bluffs (IA) Weekly Morning Bugle, August 11, 18, September 15, 1864.

Council Bluffs (IA) Weekly Nonpareil, December 17, 1864.
Crown Point (IN) Register, October 31, 1861; February 27, 1862.
Denver (CO) Post, June 8, 1930.
Denver (CO) Daily Rocky Mountain News, August 9, 10, 11, September 24, 28, November 28, 29, 1864; January 7, 9, 10, February 4, June 27, 1865; June 10, 1868; October 5, 8, 1894.
Denver (CO) Times, September 13, 1887.
Denver (CO) Republican, September 15, 1887.
De Witt (NE) Times-News, November 11, 18, 25, 1926; April 14, 23, August 25, 1927; October 2, 1930.
Ellsworth (KS) Reporter, March 23, 1899.
Grand Island (NE) Independent, July 2, 1932.
Hastings (NE) Daily Tribune, October 20, 1921; November 15, 1926; May 24, 1928.
Hastings (NE) Democrat, May 31, 1928.
Johnson's Ranch (Wood River Center) Huntsman's Echo, May 2, 1861.
Juniata (NE) Herald, June 7, 1883.
Lincoln (NE) Star, August 12, 1936; May 11, 1946.
Lincoln (NE) Sunday Journal and Star, May 29, 1932; February 18, 1996.
Marysville (KS) Big Blue Union, August 27, September 3, 10, 1864.
Nebraska City (NE) Daily Press, August 10-30, 1864.
Nebraska City (NE) News, May 18, June 6, 20, 1868; March 6, 1869; August 7, 1912.
Nelson (NE) Gazette, January 17, 1929.
North Platte (NE) Democrat, March 28, 1872.
Oak (NE) Oakleaf, June 4, 1914; June 20, 1918.
Omaha (NE) Nebraskian, April 9, 1859; July 17, 24, August 7, 14, September 18, November 20, 1863; May 6, July 1, 8, 18, 29, August 10, 17, September 1, October 28, 1864.
Omaha (NE) Weekly Herald, December 28, 1866; October 27, 1869.
Omaha (NE) Weekly Republican, July 22, August 12, 19, 26, September 3, 1864; January 13, 1865.
Omaha (NE) World-Herald, August 14, 17, 19, 21, 22, 23, September 1, 1993; July 18, 1994; June 9, 1995; March 13, 1997.
Ottumwa (IA) Democrat, April 16, 1890.
Pawnee (OK) Chief, August 20, 1959.
Quincy (IL) Weekly Herald, August 15, 22, 29, 1864.
Red Cloud (NE) Argus, February 11, 1926.
St. Joseph (MO) Morning Herald, August 12, 14, 16, 18, 19, 22, 28, September 1, 11, 19, 1864.
Seneca (KS) Nemaha Weekly Courier, June 25, July 9, August 11, 25, 1864.
United Methodist Reporter, June 26, 1992; July 5, 1996.

Indian Depredation Records

(RG 075, Bureau of Indian Affairs; RG 123, U.S. Court of Claims, National Archives and Records Administration)

Adams, Harriet Palmer Eubank. RG 123, Case #1117.

Bainter, James. RG 123, Case #1020.
Bichtold (Biktole, Biktold, Biktole), John. RG 123, Case #2505.
Comstock, George. RG 123, Case #2493, Case #5156.
Douglas, James. RG 123, Case #2337.
Douglas, James (Harriet). RG 123, Case #67.
Emery, Charles. RG 075, Case #1620.
Emery, Charles. RG 123, Case #1019.
Eubank, Joseph Sr. (Hess, Administrator). RG 123, Case #2504.
Eubank, Joseph Sr. (Walton, Administrator). RG 123, Case #2733.
Hammond, Andrew J. RG 123, Case #2579.
Lemmon, James. RG 123, Case #2331.
Marble, Ann. RG 075, Case #892.
Morton, (Stevens) Nancy. RG 075, Case #332.
Roper, Joseph (heirs). RG 123, Case #7007.
Simonton, Thomas and George Tritch. RG 123, Case #1174 consolidated with Case #3102.
Uhlig, Edmund H. RG 075, Case #2869.
Uhlig, Edmund H. RG 123, Case #2469.

Periodicals

Anderson, Tom. "Old North Channel of Platte was Key to Formation of La Grande Ile." *Prairie Pioneer Press* 24, no. 9 (September, 1990). Stuhr Museum; Grand Island, Nebraska.
—"Ownership of Cannon was Disputed for 32 Years." *Prairie Pioneer Press* 25, no. 1 (January, 1991). Stuhr Museum; Grand Island, Nebraska.
Blunt, James G. "General Blunt's Account of his Civil War Experiences." *Kansas Historical Quarterly* 1 (May, 1932).
Burnett, Finn. "History of the Western Division of the Powder River Expedition." *Annals of Wyoming* 8, no. 3 (January, 1932).
Castel, Albert. "The Price Raid of 1864." *Kansas Historical Quarterly* 24, no. 2 (1958).
Collins, Catherine Wever. "An Army Wife Comes West." *Colorado Magazine* 31 (October, 1954).
Danker, Donald F. "Columbus, a Territorial Town in the Platte Valley." *Nebraska History* 34, no. 4 (December, 1953).
"Death of Bro. J. M. Chivington." *Square and Compass (A Journal of Masonry)*, Vol. 3, no. 8, Denver, CO., (October, 1894).
"Exploring the Great Platte River Road." Lexington (NE) Chamber of Commerce and Dawson County Historical Society (1993).
Follmer, George D. "Incidents of the Early Settlement of Nuckolls County." *Collections of the NSHS* 17 (1913).
Garfield, Marvin H. "Defense of the Kansas Frontier, 1864-'65." *Kansas Historical Quarterly* 1, no. 2 (February, 1932).
Hadley, C. B. "The Plains War in 1865." *Proceedings and Collections of the NSHS*, Series 2, Vol. 5 (1902).
Hagerty, Leroy W. "Indian Raids along the Platte and Little Blue Rivers, 1864-1865." *Publications of the NSHS* 28 (1947).

Hansen, George. "True Story of Wild Bill - McCanles Affray in Jefferson County, Nebraska, July 12, 1861." *Nebraska History* X no. 2 (April-June, 1927).
Harvey, Alice G. "The Beginning of Tobias, Nebraska." *Nebraska History* XVI, no. 2 (April-June, 1935).
Henig, Gerald S. "A Neglected Cause of the Sioux Uprising." *Minnesota History* 45, no. 3 (1976).
"The History of Thayer County." *Thayer County Museum Muse* (Fall-Winter, 1976).
"The Irrepressible Conflict." *Annals of Iowa*, Series 3, Vol. 24, no. 1 (July, 1942).
Lemmon, James. "Early Days on the Little Blue." *Proceedings and Collections of the NSHS* 15 (Series 2, Vol. 10), (1907).
Lyon, Herman Robert. "Freighting in the '60s." *Proceedings and Collections of the NSHS*, Series 2, Vol. 5 (1902).
Marvin, George P. "Bull-whacking Days." *Proceedings and Collections of the NSHS*, Series 2, Vol. 5 (1902).
Mattes, Merrill, and Henderson, Paul. "The Pony Express: Across Nebraska from St. Joseph to Fort Laramie." *Nebraska History* 41, no. 2 (June, 1960).
Mattes, Merrill. "The South Platte Trail: Colorado Cutoff of the Oregon-California Trail." *Overland Journal* 10, no. 3 (Fall, 1992).
McCann, Lloyd E. "The Grattan Massacre." *Nebraska History* 37, no. 1 (March, 1956).
Merrill, Irving. "The Civil War in the West: The 1864 Trail Season." *Overland Journal* 9, no. 4 (Winter, 1991).
"Military History of Iowa." *Annals of Iowa*, Series 1, Vol. 5, no. 1 (January, 1867).
"New Light on Mrs. Lucinda Eubanks' Experiences." *The Trail* 8, no. 2 (July, 1920).
Newby, William T. "Diary of the Emigration." *Oregon Historical Quarterly* 8, (December, 1906).
North, James E. "The Elkhorn - Battle Creek Campaign." *Nebraska History* 18, no. 3 (July-September, 1939).
Palmer, Henry E. "History of the Powder River Expedition of 1865." *Transactions and Reports of the NSHS* 2 (1887).
Pattison, John. "With the U. S. Army along the Oregon Trail, 1863-1865." *Nebraska History* 15 (June, 1934).
"The Pawnee War." *Transactions and Reports of the NSHS* 2 (1887).
Reading, Pierson Barton. Journal. *Southern California Pioneers' Quarterly* 7 (September, 1930).
Sheldon, Addison E. "George A. Hunt." *Nebraska History and Record of Pioneer Days*, Vol. 2, no. 3 (July-September, 1919).
Spring, Agnes Wright. "Old Letterbook Discloses Economic History of Fort Laramie 1858-1871." *Annals of Wyoming* 13, no. 4 (October, 1941).
Stewart, Captain George H., and Captain Henry Wharton. Reports. *Transactions of the Kansas State Historical Society*, Vol. 4 (1886-1888).
"The Sting of Envy." *Annals of Iowa*, Series 3, Vol. 27, no. 4 (April, 1946).

Stolley, William. "Defense of Grand Island." *Nebraska History* 16, no. 4 (October-December, 1935).
Sydenham, Moses H. "Freighting Across the Plains in 1856–A Personal Experience." *Proceedings and Collections of the NSHS*, Series 2, Vol. 1, no. 3 (1895).
Thayer, John M. "The Pawnee War of 1859." *Proceedings and Collections of the NSHS*, Series 2, Vol. 5 (1902).
"The 1864 Overland Trail: Five Letters from Jonathan Blanchard." *Nebraska History* 63, no. 1 (Spring, 1982).
Tyson, Thornton K. "Freighting to Denver." *Proceedings and Collections of the NSHS*, Series 2, Vol. 5 (1902).
Watkins, Albert, Ed. "Incidents in the Indian Outbreak of 1864." *Publications of the NSHS* 19 (1919).
Young, Will H. "Journals of Travel of Will H. Young." *Annals of Wyoming* 7, no. 2 (October, 1930).

Books

Andreas, A. T., comp. *History of the State of Nebraska*, Vol. 2. Chicago: Western Historical Company, 1882.
Ball, George, ed. and comp. *"Go West, Young Man."* Greeley, Colorado: Republic Publishing Co., 1969.
Ball, Rev. T. H. *Lake County Indiana from 1834 to 1872.* Chicago: J. W. Goodspeed, 1872.
Barr, R. J. and A. F. Buechler, eds. *History of Hall County, Nebraska.* Lincoln: Western Publishing and Engraving Co., 1920.
Berthrong, Donald J. *The Southern Cheyennes.* Norman, Oklahoma: University of Oklahoma Press, 1963.
Biographical and Historical Memoirs of Adams, Clay, Webster, and Nuckolls Counties, Nebraska. Chicago: Goodspeed Publishing Co., 1890.
Bourne, Russell. *The Red King's Rebellion.* New York: Atheneum, 1990.
Britton, Wiley. *The Union Indian Brigade in the Civil War.* Kansas City: Franklin Hudson Publishing Co., 1922.
Buchanan, James. *Sketches of the History, Manners, and Customs of the North American Indians.* New York: Borradaile, 1824.
Burnett, Peter H. *Recollections and Opinions of an Old Pioneer.* New York: D. Appleton and Co., 1880.
Carrington, Margaret Irvin. *Absaraka C Home of the Crows.* Lincoln: University of Nebraska Press, 1983.
Catton, Bruce. *The Coming Fury.* New York: Doubleday and Co., 1961.
—*This Hallowed Ground.* New York: Doubleday and Co., 1956.
Chalfant, William Y. *Cheyennes and Horse Soldiers.* Norman: University of Oklahoma Press, 1989.
Chittenden, Hiram Martin and Alfred T. Richardson. *Life, Letters, and Travels of Father De Smet*, Vol. 2. New York: Arno Press, 1969.
Clark, Charles M. *A Trip to Pike's Peak and Notes by the Way.* San Jose, California: Talisman Press, 1958.
Clinkinbeard, Anna Dell. *Across the Plains in '64.* New York: Exposition Press, 1953.

Collins, John S. *Across the Plains in '64.* Omaha: National Printing Co., 1904.
Colorado Territory Civil War Records. Littleton, Colorado: Columbine Genealogical and Historical Society, Inc., 1994.
Craig, Reginald. *The Fighting Parson.* Los Angeles: Western Lore Press, 1959.
Creigh, Dorothy Weyer. *Tales from the Prairie.* Hastings, Nebraska: Adams County Historical Society, 1973.
Curry, Margaret. *The History of Platte County, Nebraska.* Culver City, California: Murray and Gee, 1950.
Czaplewski, Russ. *Captive of the Cheyenne.* Lexington, Nebraska: Dawson County Historical Society, 1993.
Dale, Raymond E. *Otoe County Pioneers: A Biographical Dictionary.* Lincoln: n. p. (Author's typescript), 1961.
Danker, Donald F., ed. *Man of the Plains–Recollections of Luther North, 1856 - 1882.* Lincoln: University of Nebraska Press, 1961.
Daughters of the American Revolution. *Nebraska Pioneer Reminiscences.* Cedar Rapids, Iowa: Torch Press, 1916.
Dawson, Charles. *Pioneer Tales of the Oregon Trail and of Jefferson County.* Topeka: Crane and Co., 1912.
Dobbs, Hugh. *History of Gage County, Nebraska.* Lincoln: Western Engraving and Publishing Co., 1918.
Dudley, Elmer S., comp. *Roster of Nebraska Volunteers from 1861 - 1865.* Hastings, Nebraska: Wigton and Evans, State Printers, 1888.
Echo-Hawk, Roger C., and Walter R. Echo-Hawk. *Battlefields and Burial Grounds.* Minneapolis: Lerner Publications, 1994.
Editors of Time-Life Books. *The Indians.* New York: Time-Life Books, 1973.
Ellenbecker, John. *Tragedy at the Little Blue (Indian Raids of 1860-1869).* (Edited and annotated by Lyn Ryder) Niwot, Colorado: Prairie Lark Publications, 1993.
—*The Indian Raid on the Upper Little Blue.* Beatrice, Nebraska: Beatrice Printing Co., 1962.
Ellsberry, Elizabeth Prather, comp. *Adair County, Missouri Marriage Records 1841-1870.* Chillicothe, Missouri: n.p., 1961.
Fay, George, ed. *Military Engagements between United States Troops and Plains Indians*, Vol. 27, Part 2. Greeley, Colorado: Museum of Anthropology, University of Northern Colorado, 1972.
Field, Homer, and Joseph R. Reed. *History of Pottawattamie County, Iowa,* 2 vols. Chicago: S. J. Clark Publishing Co., 1907.
Fletcher, Alice and Francis La Flesche. *The Omaha Tribe,* Vol. 2. 1911. reprint, Lincoln: University of Nebraska Press, 1972.
Franzwa, Gregory. *Maps of the Oregon Trail,* 3rd ed. St. Louis: Patrice Press, 1990.
Frederick, J. V. *Ben Holladay: The Stagecoach King.* 1940. reprint, Lincoln: University of Nebraska Press, 1968.
Frerichs, Herman, ed. and comp. *Cedar County Gleanings*, Vol. 1. Looseleaf notebook in archives, NSHS, Lincoln.

Gage County, Nebraska Marriages 1861-1892, Vol. 1. Lincoln: Nebraska State Genealogical Society, 1994.

Garraty, John A. *A History of the United States.* New York: Harper and Row, 1966.

Gilman, Musetta. *The Pump on the Prairie.* Detroit: Harlo Press, 1975.

Gregory, Annadora Foss. *Pioneer Days in Crete, Nebraska.* Lincoln: State Journal Printing Co., 1937.

Grinnell, George Bird. *The Fighting Cheyennes.* 1915. reprint, Norman: University of Oklahoma Press, 1956.

—*Two Great Scouts and their Pawnee Battalion.* 1928. reprint, Lincoln: University of Nebraska Press, 1937.

Hafen, Le Roy. *Relations with the Indians of the Plains,* Vol. 9 of the Far West and the Rockies. Glendale, California: Arthur Clark Co., 1959.

Halsey, Ashley, *Who Fired the First Shot?* New York: Fawcett Publications, 1963.

Haynes, Rev. James. *The History of the Methodist Episcopal Church in Omaha and its Suburbs.* Omaha: The Omaha Printing Co., 1895.

History of Adair, Sullivan, Putnam, and Schuyler Counties, Missouri. Chicago: Goodspeed Publishing Co., 1888.

History of Spring Ranch, 1870-1990. n.p. Archives of the NSHS, Lincoln.

The History of Wapello County, Iowa. Chicago: Western Historical Company, 1888.

Hoig, Stan. *The Battle of the Washita.* New York: Doubleday and Co., 1976.

—, *The Sand Creek Massacre.* Norman: University of Oklahoma Press, 1961.

Holmes, Kenneth, ed. *Covered Wagon Women,* Vol. 8. Spokane: Arthur H. Clark, Co., 1989.

Horowitz, David. *The First Frontier.* New York: Simon and Schuster, 1978.

Hyde, George E. *A Life of George Bent Written from his Letters.* Norman: University of Oklahoma Press, 1968.

—*The Pawnee Indians.* Norman: University of Oklahoma Press, 1974.

—*Red Cloud's Folk–A History of the Ogalala Sioux Indians.* Norman: University of Oklahoma Press, 1937.

—*Spotted Tail's Folk.* Norman: University of Oklahoma Press, 1961.

Jones, Robert Huhn. *The Civil War in the Northwest.* Norman: University of Oklahoma Press, 1960.

Kaura, J. W. *Saline County, Nebraska History.* Lincoln: Nebraska Farmer Co., 1962.

Lavender, David. *Bent's Fort.* Lincoln: University of Nebraska Press, 1954.

Manley, Robert N. *The Town Builders.* Grand Island, Nebraska: Prairie Pioneer Press, 1985.

Mattes, Merrill. *The Great Platte River Road.* Lincoln: University of Nebraska Press, 1969.

McFarling, Lloyd. *Exploring the Northern Plains, 1804-1876.* Caldwell, Idaho: Caxton Printers, 1955.

Miller, James Knox Polk. *The Road to Virginia City*, ed. by Andrew Rolle. Norman: University of Oklahoma Press, 1960.

Miller, Nina Hull. *Shutters West.* Denver: Sage Books, 1962.

Monahan, Doris. *Destination: Denver City–The South Platte Trail*. Chicago: Swallow Press/Ohio University Press, 1985.

Moore, John H. *The Cheyenne Nation*. Lincoln: University of Nebraska Press, 1987.

Morris, Maurice O'Connor. *Rambles in the Rocky Mountains*. London: Smith, Elder and Co., 1864.

Morton, J. Sterling (Albert Watkins, ed.). *Illustrated History of Nebraska*, Vol. 2. Lincoln: Jacob North and Co., 1906.

Nadeau, Remi. *Fort Laramie and the Sioux*. Lincoln: University of Nebraska Press, 1967.

Noble, Glenn. *Frontier Steamboat Town*. Lincoln: Midguard Press, 1989.

—*Historically Eventful Nebraska City*. n.p., 1981. Archives of the NSHS, Lincoln.

The Official State Atlas of Nebraska. Philadelphia: Everts and Kirk, 1885.

Our Parish: The First One Hundred Years. Columbus, Nebraska: St. Bonaventure Catholic Parish, 1977.

Phillips, G. W., ed. *Past and Present of Platte County, Nebraska*, Vol.1. Chicago: S. J. Clark Co., 1915.

Portrait and Biographical Album of Gage County, Nebraska. Chicago: Chapman Brothers, 1888.

Root, Frank A. and William E. Connelley. *The Overland Stage to California*. 1901. reprint, Columbus, Ohio: Long's College Book Co., 1950.

Ross, Alexander. *Fur Hunters of the Far West*. Chicago: Donnelley and Sons, 1945.

Sanford, Mollie Dorsey. *Mollie: The Journal of Mollie Dorsey Sanford in Nebraska and Colorado Territories, 1857-1866*. Lincoln: University of Nebraska Press, 1959.

Sharp, Abigail Gardner. *History of the Spirit Lake Massacre*. Des Moines: Homestead Printing Co., 1885.

Sheldon, Addison E. *Nebraska–The Land and the People*, 3 vols. New York: Lewis Publishing Co., 1931.

Skogen, Larry C. *Indian Depredation Claims, 1796-1920*. Norman: University of Oklahoma Press, 1996.

Smith, Sherry L. *The View from Officers' Row–Army Perceptions of Western Indians*. Tucson: University of Arizona Press, 1990.

Sorenson, Alfred. *History of Omaha from Pioneer Days to the Present Time*. Omaha: Gibson, Miller, and Richardson, Printers, 1889.

Spring, Agnes Wright. *Caspar Collins: The Life and Exploits of an Indian Fighter of the Sixties*. New York: Columbia University Press, 1927.

Standing Bear, Luther. *Land of the Spotted Eagle*. Lincoln: University of Nebraska Press, 1978.

Stanley, Henry M. *My Early Travels and Adventures in America*. 1895. reprint, Lincoln: University of Nebraska Press, 1982.

Stiles, Edward H. *Recollections and Sketches of Notable Public Men of Early Iowa*. Des Moines: Homestead Publishing Co., 1916.

Stolley, William. *History of the First Settlement of Hall County, Nebraska*. 1946. reprint, Grand Island, Nebraska: Hall County Historical Society, 1982.

Stuart, A. A. *Iowa Colonels and Regiments.* Des Moines: Mills and Co., 1865.
Taylor, I. N. *History of Platte County, Nebraska.* Columbus, Nebraska: Columbus Republican Printers, 1876.
Trail of Memories: Oak, Nebraska. Oak Centennial Committee, 1988.
Unrau, William E., ed. *Tending the Talking Wire.* Salt Lake City: University of Utah Press, 1979.
Utley, Robert M. *Frontier Regulars: The United States Army and the Indian, 1866-1891.* Bloomington, Indiana: University of Indian Press, 1973.
—Frontiersmen in Blue: The United States Army and the Indian, 1818-1865. New York: Macmillan and Co., 1967.
Walker, Henry Pickering. *The Wagonmasters.* Norman: University of Oklahoma Press, 1966.
Ware, Eugene Fitch. *The Indian War of 1864.* 1911. reprint, Lincoln: University of Nebraska Press, 1987.
Wells, Rev. Charles Wesley. *A Frontier Life.* Cincinnati: Press of Jennings and Pye, 1902.
Wilson, D. Ray. *Fort Kearny on the Platte.* Dundee, Illinois: Crossroads Communications, 1980.
Works Progress Administration. *A Military History of Nebraska.* Lincoln: Federal Writers' Project, 1939.
—Nebraska: A Guide to the Cornhusker State. 1939. reprint, Lincoln: University of Nebraska Press, 1979.
Wynkoop, Edward W. *The Tall Chief: The Unfinished Autobiography of Edward Wynkoop, 1856-1866.* (ed. Christopher Gerboth) Denver: Colorado Historical society, 1994.
Yost, Nellie Snyder, ed. *Boss Cowman: The Recollections of Ed Lemmon, 1857-1946.* Lincoln: University of Nebraska Press, 1969.

INDEX

11th Kansas Cavalry 303
11thOhio Cavalry 306, 364
16th Kansas Cavalry 105, 198, 207, 306
17th Kansas Militia 190
19th Kansas Volunteers 385
1st Colorado Cavalry 88, 320, 325, 403, 445
1st Nebraska Cavalry 185, 202, 303, 307, 372
1st New Mexico Vol. 318
2nd Colorado Cavalry 105, 108, 347
2nd Nebraska Cavalry 209, 287
6th Cavalry 387
7th Cavalry 382, 386
7th Iowa Cavalry 83, 116, 128, 248, 251, 306-308, 348, 371, 429
Adams, Joseph 415
Adobe Walls 387
Alexander, Col. Edmund 66
Alexander, Martin 431
Alexander, S.J. 383
Alkali Station 342
American Fur Co. 11
American Ranch 74
Ames, John 172
Anderson, James 62
Angell, Herman 263, 265, 267
Anthony, Maj. Scott 27, 345
Arapaho 3, 37, 70, 123, 157, 249, 316, 323, 343, 348, 362
Arnsen, Isabella 405
Artist, Isaac 412-413
Artist, Jane 136
Artist, Libby 136, 172, 187, 413
Ash Hollow 245, 308, 346
Asher, Ambrose 138, 150, 295, 314, 321, 327, 423
Assiniboin 15
Atkinson, D.F. 200, 296, 430
Augur, Gen. C.C. 388
Babbitt, Almon 40
Backus, Capt. William 107
Bad Wound 92, 122
Bainter, Elizabeth 180, 415
Bainter, Jacob 149, 152-153
Bainter, James 48, 115, 122, 129, 149-150, 165-166, 177, 179, 183-184, 192, 415, 417
Bainter, Sarah 410
Baker, Frank 136, 143, 148, 151, 166, 196, 412
Baker, Jane Artist 413
Baldwin, Lt. Frank 387
Bare, John 150
Barratt, John 136, 209, 414, 437
Barroldo, Joe 162, 295
Bartholomew, James 430
Bates, N.S. 422
Battle of the Washita 386
Baumer, Lt. Col. William 372
Beall, Capt. Roger 287
Bear Butte 34
Bear Man 344
Beardsley, Rev. Isaac 407
Beauvais Ranch 249, 365
Beaver Creek 356
Beaver Creek Ranch 118
Beaver Creek Station 118
Becker, John Peter 96
Bennett, Judge H.P. 349
Benson, Mary 143, 411
Bent's Fort 41
Bent, George 82, 89, 315-317
Bent, William 14, 22, 25, 38, 41, 43, 70, 82, 106, 122, 316, 382
Benton, Thomas H. 11, 33
Berkely, George 52
Bickle, Mary 413
Big Blue River 170, 191
Big Crow 363-364, 372
Big Horn Mountains 360
Big Sandy 181, 338
Bissonette, Joe 360, 361
Black Hawk 10
Black Hills 32
Black Kettle 88, 310, 316-317, 319, 321, 325-326, 344, 355, 385-386
Black, Gov. Samuel 57
Blackfoot 30, 370, 372-373
Blakely, William 418
Blondeau, Bernard 245
Blue Jacket, Charles 70
Blunt, General James 109
Boehl, Charles Boehl 63
Bone, Lt. Joseph 251
Boone, Albert G. 44
Bordeaux, James 33, 370
Bosse 321
Bowie, William 157, 168
Bowler, Mart 252-253, 266
Box Elder Ranch 248
Boyd, James 276
Boyer, Isidor 248
Bozeman Road 381
Bridger, Jim 15

Brown, John 55, 314
Brown, Maj. J.R. 226
Brule 15, 18, 30, 371, 380, 385
Bueler's Ranch 395
Buffalo Ranch 48, 141, 149, 164, 410
Bull Bear 319, 321, 326
Bullock, William 364, 430
Bunch of Timbers 318
Burch, John 417
Burdsal, Dr. Caleb 328
Burke, Patrick 149, 152, 165, 410
Butler, Ella 159, 437
Butler, Jonathan 150, 153, 159, 210
Butler. Charles & Preston 135
Byers, William 404
Byram and Howe 46
Cain, Charlotte 415
Calhoun, John C. 9
Camp McKean 248
Camp Rankin 395-396
Camp Shuman 365
Camp Weld 326, 344
Campbell, Peter 383
Canada, Bill 157, 195
Cantonment Loring 11
Carlyle, George 264, 266
Carney, Gov. Thomas 84
Carrington, Col. Henry B. 381
Carson, Kit 88
Castor, Tobias 136, 159-160, 187, 414
Chaffee, J.B. 349
Cherokees 69
Cherry Creek 42, 44, 346, 394
Cheyenne 3, 12, 14, 18, 37, 68, 70, 100, 204, 323, 118, 123, 125, 157, 182, 249, 263, 267, 278, 288, 295, 304, 308, 316, 321, 343, 348, 359, 380, 394, 418
Chickasaws 69
Chivington, John 84, 402, 405, 407
Chivington, Martha 404
Chivington, Thomas 404
Clark, Dr. Charles 132
Clark, Jeremiah 417
Clear Lake, Iowa, 55
Clyne, Sheriff Joe 188, 197, 203
Coast of Nebraska 242, 256, 342
Colley, Samuel 25, 79, 316, 349
Collins, Col. William O. 24, 309
Columbus 212
Comanche 14, 70
Comstock, Erastus 135, 148, 152, 161, 196, 247, 413, 418, 445
Comstock, George 136, 145, 167, 438
Comstock, James 136, 141, 149, 162, 163, 437
Comstock, John 412
Connelley, Mike 136, 148
Conquering Bear 33
Constable, George 151, 168, 171, 176, 187, 195, 197, 201, 203
Cook, Louisa 48, 115
Coons, Harry 439
Corriston, Robert 264
Cottonwood Springs 74, 128, 243
Creighton, Ed 287
Crow 15
Crow Chief 86
Curtis, Gen. S.R. 69, 83
Curtis, Henry Z. 84
Curtis, Samuel 58, 399, 400
Custer, Lt. Col. G.A. 382
Dakotas 30
Dan Smith's East Ranch 247
Dan Smith's Ranch 267
Dan Smith's West Ranch 247
Darling, Richard 248
Davenport Company 275
David, Capt. James B. 73, 94
Davis, Jefferson 34
De Smet, Fr. Pierre 15
Deer Creek Agency 35
Deer Creek Station 363
Deer Creek Treaty 65
Denver City 43, 46, 78, 81, 108, 184, 226, 242, 247, 268, 284, 290, 316, 322-323, 325, 344, 346, 348, 358
Denver Pacific Railroad 402
Denver Road 84, 249, 263, 292
Deyo, Abraham 287
Diamond Springs Station 248
Dirty Woman Ranch 244
Dobbs, Hugh 188
Dobytown 244
Dodge, Col. Henry 22
Dodge, Gen. Grenville 352, 435
Dog Soldiers 37, 107, 316, 319, 321, 346, 382, 385-386
Donald, Letitia 422
Douglas, Harriet 168
Douglas, James 136, 151, 156, 169, 172, 181, 383, 417
Dudley, Sarah Comstock 168, 445
Dull Knife 390
Eagle Head 317-318
Eayre, Lt. George 86
Ecoffey, Jules 361
Edwards, Capt. Henry 67
Eldridge, Jesse 64
Elston, Charley 371-372, 374
Emery, Bob 172-173, 176
Emery, Charles 143, 153, 164, 178, 338, 411, 417-418, 445
Eubank, Connie 423
Eubank, Dora 158, 161, 295
Eubank, Fred 138, 150, 156
Eubank, Hannah 418
Eubank, Hattie 168, 187, 415, 430

Eubank, Henry 295
Eubank, Isabelle 295, 313, 321
Eubank, Joseph 137, 155
Eubank, Joseph 415
Eubank, Lucinda 150, 207, 295, 321, 353, 355, 369, 372-373, 380, 394, 423, 430, 435
Eubank, Mary 424
Eubank, Ruth 150, 424
Eubank, Will 157-158, 195
Eubank, William 431
Evans, Gov. John 19, 84
Evans, John 78, 401
Ewing, Jesse 140
Fall Leaf 42, 45
Fire Thunder 440
Fisher, King 191
Fisk, Gen. Clinton 84
Fitchie, Elizabeth 421
Fitchie, Martha 248
Fitchie, Sam 327
Fitzpatrick, Tom 6, 14, 31
Five Civilized Tribes 10, 18, 69
Flanagan, Lt. Thomas 207
Fleming, Lt. Hugh 32
Fletcher, John 252, 258
Fletcher, Samuel & Charlotte 255
Fletcher, William 252, 258
Follmer, George 436, 445
Fort Atkinson 39
Fort Cobb 385
Fort Cottonwood 87, 90, 263, 267, 436
Fort Hall 11
Fort Independence 277
Fort Kearny 11, 31, 39, 61, 92, 118, 124, 129, 141, 149, 164, 167, 182, 192, 201, 207, 224, 232, 244, 263, 302, 306, 327, 334, 338-339, 366, 374, 411, 436
Fort Laramie 11, 14, 24, 33, 65, 68, 107, 117, 245, 359, 364, 370-371, 373, 380, 388, 394
Fort Larned 88, 106, 109, 344
Fort Leavenworth 31, 83, 171, 184, 326
Fort Lyon 79, 106, 317, 321, 344
Fort O.K. 277, 305, 450
Fort Randall 73
Fort Riley 307-308
Fort Sedgwick 375
Fort Sockittoem 302
Fortescue, William 417
Freeman Ranch 339
Freeman, Dan 149, 245, 266, 335
Freeman, Thomas 170
Fremont's Orchard 86, 118
Fremont, John C. 11
Frogue, Jennie 430
Gantt, John 38, 114
Garnett, Lt. Richard 32
Gay, Al 91 122
Gay, Will 253-254, 261-262, 266
German Settlements 62, 227, 236, 275, 305
German, John 387
Gerry, Elbridge 81, 291
Gilbert, John 137, 141, 151, 156, 169, 172-173, 181, 187, 195, 197, 201, 204, 413, 418, 437
Gillett, Capt. Lee 418
Gilman's Ranch 128, 243, 247
Gilman, Jeremiah 247
Gilman, Jeremiah 267, 420
Gilman, John 247, 264, 420-421
Gilman, Martha 263
Gilmans' Station 420
Gilpin, William 78
Gleason, Pat 280
Godfrey's Ranch 118
Grand Island City 48, 275, 277, 388
Grant, George 209
Grattan Affair 32, 39, 125
Gray Head 360
Gray, Lt. Henry 71
Graybeard Company 287
Great American Desert 25
Great Platte River Road 114, 335, 353, 436
Green, James 118, 128, 252, 262
Greenwood, A. B. 44
Griffing, Rev. J.S. 196
Grimes, Reason 93-94
Grindstone War 56
Gros Ventre 15
Guerrier, Edmond 317
Hackney Ranch 190, 383
Hackney's Station 71
Hafen, Dr. Le Roy 431
Hammond, Andrew 145, 417
Hancock, Gen. W.S. 382
Harney, Gen. William 34
Harrison, Belle 424
Hazen, Gen. W.B. 385
Heap-Of-Buffalo 321
Helvey, Frank 115
Helvey, Joel 199
Helvey, Tom 115
Hendricks, Stephen 93-94
Hess, William 417
High Forehead 32
Hinman, Washington 48, 244, 248, 420
Hitchcock, Harriet 116
Hoffman, Lan 172
Holladay, Ben 51, 114, 133, 137, 291, 309, 335, 338, 410, 435
Hollenberg, G.H. 199
Homestead Act 62
Hook's Junction Ranch 145, 182, 193, 233, 366
Horse Creek 16, 33, 375, 380
Howe, Albert 188
Hungate, Ward 101
Hunkpapa 30

Hunt, Catherine 414
Hunt, George 136, 160, 412-413, 437
Hunt, Jacob 189
Hunter, John 83
Hutchinson, Perry 415
Hynes, Thomas 191
Ikes, Bill 411
Iliff, Charles 252, 255
Indian Creek 69
Indian Hollow 151, 166, 182, 184, 196, 299
Indian Intercourse Act of 1834 211
Indian Removal Act 26
Indian Territory 84
Ingersoll, Charles 100
Inkpaduta 56
Jackson, Andrew 10
Jefferson, Thomas 9
Jewell, Henry 425, 428
Johnson, Hervey 27
Johnston, Col. Albert S. 56
Jones, H. L. 100
Jones, John 133
Julesburg 107, 128, 244, 268, 286, 334, 348, 364, 375-376, 380, 394, 396, 398, 420
Julesburg Station 394
Junction Ranch 50, 118, 299
Junction Station 118
Kansas Militia 207-208, 336
Kansas-Nebraska Act 54
Kearny, Stephen W. 11
Kelley, Allen J. 425
Kelley, Clarence 140, 425
Kelley, Marshall 139, 149, 159, 209-210, 445
Kelly, Michael 252
Key, John 423
Kinnison, John 445
Kiowa 14, 70
Kiowa Station 136, 150, 172, 176, 191, 299, 383, 416
Kirby, Sylvester S. 426
Kneeland, Dave 188
Kuhl, Capt. Henry 202
La Bonte Station 363
La Flesche, Joseph 22
La Grande Ile 224
Lakota Sioux 30, 380
Lane, James 83-84
Latagotskalahar, Chief 391
Latham Station 290, 303, 338
Laughery, Harriet 295
Lean Bear 4, 39, 80, 88, 90
Leavenworth, Jesse 80, 89
Left Hand 43, 106, 320
Lemmon, Alpharetta 412
Lemmon, Ed 199
Lemmon, James 142, 335, 383, 411-412
Leutze, Emanuel 52
Liberty Farm 129, 134, 140-142, 153, 164, 170, 178, 197, 382, 411, 418
Lincoln, Abraham 69
Little Blue River 40, 48, 50, 115, 129-130, 148, 296, 444
Little Blue Station 136, 141, 149, 162, 177, 180, 195, 201, 205, 339
Little Blue Valley 2, 74, 134, 137, 145, 212, 286, 292, 339, 382, 416, 425, 436, 441, 444
Little Crow 56, 66
Little Heart 4, 80-81
Little Horse 359-360
Little Robe 385-386
Little Thunder 35, 371
Little Whiteman 316
Livingston, Col. Robert 185, 193, 400
Lloyd, George 167
Lockwood, J.D. 252
Lone Tree Station 145, 148, 152, 184
Long Chin 33, 291
Long, Maj. Stephen 48
Looking Glass Creek 92
Loree, John 24
Lull, Almira 404
Lull, Sarah 404
Lushbaugh, Benjamin 71
Lynch, Tom 280
Majors, Alexander 133, 226
Majors, Maj. Tom 343
Man Afraid 380
Man-Shot-By-A-Ree 291
Mandan 15
Manifest Destiny 4, 51
Manning, Col. Edwin 190, 212
Marble, Ann 327, 422, 438
Marble, Danny 129, 295, 321-322, 326-327, 384
Marble, Joel 423
Marble, William 252, 255
Markham, Joe 178, 183
Marshall, Francis 68
Martin Ranch 366, 383
Martin, Anne 230, 234, 383
Martin, Beck 234
Martin, George 227, 236, 277, 421
Martin, Nathaniel 422
Martin, Robert 130, 421
Marysville 198
Mason, Col. O. P. 309
Massacre Canyon 389
Massasoit 7
Maxfield, J.B. 303
May, Maj. Charles A. 61, 275
Maynadier, Col. Henry 381
McClelland, Dr. W. F. 326
McDonald Ranch 116
McDonald, Charles 243, 248, 420
McDonald, Orra 243, 420
McFadden, James 305
McKean, Gen. T.J. 84
McKenny, Maj. T.I. 101

McLain's Battery 86, 88
Medicine Road 4, 12, 124
Metcalf, Newton 144, 180, 411-412, 416
Midway Station 247, 343
Military Road 275, 280, 302
Milligan, Joe and Sally 141
Milligan, Sallie 410
Minneconjou 30, 380
Minnesota Uprising 125
Missouri Compromise 54
Mitchell, David 15, 33
Mitchell, Gen. R.B. 24, 85, 398
Mitimonie 358, 361-362
Monroe, James 9
Moonlight, Col. Thomas 348, 372
Moore, Johnnie 253
Mormon 19, 32, 143, 253
Morrill, Lot 26
Morris, Maurice 132, 138
Morrow, Jack 50, 97, 248, 394, 396, 419
Morton, Francis Jane 357
Morton, Frank 129, 253, 255
Morton, J. Sterling 58
Morton, Nancy 224, 255, 261, 295, 312-313, 321, 353, 355, 371, 384, 394, 419, 423, 429
Morton, Thomas F. 252, 417
Mudge, Elizabeth 141
Mudge, William 141, 164, 227
Mudge, Willie 192, 410
Mullaly, Pat 245
Murphy, Capt. Edward 192
Murray's Station 118
Murray, Bridget 94, 129
Murray, Pat 92, 279, 282
Na-ta-ne 321
Nagle, Elizabeth 421
Nakota 30
Nebraska Cavalry 303
Nebraska City 11, 46, 114, 191, 194, 201, 211, 224, 263, 285, 366
Nebraska Militia 306
Needham, Herschel 282
Neva, Chief 315, 319
Nicholas, Frank 170
Nicholas, Robert 170
Nine Mile Ridge 141, 149, 164, 169, 177, 181, 197, 203,
North, Frank 97, 303-306, 308-309, 381, 388, 390
North, Luther 66, 92, 128, 282, 388, 391
North, Robert 80, 82, 103, 122
Northern Cheyennes 385, 390
Northern Pacific RR 413
Notanee, John 103
Nye, John 336
O'Brien, Maj. George 90
O'Sullivan, John L. 52
O.K. Store 276
Oak Grove 71, 135, 150, 159, 169, 187, 195, 210, 299, 437
Oak, Nebraska 3
Ogalala 15, 30, 369, 380, 385, 440
Omaha 46, 117, 201, 210, 268, 280, 285, 338, 397
One Eye 317, 344
Opechancanough 7
Oregon-California Trail 2, 4-5, 11, 26, 31, 45, 84, 132, 142, 161, 198, 263, 295, 309, 380, 435, 444, 450
Osceola 10
Ostrander, Lewis 150
Ostrander, Nelson 160
Otis, George 189
Overland Road 268
Overland Stage Line 134, 189, 244, 264, 290, 338
Oxbow Trail 208, 224, 236
Pahuk 57
Palmer, John 138, 150, 155, 168, 187, 415
Parmetar, Capt. James W. 80
Parriott, Mable 431
Pattee, Lt. Col. John 117
Patterson, Dan 133
Pawnee Agency 73, 93, 281
Pawnee Creek 382
Pawnee Killer 346
Pawnee Ranch 129, 139, 144, 152, 161, 165, 177, 193, 197, 299, 309, 339, 410-411
Pawnee Reservation 302
Pawnee Scouts 304, 306, 381, 384, 388, 391, 440
Pawnees 19, 56, 61, 100, 279, 303, 388, 390, 439, 441
Pea Ridge 69, 83, 399
Peta-Neh-Sah-Doh 389
Pike's Peak Express 133
Pike, Gen. Albert 69, 80
Pike, Zebulon 48
Platte Bridge 39
Platte Bridge Station 360, 363, 380
Platte River 5, 11
Platte River Road 242
Plum Creek 182, 299, 334, 340, 366-367, 417
Plum Creek Massacre 267, 276, 280, 295, 429
Plum Creek Station 119, 245, 251, 343, 384
Pocahontas 7
Polk, James K. 11
Pollock, Thomas 403
Pontiac 8
Pony Express 51, 85, 133, 141, 243
Poole, Leonard 417
Porcupine Ranch 366

Porter, Lt. Charles 183, 267
Powell, Lt. Col. Ludwell 49
Powhatan 7
Pratt and Clark 417, 423
Pratt, John 193, 281, 293
Pratt, Matthew 423, 429
Price, Gen. Sterling 83, 309
Quantrill, William 84, 285
Randolph, G. C. 172
Randolph, Hattie 172
Rath Ranch 90
Raynalds, Capt. William 35
Red Cloud 27
Red Cloud Tom 165
Red Leaf 33
Reynal, Antoine 292
Richard, Louis 360
Robertson, Lt. Beverly 58
Robideau, Joseph 248
Robinson, A. M. 43
Rock Creek Station 143, 190
Rocky Mountain Fur Co. 14
Rolfe, John 7
Rollins, John 172
Root, Frank 48, 74, 116
Roper, Clarence 427
Roper, Clarisa 383
Roper, Fordyce 139, 144
Roper, Fred 190
Roper, Frederick 418
Roper, Joe 139-140, 149, 169, 179, 193, 197, 202, 207, 211, 327, 424-426
Roper, Katie 426
Roper, Laura 130, 140, 149, 153, 161, 171, 181, 186, 295, 312-313, 319-320, 327, 364, 438, 446
Roper, Paulina 162, 181, 199
Rousseau, John 361
Royce, Ben 412
Russell, Majors & Waddell 46, 85, 133, 137, 141, 224, 245
Russell, William 133
Sand Creek 4, 344, 346, 348-349, 351, 353, 386, 401-402, 406, 416, 442
Sanford, Mollie 290, 328
Sans Arc 30, 380
Santa Fe Trail 11, 69, 84, 90, 100, 249
Santee 20, 30
Satanta 106
Saunders, Gov. Alvin 84, 185, 188
Schuetz, Ida Uhlig 416
Schuetz, Joseph 416
Scotts Bluff 38
Scroggin, Benjamin 436
Scroggin, Grover 444
Sedgwick, Maj. John 41
Seminoles 69
Shakespear Station 245
Sharitarish, Chief 390
Sheldon, Addison E. 436, 445
Sheridan, Gen. P.H. 385
Sherry, Gen. Byron 192
Shinn's Ferry 128
Shoshone 15
Sibley, Gen. H.H. 85
Sibley, Henry H. 67
Sioux 3, 12, 14, 71, 93, 100, 118, 123, 125, 157, 203, 263, 267, 278, 288, 304, 316, 321, 325, 343, 348, 374, 380, 418
Six Nations 9
Slim Fox 23
Slough, Col. John 85
Smith's Ranch 340
Smith, Adam 92, 94, 129, 279
Smith, Dr. A.A. 326
Smith, Fred 245, 262
Smith, Horace 129, 148, 151, 182
Smith, James 252, 255, 258
Smith, John 81, 89, 91, 97, 122
Smith, Joseph P. 62
Smith, Michael 279
Smith, William 322-323
Soper, Elijah 424
South Pass 68
Southern Cheyennes 385, 387
Spirit Lake Massacre 68, 125
Spotted Crow 344
Spotted Horse 292, 359-360
Spotted Tail 18, 33, 66, 92, 122, 346, 380-381, 388
Spring Ranch 144, 149, 165, 183, 415, 418
St. Joseph, Missouri 24
Standing-In-Water 344
Star 88
Steam Wagon Road 226, 421
Steamwagon Road 366
Stevens, George 429
Stevenson, Capt.Tom 306
Stewart, Capt. George 40
Stolley, William 276, 450
Strike-The-Ree 23
Strong, Horatio 423
Stuart, Robert 5
Sully, Capt. Alfred 61
Summers, Col. Samuel 107, 116, 192, 394
Summit Springs 386
Summit Station 145, 184, 196
Sumner, Col. Edwin Vose 40, 55, 304
Sumner, Sen. Charles 55
Sydenham's Ranch 252
Sydenham, Moses 48, 244-245, 248
Taffe, Maj. John 287
Tall Bull 386
Taylor, E. B. 381
Tecumseh 9
Thavenet, Wilhelm 277
Thayer, Gen. John 58
The Narrows 130, 138, 157, 161, 169, 173, 176, 180, 299, 438, 441, 444

Thirty-two Mile Creek 136, 144, 184
Thirty-two Mile Station 136, 144, 148, 152, 166, 184, 412
Thomas Ranch 245, 251, 256, 261
Thompson, Capt. John 62
Thompson, Capt. S.P. 189
Thomsson, John 63
Thornton, Coon 86, 108
Thorspeken, Dr. Wilhelm 277
Trail of Tears 10
Treaty of 1851 42, 125, 375
Treaty of Fort Wise 44, 79, 81
Treaty of Medicine Lodge 387
Treaty of Table Creek 57, 61
Tum-A-Tap-Um 19
Turkey Leg 384
Twenty-five Mile Ranch 245
Twiss, Thomas 35, 65
Two Face 248, 268, 369-371, 373, 439
Two Kettle 30
Two Thighs 344
Uhlig, Hugo 416-418
Uhlig, Joanna 139, 157
Uhlig, Otto 200, 416
Uhlig, Theodore 156-157
Umphrey, E. 172
Union Pacific RR 244, 402, 435
Ute 19, 79
Van Wormer Ranch 79, 101
Vance, James 427-428
Vorse, Newt 406
Wakarusa War 40, 55
Wallen, Maj. H. D. 103
Walton, Daniel 423
War Bonnet 344
Ware, Eugene 21, 438
Warren, Thurston 384
Washita River 386
Weavers, Anne 227
Wehn, John 427
Wells Fargo 435
Wells, Rev. Charles Wesley 149
Wells, Richard 177
West Wind 226
Western Stage Co. 226, 228
Weston, J.B. 139, 144, 191
Westport, Missouri 114
Whaley, Charles 93, 279
Whaley, Lizzy 302
Wharton, Henry 11
Wheeler, Ann 415
White Antelope 310, 321, 344
White Bull 41
White Turkey, Chief 70
Whitfield, John 33
Whitman, Marcus 114
Whittemore, Lucy 142
Wickham, Horace 188
Wilder, William 149, 172
Willard, Rev. O.A. 403
Willow Island Ranch 245
Winthrop, John 17
Wiscamb, Louis 245
Wiseman, Henson 72
Wiseman, Phoebe 72
Wolf Chief 88
Wolf Fire 39
Wood River 64
Wood, Maj. John 107, 117, 359, 361, 429
Wright, Col. George 84
Wynkoop, Maj. E.W. 323, 382
Yellow Shield 344
Yellow Squaw 187
Yellow Wolf 19, 344
Young, Brigham 143

The Author

Ronald Becher is a native of Nebraska, receiving his elementary and secondary education in Columbus. He earned his undergraduate and graduate degrees from Concordia Teachers College in Seward, Nebraska, and did additional study in special education at the University of Kansas at Lawrence. He has thirteen years teaching experience in regular and special education at the elementary and junior high school levels and has published several articles on education and historical events. *Massacre along the Medicine Road* is his first book. The author also is a member of the Oregon-California Trails Association and the American Guild of Organists. He currently resides in Valparaiso, Nebraska.

Recent Titles from
CAXTON PRESS

The Cabin on Sawmill Creek
A Western Walden
by Mary Jo Churchwell
ISBN 0-87004-380-3 240 pages paper $12.95

Silver Creek: Idaho's Fly Fishing Paradise
by David Clark and David Glasscock
ISBN 0-87004-382-x 224 pages paper $18.95

Pioneers of the Colorado Parks
by Richard Barth
ISBN 0-87004-381-1 276 pages paper $17.95

Encyclopedia of Western Railroad History
Vol. IV California
by Donald B. Robertson
ISBN 0-87004-385-4 354 pages cloth $42.95

On Sidesaddles to Heaven
The Women of the Rocky Mountain Mission
by Laurie Winn Carlson
ISBN 0-87004-384-6 256 pages paper $19.95

From the Grave:
A Roadside Guide to Colorado's Pioneer Cemeteries
by Linda Wommack
ISBN 0-87004-386-2 496 pages paper $24.95
ISBN 0-87004-390-0 496 pages cloth $34.95

For a free catalog of Caxton books write to:

CAXTON PRESS
312 Main Street
Caldwell, ID 83605-3299

or

Visit our Internet Website:

www.caxtonprinters.com

Caxton Press is a division of The CAXTON PRINTERS, Ltd.

WC